REFORMING
PERSONNEL PREPARATION
IN EARLY INTERVENTION

REFORMING PERSONNEL PREPARATION IN EARLY INTERVENTION

Issues, Models,
and Practical Strategies

edited by

Pamela J. Winton, Ph.D.
Frank Porter Graham Child Development Center
University of North Carolina at Chapel Hill

Jeanette A. McCollum, Ph.D.
Department of Special Education
University of Illinois
Champaign

Camille Catlett, M.A.
Frank Porter Graham Child Development Center
University of North Carolina at Chapel Hill

·P A U L·H·
BROOKES
PUBLISHING C⁰

Baltimore • London • Toronto • Sydney

Paul H. Brookes Publishing Co.
Post Office Box 10624
Baltimore, Maryland 21285-0624

Typeset by PRO-Image Corporation, Techna-Type Division, York, Pennsylvania.
Manufactured in the United States of America by
Hamilton Printing Company, Rensselaer, New York.

Partial support for the preparation of this volume was provided by the following grants from the
U.S. Department of Education: Grant #H024P2002 as administered by the Office of Special
Education Programs and Grant #R307A6004 as administered by the Office of Educational
Research and Improvement.

The case example in Chapter 17 is based on actual events and the quotations from the individuals
described in Chapter 20 are taken from conversations with actual people. All other examples in
this book are completely fictional; any similarity to actual individuals or circumstances is
coincidental and no implications should be inferred.

Library of Congress Cataloging-in-Publication Data
Reforming personnel preparation in early intervention: issues,
   models, and practical strategies/edited by Pamela J. Winton,
   Jeanette A. McCollum, Camille Catlett.
      p.   cm.
   Includes bibliographical references and index.
   ISBN 1-55766-286-X
   1. Child welfare—United States.   2. Child development—United States.   3. Child
psychotherapy—United States.   4. Social work with handicapped children—United
States.   5. Special education—United States.   6. Family social work—United
States.   7. Family psychotherapy—United States.   8. Family day care—United
States.   9. Home-based family services—United States.   10. Crisis intervention
(Psychiatry)—United States.   I. Winton, Pamela J.   II. McCollum, Jeanette A.   III. Catlett,
Camille.
HV741.R434   1997
361.7′0973—dc21   97-16420
                                                                                         CIP

British Library Cataloguing in Publication data are available from the British Library.

CONTENTS

ABOUT THE EDITORS

Pamela J. Winton, Ph.D., Research Investigator, Frank Porter Graham Child Development Center, University of North Carolina at Chapel Hill, CB#8185, Chapel Hill, North Carolina 27599-8185

Pamela J. Winton is a research fellow and investigator at the Frank Porter Graham Child Development Center, University of North Carolina at Chapel Hill. Since 1981, she has been involved in research and professional development in the area of family–professional and interprofessional collaboration within the context of early childhood intervention. She is on the faculty of the School of Education and directs several federally funded grants that focus on reforms in early childhood intervention personnel development systems. She has also served as an advocate for children and families on local, state, and national boards.

Jeanette A. McCollum, Ph.D., Professor, Department of Special Education, University of Illinois, 1310 South 6th Street, 288 Education Building, Champaign, Illinois 61820

Jeanette A. McCollum is a professor in the Department of Special Education at the University of Illinois in Champaign. She has written extensively in the area of personnel preparation of early childhood personnel and has been instrumental in the development of standards for personnel working with infants and toddlers with disabilities and their families. She coordinates the graduate program in early intervention at the University of Illinois.

Camille Catlett, M.A., Research Associate, Frank Porter Graham Child Development Center, University of North Carolina at Chapel Hill, CB#8185, Chapel Hill, North Carolina 27599-8185

Camille Catlett has played an instrumental role in four national early intervention personnel preparation projects since 1990. In her position as Research Associate at the Frank Porter Graham Child Development Center, University of North Carolina at Chapel Hill, she co-directs two federal projects designed to promote improvements in the preservice and inservice preparation of individuals serving young children and their families.

CONTRIBUTORS

Isaura Barrera, M.A., Ph.D.
Associate Professor
Department of Special Education
College of Education
University of New Mexico
Lomas Boulevard
Albuquerque, New Mexico 87131

Mary Jane Brotherson, Ph.D.
Associate Professor
Department of Human Development and
   Family Studies
Iowa State University
1086 LeBaron
Ames, Iowa 50011

Mary Beth Bruder, Ph.D.
Professor and Director
Department of Pediatrics
Division of Child and Family Studies
University of Connecticut Health Center
263 Farmington Avenue
Dowling North, MC-6222
Farmington, Connecticut 06030-6222

Virginia Buysse, Ph.D.
Frank Porter Graham Child Development
   Center
University of North Carolina at Chapel Hill
CB#8180, 105 Smith Level Road
Chapel Hill, North Carolina 27599-8180

Angela Capone, Ph.D.
Director of Early Childhood Programs
University Affiliated Program of Vermont
University of Vermont
499C Waterman Building
Burlington, Vermont 05401

Elizabeth R. Crais, Ph.D.
Division of Speech and Hearing
University of North Carolina at Chapel Hill
CB#7190, 76A Wing D. Med School
Chapel Hill, North Carolina 27599-7190

Juliann Woods Cripe, Ph.D.
Associate Professor
Valdosta State University
College of Education
Department of Special Education
   and Communication Disorders
Valdosta, Georgia 31698

Steven E. Daley, Ph.D.
Early Childhood Special Education
Child Development/Special Education
   Department
Idaho State University
Campus Box 8059
Pocatello, Idaho 83209

Karen Diamond, Ph.D.
Associate Professor and Director
Child Development Laboratory School
Department of Child Development and Family
   Studies
Purdue University
1267 Child Development and Family Studies
   Building
West Lafayette, Indiana 47907-1267

Nancy J. DiVenere, B.A.
Director
Parent to Parent of Vermont
1 Main Street
69 Champlain Mill
Winooski, Vermont 05404

Sue Forest, Ph.D.
Director
Rural Early Intervention Training Program
Department of Psychology
University of Montana
PHB 203
Missoula, Montana 59812

Adrienne Frank, M.S., O.T.R.
Co-Director
Trans/Team Outreach
Occupational Therapist
Child Development Resources
150 Point O'Woods Road
Post Office Box 280
Norge, Virginia 23127

Kathleen K. Gallacher, M.A.
Co-Director, Project PROBE
Montana University Affiliated Rural Institute
    on Disabilities
52 Corbin Hall
Missoula, Montana 59812-1588

Corinne Welt Garland, M.Ed.
Executive Director
Child Development Resources
150 Point O'Woods Road
Post Office Box 280
Norge, Virginia 23188

Ann Higgins Hains, Ph.D.
Associate Professor
Department of Exceptional Education
University of Wisconsin–Milwaukee
2400 East Harford Avenue, Room 610
Milwaukee, Wisconsin 53211

Barbara Hanft, M.A., O.T.R., F.A.O.T.A.
Developmental Consultant
1022 Woodside Parkway
Silver Spring, Maryland 20910

Mary Frances Hanline, Ph.D.
Associate Professor
Department of Special Education
Florida State University
Tallahassee, Florida 32303

Elizabeth Hecht, B.A.
Outreach Specialist
Waisman Center
Early Intervention Program
University of Wisconsin–Madison
1500 Highland Avenue
Madison, Wisconsin 53705

Mary-alayne Hughes, Ph.D.
CSPD Coordinator and Training Consultant
Ohio Department of Health
Bureau of Early Intervention Services
246 North High Street, Fifth Floor
Post Office Box 118
Columbus, Ohio 43266-0118

Karla M. Hull, Ed.D.
Associate Professor
Department of Special Education and
    Communication Disorders
Valdosta State University
1500 North Patterson Street
Valdosta, Georgia 31698-0102

Jennifer L. Kilgo, Ed.D.
Associate Professor
Department of Early Childhood Education and
    Development
University of Alabama–Birmingham
901 13th Street South
Education Building, Room 232-H
Birmingham, Alabama 35294-1250

Pamela Marsalis Kimbrough, M.Ed.
Director
Children's Services Division
Early Intervention Program
C-BARC, The Arc of Caddo-Bossier
351 Jordan Street
Shreveport, Louisiana 71101

Susan Kontos, Ph.D.
Professor
Department of Child Development and Family
    Studies
Purdue University
1269 Fowler House
West Lafayette, Indiana 47907-1269

Lucinda Kramer, Ph.D.
Instructor
Early Childhood Multicultural Special
    Education
College of Education
University of New Mexico
Hokona Hall, Room 281
Albuquerque, New Mexico 87131

Marcia S. Lobman, M.Ed.
Clinical Associate Professor
Louisiana State University Medical Center
Human Development Center
1110 Florida Avenue
Building 138
New Orleans, Louisiana 70119-2799

Kathy Matthews
Parent Consultant
2281 Pilgrim Rest Road
Doyline, Louisiana 71023

Susan L. McBride, Ph.D.
Associate Professor
Department of Human Development and
    Family Studies
Iowa State University
101 Child Development Building
Ames, Iowa 50011

Patricia Place, Ph.D.
Consultant
20 Shaw Avenue
Silver Spring, Maryland 20904

Sharon E. Rosenkoetter, Ph.D.
Associate Professor
Coordinator of Early Childhood Special
    Education
Associated Colleges of Central Kansas
210 South Main Street
McPherson, Kansas 67460

Peggy Rosin, M.S., CCC-SP
Coordinator
Pathways Service Coordination Project
Waisman Center
Early Intervention Program
University of Wisconsin–Madison
1500 Highland Avenue
Madison, Wisconsin 53705

David Sexton, Ph.D.
Professor
Early Childhood Education and Development
University of Alabama–Birmingham
901 13th Street South
Birmingham, Alabama 35294-1250

Patricia Snyder, Ph.D.
Associate Professor
Department of Occupational Therapy
Louisiana State University Medical Center
1900 Gravier Street
New Orleans, Louisiana 70112-2262

Vicki D. Stayton, Ph.D.
Professor and Chair
School of Integrative Studies in Teacher
    Education
Western Kentucky University
328 Tate C. Page Hall
Bowling Green, Kentucky 42101

Patricia W. Wesley, M.Ed.
Director
Partnerships for Inclusion
Frank Porter Graham Child Development
    Center
University of North Carolina at Chapel Hill
521 South Greensboro Street
Sheryl-Mar Suite 100
Carrboro, North Carolina 27510

Barbara L. Wolfe, Ph.D.
Assistant Professor
School of Education
University of St. Thomas
2115 Summit Avenue
St. Paul, Minnesota 55105

Tweety Yates, Ph.D.
Director
Partnerships Project and Parents Interacting
    with Infants (PIWI) Outreach
University of Illinois
61 Children's Research Center
51 Gerty Drive
Champaign, Illinois 61820

FOREWORD

Anyone associated with early intervention is well aware of the challenges of this dynamic field. The professionals and paraprofessionals who touch the lives of infants and toddlers work in interdisciplinary contexts, in diverse settings, and with children who have widely varying abilities. Early interventionists are expected to be knowledgeable about diverse disabilities, able to identify the learning and therapeutic needs of young children, and highly skilled in designing educational and therapeutic interventions. They must also work collaboratively with parents and other family members to identify and meet the needs of individual children and to support families in achieving family-identified priorities. Furthermore, they must be knowledgeable about the various agencies and programs that serve children with disabilities and their families, and they must be skilled at integrating and coordinating services.

This book frames these and other challenges facing the field of early childhood intervention within the context of ecosystems theory; but what is truly unique and useful about this book is the way that it moves beyond those challenges to thoughtful and sometimes provocative strategies for early intervention preservice preparation, inservice training, and individual interactions. Issues are delineated in interesting vignettes and examples. Activities for promoting personnel development are provided throughout the text. The authors, who have considered and implemented a variety of methods for and models of personnel preparation, share their ideas and perspectives as well as barriers to and facilitators of successful service delivery. In each case, the suggestions reflect an understanding of the complex and multiple early childhood intervention roles and the corresponding responsibility of faculty members, family members, and trainers to help prepare personnel for those roles. This volume emphasizes that learning is a lifelong process and must constantly be tied to real-life issues and challenges such as those encountered daily by practitioners.

This book's title, *Reforming Personnel Preparation in Early Intervention: Issues, Models, and Practical Strategies,* begins with the bold premise that personnel preparation in early intervention needs to be reformed. One definition of reform is to "change for the better." This book is not an attack on existing efforts, but it is an attempt to provide capable personnel with the resources with which to achieve desired changes. For early intervention program directors, it offers ideas for encouraging the development of staff in family-centered directions. For early intervention trainers, it provides ideas for increasing the repertoire of methods and materials and a set of positive examples and suggestions for how personnel preparation efforts can prepare professionals for the reality of the world of work. For new faculty members, it delineates both broad and specific suggestions for course planning and program development. For experienced faculty members, it provides ideas for revising or modifying existing courses. For family members of children with disabilities, it offers support in advocating for family–professional collaborations in personnel preparation. And, for agency representatives and policy makers, it promotes thoughtful reflection on the challenges inherent in supporting personnel through resource management and allocation.

Ultimately, providers of early intervention services (and, I would argue, all teachers as well) need to be prepared to enter and deal with situations for which they have not been specifically prepared. This challenge requires an understanding of the fundamental goals that should be achieved in the context of any helping relationship. It also requires an ability to engage in productive problem solving with family members and co-workers until an acceptable solution is achieved. This volume provides key insights into what will be required for personnel preparation efforts to be truly effective in preparing, developing, and supporting a work force for the field.

Don Bailey, Ph.D.
Director
Frank Porter Graham Child Development Center
Chapel Hill, North Carolina

PREFACE

A book about changes and reforms written in a time of rapid change presents certain inherent challenges. The terminology used in this book was one challenge. It was important to use terms that had shared meanings across diverse groups; however, the broad audience for this book (multiple disciplines, including families and agencies) did not make this an easy task. For example, terms used to define aspects of personnel preparation have different meanings for different audiences. For some the term "training" is inappropriate and offensive, conjuring up images of dogs being trained to do tricks. For others, the term "training" has a specific meaning: staff development activities for practitioners in the work force, as opposed to "education," which refers to experiences in formal institutions that result in degrees. Furthermore, some individuals make this same distinction by using the terms "inservice" and "preservice." Our goal in this book is to define personnel preparation in the broadest possible sense. Our definition includes all of these strategies (e.g., mentoring, consultation, self-study, guided decision making) and processes (e.g., personnel standards, licensure, certification, competencies, monitoring) that create a community of learners with the capacity to grow and develop in the face of ongoing changes in the field. We view personnel preparation as a part of the daily work life of practitioners, rather than as a series of events that takes place in particular environments or on particular days. Our approach to the challenge of terminology regarding personnel preparation was to heighten the chapter authors' awareness of the issue and to encourage them to use terminology that best suited their particular discussion.

A related challenge was how to consider evolving policies and laws. References to a specific component of legislation, such as Part H of IDEA, are soon dated. Policy initiatives such as welfare and health care reform, whose impact at state and local levels is still unfolding, are challenging to discuss when information is changing rapidly. Our approach was to use the term "early intervention legislation" whenever possible and to promote personnel preparation strategies and processes that enable learners and communities to grapple with rapid changes, no matter what they might be, rather than to focus exclusively on early intervention content.

The values that underlie this book are to share information in ways that promote family-centered, interdisciplinary, community-based early intervention services. The definition of what that resembles continues to evolve and must be individualized according to the needs of each community. However, what is constant if that value is to be realized is the need for a diverse, sensitive, flexible, confident, competent cadre of personnel serving young children and families. This book is designed to give those who need them the tools to do the most effective job possible in preparing such a cadre of personnel.

Chapter 1 provides an overview of the personnel preparation issues and challenges facing the field, possible solutions to those challenges, and a framework that recognizes and acknowledges the transactions and involvement of multiple systems. The framework provided in Chapter 1 is important in terms of understanding the challenges as well as moving toward solutions to those challenges. Just as problems are interrelated, so are solutions. For example, setting personnel standards as a solution to the problem of not having competent personnel can create a new problem related to shortages of personnel if the standards are difficult to achieve. This means that solutions must be considered within a broad framework to evaluate and anticipate unexpected outcomes that might result from particular approaches designed to address challenges in one part of a system. In the remaining chapters in Part I, issues, strategies, and models related to discrete aspects of the broader ecology—state systems, community systems, and higher education systems—are described in more detail.

The focus of Part II is those critical components that must be included and considered in every personnel preparation effort. Chapter 5 provides a conceptual framework for designing effective personnel preparation. Chapters 6 and 7 provide practical information and strategies related to needs assessment, evaluation, and follow-up strategies. The role that supervision, mentoring, and coaching play in ongoing professional development is the topic of Chapter 8.

Part III (Chapters 9–16) is designed to provide the reader with concrete ideas, instructional activities, frameworks, and resources related to early intervention content areas that have been shown to be of interest to university faculty and staff development specialists. These content areas are sensitivity to cultural variations, family-centered practices, service coordination, child assessment, intervention planning, team collaboration, inclusion, and early intervention legislation and policy. The array of ideas presented in each chapter should appeal to all who address this content in instruction.

Part IV (Chapters 17–21) provides more detailed information and, in some instances, specific models that have been developed to effectively deal with the key issues introduced previously in the book. These include the following: 1) the role of families as instructional resources and partners, 2) designing and implementing interdisciplinary practica, 3) strategies related to distance learning, and 4) linking preservice and inservice efforts through team-based instruction. The information presented in this part not only has application at state, community, program, and university levels and across all disciplines but also promotes linkages among these various entities. The focus is on practical information that will assist individuals and agencies in making changes that affect the way personnel preparation is implemented. Chapter 21 closes the book with practical ideas, strategies, and checklists related to implementing effective instruction. Included at the end of most chapters is an annotated bibliography of exemplary early intervention instructional resources related to the topic of the chapter, including price and ordering information.

Our hope for this edited volume is to promote and inspire continued innovation and creativity in how personnel are prepared and sustained in their early intervention roles. By focusing on practical, concrete strategies that are provided within a well-conceived theoretical framework and research base, we hope that each reader will take from this book new ideas to try that will prove effective and successful.

ACKNOWLEDGMENTS

We have been privileged to work with talented and generous colleagues (families, faculty, and practitioners) who have shared their ideas, activities, and enthusiasm for personnel preparation with us and with others. Many of these colleagues participated in the regional faculty training institutes funded from 1992 to 1995 by the Office of Special Education Programs in the U.S. Department of Education. These and others have contributed chapters to this book. We thank these colleagues for their generosity, wisdom, and creativity and express our appreciation for their willingness to be partners with us.

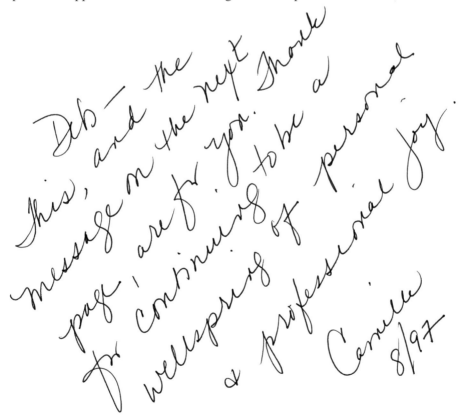

Deb — the message on this, and the next page, are for you. Thank for continuing to be a wellspring of personal & professional joy.

Camille 8/97

To families (including our own) and colleagues
who teach us every day about the value of partnerships and collaboration
in sustaining and promoting lifelong learning

I ECOSYSTEMIC PERSPECTIVES

Looking at the Big Picture

Part I sets the stage for this book by describing the personnel preparation challenges that the field of early intervention faces, with a particular focus on collaboration across agencies, institutions, disciplines, and constituents (e.g., consumers, administrators, direct service providers, faculty, consultants). The 1990s are a period of radical change in how we define the roles and competencies of early intervention stakeholders. It is critical that we analyze how our personnel preparation systems need to be reformed to effectively address the transformations that have occurred in early intervention. Chapter 1 provides a framework and guidelines for the change process. Subsequent chapters in Part I address personnel preparation issues and strategies and models from a systems change perspective at each of the following levels: state, community, and institutions of higher education.

1 ECOLOGICAL PERSPECTIVES ON PERSONNEL PREPARATION

Rationale, Framework, and Guidelines for Change

Pamela J. Winton

Jeanette A. McCollum

When families describe their experiences with early intervention, the presence of competent and caring practitioners often is the key to those experiences being positive and successful. When practitioners describe incentives to working in early intervention, additional instruction and opportunities to be mentored by a more experienced practitioner are top priorities (Pierce & Beutler, 1996). When early intervention administrators describe the challenges they face, one of the biggest is recruiting and retaining qualified practitioners (Hebbeler, 1995). Each of these constituent groups—families, direct service providers, and administrators—places a high value on competent, confident personnel. The story of Janet, a young woman who has just embarked on her career in early intervention, illustrates two major points about the status of early intervention in terms of this shared goal for personnel: 1) the personnel development system needs changing if this goal is to be realized, and 2) making the needed changes will not be simple or easy.

JANET'S STORY
Graduate School
    Janet enrolled in the master's degree program in speech-language pathology at the state university as a 23-year-old. The 2-year program was highly structured during the first year, with required courses in core subjects filling up all 13 semester hours suggested as a reasonable student load. Janet and her 11 classmates developed strong bonds, as they essentially spent most of their time together in class or working on class-related projects. Janet felt lucky that she was able to do her practicum placement at the university's Speech and Hearing Clinic for Children. She was interested in young children and was happy that she would have a chance to develop that interest. Although it was hard to develop a specialization in young children because of all of the required courses, Janet hoped that her practicum placement and her methods courses, which included some

    Portions of this chapter were completed while the first author was funded partially by U.S. Department of Education grants #H024P20002, #H024D50069, #H029K60111, and R307A6004 to the University of North Carolina. The content does not necessarily reflect the position of the U.S. Department of Education, and no official endorsement should be inferred.

early intervention content, would provide her with enough background to find a job working with young children.

Finding a Job

Janet felt very fortunate to have a number of employment possibilities when she graduated from her program. She accepted a Clinical Fellowship Year (CFY) position at a local mental health agency and arranged for a certified speech-language pathologist in the community to provide the required monitoring and supervision. She looked forward to becoming a member of the agency's early intervention team, which was designed to provide community-based services to young children with disabilities and their families. She knew that the agency would have preferred someone with more experience than she had, but because of the shortage of therapists in the community, agency staff were pleased to find a qualified speech-language pathologist to take the position.

Janet knew she had a lot to learn. The team members were all expected to do a variety of tasks: develop and implement individualized family service plans with families and children, coordinate services with other agencies and professionals, provide consultation to child care staff and preschool teachers who might serve children on the team's caseload, and work together in a transdisciplinary method to maximize their flexibility in responding to the large number of families that they served. Janet was relieved to learn that she would be allowed some time and support for staff development. She felt fairly confident of her skills in working individually with children; however, she had very little experience working with families or with other disciplines. In her coursework she had read articles about the importance of family involvement and interdisciplinary collaboration, but she had seen few of these practices in action. Because these ideas made sense to her, she believed she would be open to learning about new ways of practicing.

The First Year

Janet had no idea that her first year in practice would be as difficult as it was. She was not prepared for the gap between the "ivory tower" world of the clinic and courses at the university and the "real world" of community-based intervention. The area in which she had the most self-confidence, working individually with children, was the area in which she was able to spend the least amount of time. There were a number of factors that made it almost impossible to do more than a minimum amount of direct therapy with the children she served. The caseload was large. Although she had a reasonable number of families for whom she had direct responsibility, she found that her colleagues expected her to consult with them on their cases as well. In addition, she was expected to function as a service coordinator with many of the families; thus, she needed to keep abreast of community resources and programs and spend quite a bit of time trying to link the family with these other services. Sometimes weeks went by without her having spent any one-to-one time with some of the children she served.

One of the most frustrating aspects of her situation was her belief that she really wasn't prepared for the tasks that seemed to be the priority for her agency. She worked out elaborate plans for home therapy for parents to implement, but somehow the plans never seemed to get done. She sometimes found herself talking with families about problems that had nothing to do with speech and language and with absolutely no idea where to go with the conversation. Another major issue was that her team members did not seem very receptive to some of her ideas. Sometimes she believed that everyone on the team had a personal agenda; each person seemed to have a different priority and a different focus for intervention efforts. It was hard to get people to see that language and speech were critical aspects of development for every child. When she consulted with child care providers and preschool teachers, she often felt unsure of her role. The teachers seemed to want some ideas about how to provide therapy but never seemed to try what she suggested. They were always asking if she knew of practical strategies for embedding speech and language development activities into ongoing routines, as they had finally accepted that she did not have time for individual therapy with each child on her caseload. The day a preschool teacher said, "Could you spend 20 minutes with this group of six children and demonstrate how you think I can make this language activity work for everyone?" was her lowest point. She realized that she had no idea how to conduct in-class therapy with other children around, yet everyone expected her magically to have skills that were not part of her preservice training. This teacher's request followed on the heels of the mother of one of the children on her caseload accusing her of not providing the intensity of therapy services that her daughter needed. Because of the hectic pace maintained at her agency, there seemed to be no good way to express her frustration to her colleagues. And her clinical fellowship year (CFY) supervisor seemed more interested in observing assessment protocols and reviewing therapy plans than in discussing strategies for successful team-based community service delivery. Janet had always been successful in everything she had done; acknowledging defeat or problems was not easy. One hope she had was the promise, when she was hired, that she would be given support for staff development. She knew that the annual state convention for speech-language pathologists was coming up soon and was encouraged to attend by her supervisor. She was eager to get some continuing education units (CEUs) that she would need to keep her license updated, and the convention would also provide her with that opportunity. Maybe she could find some answers at this conference.

More Instruction

The state convention was a real eye-opener for Janet. Much of the information she heard in presentations was about the importance of interdisciplinary teamwork and professional partnerships. Many of the challenges being described were similar to her own, and she found herself volunteering her perspectives in sessions and realizing that she had learned a huge amount in 8 months. She suddenly found herself in the position of being a "voice of experience." Yet as she reflected on the conference, she realized that when she got back to work she had no concrete plans or ideas for how she could do a better job with families, with consultations with peers, or with understanding the complexities of her own community. She wondered how much longer she could keep "flying by the seat of her pants." She started sounding like the preschool teachers when she asked herself, "But what did I learn that was practical, that I could embed in my daily practices?" She wondered how other professional conventions dealt with early intervention practices. Did her teammates learn things at their professional meetings that were more practical and applicable to their daily practices? She knew that some of the Head Start teachers with whom she consulted had attended workshops on routines-based interventions. This sounded like something that she could have used, but she had not been invited to attend.

Janet also started thinking about how there was never time at work to ask these kinds of questions. When the team met, there was barely time to cope with the immediate crises around individual families. They never had time to reflect on teamwork, philosophy, models of service delivery, or any of the topics that Janet struggled with privately. Did her teammates have their own private struggles with these issues? She thought back to a home visit she had made with Ruth, the special educator on the team. Ruth confided that she was going to resign from her position at the end of the month and work for her husband's contracting company. Her decision, in part, was a financial one and in part was related to feeling "burned out." The new certification requirements established for early interventionists by the state agency would require her to take additional courses. She had decided to invest in accounting and computer courses instead so that she could become the office manager for her husband's growing business. This was a shock to Janet. She considered Ruth to be one of the most experienced interventionists she had ever met. It seemed strange that Ruth could not get certified based on her experience. Now she wished she had spent more time trying to learn from

Ruth. At the state convention one of the participants had talked about a series of workshops on family-centered practices that her entire agency had attended together. From how she described it, it was exactly the kind of experience that Janet believed her agency needed. When she tried to find out more about it, however, it turned out to be a special grant-funded project that had ended the year before. Working with teams and families might be what everyone talked about in glorified terms, but how were the professionals who were doing it making it work, and how were they finding help when they needed it? "No wonder there is so much turnover in this field," thought Janet.

It is clear that Janet will not be able to effectively serve families and children unless she can find consistent, practical support for her continued professional growth that reflects the changes under way in the field. The approaches to early intervention that Janet is encountering in her work and believes she is unprepared to implement are part of a major transformation since the mid-1980s in how recommended practices in early intervention have been defined. One force for reform is the Regular Education Initiative (Goodlad & Lovitt, 1993), through which the inclusion of young children with disabilities in general education settings (e.g., public and private preschools, child care) has become an expectation with significant implications for personnel preparation. Another reform effort relates to an empowerment approach to the provision of services across a broad spectrum of human services (Dunst, Trivette, & Deal, 1988). The goal of this approach is to strengthen families and to promote the development and competence of individuals needing services. In the early childhood community, this reform effort is best known as a family-centered approach to care and intervention (Bowman, 1995; Shelton & Stepanek, 1994). A third initiative is the movement toward service integration (Kagan, Goffin, Golub, & Pritchard, 1995); that is, the need to build community-based systems of support for young children and their families that are coordinated across multiple agencies and disciplines with practitioners working as interdisciplinary teams. A fourth reform effort relates to the emergence of a set of developmentally appropriate practices that are being disseminated (Bredekamp, 1987), debated (Carta, 1994; Mallory & New, 1994), and refined (Johnson & Johnson, 1994; Wolery & Bredekamp, 1994) to develop definitions of quality in early childhood settings.

These reforms have brought about massive changes in the definitions of competent and qualified early childhood/early intervention practitioners (Bowman, 1995; Bredekamp, 1992; Buysse & Wesley, 1993). New roles (e.g., service coordinator, family–professional partner, interdisciplinary team member) and new competencies (e.g., teamwork, communication, consultation, cultural sensitivity) are needed to deliver services, care, and education using new models of service delivery (e.g., inclusion, integrated therapy, transdisciplinary teaming, home visiting, routines-based interventions). These are not simply trends. Support for the reforms is strong. Legislative initiatives (e.g., the Americans with Disabilities Act [ADA] of 1990, PL 101-336; Part H of the Individuals with Disabilities Education Act [IDEA] of 1990, PL 101-476) promote inclusionary, family-centered, interdisciplinary approaches to serving young children with disabilities and their families. To address these changes, states have been required to reconceptualize agency and discipline boundaries and rethink relationships among agencies, disciplines, and consumers (Shonkoff & Meisels, 1990). The challenge has been compounded because early intervention is not the only system undergoing change. Whether it is because of new discoveries, new technologies, new politics, or new policies, interaction with each other and with the world is rapidly changing. It means that changes in early intervention must be considered within the context of the changes taking place within other human services, management, and information systems.

PURPOSE OF THIS BOOK

The reform initiatives have created tremendous pressure on state personnel development systems. State policy makers are beginning to recognize that no matter how progressive their early intervention service delivery systems may be, they will not be effective unless there are competent and qualified personnel to implement them. However, that is exactly what is missing—adequate numbers of competent, qualified professionals to implement quality services and programs. Research has demonstrated that many communities face the problems illustrated in the vignette about Janet. There are not enough qualified, experienced personnel who feel competent and confident in dealing with the complexities of providing early intervention services. Policy research indicates that personnel preparation is the component of early intervention legislation in which states have made the least amount of progress (Harbin, Gallagher, & Lillie, 1991). National Early Childhood Technical Assistance System (NEC*TAS), the agency funded to provide technical assistance to states as they plan and implement early intervention systems, reported that the greatest number of requests for help they received from clients in 1994 was in the area of personnel preparation (National Early Childhood Technical Assistance System, 1994); it was one of the top issues in 1995 as well (National Early Childhood Technical Assistance System, 1995). Eleanor Szanton, Executive Director of the National Center for Clinical Infant Programs, stated, "As funds are beginning to flow to programs for infants and toddlers, the personnel to create and maintain quality services are not in place. THIS IS THE MAJOR CHALLENGE OF THE NEXT DECADE" (Szanton, 1993, p. 29).

The personnel preparation system should be leading and shaping efforts to reform the early intervention system. It should be on the cutting edge of developing innovative practices and disseminating that information to the field. It is expected that an individual who has just completed a preservice program of studies or participated in continuing education will have the most updated knowledge in a particular field. Perhaps because change has happened so quickly, this is not guaranteed. The quality of instruction available for entry-level and existing early interventionists is uneven and unpredictable. Not only is it necessary to consider how to rethink the personnel development system, but it is also necessary to consider what this newly reformed system should look like so that it can better deal with the continued changes that characterize all human services systems. The system must be reformed so that it has the capacity to reform itself continuously in response to ongoing changes.

A primary purpose of this book is to set a course for rethinking how personnel in early intervention are prepared and to provide strategies for making the needed changes. Janet's story shows that simply increasing the number of existing preservice programs and inservice initiatives will not adequately address the challenges. The same kind of reconceptualization of boundaries and relationships that is happening in the early intervention service system must be made in terms of personnel development systems. Many innovative and creative models and strategies have been developed that offer solutions to the challenges faced by Janet and the early intervention community in which she works. Information about these models and strategies is shared throughout this book.

This chapter sets the context for change by providing in-depth discussion of the complex, systemic issues currently facing early intervention personnel preparation and by delineating guidelines for developing and implementing solutions. The information in this chapter includes the following:

- Presentation of an ecological framework for describing the issues
- Description of systems-level needs that are important in effectively communicating and developing solutions to these problems
- Presentation of factors that must be considered when planning systems-level reforms
- Outline of lessons learned from other reform efforts

The discussion in this chapter is based on the following assumptions about personnel preparation:

- Personnel needs are complex and are based on interrelated phenomena that cut across disciplines, agencies, institutions, and bureaucratic levels.
- Solutions to the personnel preparation needs are equally complex and must rely on input from a broad-based and diverse number of sources, including consumers, administrators, direct service providers, and policy makers.
- A comprehensive and innovative plan that includes both long- and short-term solutions to personnel preparation needs and includes linkages among the layers and players of the different relevant systems is critical as we rethink how to adequately prepare early intervention personnel.

AN ECOSYSTEMIC FRAMEWORK

An ecosystemic framework was chosen to organize this discussion because of its ability to describe complex, interrelated phenomena. The ecosystemic framework is based on the circular manner in which parts of a system regulate and affect each other. No part of a system can change without change occurring in all other parts and the system as a whole; problems and solutions related to making improvements and changes are inextricably connected. This framework has been used to explain the development, behaviors, and outcomes of a variety of human phenomena, including families and organizations (Bronfenbrenner, 1976; Darling, 1989; Winton, 1986). It is particularly relevant for examining issues related to early intervention because one of the significant features of early intervention is that it comprises multiple service systems and financial agents (e.g., health, education, mental health, social services, Head Start, consumers, Medicaid, insurance companies, health maintenance organizations, private citizens) who operate at multiple levels (i.e., federal, state, community, agency). The individuals who are employed and served by these agencies represent multiple disciplines, backgrounds, and perspectives. The personnel development systems that support these individuals are equally diverse (e.g., universities; community colleges; professional organizations; employers; local, state, and federal agencies), as shown in Figure 1.1.

An intent of the federal legislation is that these multiple systems and individuals collaborate in their efforts to serve young children. Although the personnel development systems that support their efforts should be integrated as well, this has not happened. As a result, a series of interrelated needs and complicated, unresolved challenges characterizes early intervention personnel preparation. Choosing an ecosystemic model as an underlying framework for this book and this chapter serves as a constant reminder that personnel preparation problems cannot be described or solved in a linear, simplistic, cause-and-effect fashion. A solution to one particular problem may contribute to the development of a new

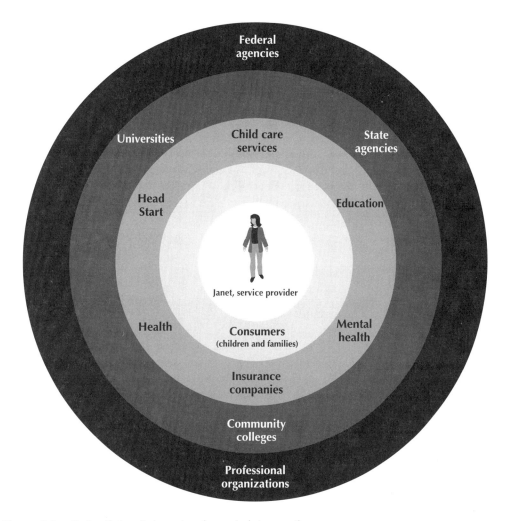

Figure 1.1. Potential collaborators in early intervention.

problem; therefore, the needs and challenges outlined in the following sections of this chapter are described as interconnected phenomena, and the relationships among the systems and individuals involved are explored. This chapter lays the groundwork for moving toward a more focused discussion and description of a variety of issues, models, strategies, and resources, the foci of subsequent chapters of this book.

PERSONNEL PREPARATION NEEDS

Janet's story demonstrates a variety of needs. Each of these is explored in more depth in the following section.

Personnel Shortages

Personnel shortages in early intervention are a serious threat to the vision of a nationwide system of services for young children with disabilities and their families (Hebbeler, 1995). The shortages are particularly acute for allied health professionals (Hebbeler, 1995; Yoder,

Coleman, & Gallagher, 1990). Those who have studied the reasons for shortages have concluded that the problem is multifaceted and involves a complicated web of political and societal factors (Hebbeler, 1995).

To use Janet as an illustration of some of the contributing factors, a typical student in a university program of studies for allied health professionals has a multitude of specialty areas (e.g., gerontology, sports medicine) from which to choose a career direction. Factors that might attract a student to select a certain area, such as interesting coursework and practica experiences or lucrative entry-level job offers, are not guaranteed in early intervention. Research has shown Janet's experience to be typical for a student in allied health; exposure to infancy and family content in coursework and interdisciplinary experiences is minimal (Bailey, Simeonsson, Yoder, & Huntington, 1990; Cochrane, Farley, & Wilhelm, 1990; Crais & Leonard, 1990; Humphry & Link, 1990). It was Janet's personal interest, not a recruitment process, special instruction, or a high salary, that attracted her to her job in the early intervention program. Starting salaries in early intervention are substantially lower than those in many of the competing specialty areas (American Occupational Therapy Association, 1990; Shewan, 1988). University administrators do not anticipate adding additional courses or specializations in early intervention to their programs of study (Gallagher & Staples, 1990). Research also has shown that these factors are unlikely to change (Hebbeler, 1995).

Attrition rates for existing staff are another factor contributing to the shortages. Studies on staff turnover in two states indicated that early intervention personnel, especially consultants, have a higher attrition rate than other occupations (Kontos, n.d.; Palsha, Bailey, Vandiviere, & Munn, 1990). Janet's waning enthusiasm and increasing frustration in her job are signs that she may soon experience the burnout that she observes in her colleague Ruth and that is becoming more common in early intervention (Krahn, Thom, Hale, & Williams, 1995). Ruth's situation also illustrates the dangers of addressing personnel preparation problems and developing solutions in an isolated manner. The certification standards set by the state for early interventionists are designed to ensure that providers are qualified; however, higher standards can drive practitioners from the field unless the certification process is carefully constructed to credit experience and on-the-job training. The problem of shortages must be addressed; however, simple solutions are not evident. More information on solutions to personnel shortages is provided in Chapter 2.

Changes in Early Intervention Roles and Competencies

Part of Janet's frustration in her job is related to her realization that her university program did not adequately prepare her for the realities of the workplace. The model for providing therapy for which she believes she is best prepared (one-to-one direct) and the skill areas in which she believes she is most competent do not match what seems to be desired by her supervisor and colleagues. Janet enjoys working with children, and that is why she chose a pediatric specialization, but her child assessment and intervention courses did not prepare her for the play-based and routines-based intervention approaches that she is expected to implement. Her university program also did not prepare her for interacting with colleagues from other disciplines, families, agencies, and broader systems. As Janet reviewed her program of studies and the syllabi from the courses she took, she saw minimal coverage of the topics that seemed most relevant to her job: understanding family and cultural contexts, understanding the roles of different disciplines, communication/ interaction/collaboration skills, knowledge about different state and community agencies and programs, transitions into and out of programs and systems, and basic knowledge of how human services systems work and change.

Janet's experience is not uncommon. Although the literature is replete with information about changing roles and emerging skills related to early intervention initiatives (Bailey, 1989; Buysse & Wesley, 1993; McCollum & Maude, 1994; McCollum, Rowan, & Thorp, 1994; Thorp & McCollum, 1994; Winton, 1988; Winton & Bailey, 1990), university programs have lagged in offering instructional experiences that match the roles and skills needed (Bailey, Palsha, & Huntington, 1990; Cochrane et al., 1990; Crais & Leonard, 1990; Holditch-Davis, 1989; Humphry & Link, 1990; Kaufman, 1989; Peterson, 1991; Roush, Harrison, Palsha, & Davidson, 1992; Teplin, Kuhn, & Palsha, 1993). It has been argued that the manner in which the various helping professions (e.g., education, social work, nursing, health, family–child studies) are organized into specialized, separate departments in colleges and universities has perpetuated the noncollaborative approaches that characterize community-based programs (Lawson & Hooper-Briar, 1994). It also has been argued that university programs and their faculty are indifferent, unresponsive, and out of touch with the real-world problems faced by communities (Lawson & Hooper-Briar, 1994). The reward system for faculty promotion and salaries in most universities is based on the production of academic publications and scholarly work. The importance of faculty, especially from human services disciplines, being involved in community service is beginning to receive some attention from university administrators; however, the balance is still heavily in favor of traditional scholarly pursuits as the measure of faculty success. Research has shown that faculty are eager for support that would enhance their abilities to effectively teach early intervention content (Winton, Catlett, & Houck, 1996); however, universities are traditionally remiss at providing faculty with this kind of opportunity. Given the important role that colleges and universities play in socializing and shaping future practitioners, changes in the higher education communities are an important aspect of any attempt to address personnel development problems. Two chapters in this book provide specific information on issues facing institutions of higher education and specific solutions being generated within those systems: Chapters 4 and 18.

Lack of a Comprehensive, Coordinated Personnel Development System

Another frustration that Janet is experiencing is related to how she can best learn the skills she needs to survive in her job. Staff development experiences are available but do not adequately address Janet's needs. The ecosystemic framework provides a way of looking at the potential resources available to Janet (see Figure 1.1).

The first concentric circle around Janet is the families she serves. It is notable that families are not mentioned in Janet's story in terms of a formal or structured personnel development role. The field increasingly is recognizing the beneficial outcomes that result from inviting families to serve in formal personnel preparation roles (Bailey, Buysse, Edmondson, & Smith, 1992; Jeppson & Thomas, 1995; Winton & DiVenere, 1995). However, this is a new direction just beginning to be implemented more broadly and is more the exception than the rule. Professional–family partnerships in personnel preparation, including effective models, are the focus of Chapter 17. This topic is also discussed in other chapters throughout the book.

The second concentric circle around Janet includes the mental health agency where she is employed. Janet's supervisor is responsible for providing Janet with ongoing staff development through individual consultation and modeling. Although Janet indicated that individual or group supervision or planning was not available at her agency in a consistent and supportive fashion, this might be an option in some early intervention programs. Janet belatedly recognized that her co-workers might be good resources. Chapter 8 has more information on the topic of mentoring and coaching as approaches to staff development. Also included in the second concentric circle are the other agencies in the community in which Janet's agency is housed. Janet mentioned that the local Head Start agency provided early intervention staff development to its teachers. Janet was not invited; however, there might be other community-based staff development opportunities sponsored by other agencies for which she might be eligible. Nonprofit agencies serving children or providing family support (e.g., United Cerebral Palsy Associations, The Arc) often sponsor community-based staff development open to a cross-section of the community. Chapter 3 provides more information on the important role that community-based instruction plays in personnel preparation. Chapter 20 describes a particular community-based model for staff development that involves families, providers, higher education faculty, and administrators in coinstruction and decision-making roles.

Staff development may also be available to Janet through statewide or regional early intervention conferences sponsored by one of the many state agencies involved in providing or advocating for early intervention services (the third concentric circle). These agencies include health, mental health, education, social service, child and family development divisions within the state government system, and statewide advocacy or parent groups. These various agencies also sometimes print and distribute relevant early intervention information (e.g., legislation, family rights, eligibility requirements). Some state agencies are taking innovative and more personalized approaches to staff development (e.g., McCollum & Yates, 1994; Wischnowski, Yates, & McCollum, 1995). Chapter 2 provides information on some of these strategies. In addition, some state agencies and universities are exploring ways that distance education strategies can be used to reach broader groups of participants with information on early intervention topics. Chapter 19 provides more information on distance education issues and strategies.

The fourth concentric circle, federal agencies and professional organizations, is well represented in Janet's professional development. The American Speech-Language-Hearing Association (ASHA) is the professional organization to which Janet belongs. Not only does she attend the state convention that the organization sponsors, but she also subscribes to the professional journal, and it is ASHA's credentialing and licensing requirements that most likely will influence some of the staff development activities that Janet seeks. The ASHA requirement for a CFY also is the reason for her continued supervision by a practicing speech-language pathologist at the community level.

As this description illustrates, a variety of public (e.g., Head Start, mental health, public school, Parent Training and Information centers) or private nonprofit (e.g., The Arc, United Cerebal Palsy Associations) federal/state/community agencies, universities, community and technical colleges, and professional organizations have personnel preparation responsibilities, resources, and authority. These various groups and individuals have different levels and types of personnel preparation responsibilities, including developing standards and competencies; developing policies; monitoring progress; providing funding for innovative personnel preparation models; designing and implementing programs of study, courses, conferences, and workshops; developing instructional materials; and supervising students and employees. The extent to which Janet continues to be effectively supported in her profession as she struggles with the ongoing, daily challenges of serving children and families depends on these various people and organizations working in a consistent and integrated fashion.

In Janet's case, the system is not fully "in sync." Janet's university experience has not supported the development of skills commensurate with those being promoted in the professional literature or at professional conferences. Her two supervisors are supporting and encouraging different approaches to service delivery—one focusing on forms and protocols and the other emphasizing family and interdisciplinary collaboration. The teachers and parents provide a somewhat different but also inconsistent set of demands on Janet's expertise and approach to service delivery. The teachers have adopted the philosophy of integrating therapy into the classroom routine, which is the one promoted by Janet's agency. However, some of the parents want intensive, one-to-one direct therapy. Opportunities for structured interactions and problem solving around the challenges of delivering early intervention services that involve all of the players (e.g., families, teachers, child care providers, administrators, therapists) and systems (e.g., schools, child care, private preschools, health, mental health) are notably absent. Each discipline and each agency seems to have its own traditions and approaches to staff development, with little connection among them.

Limited Staff Development Options

The limited options for staff development available to Janet in the vignette reflect what is typical in the field. Despite the literature refuting their effectiveness, one-shot, discipline-specific workshops continue to be the norm for what state agencies, professional organizations, and local communities provide for ongoing staff development (Goldenberg & Gallimore, 1991; Wood & Thompson, 1980). An expectation of early interventionists is that they should be able to constantly adjust and refine their practices based on the needs, backgrounds, priorities, and cultures of each individual family. This suggests the ability to spontaneously evaluate changing situations and events and engage in creative problem solving in collaboration with others around those events. These are complex skills that require ongoing support and opportunities for professional growth. It is unrealistic to think that one-shot workshops adequately address these needs. Complex abilities require more complex instruction. There is a body of literature on adult learning (Brookfield, 1993; Knowles, 1980; Moore, 1988; Wood & Thompson, 1980) that provides guidance on the kinds of staff development opportunities that are most effective for practitioners. This research asserts that instructional activities should be directly relevant to a practice context with demonstrations and models provided of the skills being taught; instructional activities should be varied and responsive to different styles of learning; each participant should develop a specific plan of action for using the information provided as part of the learning experience; and ongoing support, monitoring, feedback, and technical assistance should be provided to participants. The suggestion that participant groups should be diverse and include families, administrators, and providers across multiple disciplines also has implications for effective instructional strategies. It suggests that strategies be used that appeal to a mixed audience of learners who represent differences in educational background, discipline, learning style, and perspective. This challenges traditional approaches and options for addressing personnel preparation needs. Information on adult learning strategies and innovative approaches for engaging diverse audiences is provided in Chapter 5 (with an emphasis on theoretical frameworks) and in Chapter 21 (with an emphasis on practical strategies and applications). Follow-up strategies for providing ongoing support are described in Chapter 7.

Problems Related to Defining and Evaluating Quality

Issues and questions related to quality pervade discussions and consideration of personnel preparation. A question that has received much attention relates to the definition of a "qualified" service provider. Policy makers recognized the importance of addressing this question and made establishing personnel standards one of the required components of each state's plan for implementing early intervention legislation. Most states have taken the approach of requiring that professionals meet the highest standards of their respective disciplines. In some states, special infancy or early childhood certification standards have been adopted and competencies identified that must be mastered to receive certification (see Chapter 2 for a more thorough discussion of this topic). However, developing standards and identifying competencies do not automatically guarantee that personnel are qualified and that quality programs are in place. There are additional challenges that states must address.

One challenge is getting universities, colleges, and community colleges to use the competencies as guidelines for their programs. Janet met the highest standard for her discipline; however, she did not receive specialized instruction in working with infants, families, or other disciplines as part of her program of studies. A second challenge for states that create specialized certificates based on newly defined competencies is how to provide staff development to existing personnel who may or may not possess the new competencies that have been defined. The approach often taken is a series of statewide or regional workshops in early intervention content. However, these approaches are often underfunded and poorly evaluated. Given the extent to which many of the early intervention competencies are related to process skills (e.g., communication, consultation, collaboration) and discretionary behavior that is based on clinical judgment (e.g., individualized, culturally sensitive assessment and planning), providing meaningful staff development through workshop formats is an inadequate approach.

The other major quality issue is how to define quality personnel development activities that are consistent with research on adult learning and reform efforts and how to evaluate the extent to which personnel preparation efforts are effective. Often the "means" related to personnel preparation (i.e., conducting a certain number of workshops of courses attended by a certain number of people who received certification credits or graduated from accredited programs as a result) becomes confused with the "end." That is, we assume that because these events happened, we accomplished some kind of meaningful outcome. In reality, we do not know if we have reached the ultimate goal of personnel preparation—improving the quality of the services and supports available to families. Policy makers and funding agencies increasingly ask about the outcomes that result from money spent on personnel development. They want to know why serious shortages and issues of quality persist. They want evaluation data that will provide accurate information about effective models of personnel development so that future efforts can be more effective and efficient, but these kinds of data are scarce. Evaluation is one of the biggest challenges faced in reconceptualizing how to define "quality" in service provision and what that means in terms of defining "quality" in personnel preparation. Questions that should be asked in that regard include the following:

- Was the instruction consistent with research on effective teaching practices?
- Was the information conveyed and skills taught applied by trainees in the workplace?
- Were services and supports for children and families improved on a short-term and long-term basis as a result?
- Were consumers representing diverse perspectives included in evaluating the quality of programs and instruction?
- Was the state monitoring system supportive of and synchronized with the skills and practices being promoted and taught?

- Were responsibilities for personnel preparation efforts (i.e., financial, logistical, human) clearly defined?
- How was evaluation information shared? With whom? For what purposes? Was it used to inform and make changes in instructional approaches?
- Was it permissible to talk about personnel preparation failures? About shortcomings?

These questions imply that evaluation efforts must be longitudinal and must look at processes as well as products. To help individuals and agencies involved in personnel preparation consider questions such as these, quality indicators related to preservice and inservice instruction (Winton, 1994) have been developed and are described in Chapter 21. Chapter 6 provides more information on needs assessment and evaluation issues and strategies.

FACTORS RELATED TO REFORM EFFORTS

Four critical elements have been identified in the literature that must be considered in creating collaborative efforts in human services systems (Blank & Lombardi, 1991; Flynn & Harbin, 1987; Harbin & McNulty, 1990; Melaville & Blank, 1991). These same factors are relevant in transforming personnel preparation systems into collaborative, effective systems. The four factors are climate, policies, resources, and problem-solving structures (see Figure 1.2).

Climate

The social and political climate at the federal, state, and community levels is a factor likely to influence changes or reforms in personnel preparation efforts. States have been slow to address the personnel preparation component of the early intervention legislation; however, interest and momentum to attend to personnel preparation have increased as policy makers and planners realize the magnitude of the problem (Safer & Hamilton, 1993). But shifts in climate experienced by one group, such as policy makers, are not necessarily shared by all groups involved in personnel preparation. Professional traditions, organizational rigidities, and disciplinary loyalties are often entrenched and create a pervasive climate that supports the status quo. University structures have been described as some of the hardest to change (Eash & Lane, 1985; Gallagher & Staples, 1990). In his book on educational reform, Fullan (1993) stated that the educational institutions responsible for ensuring that practitioners possess updated, state-of-the-art knowledge and skills are themselves so hierarchical and rigid that they are more likely to perpetuate the status quo than to provide leadership in making reforms. Climate influences policies; the next section focuses on how policies affect reforms in personnel development systems.

Policies

Policies are "those sets of governing principles which have been established within and among agencies" (Flynn & Harbin, 1987, p. 38), including laws, regulations, standards, licensing, certification, and interagency agreements. Policies have a significant impact on if and how agencies, disciplines, and people plan, fund, and implement personnel preparation. For instance, personnel preparation activities are often funded through categorical funding streams that originate in separate policy initiatives at the federal level (e.g., the Department of Health and Human Services has money to train nurses, the Department of Education has money to train teachers). Each professional organization also has a set of policies governing its own license and certification systems and funding of its own discipline-specific personnel preparation initiatives. The result is that personnel preparation looks like "parallel play." In a single state there might be several different workshops on

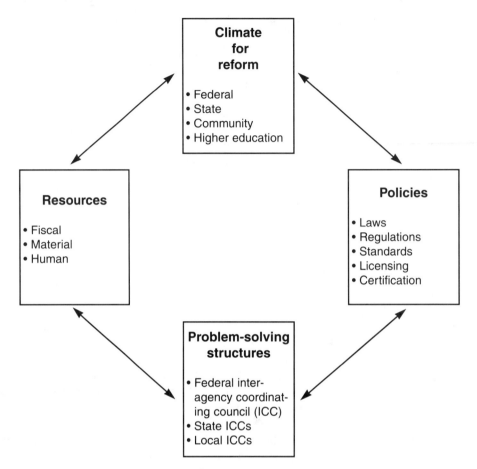

Figure 1.2. Critical elements in creating collaborative efforts.

the same topic (e.g., child assessment, service coordination), but the workshops might be sponsored by different agencies for different disciplines and may promote conflicting philosophies and contradictory approaches to the one topic. The same parallel play characterizes personnel preparation activities in institutions of higher education. A child assessment course might be offered in several different departments or divisions (e.g., nursing, psychology, special education) without any attempt to have students come together for cross-disciplinary discussions or activities. There are few policies that facilitate or provide tangible incentives for cross-agency, cross-discipline instruction.

Federal policy makers recognized this problem and tried to address it, partly by mandating that a Comprehensive System of Personnel Development (CSPD) be a required component of the state plan that each state had to submit to receive early intervention funding from the U.S. Department of Education. The CSPD was seen as a mechanism for ensuring that staff development activities in each state would be coordinated across agencies, disciplines, and institutions and would cover a variety of activities, including data collection, recruitment, preservice, inservice, technical assistance, and continuing education. However, research has indicated that most of the individuals with the power, authority, and resources to provide early intervention instruction do not even know that a CSPD plan exists in their state (Winton, 1995; Winton et al., 1996). This is an example of how policies can be ineffective if there is not a responsive climate to ensure that the spirit as well as the letter of the law is met.

Resources

The availability, nature, and management of existing human and material resources have a significant impact on reforms and improvements to personnel preparation efforts. The evidence that states have not made progress on this component of early intervention legislative mandates suggests that adequate amounts of early intervention funds have not been earmarked for personnel preparation. Chief state school officers and school superintendents in 50 states were surveyed on the barriers to providing meaningful staff development to teachers; they indicated that inadequate financial support was one of the biggest barriers (Thompson & Cooley, 1986). Policy studies suggested that finances are a barrier to staff development in early intervention as well (Gallagher, 1993). However, as Peterson (1991) pointed out, shrinking resources across all agencies could have the beneficial effect of forcing agencies to collaborate and share their scarce resources. Anecdotally, that is what some state agency personnel in North Carolina have reported as happening. The Department of Public Instruction (preschool lead agency) and the Department of Human Resources (early intervention lead agency) have sometimes blended dollars to fund joint staff development for preschool and early intervention personnel because they did not have the money to implement separate initiatives. Rather than simply advocating for more personnel preparation money, perhaps the resources should be spent in planning and implementing events that cut across agencies.

This recommendation also should apply to instructional resources and materials. Since the 1970s, a wealth of instructional materials and products has been developed under the auspices of federal grant programs, such as the Early Education Program for Children with Disabilities (EEPCD) of the Department of Education. However, many of these materials have not been widely disseminated. What typically happens is that by the time products get developed, the project has ended, and there is little time to disseminate information about the products. Thus, information about the availability of these products does not reach the university faculty and state and local staff development consultants who could use them. One of the activities of the Southeastern Institute for Faculty Training (SIFT), a regional institute funded through EEPCD (Winton, 1996), was to identify interdisciplinary, family-centered instructional resources, many of which had been developed by small grant-funded projects, and to disseminate information to faculty about them through a resource guide (Catlett & Winton, 1996) and through demonstrations and hands-on exposure. Several findings from this activity are notable (Winton, 1995). First, most faculty were unfamiliar with these materials. Second, they were excited about finding them and started using them as resources in their teaching. Third, many states have existing resource libraries, and some of these materials were in these libraries; however, faculty either did not realize this resource was available or found it hard to evaluate the materials without an opportunity to directly examine them or see them demonstrated. Regional and statewide resource libraries of various kinds exist throughout the country. Some states use early intervention money to fund resource libraries; the Office of Educational Reform and Innovation funds 10 regional educational laboratories that provide technical assistance and instructional resources to states; and each state has a Parent Training and Information Center with instructional resources. These various centers are not necessarily coordinated in their efforts to identify and publicize resources; therefore, they may be underused by consumers. The management of resources may be of equal importance to securing additional resources.

The other kind of resource that must be considered is the human one. The importance of personal relationships, personal commitment, and leadership is reported across a number of studies and projects related to making reforms that increase collaboration across systems (Blank & Lombardi, 1991; Harbin & McNulty, 1990; Harrison, Lynch, Rosander, & Borton, 1990). Research collected as part of the evaluation of SIFT indicated that support from colleagues was a major factor that helped faculty accomplish the goals they identified for themselves for improving their own personnel preparation practices (Winton, 1995). This suggests that relationships need to be nurtured and the human resources involved in personnel preparation activities need to be expanded. As one state agency official in charge of early intervention personnel development said, "Money is not my biggest problem. I need people who are knowledgeable about early intervention content and about our early intervention system, knowledgeable about good training practices, and willing to travel around the state providing technical assistance and training to providers" (G. Perotta, personal communication, February, 1993). Identifying and supporting individuals (e.g., faculty, providers, consumers) who are willing to help plan and implement staff development activities is a need for most states. Creating an infrastructure that can support their efforts is another need. Some states that participated in SIFT have created regional technical assistance teams, consisting of providers, families, and college and university faculty (Winton, 1995). These "teams" can be pulled together to respond to regional needs for staff development; the team members are reimbursed for their involvement by the state agency responsible for early intervention. Research has shown that families can be powerful and effective in personnel preparation roles when provided with support. Exploring ways to support family involvement, especially from families from diverse backgrounds, should be pursued (see Chapter 17 for more information on family participation in personnel development). In addition, nontraditional approaches to personnel development (e.g., coaching as described in Chapter 8, use of new technologies such as teleconferencing and interactive networking as described in Chapter 19) need to be explored as strategies for coping with shortages of human resources.

Problem-Solving Structures

The presence of structures that provide opportunities for agency, discipline, and constituent representatives to develop solutions to personnel preparation challenges is an important component of change. These structures are especially important because of the continuation of such problems as the financing of personnel development efforts, collaboration across agencies, personnel shortages, and the ongoing changes in all human services systems.

At the federal, state, and local levels, interagency coordinating councils (ICCs) have been mandated through the early intervention legislation to provide advice to policy makers on policy and implementation issues. The extent to which the ICCs have effectively addressed personnel preparation issues varies tremendously. In some states, personnel preparation or CSPD subcommittees of the ICCs have effectively addressed personnel needs through activities such as conducting needs assessments, securing federal grant money to address state personnel needs, providing a means for collaborative problem solving across agencies around personnel issues, and identifying competencies and standards. Some of the difficulties encountered by such groups is that their budgets are nonexistent or limited, and they depend heavily on volunteer time from providers, faculty, and families, who may live in geographically scattered parts of the state.

External projects have demonstrated that they can serve as a catalyst for problem solving and positive changes in personnel preparation efforts. For example, data collected by SIFT in 15 states demonstrated the following positive changes from the perspectives of state leaders who participated in problem solving that led to further staff development opportunities for individuals from their states: increased collaboration in personnel preparation activities across agencies, greater linkages between preservice and inservice efforts, greater involvement on the part of families in personnel development efforts, more family-centered inservice instruction, more interdisciplinary instruction at preservice and inservice levels, more instruction linked with certification, and increased knowledge on the part of key stakeholders of the CSPD (Winton, 1995). However, the long-term effectiveness of external efforts such as this one has not been established. The complexities of reforming personnel preparation systems require an ongoing, concerted effort that challenges the capacities of time-limited grants. The ultimate success for any external reform effort is state or local adoption and maintenance of the ideas and practices (see Chapter 3, which highlights the importance of change efforts being firmly rooted in the community context). A study by Rooney (1995) suggests that institutionalization of reforms should not be taken for granted. She conducted a follow-up study of 10 federally funded, interdisciplinary preservice preparation programs to determine the extent to which the interdisciplinary aspects would continue after the end of the funding period. Her results were discouraging: Eight of 10 programs reported that the interdisciplinary focus would not continue.

LESSONS LEARNED FROM OTHER REFORM EFFORTS

Other reform efforts involving human services and education systems (Bruner, 1991; Fullan, 1993; Havelock & Havelock, 1973; Kagan et al., 1995; Melaville & Blank, 1991; Peck, Odom, & Bricker, 1993; View & Amos, 1994) provide practical information that can be generalized to the efforts to rethink early intervention personnel preparation. These lessons have shaped the assumptions stated at the beginning of this chapter. The following is a brief summary of these lessons (Chapter 3 provides excellent detail about community-based approaches to reforms that illustrate these lessons):

- Integrate reform efforts into existing ecology.
- Involve all relevant stakeholders.
- Provide stakeholders with new information.
- Identify specific goals and action plans for making changes.
- Provide ongoing monitoring, evaluation, and follow-up.

Integrate Reform Efforts into Existing Ecology

Reform efforts and the reformed personnel development systems must be constructed with a sensitivity to the unique needs, priorities, traditions, and resources of particular localities (Bruner, 1991; Fullan, 1993; Peck et al., 1993). This implies that community, higher education, and state problem-solving structures must be in place and adequately supported to define local need and local solutions related to the broader personnel issues outlined in this chapter. The following are some of the questions that these groups might address on a local level:

- What are the specific personnel needs in our community, and what are the resources and strategies for meeting these needs?
- What should early interventionists in our community need to know and be able to do to effectively serve children and families?

- What are all of the ways that early interventionists can develop this knowledge and these skills?
- What needs to happen to create these learning opportunities?

Involve All Relevant Stakeholders

Another lesson learned is that a combination of "top-down" and "bottom-up" approaches to reform efforts works best (Fullan, 1993; Powers, 1988; Trohanis, 1994). Support from the highest administrative levels is important so that individuals believe it is in their best interest to participate in staff development and reform efforts that will ultimately result in improvements for children and families. Because the status quo is the natural state, active strategies (e.g., promotions, tenure, release time, CEUs) must be used to promote and reward change. However, it is not enough to have high-level administrators support change. All constituent groups, including families, direct service providers, consultants, and administrators, need to be involved in planning, developing, and participating in staff development related to making changes. The needs, strengths, and resources of individual learners as well as those of systems-level personnel must be addressed in an interrelated and simultaneous fashion (see Chapter 20 for a description of a collaborative model for instruction that includes these constituent groups).

Provide Stakeholders with New Information

Much has been written about the gap between research information and typical practices (c.f., Gersten, Vaughn, Deshler, & Schiller, 1995). Some blame the research community for failing to provide practical strategies for improving services (Gersten et al., 1995; Lovitt & Higgins, 1995; Malouf & Schiller, 1995), whereas others blame ineffective personnel development systems for failing to adequately disseminate new information (Goldenberg & Gallimore, 1991; Guskey, 1986; Smylie, 1988). A wealth of information exists on models of staff development, on new technologies for disseminating information, on instructional strategies that reflect principles of adult learning, and on innovative instructional resources; getting this information to those who need it is a critical part of the change process. The information must be imparted in ways that invite application to local issues. Solutions to personnel preparation issues developed in one community or in one university or community college cannot be transported in a wholesale fashion to other communities, but this information can generate variations that might be effective.

A second point is the importance of innovative processes for delivering the content. The importance of the instruction being delivered in a manner that models family-centered practices and behaviors has been stated in previous publications (Winton, 1990). Training strategies that mirror the family-centered practices being promoted include the following: 1) providing participants with choices that enable them to select experiences based on their perceived needs; 2) respecting individual differences in learning styles and preferences; 3) appreciating and building on existing knowledge, skills, and experiences; 4) providing opportunities for participants to learn from and build relationships with one another; and 5) including families as planners, instructors, and evaluators of instructional initiatives. Chapters 9–16 provide more information on considerations and strategies for designing and implementing effective instruction using innovative strategies to address key early intervention content areas.

Identify Specific Goals and Action Plans for Making Changes

A significant challenge in making reforms is translating broadly stated goals for change into measurable outcomes that can be achieved and monitored. Focusing on the gap between current status and ideal status and developing concrete goals and strategies for closing this gap have been identified as important components of making changes (Havelock & Havelock, 1973; Powers, 1988; Winton, 1990). In addition, it is important to make short-term, achievable goals so that participants will be motivated by their successes (Winton, 1990). Again, this suggests ongoing activities and efforts with new goals being added as accomplishments are made.

Provide Ongoing Monitoring, Evaluation, and Follow-Up

Making changes in personnel systems that ultimately benefit children and families is a slow process. Policies, resources, and other factors outside the control of those engineering the change affect structured attempts to bring about change. "Expect the unexpected" is the motto for those attempting to implement a plan for making reforms. Therefore, evaluation and monitoring efforts must be creative and multifaceted. Data must be collected from the systems being changed in an ongoing fashion so that the circuitous passages and derailments toward reform can be documented and used to modify strategies and revise directions. Learning from mistakes as well as successes is critical. We must assess the impact of our actions at all levels and with all constituent groups and must also examine what changes remain or become institutionalized in existing structures and which changes are transitory and ephemeral (i.e., dependent on a short-term grant or one person's support). This requires an intensive, longitudinal effort. Chapters 6 and 7 provide information on evaluation and follow-up strategies.

CONCLUSION

Perhaps the ultimate goal in rethinking personnel development systems is to create a flexible "learning organization," in Fullan's words (1993), capable and expert at dealing with change as a normal part of the way it works and how it prepares others. Not only should personnel development systems be flexible learning organizations, but also individuals must be prepared who are lifelong learners, capable of dealing with unpredictable changes. The solutions to the problems and challenges outlined in this chapter remain to be developed; because the challenges and needs continue to evolve and change, this must be an ongoing activity. A spirit of inquiry needs to be promoted in individuals and the systems that support those individuals; this spirit must undergird all personnel preparation efforts.

REFERENCES

American Occupational Therapy Association. (1990). *Member data survey.* Rockville, MD: Author.

Americans with Disabilities Act (ADA) of 1990, PL 101-336, 42 U.S.C. § 12101 *et seq.*

Bailey, D., Buysse, V., Edmondson, B., & Smith, T. (1992). Creating family-centered services in early intervention: Perceptions of professionals in four states. *Exceptional Children, 58*(4), 298–309.

Bailey, D., Palsha, S., & Huntington, G. (1990). Preservice preparation of special educators to serve infants with handicaps and their families: Current status and training needs. *Journal of Early Intervention, 14*(1), 43–54.

Bailey, D., Simeonsson, R., Yoder, D., & Huntington, G. (1990). Preparing professionals to serve infants and toddlers with handicaps and their families: An integrative analysis across eight disciplines. *Exceptional Children, 57*(1), 26–35.

Bailey, D.B., Jr. (1989). Issues and directions in preparing professionals to work with young handicapped children and their families. In J.J. Gallagher, P.L. Trohanis, & R.M. Clifford (Eds.), *Policy implementation and PL 99-457: Planning for young children with special needs* (pp. 97–132). Baltimore: Paul H. Brookes Publishing Co.

Blank, M., & Lombardi, J. (1991). *Towards improved services for children and families: Forging new relationships through collaboration.* White Plains, NY: A.L. Mailman Family Foundation.

Bowman, B.T. (1995). The professional development challenge: Supporting young children and families. *Young Children, 51*(1), 30–34.

Bredekamp, S. (Ed.). (1987). *Developmentally appropriate practice in early childhood programs serving children from birth through age 8.* Washington, DC: National Association for the Education of Young Children.

Bredekamp, S. (1992, September). The early childhood profession coming together. *Young Children, 36*–39.

Bronfenbrenner, U. (1976). The experimental ecology of education. *Educational Researcher, 5,* 5–15.

Brookfield, S.D. (1993). *Developing critical thinkers: Challenging adults to explore alternative ways of thinking and acting.* San Francisco: Jossey-Bass.

Bruner, C. (1991). *Thinking collaboratively.* Washington, DC: Education and Human Services Consortium.

Buysse, V., & Wesley, P. (1993). The identity crisis in early childhood special education: A call for professional role clarification. *Topics in Early Childhood Special Education, 13*(4), 418–429.

Carta, J.J. (1994). Developmentally appropriate practices: Shifting the emphasis to individual appropriateness. *Journal of Early Intervention, 18*(4), 342–348.

Catlett, C., & Winton, P. (1996). *Resource guide: Selected early intervention training materials* (5th ed.). Chapel Hill: University of North Carolina at Chapel Hill, Southeastern Institute for Faculty Training, Frank Porter Graham Child Development Center.

Cochrane, C.G., Farley, R., & Wilhelm, I.J. (1990). Preparation of physical therapists to work with handicapped infants and their families: Current status and training needs. *Physical Therapy, 70*(6), 372–380.

Crais, E.R., & Leonard, C.R. (1990). P.L. 99-457: Are speech-language pathologists prepared for the challenge? *Asha, 32,* 57–61.

Darling, R.B. (1989). Applying a systems approach to the assessment of family needs: The individualized family service plan and beyond. In M. Seligman & R.B. Darling (Eds.), *Ordinary families, special children: A systems approach to childhood disability.* New York: Guilford Press.

Dunst, C.J., Trivette, C.M., & Deal, A.G. (1988). *Enabling and empowering families: Principles and guidelines for practice.* Cambridge, MA: Brookline Books.

Eash, M.J., & Lane, J.J. (1985). Evaluation of a model for faculty development: Implications for educational policy. *Educational Evaluation and Policy Analysis, 7*(2), 127–138.

Education of the Handicapped Act Amendments of 1986, PL 99-457, 20 U.S.C. § 1400 *et seq.*

Flynn, C., & Harbin, G. (1987). Evaluating interagency coordination efforts using a multidimensional, interactional, developmental paradigm. *Remedial and Special Education, 8*(3), 35–44.

Fullan, M. (1993). *Change forces: Probing the depths of educational reform.* New York: The Falmer Press.

Gallagher, J. (1993). *The study of federal policy implementation: Infants/toddlers with disabilities and their families.* Chapel Hill: University of North Carolina at Chapel Hill, Carolina Policy Studies Program, Frank Porter Graham Child Development Center.

Gallagher, J., & Staples, A. (1990). *Available and potential resources on personnel preparation in special education: Deans survey.* Chapel Hill: University of North Carolina at Chapel Hill, Carolina Policy Studies Program, Frank Porter Graham Child Development Center.

Gersten, R., Vaughn, S., Deshler, D., & Schiller, E. (1995). *What we know (and still don't know) about utilizing research findings to improve practice: Implications for special education.* Presentation at Research Project Directors' Meeting, Office of Special Education Programs, U.S. Department of Education, Washington, DC.

Goldenberg, C., & Gallimore, R. (1991). Changing teaching takes more than a one-shot workshop. *Educational Leadership, 49*(3), 69–72.

Goodlad, J.I., & Lovitt, T.C. (1993). *Integrating general and special education.* Columbus, OH: Macmillan.

Guskey, T. (1986). Staff development and the process of teacher change. *Educational Researcher, 15*(5), 5–12.

Harbin, G., Gallagher, J., & Lillie, D. (1991). *Status of states' progress in implementing Part H of IDEA: Report #3.* Chapel Hill: University of North Carolina at Chapel Hill, Carolina Policy Studies Program, Frank Porter Graham Child Development Center.

Harbin, G., & McNulty, B. (1990). Policy implementation: Perspectives on service coordination and interagency cooperation. In S. Meisels & J. Shonkoff (Eds.), *Handbook of early intervention.* Cambridge, England: Cambridge University Press.

Harrison, P.J., Lynch, E.W., Rosander, K., & Borton, W. (1990). Determining success in interagency collaboration: An evaluation of processes and behaviors. *Infants and Young Children, 3*(1), 69–78.

Havelock, R.C., & Havelock, M.C. (1973). *Training for change agents.* Ann Arbor: University of Michigan.

Hebbeler, K. (1995). *Shortages in professions working with young children with disabilities and their families.* Chapel Hill: University of North Carolina at Chapel Hill, National Early Childhood Technical Assistance System, Frank Porter Graham Child Development Center.

Holditch-Davis, D. (1989). In light of Public Law 99-457: How well are novice nurses prepared? *In Touch, 7*(2), 5.

Humphry, R., & Link, S. (1990). Entry level preparation of occupational therapists to work in early intervention programs. *American Journal of Occupational Therapy, 44*(9), 828–833.

Individuals with Disabilities Education Act (IDEA) of 1990, PL 101-476, 20 U.S.C. § 1400 *et seq.*

Jeppson, E.S., & Thomas, J. (1995). *Essential allies: Families as advisors.* Bethesda, MD: Institute for Family-Centered Care.

Johnson, J.E., & Johnson, K.M. (1994). The applicability of developmentally appropriate practice for children with diverse abilities. *Journal of Early Intervention, 17*(1), 73–79.

Kagan, S., Goffin, S.G., Golub, S.A., & Pritchard, E. (1995). *Toward systemic reform: Service integration for young children and their families.* Falls Church, VA: National Center for Service Integration.

Kaufman, M. (1989). Are dietitians prepared to work with handicapped infants? P.L. 99-457 offers new opportunities. *Journal of American Dietetic Association, 89*(11), 1602–1605.

Knowles, M.S. (1980). *The modern practice of adult education.* Chicago: Association Press, Follett Publishing Co.

Kontos, S. (n.d.). *A profile of Indiana's early intervention workforce.* West Lafayette, IN: Purdue University.

Krahn, G., Thom, V., Hale, B., & Williams, K. (1995). Running on empty: A look at burnout in early intervention professionals. *Infants and Young Children, 7*(4), 1–11.

Lawson, H., & Hooper-Briar, K. (1994). *Expanding partnerships: Involving colleges and universities in interprofessional collaboration and service integration.* Oxford, OH: Danforth Foundation.

Lovitt, T.C., & Higgins, A.K. (1995). The gap: Research into practice. *Teaching Exceptional Children, 28*(2), 64–68.

Mallory, B.L., & New, R.S. (Eds.). (1994). *Diversity and developmentally appropriate practices.* New York: Teachers College Press.

Malouf, D.B., & Schiller, E.P. (1995). Practice and research in special education. *Exceptional Children, 61*(5), 414–424.

McCollum, J.A., & Maude, S.P. (1994). Early childhood special educators as early interventionists: Issues and emerging practice in personnel preparation. In P.L. Stafford, B. Spodek, & O.N. Saracho (Eds.), *Yearbook in early childhood education: Early childhood special education* (Vol. 5). New York: Teachers College Press.

McCollum, J.A., Rowan, L.E., & Thorp, E.K. (1994). Philosophy as framework in early intervention personnel training. *Journal for Early Intervention, 18*(2), 216–226.

McCollum, J.A., & Yates, T.J. (1994). Technical assistance for meeting early intervention personnel standards: Statewide processes based on peer review. *Topics in Early Childhood Special Education, 14*(3), 295–310.

Melaville, A.I., & Blank, M.J. (1991). *What it takes: Structuring interagency partnerships to connect children and families with comprehensive services.* Washington, DC: Education and Human Services Consortium.

Moore, J. (1988). Guidelines concerning adult learning. *Journal of Staff Development, 9*(3), 1–5.

National Early Childhood Technical Assistance System. (1994). *Annual report.* Chapel Hill, NC: Author.

National Early Childhood Technical Assistance System. (1995). *Part H updates.* Chapel Hill, NC: Author.

Palsha, S., Bailey, D., Vandiviere, P., & Munn, D. (1990). A study of employee stability and turnover in home-based early intervention. *Journal of Early Intervention, 14*(4), 342–351.

Peck, C.A., Odom, S.L., & Bricker, D.D. (Eds.). (1993). *Integrating young children with disabilities into community programs: Ecological perspectives on research and implementation.* Baltimore: Paul H. Brookes Publishing Co.

Peterson, N.L. (1991). Interagency collaboration under Part H: The key to comprehensive, multi-disciplinary, coordinated infant/toddler intervention services. *Journal of Early Intervention, 15*(1), 89–105.

Pierce, P., & Beutler, M. (1996). *Specialized therapies: Why they do or do not work with children ages birth-to-five.* Raleigh: North Carolina Department of Human Resources.

Powers, M.D. (Ed.). (1988). *Expanding systems of service delivery for persons with developmental disabilities.* Baltimore: Paul H. Brookes Publishing Co.

Rooney, R. (1995, May). *Implementation of preservice interdisciplinary personnel preparation programs*. Paper presented at the third annual Comprehensive System of Personnel Development (CSPD) conference, Arlington, VA.

Roush, J., Harrison, M., Palsha, S., & Davidson, D. (1992). Educational preparation of early intervention specialists: A national survey. *American Annals of the Deaf, 37*(5), 425–430.

Safer, N.D., & Hamilton, J.L. (1993). Legislative context for early intervention services. In W. Brown, S. Thurman, & L. Pearl (Eds.), *Family-centered early intervention with infants and toddlers: Innovative cross-disciplinary approaches* (pp. 1–19). Baltimore: Paul H. Brookes Publishing Co.

Shelton, T.L., & Stepanek, J.S. (1994). *Family-centered care for children needing specialized health and developmental services* (3rd ed.). Bethesda, MD: Association for the Care of Children's Health.

Shewan, C.M. (1988). *ASHA work force study final report*. Rockville, MD: American Speech-Language-Hearing Association.

Shonkoff, J., & Meisels, S. (1990). Early childhood intervention: The evolution of a concept. In J. Shonkoff & S. Meisels (Eds.), *Handbook of early intervention* (pp. 3–31). Cambridge, England: Cambridge University Press.

Smylie, M.A. (1988). The enhancement function of staff development: Organizational and psychological antecedents to individual teacher change. *American Educational Research Journal, 25*(1), 1–30.

Szanton, E. (1993). Zero to Three notes. *Zero to Three, 14*(2), 29.

Teplin, S., Kuhn, T., & Palsha, S. (1993). Preparing residents for P.L. 99-457: A survey of pediatric training programs. *American Journal of Diseases of Children, 147*, 175–179.

Thompson, J., & Cooley, V. (1986). A national study of outstanding staff development programs. *Educational Horizons, 64*, 94–98.

Thorp, E.K., & McCollum, J.A. (1994). Defining the infancy specialization in early childhood special education. In L.J. Johnson, R.J. Gallagher, M.J. LaMontagne, J.B. Jordan, J.J. Gallagher, P.L. Hutinger, & M.B. Karnes (Eds.), *Meeting early intervention challenges: Issues from birth to three* (2nd ed., pp. 167–183). Baltimore: Paul H. Brookes Publishing Co.

Trohanis, P. (1994). Continuing positive change through implementation of IDEA. In L.J. Johnson, R.J. Gallagher, M.J. LaMontagne, J.B. Jordan, J.J. Gallagher, P.L. Hutinger, & M.B. Karnes (Eds.), *Meeting early intervention challenges: Issues from birth to three* (2nd ed., pp. 217–233). Baltimore: Paul H. Brookes Publishing Co.

View, V.A., & Amos, K.J. (1994). *Living and testing the collaborative process: A case study of community-based services integration* (Executive Summary). Arlington, VA: ZERO TO THREE/ National Center for Clinical Infant Programs.

Winton, P. (1986). The developmentally delayed child within the family context. In B. Keogh (Ed.), *Advances in special education* (Vol. 5, pp. 219–256). Greenwich, CT: JAI Press.

Winton, P. (1988). Effective parent–professional communication. In D. Bailey & R. Simeonsson (Eds.), *Family assessment in early intervention* (pp. 207–228). Columbus, OH: Charles E. Merrill.

Winton, P. (1990). A systemic approach to in-service education related to PL 99-457. *Infants and Young Children, 3*(1), 51–60.

Winton, P. (1994). Early intervention personnel preparation: The past guides the future. *Early Childhood Report, 5*(5), 4–6.

Winton, P. (1995). *A model for promoting interprofessional collaboration and quality in early intervention personnel preparation*. Chapel Hill: University of North Carolina at Chapel Hill, Southeastern Institute for Faculty Training, Frank Porter Graham Child Development Center.

Winton, P. (1996). A model for supporting higher education faculty in their early intervention personnel preparation roles. *Infants and Young Children, 8*(3), 56–67.

Winton, P., & Bailey, D. (1990). Early intervention training related to family interviewing. *Topics in Early Childhood Education, 10*(1), 50–62.

Winton, P., & DiVenere, N. (1995). Family–professional partnerships in early intervention personnel preparation: Guidelines and strategies. *Topics in Early Childhood Special Education, 15*(3), 295–312.

Winton, P.J., Catlett, C., & Houck, A. (1996). A systems approach. In D. Bricker & A. Widerstrom (Eds.), *Preparing personnel to work with infants and young children and their families: A team approach* (pp. 295–320). Baltimore: Paul H. Brookes Publishing Co.

Wischnowski, J.W., Yates, T.J., & McCollum, J.A. (1995). Expanding training options for early intervention personnel: Developing a statewide staff mentoring system. *Infants and Young Children, 8*(4), 49–58.

Wolery, M., & Bredekamp, S. (1994). Developmentally appropriate practices and young children with disabilities: Contexual issues in the discussion. *Journal of Early Intervention, 18*(4), 331–341.

Wood, F., & Thompson, S. (1980). Guidelines for better staff development. *Educational Leadership, 37*(1), 374–378.

Yoder, D., Coleman, P., & Gallagher, J. (1990). *Personnel needs: Allied health personnel meeting the demands of Part H, PL 99-457.* Chapel Hill: University of North Carolina at Chapel Hill, Frank Porter Graham Child Development Center.

2 STATE PERSPECTIVES ON MEETING PERSONNEL CHALLENGES

Closing the Gap Between Vision and Reality

Tweety Yates
Ann Higgins Hains

The vision presented to states with the passage of early intervention legislation was of a comprehensive, multidisciplinary, interagency, coordinated service system for infants and toddlers with disabilities and their families. This called for the restructuring of service delivery systems, delegating to states the task of creating one coordinated system from many existing fragmented and disjointed systems, each with its own set of rules and policies (Harbin, 1996; Harbin, Gallagher, & Lillie, 1991). Change, in general, is not easy, but it is even more complex when the target of change is an entire state system involving groups, agencies, and individuals at different levels in the system (Apter, 1994). Bridging the gap between the vision of Part H of the Education of the Handicapped Act Amendments of 1986, PL 99-457 (Infants and Toddlers), and the reality of its implementation has proven to be a very demanding challenge for state systems (Dokecki & Heflinger, 1989; Gallagher, Harbin, Thomas, Clifford, & Wenger, 1988; Gallagher, Trohanis, & Clifford, 1989; Garwood & Sheehan, 1989; Martin, 1989; McCollum & Bailey, 1991).

As with any legislative initiative that drastically changes a service delivery system, immediate personnel needs resulted from the passage of PL 99-457. States were faced with the reality that regardless of how comprehensive the design of a system, it would not be effective without competent and qualified personnel to implement it (Gilkerson, Hilliard, Schrag, & Shonkoff, 1987; McCollum & Bailey, 1991; Winton, 1990). This presented a particularly challenging task to systems that even before the passage of PL 99-457 reported shortages in the availability of early intervention personnel (McLaughlin, Smith-Davis, & Burke, 1986; Meisels, 1989). Hence, one of the greatest challenges that states have faced has been the development of a personnel system that ensures not only availability of but also high quality in all personnel (Harbin, Gallagher, & Batista, 1992; McCollum & Bailey, 1991; Winton, Catlett, & Houck, 1996). An analysis of states' progress toward implementing Part H found personnel development to be one of the areas in which the least amount of progress had been made (Harbin et al., 1992).

Of the 14 programmatic components to be addressed by each state participating in Part H of PL 99-457, two were related to the development of a statewide personnel system: 1) the setting of professional standards and 2) the design of a Comprehensive System of Personnel Development (CSPD). The components to be included in the development of this statewide system are summarized in Figure 2.1 (McCollum & Bailey, 1991). In general, early intervention services were to be provided by qualified personnel representing a range of disciplines. If necessary, new occupational categories could be created to support the new service delivery systems. Personnel standards requiring all early intervention personnel to meet the highest entry-level degree applicable to their given profession or discipline were to be used as basic minimum standards. The overall design of the CSPD was to include qualified personnel, a preservice system, an inservice system, methods for dissemination, and technical assistance. In addition, a set of special provisions was provided to support the unique nature of working with infants and their families. For example, staff development activities were to occur on an interdisciplinary basis and respond specifically to the interrelated nature of development in infancy and the skills necessary to help families enhance the development of their child and participate in the development and implementation of the individualized family service plan (McCollum & Bailey, 1991).

Although these components represent only 2 of the required 14, they are critical to the full implementation of the services required by the law (Bruder, Klosowski, & Daguio, 1991; Gilkerson et al., 1987; Meisels, Harbin, Modigliani, & Olson, 1988; Smith & Powers, 1987). As states have moved forward in the development of statewide systems and their required components, complex issues have arisen. Different activities have been used by individual states to implement these components under the assumption that each state is different in terms of the populations served, administrative structures, delivery models, geographic boundaries, collaborative efforts, and financial situations (Campbell, Bellamy, & Bishop, 1988; Striffler, 1995).

This chapter identifies and discusses critical issues, challenges, and strategies associated with the design and implementation of statewide personnel systems and shares the findings from a national survey on the directions that individual states have taken in bridging the gap between the vision and reality of PL 99-457. This chapter is organized around a set of questions used to guide states in considering the range of personnel issues involved in the development of their comprehensive, systematic personnel plans (Bruder & McCollum, 1991; McCollum & Bailey, 1991). These questions are as follows:

   I.   Individuals included (personnel representing range of disciplines)
  II.   Personnel standards
      A.   Highest standard
      B.   Infancy specialization
      C.   Assurance of qualified personnel
         1.   Analysis of current status
         2.   Steps to meet standards
 III.   Comprehensive system of personnel development
      A.   Qualified personnel
      B.   Preservice system
      C.   Inservice system
      D.   Dissemination
      E.   Technical assistance
 IV.   Special provisions
      A.   Interdisciplinary instruction
      B.   Variety of personnel
      C.   Interrelated needs
      D.   Assistance to family

Figure 2.1.   Components of a statewide early intervention personnel system.

- What personnel configurations and occupational categories will define the early intervention service delivery system?
- What kind of credentialing systems or structure will ensure that entry-level personnel are qualified for early intervention services?
- What systems will be used to enable early intervention personnel to meet qualifications or recommendations established for the statewide early intervention system?
- What are the characteristics of a statewide preservice system that will meet long-range, entry-level personnel needs?
- What system or structure will be needed to meet ongoing inservice and professional development needs?
- How will long-term personnel needs be determined?
- What structures and processes are needed to develop and institutionalize personnel standards and establish a comprehensive system for personnel development?

Using these questions as a guide for addressing state perspectives on meeting personnel challenges, information is given on why these areas are considered to be issues for states, what the challenges have been, what the survey and other sources of information revealed, selected examples of how states are addressing some of these issues, and suggestions for future directions.

ISSUES, CHALLENGES, AND STRATEGIES IN DESIGNING PERSONNEL SYSTEMS

States have used a variety of approaches to face the challenges of developing their statewide personnel systems. Information for this chapter on individual states was gathered from a variety of resources, including information obtained in a national survey of Part H coordinators as part of a follow-up study (Bruder, Hains, & Yates, 1995) to a national review of personnel standards that was completed during the spring of 1989 (Bruder et al., 1991). In addition to obtaining information about certification, licensure, and credentialing issues, the study gathered information on broader issues that states have faced in the development of their statewide personnel systems. States were asked to comment on the development of new occupational categories, the establishment of short- and long-term structures to support personnel in meeting new standards, state CSPD linkages, and preservice and inservice activities.

The Part H coordinators were initially contacted by telephone to provide a brief explanation of the survey and determine a time for a 30-minute telephone interview. A letter confirming the interview and a copy of the questions were then sent to each coordinator. In two of the interviews, the Part H coordinators believed they were unable to provide all of the information requested, and a referral was made to other Part H staff members more involved in the day-to-day personnel preparation activities. After the information was received, a follow-up letter was sent to each state contact requesting confirmation of the accuracy of the data recorded and any necessary corrections. Forty-seven of the 50 states in addition to the District of Columbia participated in the telephone interviews.

Personnel Configurations and Occupational Categories

In addressing issues of personnel configurations and occupational categories, states had to consider first what staffing patterns would need to be established to support their early intervention service delivery systems. In addition to the disciplines listed in the law, each state was given the option of defining new occupational categories to meet the needs of their new system. Several states reported the development of new occupational categories for personnel who would provide services to infants, toddlers, and families (see Table 2.1). In response to the emphasis on family-centered services, some states added categories that recognized the importance of the role of families of young children with disabilities and developed new categories that could be filled by parents. Some examples include community resource parent (Vermont), community outreach worker (Massachusetts), family health adviser (Massachusetts), parent liaison (Illinois), and parent-to-parent specialist (Michigan). Typically, no license or certification is needed to fill these roles, although in most cases documentation of completion of specialized instruction is required. Thus, states were also faced with the development of instruction to support personnel in these new roles.

In addition to the development of roles recognizing the importance of support and coordination to families, several states have added new categories for various roles of professionals who provide early intervention services, including infant mental health specialist (Michigan), early intervention specialist (Illinois, Texas, Utah, Virginia), early interventionist (Massachusetts, Rhode Island, Vermont), child development specialist (Illinois), family support specialist (Illinois, Montana), intake specialist (Montana), and service coordinator (Illinois, Nebraska). Another approach, which was taken by Utah and Virginia, was to define occupational categories by multiple levels of preparation and experience in early intervention. For example, as shown in Figure 2.2, Utah uses the levels of EI Specialist III (individuals with licensure/certification and completion of a program of advanced studies), EI Specialist II (individuals with licensure/certification), EI Specialist I (individuals working as service coordinators and/or assistants), and EI aide (individuals working in paraprofessional roles). Other states have defined the requirements for an early interventionist at a single level. For example, Rhode Island requires a high school diploma, experience, instruction, and mentoring; Virginia requires a bachelor's degree in human services; and Illinois, Massachusetts, and North Carolina require advanced study beyond initial licensure/certification or degree. Thus, requirements for early interventionists vary considerably across states.

Credentialing Systems or Structures to Ensure Qualified Personnel

In setting new standards for early intervention personnel, many complex issues needed to be addressed to ensure that entry-level personnel were qualified for providing early intervention services. PL 99-457 required states to use the highest entry-level degree needed

TABLE 2.1.   Examples of new occupational categories

Occupational category	State(s)
Child development specialist	Illinois
Community outreach worker	Massachusetts
Community resource parent	Vermont
Early intervention specialist	Illinois, Texas, Utah, Virginia
Early interventionist	Massachusetts, Rhode Island, Vermont
Infant mental health specialist	Michigan
Intake specialist	Montana
Family health adviser	Massachusetts
Family support specialist	Illinois, Montana
Parent liaison	Illinois
Parent-to-parent specialist	Michigan
Service coordinator	Illinois, Nebraska

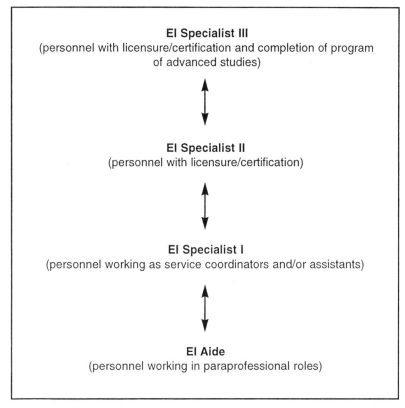

Figure 2.2. Levels of early intervention personnel in Utah.

for state credentialing (i.e., licensure, registration, certification) as a minimum standard requirement for all early intervention personnel. This forced states to reexamine their existing standards for personnel across disciplines because the development of a comprehensive, interdisciplinary system required that emphasis be placed equally on the needs of all professionals recognized under Part H (Bruder et al., 1991; Burke, McLaughlin, & Valdivieso, 1988). Consideration also had to be given to the unique knowledge and skills required to provide services to infants and toddlers and their families. The credentialing process needed to consider not only the broad experience of personnel already employed in the field but also recognize that future personnel might not have had access to specialized early intervention instruction in university programs. In addition, the process needed to apply to multiple disciplines working in different settings and different capacities (McCollum & Bailey, 1991). Two themes dominated discussions of standards: 1) how restrictive or extensive to make standards and 2) how to ensure that standards reflect inclusionary placements for young children with disabilities.

Extensiveness of Standards In establishing personnel standards, many states struggled with the conflict of whether to establish restrictive standards that would entail very extensive requirements or to add broader (more general) and less-restrictive standards. Although restrictive standards would ensure high-quality personnel, they might limit the number of available qualified service providers, whereas broader standards would allow more personnel to enter the field but result in less thoroughly prepared providers (Burke et al., 1988). This created a difficult situation for states already faced with shortages of personnel under their previous service delivery systems. Accompanying this larger issue were many other issues, ranging from determining who should actually be expected to meet the new standards to finding appropriate avenues for making early intervention personnel aware of new standards and requirements (McCollum & Yates, 1994).

In the process of developing personnel standards, most states relied on existing state or national standards for licensure or certification. When no existing standards were available for a particular category, licensure or certification of other categories typically has been used (Bruder et al., 1991). For example, states might use existing licensing or certification standards for social workers, counseling psychologists, and school psychologists to define the family therapist category. In the 1995 study (Bruder et al., 1995), most states reported personnel standards for all required disciplines except nutrition. However, the information obtained also indicated an increase in the number of states working toward development of standards in nutrition ($n = 30$) in comparison with what was reported ($n = 18$) in 1991 (Bruder et al., 1991). Although most states have completed identifying personnel standards for all required disciplines, these standards do not always require demonstration of knowledge or instruction specific to the unique needs of infants and toddlers and their families.

Inclusionary Standards   A few states, such as Illinois, Massachusetts, and North Carolina, have addressed issues related to including all disciplines by adding cross-disciplinary certification and/or credentials in early intervention. The Massachusetts Department of Health's cross-disciplinary certification is competency based for all 12 disciplines listed in PL 99-457. Personnel employed in early intervention programs must take an orientation course, and they have 3 years to achieve a set of early intervention core competencies. These competencies address infant and toddler development; program development and implementation (including family support, screening and evaluation, and intervention); collaboration (including interpersonal skills and service coordination); and policies, procedures, and advocacy. A portfolio approach is used to demonstrate the attainment of these competencies. The Massachusetts Department of Health hired a full-time staff member to oversee the certification process and the evaluation of portfolios.

Illinois developed a new early intervention credentialing system that requires all personnel working with children birth to 3 years old to have additional early intervention instruction beyond the minimum entry license required by their discipline (McCollum & Yates, 1994). This process essentially defined a new entry level for both current and future personnel. Two credentialing mechanisms were developed to assist personnel in obtaining the new early intervention specialization: 1) a portfolio review process and 2) approved university programs. The individual portfolio process was designed to meet the needs of personnel who have not completed an early intervention specialization through a university program. It also addressed the needs of personnel currently employed in early intervention programs who may not meet the new minimum degree and/or specialization requirements. Using the portfolio approach, individuals obtain a minimum number of credit points, depending on their particular roles and backgrounds. As shown in Table 2.2, credit points may be obtained through a variety of activities. Portfolios are submitted for individual review by a credentialing committee comprising early intervention providers, parents, preservice and inservice instructors, and lead agency representatives.

North Carolina has an extensive certification system. This state identified specific competencies in seven general areas relevant to working with infants and toddlers and their families. To earn the Personnel Certificate, early interventionists must participate in training and demonstrate competencies in their work settings. All interventionists are required to obtain the Personnel Certificate within a specific period of time. Personnel with degrees related to working with young children are required to complete 9 additional

TABLE 2.2.   Illinois portfolio credit points

Activity	Credit points	Maximum points
Experience in early intervention birth to 3	1 year = 1 point	4
Early intervention inservice, continuing education	10 contact hours = 1 point 1 contact hour = .10 point	5
P*TEIS[a] early intervention field training sites	8 contact hours = 1 point	5
P*TEIS staff mentoring process	8 contact hours = 1 point	5
Coursework	1 semester hour = 1.5 points	no maximum
P*TEIS validation of performance tasks	1 task = 1.5 points	no maximum
Other proposed tasks	(proposed by individual)	2

[a]P*TEIS, a federally funded Partnerships Project under the U.S. Department of Education, Office of Special Education and Rehabilitative Services, has supported a variety of training opportunities for credentialing early intervention personnel in Illinois.

instruction credits, and personnel with less relevant degrees are required to complete 18 credits. The Personnel Certificate is awarded after an examination of each individual's record by a local certifying program, in accordance with statewide standards.

Another means of addressing the development of inclusionary standards, as reflected in a number of states, is reform in the early childhood/early childhood special education certification and licensure standards. Although early childhood education/child development is not a Part H personnel category, many states are changing standards to include preparation of early childhood interventionists. States are merging general early childhood education and early childhood special education for teachers serving young children (birth to age 8 or birth to age 5) and their families. States that have adopted unified early childhood standards include Iowa, Kansas, Kentucky, and North Carolina.

The information obtained from the interviews with Part H coordinators indicates that, in general, movement continues to be slow. Although the initial response of most states to Part H was to adopt existing standards without modification (Bruder et al., 1991), there is ongoing concern that both disciplinary and cross-disciplinary competencies specific to early intervention still need to be addressed (Bruder et al., 1995). Although most states have not developed new occupational categories or changed existing standards to include specializations in early intervention, many states expressed interest in moving in this direction. Several states have a personnel committee or task force to address the issues raised when personnel do not have to meet any early intervention requirements within existing standards. Many questions and concerns have been raised about whether higher standards increase personnel shortages. States that have adopted higher standards did not believe that their systems had created personnel shortages, although specific studies had not been completed to officially address this issue. Other concerns that were raised, and that need to be addressed before these systems become institutionalized, centered around the costs and benefits of portfolio systems and inclusionary licensure processes.

COMPREHENSIVE SYSTEMS OF PERSONNEL DEVELOPMENT

The second personnel component in the development of a statewide personnel system is the design of a CSPD, which would include qualified personnel, preservice and inservice systems, methods for dissemination, technical assistance, and special provisions related to the unique nature of working with infants and toddlers and their families. These requirements mirror the CSPD provisions of Part B of the Education for All Handicapped Children Act of 1975, PL 94-142, and the Individuals with Disabilities Education Act Amendments of 1991, PL 102-119, (McCollum & Bailey, 1991) and could be included as part of the system developed for Part B. The interviews with Part H coordinators indicated that most states had separate CSPD systems for Part H and Part B. Several states (e.g., Utah, Washington) reported having a birth to 21 CSPD system including Part H and Part B. The differences in lead agencies were reported as a major personnel preparation issue in states where these two systems were separate. Many states reported that although the Part H CSPD system was separate, it shared several common committee members, exchanged meeting minutes, and held joint conferences with the Part B system. Others expressed concern over the lack of communication between the two systems and were working on building these relationships. Even states with a unified CSPD system on paper were not always unified.

As states have moved beyond the initial period of reacting to the new legislation, concern has shifted to issues of building infrastructures to support the new systems. One approach, present in most states, has been to create a system that uses existing infrastructures to support ongoing instruction and technical assistance. This goal ties into the intent of Part H in that the "new" system should be built on the strength of the already existing system. The task was not to duplicate existing instruction or other personnel development structures but to build on what was already available (Apter, 1994; Miller, 1992). Nevertheless, most states have found their existing systems to be fragmented and disjointed, creating yet another challenge in meeting the demands of developing a coordinated, statewide personnel development system.

The following section addresses issues that states have faced as they have moved forward in the development of their statewide CSPDs. Challenges include how the system would help current personnel to meet the new qualifications; how it would meet the long-range needs of personnel; and what systems or structures could be established to meet the ongoing inservice, preservice, and professional development needs.

Systems to Enable Current Personnel to Meet Standards

As stated previously, the system changes had the potential to increase an already existing personnel shortage (Meisels, 1989; Meisels et al., 1988; Yoder & Coleman, 1990). The question arose as to whether states would have staff available who met the minimum requirements for their discipline and who were also adequately prepared to meet the unique needs of infants and toddlers and their families. In addressing these issues, it became obvious that current personnel could serve as one of the best sources of recruits. Most direct service providers not only have valuable experience with infants and toddlers but have also participated in a variety of types of instruction specific to early intervention (McCollum & Bailey, 1991). Thus, states could choose to implement a short-term system to overcome current shortages by upgrading the skills of existing personnel who required additional instruction to achieve an appropriate entry level and qualify them to work with infants and toddlers and their families. In addition to these short-term solutions, current and future personnel would need to be supported by the planning and implementation of long-term systems.

The survey indicated that states vary greatly in their decisions to implement short- and/or long-term approaches to personnel development. States with a history of early intervention programs and federal- or state-funded planning efforts reported having fewer problems instituting short- and long-term plans than those that did not. Twenty-three states reported requiring the highest standard for credentialing without implementing short-term strategies to upgrade the skills of current personnel to new standards. A frequent rationale was that standards were already required for Medicaid-funded services; thus, short-term measures were not necessary. Many states that did develop short-term strategies to accommodate current personnel used emergency or provisional licenses (ranging from 2 to 5 years), reimbursement of tuition for coursework toward full qualification, grants or contracts with institutions of higher education to develop preservice programs for preparing personnel in targeted disciplines (e.g., early childhood special education, nursing, occupational therapy, physical therapy, speech-language pathology), and inservice courses offered through the lead agency (e.g., Ohio offers two early intervention courses through the Department of Health). "Grandfather" clauses for personnel already employed in early intervention were also used (e.g., in Arkansas, Iowa, Nevada, New Jersey, New Mexico, Texas). A few states provided tuition reimbursement and inservice staff development opportunities to support existing personnel in achieving new entry-level requirements (e.g., Illinois, Massachusetts, Vermont).

A number of states identified the Part H CSPD as the long-term structure supporting their standards. Many states indicated that once standards were set, they assumed they were being implemented and appropriately regulated by the licensing agencies for each discipline. States reported that at the local level programs would address the long-term structure supporting the standards by employing appropriately credentialed personnel. As an example, Arkansas was in the process of having state agencies include early intervention standards as part of the yearly employee contract agreements. Several states reported that their plan was to use the preservice personnel preparation system as part of their long-term structure by developing the capacity of university programs offering early intervention coursework across disciplines. Specific examples related to how states are accomplishing these goals at a preservice level can be found in the next section. Other states require staff to complete a certain number of hours per year of instruction specific to early intervention content.

In the short term, one of the major issues for states has been to support existing personnel as they adapt to the system changes and new approaches to service delivery, as well as to plan for preparing entry-level personnel at the college and university level. Reflecting on the issues raised in Janet's story in Chapter 1 not only reinforces the importance of designing systems that support the ongoing development of personnel but also highlights the magnitude of this task. Issues ranged from personnel feeling inadequately prepared at the preservice level to the frustrating experience of participating in statewide inservice activities as a means of "filling in the gaps," only to believe that specific needs had not been addressed.

Statewide Preservice Systems to Meet Long-Range Personnel Needs

Ensuring that a statewide preservice system is in place to support the development and supply of personnel has presented a number of challenges for states. Although it is unrealistic to expect that personnel needs can be completely met through traditional, university-based preservice programs, building the state's capacity in this area is crucial (McCollum & Bailey, 1991). However, there are few college and university preservice personnel preparation programs available that provide infancy specializations, regardless of discipline (Bailey, Simeonsson, Yoder, & Huntington, 1990; Courtnage & Smith-Davis, 1987).

One drawback is that developing new preservice programs or even integrating programmatic changes into existing programs can be a lengthy, involved process (Gallagher,

1989). Progress in this area is also affected by personnel certification and standards. Getting universities involved in the development of new programs is difficult when there are no financial incentives and a lack of certification and licensing standards for the various disciplines. Other barriers include lack of qualified faculty and lack of an identifiable job market.

A major barrier to meeting the personnel demands of early intervention has been the lack of collaboration between higher education and state agencies. Historically, the relationship between state government and higher education has been characterized by issues of autonomy and accountability (Fisher, 1988). State agencies are responsible for supplying personnel to service delivery programs, but they are not responsible for funding for universities to establish personnel preparation programs. Of the few preservice programs that offer infancy specializations, most have been funded on a short-term basis by federal grants. Universities need funding and time to initiate preservice programs. Both state agencies and universities are limited by constraints of time, funding, and authority in forging ahead with personnel preparation. Without additional incentives or external support for personnel preparation, significantly involving higher education in early intervention may continue to prove difficult.

States have taken a variety of approaches to addressing these barriers. For example, the federally funded Partnerships Project in Illinois offers small grants (minigrants) of $2,000 to assist faculty in their efforts to develop early intervention instruction options. This process has been well received, with an average of 32 colleges and universities representing nine disciplines being awarded minigrants on a yearly basis. Minigrants have been used for activities such as establishing inter-university early intervention discussion groups, developing a student library containing early intervention resources, sponsoring parents as co-teachers, and developing early intervention coursework. Another example is Wisconsin, which has developed a Parents as Presenters model in which faculty can apply for funds to pay a small stipend to parents for presenting in preservice courses. Faculty from all public and private institutions of higher education across all disciplines can apply for stipends. A strategy used by several states to support faculty in their early intervention instruction roles has been to hold faculty development institutes to upgrade faculty knowledge and skills in early intervention. Many of these institutes were inspired by regional faculty development activities funded through federal grants sponsored by the Department of Education, Early Education Program for Children and Disabilities.

Many states reported that although they do not have a systematic program within a university that specifically focuses on early intervention, they have offered individual coursework that focuses on infancy content. For example, Delaware and Rhode Island have disseminated modules to faculty as a means of encouraging integration of early intervention content into existing curricula. These modules were developed and disseminated through the Northeast Regional Faculty Training Institutes to support states in their efforts to increase personnel preparation options. Several other states have used distance learning courses and teleconferences offered for university credit as a means of reaching a larger number of early intervention personnel (e.g., Arkansas, Nevada, Utah, West Virginia). Virginia Polytechnic Institute and State University has offered child development courses via e-mail and the Internet. In Massachusetts, the Department of Public Health sponsors an award program for participants in disciplines relevant to early intervention services. Five students enrolled in degree programs from nursing, early childhood, developmental or special education, social work, physical or occupational therapy, speech-language pathology, or psychology are awarded a $2,000 stipend in their last year of training if they complete a practicum in early intervention (minimum of 250 hours). The recipients are also expected to work in a Massachusetts early intervention program for at least 1 year following their graduation. In addition, three senior fellowships are awarded for 1 year to seniors who wish to conduct research in an identified early intervention area of need. Each award for $2,000 is to be used in a 6-month period to pay for educational expenses or to support release time from the early intervention program. Many other states reported that they are working toward assisting university programs to incorporate interdisciplinary coursework, team teaching, and parents as co-instructors at the preservice level.

Systems to Meet Ongoing Inservice and Professional Development Needs

State and national standards for licensure and certification in specific disciplines do not typically include requirements for early intervention; therefore, preservice programs often do not include early intervention preparation. Based on this situation, the pattern that has emerged across states is a reliance on inservice activities for providing early intervention information to personnel. Although inservice instruction has been criticized as being ineffective (Bailey, 1989; Odom, 1987), the reality is that this continues to be a main avenue for instructing early intervention personnel. A 1996 study by Sexton and colleagues stated that part of the criticism has stemmed from the assumption that inservice instructional outcomes should result in positive practice changes within service delivery contexts, whereas in reality these service contexts are rarely taken into consideration during planning and evaluation activities. Sexton and his colleagues also pointed out that another reason for the lack of success with inservice instruction has been the immediate demand for appropriately instructed personnel, resulting in a "crisis-mentality" approach to inservice instruction. States quickly instruct large numbers of personnel in primarily didactic-type instructional situations with no follow-up system. These are major challenges to determining the best and most cost-efficient way for a statewide system to support the development of qualified personnel.

Given the range of professionals who function as early intervention personnel, states have had to be creative in ensuring that professionals continue to develop early intervention competencies (Hanson & Brekken, 1991; Trohanis, 1994). Alternatives to large, didactic instructional activities have emerged as states have begun to make training more accessible and relevant to personnel. For example, Illinois developed several field-based training alternatives to expand existing options and offer geographically and financially accessible instruction to personnel. Two examples are staff mentoring and field instruction sites, both funded through a federal partnerships grant under the Department of Education. Staff mentoring (Wischnowski, Yates, & McCollum, 1996) provides individual guidance to personnel in one or more of the following areas of competence: legislation and program models, family-centered principles, assessment, intervention, service coordination, teaming, typical/atypical development, biological risk factors, and interagency collaboration. Mentees indicate an instructional need and are matched with a mentor with expertise in that area. Each mentor–mentee partnership includes a minimum of 8 hours of contact time, with at least half of this time completed at the mentee's site. Field training sites comprise six exemplary early intervention programs per year that are willing to provide 1 day of instruction (a minimum of four times per year) to share their strategies, techniques, and ideas with other early intervention personnel. They are awarded a $2,000 minigrant to help with expenses. Both of these options not only offer a cost-effective way to meet individual instructional needs but also serve as a means of recognizing and building on the knowledge and expertise of early intervention personnel within the state (McCollum & Yates, 1994).

To coordinate instructional efforts, several states have developed inservice instructional modules that are presented statewide to ensure that all personnel receive consistent knowledge, skills, and philosophy. States such as Massachusetts and North Carolina have developed statewide orientation that includes overviews of new state systems as a means of meeting the needs of new personnel and ensuring the delivery of consistent information. Other states (e.g., Delaware, Idaho, Nebraska, Virginia) have developed instruction for specific job roles such as service coordinator. In addition, other states (e.g., Kansas, Oklahoma) have expanded their existing inservice instructional options by requiring personnel to attend instruction with the teams with whom they work. As an incentive, teams in these states are offered follow-up consultations at their worksites to assist in embedding workshop information into daily practice. Five states reported that annual statewide early intervention/early childhood conferences have supported collaborative efforts among instructional entities, accomplished through coordination and sponsorship of the conference by multiple state interagency groups. In general, the most common instructional events reported were conferences, inservice workshops, and short-term professional development activities.

Determining Personnel Needs

Another challenge for states has been the development of a systematic statewide needs assessment process to support the preservice and inservice aspects of the system (see Chapter 6 for more information on conducting needs assessment). Most states indicated that they had established a systematic means of identifying the instructional needs of personnel. These ranged from informal surveys to annual needs assessments. Some were individual needs assessments completed at the preservice level, whereas others represented a statewide, cross-agency survey of instructional needs. Several states regionalized their needs assessment process to better meet the needs of personnel in particular settings and geographic locations. Only a few states reported linkages between preservice and inservice instructional needs at the level of needs assessment information and planning; the majority of states reported no linkages at all between inservice and preservice systems. Most often two systems were in place, one charged with inservice and continuing education and the second with the preparation of new personnel at the preservice level.

Several states have moved forward in developing models that are more responsive to statewide personnel needs. For example, Maryland has an inservice model in which local and state instructional needs are assessed and met. Local programs in urban areas may indicate a continuing need for orientation of new staff, which represents a need that is not likely to be addressed at a statewide level. By assessing needs at both the local and state levels, the state is better able to meet and support the instructional needs of early intervention personnel. To further support this bilevel system, funds are allocated for both local and state instructional activities. Other states, such as Washington, contract with one of their institutions of higher education to design the statewide inservice activities based on the results of their needs assessment. This process not only serves as a means of linking preservice and inservice instructional efforts but also integrates into inservice instruction the issues being taught at the preservice level.

As states strive to meet the future needs of personnel within their systems, it also has been necessary to develop a structure for the ongoing collection of information related to the supply and demand of early intervention personnel (McCollum & Bailey, 1991). In response to the questions concerning critical shortages of personnel, 43 states reported shortages of occupational therapists, physical therapists, and speech-language pathologists. This finding is similar to information gathered in a 1990 supply-and-demand study in which substantial shortages were reported in these same three areas (Yoder & Coleman,

1990). Yoder and Coleman also documented a decline in personnel preparation programs in speech-language pathology with little indication that this situation would improve. This shortage of personnel, along with declining personnel preparation programs, creates additional barriers as states strive to meet the demands of full implementation of Part H. Many states have continued to strengthen existing personnel preparation programs; several states also expressed the desire to explore the role of community colleges in the development of early intervention personnel at the paraprofessional level. Part H coordinators also expressed concern over the retention of currently employed personnel. Forty-two states reported retention as a problem primarily due to the salary range for early intervention personnel and the unavailability of additional funds to increase salaries as an incentive to remain in the field.

Collaborative Statewide Personnel Structures

Collaboration is critical to the successful implementation of a comprehensive system that calls for instructional institutions, professional organizations, state agencies, and families to work together to develop personnel preparation opportunities (Hanson & Brekken, 1991; Rosin et al., 1996). The states surveyed for this chapter, however, identified many barriers to such collaboration. Achieving interagency collaboration and coordination has been difficult because multiple players contribute to the preparation of early intervention personnel; thus, creating linkages among the different levels of the service delivery system is critical if change is to occur. A CSPD should be representative of all key players, including institutes of higher education such as private and public universities and colleges, technical colleges, and university affiliated programs; families who have young children with special needs; people representing agencies conducting inservice instruction in the state; students who participate in preservice and inservice activities; professional associations encompassing all disciplines; service providers including early intervention direct service providers and child care providers; and state agencies including Part H and Part B. It also is critical for states to link the components of Part H and Part B under the state's CSPD plan. Differences in lead agencies and the structure of state mandates have often made articulation between these two systems difficult (Winton et al., 1996).

A significant challenge for states in building a more collaborative, linked system has been to identify, coordinate, and develop the resources necessary to accomplish this task (Winton, 1990). Questions such as who provides professional development in the state and how collaborative efforts can be facilitated across key players represent major issues. One mechanism that states have used to obtain this information has been to develop a map of the organizations and the key players. In the information obtained for a 1995 study (Bruder et al., 1995), states that were more successful in their collaborative attempts reported building broad personnel development systems that were interdisciplinary and interagency in nature. The important feature in those states was a designated group, such as a personnel committee of the state interagency council, to directly address the issues and lead, not just manage, the change process. Themes that emerged as necessary components across states included the following issues: identify the key players, identify instructional issues, set priorities and time lines, develop structures and incentives to support the retention of personnel, and identify funding sources.

CONCLUSION

The survey (Bruder et al., 1995) conducted for this chapter indicated that although states have put much energy into developing personnel systems responsive to the components described in early intervention legislation, significant work remains. Two areas that must receive priority are personnel standards and personnel shortages. In each, the experiences of other states can be a major source of guidance.

Personnel Standards

The initial study of personnel standards revealed that most states adopted existing standards without modification; few states developed new occupational categories (Bruder et al., 1991). The 1995 study replicated these findings; however, many states reported concern that disciplinary and cross-disciplinary competencies in early intervention still need to be addressed. Overall, these states reported that once existing state and national standards for licensure and certification were adopted, they turned their attention to other priorities such as expanding early intervention direct services. There is dissatisfaction with continued reliance on inservice activities, yet preservice programs continue to address existing standards. This has led to challenging situations, such as national professional standards not including early intervention; many states adopting existing national professional standards as institutes of higher education in these states provide preservice programs that meet existing standards; and new professionals entering the field without early intervention preparation.

The challenge is how to further refine existing standards to include early intervention and/or to develop new occupational categories. On examining the states that have accomplished these activities, a variety of approaches for exceeding minimum standards have been used successfully. All of these approaches require states to engage in continued development of personnel standards, and all will be influenced by each state's supply-and-demand issues, recruitment and retention efforts, and economic conditions. The assumption is that state regulatory standards for personnel are critical to the success of implementing the law and in providing guidance to institutions of higher education for their personnel preparation programs.

An additional approach is to consider national professional recognition. The professional disciplines identified in the federal legislation represent diversity in traditions, standards, levels, and models of personnel preparation. The Carolina Policy Studies Program found in a survey of 10 professional organizations that only 1 professional association (the Council for Exceptional Children) encouraged the establishment of a special certification (Gallagher & Coleman, 1990). All 10 organizations supported inservice activities and annual convention sessions on early intervention (Gallagher & Coleman, 1990). Many of these organizations planned to develop "best practice" guidelines (Gallagher & Coleman, 1990). Documents exist for early childhood special education, nursing, nutrition, occupational therapy, physical therapy, psychology, social work, and speech and language (cf. Miller & Stayton, 1996). These professional associations have delineated specific competencies required to work with infants, toddlers, and preschoolers with disabilities (Miller & Stayton, 1996); however, the documents are guidelines that are not part of the licensing or certification standards. In the future, these documents could become part of early intervention personnel standards through work within the organizations at a national level or through standards developed at the state level.

Other creative solutions also may emerge; for example, professional organizations may endorse a national early intervention standard with interstate recognition. The Interstate New Teacher Assessment and Support Consortium (1992) proposed model standards for beginning teacher licensing and development, an example of a national effort for consensus on teaching standards that cross state boundaries. The Division for Early Childhood (DEC) of the Council of Exceptional Children, National Association for the Education of Young Children (NAEYC), and Association of Teacher Education (ATE) developed a position statement (1994) and guidelines for personnel standards for early education and early intervention (DEC, NAEYC, & ATE, 1995). This work, extended to discipline-specific associations, could achieve consensus on standards for personnel working in programs for young children with and without disabilities and their families. Given the wide range of the "highest entry-level standard," professional organizations must take a leadership role in providing guidelines for state agencies and institutions of higher education, following a similar movement that exists for teachers of school-age students.

Personnel Shortages

The 1995 study reported in this chapter (Bruder et al., 1995) replicated previous research documenting the critical shortages of early intervention personnel (Bruder et al., 1991; Striffler, 1995). Although the need for personnel, especially therapists, continues, a number of states have designed creative solutions that may lend guidance to those states attempting to overcome these shortages.

The use of paraprofessionals may increasingly emerge as a means of addressing shortages. In a survey of 31 states, 8 (Hawaii, Illinois, Maine, Massachusetts, North Carolina, South Carolina, Texas, and Utah) reported establishing occupational categories at the paraprofessional level (Striffler, 1993). Fifteen states reported the use of paraprofessionals or assistants in providing service coordination, and 18 states use paraprofessionals or assistants to deliver special instruction. Striffler (1993) outlined several factors that contribute to states' decisions to develop paraprofessional and/or assistant positions:

- Including parents as service providers and service coordinators
- Providing services in rural and remote areas
- Ensuring culturally and linguistically appropriate services
- Extending services into a range of settings (e.g., inclusive, community-based programs)
- Responding to the scarcity of professional staff (especially in occupational, physical, and speech therapy)
- Responding to state budget and monetary constraints

Controversy remains over who (professional or paraprofessional) should do what under what circumstances; however, clarification of the specific role(s), job descriptions, selection and hiring criteria, and initial and continuing education expectations will increase the likelihood that paraprofessionals deliver early intervention services congruent with their states' vision of early intervention. Given the continued reports of shortages of personnel, more states undoubtedly will turn to paraprofessionals in the delivery of various early intervention services.

Another possible solution to personnel shortages is the development of career ladder or lattice strategies for promoting personnel toward full credentials. A conceptual model of a career lattice has been delineated by the NAEYC in promoting an articulated professional development system for early childhood education (Bredekamp & Willer, 1992). The lattice encompasses the concept of career ladders that assume that higher qualifications and greater levels of responsibility will translate into higher compensation (Bredekamp & Willer, 1992). For the profession as a whole, "a 'lattice' conveys the reality of early childhood education more clearly in that there are many diverse settings, roles and responsibilities in programs servicing children from birth through age eight" (Bredekamp & Willer, 1992, p. 48). The goal of a career lattice is to support movement from one system to another and to improve compensation so that increased opportunities exist for horizontal movement. In Utah, for example, a career ladder/lattice credential-level system extends credentials from personnel with a high school degree or equivalent to full licensure. Although 19 states are working in partnership with community colleges to develop programs for paraprofessionals in early intervention (Striffler, 1995), whether clear articulations exist between levels of credentials is unknown.

The steps necessary to develop personnel career ladder/lattice recruitment, instruction, and retention initiatives depend on the purpose. One important purpose should be to improve the cultural and linguistic diversity of personnel, a challenge identified by Part H coordinators in the survey by Striffler (1995). Historically, early intervention has been disproportionately dominated by young white females (Bowman, 1990; Fenichel & Eggbeer, 1991; Kontos & File, 1992). Individuals who are representative of families' home cultures and communities must be supported in entering and remaining in early intervention. Personnel who represent diversity are often employed in child care, Head Start, and other community-based programs (Garcia, McLaughlin, Spodek, & Saracho, 1995). South Carolina recognized this resource when state leaders approached the Regional Technical Schools to develop a child development associate degree program that includes the competencies for the early intervention assistant category.

States need to identify long-term, expanded ways to recognize and build on the strengths of nondegree professionals in early intervention settings. Simultaneously, states must develop alternative preservice and inservice opportunities to assist personnel in moving up educational and career ladders. New program approaches must take into account and provide proactive responses to the reality that personnel in early childhood themselves experience economic hardships, which limit the incentive and opportunity for them to gain educational experiences, and that multicultural personnel, especially in urban communities, already encounter the complex needs of families and children, including poverty, child abuse and neglect, substance abuse, and violence (Anderson & Fenichel, 1989; Arcia, Keyes, Gallagher, & Herrick, 1993; Christensen, 1992; Harry, 1992; Phillips & Crowell, 1994; Rosin et al., 1996).

High rates of staff turnover limit consistency in services and influence the quality of early intervention (Kontos & File, 1992). At a state level, one solution may be to recognize and support preservice and inservice personnel. For example, each year Massachusetts gives awards to early intervention practitioners who have completed 5 years of service in early intervention programs. This state also provides grants to a small number of preservice students during their internship or practicum experience (A. Schuman, personal communication, June 8, 1995). Both groups of recipients attend two seminars with state agency leaders and other early intervention specialists to discuss projects and experiences and emerging issues in the field. Although not specifically mentioned, professional support and recognition are also found in this award program. Through the seminars, informal support and mentorship likely occurs for both sets of recipients—either for entering or for continuing careers in early intervention. The award program also provides public recognition of personnel working in the field of early intervention.

Another solution that has been used in developing and maintaining quality personnel has been the development of program review and monitoring systems (Winton & Crais, 1996). For example, Alaska has developed a process for monitoring early intervention programs along with a 42-page program assessment tool (Alaska Early Intervention/Infant Learning Program, 1994) that includes a section addressing personnel issues. The monitoring process involves a 4-day site review conducted by parents of children with disabilities, "peers" from other early intervention programs, and representatives from area referral sources such as Head Start. Kansas has also developed a program review process that consists of three phases: planning for the upcoming review and preliminary data collection, on-site visitation by a five-member team, and the development of a plan to address any areas of concern that were identified during the site visit. Personnel issues are addressed in all three phases. Participants include parents of children served by Part H, service providers, and the local interagency coordinating council (ICC). One unique feature of this process involves the completion of an instrument, the Self-Assessment for the Community Network (Kansas Infant-Toddler Services, 1993), by the local ICC. The instrument provides a framework for self-evaluation and addresses such issues as how the community has changed its services based on annual evaluations, how community facilitates family involvement and professional collaboration, and how community facilitates opportunities for continuing education among staff members. Alaska and Kansas both use the information gathered through their review and monitoring systems to identify personnel issues and develop technical assistance plans that support the needs of early intervention staff (Winton & Crais, 1996).

Some solutions to personnel standards and personnel shortages will be found with the increasing use of technology. For example, the Internet provides inexpensive access to information and communication all day, every day (Reddick & King, 1996). Electronic mail has been found to facilitate collaborative opportunities between instructors and learners (Buchana, Rush, Krockover, & Lehman, 1993; Rush, 1993) and to support preservice students in practicum experiences (Hoover, 1994). With the emergence of the Internet, interdisciplinary gatherings of teachers and learners are no longer bound by space and time; however, structured support for personnel is necessary because the fear of computer technology still exists with faculty and students (Strudler, Quinn, McKinney, & Jones, 1995; Willis, Willis, Austin, & Colon, 1995).

Technology offers many potential supports for states. These include creating the "virtual" university where students within states, countries, or the world engage in instructional activities; extending communication globally but also across urban, rural, and remote regions within states; accessing expertise from colleagues as well as information provided by thousands of organizations, companies, and individuals all over the world at a moment's notice; conferencing with audio and video capabilities; facilitating state CSPD data gathering from institutions of higher education; and increasing networking among family members; service providers; local, state, and national organizations; and agencies (see the Appendix at the end of this chapter for selected Internet sources available as of 1996). Thus, states will be able to address many of their personnel concerns by entering into cyberspace.

States across the United States continue to address the need for personnel standards and comprehensive systems of personnel development. Many creative strategies have been developed to address the goals identified in Part H. Young children often ask on car trips, "Are we there yet?" and parents often respond, "No, not yet." Study results indicate that no state has "arrived" and that states are at varying distances depending on the destination (e.g., standards, shortages, preservice/inservice preparation). However, it is reassuring that states seem to be traveling the same road together.

RESOURCES

Division for Early Childhood, National Association for the Education of Young Children, & Association of Teacher Educators. (1995, June). Personnel standards for early education and early intervention: Guidelines for licensure in early childhood special education. *Communicator, 21*(3), 1–16.

Describes the knowledge and skills necessary for effective work with all young children, including those with special needs. This publication helps distinguish the roles of educators in both early childhood education and early childhood special education and outlines recommendations for licensure for early childhood special educators serving children with special needs in a variety of settings.

Division for Early Childhood Task Force on Recommended Practices. (1993). *DEC recommended practices: Indicators of quality in programs for infants and young children with special needs and their families.* Reston, VA: Division for Early Childhood of the Council for Exceptional Children. Cost: $20 plus shipping. (800) 232-7373.

Recommended practices for programs designed to meet the special needs of infants and young children. Aspects of early intervention that are examined include assessment; family participation; individualized family service plans and individualized education programs; interventions for children who are gifted; and interventions to foster cognitive, communication, social, adaptive behavior, and motor skills. Suggestions for service delivery models, transitions, developing personnel competence, and evaluating programs are also included.

National Early Childhood Technical Assistance System (NEC*TAS). (1996, June). *Resources from the National Early Childhood Technical Assistance System.* Chapel Hill: University of North Carolina at Chapel Hill, Frank Porter Graham Child Development Center. Cost: Free. (919) 962-2001.

A listing of the most current publications and technical assistance documents from NEC*TAS on key aspects of early intervention (e.g., assessment and eligibility, personnel issues). NEC*TAS publications are low-cost, high-quality documents designed to assist states in implementing effective early intervention programs. NEC*TAS also compiles and distributes lists of the Part H coordinators, Part B/619 coordinators, and directors of special education in each state and jurisdiction.

REFERENCES

Alaska Early Intervention/Infant Learning Program. (1994). *Monitoring tool.* Juneau, AK: Department of Health and Social Services.

Anderson, P.P., & Fenichel, E.S. (1989). *Serving culturally diverse families of infants and toddlers with disabilities.* Washington, DC: National Center for Clinical Infant Programs.

Apter, D.S. (1994). From dream to reality: A participant's view of the implementation of Part H of PL 99-457. *Journal of Early Intervention, 18*(2), 131–140.

Arcia, E., Keyes, L., Gallagher, J.J., & Herrick, H. (1993). National portrait of sociodemographic factors associated with underutilization of services: Relevance to early intervention. *Journal of Early Intervention, 17*(3), 283–297.

Bailey, D.B., Jr. (1989). Issues and directions in preparing professionals to work with young handicapped children and their families. In J.J. Gallagher, P.L. Trohanis, & R.M. Clifford (Eds.), *Policy implementation and PL 99-457: Planning for young children with special needs* (pp. 97–132). Baltimore: Paul H. Brookes Publishing Co.

Bailey, D.B., Jr., Simeonsson, R.S., Yoder, D.E., & Huntington, G.S. (1990). Infant personnel preparation across eight disciplines: An integrative analysis. *Exceptional Children, 56*(1), 26–35.

Bowman, B.T. (1990). Issues in recruitment, selection, and retention of early childhood teachers. In B. Spodek & O. Saracho (Eds.), *Early childhood teacher preparation* (pp. 153–175). New York: Teachers College Press.

Bredekamp, S., & Willer, B. (1992). Of ladders and lattices, cores and cones: Conceptualizing an early childhood professional development system. *Young Children, 47*(3), 47–50.

Bruder, M.B., Hains, A.H., & Yates, T.J. (1995). *Update on a review of personnel standards for Part H of PL 99-457.* Unpublished study, University of Connecticut Health Center, Farmington.

Bruder, M.B., Klosowski, S., & Daguio, C. (1991). A review of personnel standards for Part H of PL 99-457. *Journal of Early Intervention, 15*(1), 66–79.

Bruder, M.B., & McCollum, J.A. (1991). *Analysis of state applications for year 4; Planning for the personnel components of Part H of PL 99-457.* Chapel Hill, NC: NEC*TAS.

Buchana, P., Rush, M., Krockover, G., & Lehman, J. (1993). Project INSITE: Development of telecommunications skills for teachers and students. *Journal of Computers in Mathematics and Science Teaching, 12*(3/4), 245–260.

Burke, P., McLaughlin, M., & Valdivieso, C. (1988). Preparing professionals to educate handicapped infants and young children: Some policy considerations. *Topics in Early Childhood Special Education, 8*(1), 73–80.

Campbell, P.H., Bellamy, G.T., & Bishop, K.K. (1988). State-wide intervention systems: An overview of the new federal program for infants and toddlers with handicaps. *Journal of Special Education, 22*, 25–40.

Christensen, C.M. (1992). Multicultural competencies in early intervention: Training professionals for a pluralistic society. *Infants and Young Children, 4*(3), 49–63.

Courtnage, L., & Smith-Davis, J. (1987). Interdisciplinary team training: A national survey of special education teacher training programs. *Exceptional Children, 53*, 451–458.

Division for Early Childhood (DEC) of the Council for Exceptional Children, National Association for the Education of Young Children (NAEYC), & Association of Teacher Educators (ATE). (1994, October). *Position statement: Personnel standards for early education and early intervention.* Reston, VA: Council for Exceptional Children, Division for Early Childhood.

Division for Early Childhood (DEC) of the Council for Exceptional Children, National Association for the Education of Young Children (NAEYC), & Association of Teacher Educators (ATE). (1995). *Personnel standards for early education and early intervention: Guidelines for licensure in early childhood special education.* Reston, VA: Council for Exceptional Children, Division for Early Childhood.

Dokecki, P.R., & Heflinger, C.A. (1989). Strengthening families of young children with handicapping conditions: Mapping backward from the "street level." In J.J. Gallagher, P.L. Trohanis, & R.M. Clifford (Eds.), *Policy implementation and PL 99–457: Planning for young children with special needs* (pp. 59–84). Baltimore: Paul H. Brookes Publishing Co.

Education for All Handicapped Children Act of 1975, PL 94-142, 20 U.S.C. § 1400 *et seq.*

Education of the Handicapped Act Amendments of 1986, PL 99-457, 20 U.S.C. § 1400 *et seq.*

Fenichel, S., & Eggbeer, L. (1991). Preparing practitioners to work with infants, toddlers, and their families: Four essential elements of training. *Infants and Young Children, 4*(2), 56–62.

Fisher, L. (1988). State legislatures and the autonomy of colleges and universities. *Journal of Higher Education, 59*(2), 91–102.

Gallagher, J. (1989). *Planning for personnel preparation: A policy alert.* Chapel Hill: University of North Carolina at Chapel Hill, Carolina Policy Studies Program, Frank Porter Graham Child Development Center.

Gallagher, J.J., & Coleman, P. (1990). *Professional organizations' role in meeting the personnel demands of Part H, PL 99-457.* Chapel Hill: University of North Carolina at Chapel Hill, Carolina Policy Studies Program, Frank Porter Graham Child Development Center.

Gallagher, J.J., Harbin, G., Thomas, D., Clifford, R., & Wenger, M. (1988). *Major policy issues in implementing Part H—PL 99-457.* Chapel Hill: University of North Carolina at Chapel Hill, Carolina Policy Studies Program, Frank Porter Graham Child Development Center.

Gallagher, J.J., Trohanis, P.L., & Clifford, R.N. (Eds.). (1989). *Policy implementation and PL 99-457: Planning for young children with special needs.* Baltimore: Paul H. Brookes Publishing Co.

Garcia, E.E., McLaughlin, B., Spodek, B., & Saracho, O.N. (1995). *Yearbook in early childhood education: Meeting the challenge of linguistic and cultural diversity in early childhood education* (Vol. 6). New York: Teachers College Press.

Garwood, S.G., & Sheehan, R. (1989). *Designing a comprehensive early intervention system: The challenge of PL 99-457.* Austin, TX: PRO-ED.

Gilkerson, L., Hilliard, A.G., Schrag, E., & Shonkoff, J.P. (1987). Point of view: Commenting on PL 99-457. *Zero to Three, 10*(1), 1–7.

Hanson, M.J., & Brekken, L.J. (1991). Early intervention personnel model and standards: An interdisciplinary field-based approach. *Infants and Young Children, 4*(1), 54–61.

Harbin, G.L. (1996). The challenge of coordination. *Infants and Young Children, 8*(3), 68–76.

Harbin, G.L., Gallagher, J., & Batista, L. (1992). *Status of states' progress in implementing Part H of IDEA: Report #4.* Chapel Hill: University of North Carolina at Chapel Hill, Carolina Policy Studies Program.

Harbin, G.L., Gallagher, J., & Lillie, T. (1991). *Status of states' progress in implementing Part H of IDEA: Report #3*. Chapel Hill: University of North Carolina at Chapel Hill, Carolina Policy Studies Program, Frank Porter Graham Child Development Center.

Harry, B. (1992). *Cultural diversity, families, and the special education system: Communication and empowerment*. New York: Teachers College Press.

Hoover, L. (1994). Use of telecomputing to support group-oriented inquiry during student teaching. In D. Willis, B. Robin, & J. Willis (Eds.), *Technology and teacher education annual* (pp. 652–656). Charlottesville, VA: Association for the Advancement of Computing in Education.

Individuals with Disabilities Education Act Amendments of 1991, PL 102-119, 20 U.S.C. § 1400 *et seq.*

Interstate New Teacher Assessment and Support Consortium. (1992). *The model standards for beginning teacher licensing and development: A resource for state dialog*. Washington, DC: Council of Chief State School Officers.

Kansas Infant-Toddler Services. (1993). *Kansas Infant-Toddler Services Community Network Program review process and site visit manual*. Topeka: Kansas Department of Health and Environment.

Kontos, S., & File, N. (1992). Conditions of employment, job satisfaction, and job commitment among early intervention personnel. *Journal of Early Intervention, 16*, 155–165.

Martin, E.W. (1989). Lessons from implementing PL 94-142. In J.J. Gallagher, P.L. Trohanis, & R.M. Clifford (Eds.), *Policy implementation and PL 99-457: Planning for young children with special needs* (pp. 19–32). Baltimore: Paul H. Brookes Publishing Co.

McCollum, J.A., & Bailey, D.B. (1991). Developing comprehensive personnel systems: Issues and alternatives. *Journal of Early Intervention, 15*(1), 57–65.

McCollum, J.A., & Yates, T.J. (1994). Technical assistance for meeting early intervention personnel standards: Statewide processes based on peer review. *Topics in Early Childhood Special Education, 14*(3), 295–310.

McLaughlin, M.J., Smith-Davis, J., & Burke, P.J. (1986). *Personnel to educate the handicapped in America: A status report*. College Park: University of Maryland, Institute for the Study of Exceptional Children and Youth.

Meisels, S. (1989). Meeting the mandate of PL 99-457: Early childhood intervention in the nineties. *American Journal of Orthopsychiatry, 59*, 451–460.

Meisels, S., Harbin, G., Modigliani, K., & Olson, K. (1988). Formulating optimal state early childhood intervention policies. *Exceptional Children, 55*, 159–165.

Miller, P.S. (1992). State interagency coordination for personnel development under PL 99-457: Building teams for effective planning. *Journal of Early Intervention, 16*(2), 146–154.

Miller, P.S., & Stayton, V.D. (1996). Personnel preparation in early education and intervention: Recommended preservice and inservice practices. In S.L. Odom & M.E. McLean (Eds.), *Early intervention/early childhood special education recommended practices* (pp. 329–358). Austin, TX: PRO-ED.

Odom, S.L. (1987). The role of theory in the preparation of professionals in early childhood special education. *Topics in Early Childhood Special Education, 7*(3), 1–11.

Phillips, D., & Crowell, N.A. (1994). Cultural diversity and early education: Report of a workshop [On-line], Available: URL:http://www.nap.edu/nap/online/earlyed/

Reddick, R., & King, E. (1996). *The online student: Making the grade on the Internet*. New York: Harcourt Brace.

Rosin, P., Whitehead, A.D., Tuchman, L.I., Jesien, G.S., Begun, A.L., & Irwin, L. (1996). *Partnerships in family-centered care: A guide to collaborative early intervention*. Baltimore: Paul H. Brookes Publishing Co.

Rush, M. (1993). Breaking down barriers through telecommunications. In D. Carey, R. Carey, D. Willis, & J. Willis (Eds.), *Technology and teacher education annual* (pp. 684–687). Charlottesville, VA: Association for the Advancement of Computing in Education.

Sexton, D., Snyder, P., Wolfe, B., Lobman, M., Stricklin, S., & Akers, P. (1996). Early intervention inservice training strategies: Perceptions and suggestions from the field. *Exceptional Children, 62*(6), 485–495.

Smith, B., & Powers, C. (1987). Issues related to developing state certification policies. *Topics in Early Childhood Special Education, 7*(3), 12–23.

Striffler, N. (1993). *Current trends in the use of paraprofessionals in early intervention and preschool services.* Chapel Hill: University of North Carolina at Chapel Hill, National Early Childhood Technical Assistance System.

Striffler, N. (1995). *Selected personnel policies and practices under Part H of IDEA.* Chapel Hill: University of North Carolina, National Early Childhood Technical Assistance System.

Strudler, N., Quinn, L., McKinney, M., & Jones, W.P. (1995). From coursework to the real world: First-year teachers and technology. *Technology and Teacher Education Annual, 1995: Proceedings of SITE 1995* (pp. 244–246). Charlottesville, VA: Association for the Advancement of Computing in Education.

Trohanis, P.L. (1994). Planning for successful inservice education for local early childhood programs. *Topics in Early Childhood Special Education, 14*(3), 311–332.

Willis, J., Willis, D., Austin, L., & Colon, B. (1995). Faculty perspective on instructional technology: A national survey. *Technology and Teacher Education Annual, 1995: Proceedings of SITE 1995* (pp. 795–800). Charlottesville, VA: Association for the Advancement of Computing in Education.

Winton, P.J. (1990). A systematic approach for planning inservice training related to Public Law 99-457. *Infants and Young Children, 3*(1), 51–60.

Winton, P.J., Catlett, C., & Houck, A. (1996). A systems approach. In D. Bricker & A. Widerstrom (Eds.), *Preparing personnel to work with infants and young children and their families: A team approach* (pp. 295–320). Baltimore: Paul H. Brookes Publishing Co.

Winton, P.J., & Crais, E.R. (1996). Moving towards a family-centered approach. In P.J. McWilliam, P.J. Winton, & E.R. Crais (Eds.), *Practical strategies for family-centered early intervention: Getting down to the brass tacks* (pp. 155–193). San Diego: Singular.

Wischnowski, M.W., Yates, T.J., & McCollum, J.A. (1996). Expanding training options for early intervention personnel: Developing a statewide staff mentoring system. *Infants and Young Children, 8*(4), 49–58.

Yoder, D., & Coleman, P. (1990). *Allied health personnel: Meeting the demands of Part H, PL 99-457.* Chapel Hill: University of North Carolina at Chapel Hill, Carolina Policy Studies Program.

APPENDIX

EARLY CHILDHOOD AND
EARLY INTERVENTION–RELATED WEB LINKS

GENERAL DISABILITY

CEC: Council for Exceptional Children
http://www.cec.sped.org

Family Village
http://familyvillage.wisc.edu

Disability Resources
http://www.icdi.wvu.edu/Others.htm

The Arc, a national organization on mental retardation
http://www.metronet.com/~thearc/welcome.html

Disability-Related Resources on the Web
http://www.metronet.com/~thearc/misc/dislnkin.html

EARLY CHILDHOOD/EARLY INTERVENTION

Division for Early Childhood
http://www.soe.uwm.edu/dec/dec.html

Early Childhood Education On Line
http://www.ume.maine.edu/~cofed/eceol/welcome.html

National Association for the Education of Young Children
http://www.america-tomorrow.com/naeyc/

National Center for Early Development and Learning
http://www.fpg.unc.edu

National Early Childhood Technical Assistance System
http://www.nectas.unc.edu

The Pathways Service Coordination Project
http://www.Waisman.Wisc.Edu/earlyint/b_index.htm

This appendix was compiled by George Jesien and Ann Hains, June 1996.

Adjunct ERIC Clearinghouse for Child Care
URL:http://ericps.ed.uiuc.edu/nccic/nccichome.html

ERIC Clearinghouse on Elementary and Early Childhood Education
http://ericps.ed.uiuc.edu/npin/npinhome.html

GENERAL EDUCATION

Adjunct ERIC Clearinghouse for Art Education
http://www.indiana.edu/~ssdc/art.html

ERIC Clearinghouse on Assessment and Evaluation
http://ericir.sunsite.syr.edu

ERIC Clearinghouse on Information and Technology
http://ericir.sunsite.syr.edu

ERIC Clearinghouse on Reading, English, and Communication
http://www.indiana.edu:80/~eric_rec

ERIC Clearinghouse on Urban Education
http://eric-web.tc.columbia.edu

CHILDREN

Children's Defense Fund
http://www.tmn.com/cdf/index.html

Children Now
http://www.dnai.com/~children/

Links to other resources on children's issues
http://www.dnai.com/~children/links.html

The Future of Children
http://www.futureofchildren.org/

National Child Care Information Center
http://ericps.ed.uiuc.edu/nccic/nccichome.html

Tribal Child Care Resource Directory
http://ericps.ed.uiuc.edu/nccic/tribedir/tribe.html

PARENTS AND FAMILIES

Internet Resources for Urban/Minority Families
http://eric-web.tc.columbia.edu/families/other.html

National Parent Information Network
http://www.ericps.ed.uiuc.edu/npin/npinhome.html

NPND Home Page
http://www.npnd.org/

The Family Empowerment Pages
http://www.downsyndrome.com/

MEDICAL INFORMATION

MedWeb: Disabilities
http://www.cc.emory.edu/WHSCL/medweb.disabled.html

Medline Guide (Ovid, Grateful, Med, PaperChase, Silver Platter, McSH)
http://www.sils.umich.edu/~nscherer/Medline/MedlineGuide.html

MedWeb: Pediatrics
http://www.cc.emory.edu/WHSCL/medweb.pediatrics.html

Virtual Hospital Home Page
http://vh.radiology.uiowa.edu/

LEGISLATIVE INFORMATION

THOMAS: Legislative information and link to Library of Congress
http://rs9.loc.gov/home/thomas.html

U.S. Senate: Info on individual senators and committees
http://www.senate.gov/

LRP Publications: Information on legislation and happenings in Washington, D.C.
http://www/lrp.com/lrpnet/index.html

FEDERAL GOVERNMENT

FedWorld
http://www.fedworld.gov/#hletr

Federal Health & Human Services Agencies on the Internet
http://www.os.dhhs.gov/progorg/progorg.html

U.S. Department of Education
http://www.ed.gov

Senator Frist, Chair of Senate Subcommittee on Disability Policy
http://www.senate.gov/~frist/

GRANT INFORMATION

Federal Register (October 1995–to date) ED Announcements
http://ges.ed.gov/fedreg/announce.html

Community of Science
http://cod.gdb.org/

Grantmaker Information
http://fdncenter.org/grantmaker/contents.html

PROGRAMS AND INSTITUTES

National Institute on Early Childhood Development and Education
http://www.ed.gov/offices/OERI/ECL/

National Institute on the Education of At-Risk Students
http://www.ed.gov/offices/OERI/At-Risk/ar_page1.html

Child and Family Studies Program (CFSP) of Allegheny-Singer Institute
http://www.asri.edu/CFSP/brochure/

National Center to Improve Practice in SpEd
http://www.edc.org/FSC/NCIP/

Waisman Center Home Page
http://www.Waisman.Wise.Edu/

Culturally and Linguistically Appropriate Services Early Childhood Research Institute
http://ericps.cro.uiuc.edu/clas/clashome.html

Early Childhood Research Institute on Measuring Growth and Development
http://mail.ici.coled.umn.edu.8001/ecri/

Office of Special Education
http://www.ed.gov/offices/OSERS/OSEP/osep.html

MISCELLANEOUS

The Chronicle of Higher Education—Academe This Week
http://chronicle.merit.edu/

Switchboard
http://www.switchboard.com/

3 COMMUNITY-BASED APPROACHES TO PERSONNEL PREPARATION

Patricia W. Wesley
Virginia Buysse

The need to change the way competent early intervention personnel are instructed and maintained is perhaps most critical when the relationships among service providers and families are defined at the community level. We depend on preservice and inservice instruction to provide communities with competent professionals and paraprofessionals to serve children and, increasingly, to work effectively with other adults, including families, colleagues, professionals from other disciplines, and other community members involved in the life of the child. Because of the multiple and complex roles of personnel practicing at the community level, ongoing and varied staff development experiences are needed to address the day-to-day challenges of teamwork in the rapidly changing field (Buysse & Wesley, 1993).

Given the diversity of communities, a local approach to training is an important way to ensure that personnel are skilled in the practices that are most relevant and responsive to their own communities. This chapter discusses the following questions:

- What are the critical components, challenges, and strategies of a community-based approach to personnel preparation?
- In what ways can community-based approaches promote innovative linkages between interests and groups that have not been related in traditional approaches to personnel preparation?
- What are some examples of community-based staff development models that facilitate effective changes at the local level?
- How can we evaluate the success of a community-based approach?
- How can we help communities develop an integrated systemwide approach to personnel preparation at the local level?
- What lessons have been learned from community-based approaches, and what are possible future directions of community-based personnel preparation efforts?

It may be helpful for the reader to compare his or her experiences with Allen County's[1] experiences, presented in the following description.

---

[1]The name of this county has been changed.

ALLEN COUNTY'S EXPERIENCE

Families and professionals in Allen County depend on a hodgepodge of instructional opportunities to develop and maintain their knowledge and skills in early education and early intervention. For example, every March the local Child Care Coalition sponsors a Day for Day Care when child care providers attend workshops at the local community college. Child care training credit is offered for participation in sessions led by local child care directors or teachers. The topics are chosen based on needs assessments completed the year before and often include behavior management, developmentally appropriate practice, and resources for children with special needs. Although anyone can attend Day for Day Care, publicity is limited to the county child care network, and local center- and home-based providers are usually the only participants.

The early interventionists in the county attend a 2-day state conference every year. There they receive infant specialist licensure credit for sessions on many of the same topics offered at Day for Day Care. The topics are chosen by the conference organizing committee based on the availability of speakers. The majority of participants are early childhood special educators who provide direct services to children with disabilities and their families, with only 10% being administrators. Therapists also go to the state conference but are more likely to attend state and national meetings of their own discipline's professional organizations.

Allen County's elementary schools sponsor 3 days of inservice training for teachers seeking certificate renewal credit. Although the topic this year was early childhood inclusion, the sessions were not publicized or open to people who were not school personnel. Following the teacher training, the schools held a month-long Spring Fling of weekly workshops for parents of children 3–8 years old. This spring, the teacher-led sessions focused on home–school communication.

One of the invited session leaders was a community college instructor from the Early Childhood Department. However, the Spring Fling schedule conflicted with a night course she was teaching on early childhood curriculum, so she could not participate. The community college course provides one of several preservice opportunities available locally. There are two major universities within a 45-mile radius of Allen County offering birth to kindergarten teacher licensure programs that reflect an inclusive focus to early childhood education. Interestingly, although more inclusive practicum sites are needed, the universities do not place students in Allen County and have not explored the potential of developing sites there.

WHAT CAN BE LEARNED FROM ALLEN COUNTY'S EXPERIENCE

The field of early intervention involves multiple settings, agencies, and funding sources along with numerous stakeholders. To be effective, staff development must do more than concentrate solely on the education of individuals. Ideally, it promotes and is guided by the creative collaboration of families, professionals from various disciplines, community organizations, agencies, and universities. In many cases, diverse groups have not worked together before (e.g., child care providers and special educators working in inclusive settings). In other cases, the organizations and individuals have prior working relationships, but from their own base, while they maintain distinctive boundaries of responsibilities (e.g., early childhood educators and therapists). A community-based approach to personnel preparation targets the local level as a critical context for change and provides opportunities for diverse participants in early intervention settings to address problems and issues related to their day-to-day experience. By listening to and understanding the unique perspectives that each brings to the issues at hand, community members can develop a shared knowledge and value base. A community-based approach recognizes the motives and ideologies of local participants as powerful influences on the adoption and institutionalization of change (McLaughlin, 1991) and recruits their involvement in designing opportunities for professional growth. The participation by a broad base of stakeholders, the emphasis on collaboration, and the importance of clarifying and reconstructing values during any change process are supported in the literature on planned change and organizational development (see Bennis, Benne, & Chin, 1985; Dimock, 1993; Kettner, Daley, & Nichols, 1985; McLaughlin, 1991; Mowbray & Freddelino, 1986; Schindler-Rainman & Lippitt, 1972).

In contrast, Allen County's story is reminiscent of Janet's story in Chapter 1 and illustrates a pattern of separating people who seek staff development according to agency, discipline, job description, and whether they are engaged in preservice or inservice instruction. There is some history in Allen County of clustering events in the spring, but a systemwide view of instruction that is responsive to ongoing local needs is absent. Although training needs are similar among child care providers, early interventionists, and teachers, needs assessment is not coordinated across agencies, and training opportunities are not jointly sponsored. There is a lack of variety in instruction, resulting in only brief exposures to topics through one-time workshops that prove inadequate to support people who hope to implement changes at the local level. Although coordination with the community college is attempted, there seems to be no dialogue between community agencies and the nearby universities about either's needs regarding personnel preparation. A critical shortcoming of Allen County's experience is the lost opportunity for professionals and families from diverse backgrounds to come together through staff development to create and sustain meaningful changes where they live and work.

CRITICAL COMPONENTS, CHALLENGES, AND IMPLEMENTATION STRATEGIES OF A COMMUNITY-BASED TRAINING APPROACH

To be effective at making substantial changes at the local level, staff development activities must include critical components based on principles of how change occurs. These components include the following:

1. Community members participate in planning staff development.
2. Training emphasizes strategic planning and problem-solving skills.
3. Participants from diverse backgrounds receive training together.
4. Learning opportunities are varied.
5. Staff development promotes innovative linkages among participants.

These critical components are discussed in the following sections; a summary of the components, challenges, and examples of strategies for overcoming the challenges are presented in Table 3.1.

Community Members Participate in Planning Staff Development

Because one factor in the adoption of any innovation is the degree to which it fits with the dominant motivations, needs, and interests of the system expected to change (Domergue, 1968), participation by local stakeholders in the planning process is the hallmark of a community-based approach. Those providing and receiving instruction must work together at the local level to gather information before training activities begin to ensure

TABLE 3.1.   Critical components of a community-based approach to training

Critical components	Challenges	Examples of strategies
Collaboration across agencies and disciplines to plan, deliver, and attend training	Motivating agencies to collaborate Coordinating logistics and scheduling	Identify incentives for broad participation such as sharing costs and resources Offer a variety of training credits, with options for continuing education credit when possible Build on existing training activities or traditions
Varied learning opportunities based on adult learning theory that are responsive to participants from diverse backgrounds who have different skills, attitudes, and values	Lack of positive attitudes on the part of participants toward innovative training models Lack of knowledge on the part of trainers about instructional methods, procedures, techniques, and technology	Publicize positive changes made as a result of training Link university technical assistance with instructors at state, regional, and local levels
Emphasis in training content on planning, problem solving, collaboration, and capacity building	Participants who want "quick fixes" or have had bad experiences working together	Help participants see staff development as a developmental process with both short- and long-term goals Involve participants in planning the content and process of instruction
Promotion of innovative linkages among participants	Helping participants to see benefits in working together in nontraditional partnerships	Foster trust by creating networking opportunities Identify common needs and benefits of working together Provide follow-through that supports innovative linkages

that the activities are relevant to community needs. Because the definition of community may expand to include neighborhoods, cities and towns, entire counties, and cultural contexts, it is not always easy to identify who should be involved in planning community-based personnel preparation efforts. We propose that at least five distinct stakeholder groups be involved in planning, delivering, receiving, and evaluating community-based instruction: consumers, including families of children with and without disabilities; providers who directly and personally deliver professional services to children and families; managers and administrators of the organizations delivering direct services to clients; policy makers who are responsible for standards governing an organization but who play no direct role in administering or executing these policies with the organization's clients; and professionals outside of the direct service agencies who provide instruction, consultation, and resources to those agencies and the families they serve (Gutkin, 1993; Wesley, 1995). These groups are presented in Table 3.2 along with examples of their members at the community level.

Once key stakeholders have been identified, an organizational structure for meeting to discuss and make decisions about personnel preparation issues is needed. Existing committees or groups, such as the local interagency coordinating council, can be modified to include community members who are not traditionally members of the council but have an interest in staff development. Information addressing the following general questions adapted from Schindler-Rainman and Lippitt (1975) can be gathered from key stakeholders through preliminary meetings to plan community-based training events:

1. *What is the purpose of the learning activity?*   Purposes might include the improvement of ongoing work of staff in the early intervention and early childhood fields; the development of new professional roles, licensure, or certification renewal; or the need for new process skills for a system (e.g., a series of meetings to improve communication across agencies).
2. *Who are the learners?*   What agencies and fields do they represent? What is their age, sex, and ethnicity? What is their background in terms of education and professional experience? In what ways have they worked with or received training with each other? Are any of them instructors?
3. *What types of related instruction have the learners had previously?*   How was it designed (e.g., when, where, how many participants, what type of follow-up)? How did they rate its effectiveness?

TABLE 3.2.   Key stakeholder groups

Stakeholder groups	Community members
Consumer	Families of children with and without disabilities, adults with disabilities
Service	Early interventionists, child care providers, Head Start staff, developmental evaluation center staff, public school preschool teachers and their assistants, therapists and other specialists, service coordinators, public health nurses
Management	Child care directors, Head Start supervisors, supervisors of early intervention personnel, developmental day directors, public school principals, preschool program coordinators
Policy	City and county government departments, Head Start executive boards, boards of local education agencies, child care programs, health departments, other local governing bodies
Support	Child care resources and referral agents, family support network, advocacy groups, university and community college systems, day care consultants, other early childhood trainers, churches and synagogues, YMCA, civic groups

4. *What size should the training groups be?*   Endless options are possible, of course, depending on the content needed and the community involved: small groups of 3–15, middle-size groups of 15–30, larger groups of up to 50, and conference-like groups of hundreds. What have the past experiences of the learners been? What physical spaces are available in the community? What will be the most facilitative group size for this event?

5. *How should the instruction be designed?*   There are a variety of ways people can come together to receive training. What previous experiences have the learners had? When and for how long are they available for training? What resources are available to support a variety of instruction formats (e.g., catering, audiovisual equipment, conference calls, conference centers, teleconferencing). (See Chapter 5 for examples of other critical questions related to instructional design.)

It is not always easy to provide staff development that truly meets needs at the community level or to coordinate with existing instructional efforts in order to build on local resources and eliminate duplication. It is no single agency's responsibility at the state or local level to improve or create a community-based approach, even though it is likely that families and professionals wish local agencies would speak the same language, would agree on similar values and philosophies, and would know what the other is doing. As a prerequisite to implementing successful community-based models, we, as instructors, must begin to see total groups, organizations, and networks as our clients. We must become diagnostic about the needs of the early intervention community as a whole, expanding our emphasis beyond the isolated training session to include a range of services and activities (Wesley & Buysse, 1996). Long-term commitment on the part of participants is also important in order to assess the instructional needs across community agencies and disciplines, examine licensure and other needs for training credit, and develop the logistics of planning and implementing the instructional events. To provide effective training, it is necessary to know what motivates participation in staff development as well as the specific content needed. In some instances, this type of information can be gathered in planning meetings. In others, surveys or questionnaires can be used effectively. (See Chapter 6 for needs assessment strategies.)

Training Emphasizes Strategic Planning and Problem-Solving Skills

A second critical component to a community-based approach is the emphasis on collaboration and problem solving, not only during the process of planning instruction but also in the instruction itself. It has been our experience that community stakeholders may confuse cooperation with collaboration, a distinction made by Melaville and Blank (1991) and Peterson (1991). For example, early childhood program staff in one community reported that they often "collaborated" to sponsor local staff development for child care providers by publishing one schedule of all agency-sponsored workshops in the weekly paper. The workshops, however, were not based on a communitywide needs assessment and were not jointly planned or sponsored. Local early intervention staff in another community reported they frequently "collaborated" with child care providers to plan the delivery of special education services to preschoolers with disabilities in inclusive settings. Their definition of collaboration, however, was that the early intervention team developed and presented a schedule for visiting children on their caseload at the child care programs to the child care staff ahead of time.

A community-based approach to staff development emphasizes group processes and the skills needed to collaborate in order to reach goals together that cannot be reached singly (Bruner, 1991). At the planning stage, community members representing diverse agencies and interests jointly assess training needs and design personnel preparation activities involving stakeholders across the community. A framework such as the seven-step model of team development developed by Drexler, Sibbet, and Forrester (1992) can be used to support this planning process. This model includes recruiting and orienting participants to a planning process, building trust, assessing needs, developing a written plan to meet the needs, implementing the plan, evaluating outcomes, and providing opportunities for participant renewal. Then, the community planners make sure that instruction about collaboration and strategic planning is among the opportunities offered community-wide, so that participants may gain skills to develop new structures for coordinating activities and relating to each other.

It can be difficult to market strategic planning processes as critical content in instruction. Training participants often want "quick fixes" to their problems and find it difficult to find the time and opportunity to focus on the planning process itself. As one early childhood interventionist put it, "Our team is overwhelmed with case management issues. We're just trying to keep our heads above water and make the best decisions we can. Right now we can't afford to think about our decision-making *process*—there's too much else to do!" Practitioners and their supervisors may believe that increased attention to planning and collaboration may mean fewer direct service hours for children and families and that they cannot "bill" for planning time. When strategic planning involves multiple agencies, confusion may exist over who should lead such efforts. One effective strategy is to begin with interagency planning groups already in existence, with identified leaders and an established team culture and structure.

Participants from Diverse Backgrounds Receive Training Together

A third critical component of effective community-based training is providing opportunities for specialists, teachers, teacher assistants, families, administrators, health professionals, social workers, and others who work with young children and their families to receive training together. Depending on the content, this may mean instruction is provided for a team of personnel within a single agency or for a broader audience of different agencies and disciplines across the community. Participants who share staff development experiences can better understand each other's services, vocabulary, philosophies, and values and then form or expand supportive relationships throughout the process of acquiring and using new knowledge and skills.

Attracting and maintaining the attention of participants from different agencies, disciplines, and levels of responsibility is challenging. Although training topics and competencies that cut across community interests can be identified through needs assessment, the process of offering appropriate training credit for different disciplines and agencies requires considerable planning and documentation. There may be resistance among staff with advanced degrees to participate in joint instructional sessions with child care providers who may have far less formal education. Child care providers may have concerns that staff development activities attended by administrators or staff who have advanced degrees may not have direct relevance to their own day-to-day jobs. It could be difficult to identify presenters from diverse backgrounds who are knowledgeable about content and skilled in teaching methods that will actively involve a wide range of individuals.

Perhaps the most effective way to maintain broad participation in community-based personnel preparation is to collect in advance information that will enable instructors to design activities that are truly responsive to specific community needs. For example, before providing instruction about consultation to support early childhood inclusion, it would be helpful to know where children with disabilities and their families receive services, how consultation is used in the community to meet their needs (e.g., who provides consultation to whom), and, as mentioned previously, the types of training that consultants and consultees have received. To respond to families and agencies who want to make changes in the early intervention referral system, it is necessary first to help them determine where the problems are. Do key players need basic information about how to contact the appropriate people to make referrals, or does the process break down once the referrals are received?

Training activities should include an examination of values and roles and should be designed to promote interaction among groups of participants (e.g., small-group discussions among administrators and direct service personnel or child care providers and special educators may be helpful). In addition, instruction should provide opportunities for participants to consider how they will apply their new knowledge and skills directly to their jobs. Encouraging participants to keep journals during their training and to develop written plans for using their new skills helps them to see direct outcomes of staff development and may motivate them to seek subsequent training experiences (Everson & Moon, 1990; Peck, Furman, & Helmstetter, 1993; Winton, 1990).

Learning Opportunities Are Varied

Participation by training recipients in planning and evaluation is critical to selecting effective instructional methods. Increased identification of and interaction among instructors at the community level in order to share strategies and experiences could increase the likelihood that a variety of effective approaches is used.

A community-based approach should employ instructional methods consistent with principles of adult learning theory (Guskey, 1986; Knowles, 1978; Schindler-Rainman & Lippitt, 1972) and provide a variety of learning opportunities for participants from diverse backgrounds who may have different levels of experience and may be in different stages of development in their skills, attitudes, and values. In their discussion of a self-renewal process for community agencies, Schindler-Rainman and Lippitt (1975) presented five phases of an ideal continuous training plan:

1. *Preservice training*   Train staff before they begin work.
2. *Start-up support*   Assist staff as they begin their work.
3. *Maintenance-of-effort training*   Provide opportunities during employment for staff to ask questions and gain additional job-related knowledge and skills.
4. *Periodic review and feedback*   Provide opportunities for supervisor and staff to discuss whether goals are being accomplished and how they feel about the work being done.
5. *Transition training*   Train staff to assume new roles and responsibilities, for example, in consultation, supervision, and leadership.

Using a framework such as this is helpful in thinking about various options that could be developed through a community-based approach. For example, apprenticeships or practicum placements in the community are effective preservice options, whereas on-site consultation or special problem-solving clinics are appropriate to help personnel refine their skills on the job (Schindler-Rainman & Lippitt, 1975). The instructional content also influences the selection of a particular type of learning opportunity. For example, a 2-day intensive session followed by 4–6 months of field work and follow-up meetings may be a productive way to teach early interventionists a model for providing consultation to child care providers. An effective strategy for providing community-based training about transition may include a series of meetings with an interagency group to determine technical assistance needs, instruction, and on-site consultation to support the development of a transition plan, and follow-up technical assistance.

The lack of financial resources and positive attitudes toward innovations in staff development may present challenges. Funding may not be adequate to support multiple or intensive activities such as on-site consultation, mentorships, or technical assistance. Funding sources may place more value on traditional training practices (e.g., one-time workshops for 80–100 people). Similarly, administrators and supervisors who approve funds and work time for staff development may prefer state-level instruction because of its generally short duration and its emphasis on procedures that ensure compliance with regulations and the law.

Publicizing positive changes made at the local level as a result of training can go a long way in changing attitudes toward innovations in staff development. For example, when families comment on and other staff see the improvements made in classrooms in which teachers receive on-site consultation to improve quality, staff in other classrooms often want to participate in the consultation process also (Wesley, 1994). Administrators who at first reluctantly authorize staff time to participate in mentor programs may support their involvement enthusiastically after observing the boost in staff morale and professionalism that results in the first year.

Staff Development Promotes Innovative Linkages Among Participants

Finally, a community-based approach promotes collaboration among interests and groups that have not been traditionally related, for example, between early childhood and early childhood special education, preservice and inservice programs, families and instructors, management and direct services, and professionals and paraprofessionals. Through collaboration, maximum use is made of local resources, talents, and skills. For example, a study tour might be planned to provide general and special early childhood professionals and parents the opportunity to visit inclusive community-based programs in another part of the state or another state. Participants could be selected based on applications that identify community teams of representatives from general and special early childhood education, families of young children, allied health, and administration. The teams could agree in advance to report on their experiences during the tour at state and regional conferences when they return. Table 3.3 presents additional examples of collaborative outcomes from such nontraditional partnerships.

INNOVATIVE MODELS THAT FEATURE A COMMUNITY-BASED APPROACH

Communities and the organizations within them have their own cultures, ways of doing things, and patterns of relationships (Kanter, Stein, & Jick, 1992). Communitywide collaboration is both a means and an end in personnel preparation: We are learning to collaborate as we teach others to do so. In this section, seven innovative approaches to personnel preparation at the local level are described that address issues in early childhood intervention and that have been implemented in various communities in North Carolina.

Community Forums

One example of how representatives from the key stakeholder domains can be involved as organizers, implementers, and recipients in a community-based instruction initiative is the Community Forum on Early Childhood Inclusion (Wesley, 1995). The Community Forum was developed by the Partnerships for Inclusion (PFI) project at the Frank Porter

TABLE 3.3. Innovative linkages and outcomes

Linkages	Collaboration	Outcomes
Early childhood education and early intervention	Community colleges embed early intervention content into early childhood courses and collaborate with local child care directors to use inclusive community child care programs as practicum sites.	Graduates with associate degrees in early childhood gain knowledge and skills in special education. Their preservice experience teaching children with and without disabilities prepares them to work in inclusive child care programs.
Preservice and inservice programs	The Speech-Language Pathology Department at Georgia's Valdosta State University has increased communication with local agencies and consumers to develop long-range plans responsive to community needs.	The department has seven full-time faculty positions at a time when other departments are closing. Some faculty conduct inservice training in the field. Communities share issues and problems in day-to-day practice that help prepare speech-language pathologists for the real world.
Families and inservice programs	A North Carolina technical assistance project prepares parents of children with disabilities as public speakers about their experiences with early intervention. Parents then participate as co-presenters in various training and information sessions in their own regions.	People have opportunities to hear the perspectives of families with disabilities, often for the first time. Instructors who like the model of co-presenting with a parent are given a list of parents in their region who are interested in public speaking.
Management and direct service providers	An interagency partnership in North Carolina's Mecklenburg County requires child care directors and teachers from the same child care program to attend training together in order for their program to be eligible to receive small grants.	Administrators and teachers share ideas and jointly develop a plan for improving their program.
Professionals and paraprofessionals	A local early intervention program offers on-site consultation to early childhood classroom teachers, teaching assistants, and specialists to improve program quality.	Both professional and paraprofessional classroom staff learn strategies for solving problems together to improve services for children.

Graham Child Development Center at the University of North Carolina at Chapel Hill, a statewide project that provides technical assistance to communities as they develop and expand programs that serve children both with and without disabilities and their families. During 1992–1995, the PFI project co-sponsored 36 forums that involved 45 counties and were attended by more than 2,000 participants.

A community forum is a half-day event in which community members with diverse backgrounds gather to learn more about options for integrating children with disabilities and their families into all aspects of mainstream community life. Typically, it is sponsored by the local interagency coordinating council (ICC) or another planning group that includes members from all five stakeholder groups. PFI provides assistance in developing the agenda, recruiting speakers, and evaluating the forum. Forum organizers have found that providing continuing education and training credits, food, time for networking, comfortable accommodations, on-site child care, and door prizes are powerful incentives for community members to attend. Forum participants include child care providers and directors, parents, early interventionists, preschool teachers, school principals, doctors and nurses, staff from the county recreation department, ministers, child care resource and referral agents, Head Start staff, librarians, county commissioners, and others interested in the lives of young children. The agenda usually includes the following:

- Presentations by parents of children with disabilities
- A video about a young child with cerebral palsy who attends a child care program for typically developing children
- A panel presentation by local agencies in the community about their services
- A display about local services and resources
- Small-group discussions about planned topics
- Time for networking among participants
- Opportunities for participants to plan "next steps" of collaboration after the forum is over

Similar to a "town meeting," the forum serves as a vehicle to identify key stakeholders, their attitudes toward and roles in implementing early childhood inclusion, and the local needs of children and families relative to inclusion. During small-group discussions, participants share their visions for the future of services for young children and their families and begin to assess their local program and continued training needs related to inclusion. Packets of written information about key concepts and local resources along with sample forms that can be used to record plans for community action based on the forum experience are distributed. Because of the broad-based community participation in its planning, the forum offers information and staff development that begin where the participants are—ideologically, conceptually, and practically. As a form of personnel preparation, a community forum could be used to explore other topics such as service coordination, transition, family-centered practices, or cultural diversity.

Community Program Planning Teams

The use of interagency groups or community planning teams to plan and develop human service programs has been advocated as an approach that reduces gaps and duplication in services, makes efficient use of scarce resources, and replaces professional turfism with collaboration (Bruner, 1991; LaCour, 1982; Melaville, Blank, & Asayesh, 1993; Peterson, 1991). Through the Individuals with Disabilities Education Act (IDEA), collaborative teamwork among agencies to develop infant and toddler programs is encouraged from the top down. Other innovations develop from the bottom up as communities themselves identify needs or opportunities to change and initiate forming a local team to address them (Kettner et al., 1985). Everson and Moon (1990) described an eight-step process that has been used by community program planning teams in various localities to plan and implement changes in transition and supported employment practices: initiate a team, define the community need, identify team members, hold an initial planning meeting, define the community program planning team's mission, assess the change opportunity, set objectives and activities, and monitor and evaluate the change effort. This approach, similar to other strategic planning models in human services and business (Bailey, McWilliam, Winton, & Simeonsson, 1992; Drexler et al., 1992; Kettner et al., 1985; Melaville, Blank, & Asayesh, 1993; Weisbord, 1992), offers a decision-making framework that can be used by any group of professionals, consumers, parents, and other advocates committed to facilitating changes at the local level.

In some communities, the local ICC may expand its role beyond coordinating services for children and families to planning and implementing training opportunities. For example, one ICC worked together to plan a series of meetings at the public library for parents about IDEA. In other communities, the core group of forum organizers may continue as a community program planning team, designing and implementing subsequent activities based on needs identified during the community forum. For example, additional instruction for child care providers about inclusion was identified as a critical need in a rural county in the eastern part of North Carolina. An early interventionist, child care resource and referral agent, health department nurse, child care director, preschool teacher, and parent in that county continued to meet together after the forum to plan naptime seminars and technical assistance strategies for the child care network. Another example of a community program planning team is the Family Day Care Home Network established in the northeast region of North Carolina through the support of the Infant-Toddler Care Project at the University of North Carolina at Chapel Hill. Funded by the North Carolina Council on Developmental Disabilities, the Infant-Toddler Care Project provided on-site consultation to improve quality in child care programs serving children with and without disabilities in 17 counties. Through their relationships with professionals and parents in the local child care networks, project staff were made aware of a need for inclusive community placements for infants and toddlers with disabilities. They assisted local communities in organizing a Family Day Care Home Network of teams of key participants in early intervention, including parents, to recruit, screen, train, and provide support to family child care home providers interested in serving infants and toddlers. In meetings facilitated by Infant-Toddler Care Project staff, the leaders of these teams (usually early interventionists or child care resource and referral agents) met quarterly at the regional level to share ideas, resources, and experiences and to develop written instructional materials.

Community planning teams also represent a key component of Smart Start, North Carolina's statewide early childhood initiative. Each year since its inception in 1993, the state has awarded grants to a growing number of local communities to plan and implement early childhood services. Smart Start brings together family members, educators, human service providers, church groups, business leaders, and local government officials to focus on the needs of young children (birth to 5) and their families. A nonprofit, public–private corporation called the North Carolina Partnerships for Children was established as a part of Smart Start to set broad goals for early childhood services across the state. These goals include ensuring that every child arrives at school healthy and prepared to be successful; providing high-quality, affordable early childhood care and education programs and other critical services for every child who needs them; and supporting parents in their roles as caregivers of young children. The community planning teams decide how best to address the state goals, tailoring their plans to reflect the specific needs and resources existing within their own communities.

To support the implementation of a comprehensive service system for young children and their families in every community, many counties are including a training component in their Smart Start development plans. Smart Start funds have been used to support community-based staff development activities designed to meet systemwide needs. Training components include collaborative and ongoing features such as the following:

- Developing a countywide fund to defray registration and other training costs
- Publishing a communitywide training calendar in the spring and fall
- Disseminating one-page fliers about the types of training credit available and the application process for offering or receiving such credit through state agencies
- Organizing an annual early childhood conference sponsored by and for multiple agencies at the local level
- Organizing an annual resource fair sponsored by and for local agencies and families
- Recruiting, screening, and training a group of substitute teachers to work in local preschools, child care centers, and homes
- Identifying Spanish interpreters who could be available as needed at training events
- Identifying local parents of young children with disabilities who are interested in copresenting as instructors or panel members
- Developing an annual countywide training needs assessment
- Scheduling annual speakers at the Smart Start meetings to share information about local services and issues related to young children and families

Smart Start not only identifies specific instructional strategies as part of a community-based approach but also offers a model for communitywide collaboration on staff development issues.

On-Site Consultation

On-site consultation is another community-based instructional approach to instruction that has proved to be effective. The Inclusion Partners Project at the University of North Carolina at Chapel Hill has expanded one model of consultation developed to improve quality in community-based programs for children with and without disabilities (Wesley, 1994). Through the Inclusion Partners Project, early intervention and early childhood consultants receive training and on-site technical assistance as they collaborate with child care providers to improve center- and home-based programs for young children. The initial instruction is provided at the regional level, and follow-up support and instruction are conducted in the participants' home communities. People interested in receiving the training must complete a detailed application describing their primary professional role, their previous training and experience in consultation, and their preliminary plans for using an on-site consultation model. Individual counties within the region are encouraged to send two or three professionals from various agencies to the training, and participants include early interventionists, child care resource and referral agents, child care directors, state child care licensing consultants, and directors of exceptional children's programs in public schools. In some instances, participants are already providing consultation to support early childhood inclusion or improve quality in child care programs. Others are direct service providers moving into consulting roles, as in the case of early interventionists who visit increasing numbers of children in community settings in which they work closely with other adults providing direct services to the child.

An initial 2-day session presents consultation skills and strategies and assists participants in planning to implement the model with community programs. After the initial 2-day session, consultants work with staff in one classroom at a time to make improvements in the early childhood environment based on a joint assessment of needs using an environment rating scale. Any adults with a direct interest in the classroom (e.g., early childhood teachers, assistants, therapists, volunteers, child care directors) may participate in the consultation process as consultees. The classroom staff typically serve children with and without disabilities. Staff from the Inclusion Partners Project provide on-site consultation to help the consultants expand and refine their skills as they collaborate with the classroom staff.

The consultation process takes 4–6 months to complete and results in three innovative outcomes. First, preliminary evaluation results have demonstrated that each classroom makes significant improvements in quality as measured by postscores on The Early Childhood Environment Rating Scale (Harms & Clifford, 1980) or the Infant-Toddler Environment Rating Scale (Harms, Cryer, & Clifford, 1990). Second, the classroom serves as a model of high-quality early childhood inclusion for preservice students in the community college system who are placed in the classroom for their practicum experience. Third, the consultants attend quarterly meetings of people trained in the on-site model of consultation where they share ideas, solve problems, and plan and receive ongoing instruction related to their practice. The consultants share sponsorship and organization of the meetings and obtain technical assistance as needed through their local universities. In this way, a network of trained early intervention and early childhood consultants in the state is supported through a community-based effort.

Supervision and Mentorship

According to Fenichel (1991) and Pawl (1995), supervision and mentoring are critical components of staff development (see also Chapter 8). They defined supervision and mentoring as relationships for learning whose essential features are reflection, collaboration, and regularity. Pairing less experienced with more experienced people has been used as an instructional strategy in many fields for years. In preservice programs, intern or practicum opportunities are generally offered after classroom instruction on basic knowledge and skills. Linking supervised work experience in a variety of community settings to personnel preparation enhances the likelihood that instruction will be meaningful and relevant to the participant. Mentors 'n Mainstreaming is an example of a program in North Carolina that reflects the concept of a "continuum of professional supervision" (Willer & Bredekemp, 1993, p. 65), extending from mentees who are just acquiring specialized knowledge and rely on others to demonstrate effective practice, to those who can model effective practice and contribute to the generation of new knowledge and skills.

Mentors 'n Mainstreaming is a community staff development program for early childhood professionals sponsored by the North Carolina Division of Child Development and administered by Community Partnerships, Inc., of Wake County, in conjunction with the University of North Carolina at Greensboro. Community Partnerships, Inc., is a private, nonprofit agency that provides inclusive services for children, youth, and adults with disabilities and their families focused on their full involvement in community child care, education, leisure, and employment opportunities. The Mentors 'n Mainstreaming program trains professionals currently working in inclusive early childhood settings as mentors for early childhood student interns from community colleges who are placed in their classrooms; these mentors must have a 2- or 4-year degree in early childhood, special education, or a related field and 1 year's experience including children with disabilities in classrooms. Mentors receive 3 hours of release time each week to complete two mandatory 45-hour courses: Early Childhood Leadership and Managing Preschool Children's Environments. The second course provides credit toward the North Carolina Department of Public Instruction's Birth to Kindergarten teacher certificate. After completing the courses, mentors are awarded a 4% salary increase and a $200 bonus by combining funding from Community Partnerships, Inc., and the local child care resource and referral agency. Mentors work with community college students for 1 year, are supervised by staff of Community Partnerships, Inc., and collaborate with Child Care Resource and Referral of Wake County to coordinate placements of children with special needs into their classrooms. Evaluation data from this project's first year of operation indicate that mentors ranked the following program components from most to least important: courses, consultation received to assist in implementing course learning, recognition, salary bonus, and salary increase. This ranking suggests that the desire for professional growth and development is highly motivational and valued.

Staff Development that Responds to Diverse Cultural Needs

Communities face many challenges as they develop and provide early intervention services for ethnically and racially diverse populations. These include the need to develop understanding and respect for other cultures and may require learning another language or learning to work with interpreters. The challenges of one rural county in central North Carolina are typical of many small communities throughout the state as they attempt to respond to the needs of an increasing Latino population. Early intervention and other human services staff in Chatham County need information about the culture of immigrants from El Salvador, Guatemala, Honduras, Mexico, Nicaragua, and other Central American countries, including cultural beliefs about disability, child rearing, and community services. They need increased awareness about their own cultural background and how their beliefs and values can affect their interactions with families. Latino families may need to know about resources for financial assistance and education and may need information about other community services and child development.

The Madres-a-Madres program, funded by the local health department, has made a start at meeting the needs of both the professional and Latino groups. Through Madres-a-Madres, Latina mothers of young children in Chatham County meet weekly to share ideas and experiences and to receive instruction from Latino project coordinators related to skills and resources that support parenting. Transportation and child care are provided along with time to socialize and enjoy refreshments. Mothers are encouraged to find a "partner" among the participants with whom to continue dialogue between sessions and to expand their networks of family support as their interests and familiarity with community resources increase. From time to time, staff from various agencies make presentations, other family members are invited to attend, and special potlucks are scheduled that are open to the community. Future possibilities for Madres-a-Madres include involving the parents as mentors to professionals who want to increase their own cultural sensitivity and family-centered practices through firsthand experience with Latino families. Other members from the Latino community serve on interagency committees to identify needs and develop new services for the Latino immigrants and to plan and deliver training to raise cultural awareness and sensitivity.

Parents as Presenters

Guskey and Peterson (1996) stressed that participation by all staff members and parents is critical to developing high-quality staff in effective schools. In their work promoting family centeredness, Bailey, Buysse, Smith, and Elam (1992) found the perspectives of parents to be valuable in helping professionals perceive a need to change. In providing technical assistance to communities across North Carolina, the PFI project encourages and models copresenting with a parent of a child with disabilities in staff development activities (see also Chapter 17). The project often pairs as presenters parents of children with disabilities and parents of typically developing children who have experienced inclusion. To help communities identify parents interested in presenting, the PFI project brings 10–12 parents from across the state together for training and support during a 2-day retreat. Project consultants recruit parents from their regions who want to learn how to become effective public speakers about their own experiences in the early childhood intervention system. Depending on the interests of the parents (determined through telephone interviews prior to the retreat), objectives at the retreat generally include the following:

- Refining understanding of the early intervention service system
- Learning pointers for dynamic presentations, including how to use personal artifacts such as photographs and children's artwork
- Observing a parent give a presentation about his or her experiences
- Beginning to formulate and practice presentations in front of the group
- Developing a plan for organizing any props they wish to incorporate in their own presentations, for receiving additional training, and for meeting with other parent participants after the 2-day retreat

After the retreat, the PFI project staff distribute a written flier about the parent presenters to key state and local agencies and training organizations, which are encouraged to negotiate directly with parents about presenting. This project also assists in locating bilingual speakers to serve as translators for Latino parents who schedule presentations. Staff also copresent with the parents in various communities and organize regional meetings twice per year to provide parents who have participated in the retreat opportunities to share their experiences as presenters.

Professional Development Schools

The emphasis on providing career-long teacher education through collaboration among universities and community schools has produced a nationwide initiative, the Professional Development School (PDS) model (Fullan, 1993). The major purpose of the PDS model is to enhance children's learning through a systematic program of professional development and research related to improving practice. It is based on the need for schools of education and other instructional programs to provide more applied instruction in quality, real-world settings for preservice and inservice learners. The PDS model encourages collaboration among various stakeholders interested in the welfare of children and families. These stakeholders typically represent teacher organizations, teachers, parents, school boards, businesses and corporations, school administrators, and university faculty.

Although teachers describe their student-teaching experiences as shaping their professional practice (The Holmes Group, 1986), preservice students often are placed in practicum settings in which teachers are not trained in the methods that the preservice students are learning in their university classes. The intent of the PDS model is to create a collaborative instructional experience for preservice and inservice participants with university faculty and other participants on equal footing. It enables education professionals to contribute to the advancement of quality services for children and families by participating in practicum seminars and classes at the university as well as assisting in the preparation of new practitioners who are placed as practicum students in their classrooms.

The relationship between the community-based professionals and university personnel implementing the PDS model is governed by four principles:

- *Reciprocity*—a mutual exchange regarding recommended practices
- *Experimentation*—a willingness to try new forms of intervention or practice
- *Systematic inquiry*—the requirement that new ideas be subject to careful study and validation
- *Student diversity*—a commitment to developing intervention strategies for a broad range of children and families with different sociocultural backgrounds, abilities, and learning styles (The Holmes Group, 1986)

As a community-based approach to personnel development, the PDS model's goal to restructure both community schools and universities to develop model sites providing inservice and preservice development is daunting. Nationwide, the first published reports of implementing the PDS model have only recently been released (Darling-Hammond, 1994). As noted by Pugach and Pasch (as cited in Fullan, 1993), it is clear that, to be effective, change of this scope will take years and should be viewed in the larger context of school reform and restructuring.

A FRAMEWORK FOR EVALUATING COMMUNITY-BASED APPROACHES

Community planners frequently face a number of challenges in their attempts to evaluate innovative approaches to personnel preparation and instruction. Sometimes it is difficult to identify individuals within the community with expertise in program evaluation. Even when these individuals are available, resources that can be allocated for evaluation efforts generally are limited. Because a variety of stakeholders should be encouraged to participate in the evaluation process to enhance the cultural relevance and utilization of the evaluation results (Greene, 1987; Orlandi, 1992), another challenge is determining the evaluation agenda.

To overcome these challenges, evaluation efforts at the community level should focus on addressing three critical questions, while keeping in mind the availability of funds to support these efforts: 1) What are the goals of a coordinated community-based approach to personnel preparation? 2) What is the purpose of evaluating this effort? and 3) How will the evaluation results be used to improve future community-based personnel preparation activities?

Identifying the Goals of a
Community-Based Approach to Personnel Preparation

The first step in developing an evaluation plan is to identify the goals of the program (Branham, 1992). Although the specific goals and objectives of a coordinated system of personnel preparation will be unique to every community, most goals can be clustered under four broad areas. These include 1) increased collaboration and coordination of personnel preparation efforts; 2) increased or improved attitudes, knowledge, and skills among a diverse group of human services professionals (e.g., teachers, child care providers, early interventionists, therapists); 3) consumer satisfaction with personnel preparation activities; and 4) improved child, family, and program outcomes resulting from personnel preparation activities. Selecting the appropriate evaluation methods and measures will depend, in part, on the emphasis community planners place on each of these areas in designing their instruction initiatives and developing an evaluation plan, as well as the availability of resources to conduct the evaluation.

Identifying the Purpose of Evaluation of Personnel Preparation

In addition to identifying the goals of personnel preparation, community planners should consider the purposes for conducting the evaluation, the audience for the evaluation results, and a set of criteria for determining if personnel preparation efforts were successful (Branham, 1992; Division for Early Childhood Task Force on Recommended Practices, Council for Exceptional Children, 1993; Trohanis, 1986). Three common purposes for conducting an evaluation of personnel instruction include monitoring and accountability, documenting contexts and processes, and determining outcomes.

Monitoring and Accountability   Monitoring is a useful tool for documenting the extent to which people actually participated in personnel preparation and training activities and for projecting future training needs. Examples of monitoring activities include recording the number and nature of training requests, documenting where and when training events occurred and the number of people who attended them, and tracking instruction-related expenditures. Some communities have established computerized databases to monitor requests for instruction and utilization of project services and activities by various consumer groups.

Documenting Contexts and Processes   Another purpose for conducting an evaluation of personnel preparation efforts is to document the context and processes involved in implementing personnel preparation. Documenting the process involves delineating the steps of designing, implementing, and evaluating instruction, whereas documenting the context involves specifying the components of instruction that might mediate expected outcomes. For example, initial steps in developing community-level training may include identifying an interagency planning team, conducting an assessment of training needs, developing a training agenda, and identifying staff development resources. By documenting each stage of this process, participants create a permanent record of how training was planned and implemented and can build on this knowledge for future training activities. At the same time, it is important to recognize that training outcomes, such as participant satisfaction, can be influenced by a variety of factors including contextual variables (e.g., geography, demographics, politics, logistics), the instructional format (e.g., case method, small-group discussion, large-group presentation), the facilitator's presentation style (e.g., didactic, interactive), or the perceived relevance and usefulness of the content. To document context variables that are most likely to mediate training outcomes, community planners could gather information about participants' level of education, experience, and perceived training needs and record descriptive information about various instructional events in a personnel preparation log or registry. The emphasis should be placed on finding out how particular aspects of training or characteristics of participants affect the outcomes of training. The results of these evaluation activities can be used throughout the process to improve the ways in which community planners design and carry out personnel preparation.

Determining Program-Related Outcomes   Finally, an evaluation of community-based approaches to personnel preparation and training is essential to determine the results of these efforts for children, families, professionals, and programs. An integrated, community-based approach to personnel preparation should result in systemic accomplishments that involve the services and infrastructure of programs as well as human outcomes: improvements for children and families (Kagan, Goffin, Golub, & Pritchard, 1995). For example, as a result of integrated staff development, communities can expect to see an array of programmatic changes such as an increase in the number of qualified human services professionals; enhanced professional collaboration and coordination across programs and agencies; innovations in how personnel preparation is funded (e.g., pooling funds from various agencies) and regulated (e.g., combined early childhood and early childhood special education certification); and, most important, improved availability and quality of direct services for children and families.

How do community planners evaluate these programmatic changes? As mentioned previously, the answer depends on the goals of the personnel preparation program, the priorities of community planners and funders, and the availability of resources to conduct the evaluation. Although several methods have been developed to assess changes in program infrastructure and services as part of a comprehensive program evaluation, these have not been designed specifically to assess outcomes related to personnel preparation and training efforts. Since the late 1980s, several promising approaches have emerged. For example, network analysis can be used to document change with respect to collaboration and coordination among professionals from various agencies. Network analysis employs a questionnaire or interview format to assess the interactions and relationships among professionals from different backgrounds. The primary purposes of this approach are to assess professionals' awareness of other agencies and services, to determine the degree of influence exercised by agencies, and to describe client referral patterns (Neenan, Orthner, & Crocker, 1995). The network analysis can be administered to targeted community agency personnel during initial implementation of a coordinated personnel preparation system as a means of gathering baseline data and every year thereafter to assess change in agency collaboration over time. A second approach is to assess changes in the competence of early childhood professionals resulting from comprehensive staff development efforts on a pre- and posttest basis (Wesley & Buysse, 1994). A third approach is to evaluate the effects of an integrated system of personnel preparation on service delivery patterns within the community. Although most states are still pioneering these efforts, extant Infant-Toddler and Preschool program databases maintained by various state agencies can be used to document changes that occur regarding the nature and location of services for young children with disabilities and families who are eligible for services under IDEA (Buysse, Bernier, Tyndall, Gardner, & Munn, 1996).

Determining Child and Family Outcomes It is logical to assume that systemic changes in personnel preparation and their corresponding effects on the quality of human services personnel and service delivery programs will have a direct impact on children and families within the community. Unfortunately, it is difficult to attribute positive child and family outcomes to an isolated effort such as training (Kagan et al., 1995). Additional challenges of an outcome orientation, according to Kagan and colleagues (1995), include defining desired outcomes and determining which activities best promote them, devising methods for collecting and aggregating data across agencies, and determining the extent to which the innovative program actually takes hold within the community. Part of the difficulty in demonstrating a connection between staff development and child and family outcomes stems from a traditional focus on the behavior of the professional rather than on the outcome of professional behavior (Buckley, Albin, & Mank, 1988). In light of these challenges, efforts to evaluate child and family outcomes related to community-based training should be carried out in conjunction with ongoing, comprehensive program evaluation efforts.

Depending on their relevance to the goals of the personnel preparation program, examples of child outcome indicators that community planners may want to consider include developmental progress, immunization rates, and reports of child abuse and neglect. Indicators of family outcomes to be considered include family well-being (e.g., parenting stress indexes, family support measures), parent participation in various early childhood programs, and use of and satisfaction with other services and supports. Existing databases available through state or local agencies and other program evaluation studies may prove more useful in documenting these child and family outcomes than original data collection, which can be costly and difficult to manage. Although it is a challenging task, specifying clear outcomes from the start can be helpful to community planners in developing a vision and clarifying the purposes of a coordinated personnel preparation system.

Using Evaluation Results to
Improve Future Personnel Preparation Activities

The results of an evaluation of a community-based approach to personnel preparation can be used for several important purposes: to judge the effectiveness of training efforts, to determine how instruction can be improved, and to demonstrate to funders and other stakeholders that training was carried out in the way it was intended to be (Branham, 1992). The success of personnel preparation is determined at the end of the program or at predetermined points in time through the use of outcome data, whereas efforts to improve personnel preparation are derived from process variables collected throughout the project. The results of the evaluation should be used by community planners to understand and interpret how changes in personnel preparation occurred, to determine which aspects of the program or the community served as barriers or supports to a coordinated system of instruction, and to identify strengths and weaknesses of the personnel preparation program.

LESSONS LEARNED

Our experiences and those of other participants in the models described in this chapter offer two important lessons about developing community-based approaches to personnel training and development. First, community-based approaches in staff development that effect lasting changes are built on trusting relationships between community members and technical assistance providers who provide an array of services (Wesley & Buysse, 1996). Second, coordinated, community-based efforts are most effective when they combine external assistance in the form of training, evaluation, coordination, and consultation with internal capacity building, which is necessary to empower stakeholders and sustain change.

Trusting Relationships and an Array of Services

As change catalysts, instructors and technical assistance providers must earn the trust of community members in order to help them take the necessary risks to alter their practices. Methods of building trust include the following:

- Establishing credibility in relevant content areas
- Providing reliable information
- Involving community participants in designing and evaluating training
- Demonstrating flexibility in adapting staff development opportunities to the experiences and needs of participants
- Providing productive follow-up assistance

Bringing community stakeholders together to plan and receive training is not sufficient to promote systems change at the local level. Ongoing support is needed to expand and sustain collaborative relationships and to help refine and integrate content knowledge and process learnings in professional practice. In addition to training events, technical assistance to facilitate team development and the continued clarification of community needs and goals are required. The experience of the PFI project's staff supports the finding of other technical assistance providers: In order to meet the staff development needs across the early childhood intervention system, a wide range of instruction and technical assistance services must be offered. These include consultation, resource linking and referral, short-term advice, provision of print and audiovisual materials, and information clearinghouse services (Buckley & Mank, 1994; Trohanis, 1994; Wesley & Buysse, 1996). In addition, links with preservice efforts are important, as illustrated in the PDS model, to provide practicum and other inservice and preservice training experiences in real-world community settings.

Promoting the Community's Capacity to Help Itself

Although preservice and inservice activities at the state level will always be a valuable part of the personnel preparation system, empowering local stakeholders to implement a systemic approach to staff development within their own community is another way to promote effective and collaborative personnel preparation efforts. Many communities have access to local resources for training through child care resource and referral agencies, state child care initiatives, private–public partnerships with industry or business, child care coalitions, advocacy organizations, hospitals, and staff development sponsored by individual agencies. As in the case of Allen County, multiple activities may occur that are not coordinated across the community or facilitative of interprofessional collaboration to sustain change. Communities may need outside help to recognize this need and to develop a plan for an integrated approach to training.

Chapter 1 reviews a framework of critical factors related to reforming personnel development systems: climate, policies, resources, people, and problem-solving structures. As a springboard to collaboration about personnel preparation issues, local stakeholders need to discuss each of these factors as they think about how they want to improve the services and supports for children and families through focused personnel preparation efforts. Table 3.4 presents questions to guide such discussions. These discussions could occur through a community forum where small- and large-group dialogue, panel presentations, and question-and-answer sessions could be employed to highlight the community's organizational routines and policies, interagency relationships, and history relative to personnel preparation. Because of the complex nature of these issues, it is likely that a series of forums would be needed to adequately address them. For example, one forum might focus on raising awareness about an integrated approach to community and individual needs assessment, another would examine collaborative implementation of staff development activities, and a third would explore evaluation methods.

FUTURE DIRECTIONS

As states continue to develop and improve their comprehensive systems for personnel development, it is helpful to anticipate future issues and directions in community-based personnel preparation efforts. Following are some predictions for the 21st century:

1. The community will become an increasingly important and visible context for instruction, technical assistance, and research as human services systems become more coordinated and integrated. An increased emphasis in the future will be on training that is planned interorganizationally to use all possible resources at the state and local

TABLE 3.4.   Questions to guide planning

Climate

- What is the community's personnel preparation history? Have people from key stakeholder domains identified personnel preparation as a priority in the community? Have agencies coordinated training calendars? Have staff from various organizations and agencies attended and planned training activities together?

- What is the current climate with regard to personnel preparation? Is there a collaborative approach or even interest in one? For example, do personnel from various disciplines and organizations collaborate to plan joint presentations at training events? Are there other ways in which existing instruction practices augment feelings of trust among community stakeholders?

- Is there a systems view of instruction at the community level? In other words, is there a mechanism to identify and consider the needs of personnel from multiple agencies in planning professional growth opportunities?

- Who defines the climate? How have the interests and needs of key stakeholder domains shaped the climate? Are families, local government officials, and diverse representatives from the private and public sector involved in personnel preparation efforts related to young children and families?

- What are the formal and informal ways stakeholders identify and communicate their needs for instruction? Do personnel preparation activities reflect the current changes in the early intervention system? For example, does training content address interagency collaboration, strategic planning, or other issues related to inclusion?

Policies

- How has training in the community been funded historically?

- What policies affect personnel preparation (e.g., agency staff development requirements, personnel policies for time off, community college requirements for offering continuing education units [CEUs], recruitment of high school students into community colleges, matriculation of community college courses to higher institutions)?

- How are policies communicated across the community? For example, do early interventionists who provide instruction know how to offer child care training credit? Does training sponsored by Head Start provide credit toward credentials recognized by local mental health agencies? Do public health departments widely advertise their community training activities or offer CEUs through the local community college?

- How open are agency-sponsored staff development activities to nonagency participants? Are inservice instruction workshops offered through the local schools, for example, open to early interventionists employed by other agencies in their community?

Resources

- What resources are available to facilitate comprehensive staff development at the local level (e.g., funding; people; transportation; communication methods such as e-mail, meeting space)?

- How flexible are the resources? Who controls them? Is the community willing to rethink how it uses resources to support instruction? For example, have agencies explored ways to pool funds to support a comprehensive approach?

- Has the community surveyed local attitudes toward innovation in personnel preparation? Are local attitudes a support or barrier to providing instruction in a new way?

People

- How does the community define itself? In other words, who are the stakeholders involved in early intervention and related personnel preparation efforts? What are their roles, relationships, and allegiances?

(continued)

TABLE 3.4. (*continued*)

People—*continued*

- Do stakeholders work in teams, and if so, how do they define their teams? Do they have a model for building and maintaining team cohesion and competence?

- Who are the leaders in the field and in staff development? What is the leadership tradition and style across the community? What is the role of leadership in strategic planning regarding personnel preparation?

Problem-solving structures

- Are established mechanisms for problem solving effective to identify and meet the challenges related to personnel preparation? Do they include a systemwide understanding of the problem-solving process?

- What is the role of vertical systems (i.e., the relationship of community to state and federal agencies and to institutions of higher learning) in the problem-solving process?

- What is the role of horizontal systems (i.e., community interagency relationships, collaboration with families, private and public partnerships) in the problem-solving process? For example, is there a collaborative approach to assessing and communicating personnel preparation needs?

- Is there a trouble-shooting mechanism to identify and remove barriers to effective training? In addition, are factors that promote effective practice identified and stressed, including productive collegial relations, open communication and feedback, and leadership that supports opportunities for professional growth and development (McLaughlin, 1991)?

- How can the community replace the competitiveness that traditional personnel preparation approaches so often promote with principles of collaboration and consensus building?

Documented results

- What evaluation activities are currently conducted by agencies and other training organizations in the community? Are evaluation results shared in an ongoing way and used in future planning? How do community evaluation plans relate to regional and state evaluation efforts and personnel preparation activities?

- How should results of individual training activities be documented? For example, what methods can be used to extend evaluation beyond measures of participant satisfaction?

- How should an integrated approach to communitywide personnel preparation be evaluated? What are the desired outcomes of such an approach? What are the implications for providing documented results when training content is related to collaboration and systems change? How can the relationship of staff competence to program competence to system integrity at the community level be assessed? For example, what are the effects on the individual programs and interagency service delivery system of training staff from community agencies together on collaboration?

- Who needs the evaluation results and why?

- Who will carry out the evaluation and who will pay for it?

- What is the community's commitment to the evaluation process, particularly if it is longitudinal? What qualitative evaluation methods are practical at the community level? In what areas can self-assessments be used to measure change?

- What do artifacts tell us about collaboration, role changes, and systems approaches to service delivery and training (e.g., written agency policies, individualized family service plans, individualized education programs, job descriptions)?

levels. Communities may show increased initiative to develop an infrastructure to support ongoing staff development activities at the local level, resulting in new technical assistance relationships between communities and institutions of higher learning. A variety of forces lead to this development: the recent emphasis on technical assistance to support school reform; the implementation of the Americans with Disabilities Act; a widespread local need for training about disabilities, inclusion, family-centered culturally sensitive practices, and transition; the press in many states for a career ladder for child care providers; and the expansion of community Head Start programs to include infants and toddlers.

2. As funding systems such as block grants from the federal government are restructured, states may have more decision-making responsibility about how money is spent. Competition for limited funds may increase between direct service and personnel preparation interests, promoting the blending (for economic reasons) of preservice and inservice training efforts that are somewhat disjointed. Training and technical assistance providers may feel pressure from funders to demonstrate third-party outcomes (e.g., to show that training of child care providers has improved developmental outcomes of children).

3. We will see an increased emphasis in professional development programs on knowledge pertaining to community resources (e.g., Family Resource Centers, transportation services, family literacy programs, teen parent support groups, pregnancy prevention programs, English as a second language courses).

4. There will be an increased focus in staff development content on working with poor, ethnically diverse, and underserved groups of people, and we will experience a growing need to include representatives from these groups in our planning and training efforts as well as in leadership roles.

5. There will be an increased need to prepare personnel at the local level to coordinate health and development needs of children, with a focus on human immunodeficiency virus and ongoing health conditions, and to identify and reduce environmental factors placing children and families at risk for violence, substance abuse, and poverty.

6. There will be a continued need for theory testing in personnel preparation and for an empirical base to guide practice. Yet because studying personnel preparation is complex and does not lend itself readily to traditional approaches to research, an increased interest in the academic community for studying training and technical assistance as a scholarly pursuit is not likely. However, there could be more emphasis on preparing people to provide training in the community (e.g., the development of a "training track" at state and regional conferences for practitioners who also provide inservice training to their own and other agencies, the establishment of regional lending libraries of staff development resources, an increase in courses on consultation and technical assistance in early childhood intervention degree programs at universities, an increase in the number of professional organizations related to personnel preparation).

Opportunities to attain the highest possible level of skill during training are enhanced when staff development activities, whether preservice or inservice, mimic or occur in natural work environments. Compared with state-level instruction, which may lack continuity and relevance to local communities, personnel preparation at the community level involving diverse local stakeholders as planners and recipients has the potential to create effective and lasting changes in practices. In addition, a community-based approach to training provides opportunities to blend local funding, materials, talent, and other resources to promote long-term, collaborative relationships.

RESOURCES

Blank, M.J., & Melaville, A.I. (1991). *What it takes: Structuring interagency partnerships to connect children and families with comprehensive services.* Washington, DC: Education and Human Services Consortium. Cost: $3. (202) 822-8405.

This monograph contains sections on guidelines for new partners and assessment of the need for interagency partnerships that could easily be converted into effective instructional activities.

Bruner, C. (1991). *Thinking collaboratively: Ten questions and answers to help policy makers improve children's services.* Washington, DC: The Education and Human Services Consortium. Cost: $3. (202) 822-8405.

This document includes excellent applications for instruction, especially with interagency audiences. Each of the 10 questions probes an aspect of collaboration (e.g., How do we know if collaboration is happening and if it is working?) and provides possible responses, along with lists of resources for additional consideration.

Dunst, C.J. (1990). Family support principles: Checklists for program builders and practitioners. *Family Systems Intervention Monograph Series, 2*(5). Morganton, NC: Family, Infant and Preschool Program, Western Carolina Center. Cost: $11. (704) 433-2690.

Six sets of family support principles are described (e.g., enhancing a sense of community, mobilizing resources and supports) and then presented in a rating scale format. In training, scales could be used to describe preferred practices, assess current practices, or target desired changes.

Harms, T., & Clifford, D. (1980). *The Early Childhood Environment Rating Scale (ECERS).* New York: Teachers College Press. Cost: $8.95. (800) 575-6566.

This easy-to-use instrument is designed to assist teachers, administrators, family members, and trainers in examining the quality features of early intervention. It defines quality through a scale of 37 items in seven categories (e.g., personal care routines, furnishings, gross and fine motor activities, language and reasoning). Companion instruments from the same publisher include the Family Day Care Rating Scale (FDCRS) (Harms & Clifford, 1993), Infant/Toddler Environment Rating Scale (ITERS) (Harms, Cryer, & Clifford, 1990), and School-Age Care Environment Rating Scale (SACERS) (Harms, Jacob, & White, 1992).

Melaville, A.I., Blank, M.J., & Asayesh, G. (1993). *Together we can: A guide for crafting a pro-family system of education and human services.* Washington, DC: U.S. Government Printing Office. Cost: Free. (202) 219-2129.

This monograph leads users through a five-stage collaborative process with milestones and land mines portrayed through vignettes and case studies. It is easily adaptable for instruction on aspects of community-based service delivery and collaboration.

Regional Educational Laboratories' Early Childhood Collaboration Network. (1995). *Continuity in early childhood: A framework for home, school, and community linkages.* Tallahassee, FL: SouthEastern Regional Vision for Education (SERVE). Cost: Free. (800) 352-6001.

This document defines key elements in a framework for linkages among community programs and agencies. In instruction, these materials could be used to explore existing resources and new possibilities for linkages among people, resources, and services.

Rosenkoetter, S.E., Hains, A.H., & Fowler, S.A. (1994). *Bridging early services for children with special needs and their families: A practical guide for transition planning.* Baltimore: Paul H. Brookes Publishing Co. Cost: $24. (800) 638-3775.

This book presents models that demonstrate how community-based planning benefits all involved in early intervention. Strategies and materials for teaching about and promoting successful transitions are included.

Swan, W.W., & Morgan, J.L. (1993). *Collaborating for comprehensive services for young children and their families: The local interagency coordinating council.* Baltimore: Paul H. Brookes Publishing Co. Cost: $37. (800) 638-3775.

This unique guidebook with more than 70 sample checklists, charts, letters, contracts, tips, and strategies for promoting quality, effective services drawn from the authors' experiences in interagency work in communities.

REFERENCES

Bailey, D.B., Buysse, V., Smith, T., & Elam, J. (1992). The effects and perceptions of family involvement in program decisions about family-centered practices. *Evaluation and Program Planning, 15,* 23–32.

Bailey, D.B., McWilliam, P.J., Winton, P.J., & Simeonsson, R.J. (1992). Building family-centered practices in early intervention: A team-based model for change. *Infants and Young Children, 5*(1), 73–82.

Bennis, W.G., Benne, K.D., & Chin, R. (1985). *The planning of change.* New York: Holt, Rinehart & Winston.

Blank, M.J., & Melaville, A.I. (1991). *What it takes: Structuring interagency partnerships to connect children and families with comprehensive services.* Washington, DC: Education and Human Services Consortium.

Branham, L.A. (1992). An update on staff development evaluation. *Staff Development Practices, 13*(4), 24–28.

Bruner, C. (1991). *Thinking collaboratively: Ten questions and answers to help policy makers improve children's services.* Washington, DC: The Education and Human Services Consortium.

Buckley, J., Albin, J.M., & Mank, D.M. (1988). Competency-based staff training for supported employment. In G.T. Bellamy, L.E. Rhodes, D.M. Mank, & J.M. Albin (Eds.), *Supported employment: A community implementation guide* (pp. 229–245). Baltimore: Paul H. Brookes Publishing Co.

Buckley, J., & Mank, D. (1994). New perspectives on training and technical assistance: Moving from assumptions to a focus on quality. *Journal of The Association for Persons with Severe Handicaps, 19*(3), 223–232.

Buysse, V., Bernier, K., Tyndall, S., Gardner, D., & Munn, D. (1997). *A statewide profile of early intervention services using the Part H data system.* Manuscript submitted for publication.

Buysse, V., & Wesley, P. (1993). The identity crisis in early childhood special education: A call for professional role clarification. *Topics in Early Childhood Special Education, 13,* 418–429.

Darling-Hammond, L. (1994). *Professional development schools.* New York: Teachers College Press.

Dimock, H.G. (1993). *Intervention and collaboration: Helping organizations to change.* San Diego, CA: Pfeiffer.

Division for Early Childhood Task Force on Recommended Practices, Council for Exceptional Children. (1993). *DEC recommended practices: Indicators of quality in programs for infants and young children with special needs and their families.* Reston, VA: Author.

Domergue, M. (1968). *Technical assistance.* New York: Praeger.

Drexler, A., Sibbet, D., & Forrester, R. (1992). The team performance model. In *Team building: Blueprints for productivity and satisfaction.* NTL Institute and University Associates.

Dunst, C.J. (1990). Family support principles: Checklists for program builders and practitioners. *Family Systems Intervention Monograph Series, 2*(5). Morganton, NC: Family, Infant and Preschool Program, Western Carolina Center.

Everson, J.M., & Moon, M.S. (1990). Developing community program planning and service delivery teams. In F.R. Rusch (Ed.), *Supported employment: Models, methods, and issues* (pp. 381–394). Sycamore, IL: Sycamore Publishing Co.

Fenichel, E. (1991). Learning through supervision and mentorship to support the development of infants, toddlers, and their families. *ZERO TO THREE, 12*(2), 1–8.

Fullan, M. (1993). *Change forces: Probing the depths of educational reform.* London: Falmer Press.

Greene, J.C. (1987). Stakeholder participation in evaluation design: Is it worth the effort? *Evaluation and Program Planning, 10,* 379–394.

Guskey, T.R. (1986). Staff development and the process of teacher change. *Education Researcher, 15*(5), 5–11.

Guskey, T.R., & Peterson, K.D. (1996). The road to classroom change. *Educational Leadership, 53*(4), 10–14.

Gutkin, T.B. (1993). Demonstrating the efficacy of collaborative consultation services: Theoretical and practical perspectives. *Topics in Language Disorders, 14*(1), 81–90.

Harms, T., & Clifford, R.M. (1980). *Early Childhood Environment Rating Scale.* New York: Teachers College Press.

Harms, T., & Clifford, R.M. (1993). *Family Day Care Rating Scale.* New York: Teachers College Press.

Harms, T., Cryer, D., & Clifford, R.M. (1990). *Infant/Toddler Environment Rating Scale.* New York: Teachers College Press.

Harms, T., Jacobs, E.V., & White, D.R. (1996). *School-Age Care Environment Rating Scale.* New York: Teachers College Press.

Kagan, S.L., Goffin, S.G., Golub, S.A., & Pritchard, E. (1995). *Toward systemic reform: Service integration for young children and their families.* Falls Church, VA: National Center for Service Integration.

Kanter, R.M., Stein, B.A., & Jick, T.D. (1992). *The challenge of organizational change: How companies experience it and leaders guide it.* New York: The Free Press.

Kettner, P.M., Daley, J.M., & Nichols, A.W. (1985). *Initiating change in organizations and communities.* Monterey, CA: Brooks/Cole.

Knowles, M. (1978). *The adult learner: A neglected species* (2nd ed.). Houston: Gulf Publishing Co.

LaCour, J.A. (1982). Interagency agreement: A rational response to an irrational system. *Exceptional Children, 49,* 265–267.

McLaughlin, M.W. (1991). The Rand change agent study: Ten years later. In A.R. Odden (Ed.), *Education policy implementation* (pp. 143–155). Albany: State University of New York.

Melaville, A., & Blank, M. (1991). *What it takes: Structuring interagency partnerships to connect children and families with comprehensive services.* Washington, DC: Education and Human Services Consortium.

Melaville, A.I., Blank, M.J., & Asayesh, G. (1993). *Together we can: A guide for crafting a pro-family system of education and human services.* Washington, DC: U.S. Government Printing Office.

Mowbray, C.T., & Freddelino, P.P. (1986). Consulting to implement nontraditional community programs for the long-term mentally disabled. *Administration in Mental Health, 14*(2), 122–134.

Neenan, P., Orthner, D., & Crocker, H. (1995). *Network analysis.* Unpublished instrument, Chapel Hill, University of North Carolina at Chapel Hill, School of Social Work.

Orlandi, M.A. (1992). The challenge of evaluating community-based prevention programs: A cross-cultural perspective. In M.A. Orlandi, R. Weston, & L.G. Epstein (Eds.), *Cultural competence for evaluators: A guide for alcohol and other drug abuse prevention practitioners working with ethnic/racial communities* (DHHS Publication No. 92–1884, pp. 1–22). Rockville, MD: Author.

Pawl, J.H. (1995). On supervision. In L. Eggbeer & E. Fenichel (Eds.), Educating and supporting the infant/family work force: Models, methods and materials. *ZERO TO THREE, 15*(3), 21–29.

Peck, C.A., Furman, G.C., & Helmstetter, E. (1993). Integrated early childhood programs: Research on the implementation of change in organizational contexts. In C.A. Peck, S.L. Odom, & D.D. Bricker (Eds.), *Integrating young children with disabilities into community programs: Ecological perspectives on research and implementation* (pp. 187–205). Baltimore: Paul H. Brookes Publishing Co.

Peterson, N.L. (1991). Interagency collaboration under Part H: The key to comprehensive, multidisciplinary, coordinated infant/toddler intervention services. *Journal of Early Intervention, 15*(19), 89–105.

Regional Educational Laboratories' Early Childhood Collaboration Network. (1995). *Continuity in early childhood: A framework for home, school, and community linkages.* Tallahassee, FL: SouthEastern Regional Vision for Education (SERVE).

Rosenkoetter, S.E., Hains, A.H., & Fowler, S.A. (1994). *Bridging early services for children with special needs and their families: A practical guide for transition planning.* Baltimore: Paul H. Brookes Publishing Co.

Schindler-Rainman, E., & Lippitt, R. (1972). *Team training for community change: Concepts, goals, strategies, and skills.* Riverside: University of California Extension.

Schindler-Rainman, E., & Lippitt, R. (1975). *The volunteer community: Creative use of human resources* (2nd ed.). San Diego: University Associates.

Swan, W.W., & Morgan, J.L. (1993). *Collaborating for comprehensive services for young children and their families: The local interagency coordinating council.* Baltimore: Paul H. Brookes Publishing Co.

The Holmes Group. (1986). *Tomorrow's teachers.* East Lansing, MI: Author.

Trohanis, P.L. (1986). *Improving state technical assistance programs.* Chapel Hill: University of North Carolina at Chapel Hill, Frank Porter Graham Child Development Center.

Trohanis, P.L. (1994). Planning for successful inservice education for local early childhood programs. *Topics in Early Childhood Special Education, 14*(3), 311–332.

Weisbord, M.R. (1992). *Discovering common ground.* San Francisco: Barrett-Koehler.

Wesley, P.W. (1994). Providing on-site consultation to promote quality in integrated child care programs. *Journal of Early Intervention, 18*(4), 391–402.

Wesley, P.W. (1995). Community forums: Finding common ground for change. *Journal of Early Intervention, 20*(1), 79–108.

Wesley, P.W., & Buysse, V. (1994). *Self-assessment for child care professionals.* Unpublished instrument. Chapel Hill: University of North Carolina at Chapel Hill, Frank Porter Graham Child Development Center.

Wesley, P.W., & Buysse, V. (1996). Supporting early childhood inclusion: Lessons learned through a statewide technical assistance project. *Topics in Early Childhood Special Education, 16,* 476–499.

Westby, C.E., & Ford, V. (1993). The role of team culture in assessment and intervention. *Journal of Educational and Psychological Consultation, 4*(4), 319–341.

Willer, B., & Bredekemp, S. (1993, May). A "new" paradigm of early childhood professional development. *Young Children,* 63–66.

Winton, P.J. (1990). A systemic approach for planning inservice training related to Public Law 99-457. *Infants and Young Children, 3*(1), 51–60.

4 CREATING NEW VISIONS IN INSTITUTIONS OF HIGHER EDUCATION

Interdisciplinary Approaches to Personnel Preparation in Early Intervention

Jennifer L. Kilgo
Mary Beth Bruder

Adequately prepared personnel are central to the successful implementation of the Infant and Toddler Program (Part H) of the Individuals with Disabilities Education Act (IDEA). As the field of early intervention has evolved, however, personnel preparation is an area in which limited progress has been made. There is general agreement among those engaged in personnel preparation that institutions of higher education (IHEs) are not adequately meeting the personnel needs in early intervention (Winton, 1996). Furthermore, there is growing consensus that major reform is needed in IHEs, with the recommendation that traditional unidisciplinary instructional approaches be replaced with innovative interdisciplinary models to meet the demand for adequately prepared personnel across disciplines.

This chapter describes new visions and strategies for changes in higher education with the promise of better preparing professionals to fill interdisciplinary roles in early intervention. The term *interdisciplinary* is used throughout this chapter to refer to personnel preparation that incorporates two or more disciplines, including early childhood special education, general early childhood education, occupational therapy, physical therapy, social work, speech-language pathology, psychology, nursing, and others. The term *higher education interdisciplinary programs* is used to refer to those programs that provide coursework, practical, or other preservice credit experiences to students from more than one professional discipline.

Higher education interdisciplinary programs are most likely to occur in one of the following settings: 1) community colleges, 2) comprehensive colleges and universities (i.e., institutions that include 4-year undergraduate-, graduate-, and/or doctoral-level preparation), or 3) university affiliated programs (UAPs). Community colleges serve the community in which they are located and provide career instruction, occupational retraining, freshman- and sophomore-level coursework for students who will transfer to 4-year colleges and universities, continuing education programs, and other educational offerings for special populations. Comprehensive IHEs focus on the areas of teaching, scholarship, and service. Within the area of teaching, the emphasis is typically on unidisciplinary preservice preparation programs that comprise hierarchical ordering of coursework from the introductory to advanced content, leading to a degree in a single discipline (or area). Related content (e.g., education specialties) usually is grouped within a specific school or college. Most faculty are assigned to a particular program or area of expertise and have primary responsibility for students enrolled in that program. UAPs, mandated in the 1960s by the Administration on Developmental Disabilities, are university organizational units that are well suited for early intervention personnel preparation. UAPs focus on developmental disabilities and emphasize an interdisciplinary approach to instruction for professionals and paraprofessionals, technical assistance, exemplary service programs, research, and information dissemination. Thus, UAPs provide resources that cross many disciplines, types of disabilities, and age groups of consumers; moreover, many activities provided by UAPs are directly related to the implementation of Part H of IDEA.

In this chapter, the role of various higher education settings in the provision of early intervention instruction, the rationale for interdisciplinary instruction, potential issues and challenges, various models of and approaches to instruction, and strategies for moving forward are discussed. Examples of early intervention instructional programs that have been developed throughout the United States are highlighted and future challenges delineated.

THE ROLE OF HIGHER EDUCATION IN EARLY INTERVENTION INSTRUCTION

Early intervention efforts are taking place in various forms in IHEs throughout the United States. However, many IHEs have been reluctant to begin new programs in early intervention or expand existing programs as a result of the overall climate of retrenchment (Bailey, 1989; Gallagher & Staples, 1990; Rooney, 1995). Due to budget reductions and scarce resources in higher education, many departments have been forced to emphasize cost-effectiveness over the provision of quality programs and recommended instructional practices. Thus, new, innovative ideas are necessary for achieving collaboration across departments and disciplines in order to provide quality instructional programs in early intervention.

Traditionally, community colleges have not been part of the mainstream of early intervention instruction. The reasons often cited for this lack of involvement include the insufficient linkages between 4-year institutions and community colleges; limited resources; inadequately prepared faculty; lack of knowledge of personnel needs and trends in early intervention; and problems with student recruitment, support, and retention. Beginning in the 1980s, however, instructional programs have been developed, often with federal support, to provide innovative instructional opportunities focused on early intervention through the community college system. It is anticipated that community colleges will play an increasingly important role in early intervention instruction. In comprehensive IHEs, there has been a shift toward offering more specialized early intervention instruction at the preservice level. These programs have tended to be unidisciplinary (Bailey, Palsha, & Huntington, 1990), even though interdisciplinary instruction has been supported by a number of professional organizations, including occupational therapy (American Occupational Therapy Association, 1989), speech-language pathology (American Speech-Language-Hearing Association, 1989), physical therapy (American Physical Therapy Association, 1990), and early childhood special education (Odom, McLean, Johnson, & LaMontagne, 1995). Some comprehensive colleges and universities have instituted interdisciplinary early intervention instructional programs; however, many of these programs have had external funding to support their efforts and have experienced difficulty in continuing implementation after the funding ended (Rooney, 1995).

UAPs or similar interdisciplinary structures are considered by many to be ideal mechanisms for facilitating interdisciplinary instruction because they are organizational units with a precedent for interdisciplinary activities. However, UAPs have a life-span focus, and some UAPs may not focus as strongly as others on early intervention. Another factor is that some UAPs place greater emphasis on inservice rather than on preservice instruction for a variety of reasons (e.g., needs of currently employed personnel working in the field of developmental disabilities). There have been suggestions that UAPs are unrealistic as models of interdisciplinary personnel preparation and may even be partly responsible for maintaining the status quo in interdisciplinary instruction in early intervention and other areas (e.g., the preparation of personnel to serve preschool- and school-age children with disabilities). Nonetheless, UAPs have the infrastructure to support interdisciplinary instruction and create models for other IHEs to follow.

RATIONALE FOR AN INTERDISCIPLINARY
APPROACH TO HIGHER EDUCATION INSTRUCTION

The delivery of effective early intervention necessitates an approach in which professionals collaborate with a child's family and with other professionals and agencies that also provide services to the family. As illustrated by the story of Janet (see Chapter 1), early intervention, by definition, is comprehensive and multidisciplinary. A lack of collaboration can result in children and their families being served by a multitude of professionals with differing philosophies of intervention and differing treatment goals (Bruder, 1994).

Although other models are being used in some IHEs, interdisciplinary instruction represents the most appropriate type for early intervention professionals. There are many reasons to provide interdisciplinary instructional experiences to individuals pursuing careers in early intervention. The first reason stems from legislative mandates. The Education of the Handicapped Act Amendments of 1986, PL 99-457, established statewide systems of early intervention services for eligible infants and toddlers and their families. There are a number of requirements in this legislation that include the use of more than one professional discipline, including the following:

- *The development of interagency and multidisciplinary models of service delivery for eligible infants and toddlers and their families as specified in the individualized family service plan (IFSP), which is directed by the family.* "Multidisciplinary" has been further defined by the U.S. Department of Education to mean efforts involving people representing at least two disciplines.
- *The appointment of a service coordinator to facilitate and ensure the implementation of the IFSP.* The service coordinator is responsible for the implementation of the IFSP and for ongoing coordination with other agencies and individuals to ensure the timely and effective delivery of services.

Thus, through interdisciplinary instruction, interventionists should be prepared for working with other professionals. A second reason to provide interdisciplinary instruction is in response to the new interdisciplinary job categories created to alleviate personnel shortages. A number of states have created new occupational categories for personnel who deliver early intervention. These occupational categories (e.g., infant specialists, early intervention generalists) represent a cross-disciplinary focus and are used to create a work force within states that is responsive to the integrated needs of infants and toddlers and their families.

A third reason is the need to decrease the number of interventionists interacting with infants and toddlers and their families at any one time. Many families have expressed concern about receiving different messages about differing priorities from the various discipline-specific interventionists. This makes early intervention unnecessarily fragmented and ineffective for a family trying to adapt to the multiple needs of their child. In 1978, the United Cerebral Palsy National Collaborative Infant Project (Hutchinson, 1978) developed an intervention model specifically to meet the needs of infants with disabilities and their families. Termed the transdisciplinary model, it comprised a primary interventionist with responsibility for coordinating input from all other relevant professionals and delivering intervention using a cohesive and holistic approach (see Chapter 14). Two fundamental assumptions of this model are that children's development must be viewed as integrated and interactive and that children must be served within the context of the family (McGonigel, Woodruff, & Roszmann-Millican, 1994). The concept of primary interventionist has been reinforced by the Head Start Advisory Committee on Services for Families with Infants and Toddlers. In particular, a number of principles for programming were identified, including a principle for positive relationships and continuity:

> Programs will support and enhance strong, caring, continuous relationships among the child, parents, family, and caregiving staff. Programs will support the mother–child/father–child bond by recognizing each parent as his or her child's first and primary source of love, nurturance and guidance. Programs will ensure that relationships between caregiving staff and young children support infant and toddler attachment to a limited number of skilled and caring individuals, thus maintaining relationships with caregivers over time and avoiding the trauma of loss experienced with frequent turnover of key people in the child's life. (*Federal Register*, 1995, p. 14550)

Finally, personnel who graduate from unidisciplinary preservice instructional programs are at a disadvantage in early intervention. A single-discipline focus, for example, can mask the interrelationship of development of and subsequent interventions with children, which can result in an inefficient and narrow application of early intervention. Furthermore, a single-discipline background can preclude any opportunity for students to have dialogue about, negotiate, and jointly develop an intervention plan with personnel from other disciplines as part of a structured supervised experience, resulting in an absence of cross-disciplinary team competence.

If supported at all levels, interdisciplinary instructional programs can provide critical opportunities to improve the content, processes, and experiences of early intervention instruction. Within IHEs, programs, faculty, and students can benefit from an interdisciplinary approach to instruction, as can the agencies that employ the graduates of an interdisciplinary early intervention program. Perhaps the greatest benefit of a genuine commitment in higher education to interdisciplinary personnel preparation will be substantive long-term reform in early intervention services for infants and toddlers and their families. The potential benefits of interdisciplinary instruction are summarized in Table 4.1.

CHALLENGES TO INTERDISCIPLINARY EARLY INTERVENTION INSTRUCTION

Historically, there have been few programs of study throughout the United States to prepare personnel in education, related services, and health professions to work with young

TABLE 4.1. Benefits of an interdisciplinary approach to personnel preparation

Training programs

- Draws on the expertise of faculty from various disciplines across the college or university
- Develops interdisciplinary content, processes, and experiences
- Infuses early intervention content into existing courses across departments
- Provides for continuity in instructional content and procedures across departments
- Assists in collaboratively meeting statewide personnel needs and shortages
- Helps in modifying and meeting certification and licensure requirements across disciplines
- Provides or increases visibility and impact within the community, college or university, and state
- Enhances probability of obtaining external funding

Faculty

- Provides access to instructional resources across disciplines
- Encourages the exchange of information across disciplines (e.g., state and federal initiatives, personnel shortages, recommended practices)
- Builds interdisciplinary alliances to promote and achieve mutual objectives
- Provides a forum for issues and ideas among professional peers with similar interests
- Facilitates collegial support among faculty members across disciplines
- Generates interdisciplinary opportunities (e.g., research, instruction, publication, presentations)
- Promotes team collaboration with colleagues
- Reduces potentially negative turf issues and unproductive competitiveness among faculty members

Students

- Expands students' knowledge of early intervention activities within the university (e.g., research projects, grants) and the community
- Enhances access to professionals across disciplines who are active in the field of early intervention
- If external funding received, provides opportunities for tuition support
- Provides formal and informal network of contacts that is likely to provide leads for employment opportunities upon graduation
- Affords opportunities for students to observe team collaboration modeled by faculty members across disciplines
- Provides opportunities for students to have a dialogue, negotiate, and learn with students from other disciplines

Administration

- Promotes awareness of and a commitment to the interdisciplinary mission and goals associated with early intervention instruction
- Builds on the strengths of faculty members from a variety of disciplines
- Establishes linkages and collaborative activities across departments
- Maximizes the use of resources across departments and programs
- Results in the provision of high-quality instructional programs and recommended practices
- Provides cost-effective strategies for addressing personnel needs

children with disabilities and their families (Smith, 1988; Styles, Abernathy, Pettibone, & Wachtel, 1984). If the rationale for interdisciplinary instruction in early intervention is so strong, the benefits so numerous, and the need for adequately prepared early intervention personnel so great, then what factors have contributed to the slow progress in this area? Traditional structures and processes within colleges and universities do not lend themselves to collaboration across divisions, departments, or disciplines. The next section discusses a number of institutional issues and challenges associated with interdisciplinary instruction in early intervention, including structural and organizational issues, administrative issues, faculty issues, curricular issues, and student-related issues (see Table 4.2).

Structural and Organizational Issues

Interdisciplinary instructional programs that prepare professionals to deliver interdisciplinary early intervention services are not facilitated by existing higher education structures. Departmental or divisional structures actually tend to discourage collaborative activities. A major problem is that interdisciplinary collaboration is hindered by the lack of organizational mechanisms or formats for interdisciplinary communication and information exchange across departments and divisions. Interdisciplinary meetings, seminars, and instructional activities are rare and tend to be given lower priority than discipline-specific or departmental activities. The overall effect is that faculty members frequently do not know or collaborate with faculty from other disciplines. This is particularly unfortunate when faculty members across disciplines share interests and engage in similar activities related to early intervention. For example, at one university there were three faculty members from different disciplines (i.e., nursing, psychology, early childhood special education) who shared many areas of interest and expertise. All three faculty members had research and direct experience with premature infants in the neonatal intensive care unit (NICU). In this example, these faculty members were conducting research in the same area, delivering similar course content, and placing students in the NICU for their clinical experiences. Although each of these professionals had been at the same university for more than 10 years, they had never engaged in collaborative activities with one another. Similar situations are common in colleges and universities throughout the United States.

The problem of limited opportunities for collaboration across disciplines is compounded when departments are not in physical proximity to one another. In some instances, disciplines with strong potential for collaboration may not even have programs at the same institution/site; therefore, geographic isolation may inhibit collaboration. As many IHEs have become more committed to providing interdisciplinary early intervention personnel preparation, however, a number of the structural or organizational barriers have been circumvented, as is demonstrated in this chapter.

Administrative Issues

For interdisciplinary early intervention efforts to flourish, faculty members need administrative support. However, faculty members often report that insufficient administrative support exists for interdisciplinary early intervention teaching and other activities. For example, in a study conducted with 249 deans of colleges of education (Gallagher & Staples, 1990), 162 reportedly had no plans to institute interdisciplinary early intervention programs.

Faculty members also report that the lack of advocacy by administrators tends to prohibit interdisciplinary faculty-related activities (e.g., the arrangement of faculty schedules for interdisciplinary meetings, time allotted for program planning and implementation, flexible scheduling of course and practicum assignments to accommodate the schedules

TABLE 4.2. Issues in planning, implementing, and maintaining an interdisciplinary effort

Structural and organizational issues

- Departmental/divisional organization
- Organizational mechanisms for interdisciplinary communication/interaction
- Geographic isolation (e.g., medical and academic campuses, departments located great distances from one another)

Administrative issues

- Mission that values interdisciplinary endeavors
- Budget reductions and scarce resources
- Support and encouragement from deans and administrators
- Administrative reward for interdisciplinary efforts
- Administrative advocacy for interdisciplinary efforts
- Flexibility in course offerings and scheduling
- Financial resources for faculty (e.g., faculty load release time)

Faculty issues

- Commitment of additional time and effort
- Faculty driven by promotion and tenure requirements that do not emphasize interdisciplinary efforts
- Teaming without "turf" or "territorial" issues
- Faculty personality and style (e.g., flexibility, communication, team player)
- Terminology and philosophy differences
- Scheduling and logistics of meetings (e.g., times, location, parking)
- Limited expertise in infant, family, and interdisciplinary content and processes

Curricular issues

- Accreditation and licensure standards of each discipline
- Inclusion of discipline-specific and interdisciplinary competencies within a reasonable program sequence
- Scheduling and logistics of training (e.g., courses, seminars)
- Clinical experiences (e.g., scheduling, supervision, availability of appropriate sites)
- Interdisciplinary course offerings (e.g., cross-listing of courses)

Student-related issues

- Recruitment and selection criteria
- Equity across disciplines
- Students from some disciplines are recruited to work in other settings or with other age ranges
- Involvement of students across disciplines (e.g., flexibility, creativity, individualization)
- Development of positive support system

of faculty and students from across disciplines). Innovation in interdisciplinary instruction requires administrative support for flexible financial arrangements across departments. When planning interdisciplinary coursework, simple issues tend to create barriers such as which department will receive credit for a team-taught course or which department will pay for photocopying. The extra effort in developing interdisciplinary early intervention instruction may be seen as an unnecessary commitment of time and resources. However, as interdisciplinary institutional programs have evolved, it seems that interdisciplinary instruction is being used as a way to consolidate resources and avoid duplication in some IHEs.

Faculty Issues

There are many challenges in implementing interdisciplinary instructional efforts that are related to faculty members' association with a specific discipline. Faculty members across disciplines have been socialized in discipline-specific ways that affect how they process information and address problems. For instance, each discipline develops its own language, concepts, and practices; these may be difficult to understand unless trained in that particular discipline. Discipline-specific philosophy and terminology make communication and instruction across disciplines difficult. Faculty members may be uncomfortable providing instruction that incorporates concepts or methods traditionally associated with another discipline. A related challenge is the difficulty that some professionals have with sharing their content and practices with professionals from other disciplines. This has been referred to as a "turf issue" in which professionals from a particular discipline guard the content and practices associated with their particular field. However, many faculty members need to learn not only how to teach interdisciplinary content but also how to model interdisciplinary practices in their teaching.

Another factor is that few faculty members across disciplines have been instructed or are skilled in delivering interdisciplinary early intervention content (Winton, 1996). Because early intervention is a relatively new and rapidly changing field, faculty members may be uncomfortable with the content, particularly if they have had limited experience applying the practices they are expected to teach. Many faculty members must retrain or retool to better prepare themselves to meet the preservice and inservice instructional needs in the field of early intervention.

A frequently cited barrier to interdisciplinary instruction is that many faculty members have limited awareness of and access to the resources necessary to support them in implementing innovative interdisciplinary approaches to early intervention instruction. Many of the already available early intervention curricula and instructional materials have not been readily accessible to faculty members. The human resources in the broader community (e.g., service providers, family members) who might collaborate in instructional programs may be unknown or underused by faculty. Furthermore, faculty members may have had limited exposure to instructional resources available in other departments, institutions, agencies, or the broader community; and, as a result, coordinated utilization has been unrealized (Winton, 1996).

Perhaps most important, there have been few rewards from the administration for faculty who engage in interdisciplinary efforts. Procedures governing promotion and academic advancement typically do not highly value interdisciplinary efforts. Research and publication outside a professional discipline has not been evaluated as highly as discipline-specific scholarly endeavors. With the need to meet the basic expectations for career advancement, such as scholarly activities and departmental or discipline-specific responsibilities, faculty often find that there is limited time for interdisciplinary collaboration. Concerted efforts are necessary to help administrators and other faculty members understand the need for and value of interdisciplinary early intervention activities. As administrators learn more about the field of early intervention and its recommended practices, it is anticipated that there will be increased support for interdisciplinary instruction in this area.

Curricular Issues

A major issue related to curriculum is the status of state personnel standards for instructing and licensing professionals within a single disciplinary area without regard to the inherent overlap of a child's needs across areas. For example, a physical therapist is instructed and licensed to provide interventions that affect motor development; a speech-language pathologist is instructed and licensed to provide interventions that affect communication. Yet when both of these professionals are hired to provide early intervention, they will be required to provide these services in compliance with legislation and recommended practices that demand an integrated, family-centered, interdisciplinary approach.

A constraint on interdisciplinary instruction is the intensity of the basic curriculum and sequence of instructional activities within each discipline. The curriculum within specific disciplines is often quite rigid, allowing minimal flexibility. Furthermore, discipline-specific instructional programs are tied to the certification, accreditation, and licensing demands of their discipline and must adhere to a number of program standards. Because of the volume of information that must be covered to prepare students within a particular discipline, cross-disciplinary competencies are not always included in lists of standards and competencies or in certification and licensing requirements of each discipline. As a result, faculty members across disciplines have focused on those skills associated with the outcomes for which their students are preparing. However, an interdisciplinary focus on early intervention does not require instructional programs within IHEs to minimize or deemphasize the discipline-specific content. Instead, the cross-disciplinary focus can augment and extend the discipline-specific knowledge and skills. Rooney (1995) recommended that the time has come for instructional programs to move away from "categorical, discipline-specific, competency and certification driven" (p. 1) approaches toward models of collaboration across disciplines.

Student-Related Issues

There also are challenges associated with the recruitment and retention of students across disciplines to participate in early intervention courses, practica, or programs. One contributing factor is that discipline-specific program requirements may be so extensive that there is a natural disinclination for students to expend additional energy or prolong their instruction to meet early intervention requirements. Another factor is that many disciplines find it difficult to recruit to early intervention. The incentives often are greater for professionals from some disciplines to work in fields other than early intervention and with other populations. For example, physical therapists often are recruited to fields such as sports medicine or rehabilitation. Similarly, many professionals across disciplines (e.g., physical therapists, occupational therapists, speech-language pathologists) are employed through contractual agreements to work with multiple populations. Often, the greatest incentive for professionals to pursue options other than early intervention is the salary differentiation between early intervention and other fields.

The backgrounds, experiences, and needs of students enrolled in early intervention personnel preparation can vary tremendously. To address these needs and concerns, individualization and flexibility are critical. Students may even be intimidated when they are evaluated by a faculty member from another discipline. Certain instructional methods, reflecting principles of adult learning, have been described as being effective in accommodating the student diversity associated with interdisciplinary instruction (Winton, 1991; see also Chapter 5).

APPROACHES TO INTERDISCIPLINARY INSTRUCTION

This section focuses on interdisciplinary approaches to instruction. The following strategies for program development are included: 1) developing interdisciplinary competencies, 2) creating interdisciplinary courses, 3) infusing interdisciplinary content, 4) requiring applied interdisciplinary field experiences, and 5) using interdisciplinary teaching processes. In addition, organizational frameworks for interdisciplinary programs are discussed.

Strategies for Program Development

Based on their research, Bailey, Simeonsson, Yoder, and Huntington (1990) generated the following recommendations for preservice programs that want to add an interdisciplinary early intervention focus:

- Students should be provided with content related to legislative mandates that affect young children and their families, as well as an overview of available early intervention programs and services.
- Students should have applied experiences through which they are exposed to programs and services for young children and their families through field experiences.
- The content and training related to working with families should be expanded.
- The amount of emphasis within programs on the process of working in teams with professionals from other disciplines should be increased.

Developing Interdisciplinary Competencies   Personnel preparation programs for the professional disciplines involved in providing early intervention should include both discipline-specific competencies in infant and family development and a knowledge base built on a framework of concepts common to all disciplines working with infants and toddlers with disabilities and their families. Thorp and McCollum (1994) identified four areas of competence that are common across disciplines:

1. Infant related (e.g., understanding typical and atypical development, interaction patterns, and the application of age-appropriate and individually appropriate interventions)
2. Family related (e.g., understanding family systems, family support, and diversity; developing and implementing IFSPs)
3. Team related (e.g., knowledge of team processes, team models of service delivery)
4. Interagency advocacy related (e.g., knowledge of federal and state legislation, coordination of IFSPs across agencies, development of coordination across agencies)

These content areas have been addressed within early intervention instructional programs in a variety of ways (Davis, Thurman, & Mauro, 1995; cf. McCollum & Thorp, 1988; Winton, 1990). At the University of Illinois, for example, the total array of competencies incudes both cross-disciplinary areas and within-discipline areas.

   Cross-discipline competencies also have been developed for early childhood education and early childhood special education. Three professional organizations, the Division for Early Childhood of the Council for Exceptional Children, the National Association for the Education of Young Children, and the Association of Teacher Educators, have collaborated in developing competencies for working with young children that bridge the traditional special education and general education division. These inclusionary competencies have been widely disseminated by the professional organizations. Certain states also have initiated the development of interdisciplinary competencies. For example, in North Carolina, the development of an inclusionary birth-through-kindergarten license was the catalyst for the formation of a Higher Education Consortium, consisting of community college and university faculty and administrators, parents, and state agency representatives, who developed competencies to accompany the license (Miller, 1993). These competencies provide guidelines for preservice instructional programs seeking approval from the Department of Public Instruction to grant licenses to graduating students.

Creating Interdisciplinary Courses   To address interdisciplinary content, faculty members across disciplines have developed special interdisciplinary courses, modules within existing courses, or seminars. At some colleges and universities, for example, students from several disciplines take interdisciplinary early intervention courses in such content areas as interdisciplinary teamwork, interdisciplinary intervention, and family-centered practices. These courses may be augmented with interdisciplinary field experiences and practicum seminars.

Perhaps the most important considerations are those of a practical nature. Due to various disciplines and departments being involved, course scheduling must be coordinated across departments, and courses must be convenient for faculty and students. Courses can be assigned interdisciplinary course numbers and cross-listed in various departments using interdisciplinary prefixes (e.g., IDS 600 Interdisciplinary Teaming). In this way, courses can be offered at the same time by different departments with the departments receiving credit for the students who enroll in the courses from their department. The following examples illustrate some ways in which IHEs have developed interdisciplinary courses.

At Virginia Commonwealth University (VCU) in Richmond, Virginia, an interdisciplinary specialty sequence of coursework and practica for students from six professional disciplines has been operating since 1985. Offered as the first sponsored program of the Virginia Institute for Developmental Disabilities (a UAP), the program was designed to unite the multiple professional instructional programs at VCU and better prepare those students focusing on early intervention. The sequence is offered as part of a post-bachelor's or post-master's certification program, and faculty from six disciplines participate in teaching seminars and coursework and in supervising practica. These interdisciplinary efforts have been perpetuated through a variety of funding sources, including university funding for the pilot project, federal funding from the U.S. Department of Education and the Administration on Developmental Disabilities, and state funding. (Readers may contact the first author of this chapter for more information.)

Another example is the interdisciplinary master's degree program in early intervention that is offered at New York Medical College. The program consisted of 36 credit hours of coursework, practica, thesis, and competency-based tasks and was directed toward students who had already attained their professional certification or license. Students from any discipline involved in early intervention were accepted. The faculty also represented multiple disciplines, including two parents of children with disabilities, and all courses were team taught. Coursework included assessment, intervention, team process, families, service delivery design, medical issues, assistive technology, research methods, and statistics. Students completing the program represented the disciplines of education, occupational therapy, physical therapy, nursing, and speech-language pathology.

Another type of interdisciplinary program was established at the University of Connecticut and provided a multi-institutional, interdisciplinary certificate program for post-bachelor's or post-master's degree students (depending on the discipline). Students attended an intensive summer institute of 6 weeks and received follow-up support for 1 year. The students could be enrolled in any of Connecticut's colleges and universities and had to be nominated for attendance by their faculty advisers. Each institute enrolled approximately 15 students who participated in coursework, practica, research seminars, and the completion of competency-based tasks. Interdisciplinary faculty from Connecticut colleges and universities participated as guest faculty during the summer and co-supervised their students with the institute faculty team during the follow-up year. Faculty also served on a statewide higher education council in early intervention. Case study methodology was used throughout the instruction to teach content related to families, medical issues, physical management, educational issues, teams, and service delivery in community environments. Family members also co-taught the program's coursework. During the program's operation, 46 students completed the certificate, the majority being special educators ($n = 20$), followed by occupational therapists ($n = 8$), physical therapists ($n = 6$), speech-language pathologists ($n = 6$), psychologists ($n = 3$), and nurses ($n = 3$). (For more information on the programs at New York Medical College or the University of Connecticut, readers may contact the second author of this chapter.)

Infusing Interdisciplinary Content   Rather than creating new interdisciplinary programs or courses, an alternative approach is to embed or infuse interdisciplinary perspectives into existing courses and instructional experiences. This infusion approach does not require significant alteration of the curricula but instead relies on creative ways of integrating the interdisciplinary perspective. Examples of content that could be infused are the ideas and concepts associated with interdisciplinary teamwork. Courses such as assessment and intervention would address within each content area the information on interdisciplinary teamwork and the implications for practice across disciplines. The importance of multidisciplinary perspectives would be emphasized throughout the instructional experiences.

An infusion model for integrating interdisciplinary family-centered content has been developed through the Carolina Institute for Research on Infant Personnel Preparation (Winton, 1990). Initially, faculty and graduate students from 10 disciplines participated together in a semester-long course on family-centered early intervention. After participating in this interdisciplinary experience, faculty and their associates in speech-language pathology (Crais, 1992), physical therapy (Sparling, 1992), and occupational therapy (Hanft, Burke, Cahill, Swenson-Miller, & Humphrey, 1992) developed discipline-specific curricula on family-centered practices in early intervention. (These curricula were disseminated to faculty in their respective disciplines.)

Requiring Applied Interdisciplinary Field Experiences   Interdisciplinary field-based experiences are essential to successful interdisciplinary instruction. Students must have the opportunity to directly observe and interact with young children and their families, as well as students and practicing professionals across disciplines. Through practica that are coordinated across disciplines, students can observe, model, and apply the interdisciplinary content gleaned through their coursework (McCollum & Stayton, 1996; also see Chapter 18).

Faculty members often report that arranging interdisciplinary field experiences for students can be labor intensive because of the limited number of early intervention sites that employ professionals from all of the disciplines and the lack of sites that demonstrate exemplary interdisciplinary practices. If interdisciplinary sites are unavailable, faculty members can work over time with professionals within available sites to establish the kinds of instructional opportunities that the students need. Community-based sites can provide learning experiences that range from brief observations to site-based seminars to supervised practica. When faculty members successfully collaborate with professionals across disciplines within community sites, the end result can be the establishment and maintenance of collegial support, both within and across disciplines, from which students can benefit greatly. Alternatively, faculty may choose to develop new instructional sites (McCollum & Stayton, 1996). In all settings individualized supervision related to teaming and family-centered practice is essential to enable students to reflect on their experiences.

Greater use of nontraditional practicum locations also can extend the discipline-specific learning that occurs in more traditional practicum sites. Such nontraditional practicum sites can include policy-making or applied research settings, community-based/ inclusive settings, family-centered settings (e.g., family support or advocacy programs), and settings in which the student's discipline has not been prominent. In such settings, there needs to be an emphasis on developing skills that transcend single disciplines such as those in the areas of teaming and family-centered practices. Negotiations can be undertaken with more traditional practicum sites about the advisability and potential for blending such characteristics into their ongoing expectations for students.

Using Interdisciplinary Teaching Processes   Faculty commitment to interdisciplinary instruction is critical to the success of any interdisciplinary program. When faculty members decide to provide interdisciplinary early intervention instruction, they make a commitment to recognize the strengths that each discipline contributes to the growth and development of preservice students across disciplines. The primary goal should be a joint effort to implement the most effective knowledge and abilities in early intervention.

To enhance interdisciplinary skills, it is recommended that students be exposed to a broad range of perspectives and experiences that influence the lives of young children, including the perspectives of professionals from other disciplines, family members, students from other disciplines, and community-based professionals. Many innovative teaching techniques have been developed that support interdisciplinary instruction. These instructional methodologies include a case study approach, role play, simulation, problem-focused learning, and other activities in which students apply their knowledge and skills to individual cases of infants and toddlers with varying abilities and needs and their families. Team teaching of courses by faculty across disciplines is suggested for courses to be truly interdisciplinary. Joint planning and teaching allows faculty and students across disciplines to interact in all aspects of the learning process. Students can learn from the combined perspectives of faculty members. As discussed in Chapter 17, another recommendation is that family members serve as coinstructors with faculty members. Families add content and expertise that only they are capable of providing.

The commitment to interdisciplinary personnel preparation should not be approached with the goal of changing everything at once but rather should address specific goals. The commitment may begin with the involvement of only two or three disciplines that want to focus on early intervention instruction, and gradually faculty members and students may be recruited from other disciplines. Or it may start with one interdisciplinary course and gradually add others, or address interdisciplinary coursework first and then move to interdisciplinary practicum experiences. Development of an interdisciplinary program takes time and is best built on a small, but firm, foundation.

Organizational Frameworks

Campbell and Leifield (1995) surveyed 100 federally funded personnel preparation programs for early interventionists. A total of 82 of the programs, representing six disciplines, reported having an interdisciplinary focus. However, a range of experiences was used to define the interdisciplinary aspect of the program. Thirty-nine programs offered interdisciplinary seminars taught by two or more faculty from different disciplines, and 53 programs reported offering an interdisciplinary seminar taught by one person with guest speakers from a variety of disciplines. Sixty-three programs allowed students to take coursework in more than one department, and 46 programs offered interdisciplinary practicum experiences to students.

Overall, 21 respondents identified the interdisciplinary focus as an area of program strength. Because establishing an interdisciplinary instructional approach often requires changes in the traditional organizational structures and processes of personnel preparation systems (Meisels, 1992; Rooney, 1995), a detailed review of early intervention personnel preparation instructional programs with an interdisciplinary focus was conducted by Rooney (1995) to identify supports and barriers to this process. This qualitative study examined 10 federally funded preservice personnel preparation programs. Five programs were operated by UAPs, and 2 of the 10 had multicampus involvement. Seven programs offered a master's degree, two an add-on specialization to a master's program, and one a bachelor's degree. All programs had faculty representing at least two disciplines (one always being education) and students from at least two disciplines. Based on this study, Rooney (1995) identified a number of factors that appear to support the expansion and institutionalization of early intervention interdisciplinary personnel preparation models. One factor is the presence of faculty with special interest in early childhood and collaborative team models. Another factor is that faculty model collaboration in their teaching and in their work. The teaching also might be shared with a professional from the service delivery community or with parents. Table 4.3 contains a list of recommendations for interdisciplinary personnel preparation programs as detailed by Rooney (1995).

Some of the most immediate steps to be taken within IHEs to effectively implement an interdisciplinary instructional approach include the following, each of which is discussed in more detail here:

- Creating institutional structures, organizations, and processes that facilitate interdisciplinary efforts
- Developing institutional missions and standards of excellence that recognize and maintain the interdependence of various disciplines and departments
- Providing support systems for faculty in their interdisciplinary roles
- Establishing linkages and support, both internally and externally

TABLE 4.3. Policy implications for interdisciplinary personnel preparation program implementation

Structure	• House program in organizational unit where precedent has been established for interdisciplinary instruction. • Establish interdepartmental structure.
Operations	• Collaboratively create guidelines and agreements that outline expectations for program participants.
People	• Individualize programs to meet needs of students.
Context	• Establish and maintain mechanisms for collaborative interactions with academic and service delivery communities. • Funding agencies should secure a commitment from the universities for partial financial support to continue interdisciplinary efforts at the conclusion of federal funding. • Explore funding options in the environment of the organization to diversify financial support for the programs.

Source: Rooney (1995, May).

Structures and Processes   Interdisciplinary instruction places a premium on flexibility in academic and administrative matters. Rooney (1995) recommended that one mechanism for overcoming many of the potential barriers associated with interdisciplinary instruction is to house the programs, when possible, within existing interdisciplinary structures. Interdisciplinary programs are frequently affiliated with or supported by UAPs, many of which have extensive experience establishing linkages across departments and agencies, as well as experience in nontraditional programming. In many instances, UAPs have existing mechanisms for circumventing the problems associated with interdisciplinary instruction and activities (e.g., interdisciplinary course offerings, preservice instructional directors to coordinate efforts). When interdisciplinary structures are not already available within institutions, then some form of interdisciplinary organizational structure or mechanism that is flexible and suitable to interdisciplinary efforts must be created. Within IHEs, bridges must be built among departments and divisions to support interdisciplinary efforts and to facilitate communication, information exchange, and joint instructional activities. Centers established at various IHEs, with both internal and external funding, have played a major role in establishing linkages across departments and divisions to support collaborative activities (e.g., the Frank Porter Graham Child Development Center at the University of North Carolina at Chapel Hill, the Kennedy Center at Peabody University in Nashville, the Center for Early Education and Development at the University of Minnesota).

In an effort to support interdisciplinary efforts, the Maternal and Child Health Bureau, the American Academy of Pediatrics, and the American Association of Colleges for Teacher Education have sponsored the National Commission on Leadership in Interprofessional Education. Three specific projects (funded by the Maternal and Child Health Bureau) are focusing on improving opportunities for interprofessional education. The first project, the Health and Education Collaborative Project in Hawaii, is developing a collaborative service delivery model of health, education, and social services. A personnel preparation model for professional instruction is being developed to provide family-centered, community-based, coordinated care. The preservice model will jointly offer instructional opportunities for pediatric and OB/GYN residents and graduate students in education and social service. The second project, the Partnership for Change Project at the University of Vermont, is focusing on improving service delivery to children with special health care needs and their families by compiling, evaluating, and disseminating exemplary models of community-based services; and by compiling, evaluating, and disseminating exemplary models of interprofessional education. This second project is directly related to the third project in Oregon, the Higher Education Service Integration Curricula Project. This project is funded to assist selected colleges and universities to develop educational offerings that will cross-instruct students in the various disciplines so that they can affect integrated services at the local level.

Missions and Standards of Excellence   Interdisciplinary efforts must be considered high-priority activities within IHEs. Although UAPs enjoy an interdisciplinary mission, many IHEs are burdened with institutional or departmental missions that do not emphasize interdisciplinary endeavors. IHEs, as well as the various divisions and departments, should include interdisciplinary instructions and activities as part of their overall mission, which will increase the likelihood of their occurrence.

Institutional commitment to the interdisciplinary perspective is essential to providing quality instructional programs in early intervention. Thus, those in positions to influence policy within institutions must understand that interdisciplinary personnel preparation represents recommended practice in early intervention. Faculty commitment is also critical to the success of the program. When faculty members decide to provide interdisciplinary early intervention instruction, they make a commitment to recognize the strengths that each discipline contributes to the growth and development of preservice students across disciplines. The primary goal should be a joint effort to implement the most effective knowledge and skills in early intervention.

Support Systems for Faculty   Interdisciplinary efforts are likely to be enhanced by strong leadership and commitment from individual faculty members with support provided by other faculty members and the administration. Faculty from various disciplines across departments often provide mutual support as they engage in collaborative endeavors. Therefore, faculty members across disciplines must work out the particulars of program changes (e.g., competencies, curriculum, practicum, evaluation) and provide support to one another as interdisciplinary efforts evolve. According to data collected through the Southeastern Institute for Faculty Training (SIFT), one of the four regional faculty training institutes funded by the Early Education Program for Children with Disabilities of the U.S. Department of Education from 1992 to 1995, faculty indicated that the support of colleagues was integral to their individual success in making positive changes in their early intervention training (Winton, 1996).

Similarly, administrative commitment and support are of critical importance. Ideally, procedures governing promotion and academic advancement also will enhance the value placed on this area by specifically recognizing skills in interdisciplinary early intervention practices. When interdisciplinary programs are implemented successfully, faculty members should be rewarded for the extensive amount of effort required.

Because of the evolving nature of early intervention and the complex processes involved in interdisciplinary training, the skills are never fully learned; therefore, it has been recommended that professional development opportunities be provided for faculty to encourage and enable them to develop interdisciplinary instructional programs (e.g., coursework, practica) in early intervention (Gallagher & Staples, 1990). One federally funded project that succeeded in facilitating the development of interdisciplinary early intervention programs among college and university faculty was described by Bruder, Lippman, and Bologna (1994). Funded to increase the capacity of IHEs to provide early intervention instruction, the program provided instruction and support to 38 faculty representing 12 professional disciplines at 15 universities and colleges. The faculty who participated attended a week-long seminar in a cross-disciplinary, cross-university group. The seminar was facilitated by two faculty of different disciplines and a parent of a child with disabilities. Upon conclusion of the seminar, participants received up to 1 year of individualized technical assistance and support by a project faculty. The participants all made significant changes in their own programs. Thirty-one infused new interdisciplinary early intervention information into existing coursework; 5 designed new courses; 3 designed an early intervention sequence within their disciplinary program; 15 designed a cross-disciplinary specialty sequence across disciplines; and 24 instituted interdisciplinary practicum experiences within their programs.

Four regional faculty training institutes were funded from 1992 to 1995 through the U.S. Department of Education to enhance the capacity of higher education to adequately prepare early intervention personnel. Each of the four institutes was interdisciplinary and focused on linkages between higher education and statewide service delivery systems, but each of the institutes approached the task differently. In the SIFT, for example, the following outcomes were achieved: 1) collaboration was increased among state agencies, families, IHEs, and other institutions with training dollars, responsibilities, and authority for personnel preparation in early intervention; 2) knowledge and skill levels of the professionals who provided the training within those contexts were increased; and 3) participants were assisted in applying what they learned through the institute to the training they provided to others (Winton, 1996).

Linkages and Support External to IHEs   Actually implementing a coherent interdisciplinary instructional program in early intervention depends on the efforts of all those currently and potentially affected by the instruction. Linkages among faculty within and across IHEs, administrators, community leaders, state agency representatives, existing and past students, family members, and service providers are critical to the success of interdisciplinary instructional efforts. In some cases, faculty members across colleges and universities and agencies have formed regional, statewide, or multistate consortia or councils to support one another in their interdisciplinary instruction efforts. In Virginia, for example, an Institutions of Higher Education Training Council has been in existence for more than 10 years. Funding for the council was initially provided by a U.S. Department of Education personnel preparation project at VCU in conjunction with funding through Part B of the Virginia Department of Education. Eventually, Part H funds were used to provide additional support for council activities. In Georgia, Part H funds have been used to establish the higher education consortia. Louisiana is another state that has blended resources to support a higher education council. These linkages between state agencies and IHEs have been very successful in supporting faculty engaged in early intervention instruction and facilitating the institutionalization of instructional procedures into existing program frameworks. Another positive outcome of the higher education councils has been the increased efforts to provide inservice programming that appeals to and includes higher education personnel as presenters and participants. The success of higher education consortia and councils may be a spillover from the regional faculty institutes that targeted increased collaboration across state agencies and IHEs in the area of early intervention.

In addition to external linkages, external funding from a variety of sources (e.g., state, federal) can be instrumental in establishing interdisciplinary instructional programs. In 1985, federal funding was made available through the Division of Personnel Preparation of the U.S. Office of Special Education Programs for IHEs preparing personnel to work with children with disabilities ages birth to 3 and their families. Programs that received these grants have used the funds to develop their instructional programs and to offset tuition costs for students enrolled in an early intervention program. In some states federal early intervention and/or preschool funds have been used to support early intervention instructional efforts. For example, in Virginia, these funds have been used to support existing employed early intervention personnel who enroll in coursework related to early intervention.

A special population that community colleges have targeted is paraprofessionals, who are needed to serve young children and their families in community-based programs. The preparation of qualified paraprofessionals has helped to meet the employment needs of their communities, provide community-based programs with paraprofessionals who represent the community being served, and create career paths for individuals who might otherwise not be employed in early intervention. In addition, instructional programs have focused on the preparation of physical therapy assistants and occupational therapy assistants. The disciplines of physical therapy and occupational therapy are experiencing critical personnel shortages (Hebbeler, 1994), with one solution being the preparation of assistants who can help to fill critical needs in these areas. Still another group of professionals that has received instruction in technical and community colleges is child care providers. Appropriately prepared child care providers are central to successful inclusion of young children with disabilities and their families. There are increasing examples of efforts in states to promote articulation agreements between community colleges and IHEs. One example is New Mexico's Higher Education Early Childhood Articulation Task Force, which was established to facilitate collaborative activities between community colleges and comprehensive IHEs with the goal of preparing personnel across disciplines to provide early intervention services. (Contact the third editor of this book for additional information.)

CONCLUSION

IHEs have a tremendous role to play in helping early intervention services to move forward. Early intervention services are directly influenced by the personnel who provide them; therefore, graduates must be prepared for interdisciplinary roles and responsibilities in early intervention.

The reasons stated in this chapter in support of interdisciplinary instruction have not resulted in an abundance of available interdisciplinary programs. Most colleges and universities provide unidisciplinary programs. Those that have developed interdisciplinary models usually have done so with the assistance of external funding. However, to guarantee that the model is institutionalized beyond the period of external funding, attention must be given to those variables that represent a true adoption of the model. This necessitates a system change perspective to college and university planning. Rooney (1995) conducted a follow-up study of 10 federally funded preservice personnel preparation programs in early intervention with findings indicating that the interdisciplinary focus of the majority of the programs had dissipated after the grant ended. Programs had returned to a traditional unidisciplinary focus for reasons such as budget cuts and scarce resources, lack of fit between the interdisciplinary programs and the university settings, and insufficient integration within the community.

There are three interrelated areas that contribute to the institutionalization of interdisciplinary programs. The first is organizational. There are a variety of structures that can accommodate interdisciplinary instructional efforts, most of which consist of unidisciplinary support (e.g., college of education, college of nursing) through which the interdisciplinary instruction occurs. Another structure is interdisciplinary, that is, an independent entity provides the support for the interdisciplinary instruction. Usually these are UAPs, although a number of non-UAP interdisciplinary structures are beginning to be facilitated by colleges and universities. Of primary importance to the institutionalization process is the permanency of the structural supports in place to maintain the instructional model. These supports can be as formal as the designation of an institutional unit within the college or university or as informal as allowing students from different disciplines to enroll in a discipline-specific course in early intervention. What is most important about the structure is that it maintains the opportunity for interdisciplinary instruction to occur over time.

A second key to institutional commitment is a funding base to support the interdisciplinary unit. Although external funding can provide the incentive for a college or university to initiate an interdisciplinary structure, only units such as UAPs can depend on such a funding base for long-term support. Another mechanism that can be used is an internal commitment by the college or university to continue to fund the interdisciplinary program because it facilitates the mission of the IHE. This allows general funds to be used to support the program. Another related strategy is the development of internal funding mechanisms for long-term program support. This may include the establishment of policies and procedures for student tuition to support interdisciplinary credit hours or the faculty of a particular course that enrolls students from different disciplines. An additional mechanism is the allocation of indirect costs (i.e., from any external source) to support the interdisciplinary effort of faculty.

A third important key to the institutionalization process is the commitment of qualified faculty to maintain the interdisciplinary program. Faculty are crucial to continuation of such instructional efforts. Once an interdisciplinary structure has been initiated, the involved faculty usually have a difficult time returning to a unidisciplinary model of instruction. However, their commitment must be supported and reinforced to ensure continuity with the program. As with the first two areas, faculty commitment contributes to the institutionalization of an interdisciplinary program. All these areas, however, must be addressed equally to institutionalize an interdisciplinary instructional model.

There are a number of levels of impact to consider when evaluating the effects of any instructional program. The first level should be the consumer of the instruction, that is, the student who receives the instruction. A second level should be the consumer of the intervention, that is, the families and children receiving early intervention; progress and satisfaction with the student should be assessed by the family. A third level should include the college or university faculty and administration, covering student perceptions of the effectiveness of the teaching and supervision, as well as self-assessments conducted by the faculty themselves.

Evaluation also should include the early intervention system. Measures of performance and satisfaction should be completed by early intervention programs and by administrators who supervise students or hire graduates of the programs. It is critical that the interdisciplinary competencies or performance standards of the early intervention students be considered at all levels of the evaluation. Thus, the instructional program must be clear about its mission and the outcomes expected of its students, and this must be communicated to all involved.

Linkage between the state's system of early intervention and higher education is critical, as discussed in Chapter 2. Administrators from both programs must educate each other about the requirements of each system. If college and university administrators are able to reconceptualize their instructional programs to meet early intervention requirements, then interdisciplinary models should result. Likewise, the state system must understand the many constraints and priorities facing higher education so that it may effectively facilitate and reward interdisciplinary efforts. Interdisciplinary instructional models must be expanded. Despite its many challenges, early intervention practice demands that unidisciplinary options be replaced by a more effective, holistic approach to preservice personnel preparation.

RESOURCES

Crais, E. (1992). *A practical guide to embedding family-centered content into existing speech-language pathology coursework.* Chapel Hill: University of North Carolina at Chapel Hill, Frank Porter Graham Child Development Center. Cost: $10. (919) 966-4221.

Four modules, each designed for presentation within a $1\frac{1}{2}$-hour class, introduce students to issues, beliefs, and practices related to using a family-centered approach to working with families of clients with special needs. Modules include student objectives, course outlines, suggested in- and out-of-class activities, recommended readings for instructors and students, materials for producing handouts and transparencies, and alternative activities and readings.

Hanft, B., Burke, J., Cahill, M., Swenson-Miller, K., & Humphrey, R. (1992). *Working with families: A curriculum guide for pediatric occupational therapists.* Chapel Hill: University of North Carolina at Chapel Hill, Frank Porter Graham Child Development Center. Cost: $10. (919) 966-4221.

Nine-module curriculum addressing issues that therapists need to know to work effectively with families who have children with special needs. Each unit contains learning objectives, discussion points including implications for practice, teaching activities, recommended readings, and teaching resources.

Sparling, J. (1992). *A guide for embedding family information in an entry-level physical therapy curriculum.* Chapel Hill: University of North Carolina at Chapel Hill, Frank Porter Graham Child Development Center. Cost: $15. (919) 966-4221.

Spiral-bound compilation that includes goals, objectives, and strategies (with readings and overhead materials) for embedding family-centered content in four courses ("Human Growth and Development," "Clinical Education I," "Pediatrics," and "Psychiatry and Mental Health").

Winton, P. (1991). *Working with families in early intervention: An interdisciplinary preservice curriculum.* Chapel Hill: University of North Carolina at Chapel Hill, Frank Porter Graham Child Development Center. Cost: $15. (919) 966-4221.

A preservice curriculum for graduate students consisting of eleven 3-hour modules or a semester-long course. Module topics focus on aspects of family-centered practice (e.g., "Communication Strategies for Assessment and Goal-Setting"), and each module includes teaching objectives, suggested student activities, references, and resources.

REFERENCES

American Occupational Therapy Association. (1989). *Guidelines for occupational therapy services in early intervention and preschool services.* Rockville, MD: Author.

American Physical Therapy Association. (1990). *Competencies for physical therapists in early intervention.* Alexandria, VA: Author.

American Speech-Language-Hearing Association. (1989). Communication-based services for infants, toddlers, and their families. *Asha, 31*(5), 32–34.

Bailey, D., Palsha, S., & Huntington, G. (1990). Preservice preparation of special educators to serve infants with handicaps and their families: Current status and training needs. *Journal of Early Intervention, 14,* 43–54.

Bailey, D., Simeonsson, R., Yoder, D., & Huntington, G. (1990). Preparing professionals to serve infants and toddlers with handicaps and their families: An integrative analysis across eight disciplines. *Exceptional Children, 57*(1), 26–34.

Bailey, D.B., Jr. (1989). Issues and directions in preparing professionals to work with young handicapped children and their families. In J.J. Gallagher, P.L. Tohanis, & R.M. Clifford (Eds.), *Policy implementation and PL 99-457: Planning for young children with special needs* (pp. 97–132). Baltimore: Paul H. Brookes Publishing Co.

Bruder, M. (1994). Working with members of other disciplines. Collaboration for success. In M. Wolery & J.S. Wilbers (Eds.), *Including children with special needs in early childhood programs* (pp. 45–70).Washington, DC: National Association for the Education of Young Children.

Bruder, M., Lippman, C., & Bologna, T. (1994). Personnel preparation in early intervention: Building capacity for program expansion within institutions of higher education. *Journal of Early Intervention, 18*(1), 103–110.

Campbell, P., & Leifield, L. (1995). *National status of early intervention personnel preparation programs.* Unpublished manuscript, Temple University, Philadelphia.

Crais, E. (1992). *A practical guide to embedding family-centered content into existing speech-language pathology coursework.* Chapel Hill: University of North Carolina at Chapel Hill, Frank Porter Graham Child Development Center.

Davis, L., Thurman, S., & Mauro, L. (1995). Meeting the challenge of establishing interdisciplinary preservice preparation for infant personnel. *Infants and Young Children, 8*(2), 65–70.

Education of the Handicapped Act Amendments of 1986, PL 99-457, 20 U.S.C. §1400 *et seq.*

Federal Register, 60 14550 (March 17, 1995).

Gallagher, J., & Staples, A. (1990). *Available and potential resources for personnel preparation in special education: Deans' survey.* Chapel Hill: University of North Carolina at Chapel Hill, Frank Porter Graham Child Development Center.

Hanft, B., Burke, J., Cahill, M., Swenson-Miller, K., & Humphrey, R. (1992). *Working with families: A curriculum guide for pediatric occupational therapists.* Chapel Hill: University of North Carolina at Chapel Hill, Frank Porter Graham Child Development Center.

Hebbeler, K. (1994). *Shortages in professions working with young children with disabilities and their families.* Chapel Hill: University of North Carolina at Chapel Hill, National Early Childhood Technical Assistance System.

Hutchinson, D. (1978). The transdisciplinary approach. In J. Curry & K. Peppe (Eds.), *Mental retardation: Nursing approaches to care* (pp. 65–74). St. Louis: C.V. Mosby.

McCollum, J.A., & Stayton, V.D. (1996). Preparing early childhood special educators. In D. Bricker & A. Widerstrom (Eds.), *Preparing personnel to work with infants and young children and their families: A team approach* (pp. 67–90). Baltimore: Paul H. Brookes Publishing Co.

McCollum, J.A., & Thorp, E. (1988). Training to infant specialists: A look at the future. *Infants and Young Children, 1*(2), 55–65.

McGonigel, M.J., Woodruff, G., & Roszmann-Millican, M. (1994). The transdisciplinary team: A model for family-centered early intervention. In L.J. Johnson, R.J. Gallagher, M.J. LaMontagne, J.B. Jordan, J.J. Gallagher, P.L. Hutinger, & M.B. Karnes (Eds.), *Meeting early intervention challenges: Issues from birth to three* (2nd ed., pp. 95–131). Baltimore: Paul H. Brookes Publishing Co.

Meisels, S. (1992). Early intervention: A matter of context. *Bulletin of National Center for Clinical Infant Programs, XII,* 3.

Miller, P. (1993). *Building quality teacher education programs in early education and early intervention (birth through kindergarten): A state planning conference for interdisciplinary teams in higher education.* Raleigh: North Carolina Interagency Coordinating Council for Services to Infants, Toddlers, and Preschoolers with Special Needs and Their Families.

Odom, S.L., McLean, M.E., Johnson, L.J., & LaMontagne, M.J. (1995). Recommended practices in early childhood special education: Validation and current use. *Journal of Early Intervention, 19*(1), 1–17.

Rooney, R. (1995, May). *Implementation of interdisciplinary personnel preparation programs for early intervention.* Paper presented at the annual Comprehensive System for Personnel Development (CSPD) meeting, Washington, DC.

Smith, B. (1988). Early intervention public policy: Past, present, and future. In J.B. Jordan, J.J. Gallagher, P.L. Hutinger, & M.B. Karnes (Eds.), *Early childhood special education: Birth to three* (pp. 213–228). Reston, VA: Council for Exceptional Children.

Sparling, J. (1992). *A guide for embedding family information in an entry-level physical therapy curriculum.* Chapel Hill: University of North Carolina at Chapel Hill, Frank Porter Graham Child Development Center.

Styles, S., Abernathy, S., Pettibone, T., & Wachtel, W. (1984). Training and certification for early childhood special education personnel: A six-year follow-up study. *Journal of the Division for Early Childhood, 8,* 69–73.

Thorp, E.K., & McCollum, J.A. (1994). Personnel in early intervention programs: Areas of needed competence. In L.J. Johnson, R.J. Gallagher, M.J. LaMontagne, J.B. Jordan, J.J. Gallagher, P.L. Hutinger, & M.B. Karnes (Eds.), *Meeting early intervention challenges: Issues from birth to three* (2nd ed., pp. 167–184). Baltimore: Paul H. Brookes Publishing Co.

Winton, P. (1990). A systemic approach for planning inservice training related to Public Law 99-457. *Infants and Young Children, 3*(1), 51–60.

Winton, P. (1991). *Working with families in early intervention: An interdisciplinary preservice curriculum.* Chapel Hill: University of North Carolina at Chapel Hill, Frank Porter Graham Child Development Center.

Winton, P. (1996). A model for supporting higher education faculty in their early intervention personnel preparation roles. *Infants and Young Children, 8*(3), 56–67.

II CRITICAL COMPONENTS OF PERSONNEL PREPARATION

Certain elements are often described as the "givens" in effective personnel preparation, regardless of the content or the target audience. These include the importance of an overall design plan that encompasses needs assessment, evaluation, follow-up, and the promotion of lifelong learning through collegial support and supervision. This section provides practical information and strategies related to these key elements of personnel preparation.

5 DESIGNING EFFECTIVE PERSONNEL PREPARATION FOR EARLY INTERVENTION

Theoretical Frameworks

Jeanette A. McCollum
Camille Catlett

Every personnel preparation program, whether preservice or inservice, is at the interface between the organizational and ecological realities and the individuals whom the program serves. Chapters 1–4 firmly establish that training is embedded within a broad ecosystem formed by mutual influences among recommended practice, federal and state law and policy, actual practice in the state and community, and each training program's own history and traditions. The interdependence within and among system levels is clear; early intervention training will have little effect except when viewed as part of a complex, ongoing change process across components of each training program's ecosystem. Similarly, individual participants bring to the training program their own unique sets of characteristics and ecologies. The designers of personnel training programs must acknowledge both context and participants, with the goal of delivering the desired content through program processes that maximize the balance between the two.

As used in this chapter, the term *training program* describes a planned array of learning opportunities designed to increase the match between personnel performance and the roles that personnel fill. Any program, whether preservice or inservice, incorporates learning structures, events, and activities developed to achieve specific learning outcomes. Programs may be short or long term, single or multifaceted, and they may occur at any point in the course of the participant's professional development. The central defining feature of a personnel training program is that it is implemented with the intent of developing or altering the professional behaviors and characteristics of its participants. This chapter addresses issues confronted by designers of both preservice and inservice programs, with an emphasis on the selection and design of training contents and processes.

Generally, the term *preservice* refers to professional development efforts that prepare individuals to perform the entry-level functions of their disciplines or professions, whereas *inservice* refers to professional development activities undertaken to assist the more experienced professional in expanding and growing within the profession. The distinctions between preservice and inservice ordinarily carry with them some important assumptions that influence program design decisions. For instance, assumptions about preservice and inservice are relatively automatic with regard to the purposes of training, the amount of professional knowledge and experience that participants already hold, the importance of training within the participants' life contexts, and the amount of time available for training. Assumptions also are made about the source of the training (university or non–university based) and the temporal relationship between training and application (future application or simultaneous application).

When broad change in practice is occurring, requiring that individuals already in or entering a field of service be extensively retrained, distinctions between the functions and audiences of preservice and inservice programs are likely to become blurred. In such times, both preservice and inservice programs are likely to enroll participants with a much broader range of characteristics and professional goals and to be wider in scope and purpose than is implied by their traditional definitions; this point is examined in greater depth later in this chapter.

Early intervention training may present some unique challenges to both preservice and inservice program designers. As illustrated in Janet's story in Chapter 1, the knowledge, skills, and attitudes desired for early intervention may be qualitatively different from those of the individuals who emerge from disciplinary training programs. The roles of early interventionists are still unfolding, yet it is clear that these roles are quite complex, blending the content of many disciplines and changing the ways in which service delivery is planned and implemented by a member of any discipline (Winton, 1990). Another layer of complexity is added by the multiple configurations of settings, policies, and people that compose early intervention services within and across states (McCollum & Bailey, 1991; McCollum & Hughes, 1988); in many ways, early intervention training must prepare personnel for the unknown. In addition to conveying specialized content, training must accomplish each of the following:

• Foster the values and attitudes that undergird recommended practice in early intervention
• Address interdisciplinary audiences and include interdisciplinary perspectives
• Be relevant and practical in an everchanging system
• Address uncertainties and fears associated with rapidly changing systems

Components common to all training programs include input variables such as program settings, characteristics of trainers, and characteristics of participants; program content, including desired outcomes and the curriculum to be presented; and program process, including program structure and organization as well as specific instructional strategies employed within the larger structural elements (Cruickshank, 1984; Katz & Raths, 1985; McCollum & McCartan, 1988). As is demonstrated in this chapter and in Chapter 21, the process of program design in both preservice and inservice may be viewed as an interrelated series of decision points, each with its own alternatives. There are no easy routes to making these decisions, as solutions depend on the unique configuration of needs, resources, and contexts of the particular program, as well as on anticipated or known characteristics of potential participants. Contextual factors in particular may constrain the range of options open to program designers, influencing the specific options selected and the ways in which these are linked to one another to form the total program. As discussed in other chapters of this book (see particularly Chapters 1–4 and 17–21), such factors might include the licensing and practice guidelines of the particular discipline, the historical and anticipated relation of the projected program to these guidelines, and the historical mission and function of the training program in the state. The availability of resources within the organization or agency offering the training and the priority given to early intervention training compared with other areas of focus are additional contextual variables influencing these decisions. Fortunately, many of these constraints and parameters are known, and guidance is available from multiple sources, as illustrated throughout this book.

This chapter emphasizes program content and process, as these compose the core of program design; outlines decisions and options within each of these two components as they apply to both preservice and inservice; and offers a framework for making design decisions. Finally, the implications for program design when the lines between the traditional purposes of preservice and inservice training blur are considered.

COMPONENTS OF PROGRAM DESIGN: CONTENT AND PROCESS

In early intervention, new roles and new visions of service delivery directly influence both what early interventionists do and how they do it (McCollum & Thorp, 1988; Winton, 1990). For instance, early interventionists must know not only how to perform an assessment but also how to do so in a manner that includes the family as a central player. Therefore, the curriculum content must include values and early intervention philosophy in addition to specific bodies of knowledge and skill. This range of content in turn requires a systematically planned training process.

Choosing and Organizing Early Intervention Training Content

Each program selects early intervention content within the parameters and constraints defined by its own traditions and contexts. However, traditional sources of content may not be sufficient when new approaches to practice are emerging or when new populations, such as infants and toddlers and their families, become part of the population to be served. As early intervention is further defined and understood, various sources of content must be examined critically to determine whether they are compatible with new roles that interventionists are experiencing and with new visions of service delivery. In every discipline providing early intervention services, new roles and visions will inevitably create tension with existing instructional content.

Table 5.1 contains a set of guiding questions that may be useful in making decisions about content. At a broader level, delineating curriculum content involves two highly interrelated decisions, to be addressed in the following sections: 1) determining important knowledge, skill, and attitudinal outcomes to be developed, derived from an understanding of the roles and functions to be performed; and 2) delineating the breadth and depth of content required to address the desired instruction outcomes.

Early Intervention Roles and Training Content Desired outcomes of instruction are those characteristics and abilities that allow existing and future early interventionists to fill their roles in accordance with emerging visions of recommended practice. A significant amount of attention has been given to the roles of early interventionists, to how these roles differ from and are similar to roles traditionally performed by individuals from various disciplines, and to how roles compare across disciplines. From this examination has emerged a vision of early intervention service delivery and of the professional orientations, attitudes, knowledge, and skills needed to achieve this vision (Bailey, 1989; Fenichel & Eggbeer, 1990). Professional organizations interested in early intervention (e.g., Division for Early Childhood of the Council for Exceptional Children, National Association for the Education of Young Children, & Association of Teacher Educators,

TABLE 5.1.   Guiding questions for determining content

1. Do desired knowledge and skill outcomes reflect current and expected early intervention roles and functions?

2. Do desired outcomes include professional orientations and attitudes reflective of recommended practice in early intervention?

3. Do desired outcomes include processes such as decision making, problem solving, and reflection on practice?

4. Are similarities and differences between within- and cross-discipline roles and desired outcomes clear?

5. Do the array and organization of content areas match desired outcomes?

6. Do the breadth and depth of content match desired outcomes?

7. Is content organized to maximize linkages among knowledge, skills, and professional dispositions?

8. Are areas of content organized to maximize linkages among them, as well as with existing knowledge?

9. Does the sequencing of content reflect systematic building toward desired outcomes?

10. Is transfer of desired outcomes to practice reflected in the selection, organization, and sequencing of content?

1995), as well as some states (e.g., Zervigon-Hakes, 1991), have developed lists of competencies needed by individuals delivering early intervention services. As desired outcomes, such listings can lend significant guidance to the selection of training content.

Early intervention personnel fill a broader range of roles with respect to children, families, other team members, and participating agencies than might be expected solely from their respective disciplinary backgrounds (Bailey, 1989). These roles also may be configured differently depending on the particular system in which the individual works, and many roles are shared among disciplines (McCollum & Hughes, 1988). Even traditional disciplinary roles often require new skills related to the developmental status of the very young child and to the centrality of the family to the early intervention process (Thorp & McCollum, 1994).

A distinction between within-discipline and cross-discipline roles places early intervention content within the context of larger bodies of disciplinary knowledge (McCollum & Thorp, 1988). For instance, a physical therapist may need to learn new approaches to assessment that take into account qualitatively different motor development during the infancy period (a within-discipline role). The same physical therapist may need to learn to perform a play-based assessment in partnership with the family (a cross-discipline role), an outcome important for all disciplines. Some training outcomes thus represent an expansion and deepening of traditional areas of disciplinary knowledge, whereas others represent areas of knowledge or new ways of thinking, many common across all disciplines with early intervention roles.

Thorp and McCollum (1994) organized content important for the provision of early intervention services into five broad areas: 1) children, 2) families, 3) team functioning, 4) interagency and advocacy functioning, and 5) personal and professional qualities and values. Cross-discipline training content can be identified in each of these areas. As discussed in Thorp and McCollum, infant-related content identified as important for all disciplines includes the ability to learn from observation, whereas important family-related content includes the ability to recognize and support family strengths. Team content needed by all disciplines includes knowing a common vocabulary and having skills for working with others as a decision-making unit, whereas interagency and advocacy content ensures that professionals from all disciplines use existing resources and advocate for additional ones when needed. Personal and professional qualities and values encompass at least two aspects of professional competence: relationships with other individuals and ways of thinking and approaching tasks and issues. The process of performing early intervention is grounded in relationships (Fenichel & Eggbeer, 1990) and in how early intervention roles are performed. The ability to build healthy relationships with others and the ability to reflect on oneself as a partner in relationships are critical to the implementation of early intervention roles (Fenichel & Eggbeer, 1990). Qualities and values needed by members of all disciplines also include respect for the collaborative nature of early intervention service delivery. Therefore, beliefs and values must become an explicit focus of training for all early intervention personnel. Dispositions and strategies for handling change also may be relevant in a rapidly changing field, particularly if traditional practice and early intervention practice are not congruent. The ability to make reasonable hypotheses, to guide one's own professional behavior based on these hypotheses, and then to reflect on the outcome are critical to all aspects of intervention. The crucial point for early intervention training, in which processes, values, and relationships are the core of service delivery, is that these must become an explicit part of the curriculum.

Early intervention content specific to each early intervention discipline is also apparent in the first four of these same broad areas (i.e., child, family, team, interagency). For disciplines that are traditionally child focused, changes in within-discipline competencies are most likely to be found in roles related to children. For disciplines with a traditional family focus, new assessment and intervention techniques appropriate for addressing the unique concerns and strengths of families with children with disabilities will be required. For both child- and family-focused disciplines, new perspectives on families may have to be learned. Thorp and McCollum's (1994) analysis of the within-discipline content needed by early childhood special educators demonstrates this process of clarifying desired areas of content. For instance, expectations of the functions to be performed by this discipline in relation to infants and toddlers would include applying observational skills toward understanding the infant's cognitive, social, and emotional development, as well as the interrelationships among these domains. To the process of intervention planning, this discipline would bring expertise in assessing and designing environments to support the infant's development, including specific environmental adaptations to allow infants with disabilities to interact with their environments.

Identifying broad areas of competence, supported by listings of more specific outcomes, suggests subareas of training content (Thorp & McCollum, 1994). For instance, supporting family strengths is based on having knowledge of family systems theory, on valuing diverse strengths, and on using family strengths toward early intervention goals. Each subarea contains its own set of knowledge and skills.

As demonstrated by the chapters in the third part of this book, some areas of content can readily be organized into teaching units or courses. Other areas, often representing the values and professional dispositions that undergird all areas of content, must be embedded throughout the instruction curriculum.

Desired Outcomes: Guidance to Curriculum Breadth and Depth   The extent to which early intervention content can be included within any preservice or inservice training program will depend on the contexts and purposes of the particular program, as well as on the early intervention roles to be filled by its participants. Some disciplines, and some programs within disciplines, although recognizing a need for specialized preparation, may choose not to offer it based on a variety of contextual barriers (Bailey, Simeonsson, Yoder, & Huntington, 1990) or because it is already available through other avenues of training. In contrast, other programs may emphasize early intervention as a specialized focus or even create new programs directed specifically toward this population. Most disciplines will fall somewhere between these extremes, addressing early intervention content to some extent within their preservice and inservice programs by offering content related to one or two subareas of content or by providing introductory content across a larger range of areas.

A number of important decisions lie between identifying an overall array of early intervention content and delineating the breadth and depth of early intervention content to be included within the curriculum of the particular preservice or inservice program. *Breadth* refers to the number of early intervention content areas or *subareas* to be included and to the amount of information to be included from each. *Depth* refers to the extent to which each area, or selected subunits of an area, will be expected to be part of the working repertoire of participants at the conclusion of the program. Breadth and depth relate to time in the same way: Given desired outcomes of greater breadth or depth, more time in training is indicated. Within given time limitations, however, breadth and depth have an inverse relationship, and a balance will have to be achieved between providing broad information at a more superficial level or more narrowly focused information at greater depth. Decisions about breadth will influence the depth that can be achieved and vice versa. By definition, preservice programs are expected to address both breadth and depth to the extent needed for entry into the professional discipline. Inservice programs, responding to a more delimited content focus and a more restricted time frame, are likely to struggle more with depth than with breadth.

A useful distinction that may lend some guidance to making decisions about *breadth* is made by Havelock and Havelock (1973) among whole-role training, training for skill sets and functions, and training for specific skills. The extent to which early intervention instruction represents any one of these three purposes may be specific to each discipline and may define the extent to which early intervention content, as opposed to other disciplinary content, must be provided to prepare participants for their roles. For some disciplines, early intervention roles may represent considerable variation in knowledge, skills, and attitudes from what is included in existing disciplinary training, to the extent that whole-role training is required. For others, broad awareness combined with a limited number of targeted skills or skill areas may be indicated. Similarities with and differences from traditional roles are an important contributor to decisions regarding the breadth and depth of early intervention content needed by participants within any particular area. The greater the difference from traditional roles, the more a whole-role curriculum may be necessary. Making this determination is not straightforward; when values and processes are the desired outcomes, it is not always easy to determine the extent to which new roles differ from old (Winton, 1990). For instance, individuals working in disciplines that have always worked closely with families may have difficulty understanding the difference between their actual practice and the way their practice would look given the values of family-centered care.

In early intervention, the discipline of special education has tended to take a whole-role perspective because of the pervasive differences in roles filled by special educators who work in early intervention contexts compared with those who work with older children in school settings (McCollum & Maude, 1994). The therapies, in contrast, have tended to take a skill set approach, based on the rationale that the major functions and practice principles of their disciplines remain constant across populations but must be supplemented by information and skills related to the birth-to-3 age period. In early intervention, single-skill training is the exception rather than the rule because few disciplines have failed to recognize the often extensive changes in disciplinary practice needed for working with this population.

Another useful distinction, lending guidance to making decisions about *depth*, relates to the level at which participants will be expected to apply the competencies gained from training. Types of learning outcomes have been represented on a continuum portraying increasingly greater depth of application, beginning with general awareness, proceeding through knowledge and understanding, to skill application, and finally to bringing appropriate attitudinal dispositions to application of knowledge and skills (Harris, 1980). One guideline for making decisions about the depth of content needed is to consider the level at which the unit of content needs to become integrated into the participant's professional thinking and behavior to perform anticipated early intervention tasks. For instance, is it enough that participants be aware of the values underlying family-centered practice, or should they recognize such practice when they see it? Should they be able to evaluate their own values and their own practice against this standard and change their practice to be congruent with a family-centered perspective? Harris (1980) recommended that, within training, participants experience content at the level at which they will need to apply it in their work.

The need to balance breadth and depth applies to both preservice and inservice. Although content for both is likely to be derived from the same delineations of early intervention roles and recommended practice, preservice and inservice providers must determine what outcomes are needed and can reasonably be achieved from their training, given the unique strengths and constraints of the particular preservice or inservice setting. Depth can be achieved only with time; furthermore, the time dimension must allow application and subsequent reflection. Breadth can be achieved only with multiple training opportunities directed toward the same role or task as part of a holistic view of early intervention practice.

Because preservice and inservice training traditionally address different purposes and use different configurations of time and place, decisions related to breadth and depth also may be different. For inservice training, content is likely to be delimited by inservice education's traditional role in responding to particular needs at particular times. Content may be derived from the needs of a larger system or directly from potential inservice participants in relation to a particular outcome they wish to achieve. Inservice programs may find it difficult to maintain coherence with a larger body of knowledge or to focus on outcomes that require greater depth of application and reflection. For preservice planners, in contrast, the curriculum needs to be narrowed from the whole range of important content to that which is most essential for entry into the profession, while still achieving the breadth of information expected and the depth of learning to facilitate transfer of new abilities and characteristics to future roles.

The balance between breadth and depth may be a particular challenge for disciplines in which early intervention represents only one portion of the roles for which participants are being prepared. Training for early intervention services requires attention not only to new skills but also to how old and new skills are employed with children and families. This appears to call for both a whole-role perspective and for a depth of training necessary for addressing professional dispositions. Integrating new content into an already full inservice or preservice agenda may prove difficult, and both preservice and inservice planners face dilemmas in balancing breadth and depth. Different ways of organizing content may need to be used to achieve this balance. For instance, knowledge areas might be organized into areas and subareas to be taught as courses, sections of courses, or classes. In contrast, values and dispositions such as those associated with family-centered practice or with transdisciplinary team interaction might be better embedded across courses (e.g., Crais, 1991), as they have implications for how intervention is carried out across multiple areas of content.

In the previous sections of this chapter, learning content has been approached from the perspective of broad program design. In matching the content to the needs of particular learners, additional considerations must include the status of the learners with respect to the content and the overall purpose of the training. Chapter 21 contains additional guidelines for accomplishing this match.

Program Process: How Should Content Be Delivered?

Whereas program content describes *what* is taught, program process refers to *how* content is delivered. As shown in Table 5.2, program process includes making decisions at two levels: 1) the overall program structure and organization and 2) the training strategies used within this larger context. At the preservice level, courses and field experiences are typical structural elements; at the inservice level, workshops and conferences are the most typical structures. Demonstration, small-group work, and lecture are typical examples of teaching strategies. Important decisions with regard to each level of process include the specific elements to be used; the number, length, and order of elements; and the establishment of interelement linkages.

The functions of both levels of training program process, alone and together, are to convey to the learner the outcomes intended by the program, support the learner in developing a professional identity compatible with the provision of early intervention services, and facilitate the transfer of these outcomes to employment. A careful look at the training process is important for at least two reasons. First, there are indications that traditional processes used in preservice and inservice education may not yield the outcomes desired in terms of characteristics and abilities of personnel. The following are process elements to which these unintended outcomes have been attributed in preservice (McCollum & McCartan, 1988) and inservice (Guskey, 1986) training:

- Episodic, disconnected training components
- Lack of opportunities to ground content in everyday experience
- Lack of opportunity to reflect on old and new visions of practice
- Lack of opportunity to build and reinforce new norms of behavior compatible with desired outcomes

A second reason is that the early intervention literature has called for some fairly specific training processes. Fenichel and Eggbeer (1990) identified four elements as essential to preparing competent early interventionists. Three of these reflect characteristics of program structure: 1) opportunities for direct observation of and interaction with a variety of children less than the age of 3 years and their families; 2) individualized supervision that allows the participant to reflect on all aspects of work with infants, families, and colleagues from a range of disciplines; and 3) collegial support, both within and across disciplines, that begins early in training and continues throughout the practitioner's professional life. Other authors have reinforced these same themes. McCollum and Stayton

TABLE 5.2.   Guiding questions for determining training process

Training program structure and organization

1. Has a written philosophy about early intervention practice been used to guide development of the training program?

2. Does the program mirror a collaborative approach to services?

3. Do structural elements make use of real situations as part of training program design?

4. Are structural elements sequenced to foster increasing complexity and integration of information?

5. Does the training structure include opportunities to apply and reflect on learning outcomes at levels the same as or close to those at which they will be used?

6. Does the training structure support the development of collegial norms with regard to early intervention practice?

7. Do structural elements match the types of learning outcomes to which they are attached?

8. Do structural elements recognize/allow/expand on individual differences in learners?

9. Are structural elements linked together to support reflection on action?

Training strategies

1. Do participants interact with content in the ways required in early intervention roles and functions?

2. Do participants reflect on process and on self as implementer, as well as on practice?

3. Do participants interact with receivers of early intervention services with the goal of understanding their perspectives?

4. Are training strategies matched to different types of outcomes?

5. Are training strategies matched to different goals and styles of learners?

6. Are common themes and principles reinforced by multiple strategies?

7. Do strategies support linkages among outcomes and with existing skills and knowledge?

(1996), for example, noted the importance of interdisciplinary interaction during preservice preparation for developing a shared value base and for achieving the collaboration intended in early intervention. Co-teaching by faculty from different disciplines and co-teaching by faculty and parents have both been recommended to support the development of skills and dispositions for collaboration (see Chapters 4, 10, 17, and 18).

Undergirding these training guidelines are two themes: 1) having opportunities within training to develop a value base consistent with knowledge of family systems and early development; and 2) experiencing, within the context of training, the processes inherent in collaboration, problem solving, and self-analysis. These recommendations imply that what is needed are training structures and strategies that will convey how early intervention services are to be delivered, as well as what is to be done, by establishing a close link between content and process. Early intervention training at its best will emulate the collaborative nature of the services that participants are preparing to provide by demonstrating collaborative relationships with families and among disciplines.

Literature on adult learning is another source of information on the process of training. Principles of adult learning yield the following guidelines to designing process (e.g., Knowles, 1987; Margolis & Bell, 1984; Moore, 1988):

- Relate new information to what is familiar and salient to the learner, building on experience and perceptions of need.
- Establish training conditions that create dissonance between existing practice and desired learning outcomes.
- Involve participants in learning experiences that nurture the development of new group norms consistent with desired learning outcomes.
- Link content to existing and future application.
- Provide opportunities for practice and reflection on practice within the context of training.
- Involve participants actively in their own learning process, letting knowledge and understanding grow from mutual investigation of real problems and issues.

These guidelines, although applied in the literature primarily to inservice planning, are equally applicable and useful for preservice design and are highly compatible with the recommendations for early intervention training. All of these conditions may be critical to acquiring and transferring new thinking and new behavior to the workplace, whether that workplace be current or future (Broad & Newstrom, 1992; Brookfield, 1986; Davis & McCallon, 1974; Fitzpatrick, 1989; Winton, 1990). Also needed are time and support for integrating new information into the participant's overall repertoire of professional behavior. (Chapter 7 contains a more detailed discussion of approaches for supporting transfer of training to the workplace.)

These guidelines connote multielement structures and strategies, as well as linkages among elements across time, and apply to both preservice and inservice training. The conditions necessary for reflection are contained in Brookfield's (1986) admonition to structure learning around an ongoing cycle of exploration–action–reflection. Placed within the context of more complex application, this also addresses Calderhead's (1988) observation that increasingly more complex interactions between participant and task become available for reflection as additional experience is gained. Both authors emphasized the parallel processes of acting and reflecting that are inherent in the broad guidelines previously outlined.

There are important differences between experienced and inexperienced learners, the traditional participants of inservice and preservice programs, respectively. First, older learners ordinarily have a fund of professional and life experience that is unlikely to be present in younger learners. Second, older learners may not be receptive to training that is not relevant to current issues in their lives and may be highly motivated to participate in training that is relevant. These two differences are important not only for the guidance they provide to the processes to be used with adult learners but also because they point to an important condition that may need to be established when teaching younger, less experienced learners: forming links with what each participant brings to the learning situation. How opportunities for reflection in complex action contexts can be accomplished within the preservice context is an important question. For instance, an experiential base can be created by providing field experience concurrent with courses or simulated through videotapes or case studies. In addition, however, personal experiences may be particularly important for formulating values compatible with early intervention services; these values represent experiences on which all participants, regardless of experience, can reflect.

The work situations and experiences of older participants may not always provide an advantage. Brookfield (1986) noted that a person's past may sometimes interfere with his or her openness to new information. Winton (1990) also emphasized the importance of using training strategies that assist learners in recognizing gaps between their practices and beliefs and those needed in early intervention settings. Nevertheless, for both inexperienced and experienced participants, past and current personal and professional experiences provide the grounding for learning.

A MODEL FOR PROGRAM DESIGN: COMBINING CONTENT AND PROCESS

Given recommendations derived from the early intervention and adult learning literatures, the question remains of how to match specific training options to specific types of desired outcomes. The next section presents a model for making this type of decision. Two examples of early intervention training are then discussed using the criteria implied by this model and the guidelines previously outlined. Additional examples of practical applications of the principles of training design may be found in Chapter 21.

Description of the Model

A model outlined by Harris (1980) and expanded on by Walker (1982) in relation to preparing early childhood special education teachers provides a framework for matching process to content, based on the congruence between the types of outcomes desired and the depth of impact likely to be achieved using different approaches. Harris's model uses the level and complexity of desired outcomes as a guide for selecting training structures and strategies.

Three basic components, each representing a different continuum, compose Harris's model; the relationship among these is shown in Figure 5.1. The first two components relate to the outcomes desired from the training. On the vertical continuum, different types of outcomes are conceived as representing differing degrees of change required of the learner, with awareness outcomes requiring the least change and attitude outcomes requiring the most. A second (horizontal) continuum, representing complexity of the outcome, expands on the first and represents the extent to which different outcomes must be integrated with other outcomes or units of information and then applied within the context of the particular workplace. The third (diagonal) continuum organizes training processes according to their match with desired levels of impact and differing levels of complexity and synthesis necessary for application to early intervention settings. The degree of impact is assumed to be related to the degree of active involvement that the participant has in the training process, with active involvement defined as the extent to which the learning activity allows the participant to experience knowledge, skills, and attitudes in the same way they will be required in the work setting. For instance, if the participant will need to lead an interdisciplinary team through the process of developing individualized family service plans, then the participant should engage in (and reflect on) this role within the context of the training. The greater the personal involvement, the more the impact. As shown in Figure 5.1, lectures might be expected to have the least impact, approaches such as role play and guided practice to have more, and learning situated in everyday experience the most. Also illustrated is the need to include among the training processes specific approaches for facilitating transfer of training (see Chapter 7).

Combining these continua allows planners to achieve a balance of efficiency and effectiveness for the range of approaches included and the types of outcomes desired. With regard to effectiveness, for example, although reading may be an efficient use of

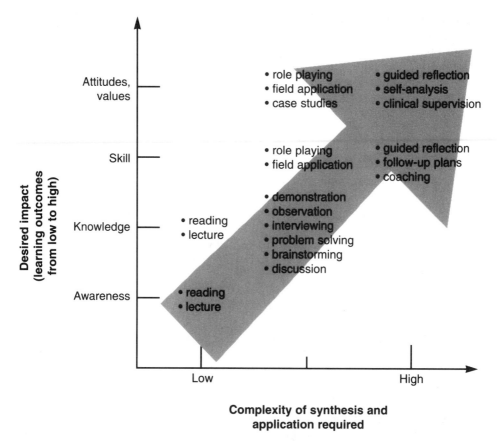

Figure 5.1. A model for matching training approach to desired training outcomes and complexity of application. (Adapted from Harris [1980].)

actual training time, it is unlikely to bring about changes in skills or attitudes; knowledge outcomes, in contrast, may be achieved quite well with reading or other relatively lower-impact approaches such as lecture. Skill or attitude outcomes would require active approaches to training such as guided practice and self-analysis, which also may take up more of the available training time. With regard to efficiency, highly active approaches, which take more training time, may be unnecessary for gaining basic knowledge that can be acquired through reading or lecture. Complex tasks and functions, requiring integrated knowledge, skill, and dispositional outcomes across multiple areas, would require a combination of training approaches with different levels of impact. For instance, as shown in Chapter 14, an inservice or preservice session on teams and teamwork might include a videotape, family story, or self-analysis survey to raise awareness; an activity for recognizing and learning the stages of team development; and an applied activity in which participants evaluate a videotaped team meeting from the perspective of principles of team practice (Project Vision, 1994; Virginia Institute for Developmental Disabilities, 1990). Complex learning outcomes likely would also require guided practice and opportunities for reflection across time, using methods such as peer coaching or clinical supervision (as described in Chapters 7 and 8).

The concept of differing levels of impact can be applied both to the larger program structure and to the strategies used for teaching. In addition, it applies to both preservice and inservice settings. For instance, at the preservice level, close structural linkages between coursework and field experience would facilitate the integration of multiple outcomes and provide opportunities for transfer, implementation, and reflection (Walker, 1982). To accomplish this, field experiences would need to be concurrent with or embedded within courses; if concurrent, then specific linkages would need to be made between them, perhaps in the form of field-based course assignments. At the inservice level, application of training content within the workplace might be parallel or subsequent to workshops or other training events or be supported by follow-up technical assistance. Within a single class session or inservice session, multiple activities might be used to provide information, allow participants to apply the information by analyzing case studies, and develop plans for implementation within a real or simulated work setting. To the extent possible, the level at which the outcome is to be applied on the job is the level at which the participant should interact with the information within the context of the training situation. Thus, if implementation of a certain skill is the outcome, then implementation should occur within the context of training, so that practice and reflection go hand-in-hand. If application of a certain value base to the planning of services is the outcome, then the value base should be applied to multiple relevant situations within the context of the training. Ideally, training would carry over into the workplace itself as part of the continuing cycle of action, exploration, and reflection (Calderhead, 1988).

The guidelines provided by this model are highly compatible with those derived from the literature on adult learning and with recommendations in the early intervention training literature related to collaborative training and to an explicit focus on values and self-reflection. What the model offers is a systematic way of thinking about the match between desired outcome and process.

Sample Applications

A number of specific approaches for teaching particular areas of content have been described in the early intervention literature and also appear throughout this book. This section applies the guidelines in the previous sections to two selected training approaches to illustrate how this process might be useful to trainers evaluating their own approaches. For the purposes of this chapter, the examples selected for discussion illustrate training efforts focused on preparing participants for collaboration with families and other team members (for more discussion of training methods related to these two topics, see Chapters 10, 14, and 17).

The Family-Based Practicum   Desired outcomes related to collaboration with families include, among others, understanding family systems, identifying family strengths, valuing family perspectives and diversity, and using skills that foster confidence and competence in family members. Professional and personal values are conveyed to families in many ways. Therefore, it is necessary for participants in early intervention training to have the opportunity to learn about the diversity of family life and to confront and examine their own feelings about families (Fenichel & Eggbeer, 1990).

One structure that has been used in several preservice programs to provide this opportunity is a family-based practicum (see Chapter 17). In this type of practicum, participants are required to spend a specified period with a family from the local community. The intent is that the participant will come to perceive daily life, including early intervention, from the family's point of view and become better able to interpret the world through the eyes of families different from his or her own. In so doing, participants confront their own values about families and how these may influence their own existing or future early intervention practice. Although family-based practica range considerably in the amount of time spent with the family, the specific activities in which participants engage with the family, and the extent to which interactions with families are accompanied by a simultaneous opportunity for ongoing reflection, they have in common the view of family as teacher and participant as learner, as well as desired outcomes related to values.

As a structural solution to providing specific early intervention content, a family practicum meets many of the guidelines previously outlined, particularly if ongoing reflection is built into the practicum through a mechanism such as supervision or keeping a journal. The need and motivation for acquiring knowledge and skills are grounded in the experience of being with the family, and experience provides the arena for application and further reflection. Questioning one's own perceptions of families, one's role with families, and one's interactions with families should be a natural outgrowth of the experience. Participants should come to question the source of their values and behaviors and be better able to interpret how these might influence their interactions with and feelings about families. Given that information is available to meet emerging questions and dilemmas and ongoing opportunities for reflection are provided, the participant becomes active in the learning process.

Although a family-based practicum has been used most with preservice participants, it also may be used with those already employed in early intervention positions. Many of the processes previously described mirror those recommended for ongoing clinical supervision of early intervention personnel (Fenichel, 1992). In addition, similar benefits could be derived from assigning currently employed participants to families external to their work settings in conjunction with coursework or as a follow-up activity to inservice training.

Strategies directed toward similar outcomes, but more limited in scope, might include the use of case studies (McWilliam, 1992). As illustrated in Chapter 17, co-teaching preservice or inservice programs with families represents another powerful strategy for modeling the values and processes that are goals for the participants.

Team Training   Interdisciplinary team training is another structure that supports the goals of early intervention training and demonstrates attention to many of the guidelines previously stated. Team training models are based on the assumption that if any team member is to change in accordance with the goals of training and transfer this change back to the work setting, the team must participate as a functional unit. For instance, in one team training model (Bailey, McWilliam, & Winton, 1992; Winton, McWilliam, Harrison, Owens, & Bailey, 1992), functioning teams were brought together to participate jointly in a 3-day workshop, with administrators present as well. The primary instructional strategies used were self-examination, decision making, and goal setting, with the ultimate goal of the workshop being the creation of a team plan for becoming more family centered in their practices and policies. The teams assessed their current practice by responding to a series of self-assessment questions and set goals for change based on what they discovered and what they were learning from case studies, presentations, and large-group discussion embedded within sections of the workshop devoted to each question. Teams then engaged in a process of structured discussion and decision making to generate a course of action (see Chapter 14 for strategies for team training and Chapter 20 for information on the use of the team training model within a community context).

Viewed from the perspective of the training guidelines, participants learned and practiced new ways of interacting with one another; in addition, teams as functioning systems developed new norms for team goals and practices to be carried back to their workplace. Training was grounded in the team's common experience, different perceptions of reality were made explicit through the use and sharing of self-assessment information, and support and new skills were provided for developing new peer group expectations. Knowledge, skills, and values are linked together as participants engaged in action and reflection (Brookfield, 1986). Strategies incorporating active problem solving were used to achieve psychological engagement with the material, and information and skills are linked to needs arising from work and within-instruction experiences. In accordance with the levels of impact guidelines, the team used its new knowledge and skills to engage in practice and evaluate this practice from the perspective of its congruence with new collegial norms. A team plan was then developed to facilitate the transfer of new behaviors and attitudes to the team's workplace. Given follow-up assistance from the instructor and from other team members, opportunities were available to engage in action and reflection, ensuring that new norms of behavior were integrated within the systems that were in place. In this approach, structure and strategy are intertwined.

Portions of this framework seem applicable across preservice and inservice. Preservice practica also can be designed around an interdisciplinary team process (McCollum & Stayton, 1996; also see Chapter 18). Within courses, teams can be created with constant membership to last throughout a semester, and simulations of field-based dilemmas and decisions can be used as the content of interaction (Winton, 1992). The critical element is that the team then reflects on its own interactions, developing and subsequently evaluating rules and agendas for its own functioning. These processes, although grounded in simulated situations, nevertheless take team members through common experiences, providing processes to be used in future team situations.

Some of the elements found within these models are also useful in and of themselves as strategies that can be applied within other training structures. For instance, self-assessment has been recommended as a strategy that can be directed toward many areas of content. Self-assessment as a training tool offers an active participation approach to providing the participant with information about recommended practice, creating dissonance (and motivation for learning) as participants compare their current practice (or what they have observed) with recommended practice. Therefore, self-assessment is a generalizable tool that may be useful across many areas of content and is applicable to both preservice and inservice settings.

At both the preservice and inservice levels, internal and external constraints and parameters influence the design of early intervention training systems. Nevertheless, there are choices to be made and creative options to be pursued. The big questions for program planners relate to which structural elements and strategies, for how long, and in what configurations will support acquisition of desired outcomes and facilitate transfer to nontraining situations. The minimum appears to be opportunities to develop relationships and to experience interactions with infants and toddlers, families, and members of multiple disciplines. Process goes far beyond mere exposure, however. The two previous examples were based on guiding principles related to the following: 1) experience, as a part of training, with the processes that will enable application and continued development, including collaboration and clarification of values; 2) training structures that match existing or future work settings as closely as possible, including using real and simulated situations and dilemmas; 3) training strategies that link understanding to experience, whether professional or personal; and 4) strategies that enhance self-directed learning, including self-assessment and peer supervision. Making decisions about how content will be conveyed to learners requires attention to how different structures and strategies relate to different types of outcomes to be achieved and to how outcomes become integrated within a single frame of reference achieved by the individual participant.

BLURRING THE LINES BETWEEN PRESERVICE AND INSERVICE

Rethinking Definitions

In the first section of this chapter, it was noted that traditional distinctions between preservice and inservice education carry a set of assumptions with regard to the purveyors and recipients of training, the degree of experience and professional knowledge that participants bring to the training process, the centrality of the training program within the participants' current life contexts, the amount of time available for training, and the temporal relationship between training and application.

New issues are raised for preservice and inservice programs when changes such as those occurring in early intervention require pervasive, rapid change in personnel. New preservice graduates may have received little preparation for entry into early intervention positions, as demonstrated in Janet's story in Chapter 1, and may need further entry-level training across many content areas. Although some experienced professionals may have considerable expertise and seek further training to broaden their skills and knowledge, others may need to make pervasive changes in what they do and believe or even in their anticipated career paths. As a consequence, both preservice and inservice programs are likely to have a broad mix of participants who differ in age, professional experience, and experience with infants and toddlers with disabilities and their families. Preservice programs that address early intervention may serve larger numbers of individuals in mid-career, who bring with them characteristics and goals that may not match those of the young learners for whom the programs were designed. Inservice programs, in contrast, are increasingly likely to serve individuals with little experience or training related to early intervention and who need a great deal of additional entry-level preparation. Thus, both preservice and inservice programs are faced with addressing functions not traditionally viewed as their mission: Inservice structures are apt to be used increasingly to address entry-level scope and depth, whereas preservice structures are apt to attract individuals whose motivation is to expand and grow in their profession rather than to learn entry-level skills and knowledge. This presents profound dilemmas for both preservice and inservice programs, as traditional sructures and assumptions are likely to be severely challenged.

The blurring of traditional preservice and inservice audiences and purposes is a reality, yet little consideration has been given to how violation of these assumptions may influence the expected outcomes of preservice and inservice programs (McCollum & Bailey, 1991). The important question for preservice and inservice planners is what implications the blend of audiences and functions has for making decisions about the content and process of training. Alternatives for addressing these dilemmas must be pursued both by the individual preservice or inservice training program and by each state's early intervention training system, which, ideally, would be closely related. Although some colleges and universities have responded to the need for early intervention training by developing preservice training options, these are few in number and often limited to adding a class session or module related to early intervention (Bailey et al., 1990). Moreover, few preservice programs involved in early intervention training appear to have direct linkages to their states' early intervention personnel systems, although they may be known to the state and recognized as benefiting the state. At the inservice level, many states have established training arms responsible for providing early intervention training. Nevertheless, inservice training opportunities, although more available and more targeted toward early intervention, tend to be separate from one another in content and structure. There also are likely to be separate agencies and professional organizations that provide substantial amounts of early intervention training and that may not be linked to the state's early intervention system. In any of these settings, traditional assumptions about characteristics of participants and purposes of training may therefore not necessarily be met. These points are discussed from the perspectives of the options open to individual training programs for addressing these dilemmas and recommendations for the state personnel training system as a whole.

Changing Roles of Training Programs

Responses made by individual training programs to the array of audiences increasingly seen in both preservice and inservice can be arranged along a continuum of most change in traditional program practice to least change. On the side of most structural discrepancy from traditional approaches to training, programs may develop and depend on self-instruction modules or other alternatives to face-to-face training. However, such options may require considerable resources and expertise not available to every program. At a slightly less intense level, the same training structures may be maintained for all participants but with individualized options. For instance, preservice participants may have individualized assignments or application plans specific to their own situations or based on the results of self-analysis or may be asked to take different roles (e.g., peer coaching) within the context of the training. A third strategy is to maintain the traditional approaches while creating common frames of reference that cross diverse participants by using strategies such as case studies or activities designed for self-examination. The latter may be particularly useful because such activities are often based on personal as well as professional experience. All learners, regardless of training or work experience, bring to the training program a background of personal experience that may be of crucial importance to their ability to relate to early intervention content. Particularly salient to early intervention training may be personal experiences related to culture or to the development of interpersonal relationships. Personal stories of all participants are relevant for reflection and analysis.

Many of the same options that appear to accommodate the increasingly diverse characteristics of participants also may respond, at least partially, to changes in function when participants with different levels of ability in early intervention content participate together in the preservice or inservice program. For instance, preservice programs, although providing broad-based training to their more traditional students, also can make individual courses available to working professionals by offering weekend formats or by including an option for supervised practicum at the individual's worksite. Other distance learning options (see Chapter 19) also can accomplish the same functions. Alternatively, inservice programs addressing the broader entry-level training needs of practicing early interventionists can develop linkages among content areas across inservice sessions, as well as multielement options such as follow-up consultation and opportunity for reflection on the results of a take-home plan.

State Support for Blending Preservice and Inservice

Both preservice and inservice programs can obtain greater coherence of content and process by linking what they provide to an overall state plan for personnel training. States that have made the most progress in addressing early intervention personnel issues are those in which state agencies and universities are closely linked (Rooney, Gallagher, Fullagar, Eckland, & Huntington, 1992). The concern is with what state training systems can do to enhance the ability of preservice and inservice programs to accommodate the unique combinations of audiences and expected training outcomes in the new field of early intervention. Although there are no definitive answers, there are many steps open to state planners.

First, each state should consider the assumptions that underlie preservice and inservice training in terms of who and what they traditionally are designed for and the unique features that allow these purposes to be achieved. The purposes of preservice and inservice programs as they relate to early intervention training within the state can be clarified and made explicit. If an inservice system is to be used for broad-based training, a purpose generally filled by preservice programs, then attention should be given to achieving the characteristics that allow preservice programs to offer breadth and depth of training. If preservice programs are expected to fill this function in relation to the specialized area of early intervention, then this should be made explicit. If preservice programs are to be encouraged to provide an inservice function, then attention should be given to the approaches and options that would assist preservice programs in reaching currently working personnel.

These deliberations presume that there is an undergirding system in place for personnel development in the state that provides a core vision and philosophy from which approaches to preservice and inservice training both derive. If both approaches are used to address both functions, credentialing or other recognition structures can be developed to legitimize these efforts. For instance, a set of common training outcomes, to be used in both preservice and inservice settings, would allow both types of programs to be linked to the same credentialing or certification system. Such a system would also support crossover by both participants and trainers, thereby maximizing the training resources within the state.

To achieve this level of cohesion, it is also necessary for state systems to provide concrete support for early intervention training. There are many barriers to providing training, including availability of instructors with expertise in early intervention and extra dollars to support programs. A first step is to survey resources for training already present within the state and to combine these resources into a linked system; this can occur only with commitment to collaboration by agencies and disciplines. A process for accomplishing this blending must itself receive the support and commitment of multiple players (Winton, Catlett, & Houck, 1996). Attention also needs to be given to providing monetary and moral support for the development of a broader array of options within or instead of more traditional preservice and inservice programs. Demonstration sites, supervision at the worksite, and distance learning all represent options beyond the resources usually available to trainers.

Many states are recognizing the importance of instructing preservice and inservice faculty in both the content and the process of early intervention personnel preparation and of using preservice and inservice trainers across their traditional boundaries (Winton et al., 1996); community-based team training, described in Chapter 20, is one way of approaching this blending. Recommended training practices can be modeled within training-of-trainers events to assist faculty in visualizing and practicing processes to use in their own work including take-home plans complete with follow-up consultation (Winton, 1996; see also Chapter 7). Consortia of experienced trainers also can assist newly prepared trainers in implementing what they have learned. Especially encouraging are the increasing linkages among trainers and the early intervention providers and families who want to assist in training. States can support and legitimize these linkages with flexible funding mechanisms, thereby maximizing the training expertise available.

A redefinition of the preservice–inservice continuum, based not on a temporal relationship between the two, on younger versus older learner, on nondegreed versus degreed, or on not yet employed versus employed, but rather on where individuals stand in relation to desired early intervention training outcomes, may better meet the needs inherent in developing a cohesive early intervention training system. Applications of adult learning to the design of training are based on the assumption that individuals differ in how they approach and benefit from learning, depending on their stage of development. What is important about stage models for program development is their implication that individuals may relate to content differently at different stages and that various training processes may be more or less effective at different stages. A complicating factor, however, is that life stages have not been clearly separated from career stages. Although younger learners presumably do not have much experience, it is not clear how the concept of career stages applies to older learners who have made major shifts in their careers or whose previous practices do not match recommended practice. How do these learners match the assumptions for typical participants in preservice and inservice training? Presuming that they vary considerably in early intervention experience, can either preservice or inservice programs, as traditionally defined, meet their needs? With redefinition, traditional inservice programs may serve preservice functions and vice versa; the important difference between preservice and inservice programs may not be who participates in them or when but rather how they serve the functions necessary within the particular state.

It also may be useful to recognize and support within the state system an induction period to serve functions that fall between preservice and inservice programs. As defined in the teacher education literature (Christensen, Burke, Fessler, & Hagstrom, 1983), induction represents the first 1- to 2-year period on the job, following completion of preservice training. It is a time of application, integration, and exploration; a time of critical importance in the development of a professional identity; and a time when professionals have particular needs for support and training (Christensen et al., 1983). The themes previously explored as undergirding broad-based training can lend guidance to processes that might be appropriate during this time. Important content during induction includes a value base and the collaborative processes consistent with early intervention. This content points toward a structure to assist individuals who have just completed entry-level training in transferring to the workplace the *how* of early intervention services as well as the *what*. Mentoring, peer support, and consultation may all be appropriate processes for meeting this purpose. At a less comprehensive level, a state may provide orientation training to newly hired early intervention providers. If viewed as a joint responsibility between programs offering entry-level training (whether in colleges and universities) and those offering training for professional expansion and growth (regardless of setting), a recognized induction period could serve an important function in the transfer of learning.

The dilemmas that arise with the blurring of lines between preservice and inservice programs cannot be easily solved. Nevertheless, some creative ways of using the guidelines outlined in this chapter might assist in this process. At the least, it is a given that each individual, whether experienced in early intervention or not, will relate to content in different ways at different levels, depending on his or her personal and professional histories and characteristics; in essence, each individual will derive his or her own curriculum from what is offered by the training program. Building training components that bring these differences to light and using them as part of the process will make it more likely that the curriculum intended is the curriculum learned.

REFERENCES

Bailey, D.B., McWilliam, P.J., & Winton, P.J. (1992). Building family-centered practices in early intervention: A team-based model for change. *Infants and Young Children, 5*(1), 73–82.

Bailey, D.B., Simeonsson, R.J., Yoder, D.E., & Huntington, B.S. (1990). Infant personnel preparation across eight disciplines: An integrative analysis. *Exceptional Children, 57*(6), 26–35.

Bailey, D.B., Jr. (1989). Issues and directions in preparing professionals to work with young handicapped children and their families. In J.J. Gallagher, P.L. Trohanis, & R.M. Clifford (Eds.), *Policy implementation and PL 99-457: Planning for young children with special needs* (pp. 97–132). Baltimore: Paul H. Brookes Publishing Co.

Broad, M.L., & Newstrom, J.W. (1992). *Transfer of training: Action-packed strategies to ensure high payoff from training investments.* Reading, MA: Addison-Wesley.

Brookfield, S.D. (1986). *Understanding and facilitating adult learning.* San Francisco: Jossey-Bass.

Calderhead, J. (1988, April). *Reflective teaching and teacher education.* Paper presented at the annual meeting of the American Educational Research Association, New Orleans.

Christensen, J., Burke, P., Fessler, R., & Hagstrom, D. (1983). *Stages of teachers' careers: Implications for professional development.* Washington, DC: ERIC Clearinghouse on Teacher Education. (ERIC #SP 021 495)

Crais, E.R. (1991). *A practical guide to embedding family-centered content into existing speech-language pathology coursework.* Chapel Hill: University of North Carolina at Chapel Hill, Carolina Institute for Research on Infant Personnel Preparation.

Cruickshank, D.R. (1984, November–December). Toward a model to guide inquiry in preservice teacher education. *Journal of Teacher Education, 43*–48.

Davis, L.N., & McCallon, E. (1974). *Planning, conducting, and evaluating workshops: A practitioner's guide to adult education.* Austin, TX: Learning Concepts.

Division for Early Childhood of the Council for Exceptional Children, National Association for the Education of Young Children, & Association of Teacher Educators. (1995). *Personnel standards for early education and early intervention: Guidelines for licensure in Early Childhood Special Education.* Denver, CO: Division for Early Childhood.

Fenichel, E.S. (Ed.). (1992). *Learning through supervision and mentorship to support the development of infants, toddlers and their families: A sourcebook.* Arlington, VA: National Center for Clinical Infant Programs.

Fenichel, E.S., & Eggbeer, L. (1990). *Preparing practitioners to work with infants, toddlers and their families: Issues and recommendations for educators and trainers.* Arlington, VA: National Center for Clinical Infant Programs.

Fitzpatrick, A.R. (1989). Social influences in standard setting: The effects of social interaction on group judgment. *Review of Educational Research, 59*(3), 315–328.

Guskey, T.R. (1986). Staff development and the process of teacher change. *Educational Researcher, 15*(5), 5–12.

Harris, B.M. (1980). *Improving staff performance through in-service education.* Needham, MA: Allyn & Bacon.

Havelock, R.G., & Havelock, M.C. (1973). *Training for change agents: A guide to the design of training programs in education and other fields.* Ann Arbor: University of Michigan, Institute for Social Research.

Katz, L.G., & Raths, J.D. (1985, November–December). A framework for research on teacher education programs. *Journal of Teacher Education, 9*–15.

Knowles, M.S. (1987). Adult learning. In R.L. Craig (Ed.), *Training and development handbook: A guide to human resource development.* New York: McGraw-Hill.

Margolis, F.H., & Bell, C.R. (1984). *Managing the learning process.* Minneapolis, MN: Training Books, Lakewood Publications.

McCollum, J., & McCartan, K. (1988). Research in teacher education: Issues and future directions for early childhood special education. In S.L. Odom & M.B. Karnes (Eds.), *Early intervention for infants and children with handicaps: An empirical base* (pp. 268–286). Baltimore: Paul H. Brookes Publishing Co.

McCollum, J.A., & Bailey, D.B. (1991). Developing comprehensive personnel systems: Issues and alternatives. *Journal of Early Intervention, 15*(1), 51–56.

McCollum, J.A., & Hughes, M. (1988). Staffing patterns and team models in infancy programs. In J.B. Jordan, J.J. Gallagher, & P.L. Hutinger (Eds.), *Early childhood special education: Birth–three* (pp. 128–146). Reston, VA: Council for Exceptional Children.

McCollum, J.A., & Maude, S.P. (1994). Issues and emerging practice in preparing educators to be early interventionists. In P.L. Safford, B. Spodek, & O.N. Saracho (Eds.), *Yearbook in early childhood education: Early childhood special education* (Vol. 5, pp. 218–241). New York: Teachers College Press.

McCollum, J.A., & Stayton, V.D. (1996). Preparing early childhood special educators. In D. Bricker & A. Widerstrom (Eds.), *Preparing personnel to work with infants and young children and their families: A team approach* (pp. 67–90). Baltimore: Paul H. Brookes Publishing Co.

McCollum, J.A., & Thorp, E.K. (1988). Training of infant specialists: A look to the future. *Infants and Young Children, 1*(2), 55–65.

McWilliam, P.J. (1992). The case method of instruction: Teaching application and problem-solving skills to early interventionists. *Journal of Early Intervention, 16*(4), 360–373.

Moore, J. (1988). Guidelines concerning adult learning. *Journal of Staff Development, 9*(3), 1–5.

Project Vision. (1994). *Stages of team development* [Videotape]. Moscow, ID: Idaho Center on Developmental Disabilities.

Rooney, R., Gallagher, J., Fullagar, P., Eckland, J., & Huntington, G. (1992). *Higher education and state agency cooperation for Part H personnel preparation.* Chapel Hill: University of North Carolina at Chapel Hill, Frank Parker Graham Child Development Center, Carolina Policy Studies Program.

Thorp, E.K., & McCollum, J.A. (1994). Personnel in early intervention programs: Areas of needed competence. In L.J. Johnson, R.J. Gallagher, M.J. LaMontagne, J.B. Jordan, J.J. Gallagher, P.L. Hutinger, & M.B. Karnes (Eds.), *Meeting early intervention challenges: Issues from birth to three* (2nd ed., pp. 167–184). Baltimore: Paul H. Brookes Publishing Co.

Virginia Institute for Developmental Disabilities. (1990). *Interdisciplinary teamwork: A guide for trainers and viewers.* Van Nuys, CA: Child Development Media Inc. (CHADEM).

Walker, J.A. (1982). Teaching teachers to teach: A framework for program planning. *Journal of the Division for Early Childhood, 5*(2), 52–59.

Winton, P.J. (1990). A systematic approach for planning inservice training related to Public Law 99-457. *Infants and Young Children, 3*(1), 51–60.

Winton, P.J. (1992). *Working with families in early intervention: An interdisciplinary preservice curriculum* (2nd ed.). Chapel Hill, NC: University of North Carolina at Chapel Hill, Frank Porter Graham Child Development Center.

Winton, P.J. (1996). A model for supporting higher education faculty in their early intervention personnel preparation roles. *Infants and Young Children, 8*(3), 56–67.

Winton, P.J., Catlett, C., & Houck, A. (1996). A systems approach. In D. Bricker & A. Widerstrom (Eds.), *Preparing personnel to work with infants and young children and their families: A team approach* (pp. 295–320). Baltimore: Paul H. Brookes Publishing Co.

Winton, P.J., McWilliam, P.J., Harrison, T., Owens, A.M., & Bailey, D.B. (1992). Lessons learned from implementing a team-based model for change. *Infants and Young Children, 5*(1), 49–57.

Zervigon-Hakes, A. (1991). *Competencies for professions serving at-risk and disabled infants, toddlers and their families.* Tallahassee: Florida Department of Education.

6 NEEDS ASSESSMENT AND EVALUATION IN EARLY INTERVENTION PERSONNEL PREPARATION

Opportunities and Challenges

Patricia Snyder
Barbara L. Wolfe

Janet's Story Continues

It has been 6 months since Janet attended the annual state convention for speech-language pathologists. She still would like to learn more about routines-based intervention and integrated therapy. She indicated these needs on a survey she received from the early intervention lead agency in her state. About 3 months after Janet returned her needs assessment survey, she received a brochure announcing a 3-day intensive workshop on integrated therapy. Janet read the brochure and was really excited. This was the workshop she had been waiting for! Participants would learn how to embed related service goals into routine activities. They also would learn how to work as team members to plan integrated therapy programs for young children with disabilities. She hoped learning about these techniques would make her feel better about her role in the early intervention program.

The following week, Janet went to the workshop, which was held in the ballroom of a hotel about an hour from her home. Janet arrived at the site and was amazed to see that 75 people from all over the state were in attendance. She recognized a few people, including some of the preschool and Head Start teachers with whom she had worked in the past year. Over the 3 days, she got to know some other teachers in her county and some speech-language pathologists from other counties whose jobs were similar to her job.

Janet was surprised at the various reactions that different people had to the workshop over the course of the 3 days. The reasons people had come were so varied. Many of the teachers were there because they needed a specialized certificate to keep their jobs, and credit toward the certificate could be obtained by participating in the workshop. Janet was surprised that some of the participants did not seem to know (or care) about the topic. Their main interest seemed to be how to fit shopping expeditions into the schedule. Over the 3 days she noticed that attendance at the sessions seemed to lag, especially after the lunch break, which seemed to serve as a time for excursions to the nearby mall.

Other people she talked with were there because of pressure from their supervisors to attend. Some of these participants seemed to have the attitude that routines-based intervention and integrated therapy were fads like many of the others that had "come down the pike." It would fade away like other fads, once people got over the initial excitement and realized the impracticality and unrealistic nature of the ideas. She talked with a few people who felt misled by the topic. They had filled out the same needs assessment that Janet had completed. However, they had interpreted integrated therapy to mean behavioral approaches to children with challenging behaviors. These people decided to leave after 1 day, when the agenda clearly was not meeting their needs.

Janet thought the presenters were excellent. During the breaks, she overheard many positive comments from others about the ways the presenters explained integrated therapy and routines-based intervention. They used videotapes and case studies to illustrate how these techniques could be used in early intervention programs. Janet learned that the presenters were nationally known early childhood special educators. She was surprised when some of her speech-language pathology colleagues were disgruntled by what they perceived to be a bias against therapists in the presentations. She agreed with them that it would have been nice to have a therapist as part of the instructor team.

Overall, however, Janet was satisfied with the workshop. She expressed this on the evaluation form she filled out at the end of the third day. As she read each question on the evaluation form, she realized what satisfied her about the workshop, at least in terms of the presenters and the facility: The presenters were well-prepared and knowledgeable (one had a great sense of humor), the room in which the event took place was comfortable, and it was nice to have refreshments served at the breaks.

Janet was pleased with her performance on the knowledge test, administered to all participants on the final day of the workshop. She answered 45 of 50 questions correctly. She bought a book one of the presenters wrote on routines-based intervention and left the workshop thinking that she now understood what was meant by routines-based intervention and integrated therapy.

She still had concerns, however, about how she would apply what she had learned to her work. Janet believed she was somewhat prepared to incorporate new ideas into her individual practices but was concerned about how she could influence her team members. After all, the workshop time scheduled for team planning had not been very helpful for addressing team concerns because her team members were not there. Perhaps she should have mentioned her concerns to the presenters. She decided that it probably was best that she didn't say anything. She wouldn't want the presenters to think she was a complainer.

As she was driving home after the final day of the workshop, Janet wondered how she would apply all she had learned on Monday morning. "Maybe if I were smarter, I could figure this out," thought Janet.

Janet's story is not that unusual. Many early interventionists have had similar workshop experiences. Janet completed a needs assessment and subsequently participated in an instructional event purportedly designed to meet her expressed needs. The instructors used a variety of active and passive strategies to engage Janet as a learner, and their presentation styles pleased her. Two types of evaluation data, satisfaction and knowledge, were gathered from Janet. She generally was satisfied with the instruction. Her performance on the exam indicated that the instruction had a measurable impact on her knowledge about integrated therapy and routines-based intervention.

Yet how meaningful will the instruction be for Janet on the job? Will she be able to apply what she learned to the work she performs every day with children and families? How will Janet incorporate what she learned into her ongoing interactions with team members?

Janet's story represents an example of a personnel preparation effort in which needs assessment and evaluation data were gathered; however, the extent to which these activities were useful and meaningful could be questioned. The instructors used videotapes and case studies to illustrate how early interventionists apply routines-based intervention and integrated therapy in early intervention. They did not, however, evaluate Janet's application skills during or after the workshop. There were no activities related to follow-up after the workshop. The organizers of this event relied on a "train and hope" approach. They instructed Janet and hoped she would be able to apply the knowledge, skills, and attitudes she gained during instruction to her real-world situation.

In this chapter and in Chapter 7, needs assessment, evaluation, and follow-up are described, and the importance of these activities to successful personnel preparation efforts in early intervention is highlighted. Personnel preparation is defined as any activity on the part of an individual that is intended to advance the individual's professional stature or performance on the job (Elam, Cramer, & Brodinsky, 1986). To be consistent with the ecosystemic framework outlined in Chapter 1, we believe early intervention staff developers should rethink how they assess needs, evaluate processes and outcomes, and implement follow-up.

This chapter shares ideas and strategies about needs assessment and evaluation activities. It offers rationales for the importance of needs assessment and evaluation as crucial, interrelated features of personnel preparation efforts. An array of strategies is described that can be used to conduct needs assessment and evaluation activities, while acknowledging complexities and challenges surrounding implementation. Our goal is to provide early intervention staff developers with practical guidance for selecting needs assessment and evaluation strategies appropriate for their circumstances. We do not believe in a "one-size-fits-all approach" to needs assessment and evaluation; therefore, we provide guidance not prescription.

This chapter begins with a discussion of the rationale for focusing on needs assessment and evaluation in personnel preparation. This discussion is followed by the presentation of a framework that might be used by staff developers to guide them in making decisions about needs assessment and evaluation approaches.

RATIONALE FOR A FOCUS ON NEEDS
ASSESSMENT AND EVALUATION IN PERSONNEL PREPARATION

Many models exist that offer guidance on planning successful personnel preparation programs for adult learners (e.g., Bertcher, 1988; Bille, 1982; Caffarella, 1994; Cervero, 1988; Harris, 1989; Houle, 1972; Knowles, 1980; Laird, 1985; Phillips, 1991; Tracey, 1992; Trohanis, 1994). All of these personnel preparation models contain explicit or implicit assumptions related to how adults learn; the importance of involving learners in the identification of personnel preparation needs; how transfer of attitudes, knowledge, or skills to practice contexts is best accomplished; and the necessity of evaluating the effects of personnel preparation efforts. The terms *needs assessment, evaluation,* and *follow-up* frequently are used to organize these assumptions, and reciprocal linkages among these terms are acknowledged or implied in the majority of these models. Staff developers probably would refer to these concepts, and the processes associated with them, as "givens."

In reality, however, Janet's experiences illustrate that these givens often receive "lip service" but not serious consideration, time, or resources. Needs usually are defined globally, evaluations often are limited to satisfaction and knowledge acquisition measures, and follow-up activities rarely occur. These superficial approaches result in instruction that is characterized as being generally unresponsive to individual needs and largely ineffective, particularly for achieving changes in practice contexts (e.g., Winton, 1990; Wood & Thompson, 1980).

The pressing need created by early intervention legislation to instruct large numbers of participants from different disciplines and geographic areas has resulted in a "crisis mentality" in early intervention personnel preparation (Winton, 1990). Large numbers of people are being instructed without adequate attention given to needs assessment, evaluation, and follow-up activities, which are costly and time consuming to implement. When resources are limited, demands for accountability in these three important areas may be reduced. In Janet's story, for example, the staff developers could produce outcome data related only to participant satisfaction and knowledge acquisition. There was no accountability for evaluating learning transfer, even though Janet spent 3 days in an intensive workshop to learn skills she wanted to apply in her daily interactions with children, families, and other team members.

Given the cost, time, and complexities involved, why should staff developers give priority to needs assessment and evaluation activities? A number of important rationales have been offered in the personnel preparation literature. Needs assessments are important because they can give the learner a sense of ownership in the personnel preparation process (Knowles, 1980). Adults are more likely to commit to learning something when the goals and objectives of instruction are considered realistic and important to them (Bruder & Nikitas, 1992; Wood & Thompson, 1980). Needs assessments can help clarify and verify needs from a variety of perspectives (e.g., the learner, the administrator, the instructor). Learners are less likely to leave an instructional session because they misunderstood the term *integrated therapy* when needs are clarified and verified (Gallegos, 1979). Clarification and verification of needs across teams composed of multiple stakeholders is a key for obtaining consensus about focus and direction for agency- or communitywide personnel preparation initiatives (Buckley & Mank, 1994). Needs assessment information can provide baseline data useful for subsequent program evaluation efforts. Finally, needs assessment data can be used to provide a shared focus and agreed-upon agenda for participants and instructors.

Evaluation data are important for determining the extent to which personnel preparation outcomes are met, supporting modifications in the personnel preparation program, and providing direction for future personnel preparation efforts (Grotelueschen, 1986). Program evaluation data can be used by policy makers, funders, program planners, participants, administrators, and other interested people for planning, decision making, and allocating resources. Although judging the value, worth, or effect of a program is difficult, there are several interrelated reasons why systematic evaluation efforts are crucial to personnel preparation. According to Caffarella (1994),

> The process (1) helps keep staff focused on the goals and objectives of the program, (2) provides information for decision-making on all aspects of the program, (3) identifies improvements in the design and delivery of learning events, (4) increases application of the learning by participants, (5) allows for program accountability, (6) provides data on the major accomplishments of the program, and (7) identifies ways of improving future programs. (p. 120)

FRAMEWORK FOR MAKING NEEDS ASSESSMENT AND EVALUATION DECISIONS

The ecosystemic orientation given in Chapter 1 provides a framework for guiding decisions about needs assessment and evaluation activities. Interrelated factors, derived from the framework, that affect needs assessment and evaluation decisions include instructional context, target audience, and target outcomes. Each of these factors is discussed briefly in this section, followed by vignettes that show real-world examples of these factors and their interactions. These factors are explored in greater depth later in this chapter as strategies and challenges associated with needs assessment and evaluation are described.

Instructional Context

Needs assessment and evaluation strategies described in this chapter and follow-up activities described in Chapter 7 should be adopted for use only after careful consideration is given to the specific environments in which personnel preparation activities will occur. This premise requires that a variety of contextual variables (e.g., "political" climate; policies; resources; instructors; participants; those affected by the instruction, such as children, families, other team members, and administrators) be considered in planning and implementing needs assessment and evaluation activities.

Target Audience

The nested arrangement of structures described in the ecosystemic framework illustrates that needs assessment and evaluation efforts can be targeted at one or more levels (e.g., individuals, agencies, communities, states, nation). Needs of the individual, agency, or community can be assessed, and evaluation can be targeted at these levels. Reciprocal or transactional relationships that exist across levels mean that strategies implemented at one level are likely to affect other levels. A needs assessment targeted at a statewide level, for example, can exert positive or negative influence at the individual level. Personnel preparation decisions based on a statewide needs assessment may meet needs of some individuals, but it is unlikely that the needs of all individuals will be addressed.

Target Outcomes

The identified problem and target outcomes to be addressed by personnel preparation influence the types of needs assessment, evaluation, and follow-up activities that are conducted. Activities should be congruent with the purpose and scope of the personnel preparation effort. For example, knowledge-oriented needs assessment and evaluation strategies should be used when the desired outcome is knowledge acquisition. The following vignettes illustrate how context, target audience, and target outcomes influence the needs assessment, evaluation, and follow-up approaches used by individuals or groups.

Vignette 1: Personnel from the university affiliated program (UAP) in a southern state are asked by the early intervention lead agency to conduct a 6-hour workshop in each of eight regions. The lead agency must provide assurances to the federal government that it instructs all primary referral sources about the Part H program. The instruction, therefore, will meet an objective specified in the Comprehensive System for Personnel Development section of the 9th-year Part H application. The awareness-level instructional content includes an overview of the Part H system in the state, a description of the required components of the Part H system, and the procedures that should be followed by primary referral sources. Participants in the instruction will come from multiple disciplines and agencies. Attendance at the workshops is expected to range from 50 to more than 200 people at each site. The lead agency wants documentation related to how many people were instructed, what disciplines and agencies were represented at the workshops, and whether increases in participant knowledge about the Part H system and the responsibilities of primary referral sources occurred as a result of the instruction. These data will be submitted in the 10th-year application to the federal government.

Vignette 2: A faculty member from a university in the Midwest is asked to assist an early intervention program in her community as it develops and implements a comprehensive personnel preparation plan. Agency personnel engage in an extensive self-study process over a period of several months and, with the assistance of the faculty member, produce a plan for personnel preparation. The plan specifies outcomes, activities, resources, time lines, and evaluation procedures. A major personnel preparation outcome desired by program personnel is to ensure that, within the next year, all teachers are using an activity-based instruction (ABI) approach in their classrooms. The group that developed the personnel preparation plan recognized that simply providing one-shot inservice training sessions on ABI may not lead to the teachers' successfully implementing this approach

within their classrooms. Agency personnel, including administrators, teachers, therapists, and families, are committed to working collaboratively over time to reach the desired outcome. Teams composed of teachers, therapists, families, and administrators will attend five 3-hour workshop sessions conducted by the university faculty member, teachers, and families who have been using this approach. During the workshop session, participants will learn about and practice ABI. Teachers will team in pairs after the sessions to provide ongoing support and constructive feedback to one another as they implement this approach in their respective classrooms. Family members will be encouraged to participate in classrooms as the teachers implement ABI. The university faculty member and teachers experienced with ABI will be available for consultation once a month. The personnel preparation plan includes attention to obtaining process and outcome data that document achievement of the desired outcome. These data will be used to assist in the ongoing refinement and expansion of the personnel preparation plan.

Vignette 3: A committee composed of families and personnel from various agencies meets each month in a local community. This committee oversees implementation of the comprehensive, coordinated, multidisciplinary, interagency system of services available to all eligible Part H children and families. One major issue that continues to be raised in the committee is the lack of opportunities for children with disabilities to receive services in natural environments. Some members of the committee believe that there is a need to modify the attitudes of community providers about inclusion. Other members believe that attitudes are not the issue, that inservice instruction on implementing inclusive practices is needed. Still other members of the committee believe that funds should be made available to provide on-site consultation to teachers who are working with young children with disabilities in natural environments. A committee member suggests that a subcommittee be formed to develop a comprehensive, communitywide personnel preparation plan to address the issue. Five people volunteer to serve on this subcommittee, which will meet next week to begin its work.

These vignettes illustrate that early intervention personnel preparation efforts can be characterized by a variety of purposes, audiences, contexts, methods, constraints, and desired outcomes. Approaches to needs assessment, evaluation, and follow-up should reflect and be responsive to different personnel preparation circumstances.

In Vignette 1, a formal needs assessment at the individual level may not be necessary or even useful if the instruction is mandated as part of state or federal guidelines (Caffarella, 1994). In this example, needs have been determined at state and federal levels. Individual personnel preparation needs do not receive priority. Outcomes, however, are targeted at the individual level. The lead agency wants each participant to be aware of the early intervention system and knowledgeable about the roles of primary referral sources. Korinek, Schmid, and McAdams (1985) characterized this type of personnel preparation effort as "information transmission." The major purpose of this type of instruction is to increase the knowledge of a specific group. Information transmission instruction will not necessarily change participant behavior in application contexts.

Vignette 2 illustrates personnel preparation aimed at changing teachers' instructional approaches. Korinek et al. (1985) labeled this type of instruction as "behavior change," which involves ongoing, in-depth attention to needs assessment, follow-up, and process and impact evaluation, at individual and organizational levels. Instruction is based on identified needs of individuals and the agency as a whole. Systematic follow-up strategies are built into the personnel preparation plan to facilitate transfer of learning. A variety of data are gathered to evaluate the personnel preparation effort and are used to assist in the ongoing refinement or expansion of the personnel preparation plan. Korinek and colleagues noted that this type of instruction is the most costly and time consuming and requires ongoing commitment from all concerned. These authors stated, "Not surprisingly, it is the inservice type least used, yet the only one which provides a reasonable chance of changing teacher practice" (Korinek et al., 1985, p. 36).

Vignette 3 shows the complexity that surrounds community-based personnel preparation efforts. Members of the committee have different perceptions of needs and suggest varied approaches to addressing the natural environment issue. Needs assessment, evaluation, and follow-up efforts will need to be embedded within a broad ecological context. In Chapter 3, strategies are offered for conducting needs assessment and evaluation in community-based personnel preparation efforts.

These vignettes illustrate that conducting *meaningful* needs assessment, evaluation, and follow-up in early intervention personnel preparation efforts often is easier said than done. A variety of factors related to the ecosystemic framework must be considered as these efforts are undertaken.

The next sections of this chapter consider needs assessment and evaluation in more detail and offer examples of strategies to address these two personnel preparation components. Challenges are raised, and some potential options are posed for meeting these challenges. Throughout the sections Janet's story and the vignettes are used to illustrate key points.

NEEDS ASSESSMENT

Needs assessment frequently describes the processes of gathering information about what people, organizations, or communities perceive as important topics to learn and of prioritizing personnel preparation activities based on this information (Caffarella, 1994). This definition implies two interrelated activities: 1) gathering of data, which assists in the identification of needs; and 2) applying judgment to assess the significance of the data gathered to determine priorities for personnel preparation (Cooper & Jones, 1984; Siegel, Attkisson, & Carson, 1978).

Needs arise when there is a "discrepancy between what individuals (or organizations or society) want themselves to be and what they are; the distance between an aspiration and a reality" (Knowles, 1980, p. 88). Needs assessments typically are designed to identify the gap between what is and what should be in terms of program practices (Wood, Thompson, & Russell, 1981).

Bertcher (1988) characterized the personnel preparation process as following a typical problem-solving model that can be stated in terms of need: recognition of need, a decision to do something about the need, an analysis of factors causing the need, generation of a strategy to reduce the need, implementation of the strategy, and evaluation of the degree to which the strategy reduced the need. Winton (1990) noted that this process is similar to the model used to address family needs, values, and goals in early intervention.

Methods and Strategies for Identifying Needs

Needs assessment information is integral to the design and implementation of meaningful personnel preparation activities. Needs data can be obtained in a variety of ways, such as by using instruments, analyzing documents, conducting observations or interviews, or employing consensus techniques (see Table 6.1). Selected strategies associated with each of these data collection methods are listed in the table. For example, the nominal group technique is a strategy associated with the consensus method; portfolio review is a strategy

TABLE 6.1. Needs assessment methods and strategies

Methods and strategies	Description	Potential advantages	Potential disadvantages	Recommendations for use
Instruments • Questionnaires • Checklists • Surveys • Scales	Gathering data from individuals, groups, or entire constituencies using structured, written formats	• They are quick. • They are low cost. • They are easy to distribute. • Data collection efforts can be directed at large numbers of respondents. • Respondents complete the same items. • They assess the needs from the learner's perspective. • Respondents can think about answers, access records, and so forth before answering. • They provide anonymity. • Respondents can choose to omit responses.	• Different meanings may be applied to items. • Single-source, self-report data may be incomplete or inaccurate. • There may be limited identification of specific content and processes to address individual needs. • There may be a tendency for people to indicate need in topic areas familiar to them. • Low return rates result in inaccurate portrayal of need. • They may not be appropriate for people with low literacy.	• Consider word choice, tone, and format prior to use. • Make sure instruments are brief, space is provided for comments, and items are grouped into logical categories. • Pilot-test instrument with individuals who are representative of respondent group. • Avoid use of double-barreled questions. • Explain purpose of needs assessment and planned use for data on the instrument. • Share summary of results with respondents. • Target individuals or groups to complete instrument, and limit generalizations of need to these people. • Format instructions for completion and return on the instrument.

Document analyses

- Records
- Reports
- Planning documents
- Audits
- Work samples
- Written policies and procedures

Compiling and making inferences of need from descriptive statistics or narratives found in documents

- They are unobtrusive.
- They are nonreactive.
- They are grounded in the context under study.
- They can be used to verify information generated by other assessment methods.
- Data are already available.
- They provide historical context against which need may be evaluated.
- Data can be accumulated with a relatively low response cost to targeted individuals or agencies.

- Documents may be incomplete or contain inaccurate information.
- Documents are limited to a historical focus and may not reflect current need.
- Causes of problems or needs may not be discernible from documents.
- Access to documents may be limited as a result of legal or logistical constraints.
- Documents may be adjusted or selectively edited prior to review.

- Delimit the scope and nature of the document analysis.
- Search for patterns and trends of need that emerge across documents.
- Request that materials for document analysis be easily accessible to reduce time required for locating and examining documents.
- Obtain consent to examine documents, when appropriate.
- Use procedures for recording data that permit separation of specific indications of need from conclusions about need.
- Seek other sources of data to verify need data gathered from documents.

(continued)

TABLE 6.1. *(continued)*

Methods and strategies	Description	Potential advantages	Potential disadvantages	Recommendations for use
Observations	Watching people doing actual or simulated tasks or activities—individuals or groups of people can be observed			
• Behavioral frequency counts	Capturing rate of occurrence of specific behaviors to identify need to acquire, modify, or change behaviors of individuals or groups	• They help put importance or impact of specific behaviors into perspective. • They can be used to clarify or verify needs of individuals or groups when used in conjunction with self-report need techniques. • They can be used to quantify need.	• It may be difficult to develop behavioral definitions. • Behaviors quantified may not be appropriate; can lead to misspecification of needs. • Observer's presence may change behavior of person being observed. • Watching people or groups generates attributed need data, not necessarily felt need data.	• Carefully select and clearly define behaviors to be observed. • Standardize data recording sheet and preserve anonymity. • Institute steps to evaluate consistency of observations and data collection procedures across observers. • Spend time observing in a natural setting prior to selecting and defining behaviors to be observed. • Chart antecedents and consequences of targeted behaviors, whenever possible. • Use low-key, nonassertive demeanor when observing.

- Critical incident observations

Observing and recording specific tasks or activities in defined situations to generate need data

- They collect data that reflect observable tasks or activities rather than ratings and opinions based on general impressions.
- Incidents can be analyzed singularly or in combination with one another.
- Accumulated critical incident observations can be used to make summative inferences about need.

- Precision of observations is heavily dependent on the competence of observer and the specificity with which the characteristic to be observed has been defined.
- They are a time-consuming, costly strategy for gathering need data.
- Gathering enough critical observations for need determination may be difficult.
- It is often difficult to make judgments about whether observed incident is "critical."

- Specify clearly the general parameters of the task or activity to be observed.
- Delimit the situations to be observed, including place, people, conditions, and activities or tasks.
- Provide examples of incidents that should be observed and recorded because of their relationships to the general parameters.
- Define an incident as critical if it makes a positive or negative contribution to the general parameters of the activity or task.
- Have recording sheets that reflect what you observed the individual or group doing and the outcome of what they did.
- Institute procedures for sorting observed incidents into piles of similar indicators of need.

(continued)

TABLE 6.1. (continued)

Methods and strategies	Description	Potential advantages	Potential disadvantages	Recommendations for use
Interviews	Talking to people to gather their perspectives related to need identification			
• Focus groups	Process of acquiring need data from a group of 5–12 people familiar with topic, service, or experience being discussed; usually a facilitator who presides over group activities; focus group guide may be developed for use by facilitator	• They have an informal structure. • Gathering need data in group form benefits from group dynamics. • They offer a rich, permanent data source. • They generate need statements for use on instruments or for verification with observational techniques. • They add qualitative dimension to need analysis. • They are an efficient means for gathering significant amount of data in a relatively short period of time. • They are unhindered by requirements for group consensus.	• There is a danger of getting off topic during discussions. • Transcribing, summarizing, and analyzing focus group data are time consuming and costly for the group sponsor. • The groups may not be representative of those to be involved in instruction. • The specific needs of individuals may be lost. • There is a possibility of bias in interpreting data. • More opinionated participants may dominate the group. • Participants may have concerns about confidentiality of comments made in focus group.	• Keep the group size "manageable." • Keep the length of group to less than 3 hours. • Verbatim recordings (either by audiotape or transcriber) are most helpful for later analysis. • Ensure participation of appropriate stakeholders in group. • Conduct the focus group at a neutral site. • Conduct the focus group around a comfortable table and have refreshments available. • Make the purpose of the focus group explicit. • Have participants identify themselves; nameplates on table helpful reminders. • Move from general to specific questions; ask open-ended questions whenever possible.

		• They can facilitate identification of shared need among participants.		• Keep comments non-judgmental and probe questions focused on information clarification; do not overfocus or overfacilitate a group. • Ask for clarification of technical terms, local jargon, and complex ideas to keep record clear. • Be ready to invest up to five times the length of the focus group in data analysis. • Follow up with focus group participants because it is critical to conduct member checks of focus group summaries.
• One-to-one interviews	Gathering information from individuals about need by talking directly with them	• They offer a rich data source. • Felt need data can be obtained directly from individuals. • Need can be clarified and verified during the interview. • Felt and attributed needs can be examined by interviewing people who hold different roles.	• They can be a time-consuming and costly process for interviewer. • Data collection and analysis can be complex. • Some individuals may not feel comfortable expressing needs in one-to-one context. • There is no protection from group members.	• Clarify the purpose of the interview for interviewee. • Develop a protocol to guide the interview. • Interview individuals from various constituencies involved in staff development. • Provide feedback to individuals about need data gathered through interviews. • Set reasonable time limits for the interview.

(continued)

TABLE 6.1. (continued)

Methods and strategies	Description	Potential advantages	Potential disadvantages	Recommendations for use
		• They can validate needs expressed by interviewees. • They can provide each person with a sense of ownership about need data.	• Interviewees may feel pressured to respond to interview questions. • It may be difficult to establish rapport between interviewer and interviewee in a limited time period. • Self-reported needs may be inaccurate or at odds with attributed needs. • Respondent effects may be present (e.g., self-preservation bias).	• Avoid yes/no questions; ask open-ended, problem-solving questions. • Give interviewees time to think about responses. This may be the first time they have been asked to identify/clarify/verify their need. • Pilot interview protocol with people similar to those to be interviewed. • Always conclude with open-ended question (e.g., "What haven't I asked about?" "Are there other needs we haven't discussed?"). • Use consistent recording strategy (e.g., audiotape recording, notetaking transcriptions). • Possibly ask interviewees to rank identified needs at the end of the interview. • Let interviewees know whether interview data will be kept confidential.

- Critical incident interviews

Procedure for gathering need data in an interview format by asking individuals to describe incidents that specifically demonstrate need based on their own experiences or observations

- Structure is provided for the interview by focusing on the identification of relevant critical incidents.

- Incidents described during the interview can take the form of stories, reports, or observations.

- Interviews can be conducted with individuals or groups.

- Incidents described in interviews can be analyzed singularly or in combination with one another.

- Accumulated critical incident interviews can be used to make summative inferences about need.

- Precision of incidents described during the interview are heavily dependent on competence of interviewee.

- They are a time-consuming, costly strategy for gathering need data.

- Gathering enough critical incidents during interviews for need determination may be difficult.

- It may be difficult to make judgments about whether reported incidents are "critical."

- Clarify purpose of the interview for interviewee.

- Describe to interviewees why they are "qualified" to describe critical incidents.

- Provide assurances that all incidents described will be kept confidential and that names of people involved in incidents will be changed to preserve anonymity.

- Pilot-test the critical incident protocol with people similar to those who will be interviewed.

- Encourage interviewees to be factual, not interpretive, in their descriptions of critical incidents.

- Avoid leading questions.

- Be sure actual behavior(s) is reported when the incident is described.

- Ask interviewees if they directly observed the incident.

- Probe for complete descriptions of incidents.

(continued)

TABLE 6.1. (continued)

Methods and strategies	Description	Potential advantages	Potential disadvantages	Recommendations for use
				• Ask interviewees to state why they believe the reported incident is "critical."
				• Have forms that can be used to record critical incidents described during the interview.
				• Institute procedures for sorting identified incidents into piles of similar indicators of need.
Consensus techniques	Bringing knowledgeable people together "jury fashion" and tapping their collective opinions to guide identification of need			
• Delphi technique	Procedure that uses sequential steps to solicit and collect informed judgments on a particular topic	• Typology of needs can be determined or developed.	• There are many different versions of the Delphi technique described in the literature. It is difficult to find precise, consistent guidance about implementation.	• Develop relevant need scenarios for the questionnaire to which Delphi panelists can respond.
	Judgments usually solicited through a set of carefully designed sequential questionnaires or on-line computer communications	• Technique allows for the exploration of underlying assumptions or information leading to different judgments about need.	• There is a lack of guidance about number of iterations required for closure.	• Have a panel of experts to assist with questionnaire development and refinement.
				• Implement retention strategies to keep all members of the Delphi group involved in successive iterations.

Technique	Description	Advantages	Considerations	Guidelines
	• Each successive questionnaire contains summarized information and feedback from earlier questionnaires provided in the form of measures of central tendency or percent agreement • Takes form of structured dialogue between people who may not meet but whose opinions about need are shared through questionnaires	• Technique can be used to educate respondent group about similarities and differences in needs. • Participant responses can be kept anonymous. • Sequential feedback is useful for refining and clarifying needs. • It is relatively efficient for respondents. • Technique can be done independently or in groups.	• Extreme positions may be lost through the iterative process. • "Group think" may occur. • "Risky shifts" may occur. • Technique requires that Delphi leaders have skills in developing and modifying questionnaires. • Highly structured emphasis may disillusion some participants. • Time and effort involved in the iterative process is great. • "Invisible" group if it does not meet face-to-face; loses advantages of social interactions among group members.	• Arrange for computerized data entry and analysis to expedite processing, feedback, and revisions of questionnaires.
• Priority matrix	• A procedure in which identified needs are set against each other in a correlation-type matrix • Respondents indicate their priority for each pair of off-diagonal needs, which is recorded in each off-diagonal cell	• The matrix is quick and easy to complete. • It uses forced-choice format to prioritize needs. • It can be used by individuals or groups.	• The matrix is useful for prioritizing, not identifying, needs. • Forced-choice format reduces opportunities for variations in need identification.	• Use to rank identified needs, not generate needs. • Best used when the number of needs to be prioritized is relatively few. • Provide clear instructions to respondents about how to complete the matrix.

(continued)

143

TABLE 6.1. (continued)

Methods and strategies	Description	Potential advantages	Potential disadvantages	Recommendations for use
	After all pairs are ranked, the needs with the highest number of priority ranks in the matrix are identified as the "priority needs" Needs can be weighted	• It offers an objective format for gathering subjective rankings. • Need data are summarized in an efficient format. • The facilitator can use successive matrixes to refine need priorities.	• Respondents may apply different interpretations to need areas represented on the matrix. • Procedure is difficult to use when large number of needs contained in the matrix. • The matrix is not conducive to prioritizing needs when there is high disagreement among group members.	• Be sure respondents understand that only one priority can be reflected in each cell (no ties).
• Nominal group technique	Silent, individual, need identification, usually written, in a group setting followed by sharing individual ideas with the total group Group leader in round-robin fashion asks each participant to "nominate" one need Each need recorded, typically on large worksheets of paper displayed for entire group Need nomination process continues until all unique individual needs are reflected on worksheets	• Nominal group technique allows for individual and group identification of needs. • Each participant given opportunity to rank individual and group needs. • It encourages the presentation of all needs, not just majority needs. • Each member of the group participates in need identification and prioritization.	• Voting or rankings can be made without careful consideration. • Nominal group technique can be too structured for some participants. • "Group think" can occur. • "Risky shifts" can occur. • It may be difficult to reach consensus during need clarification process. • Process can become time consuming, and participants may lose interest or become	• Set aside adequate time to complete entire nominal group process. • Arrange for a comfortable setting; have refreshments available and provide opportunities for participants to take short breaks. • Have an experienced recorder available who is not a member of the target group, if possible. • Remain nonjudgmental about identified needs. • Record need statements verbatim. • Maintain privacy of individual rankings, if participants so desire.

144

- Keep all data for potential future use (e.g., worksheets, individual rankings).

- Discussion follows initial nominal activity to elaborate, add, eliminate, or combine needs

  - Individual members may benefit from hearing other members' perspectives about needs.

- Following discussion, group leader asks each participant to rank needs from most to least important

  - Group members given opportunities to question, clarify, modify, combine, or eliminate needs.

- Group leader tallies individual rankings and presents results to group

  - Recording format provides permanent record of the need identification and prioritization process.

- Brainstorming

  - Relatively unstructured group process for need identification that encourages free expression of ideas about needs

    - Brainstorming encourages group members to generate as many ideas as possible, whether good or bad.

      - Some participants may not be inclined to brainstorm.

        - Encourage expression of all needs that come to mind.

  - Ideas are recorded in written or taped formats for later reference

    - Can stimulate creative identification of needs.

      - Lack of formalized structure in the group may lead to inefficient use of time and poor dynamics.

        - Consider all expressed needs valuable; don't apply judgments during brainstorming.

  - May or may not be formally facilitated

    - Nonthreatening, open-ended, and evaluative judgments are avoided.

      - Group members may condemn, verbally or nonverbally, novel or unique ideas.

        - Record need statements verbatim.

    - It may lead to the generation of novel needs.

      - Needs generated by the group may be unfocused.

        - Publicly post generated needs to stimulate further need identification.

    - It is a nontechnical process.

      - It does not identify need priorities.

        - Follow up activity to analyze and to prioritize needs identified during brainstorming activity is critical.

    - It is relatively time and cost efficient.

(continued)

TABLE 6.1. (continued)

Methods and strategies	Description	Potential advantages	Potential disadvantages	Recommendations for use
• Community forum	Open meeting to which all members of community are invited and at which all participants are encouraged to present views regarding needs	• Forum involves numerous stakeholders. • Views about needs based on perspectives obtained from a variety of people. • It is economical. • It facilitates the establishment of networks of individuals who share interests in particular need areas.	• Need identification and prioritization can become diffuse. • Forum involves need identification, but decisions about how needs will be addressed usually take place outside the forum context. • If forum is well attended, not every participant may have an opportunity to express needs. • Those individuals or groups not represented at the forum may not have needs represented.	• Invite participation of all relevant stakeholders at the forum by publicizing forum and issuing invitations. • Develop incentives for individuals or groups to be represented at the forum. • Allot time to be certain each individual or group who desires to speak can have an opportunity to share perspectives about need. • Clarify expectations about time limits at the beginning of and as needed during the forum. • Appoint a forum facilitator to moderate. • Hold the forum in a location viewed as "accessible" and "neutral" for participants. • Facilitator should reiterate the focus of the forum at selected intervals to keep participants focused. • Arrange for verbatim recordings (either by audiotape or transcriber) for later analysis.

Adapted from Zemke & Kramlinger (1982).

146

associated with the document analysis method. Table 6.1 also shows potential advantages, disadvantages, and selected recommendations for using each of the methods or strategies.

Instruments   Instruments can reach large numbers of and widely dispersed respondents. Factual or subjective needs data can be gathered with relative ease once the instrument has been developed or obtained. Respondents have an opportunity to indicate their perspectives about needs; however, they often are required to share these views in a predetermined format. The structure imposed by most instruments can reduce opportunities for identifying idiosyncratic needs. Respondents completing the instruments often do not have an opportunity to talk directly with needs assessors to clarify or verify their needs. Low return rates and inappropriate responses can limit the accuracy of the needs assessment data obtained from instruments (American Society for Training and Development, 1985).

Document Analysis   Document analysis strategies are useful when the identified problem might be reflected in permanent products or records of performance by those potentially targeted for personnel preparation. For example, if the problem is lack of sufficient family-centered focus in an agency, individualized family service plans (IFSPs) could be reviewed to analyze the extent to which they reflect family-centered principles and recommended intervention practices. Patterns and themes that emerge from document analysis provide staff developers with contextually relevant needs data based on stable products or records. Documents, however, may be incomplete or contain inaccurate information. The information in documents is constrained by legal requirements, agency policies and procedures, or the types of products individuals choose to place in portfolios. Although participants usually are involved in the production of documents or records, they are not necessarily directly involved in the document review process. This lack of involvement may prohibit participants from explaining or extending the data staff developers gather from documents.

Observational Strategies   Observational strategies, such as frequency counts and critical incident observations, are useful when the identified problem can be observed under natural conditions and when most of the needs information sought is visible (Zemke & Kramlinger, 1982). Observational strategies usually require a minimal level of involvement by those being observed. These strategies, however, require that the needs assessor devote a significant amount of time and resources to data collection and analysis. Another limitation of observational strategies is the potential for decreased participant commitment to the personnel preparation process because needs have been identified by an observer and not by the learners themselves. Finally, individuals may exhibit reactivity in the presence of observers and behave differently than they would under typical circumstances.

Interviews   Interviews, whether conducted with individuals or groups, provide the learners with direct opportunities to express their needs. Needs can be clarified and verified during the interview process through the use of probes, open-ended questioning, and requests for examples. Individual or group interviews can be conducted face-to-face or over the telephone or Internet. Interviews are flexible methods for gathering needs data, but the quality of the data depends largely on the skills and sensitivities of interviewers. Each of the interview strategies listed in Table 6.1 requires a large investment of personnel time for conducting the interviews and analyzing and interpreting the data.

Consensus Techniques   Consensus techniques are most useful when staff developers encounter groups of individuals with strong or discrepant opinions about needs. These strategies can be used to foster cooperation and commitment while reaching some degree of agreement about individual or group needs. A variety of consensus strategies are listed in Table 6.1. Each takes a slightly different approach to building consensus and determining needs. Most of the strategies require a significant investment of time on the part of learners. Another limitation is that idiosyncratic needs of individuals may be lost to the group when these strategies are used.

Other Formal Methods   There are other methods not described in Table 6.1 that can be used to gather needs data. These include network analysis (Neenan, Orthner, & Crocker, 1995), job and task analysis (Zemke & Kramlinger, 1982), and written performance tests designed to evaluate an individual's knowledge, skill, or attitudes.

Network analysis can be used to illustrate interactions and relationships among individuals or agencies. Data for the network analysis can be gathered by using instruments or by conducting interviews or observations. In network analysis, individuals or groups may be asked to describe the roles or functions of other individuals, groups, or agencies; the interrelationships among individuals, groups, or agencies; or typical patterns of service used by consumers across various professionals, groups, or agencies. Needs for community-based personnel preparation efforts, as described in Vignette 3, could be clarified and verified from a network analysis.

Job and task analysis involves "collecting, tabulating, grouping, analyzing, interpreting, and reporting on the duties, tasks, and activities that make up a job" (Caffarella, 1994, p. 74). Many of the methods described in Table 6.1 can be used to gather data about a job or task (e.g., observations, document analyses, interviews, instruments). This method of needs determination is accomplished most easily when the job or task occurs repeatedly, has a specific purpose and a defined beginning and end, involves people's interaction with equipment or other people, and results in a meaningful outcome (Zemke & Kramlinger, 1982). For example, in Janet's story, the workshop leaders could have analyzed the tasks or activities involved in teachers' or therapists' implementing a routines-based approach to early intervention in preschool settings. Results from this analysis could be used to guide decision making about workshop content and format and to structure evaluation and follow-up activities.

Written performance tests are used to evaluate an individual's knowledge, skill, or attitudes. Needs data are generated based on information about current performance levels. Staff developers who use these types of tests to gather needs data should ensure that the measure yields adequate indexes of reliability and validity based on data obtained from the respondent sample. The measure should be matched to the identified problem. In Vignette 1, a knowledge test on the Part H referral process might be an appropriate performance measure; a test of skill would be inappropriate given the identified problem.

Informal Strategies   There are a variety of informal, on-the-spot pre- or during-instruction strategies that staff developers can use when they are unable to conduct comprehensive needs assessments before the personnel preparation event. Several commonly used pre- or during-instruction strategies are listed in Table 6.2. The purpose of using these strategies is to ensure that participants feel a sense of ownership in the personnel preparation process, even though their individual or collective needs were not necessarily considered before the instructional event. Several of these strategies can form the basis for subsequent evaluation or follow-up activities (Zemke & Gunkler, 1985).

Guiding Questions Related to Selecting Needs Assessment Strategies

Knowing which needs assessment strategies to choose for a given personnel preparation circumstance is a major decision staff developers must make. Newstrom and Lilyquist (1979) offered six criteria to consider when selecting needs assessment strategies. First, what level of learner involvement is desired? There is consensus in the personnel preparation literature that, whenever possible, learners should be involved in the needs assess-

TABLE 6.2.   Pre- or during-instruction informal needs assessment strategies

Strategy	Description
Executive memo	Instructor or supervisor sends a letter to participant describing the purpose, structure, and desired outcomes from the staff development event; indicates the significance of the event for the individual or organization; and communicates attributed needs to participant.
Self-assessments	Simple pretests or self-assessment instruments are used to prepare participants for instruction. Participants are provided with the opportunity to preview instructional content, and insight is given into what they do or do not know about a topic.
Supervisory briefing	If administrators or supervisors cannot attend the instruction, a briefing is conducted for these individuals to familiarize them with what the participants will be learning in the staff development activity. Strategies they can use to support participants' transfer of learning after the instructional event are suggested. Participants are told about the supervisory briefing at the beginning of their instruction event.
Expectations opener	Participants are asked to generate, individually or in groups, two or three things they want to be able to do or know as a result of the instruction. The instructor records the expectations on a flipchart. When all expectations have been voiced, the instructor either describes which expectations will and will not be met or modifies the instructional event to meet identified expectations.
Objectives opener	Instructors hand out a list of objectives to participants. Instructors discuss the objectives. They may provide participants with opportunities to modify objectives or to generate additional objectives.
Clarifying the agenda	Instructors distribute copies of an agenda to participants. Instructors discuss the agenda. They may provide participants with opportunities to modify the agenda or generate additional agenda content.
Burning questions	At the beginning of the instructional session and throughout it instructors can ask participants to generate burning questions. Time can be reserved to address burning questions at selected points during the instruction or the instructor can review the burning questions during breaks and modify instructional content in response to these questions. Participants also can be encouraged to find answers on their own, by talking with other participants or conducting follow-up activities after the workshop.

ment process and programs should be planned in response to their assessed needs (e.g., Buckley & Mank, 1994; King, Hayes, & Newman, 1977; Thompson & Cooley, 1986; Winton, 1990). Second, what levels of organizational needs should be recognized? Strategies should facilitate, when possible, the gathering of multisource needs data from supervisors and other people in the organizational setting. Third, what are the time requirements for gathering the information? Individual interviews with potential participants, for example, consume more time than nominal group techniques. Fourth, what is the cost of using various methods or strategies? Using existing instruments to gather needs data is less costly than conducting on-site observations. Fifth, what types of data are required? Different strategies may be appropriate if the focus is broad-based group consensus versus more narrow assessments of the needs of targeted individuals. Sixth, how can the relevance and quantifiability of the data be ensured? Questionnaires may not be a relevant needs assessment strategy when highly individualized data are needed.

No one method or strategy for gathering needs data is inherently better than another (Caffarella, 1994). As illustrated in Table 6.1, each of the techniques has strengths and weaknesses. Data collection options include formal and informal methods, broad-based and narrow assessments, and group and individual techniques. Use of multisource, multimethod data-gathering strategies is preferred to capitalize on the strengths and reduce the impact of the limitations associated with each of the methods. Regardless of the needs assessment method or strategies chosen, a formal needs assessment should involve the interrelated processes of defining objectives for the needs assessment; determining who will be involved in planning and conducting the needs assessment; determining a time frame and budget for the needs assessment process; choosing a design and methods or strategies for gathering data, considering the instructional context, target audience, and target outcomes; collecting data; analyzing data; and reporting results of the needs assessment to appropriate individuals and groups (Caffarella, 1982, 1994; Tracey, 1992).

Using Needs Assessment Data   Once gathered, needs data can be used for a variety of purposes. Trohanis (1994) noted that needs assessment data are tabulated, analyzed, and interpreted so that priorities and a focus for personnel preparation content become clear. Needs data can assist with the identification of who training participants are, clarify the roles participants assume relative to the personnel preparation topic, and illuminate expectations of participants for how a personnel preparation event can benefit them. Data can be analyzed to identify incentives for participation in instructional events. Needs data also can be used as a basis for evaluating the impact of personnel preparation efforts. Results from a needs assessment should be shared with those who participated in the needs assessment process. This can involve making presentations to targeted audiences, writing reports that summarize findings, or describing in subsequent personnel preparation events how needs data were used to design programs.

Challenges Related to Conducting Needs Assessment

Although Table 6.1 shows a variety of strategies available for gathering data, challenges remain for early intervention staff developers who want to conduct meaningful needs assessments. The following sections describe several of these challenges and offer possible options to address them.

Whose Needs Are We Talking About?   One challenge surrounding needs assessment is difficulty in defining the term *needs* to effectively assess them. "Need is at best a relative concept and the definition of need depends primarily upon those who undertake the identification and assessment process" (Siegel et al., 1978, p. 216).

Bertcher (1988) defined three types of needs that might be assessed: 1) felt, 2) attributed, and 3) organizational. *Felt needs* arise in situations where individuals sense the absence of something important to them in doing their job. Janet had a felt need to learn more about integrated therapy and routines-based intervention because she believed it was important to her job. Needs assessment surveys administered to an individual or group usually assess felt needs (Timms, 1995). *Attributed needs* originate when one individual believes another individual has a particular need; for example, an early intervention supervisor believes that a teacher has a need for learning about family-centered intervention.

When only attributed needs are assessed, resulting decisions about personnel preparation are made by people other than the learner. *Organizational needs,* according to Bertcher, are those things the organization must have or must do to continue to exist and fulfill its mission. For example, early intervention program administrators may need all agency employees to learn about Medicaid reimbursement procedures to continue service delivery.

Knowles (1980) described another type of need—educational. He suggested these needs are most commonly assessed when planning programs for adult learners. Educational needs, according to Knowles, are those things that people ought to learn for their own good, for the good of an organization, or for the good of society.

To address the challenge of defining needs from an ecological perspective, Bertcher's and Knowles' conceptualizations of needs could be combined. Bertcher's three types of needs might exist within and across the nested levels described by Knowles (e.g., individual, group, community, state, nation). Members of the community in Vignette 3, for example, expressed a felt need related to establishing service delivery in natural environments for young children with disabilities. They each felt differently, however, about how this need should be addressed. Outside technical assistance consultants may attribute needs to this community or to groups within the community. State policies related to the early intervention program may create organizational needs for the community.

As needs assessments are undertaken, staff developers should be aware of the types of needs they are assessing and at which levels they are assessing them. Various levels and categories of needs can be defined, and no one definition probably is adequate or complete for every use (Timms, 1995).

How Can Needs Be Clarified and Verified?   A second challenge involves clarifying and verifying expressed needs, whether felt, attributed, or organizational. If two early interventionists state that they feel a need for instruction in family service coordination, do they mean the same thing? One interventionist might mean that she has a felt need to learn what service coordination is, whereas the other may want to learn better strategies for coordinating services across agencies. In Janet's story, for example, interventionists applied different meanings to the terms *integrated therapy* and *routines-based intervention.*

If an early intervention program director states that her staff need instruction in principles of family-centered service delivery, what does this mean? Furthermore, once her attributed need is clarified, it could be verified with staff members and families.

Gallegos (1979) recommended that needs, however defined, should be clarified and verified. He noted that assessing gross categories of needs does not provide adequate data from which to make informed personnel preparation decisions. Gallegos proposed that "more should be done to develop and refine multilevel, cross-validated assessment techniques . . . so that single level or single source 'needs' are not the sole basis for inservice efforts" (p. 23). Judgments about needs are most valid when multiple sources and methods are used and when adult learners themselves, and relevant others, contribute to the needs identification process (Knox, 1986).

How Can Agreement About Needs Be Achieved?   Felt, attributed, or organizational needs across various levels may not be congruent. What teachers say they need may or may not conform to what supervisors believe is needed. Observations of performance by outsiders may reveal needs not identified by teachers or supervisors. Family members might have an entirely different perspective about needs. Knowles (1980) stated,

The more congruent the needs of individuals are with the aspirations their organizations and society have for them (or the other way around—the more congruent the aspirations of organizations and society are with the educational needs of individuals), the more likely effective learning will take place. (p. 88)

Knowles believed that an important role for the staff developer is to use skill and sensitivity to help groups assess the needs of individuals, organizations, and society; negotiate congruence among them; and stimulate the translation of needs into personnel preparation goals. The consensus strategies described in Table 6.1 may be used to help reach congruence.

Another promising approach for fostering congruence of needs is the team-based model for change (Bailey, McWilliam, & Winton, 1992; Bailey, McWilliam, Winton, & Simeonsson, 1992; Winton, McWilliam, Harrison, Owens, & Bailey, 1992). This model is described in Chapter 20, which contains a detailed account of how this approach to needs assessment is being used in early intervention. A major feature of the team-based model is gaining consensus about organizational needs while considering interventionist and family needs. This aspect of the model is accomplished by providing teams, composed of a variety of stakeholders, with the opportunity to rate actual and desired levels of family-centered practices at individual and organizational levels.

Similar to the needs discrepancy model described by Knowles (1980), emphasis in the team-based model is placed on assisting individuals and groups to self-diagnose needs. Competencies or characteristics required to achieve a given model of performance associated with family-centered service delivery are indicated in a set of instruments (FOCAS [Bailey, 1991]; Brass Tacks [McWilliam & Winton, 1990a]; The Family Report [McWilliam & Winton, 1990b]). Teams and individuals are provided with the opportunity to assess their policies and practices compared with those portrayed on the instruments. This process assists individuals and teams to measure the gaps between their actual and desired practices.

Two perspectives related to congruence may emerge from this team-based process: First, the level of congruence between the actual and desired practices at the individual and agency level surfaces; and second, congruence, or lack of congruence, between individual and organizational needs emerges. The discrepancy model is successful because "the more concretely individuals can identify their aspirations and assess their present levels of competencies in relation to them—the more exactly they can define their educational needs—the more intensely they will be motivated to learn [reduce the gap]" (Knowles, 1980, p. 88). The team-based model provides a concrete way to assess needs and gives many diverse stakeholders a voice in the process.

When individuals with diverse needs are provided with the opportunity to express felt needs and collectively review organizational needs, they are more likely to remain interested in and supportive of priorities targeted for personnel preparation. This seems to be the case even when these targets do not specifically meet their individual needs. The needs assessment process in the team-based model also can keep individuals aware of linkages between the assessment process itself, what was learned from the process, and how needs assessment priorities eventually are linked to personnel preparation activities.

How Are Values Accommodated in the Needs Assessment Process? The definition of needs assessment given previously noted that the process involves application of judgment. An individual or group makes value-based judgments during each phase of the process. Regardless of how needs are defined, whose needs are assessed, and at what levels needs are determined, the identified needs are filtered through and influenced by the perspectives of individuals responsible for translating information into personnel preparation priorities (Siegel et al., 1978).

McKillip (1987) and Monette (1977) noted that it is important for personnel developers to acknowledge that the needs assessment process is value laden. Needs analysis is more meaningful when the contributions of values to the process are made explicit rather than left implicit. Value-based choices may facilitate or impede the needs assessment process. For example, during the construction of a needs assessment survey, the values of the developers of the instrument influence the content and structure of the measure. The effect of this set of value-based choices could be to enhance needs identification for those whose values are congruent with the developers' values or to hamper needs description for those who have different values.

Can People Always Recognize Their Needs?   People may not always have sufficient knowledge about a topic area at a particular point in time to participate adequately in needs assessment activities. Janet, for example, had limited knowledge about integrated therapy. Although she identified a general need to know more about this approach, she probably could not have diagnosed her specific learning needs before attending the workshop. Cameron (1988) defined the tendency for an individual or group to base perceptions of needs on what is available or known to them as "bounded rationality."

Winton (1990) suggested a strategy to overcome this problem. She described a process in which specific information about an innovation is presented. This information is accompanied by a series of guided questions that could be used to stimulate discussion of needs. In her example, the mandated components of an IFSP were specified. A series of questions related to each mandated component was posed. This format could be used to inform individuals about the innovation while simultaneously involving them in needs assessment.

How Might the Scope of the Needs Assessment Be Determined?   How broad should a needs assessment be? Needs assessment can occur across multiple levels (e.g., individual, group, organization, community, state, nation). Multilevel needs assessment can be informative, necessary, appropriate, and feasible. Often, however, the scope of the needs assessment is limited to one or two levels as a result of economic or resource constraints. Determining which levels of need to assess in these circumstances should be tied directly to the ecology in which personnel preparation activities will be implemented.

Personnel preparation activities resulting from a broad-based, statewide needs assessment survey concerned with instructional needs in topics of infant mental health, for example, are unlikely to reflect specific organizational needs or felt needs of individuals. The more broad based and distal the assessment is from the personnel preparation ecology, the less likely that personnel preparation activities will meet needs and result in meaningful change at the individual or organizational level.

Is Needs Assessment Always Necessary in Personnel Preparation?   Assessments of felt needs may not be necessary if what people need to learn about are practices mandated from more distal systems. The lead agency in Vignette 1 had an organizational need that arose from federal mandates for individuals to learn about the early intervention system and the role of primary referral sources. A needs assessment, conducted to identify individual felt needs, probably would not be necessary or useful in this situation. People participating in the personnel preparation activities, however, should be told why the need to know has been imposed on them.

Participation in group assessments represents only one way individuals may identify needs and engage in the personnel preparation process. In some cases, needs are better addressed by individual assessment and personnel preparation initiatives instead of through formal needs assessments involving groups of individuals. Self-study, continuing education, journal reading, team-based interactions, and other forms of learning also contribute to individual needs identification and development.

Summary of Needs Assessment Issues

The ultimate goal of the needs assessment process is to ensure that needs assessment data are meaningful. Needs are not static; thus, needs assessment data can become obsolete rapidly. Instruction must be based on up-to-date needs assessment data if meaningful outcomes for personnel preparation participants are to occur. Options for maintaining the meaningfulness of needs assessment data include repeating needs assessments at regular intervals, verifying previously compiled needs data immediately before a personnel preparation event, and having participants state instructional needs or goals during a workshop (Corbett, 1992).

Although the challenges described related to conducting needs assessments may appear formidable, there are strategies and options for addressing these challenges. Meaningful activities will be more likely to occur if people involved in early intervention personnel preparation evaluate the strategies outlined in Table 6.1 in a context that considers the challenges and options. No one model or strategy should be used across all contexts. Needs assessments are characterized by a variety of purposes, strategies, and outcomes. Strategies used in personnel preparation efforts should reflect an appreciation for these variations.

The majority of instructional activities in early intervention would benefit from more systematic attention to the needs assessment process, both at individual and group levels. Carefully designed and applied needs determination procedures contribute direction to personnel preparation efforts not otherwise available. The nature of felt, attributed, and organizational needs can be discovered and meaningfully displayed by well-conceived and executed needs assessments.

EVALUATION

Since the 1970s, the emphasis on evaluation in the personnel preparation literature has expanded greatly. Personnel instructors are asked to demonstrate the effectiveness of their programs by a wide variety of constituency groups. Effectiveness, however, is a relative term. Personnel preparation can be considered effective if it satisfies participants, encourages their knowledge acquisition, results in skill acquisition or refinement, or modifies their attitudes. Two other types of effectiveness receiving increased attention are measuring the degree to which instruction enhances participant performance beyond the instructional context and demonstrating linkages between personnel preparation efforts directed toward participants and positive changes in children or consumers of services (Bertcher, 1988).

Yet as Knox (1986) noted, few aspects of personnel preparation generate more concern and less action than program evaluation. One reason for inaction may be explained by the difficulties in documenting that positive changes in participants or consumers of services are related directly to instructional efforts. These types of program evaluation questions are difficult to answer.

In this section, evaluation is considered as a separate component of personnel preparation. This section defines evaluation, describes major purposes for conducting evaluation, provides a brief review of evaluation emphases, suggests concrete evaluation guidelines and strategies, and identifies challenges associated with designing and implementing meaningful evaluation. In exploring evaluation issues in personnel preparation, the conclusion that evaluation is inextricably linked to needs assessment and follow-up will emerge. Staff developers generally agree that effective evaluation should be part of each component of planning personnel preparation and all aspects of the teaching–learning transaction.

Definitions of Evaluation

Many definitions of evaluation have been offered in the personnel preparation literature. There are more than 100 definitions of program evaluation (Steele, 1988). Grotelueschen (1986) stated that the definitions used for evaluation vary depending on the intended use of acquired information. Definitions of evaluation also can vary according to the scope of the evaluation (e.g., evaluation of a single instructional session versus evaluation of a cluster of educational activities such as a course). Finally, the literature related to evaluation of instruction and program evaluation do not always use the same definitions.

Nevertheless, several definitions can be proposed. Caffarella (1994) defined evaluation as "a process used to determine whether the design and delivery of a program were effective and whether the proposed outcomes were met" (p. 119). According to Caffarella, the heart of program evaluation is judging the value or worth of the program. Stufflebeam (1973) described evaluation as the process of delineating, obtaining, and providing useful information for judging decision alternatives. Finally, Steele (1988) noted four definitions of evaluation useful for staff developers. These include defining evaluation as the process of 1) describing a program, 2) judging a program against criteria, 3) answering critical questions about a program, and 4) determining the value of a program. She stated that program evaluation efforts can aim at one or all of these definitions.

Knox (1986) noted several common elements expressed in the definitions. First, most call for a description of the educational program, including the purpose of the evaluation, needs and preferences of the audience, nature of the program, and the context in which it operates. Second, judging worth or determining value implies gathering data to make value judgments. Like needs assessment, evaluation is value based, and values should be acknowledged explicitly in program evaluation efforts. Third, most definitions suggest data are gathered to make decisions; however, decisions can be made at many levels. For example, participants can decide if the program is worthwhile, instructors can decide how they would like to modify their instructional activities, and administrators can decide if instruction results in practice changes.

In addition to defining evaluation generally, program evaluators distinguish formative and summative evaluation. Dick (1987) described formative evaluation as a process employed to collect data and information to revise instruction. Formative evaluation, therefore, is performed to improve or change a program. Formative evaluation can focus on evaluating instructional questions, examples, practices, sequences, pacing, and reinforcement. Summative evaluation efforts focus on results or outcomes of the personnel preparation program. For example, participant satisfaction, effects on learner performance, changes in attitudes of participants, and benefits to others are types of outcome evaluations.

In practice, a combination of formative and summative evaluation efforts is most useful (Knox, 1986). Summative evaluation provides the most convincing evidence of outcomes. This information is of limited value, however, without knowing what practices or products contributed to program successes or failures.

Purposes of Evaluation

There are several major purposes for evaluation. One is to provide feedback to instructors, participants, and decision makers to guide program decisions. Evaluation decisions encompass program planning, improvement, and justification activities. Proof of causality, demonstrating that a program produced certain effects, is another major purpose of program evaluation (Steele, 1988). Steele noted that program evaluators typically focus evaluation efforts around proof of causality and not program improvement and stated that both purposes are relevant for program evaluation.

Grotelueschen (1986) characterized the purposes of evaluation according to three categories, which correspond to the timing of the evaluation. When evaluation activities focus on past activities or outcomes, the purpose usually is justification or accountability. This is synonymous with what Scriven (1967) called summative evaluation. A focus on current program activities typically is for the purpose of program improvement and is known as formative evaluation. Finally, when the focus is on possible future actions, sometimes known as evaluation in advance, the purpose of evaluation is similar to a needs assessment. Walsh and Green (1982) characterized evaluations performed to contribute to planning as needs assessments, evaluations performed to improve present practices or products as formative evaluation, and evaluations performed to justify a practice or program as summative or impact evaluation. Integrated needs assessment, follow-up, and evaluation efforts, therefore, produce formative and summative evaluation data.

Types of Evaluation Emphases

Early efforts in personnel preparation evaluation were characterized mainly by gathering satisfaction data from learners. Buckley and Mank (1994) noted that end-of-session recipient satisfaction measures still are being used as "defaults" in many instruction and technical assistance contexts. Satisfaction measures can include assessments of the instruction site, logistics (including food and room temperature!), presenter's delivery and knowledge, the degree to which content matches learner expectations, and learner satisfaction with instructional content. Satisfaction evaluations can be used to shape future instruction, and the data provided can be useful in many evaluation contexts. Placing sole reliance on these measures is problematic, however, because high satisfaction is not guaranteed to translate into quality outcomes for participants, agencies, children, and families (Buckley & Mank, 1994). Most program evaluation experts recommend the use of broader and more detailed conceptions of evaluation in personnel preparation efforts (e.g., Cervero, 1984; Knox, 1986).

Young and Willie (1984) conducted a literature review to examine how staff developers evaluated the effectiveness of continuing education programs for allied health professionals. These authors discerned four levels of evaluation across the reviewed studies. The first level of evaluation, prominent in the 1960s and 1970s, was participant satisfaction. A second level of evaluation, prominent in the 1970s, focused on acquisition and retention of knowledge, formation and modification of attitudes, and development of skills. During the 1980s, program evaluators in allied health moved to a third level where they evaluated whether changes in knowledge, skill, or attitudes ensured application to practice. Finally, a fourth level of evaluation involved examination of the impact of instruction on consumers. Compelling arguments for broadening evaluation efforts to encompass all four levels, when appropriate, are being raised in the personnel preparation literature. Young and Willie (1984) documented that these efforts are beginning in allied health continuing education; however, they acknowledged that most evaluation efforts continue to be characterized by poor attention to using an array of evaluation levels or strategies. This statement is supported by a number of authors who reviewed evaluation studies in medicine (Bertram & Brooks-Bertram, 1977), allied health (Turnbull & Holt, 1993; Walsh & Green, 1982), nursing (Faulk, 1984), and education (Daresh, 1987; Edelfelt, 1981).

Evaluation Strategies

Early intervention personnel instructors should view evaluation as a circular process that begins in the planning phase of personnel preparation. Follow-up and impact data, for example, become needs assessment data to guide future personnel preparation efforts. Through each phase of the personnel preparation process, early intervention instructors should state clearly and understand fully the purposes and scope of their evaluation. Planned evaluation strategies should be matched to the goals established for personnel preparation. Goals can include specification of desired participant outcomes. Instructors and the instructional context also can be evaluated. Staff developers should plan, whenever feasible, to gather evaluation data at different levels of the system (e.g., individual, agency). Multisource, multidomain, multimethod data collection strategies are superior to strategies that focus on a single source, domain, or method.

A variety of evaluation strategies are proposed in the personnel preparation literature. Table 6.3 lists example evaluation strategies that could be used in early intervention efforts. These strategies are discussed according to a conceptual framework proposed by Cervero (1988), which includes seven categories of evaluation: 1) program design and implementation; 2) learner participation; 3) learner satisfaction; 4) change in learner knowledge, skills, and attitudes; 5) application of learning after the program; 6) impact of application of learning; and 7) program characteristics associated with the outcomes. Within each of these categories, evaluation questions can be posed, and a variety of evaluation methods or strategies can be used to gather data.

Program Design and Implementation   This category of evaluation includes factors related to how the program is designed and implemented, including activities of learners or instructors, characteristics of the setting, and the nature of the teaching–learning transaction (Cervero, 1988). Sample evaluation questions that might be asked in this category are, "What methods were used to deliver program content?" "How comfortable was the room arrangement for participants and instructors?" or "How much time did the instructors allow for skill practice?" Instructors, participants, and other program planners can be sources of data for this category of evaluation. For example, participants, instructors, and observers could be asked to evaluate whether planned topics were covered. These three sources of evaluation data could be analyzed for areas of agreement or disagreement. Instrument, observation, and interview methods could be used to gather data in this category. Cervero (1988) noted that evaluations in this category usually require a minimal amount of effort, yet produce quite useful evaluation data. Data gathered in this category offer evaluations of current program design and implementation efforts and also could be used to plan future personnel preparation activities.

Learner Participation   This category of evaluation is concerned with issues such as the number of people who participated in the personnel preparation event, participation of various stakeholder groups in the instruction (if appropriate), and levels of learner participation across activities. For example, for Janet's story, learner participation data would identify that some individuals left the instruction for the mall. Relatively simple data collection strategies can be used to gather learner participation data, including head counts and data gathered from attendance rosters. Perspectives about learner participation can be gathered from participants and instructors using rating scales or tally sheets. A participant observer could conduct observational scans to determine learner participation throughout the instruction session. Cervero (1988) noted that learner participation data, although often overemphasized at the expense of other evaluation alternatives, are impor-

TABLE 6.3. Examples of evaluation strategies

Evaluation strategy	Description	Rationale for the strategy	Options for gathering data	Formats for data collection
Satisfaction measurement	Any evaluation procedure in which individuals (instructors or participants) rate their level of satisfaction with the overall instructional experiences or components of the instruction	These are judgments based on the subjective impressions of raters. These measures are generally easy to develop and administer, cost-effective, and straightforward in their interpretation. Satisfaction measures can be used in formative evaluation for further development of instruction and as summative evaluation data to help describe instructional outcomes (e.g., levels of satisfaction).	• Information about instructional content, educational process, the instructor, physical facilities, and cost can be obtained. • Satisfaction data can be obtained on the spot while instruction is occurring to determine whether modifications to program should be made. • Satisfaction data can be gathered at the end of various sections of the instructional event, at the conclusion of the instructional event, or days or weeks after the instructional event.	• Instruments • Informal conversational approach • Semistructured interview using guiding questions • Standardized open-ended interview • Telephone interviews • Critical incident interviews
Self-ratings of knowledge, skills, or effectiveness	Any evaluation procedure in which individuals (instructors or participants) rate current levels of their skills, knowledge, or effectiveness	A major goal of many instructional experiences is to increase the skills, knowledge, or effectiveness of participants. Self-ratings are useful for gathering data about the participants' perspectives about change. Ratings scales generally are economical to develop and administer. Self-rating may help the participants reflect on their experiences and gains.	• Instructors or participants can be asked to rate their current knowledge about certain practices, their skill in implementing practices, or the efficacy of their skill implementation. • Self-rating data can be gathered before instruction, during instruction, at the conclusion of instruction, or during follow-up.	• Instruments • Interviews • Role playing/discussion • Case discussions

(continued)

| Attitude measures | Any evaluation procedure in which individuals (instructors or participants) indicate the direction of their feelings about something | Four change areas frequently are targeted in instruction: attitude, knowledge, skill, and practice. The interrelationships of these areas are acknowledged, but the order in which changes occur is debatable. Whether changed attitudes foster skill change or vice versa is one issue. Attitude change is considered important for maintaining or using new skills over time. Attitude measures can be relatively inexpensive to develop and administer. These measures can assist people to reflect on current attitudes and the relationships of these to information presented during staff development. | • Words typically used in attitude questions can include *favor* versus *oppose, prefer* versus *not prefer, should* versus *should not, good* versus *bad, right* versus *wrong,* and *agree* versus *disagree.*

• Free- or fixed-response questions can be used on attitude measures.

• Likert scales or Likert-type scales can be used to quantify dimensions of attitude.

• Other scaling options can include semantic differential, Thurstone, or Guttman scales. | • Instruments
• Interviews |

TABLE 6.3. *(continued)*

Evaluation strategy	Description	Rationale for the strategy	Options for gathering data	Formats for data collection
Knowledge and skill acquisition measures	Evaluation procedures used to quantify or qualify changes in knowledge or skill related to staff development	Two primary interests in many staff development contexts are knowledge or skill acquisition. This category of evaluation focuses on what the learner or instructor is expected to know or be able to do at the end of the instructional event.	• Direct or indirect measurements can be used to confirm or infer changes in knowledge or skills. • Knowledge measurement can involve assessment of knowledge, comprehension, application, analysis, or synthesis. • Skills can be assessed in simulated or actual situations. • Skill acquisition can be evaluated by assessing live performance or by reviewing portfolios or taped samples.	• Instruments • Portfolio review • Performance rating scales • Observational methods • Interviews • Role play/discussion • Case discussions

| Observational measures | Data collected through observing the processes or outcomes of instruction; data may be collected on performance of individual participants or instructors, groups of participants or co-workers, instructional context variables, and child or family impact variables | Observational assessments permit evaluations of actual practices rather than relying on self-ratings, knowledge, or attitude measures. Specific barriers related to transfer of instruction can be identified through observational assessments. Observers can provide feedback to the learner in the performance environment. Observations can be made by a variety of people, including supervisors, co-workers, the evaluator, or those affected by the individual's performance. Observations require a large investment of time, and the costs associated with this evaluation strategy must be weighed against the potential benefits. | • Behaviors can be counted, timed, or compared with a standard.

• Behaviors can be observed over time and circumstances to assess acquisition, generalization, and maintenance.

• Observations can be live or based on recorded performance.

• Observations can be continuous, time sampled, or momentary.

• Recorded performances can be reviewed repeatedly by different observers (e.g., instructors, family members).

• Qualitative criteria can be included in the observation system. | • Performance checklists
• Environmental rating scales
• Child and family observational measures related to participant performance
• Critical incident observations
• Frequency counts
• Duration measures
• Observation coding systems |

(continued)

TABLE 6.3. *(continued)*

Evaluation strategy	Description	Rationale for the strategy	Options for gathering data	Formats for data collection
Evaluating planned outcomes	Procedures specifically used to document projected versus actual outcomes of staff development	Generating statements of goals or behavioral objectives to be achieved is common practice in staff development. Using these goals or objectives as benchmarks to evaluate outcomes contributes direction to current and future staff development efforts. Evaluating planned outcomes focuses attention on the overall processes and effects of staff development.	• If goals and objectives for staff development are set at specific target levels, planned outcomes are evaluated in a binary fashion (e.g., achieved, not achieved). • If goals and objectives for staff development are stated in terms of variable outcome levels, then evaluation of planned change can be documented (e.g., worse than expected outcome, expected outcome, better than expected outcome).	• Record sheets • Goal attainment scaling forms

Measurement of program or community practices	Procedure by which participants or instructors, family members, or other stakeholders provide their perspectives about program or community practices related to staff development activities	Many staff development experiences are designed to affect program or community practices and are not limited to altering knowledge, skills, or efficacy of individuals. Evaluation data focused on collective changes at the agency or community level. These data can provide a contextual perspective and assist with agency- or community-level decision making about staff development.	• Agency policies, procedures, and records can be reviewed. • Interrelationships among various community agencies can be analyzed. • Selected representative individuals can be asked to describe program or community practices. • Individuals can observe agency or community teams doing their work. • Selected representative individuals can complete rating scales that quantify program or community characteristics. • Agency or community funding patterns, levels, and cost centers can be analyzed.	• Document analysis • Network analysis • Consensus techniques • Critical incident observations or interviews • Instruments • Focus groups • Community forum

Adapted from Bailey, Geissinger, McWilliam, McWilliam, & Simeonsson (1989).

tant for three reasons: 1) a minimum level of participation may be necessary to justify offering the program, 2) the number of participants in an instructional session can affect its quality, and 3) the extent to which participants are actively involved in the workshop can influence its effectiveness.

Learner Satisfaction   The most common category of evaluation is learner satisfaction. This category is based on the subjective perspectives of participants about instructional content, instructional processes, instructors, physical facilities, and ancillary factors such as registration procedures, materials, and cost. Satisfaction data can be gathered from all participants or from a representative sample. Data can be obtained at selected points throughout the instructional event or at the end of the session. Instrument or interview methods can be used to gather satisfaction data. A unique approach for collecting satisfaction data is to post three sheets of flipchart paper labeled "What did you like?" "What would you change?" and "What do you want more instruction and information about?" on the wall outside the room where the instruction is taking place. Each participant is given pages from a self-sticking notepad and invited to write comments on the pages and post their responses on the appropriate flipchart page (C. Catlett, personal communication, November 1992).

Although not often discussed, instructor satisfaction data can be obtained using strategies similar to those used with participants. For example, instructors could be asked to evaluate overall satisfaction with their session, including what they might alter in future sessions.

Satisfaction data from participants and instructors may be useful for decision making about alternative formats, locations, and other aspects of personnel preparation. The importance of satisfaction data, however, can be overemphasized. High levels of satisfaction do not guarantee knowledge or skill gains or transfer of skills to practice contexts.

Change in Learner Knowledge, Skills, and Attitudes   This category of evaluation involves documenting changes in knowledge, skills, or attitudes. Baseline and at least one or more repeated measurements are needed to evaluate change. Table 6.3 shows several methods or strategies that can be used to evaluate knowledge, skills, and attitudes. Staff developers who evaluate knowledge, skills, or attitudes may observe change from pre- to posttest. However, without appropriate experimental controls in place, evaluators cannot necessarily attribute the change directly to the personnel preparation activity. People may change simply because they grow wiser or succumb to peer influences. These and other internal and external validity threats are present in most personnel preparation circumstances. Evaluators should refrain from making unsubstantiated claims about why changes in knowledge, skills, or attitudes occur.

Application of Learning After the Program   This category of evaluation is concerned with the extent to which the knowledge, skills, and attitudes learned during instruction transfer to practice contexts. A variety of follow-up evaluation strategies are described in Chapter 7. Follow-up evaluation data are central to the personnel preparation process, particularly when the goals of personnel preparation involve transfer of learning.

Impact of Application of Learning   This category focuses on the evaluation of second-order outcomes. First-order outcomes evaluate impact on individuals who participate directly in the personnel preparation activity (e.g., learners, instructors). For example, in Janet's story, changes in her knowledge about routines-based intervention is a first-order outcome. Second-order outcomes relate to effects realized by people who do not participate directly in the personnel preparation activity. For example, children and families in the program where Janet works may realize a benefit from her participation in the workshop. Second-order evaluation data are sought actively by staff developers, funders, and policy makers because these data are believed to offer convincing evidence about the "worth" of personnel preparation programs. In many contexts, the ultimate goal of personnel preparation is to improve services for children and families.

Most of the evaluation formats listed in Table 6.3 could be used to evaluate second-order effects. However, demonstrations of second-order effects do not necessarily offer conclusive evidence that the personnel preparation activity was responsible for the effects. Internal and external validity design threats may limit conclusions that can be drawn about the impact of training. Staff developers should evaluate second-order effects, when appropriate, but they should use caution in attributing them solely to personnel preparation activities.

Program Characteristics Associated with Outcomes   This category of evaluation attempts to link workshop implementation and outcome data (Cervero, 1984). This level focuses on explicating relationships between workshop characteristics and outcomes. Questions that might be asked include, "Is there a statistically significant or noteworthy relationship between the amount of instructional time devoted to active instructional methods and participants' satisfaction ratings?" or "Are levels of participation by individuals during the personnel preparation activity related to skill proficiency in their practice contexts?"

Similar to other categories of evaluation, making definitive statements that imply the existence of direct relationships between program characteristics and program outcomes may be problematic. However, as Cervero (1984) noted, "The alternative is to use the workshop title as the explanatory variable. . . . It seems obvious that some information is better than none, as long as we recognize the limitations of the data" (p. 65).

Beyond the strategies listed in Table 6.3 and previously discussed, many of the same data collection methods and strategies listed in Table 6.1 for gathering needs assessment information are recommended for use in evaluation. Caffarella (1994) noted that this overlap is not unexpected because needs assessment information often serves as baseline data for evaluations that occur during or after the instruction.

Use of the Strategies in Early Intervention Personnel Preparation Efforts

Janet's story and two vignettes are used to examine how Cervero's (1984) framework and strategies presented in Table 6.3 could guide program evaluation efforts. In Vignette 1, the goals for instruction included demonstrating that primary referral sources receive awareness-level instruction about the early intervention program and increasing participants' knowledge about the early intervention systems and the responsibilities of primary referral sources. Evaluation data must include documentation of the numbers of participants, their disciplines, and the agencies they represent. Participants' knowledge acquisition also must be evaluated. Personnel from the UAP could provide the lead agency with formative data, specifying how instruction was planned, implemented, and modified based on feedback from participants.

The personnel preparation plan specified in Vignette 2 includes attention to obtaining multilevel process and impact data that document achievement of a desired outcome. The goal is to have all teachers learn about and use ABI in their classrooms. If this goal is achieved, then effects on teachers, children, families, and the agency as a whole would be expected. Each category specified in Table 6.3 could become part of a comprehensive evaluation plan. Decisions about which specific evaluation strategies to use should be made after team members consider their major goals for the personnel preparation efforts over time, the resources and climate in the agency, and the expertise available to them from university personnel.

In Janet's story, two types of evaluation data were gathered: satisfaction and knowledge. Although these were matched to the goals of instruction, how meaningful were these data for Janet? She wanted to learn about routines-based intervention and integrated therapy so she could apply it in the work setting. Without program implementation and follow-up evaluation data, the instructors will never know the extent to which their efforts affected Janet's performance in the work setting.

Deciding on a Strategy

Decisions about specific evaluation strategies should be based on availability of data, relevance of data to personnel preparation goals, reliability of the data source, availability of methods to collect data, degree to which data collection methods intrude, trade-offs between effort expended and information yielded, and resources available for use (Walsh & Green, 1982). Additional criteria that early intervention staff developers can use to guide evaluation decisions can be found in Grotelueschen (1986) and Knox (1986).

Challenges in Evaluation

As staff developers plan for and implement evaluation, they face a variety of challenges. These challenges include specifying the focus of the evaluation, ensuring that evaluation corresponds to the intended outcomes of personnel preparation, evaluating informal or unplanned outcomes, planning evaluation so results are used, securing resources, using measures that produce reliable and valid data when used with various samples of participants, considering ethical and practical constraints on evaluation, and recognizing the role values and preferences play in the evaluation process. These challenges are described, and potential options to address them are offered.

How Is the Focus of the Evaluation Specified?   Evaluators can focus their efforts on program elements such as the instructor, participant, topic, and context. They also can evaluate program characteristics, including goals, design, implementation, and outcomes. Specific evaluation models, such as Stufflebeam's Context, Input, Process, and Product (CIPP) model (1973), can frame evaluation efforts. A review by Cervero (1984) reinforced the conclusion that there is no shortage of evaluation models available to guide program evaluation efforts. He found more than 40 formal evaluation models represented in the published literature. The challenge most staff developers face is how to specify a focus given the many possible directions evaluation can take. Becker, McCarthy, and Kirkhart (1992) suggested that five basic questions (see Table 6.4) be asked when deciding on a

TABLE 6.4.   Criteria for deciding what to evaluate

- **What's worth knowing?**   In other words, what information can be used to guide and evaluate personnel preparation efforts?

- **Who wants to know?**   Some evaluation questions are worth asking because they are important to certain key stakeholders or funders.

- **What are the most important program goals?**   State the goals and objectives for the personnel preparation effort, and identify the most important ones. This may provide a logical starting place for planning evaluation activities.

- **What is the program's stage of development?**   Certain evaluation questions may be more critical at one point than at another in the personnel preparation process.

- **What is feasible to evaluate?**   Some questions require more resources, time, and expertise than others. Some questions cannot be investigated due to ethical considerations or the undue burden placed on learners, instructors, or consumers of services.

Adapted from Becker et al. (1992).

focus for the evaluation: 1) What's worth knowing? 2) Who wants to know? 3) What are the most important program goals? 4) What is the program's stage of development? and 5) What is feasible to evaluate?

How Should Evaluation Correspond to the Intended Outcomes of the Personnel Preparation Effort? Personnel preparation efforts can be characterized by a variety of purposes or intended outcomes. These include increasing participant knowledge, modifying attitudes, or changing practices. Evaluation strategies should correspond to these desired outcomes. If personnel preparation is intended to change participants' performance in the workplace, a primary evaluation focus should be on application of learning after the instructional event. Evaluation of knowledge acquisition would correspond to a stated purpose of increasing participants' knowledge about a particular topic. Different types of evaluation are better than others only to the extent that they correspond to the intended outcome of the personnel preparation effort (Cervero, 1984).

How Are Informal or Unplanned Outcomes Evaluated? Personnel preparation efforts can be expected to produce informal or unplanned outcomes. The evaluation plan should be structured so that side effects and opportunity costs, as well as intended outcomes, are measured. Informal or unplanned outcome evaluation opportunities arise, for example, when instructors notice that participants either remain in the instructional session or make a decision to go shopping instead. This is a powerful type of participation data that might not be captured in a formal evaluation plan. Informal or unplanned evaluation might occur during the lunch break when instructors meet with three participants to get their reactions to the morning session. This type of learner satisfaction data, obtained during the instructional event, could alter the remainder of the program.

How Can Evaluation Be Planned So Results Are Used for Decision Making? Program planners might devote time and resources to developing and implementing a model evaluation plan only to find the data not used for current or future decision making. To increase the likelihood of use, Cervero (1984) advised staff developers to determine who would use the information and what kind of information they would need. He recommended that these people be involved, as much as possible, in the evaluation design, implementation, analysis, and reporting. Information users might include participants, program planners, instructors, those who finance the personnel preparation activity, and administrators. These users might have different evaluation needs. Satisfaction data, for example, might be important to the instructor, whereas administrators might be interested in application outcomes. Each of these users and their needs may need to be addressed in the evaluation plan. The constraints of monetary and human resources also must be considered with the needs of these users.

How Important Are Resources for Evaluation? Resources should be assessed continually while the evaluation plan is being formulated. Resources include available money, time, expertise, and contextual factors to support evaluation efforts (e.g., instructor who is willing to devote part of a workshop session to administering pre- and postknowledge assessments). Quality evaluation is time consuming, labor intensive, and expensive. As resource availability usually is limited, staff developers in early intervention can no longer justify single source, method, or domain evaluations. Some form of multisource, multidomain, and multimethod evaluation must appear in every program evaluation effort, and efforts must be made to secure the resources to perform these types of evaluations.

How Important to the Evaluation Process Are Measures that Produce Reliable and Valid Data? Measures used to gather evaluation data from instructional participants must produce reliable and valid data. Reliability and validity, however, are not static properties of a measure. Reported indexes of reliability and validity relate to data obtained from samples of participants in specific instructional contexts. These indexes may fluctuate from one evaluation context to another. For example, estimates of internal consistency reliability for an instrument that purports to operationalize attitudes toward family-centered early intervention may change across evaluation contexts when different samples of interventionists complete the measure. Evaluators should examine the reliability and validity of the instruments they select for program evaluation efforts using data gathered from participants in their program. These analyses provide the evaluator with important information about how the instrument performed in a particular evaluation context and whether substantive evaluation questions can be asked and answered with confidence (see Snyder, Lawson, Thompson, Stricklin, & Sexton, 1993).

How Do Ethical and Practical Constraints Affect Evaluation?   Many of the same ethical considerations used to guide organized research activities apply in the evaluation context. For example, individuals cannot be forced to participate in evaluation activities. Evaluators must ensure that the privacy of participants is protected when reporting results. Evaluation data obtained from participants should not be used to make hiring or retention decisions. These and other ethical considerations present constraints on evaluation that staff developers must consider. Practical constraints also affect evaluation efforts; for example, it may not be feasible for participants to be observed by instructors in the workplace. The practicality of having people with limited reading proficiency complete written surveys should be questioned. Staff developers should make every effort to identify ethical and practical constraints during the formulation of evaluation plans.

How Can the Roles of Values and Preferences Be Considered?   The evaluation process involves application of judgment. An individual or group makes value-based judgments during each phase of the evaluation process. Decisions are filtered through and influenced by the perspectives of individuals responsible for developing the evaluation plan. For example, an evaluator may prefer certain instruments because the measures have yielded reliable and valid data when administered to samples of early interventionists. Values and preferences should be acknowledged explicitly so that everyone involved in the evaluation process is aware of their influence (Cervero, 1984).

Summary of Evaluation Issues

The evaluation plans described in Vignette 1 and in Janet's story are too common in early intervention. More extensive evaluation data should be gathered and used in personnel preparation efforts. Bailey (1989) stated that these data are desperately needed. Without data to document the impact or worth of personnel preparation, these efforts will continue to be characterized as "irrelevant and ineffective, a waste of time and money" (Wood & Thompson, 1980, p. 374). Bailey urged early intervention personnel instructors to conduct evaluations that focus on the process of personnel preparation and on the various outcome domains (described in Table 6.3), including participant satisfaction, change in participant behavior and attitudes, and, ultimately, benefits for children and families served by individuals who participate in personnel preparation.

There are many challenges that staff developers face as they attempt to design and implement comprehensive and meaningful evaluation. Although these difficulties can appear overwhelming, evaluation efforts in early intervention must move beyond participant satisfaction and knowledge acquisition.

CONCLUSION

This chapter has presented concrete strategies and decision-making guidelines that could be used to enhance the quality of needs assessment and evaluation efforts in early intervention and has raised challenges associated with these two personnel preparation components. Chapter 7 addresses follow-up, a third critical component of personnel preparation efforts, and concludes with several important guidelines for linking needs assessment, follow-up, and evaluation in early intervention.

REFERENCES

American Society for Training and Development. (1985). *Be a better needs analyst.* Alexandria, VA: Author.

Bailey, D.B. (1991). *FOCAS: Family Orientation of Community and Agency Services.* Chapel Hill: University of North Carolina at Chapel Hill, Frank Porter Graham Child Development Center.

Bailey, D.B., Geissinger, S., McWilliam, P.J., McWilliam, R.A., & Simeonsson, R. (1989, October). *Evaluating in-service education in early intervention: Issues and alternatives.* Preconference workshop at International Division for Early Childhood Conference, Minneapolis, MN.

Bailey, D.B., McWilliam, P.J., & Winton, P.J. (1992). Building family-centered practices in early intervention: A team-based model for change. *Infants and Young Children, 5*(1), 73–82.

Bailey, D.B., McWilliam, P.J., Winton, P.J., & Simeonsson, R.J. (1992). *Implementing family-centered practices in early intervention: A team-based model for change.* Cambridge, MA: Brookline.

Bailey, D.B., Jr. (1989). Issues and directions in preparing professionals to work with young handicapped children and their families. In J.J. Gallagher, P.L. Trohanis, & R.M. Clifford (Eds.), *Policy implementation and PL 99-457: Planning for young children with special needs* (pp. 97–132). Baltimore: Paul H. Brookes Publishing Co.

Becker, H.A., McCarthy, M., & Kirkhart, K.E. (1992). *Making evaluation work for you: A guidebook for programs that serve persons with developmental disabilities.* (Available from Texas Consortium for Developmental Disabilities: A University Affiliated Program, University of Texas at Austin)

Bertcher, H.J. (1988). *Staff development in human service organizations.* Englewood Cliffs, NJ: Prentice Hall.

Bertram, D.A., & Brooks-Bertram, P.A. (1977). The evaluation of continuing medical education: A literature review. *Health Education Monographs, 5*(4), 330–362.

Bille, D.A. (1982). *Staff development: A systems approach.* Thorofare, NJ: Slack.

Bruder, M.B., & Nikitas, T. (1992). Changing the professional practice of early interventionists: An inservice model to meet the service needs of Public Law 99-457. *Journal of Early Intervention, 16,* 173–180.

Buckley, J., & Mank, D. (1994). New perspectives on training and technical assistance: Moving from assumptions to a focus on quality. *Journal of The Association for Persons with Severe Handicaps, 19,* 223–232.

Caffarella, R.S. (1982). Identifying client needs. *Journal of Extension, 20,* 5–11.

Caffarella, R.S. (1994). *Planning programs for adult learners: A practical guide for educators, trainers, and staff developers.* San Francisco: Jossey-Bass.

Cameron, C. (1988). Identifying learners' needs: Six methods adult educators can use. *Lifelong Learning, 11*(4), 25–29.

Cervero, R.M. (1984). Evaluating workshop implementation and outcomes. In T.J. Sork (Ed.), *Designing and implementing effective workshops: New directions for continuing education* (pp. 55–67). San Francisco: Jossey-Bass.

Cervero, R.M. (1988). *Effective continuing education for professionals.* San Francisco: Jossey-Bass.

Cooper, C.M., & Jones, E.V. (1984, November). *The state of the art in inservice education: A review of the literature.* Paper presented at the annual meeting of the National Council of States on Inservice Education, Orlando, FL. (ERIC Document Reproduction Service No. ED 258 343)

Corbett, A.H. (1992). Give participants responsibility for learning: Techniques for opening a workshop. *Journal of Staff Development, 13,* 40–43.

Daresh, J.C. (1987). Research trends in staff development and inservice education. *Journal of Education for Teaching, 13*(1), 3–11.

Dick, W. (1987). Formative evaluation: Prospects for the future. *Educational Technology, 27*(10), 55–57.

Edelfelt, R. (1981). Six years of progress in in-service education. *Journal of Research and Development in Education, 14*(2), 113–119.

Elam, S.E., Cramer, J., & Brodinsky, B. (1986). *Staff development: Problems and solutions.* Arlington, VA: American Association of School Administrators.

Faulk, L.G. (1984). Continuing education program evaluation for course improvement, participant effect, and utilization in clinical practice. *Journal of Nursing Education, 23*(4), 139–146.

Gallegos, A.M. (1979). Some critical issues for in-service education. *Journal of Teacher Education, 30*(1), 23.

Grotelueschen, A.D. (1986). Program evaluation. In A.B. Knox (Ed.), *Developing, administering, and evaluating adult education* (pp. 75–123). San Francisco: Jossey-Bass.

Harris, B.M. (1989). *In-service education for staff development.* Needham, MA: Allyn & Bacon.

Houle, C.O. (1972). *The design of education.* San Francisco: Jossey-Bass.

King, J.C., Hayes, P.C., & Newman, I. (1977). Some requirements for successful inservice education. *Phi Delta Kappan, 58,* 686–687.

Knowles, M.S. (1980). *The modern practice of adult education.* New York: Cambridge.

Knox, A.B. (1986). *Helping adults learn: A guide to planning, implementing, and conducting programs.* San Francisco: Jossey-Bass.

Korinek, L., Schmid, R., & McAdams, M. (1985). Inservice types and best practices. *Journal of Research and Development in Education, 18*(2), 33–38.

Laird, D. (1985). *Approaches to training and development* (2nd ed.). Reading, MA: Addison-Wesley.

McKillip, J. (1987). *Need analysis: Tools for the human services and education.* Beverly Hills: Sage Publications.

McWilliam, P.J., & Winton, P.J. (1990a). *Brass Tacks.* Chapel Hill: University of North Carolina at Chapel Hill, Frank Porter Graham Child Development Center.

McWilliam, P.J., & Winton, P.J. (1990b). *The Family Report.* Chapel Hill: University of North Carolina at Chapel Hill, Frank Porter Graham Child Development Center.

Monette, M.L. (1977). The concept of educational need: An analysis of selected literature. *Adult Education, 27*(2), 116–127.

Neenan, O., Orthner, D., & Crocker, H. (1995). *Network analysis.* Unpublished instrument. Chapel Hill: University of North Carolina at Chapel Hill, School of Social Work.

Newstrom, J.W., & Lilyquist, J.M. (1979). Selecting needs analysis methods. *Training and Development Journal, 33*(10), 52–56.

Phillips, J.J. (1991). *Handbook of training evaluation and measurement methods.* Houston, TX: Gulf.

Scriven, M. (1967). The methodology of evaluation. In R. Tyler, R.M. Gagne, & M. Scriven (Eds.), *Perspectives of curriculum evaluation* (pp. 39–83). Chicago: Rand McNally.

Siegel, L.M., Attkisson, C., & Carson, L.G. (1978). Need identification and program planning in the community context. In C.C. Attkisson, W.A. Hargreaves, & M.J. Horowitz (Eds.), *Evaluation of human service programs* (pp. 215–252). New York: Academic Press.

Snyder, P., Lawson, S., Thompson, B., Stricklin, S., & Sexton, D. (1993). Evaluating the psychometric integrity of instruments used in early intervention research: The Battelle Developmental Inventory. *Topics in Early Childhood Special Education, 13*(2), 216–232.

Steele, S.M. (1988, January). *Evaluation as a mental process.* Class notes for 268–602. Madison: University of Wisconsin, Department of Continuing and Vocational Education.

Stufflebeam, D.L. (1973). Educational evaluation and decision making. In B. Worthen & J.R. Sanders (Eds.), *Educational evaluation: Theory and practice* (pp. 128–142). Belmont, CA: Wadsworth.

Thompson, J.C., & Cooley, V.E. (1986). A national study of outstanding staff development programs. *Educational Horizons, 64,* 94–98.

Timms, J. (1995). Needs assessment surveys in gerontological nursing: Are we really assessing continuing education needs and priorities? *Journal of Continuing Education in Nursing, 26,* 84–88.

Tracey, W.R. (1992). *Designing training and development systems* (3rd ed.). New York: AMACOM.

Trohanis, P.L. (1994). Planning for successful in-service education for local early childhood programs. *Topics in Early Childhood Special Education, 14*(3), 311–332.

Turnbull, D.C., & Holt, M.E. (1993). Conceptual frameworks for evaluating continuing education in allied health. *Journal of Continuing Education in the Health Professions, 13,* 177–186.

Walsh, P.L., & Green, J.S. (1982). Pathways to impact evaluation in continuing education in the health professions. *Journal of Allied Health, 11,* 115–123.

Winton, P.J. (1990). A systemic approach for planning in-service training related to Public Law 99-457. *Infants and Young Children, 3*(1), 51–60.

Winton, P.J., McWilliam, P.J., Harrison, T., Owens, A.M., & Bailey, D.B. (1992). Lessons learned from implementing a team-based model for change. *Infants and Young Children, 5*(1), 49–57.

Wood, F.H., & Thompson, S.R. (1980). Guidelines for better staff development. *Educational Leadership, 37,* 374–378.

Wood, F.H., Thompson, S.R., & Russell, S.F. (1981). Designing effective staff development programs. In B. Dillon-Peterson (Ed.), *Staff development/organization development* (pp. 59–91). Alexandria, VA: Association for Supervision and Curriculum Development.

Young, L.J., & Willie, R. (1984). Effectiveness of continuing education for health professionals: A literature review. *Journal of Allied Health, 13*(2), 112–123.

Zemke, R., & Gunkler, J. (1985). 28 techniques for transforming training into performance. *Training, 22*(4), 48–54.

Zemke, R., & Kramlinger, T. (1982). *Figuring things out: A trainer's guide to needs and task analysis.* Reading, MA: Addison-Wesley.

7 FOLLOW-UP STRATEGIES

Ensuring that Instruction Makes a Difference

Barbara L. Wolfe
Patricia Snyder

Janet's Story Continues

Janet is back at work the Monday following the workshop on integrated therapy. At the beginning of the day, a few colleagues asked how she had liked the workshop and if she'd gotten any shopping done at the mall. Janet started to explain how much she'd learned, but it seemed to fall on very uninterested ears. Her colleagues were certainly competent but were not familiar with the approaches she now wanted to implement—approaches that were a significant departure from existing practices in the agency. Undaunted, Janet went to her boss to outline her new ideas and ask for support. Her boss listened politely and told her how glad she was that the seminar had been worthwhile given the amount of money it had cost but informed her that there were many other, more pressing priorities that needed attention. Janet was free to do as she pleased in terms of implementation, but it would have to be on her own.

Janet decided to try another strategy to gain support; she asked the staff to join her for a "brown bag" luncheon at which time she would more fully explain the procedures. A few staff members came, but they seemed to be full of "yeah, buts" and the discussion quickly moved into more immediate concerns, such as upcoming individualized family service plan meetings and a family in crisis. It seemed she was going to have to do this alone. She wondered if that was even possible. And what was also frustrating was that she so quickly became wrapped up in the usual frenzy of her job. She had little time to even think about the many things she'd learned, much less implement them! She had another idea: The instructors had offered to lend telephone support to participants and had given their telephone numbers. It seemed like an intrusion, but they were nice people and she really did need ideas about how to proceed, so Janet swallowed hard and made the call. She was informed that the instructors were "on the road" and would be hard to reach for the next couple of weeks.

One last try. She decided to contact a fellow speech-language clinician from the workshop who had been equally enthusiastic about the procedures. Janet was met with a similar discouraging tale of implementation woes. It seemed they were both in the same very frustrating and discouraging place. After a few minutes of commiserating, Janet hung up and decided to give up. It was just too hard to implement innovative ideas with so little support, so few resources, and so little time. If only the workshop had included follow-up strategies; if only other members of her team had attended with her; if only she'd thought about and prioritized what she wanted to do on the job before she'd left the workshop; if only she'd had a chance to anticipate the barriers and strategize solutions; if only

they'd gotten better handouts that she could share with colleagues; if only a follow-up session had been planned; if only. . . .

Janet's story is a common tale. Implementation of suggested procedures on the job is the most difficult and complex outcome of training, requiring the most intensive instructional design. Training, whether preservice or inservice, addresses the knowledge or awareness of participants related to the topic, changes in attitudes toward the topic, and development of skill in the content area (Joyce & Showers, 1995; Knox, 1986; Wood, McQuarrie, & Thompson, 1982). Joyce and Showers (1988) suggested an additional aim: "transfer of training and executive control (the consistent and appropriate use of new skills and strategies)" (p. 68). Caffarella (1994) defined transfer of learning as the effective application by program participants of what they learned as a result of attending an educational program. It is the "so what" or "now what" phase of the personnel development process. This chapter describes follow-up procedures that can help ensure transfer of learning to the job.

WHY DO FOLLOW-UP?

Harris (1980) and Showers, Joyce, and Bennett (1987) suggested that different types of instructional objectives require different degrees of change in the learner. The most complex objectives, those that require transfer and mediation of learning in the applied setting, require a combination of activities, including follow-up strategies. Personnel preparation experts highlight the critical role follow-up strategies play in facilitating transfer of learning (Caffarella, 1994; Winton, 1990). Yet in planning instructional programs, until fairly recently, it was assumed that transfer of learning would somehow just happen. Instructors paid little attention to planning systematically for integration of content in the workplace. It primarily was left to participants to apply what they had learned as they saw fit (Caffarella, 1994). It was the "train-and-hope" approach illustrated in Janet's story.

There are at least three primary reasons why planning for learning transfer is receiving increased emphasis. First, in staff development efforts, participants, their administrators, and even members of the community-at-large are demanding results-oriented outcomes from instructors. The results these individuals usually desire is transfer of knowledge, skills, or attitudes from the training context to the workplace. Planning for transfer of learning may ensure that inservice training efforts do not continue to be characterized as "the slum of American education" and "a waste of time and money" (Wood & Thompson, 1980, p. 374). Second, instructors recognize that installing complex, innovative service delivery models requires more than the train-and-hope approach described in Janet's story. This approach leaves the transfer of learning to chance. Early interventionists need systematic assistance to transfer newly acquired knowledge, skills, or attitudes about team processes, family-centered service models, routines-based intervention, and integrated therapy (Winton, 1990). Finally, there is consensus that instructional efforts should address how knowledge, skills, or attitudes developed in training mesh with the realities of the workplace, including not only individuals but also administrators, children, family members, and organizational policies and procedures. For inservice participants, the full cooperation and support of administrators and organizational policies and procedures that support transfer are critical features of staff development programs (Ingvarson & Mackenzie, 1988). For preservice participants, in preparing for some future role, an awareness of how these programmatic elements serve as supports is critical.

Enabling people to make changes—changes in themselves, in their practices, in the children and families they serve, in their organizations, and even in their communities—is what learning transfer is all about. Many reasons are offered to explain why participants do or do not apply what they have learned. Examples include whether participants considered the training relevant and practical, whether the instructor was effective, the presence or absence of demonstration and practice activities during training, the opportunity to receive supportive and corrective feedback on site during or following the seminar, and the support of colleagues and administrators following instruction (Wolfe, 1990). Caffarella (1994) organized factors affecting learning transfer into six categories: 1) program participants, 2) program design and execution, 3) program content, 4) changes required to apply learning, 5) organizational context, and 6) community/societal forces. These factors can be barriers or enhancers to the learning transfer process. Examples of specific barriers and enhancers associated with each of these factors appear in Table 7.1. Although developed from the perspective of inservice training, similar barriers and enhancers will be present for the new graduate of a preservice program as well.

Examination of the factors and associated examples reveals that learning transfer is a complex issue. Complexity increases when training and development aims are complex, large numbers of people are targeted for instruction, great magnitudes of change are desired, and the developer and participants have limited control over organizational and community forces (Caffarella, 1994). Regardless of complexity, however, the factors listed in Table 7.1 reinforce the point that a single approach to addressing transfer of learning is not likely to be effective. Characteristics of the participants, the instructional program, the organizational context, and the community all interact to facilitate or impede transfer.

One of the most widely cited sources highlighting the importance of follow-up support is a report published by the Rand Corporation, which is an examination of federally funded staff development programs designed to spread innovations in the public schools. Milbrey and McLaughlin (1978), the authors of this report, found that programs making a lasting difference emphasized concrete, teacher-specified, extended training. The combination of classroom assistance by resource personnel and follow-up meetings had positive effects on the percentage of staff development goals achieved, students' performance, and implementation and continued use of the innovation by teachers. These authors also found that quality, not quantity, of follow-up resource assistance was critical for success. Good consultants, whether local or outside resources, provided concrete, practical advice to teachers. The consultants assisted teachers in learning to solve problems for themselves, rather than solving problems for them.

Other authors have similarly endorsed on-site support from administrators and colleagues following instruction as an important component of staff development efforts. Sparks (1983) cited the importance of discussion and peer observation as follow-up activities. She noted that discussion is useful as a problem-solving tool after teachers have had an opportunity to try new strategies. Hinson, Caldwell, and Landrum (1989) recommended the formation of support teams (teams of workshop participants) to enhance follow-up efforts. Glatthorn (1987) identified four ways small teams of teachers could work together for cooperative professional development: 1) professional dialogue, 2) curriculum development, 3) peer supervision, and 4) peer coaching.

Professionals working with young children with and without disabilities also perceive follow-up support to be an important component of staff development. Sexton, Snyder, Wolfe, Lobman, and Akers (1996) and Wolfe (1990) asked 241 early intervention and 122 early childhood inservice participants, respectively, to rank 22 training and follow-up strategies according to the amount of change each fostered on the job. For each group of respondents, follow-up job assistance (defined as on-the-job help and feedback on current activities related to an inservice topic) ranked second only to observing actual practice. These respondents ranked follow-up meetings (sessions following the inservice to discuss

TABLE 7.1.   Factors associated with learning transfer

Barriers	Enhancers
Program participants	

Barriers	Enhancers
Do not have a voice in the planning process	Assist with planning via needs assessment
Do not possess necessary prerequisite knowledge or experience	Have useful prior knowledge and experiences that can be linked to new learning
Do not believe they will be successful in making changes	Have had prior success in making changes
Do not have time to incorporate new practices	Are risk takers
Are not persistent	Realize that change takes time and effort and work to carve out time to try new things
Are not self-confident in their teaching abilities	Are able to drive through initial trials when performance is awkward and effect minimal
Are not motivated to change	Have a positive self-concept about teaching skills, abilities, and impact
Have interfering life issues (e.g., financial worries, divorce)	View the changes as relevant and practical
	See benefits in the change

Program design and execution	
Lacks emphasis on application in terms of instructional methods	Incorporates application strategies such as demonstration, practice with feedback, group discussion, and back-home planning
Includes no follow-up strategies	Recognizes that when transfer of learning is the desired result, follow-up strategies such as coaching, teaching others, assignments, peer support groups, refresher courses, or administrative support are likely to enhance outcomes
Does not emphasize problem solving	
Is not delivered by an effective instructor	
Is not enjoyable for participants	
Is a "one-shot" activity	Includes opportunities for problem identification and solving
Does not include resources to support change	Is delivered by an instructor who is well prepared, knowledgeable, and enthusiastic and who uses a variety of active learning techniques
	Is part of a multiphase program
	Includes human and written resources to enhance and support the change process
	Incorporates practices to encourage reflection and critical thinking, such as keeping a journal, using case methods, role-playing, and so forth

(continued)

TABLE 7.1. *(continued)*

Barriers	Enhancers
Program content	

Barriers	Enhancers
Is not based on participant needs	Is based on the assessed needs of participants
Does not consider learners' experiences as a point of departure	Builds on previous knowledge and experience of participants and recognizes that sometimes new learning requires unlearning
Does not encourage reflective thinking about experiences, values, assumptions	
Is not practical/readily applicable	Is driven by clear, specific goals and shaped by evaluation data
Has unclear goals	Content is up to date and supported by research
Is not driven by evaluation data based on application of practices	
	Is relevant and practical and includes ideas to implement immediately and opportunity to develop back-home plans

Changes required to apply learning

Barriers	Enhancers
Do not give learners an opportunity to grow	Are challenging but realistic and possible
Changes expected are unrealistic	Given time, are an extension or modification of current practice and are approached incrementally
Are too disruptive to existing routines and practices	
Are not supported in the program	Are supported by norms of collegiality and experimentation

Organizational context

Barriers	Enhancers
Does not have an ongoing problem-solving and improvement process	Has an atmosphere of equity in problem solving and program improvement
Staff members do not have a good working relationship	Staff members work well together and provide technical help and support to one another
Agency administrators do not support change or are unaware of the changes suggested	Administrators understand, support, and encourage changes
Administrators do not provide time or follow-up support	Administrators provide time and resources to support change
Organization does not provide incentives to change	Organization provides recognition, affiliation opportunities, support for making changes, and opportunities for leadership

Community/societal forces

Barriers	Enhancers
Includes key leaders who are hostile to proposed change	Key leaders support change
Does not offer policies or financial resources to support change	Policies and financial resources direct and/or support change
Societal norms or values impede change	Receptive political climate

Adapted from Caffarella (1994).

progress and problems related to content) sixth and ninth, respectively, with mean scores of 2.82 and 2.78 on a 4.0 Likert-type scale. The perspectives of early intervention personnel support the incorporation of on-site follow-up from administrators or peers into staff development efforts. In the next section, several follow-up strategies are described in more detail.

Despite fairly widespread agreement about the importance of follow-up in staff development, especially when the goals of instruction include application and problem solving on the job, Wood and Thompson (1980) noted that the lack of follow-up in the job setting after instruction takes place is almost universal. Fullan (1982) stated: "The absence of follow-up after workshops is without doubt the greatest single problem in contemporary professional development" (p. 287). Thompson and Cooley (1986) offered data to support these assertions. They conducted a descriptive study to gather data about the perceived importance and the actual practices of ongoing staff development programs in local school districts. The authors received responses to a mail survey from representatives of 267 school districts throughout the United States. Of the respondents, 90% believed that follow-up sessions after instruction were important, but only 33% reported that sessions typically were scheduled.

FOLLOW-UP STRATEGIES

Follow-up strategies have been offered as one way to influence transfer of learning. These strategies, part of program design and execution, are defined as transfer strategies employed after the educational program is completed. Examples are back-home plans, individualized learning contracts, support groups, coaching, assignments, and telephone calls. Follow-up strategies are receiving increased attention in the staff development literature as powerful methods for enhancing learning transfer (e.g., Duttweiler, 1989; Hinson et al., 1989).

Although follow-up strategies are believed to be important for transfer of learning, there is a notable absence of empirical research to support many of these methods. The two exceptions are support groups and coaching. There is a significant amount of literature that documents the efficacy of these two approaches (e.g., Ingvarson & Mackenzie, 1988; Johnson & Johnson, 1987; Joyce & Showers, 1983; McLaughlin & Marsh, 1978; Miller, Harris, & Watanabe, 1991; Pasch & Harberts, 1992; Phillips & Glickman, 1991; Showers, 1985; Showers et al., 1987; Sparks, 1983, 1986).

Peer Support Groups

Peer support groups provide opportunities to extend learning beyond the instructional program. The purposes of the support group are to help participants work through the various stages of implementation, to develop collegiality, to provide assistance with problems, to develop common language and understandings, and to learn from members' experiences (Killion & Kaylor, 1991). Ongoing support from colleagues maintains the excitement and momentum of the new learning long after the training ends.

A collegial or peer support group is a group of colleagues that meets periodically following a seminar to help and support each other in making desired changes. Peer support groups should be small (5–12 members) and should be safe places where 1) members volunteer to be, 2) topics for discussion are generated by group members, 3) the group works together to establish norms for behavior within the support group meeting (e.g., confidentiality, equal participation time, honest feedback), and 4) the primary goal of improving each other's competence in specific teaching strategies or practices is never lost (Killion & Kaylor, 1991).

Peer support groups succeed when they are carefully structured to provide support and encouragement, to produce concrete products (e.g., lesson plans or materials) that members can actually use, and/or to provide opportunities for problem solving and practice (Johnson & Johnson, 1994; Parry, 1990). The structure must clearly point members toward increasing each other's expertise. Participants must ensure that considerable face-to-face discussion and assistance takes place, hold each other accountable to implement their plans between meetings, learn and use interpersonal small-group skills required to make meetings productive, and periodically initiate a discussion of how effective the group is in carrying out its mission (Johnson & Johnson, 1994).

According to Johnson and Johnson (1994), there are four key activities of a peer support group:

1. Discussion concerning the topic being implemented: This may include introduction of new material or review of previously covered information. For example, if members of the peer support group have attended a workshop on integrated therapy, there may be review of a skill, such as embedding goals, or a new strategy might be introduced, such as conducting structured play sessions.
2. Sharing of successes related to instructional content: For example, a therapist who left a seminar with the goal of using language facilitation strategies in the classroom with two target children during choice time might share what he or she did, how well it worked, and even how the children reacted.
3. Problem solving specific issues and concerns related to instructional content: For example, problem posers clearly delineate the instruction-related problem they have encountered and what they have already done to try and solve it. Group members then brainstorm potential solutions, which are recorded. The problem poser then selects a solution to try from the options given. Figure 7.1 illustrates a form that can be helpful in this problem-solving process.
4. Coplanning new goals and strategies for future implementation: This may include activities such as revising back-home plans, jointly writing lesson plans, or preparing materials that incorporate suggested strategies. For example, group members might prepare lessons for structured play sessions that facilitate specific language skills.

Peer support groups typically meet for 1–1½ hours on a regular basis. The length of the meetings will depend on the size of the group and familiarity of members with one another. The agenda of each meeting should be negotiated so that members are satisfied with the time set for each task. Leadership of peer support groups may be fixed or fluid. The more the group takes over its own leadership responsibilities, the more individually accountable members will be. Groups may be organized following an instructional event or series of events. It is important that all group members have attended the same workshop to have a similar knowledge base. It is also essential that group members prepare back-home plans following instruction as a point of departure for peer support group activities. Figure 7.2 illustrates a sample back-home plan form.

Coaching

Coaching involves helping participants implement newly acquired skills, strategies, or models on the job. It has four major functions: 1) provide companionship, 2) provide technical feedback, 3) analyze application, and 4) adapt the results to students (Showers, 1985). Coaching can be guided by experts or fellow learners in pairs or teams. Peer coaching involves companion functions of peer observations and small teacher support groups. For instance, teachers might observe each other's classrooms, receive feedback

Date	Description of problem	Potential solutions	Decisions	Individual responsibilities and time lines

Figure 7.1. An example of a form that may be used to record peer support group problem solving. (Adapted from Portland State University [1982].)

Instructions: In the spaces provided, develop a plan of action for yourself that details what you intend to do as a result of this workshop. Write goals that are clear, specific, and action oriented. Next, think of the steps involved in accomplishing these goals. Then, think of people and resources that might help you in reaching these goals. Finally, decide on a time line for accomplishing your goals.

Goal I want to achieve: _____

Date by which I want to achieve this goal: _____

Steps to take	Resources and people who could help me accomplish this step
1. _____	_____
2. _____	_____
3. _____	_____
4. _____	_____
5. _____	_____

Goal I want to achieve: _____

Date by which I want to achieve this goal: _____

Steps to take	Resources and people who could help me accomplish this step
1. _____	_____
2. _____	_____
3. _____	_____
4. _____	_____
5. _____	_____

Figure 7.2. A sample of a back-home plan form. (From Winton, P.J., & Catlett, C. [1996, June]. *My plan for back home.* Unpublished handout, Southeastern Institute for Faculty Training Outreach [SIFT-OUT] Faculty institute. Flat Rock, NC: Authors; originally adapted from Group Child Care Consulting Services, School of Social Work, University of North Carolina [1982].)

181

about their teaching, implement improved or new techniques, and receive ongoing support from members of their group. Teacher support groups typically consist of three to five individuals who meet regularly to solve problems and provide professional stimulation. Ackland (1991) listed three characteristics common to all coaching programs: 1) non-evaluative, 2) based on the observation of classroom teaching followed by constructive feedback, and 3) aimed to improve instructional techniques.

Empirical research in teacher education supports the value of coaching as a follow-up strategy. Showers (1985) reported that coaching provided the necessary follow-up for learning new skills. Moreover, teachers who were coached by peers transferred learning at a greater rate than uncoached teachers (Showers, 1984). Miller et al. (1991) found that two coaching sessions in a 5-week period were effective for improving teacher performance, and use of the newly acquired skills was demonstrated 3 months later. Ackland (1991) cited 29 studies that demonstrated the effectiveness of two types of coaching: coaching by experts and reciprocal coaching.

Duttweiler (1989) concluded that, regardless of type, successful coaching programs were characterized by several elements. First, the process was removed from summative teacher evaluation. Second, participation was voluntary. Third, there was structure in the process usually involving goal setting, observation, and a format for sharing information. Finally, the school climate was conducive to collegiality and instructional improvement (see also Chapter 8). Effective models for peer-coaching continue to evolve (see Joyce & Showers, 1995, for more information).

Other Follow-Up Strategies

Numerous follow-up strategies beyond peer support groups and coaching have been suggested in the literature and used in practice (e.g., Killion & Kaylor, 1991; Parry, 1990). Although many of these approaches have not been examined empirically, it is useful to know what these strategies are and to consider their potential advantages and disadvantages. Each of these strategies addresses application of skills, whether serving as a reminder or providing more comprehensive assistance. Table 7.2 illustrates additional follow-up strategies and posits several advantages and disadvantages for each. The list is not exhaustive; however, it illustrates possible approaches that early intervention personnel instructors might include in the design, implementation, and evaluation of teacher development activities.

In inservice settings, follow-up strategies have a greater chance of success in facilitating transfer of learning when other personal, instructional, and organizational factors (see Table 7.1) are part of the staff development plan. Guskey (1986) concluded that continued support and follow-up after initial instruction is critical to success. He maintained that support and follow-up will be effective only when they are implemented in a supportive context and where there are ongoing opportunities for participants to share ideas in an atmosphere of collegiality.

CHALLENGES ASSOCIATED WITH FOLLOW-UP

Three of the most commonly cited challenges associated with implementing follow-up are time, monetary expense, and disruption (Wenz & Adams, 1991). Participants in peer coaching programs, for example, need to have time available for peer observation and support group meetings. Follow-up is expensive. Wenz and Adams noted that many inservice developers spend hours figuring out how to provide follow-up without breaking their budgets. Finally, follow-up can be disruptive. Some participants may not want to

TABLE 7.2.   Follow-up strategies

Strategy	Description	Advantages/ideas	Disadvantages
Back-home plans	An action plan that spells out one to three goals with action steps to be accomplished following instruction; can be derived from an ongoing "to do" list that is part of instruction (see Figure 7.2)	Can be shared with supervisors or peers during or following instruction to gain support for changes	Typically completed at the conclusion of training when participants are eager to leave
		Offers an opportunity to reflect on content and determine where to begin implementation	Participants have reported in two studies that back-home plans only moderately effective in promoting changes
		Can be combined with a problem-solving process in training that identifies potential barriers to goal attainment and suggests possible solutions	
		Quick and easy	
		Can be used in evaluation; can be self-duplicating paper for multiple copies and used in follow-up telephone calls to discuss progress	
Mentors	An experienced peer or trusted counselor who provides feedback and support on an ongoing basis	Connects mentees to resources	Is time consuming and labor intensive
		Develops a support base for mentees	Is constrained by attitudes and skills of mentors
		Mentors polish skills and reflect on their own practices	Can create dependence
		Is individualized	Must be supported by the school or agency

(continued)

TABLE 7.2. (continued)

Strategy	Description	Advantages/Ideas	Disadvantages
Support groups	Small groups of teachers meet on an ongoing basis to discuss progress, solve problems, analyze and discuss cases, and extend learning	Best if voluntary	Can become a gripe session if not focused and partially structured
		Ongoing support, feedback, and discussion can maintain enthusiasm and momentum and help push through first difficult stages of implementation	Needs support of administration
			Effectiveness data are limited but indicate positive results
		May be used to target and pursue new learning, conduct action research, develop materials or curriculum	Relies on team participation/instruction
		Develops collegiality and independence from instructor	Depends on collegiality and trust in group members
		Needs to balance structure and open-endedness	
		Inexpensive and site based; places responsibility for implementation on learner	
		Can be used in evaluation	
Coaching	Practitioners observed in the classroom and given feedback by "experts" or peers on an ongoing basis	Assessment should be collaborative and objective	Assessment that may become evaluative
		Targets for observation should be selected by person being observed	Time consuming and labor intensive
		Research supports effectiveness	Needs support of administration
		Develops collegiality and partnerships in growth	Can create "hard feelings" when done poorly
		Can be implemented in small groups	
		Assessment should be reciprocal	
		Is individualized	
		Encourages reciprocal reflection	

	Description	Advantages	Disadvantages
Assignments	Training-related tasks to do back home	Works best when paired with feedback and credit Participants need to have choices and may be encouraged to develop their own assignments Needs to be related to practice If carefully chosen and implemented, may encourage transfer to the workplace May be used in evaluation	"School-like" and not perceived as effective by inservice participants in two studies Does not promote collegiality and support May be "busy work" and irrelevant Motivation may be a problem
Job aids	Planning sheets, forms, flowcharts, checklists, "how-to" or "reminder" posters, and so forth, that can be used in the workplace to reinforce content/practices	Cost and time efficient Provide a simple reinforcement of training content/practices Easy to use Can be commercially available instruments or can be generated by the instructor and/or participants	Limited scope—few subjects lend themselves to such a simple "how-to" approach No effectiveness data available
Handouts	Blank copies of handouts for further use; ongong "ideas to try" sheets to be used in back-home planning	Empty handouts can be used by participants to train others Simple to implement Cost and time efficient Participants claimed handouts were effective for learning transfer in two studies	Impersonal Noninteractive Reinforces knowledge but not practice or skill

(continued)

TABLE 7.2. *(continued)*

Strategy	Description	Advantages/Ideas	Disadvantages
Refresher sessions	Participants reconvene with the instructor to review and extend their understandings and practices	Promotes collegiality and recognizes learning as an ongoing process Can be used to clear up misunderstandings and as a vehicle for problem solving May be used in evaluations	May be costly and difficult to implement when participants and/or instructor are geographically distant May encourage dependence on instructor No effectiveness data available
Follow-up letters/ packets of information	A letter and/or follow-up materials (e.g., related articles, resources) sent by instructor after the session(s)	Can serve as a reminder and extension of training content Can be a vehicle for distributing "personal requests" that arise in the workshop Cost and time efficient May be individualized to individual participants and tied to back-home plans	Impersonal Noninteractive "One-shot" Reinforces knowledge but not necessarily practice or skills
Follow-up telephone call	A telephone contact after the training from the instructor or fellow participant to discuss progress and problems	Can be used in evaluation if conducted by instructor Simple to implement Provides a small measure of accountability and support Individualized and personal Deemed moderately effective by inservice participants in two studies	May involve considerable time and cost expenditure if conducted by instructor "One-shot" Only slightly interactive

186

interact with peers because they believe the natural flow of events in an intervention context may be interrupted by having another person in the setting.

There are several other challenges in implementing follow-up that have been raised in the literature. These include defining the focus of follow-up, scheduling the timing of follow-up, maintaining follow-up, and determining who is involved in planning follow-up.

Defining the Focus of Follow-Up

Follow-up activities usually focus on the individual. Staff developers recognize, however, that follow-up activities often need to be implemented at team, organizational, or community levels for successful learning transfer to occur. For example, follow-up activities focused only on Janet may not be sufficient to support learning transfer. Janet's team members may need follow-up to ensure they understand the principles and practices associated with routines-based intervention and integrated therapy. Her administrator might be asked to review existing operating policies and procedures to determine if barriers exist related to the provision of integrated therapy services.

Scheduling the Timing of Follow-Up

Transfer of learning strategies can be used before, during, or after an instructional event occurs. A challenge for developers is to determine when follow-up activities should begin. Although implemented after the workshop, should planning for follow-up begin earlier? How much time should elapse, if any, between the workshop and the implementation of follow-up activities? Parry (1990) recommended that instructors and administrators share responsibility for a seamless maintenance system, one that will support and reinforce learners as they attempt to apply at work what they learned in the workshop. This means planning for learning transfer and follow-up should begin early, as part of the needs assessment process. As needs for professional development are identified, early intervention instructors should ask, "What supports will participants need on the job to apply instructional content?" For inservice participants, the personnel development plan should include specification of how and when these supports will be put in place. Some follow-up activities, such as telephone calls, may occur several weeks after the seminar. Other transfer of learning or follow-up supports could begin immediately after training (e.g., support groups, administrative endorsement).

Maintaining Follow-Up

Who should be responsible for maintaining follow-up? At the inservice level, instructors, administrators, and participants initially may share, equally or unequally, the responsibility for follow-up. Over time, however, follow-up should become the responsibility of agency personnel, including administrators and participants. This approach focuses attention on the importance of helping administrators and participants identify and use existing resources so that the formal support offered by instructors becomes less important and not always a necessary condition for ongoing staff development (Winton, 1990).

Determining Who Is Involved in Planning Follow-Up

In addition to the educator, who else should be involved in planning follow-up? Broad and Newstrom (1992) suggested that key players should be involved in planning. They characterized key players as the people or groups that need to be involved to have the transfer of learning actually happen. Key players in early intervention could include the participants, their colleagues, administrators, and family members. Havelock and Havelock (1973) referred to these individuals as organizational families and noted that they have a direct effect on one another in the workplace. Therefore, their involvement in planning for follow-up may be critical for learning transfer to occur at both the preservice and the inservice levels.

CONCLUSION

Planning for transfer and implementing follow-up after instruction is expensive, time consuming, and challenging. The train-and-hope approach, however, does not appear to be a viable alternative. Instructional developers in early intervention can no longer ignore the critical role that follow-up plays in transfer. If the desired outcome of staff development is on-the-job application of knowledge, attitudes, or skills, then follow-up and other transfer strategies must be used. Early intervention personnel instructors who ignore follow-up in application circumstances are likely to find their staff development efforts characterized as irrelevant and ineffective, a waste of time and money (Wood & Thompson, 1980).

This chapter has presented concrete strategies for follow-up. However, none of these strategies should be used without consideration of the goals for staff development, the larger contexts in which instruction and implementation are to occur, and data collected in the other two parts of the instructional triad—needs assessment and evaluation.

Personnel development comes in a variety of forms in early intervention. In the inservice context, it can be an awareness-level workshop on the early intervention system, a comprehensive agencywide initiative to install an innovative practice, or a community-based examination of inclusive practices. In the preservice context it can be a comprehensive course on assessment methods, fieldwork experiences with a team of early interventionists, or a personal learning project that examines transition practices in the community. Only rarely are personnel development goals meaningfully accomplished through brief, episodic workshops or classes. In both contexts, teaching should be an ongoing process, where people interact with one another in particular contexts to implement change for the benefit of themselves, their organization, and the consumers of their services.

An important first step is to ask a simple question: "What is the goal for the instructional program?" If transfer of learning is a goal, then follow-up plans must be developed and implemented. At the inservice level, these plans will apply to the existing work situation, whereas at the preservice level, projects, papers, observations, and other class activities or assignments should be made as relevant as possible to potential work contexts. Organizational supports and resources should be present to support learning transfer. Evaluation should document how transfer occurred and what impact it had on the learner and, if possible, on the organization and the consumers of services. Needs assessment, follow-up, and evaluation activities should be matched to the goals of the effort.

For too long, the train-and-hope mentality has guided staff development in early intervention. Most training and development goals cannot be addressed through this approach. Isolated and cursory needs assessments, limited follow-up, satisfaction measures, and frequency counts of how many people received instruction should no longer dominate the early intervention personnel development landscape. Personnel instructors in early intervention should use the growing body of empirical research on staff development and individual and organizational change as well as principles of adult learning to guide their efforts. Economic and knowledge barriers exist, but how successfully these barriers are overcome will determine the health of early intervention personnel development in the 21st century (cf. Bricker, 1988).

REFERENCES

Ackland, R. (1991). A review of the peer coaching literature. *Journal of Staff Development, 12*(1), 22–27.

Bricker, D. (1988). Commentary: The future of early childhood/special education. *Journal of the Division for Early Childhood, 12,* 276–278.

Broad, M.L., & Newstrom, J.W. (1992). *Transfer of training: Action-packed strategies to ensure high payoffs from training investments.* Reading, MA: Addison-Wesley.

Caffarella, R.S. (1994). *Planning programs for adult learners: A practical guide for educators, trainers, and staff developers.* San Francisco: Jossey-Bass.

Duttweiler, P.C. (1989). Components of an effective professional development program. *Journal of Staff Development, 10*(2), 2–7.

Fullan, M. (1982). *The meaning of educational change.* New York: Teachers College Press.

Glatthorn, A.A. (1987). Cooperative professional development: Peer-centered options for teacher growth. *Educational Leadership, 45*(8), 31–35.

Group Child Care Consulting Services, School of Social Work, University of North Carolina. (1982). *Special needs adoption curriculum.* Chapel Hill, NC: Author.

Guskey, T.R. (1986). Staff development and the process of teacher change. *Educational Researcher, 15*(5), 5–11.

Harris, B.M. (1980). *Improving staff performance through inservice education.* Needham, MA: Allyn & Bacon.

Havelock, R.G., & Havelock, M.C. (1973). *Training for change agents.* Ann Arbor: University of Michigan.

Hinson, S., Caldwell, M.S., & Landrum, M. (1989). Characteristics of effective staff development programs. *Journal of Staff Development, 10*(2), 48–52.

Ingvarson, L., & Mackenzie, D. (1988). Factors affecting the impact of inservice courses for teachers: Implications for policy. *Teaching and Teacher Education, 4,* 139–155.

Johnson, D., & Johnson, R. (1987). Research shows the benefits of adult cooperation. *Educational Leadership, 45*(3), 27–30.

Johnson, D., & Johnson, R. (1994). *Joining together* (5th ed.). Needham, MA: Allyn & Bacon.

Joyce, B.R., & Showers, B. (1983). *Power in staff development through research on training.* Alexandria, VA: Association for Supervision and Curriculum Development.

Joyce, B.R., & Showers, B. (1995). *Student achievement through staff development* (2nd ed.). White Plains, NY: Longman.

Killion, J.P., & Kaylor, B. (1991). Follow-up: The key to training for transfer. *Journal of Staff Development, 12*(1), 64–67.

Knox, A.B. (1986). *Helping adults learn: A guide to planning, implementing, and conducting programs.* San Francisco: Jossey-Bass.

McLaughlin, M., & Marsh, D. (1978). Staff development and school change. *Teachers College Record, 80*(1), 69–94.

Milbrey, P.B., & McLaughlin, M. (1978). *Federal programs supporting educational change VIII: Implementing and sustaining innovations.* Santa Monica, CA: Rand Corporation.

Miller, S., Harris, C., & Watanabe, C. (1991). Professional coaching: A method for increasing effective and decreasing ineffective teacher behaviors. *Teacher Education and Special Education, 14*(3), 183–191.

Parry, S. (1990, May). Ideas for improving transfer of training. *Adult Learning,* 19–23.

Pasch, M., & Harberts, J.C. (1992). Does coaching enhance instructional thought? *Journal of Staff Development, 13*(3), 38–44.

Phillips, M.D., & Glickman, C.D. (1991). Peer coaching: Developmental approach to enhancing teacher thinking. *Journal of Staff Development, 12*(2), 20–25.

Portland State University. (1982). *Education coordinator's handbook.* Portland, OR: Author.

Sexton, D., Snyder, P., Wolfe, B., Lobman, M., & Akers, P. (1996). Early intervention inservice training strategies: Perceptions and suggestions from the field. *Exceptional Children, 62*(6), 485–495.

Showers, B. (1984). *Peer coaching: A strategy for facilitating transfer of training.* Report to the U.S. Department of Education. Eugene: University of Oregon, Center for Educational Policy and Management. (ERIC Document Reproduction Service No. ED 271 849)

Showers, B. (1985). Teachers coaching teachers. *Educational Leadership, 42*(7), 43–48.

Showers, B., Joyce, B., & Bennett, B. (1987). Synthesis of research on staff development: A framework for future study and a state-of-the-art analysis. *Educational Leadership, 45*(3), 77–87.

Sparks, G. (1983). Synthesis of research on staff development for effective teaching. *Educational Leadership, 40,* 65–72.

Sparks, G.M. (1986). The effectiveness of alternative training activities in changing teacher practices. *American Educational Research Journal, 23,* 217–225.

Thompson, J., & Cooley, V. (1986). A national study of outstanding staff development programs. *Educational Horizons, 64,* 94–98.

Wenz, A., & Adams, C.D. (1991). Life after training: A look at follow-up. *Journal of Staff Development, 12*(1), 60–62.

Winton, P.J. (1990). A systemic approach for planning inservice training related to Public Law 99-457. *Infants and Young Children, 3*(1), 51–60.

Winton, P.J., & Catlett, C. (1996, June). *My plan for back home.* Unpublished handout, Southeastern Institute for Faculty Training Outreach (SIFT-OUT) Faculty Institute. Flat Rock, NC: Authors.

Wolfe, B. (1990). *Effective practices in inservice education: An exploratory study of the perceptions of Head Start participants.* Unpublished doctoral dissertation, University of Wisconsin–Madison.

Wood, F.H., McQuarrie, F.O., & Thompson, S.R. (1982). Practitioners and professors agree on effective staff development practices. *Educational Leadership, 40*(1), 28–31.

Wood, F.H., & Thompson, S.R. (1980). Guidelines for better staff development. *Educational Leadership, 37*(5), 374–378.

8

SUPERVISION, MENTORING, AND COACHING

Methods for Supporting Personnel Development

Kathleen K. Gallacher

The need for supervision, mentoring, and coaching is driven by several issues related to personnel development in early intervention. First, because of the demand for early intervention personnel in many states (Burke, McLaughlin, & Valdiviesco, 1988; Meisels, Harbin, Modigliani, & Olson, 1988; U.S. Department of Education, 1992; Yoder, Coleman, & Gallagher, 1990), professionals are often faced with the challenge of acquiring or refining the competencies needed to deliver early intervention services. Key features of IDEA, specifically of Part H, directly influence the specific competencies that professionals must possess. Many of these competencies (e.g., building relationships, collaboration, teamwork, service coordination) are required across a range of early intervention roles, settings, and tasks (Kontos & File, 1992).

Second, the delivery of early intervention services is a complex task requiring problem solving, divergent thinking, creativity, and critical thinking. Practitioners are required to make informed judgments and perform complicated tasks in complex environments (Howey, 1988). Fenichel and Eggbeer (1990) argued that early intervention professionals are competent when they possess a combination of knowledge, skills, and experience that enables them to analyze a situation, consider alternative approaches, select and skillfully use the best intervention techniques, evaluate the outcome, and articulate their rationale. Other fundamental competencies required to deliver early intervention services include communication, advocacy, problem solving (Able-Boone, Sandall, & Loughry, 1989; McCollum & McCartan, 1988; Thurman et al., 1992), reflection (Brown, Hanft, & Browne, 1993; Fenichel, 1991; McCollum & McCartan, 1988), and self-direction (Division for Early Childhood Task Force on Recommended Practices, 1993; McCollum & McCartan, 1988; Reid & Bross, 1993; Rowan, Thorp, & McCollum, 1990).

Third, personnel demands are likely to continue (Bogenschild, Lauritzen, & Metzke, 1988; Howey & Zimpher, 1987; Kontos & Dunn, 1989; Lawrenson & McKinnon, 1982; Mark & Anderson, 1985; Palsha, Bailey, Vandiviere, & Munn, 1990; Schlechty & Vance, 1981; Seyforth & Bost, 1986). In early intervention, low salaries, lack of opportunity for career advancement, and lack of benefits contribute to the attrition rates (Kontos & File, 1992; Palsha et al., 1990). In education, the high attrition rates are also linked to difficult work assignments, unclear expectations, inadequate resources, isolation, role conflicts, and "reality shock" (Gordon, 1991; Morey & Murphy, 1990). The factors that influence attrition rates of new teachers also may affect attrition in early intervention.

Finally, the field continues to evolve in terms of those techniques, processes, and strategies that can be considered recommended practice. Early intervention practitioners must consider which attitudes, behaviors, and skills facilitate learning within new models of service delivery. Daloz and Edelson (1992) articulated that "in today's work place what matters is not so much the skills and attributes that a person already brings to the job but rather those that they will need to learn and develop" (p. 31).

To address these personnel challenges, a variety of strategies for continued personnel development must be considered. Although personnel development typically has been provided through short-term conferences, workshops, consultations with visiting experts, or other episodic events, the effectiveness of these strategies has been questioned (Burke et al., 1988; Campbell, 1990; Guskey, 1986). Alternatively, supervision, mentoring, and coaching have been described in the literature as strategies for building or refining specific early intervention skills, providing support, and encouraging continued professional growth. For example, Fenichel and Eggbeer (1993) suggested that supervision and mentoring relationships that allow individuals to reflect on all aspects of work with young children with disabilities, their families, and colleagues are an essential element of becoming competent infant and family practitioners.

This chapter summarizes the extensive information available on supervision, mentoring, and coaching. It includes a description of each of these processes, practical information and strategies for administrators and professionals who want to explore these supports for staff development, and an overview of the challenges these approaches present for individuals and organizations. Finally, this chapter reviews features of particular mentoring and coaching models.

Supervision, mentoring, and individualized personnel development strategies such as coaching are processes that share foundations and whose purposes, elements, and competencies overlap. The lines between these processes are often blurred. Throughout this chapter, the following distinctions are used. All three support personnel development; however, supervision is broader in scope, incorporates administrative functions, and may entail performance evaluation. Mentoring often is an informal process, narrower in scope than supervision, and does not include the evaluative function. Although it may be one strategy by which the organization accomplishes professional development and promotes assimilation of new practitioners, a supervisor typically is not an individual's mentor. Both a supervisor and a mentor may employ coaching to help a practitioner refine his or her technical competencies or extend the professional's knowledge base. Coaching is narrower in scope than either supervision or mentoring because its primary purpose is refining specific practices. Coaching is conceptualized in this chapter as a process that occurs between peers or colleagues and is typically more structured and systematic than mentoring. Each of these processes is discussed separately in this chapter. However, as organizations adopt more structured approaches such as facilitated mentoring, mentoring and coaching may appear similar.

SUPERVISION

In the education and organizational theory literature, supervision is the process of directing or guiding people to accomplish the goals of the organization in which they work (Daresh, 1989), the ultimate objective of supervision is offering the agency's service to the consumer in the most efficient and effective manner possible (Kadushin, 1985). Effective supervision accomplishes three broad purposes (Sergiovanni, 1991): 1) quality control in which the supervisor is responsible for monitoring employee performance; 2) personnel development in which the supervisor is responsible for helping practitioners refine their skills and elaborate both their discipline-specific knowledge and their technical competencies; and 3) promoting commitment to the field and position, which, in turn, enhances motivation. To accomplish these purposes, supervision involves defining and communicating job requirements; counseling and coaching for improved performance; providing job-related instruction; planning, organizing, and delegating work; evaluating performance; providing corrective and formative feedback; providing consequences for poor performance; and arranging the environment to support performance (Professional Development Center, 1994). For personnel development, Arredondo, Brody, Zimmerman, and Moffett (1995) added that effective supervision helps professionals construct meaning by using what they already know to learn new strategies and techniques. It establishes an environment that is conducive to learning and supports practitioners' acquisition of both skills and knowledge.

Different models of supervision can be found across disciplines, including education, social work, counseling, and psychotherapy. Some of the models of supervision relevant to early intervention settings are shown in Table 8.1. Several themes are evident across these models of supervision. First, several of the functions of supervision are similar: improving service delivery or instruction, supporting personnel development, and accomplishing administrative tasks to achieve organizational goals. Second, the leadership and interpersonal skills needed for effective supervision are evident; many models also incorporate specific technical skills and procedures needed to accomplish intended outcomes of a particular model. The leadership practices outlined in many models include recognizing and being sensitive to the needs of others, building trust, articulating a vision based on shared values, and demonstrating various methods to accomplish the vision (Sergiovanni, 1991). Other important leadership practices include building a supportive climate that empowers others, fostering collegiality, and enabling practitioners to function independently while achieving shared purposes (Sergiovanni, 1991). Interpersonal skills emphasized include listening, paraphrasing, giving descriptive feedback, reflecting, clarifying, encouraging, problem solving, managing conflict, and providing direction (Acheson & Gall, 1987; Garmston, 1989; Glickman, 1985).

Several challenges for supervisors are also outlined in the literature. Acheson and Gall (1987), Carter and Curtis (1994), and Fenichel (1992) described the fundamental concern that individuals must have instructional support and practice to execute effectively the roles and functions of supervision. In some states supervisors are now required to obtain specific instruction in supervisory models, performance evaluation, staff development, and analysis of instruction (Borders et al., 1991; Daresh, 1989). However, many supervisors were promoted to a supervisory position because of their technical skills and experience; many were clinicians who made the transition to supervisor after providing direct services. Most have not received specific instruction and coaching on how to supervise effectively (Robiner & Schofield, 1990). This may represent a challenge if early intervention programs have chosen a clinical supervision model from the social work literature (e.g., Fenichel, 1992). Unlike clinical supervision as defined in the education literature, in which the focus is on fostering self-reflection and self-growth in relation to professional skills, the more therapeutic clinical supervision model focuses on fostering self-reflection in relation to one's understanding of self and the use of self as a tool in the intervention process. Thus, this approach to clinical supervision is much less concrete in the skills required for its implementation.

TABLE 8.1.   Supervision models

Author	Model	Focus
Sergiovanni (1991)	Organizational supervision	A human resources approach that addresses the following: • Administrative and supervisory organizational style • Organizational style, climate, and systems • Approaches to organizational change
Glatthorn (1990)	Differentiated supervision	An approach that offers practitioners choices in the type of supervision they prefer: • Clinical supervision • Collegial supervision • Self-directed supervision
Glickman (1985)	Developmental supervision	An individualized approach in which the supervisor selects techniques to match the developmental stage of a professional: • Directive supervision • Collaborative supervision • Nondirective supervision
Cogan (1973); Goldhammer (1969); Krajewski (1993)	Clinical supervision	A process that offers practitioners feedback regarding their skills and practices through a cycle of several steps: • Preobservation conference • Observation of teaching • Analysis and strategy • Postobservation conference • Postconference analysis
Glatthorn (1987)	Peer supervision/ collegial supervision	Cooperative professional development in which teams of teachers serve as informal observers and consultants for each other; techniques range from those employed in clinical supervision to informal discussion and feedback

(continued)

TABLE 8.1. *(continued)*

Author	Model	Focus
Anderson (1993); Hersey and Blanchard (1988)	Contingency supervision	A situational leadership approach that matches the supportive or directive behaviors of a supervisor to the maturity level, style, and level of experience of the practitioner being supervised
Hunter (1984)	Skills-focused supervision/ scientific supervision	An approach emphasizing review of teacher–student interactions and the process of designing lessons
Costa and Garmston (1985); Garman (1986)	Cognitive-based supervision	Specific models of clinical supervision that stress refinement of a practitioner's thinking: • Costa and Garmston's model is designed to enhance teachers' perceptions, judgments, and decision making • Garman's model is designed to promote the practitioner's reflection and individual construction of knowledge
Glatthorn (1984)	Self-directed supervision	An individualized process in which the practitioner sets his or her own targets or goals, plans and implements activities, and evaluates progress with a supervisor through review of a portfolio, classroom artifacts, or videotaping
Kadushin (1985)	Social work supervision	An eclectic approach that incorporates a variety of techniques to address the administrative, supportive, and educational components of supervision
Munson (1993)	Clinical social work supervision	An interactional approach to supervision based on the styles that emerge from interaction and that incorporates personality, situational, and organizational perspectives regarding supervision

Another challenge is the frequent need for supervisors to fulfill roles involving both education and evaluation. Because the supervisor is involved in making decisions about a practitioner's performance, promotion, or retention, it is difficult to separate the evaluative role and its related function of quality control from the educational role of promoting personnel development. In supporting personnel development, establishing trust and an atmosphere of collegiality is particularly important (Arredondo et al., 1995). Supervisors must be aware of their own beliefs, be consistent in their behavior, observe and analyze patterns of behavior, consider alternative perspectives and approaches, understand their organization, and recognize that supervision is ongoing rather than periodic (Daresh, 1989).

A third challenge for supervisors is accomplishing supervision within diverse programs in diverse settings. Frequently, practitioners in early intervention operate autonomously in delivering services, and finding time for supervision is difficult. Both administrators and practitioners resist devoting resources, including time, to supervision, even though they recognize the value of regular supervision (Fenichel, 1991). In addition, supervision of and by staff from multicultural backgrounds requires establishing a safe and accepting climate for supervision (Bernard, 1994). To be effective, a supervisor in a multicultural setting must interact with supervisees with respect, support, and openness to cultural issues (Fukuyama, 1994).

Individualizing methods of supervision to match the needs of novices and experienced practitioners is another challenge. Some supervisory models may be more appropriate for practitioners with particular qualities. For example, developmental or contingency models of supervision suggest that more directive styles may be appropriate with less mature or less experienced practitioners and with individuals whose thinking is more concrete. Clinical supervision (Cogan, 1973) may be more effective when professionals are experienced, reflective, and generally competent (Daresh, 1989). Furthermore, experienced and competent practitioners may benefit from increased opportunities to direct their own learning and from having more options in the supervision they receive (Glatthorn, 1990). Selecting a model of supervision that matches the experience and needs of paraprofessionals or paraeducators is a challenge as well. Developmental or contingency models of supervision may offer flexible alternatives in addressing supervision issues with paraprofessionals and novice professionals.

Effective supervisors in early intervention also must facilitate organizational change and support staff during the change process. Continued improvement in methods of delivering services to families and young children with disabilities requires that organizations devote resources to adopting innovations and infusing them throughout the organization. Successful implementation of new processes and procedures requires commitment of time, personnel, and material resources, as well as attention to individuals' concerns regarding what the change means for them. Supervisors play a key role in providing information and instruction that will enable practitioners to implement innovations. Providing support and assistance that matches the concerns of professionals necessitates that supervisors understand the change process, models for facilitating change, and their own change facilitator style (Hall & Hord, 1987; Hord, Rutherford, Huling-Austin, & Hall, 1987; Sergiovanni, 1991). Gordon (1992) argued that, in the 1990s, the paradigm in supervision is shifting to one that empowers practitioners, integrates the functions and activities of supervision, and recognizes the diversity of practitioners (i.e., their unique levels, needs, interests, and abilities). The new paradigm supports the development of collegial networks, encourages inquiry, and compares organizational change to the growth and development of a complex organism. Some models of supervision (e.g., Glatthorn, 1990; Glickman, 1985) offer multifaceted approaches that will be useful as the paradigm for supervision evolves; however, new models of supervision also will be necessary.

MENTORING

Mentoring may be defined as a caring and supportive interpersonal relationship between an experienced, more knowledgeable practitioner (mentor) and a less experienced, less knowledgeable individual (protégé or mentee) in which the protégé receives career-related and personal benefits (Henry, Stockdale, Hall, & Deniston, 1994). Mentoring facilitates the transfer of knowledge, skills, attitudes, beliefs, and values between an experienced and a less experienced practitioner. The essence of the relationship is that the experienced practitioner takes a direct and personal interest in the education and development of the younger or less experienced individual (Krupp, 1985).

Some early intervention programs have made efforts to facilitate the development of formal mentoring relationships. In Colorado, graduate students in speech, language, and audiology training programs are matched with mentors in public school settings (S.M. Moore, personal communication, October 8, 1995). The mentor models professional practices, shares resources, and supervises the graduate student's internship. Mentors meet together in a collegial group to obtain instruction on and support for issues of mentoring and supervision. They receive honoraria, provided through federal funding of personnel preparation projects, as an incentive. This federal funding also helps support other mentoring activities.

Professionals in the Colorado Speech and Hearing Association (CSHA) also are encouraged to pursue mentoring opportunities (CSHA, n.d.). In this informal mentoring model, practitioners are matched on the basis of similar aspirations and interests. Contact between the mentor and protégé occurs face to face at specifically arranged meetings or at other events and through telephone contact, correspondence, audio- or videotape, computer networks, or fax transmission. The CSHA vice president for education and the vice president for membership coordinate the association's mentoring activities. The American Occupational Therapy Association's publication *Find a Mentor or Be One* (Robertson, 1992) provides a framework for professionals interested in becoming mentors or protégés. The mentoring subcommittee also offers additional information on mentoring principles, strategies, and challenges to members of the CSHA. Expectations for participants, roles, and procedures for developing a mentoring agreement are described in writing for prospective mentors and protégés. Another resource, *The Early Childhood Mentoring Curriculum* (Bellm, Whitebook, & Hnatiuk, 1997), has been developed by the National Center for the Early Childhood Workforce, with strategies and materials targeted to both mentors and trainers. (See Chapter 3 for an example of a higher education mentoring project in North Carolina.)

The Partnership Project in Illinois (McCollum, Yates, & Lueke, 1995) provides an opportunity for practicing early intervention professionals to obtain mentoring as one method for completing state credentialing requirements. In this program, mentors and protégés are matched based on the topic of the protégé's request. The mentor and protégé interact across approximately 8 hours by telephone and face to face at the protégé's site. Their interaction is designed to accomplish individualized learning objectives that have been specified in an instructional action plan. Benefits for the protégé include individualized instruction and technical assistance, as well as credit earned toward credentialing. Benefits for the mentor include development of a reciprocal collegial relationship and direct reimbursement.

As demonstrated by these examples, the goals of mentoring may include assimilating new practitioners into an organization; maximizing the effectiveness of the practitioner's first year; facilitating continued professional growth and development; improving professional practices and, thus, benefiting consumers of services through improved programs or products; and increasing the retention of promising new practitioners (Huling-Austin, 1989; Murray, 1991).

Many benefits for both the protégé and the mentor result from the mentoring process. The mentoring relationship offers a protégé the opportunity for support, protection, and guidance (Henry et al., 1994). Specifically, the benefits for the protégé include improved performance and productivity, development of new skills, increased likelihood of promotion and success on the job, greater likelihood that the protégé will be directed to positions in the organization that match his or her interests and skills, increased social and emotional support, and increased awareness of the organization (Gordon, 1991; Murray, 1991). Mentoring improves the protégé's discipline-specific competencies, increases knowledge, encourages risk taking, promotes leadership skills, enhances communication skills, and increases experience (Kasunic, 1993).

Mentoring also provides a variety of intrinsic rewards and benefits for mentors. These include a recognition of the value of the mentor's experience, creation of a close relationship with the protégé, a renewed interest in work resulting from the opportunity to review and reflect on his or her own professional practices, an opportunity to learn new skills, more perceived control of the work environment, and personal satisfaction from aiding a colleague (Graham, 1994; Hutto, Holden, & Haynes, 1991). Although mentors derive intrinsic benefits from the mentoring relationship, most organizations use additional strategies to retain mentors (Gordon, 1991; Murray, 1991; Newby & Heide, 1992). Typically, mentors are given time to participate in the mentoring process and are afforded ongoing learning opportunities to refine their own skills. Public recognition of the mentor's efforts and an opportunity to shape the organization's culture and practices frequently are offered. The protégé's assistance with work projects also furnishes increased resources for the mentor. Finally, many organizations provide financial rewards or incentives to mentors, such as bonuses or differential compensation, awards for innovative projects, or stipends for travel or personal development.

The mentoring relationship typically unfolds across three or four stages (Kram, 1983; Newby & Heide, 1992). The first stage is the *initiation* stage, during which the protégé recognizes the mentor as a competent individual from whom he or she would like support and assistance. Concurrently, the mentor notices the protégé as someone deserving of encouragement and special attention. As the individuals develop a rapport and establish a relationship, they consider what support and guidance the protégé desires. During the second stage, the *cultivation* stage, the protégé and mentor become better acquainted, and the mentor provides the bulk of his or her assistance to accomplish the protégé's specific career goals. As the relationship develops, the mentor provides increased social-emotional support for the protégé. During the third stage, the *separation* stage, the protégé becomes more independent and autonomous, although the mentor still offers some assistance. Separation may occur as the protégé moves to a different position or when the relationship no longer meets his or her psychosocial needs. The last stage is the *redefinition* stage, during which the relationship between the protégé and the mentor evolves into a more collegial relationship. The individuals relate to each other as peers or as friends, and the former mentor no longer influences the protégé's career directly. The mentor advances the protégé's career through various functions or activities that are summarized in Table 8.2 (Geiger-DuMond & Boyle, 1995; Kram, 1983; Wright, 1992).

The characteristics, qualities, and skills of effective mentors are consistently described in the literature (Daresh & Playko, 1991; Hutto et al., 1991; Murray, 1991; Stott & Walker, 1992; Wildman, Magliaro, Niles, & Niles, 1992). The most fundamental attribute is the willingness to serve as a mentor. However, effective mentors also are encouraging and supportive, committed to their protégé, sensitive, helpful but not authoritative, flexible, respectful, enthusiastic about the profession, diplomatic, patient, willing to share information, willing to share credit or recognition, and willing to take risks. Successful mentors generally are experienced practitioners who are knowledgeable about the organization, are effective leaders in the organization, reflect the organization's culture and values, and are

TABLE 8.2.   Mentoring functions

Function	Action
Coaching	• Teaching technical skills
	• Helping clarify performance goals and learning objectives
	• Suggesting strategies for achieving goals and objectives or meeting job performance requirements
	• Reinforcing effective on-the-job performance
Increasing exposure and visibility	• Providing opportunities for the protégé to demonstrate competencies and special talents
	• Representing the protégé's competencies and concerns to higher-level administrators
Protecting	• Minimizing the protégé's involvement in controversial situations
	• Helping the protégé avoid costly career mistakes
	• Offering warnings of various pitfalls in the organization
Sponsoring	• Nominating the protégé for promotion, specific positions, or special assignments
	• Expanding the protégé's network of professional contacts
	• Linking the protégé with educational opportunities
Role modeling	• Stimulating growth and development of the protégé
	• Demonstrating successful professional behaviors
Encouraging	• Providing acceptance, validation, confirmation, and friendship
	• Bringing together several protégés who may help each other
Advising	• Helping the protégé clarify and achieve career goals
	• Helping the protégé evaluate career options
	• Recommending strategies for career development
Explaining	• Providing the protégé with information on policies and procedures in the organization
	• Clarifying organizational goals and objectives
	• Identifying resources to help with specific problems

Adapted from Geiger-DuMond & Boyle (1995).

high performers. To accomplish desired outcomes and execute their roles, mentors employ a variety of skills, including interviewing, observing, communicating effectively (e.g., listening, paraphrasing, clarifying, reflecting, summarizing, validating), coaching, problem solving, consulting, negotiating, maintaining trust, and developing rapport. In addition, mentors adapt their support behaviors to the protégé's developmental stage, learning style, and personal (behavioral) style. Finally, mentors encourage and promote protégé independence so that the mentoring relationship can be concluded successfully (Henry et al., 1994).

The program administrator also must attend to the characteristics of potential protégés. Protégés must be willing to assume responsibility for their own growth and development (be self-directed), be receptive to feedback and ideas, recognize that professional development requires an enduring commitment, and ask questions or seek guidance to better understand professional practices and their impact. Furthermore, mentoring relationships require that protégés demonstrate many of the same characteristics, attributes, and skills that effective mentors possess, such as a willingness to take risks, flexibility, enthusiasm, effective communication skills, a systematic approach to problem solving, a positive attitude, and a collaborative style (Henry et al., 1994; Hunton et al., 1993; Hutto et al., 1991).

Components of a Mentoring Program

Although a mentoring relationship ordinarily evolves gradually, mentoring incorporates several systematic steps: 1) identifying the protégé's interests and needs, 2) developing a mentoring plan or agreement, 3) providing assistance as the mentoring plan is executed, and 4) evaluating the mentoring plan's effectiveness. Identification of the protégé's interests or wants occurs through informal discussion, self-assessment, semistructured interviews, observations, or written questionnaires (Gordon, 1991). Because each method has advantages and disadvantages, a comprehensive approach incorporates a variety of techniques. However, an organization may select a specific method(s) based on the goals of the organization's mentoring program, the degree of structure or formality the organization adopts for mentoring, and the scope of mentoring in the organization.

A clear agreement between the protégé and the mentor about the goals of the relationship is an essential foundation for a good mentoring relationship. The agreement can be delineated formally in a short, written "contract" or plan, or it may be simply outlined during an informal discussion that culminates with a joint verbal agreement. The protégé and mentor agree what support and assistance is desired, formulate realistic expectations for the relationship, and pinpoint the concrete skills and information that the protégé hopes to learn as well as the intangibles he or she would like to be exposed to or receive (Bozarjian et al., 1993). As with other planning processes, the protégé and the mentor consider what specific actions are needed to accomplish the protégé's goals, time lines for each targeted action, and the resources needed to accomplish desired goals. They also agree to maintain confidentiality and discuss the duration of the mentoring relationship, the frequency of meetings or contact by telephone, the time commitment each will invest in the relationship, and the roles of the protégé and the mentor (Murray, 1991).

Challenges to the Mentoring Process

Although mentoring and facilitated mentoring programs have gained widespread acceptance since the 1980s, some challenges have been documented (Fenichel, 1992; Graham, 1994; Murray, 1991; Smith, 1993; Stott & Walker, 1992; Wildman et al., 1992). First, finding the time necessary to accomplish mentoring activities frequently is difficult. Both mentors and protégés feel guilty about taking time from their regular positions for mentoring (Fenichel, 1992; Wildman et al., 1992). Mentors ordinarily have numerous other responsibilities and demands that create conflict with the time required for mentoring. Likewise, as new professionals, protégés often are overwhelmed by accomplishing the basic tasks of their position and believe they have little time for mentoring. In some cases protégés neither maintain regular contact nor actively pursue mentoring relationships.

Many programs deal with the challenge of time by building mentoring into work schedules (B. Quackenbush, personal communication, September 15, 1995). Others encourage telephone contact or dialogue journals as an alternative to face-to-face meetings (Killion & Todnem, 1989; McCollum et al., 1995).

Second, role confusion presents a challenge, especially if the roles of supervisor and mentor are not separate (Graham, 1994). If dual roles occur, particular attention must be directed to separating the performance appraisal functions of supervision from the support functions of mentoring.

In some programs the selection of mentors and matching of protégés and mentors have proved problematic. Systematic screening processes and clear criteria are necessary for successful selection of mentors. Matching that occurs through consideration of the needs and strengths of protégés, mentors, and the organization has been recommended (Daresh & Playko, 1991; Stott & Walker, 1992).

Third, mentors and protégés who are involved in successful mentoring relationships or programs sometimes receive negative feedback from other practitioners who have not been involved in mentoring (Hutto et al., 1991; Murray, 1991; Smith, 1993). Strategies for minimizing negative feedback include widely disseminating information about mentoring or the mentoring program, making parameters for the program and selection criteria clear, and encouraging many individuals to become involved.

Finally, many mentors are apprehensive about the mentoring role and the necessary skills. Frequently, the amount of instruction and support provided to mentors is correlated with their satisfaction with mentoring (Smith, 1993). Specific instruction and continued support help mentors refine their skills to create effective mentoring relationships and assist them in problem-solving any difficulties they encounter during mentoring.

COACHING

Coaching evolved from athletic training models, clinical supervision in education, and staff development with educators. It has been used as a method for improving instruction and teaching strategies, experimenting with new approaches and techniques, problem solving, and building collegial relationships. As described in Joyce and Showers (1983), Mello (1984), and Smith and Acheson (1991), coaching provides professionals with the following opportunities:

- To receive support and encouragement through the opportunity to review experiences, discuss feelings, describe frustrations, and check perceptions with a partner
- To fine-tune skills or strategies through technical feedback and technical assistance from a coaching partner
- To analyze practices and decision making at a conscious level
- To adapt or generalize skills or strategies by considering what is needed to facilitate particular outcomes, how to modify the skill or practice to better fit interactions with specific families or practitioners, or what results may occur from using the skill or practice in different ways
- To reflect on what they perceive or how they make decisions, which helps improve their knowledge and understanding of professional practices and activities

Through the 1980s, various models of coaching were developed: expert coaching, peer coaching, peer consultation, team coaching, technical coaching, collegial coaching, reflective coaching, cognitive coaching, and challenge coaching (Ackland, 1991; Costa &

Garmston, 1985; Fenichel, 1992; Garmston, 1987; Joyce & Showers, 1983; Mello, 1984; Smith & Acheson, 1991; Wolfe & Robbins, 1989). Coaching models vary along several dimensions: 1) whether the coaching occurs between an expert and a novice or between peers in a reciprocal relationship, 2) whether the coaching occurs between individuals or among members of a team of practitioners, and 3) whether the focus is on the performance of specific skills or on the decision making involved during intervention. Along these dimensions, the major differences among coaching models include the primary objective or purpose(s) for coaching, who defines the focus of the coaching (i.e., learner, coach, administrator), the coach's role, the degree of structure in the coaching process, and whether the coaching involves a dyad or a group. For example, *technical coaching* is intended to help teachers transfer new skills from staff development workshops to actual practice in classrooms. *Cognitive coaching,* in contrast, is designed to stimulate the teachers' thinking about the judgments they make regarding instruction and about the decisions they make in selecting specific instructional techniques. *Challenge coaching* involves teams of professionals generating solutions to persistent instructional problems through use of a systematic problem-solving approach.

Regardless of the model, coaching has several common, important characteristics: 1) it is most successful when it is voluntary, 2) it flourishes when it is separated from supervision and/or performance evaluation, 3) it is an ongoing process, 4) it is based on collaborative (collegial) relationships, and 5) it requires an atmosphere of trust and experimentation (Wolfe, 1994).

A coaching model for early intervention professionals in Montana was developed between 1991 and 1994 through Project CLASS (Cooperative Learning: Acquiring Specialized Skills), an inservice project funded by the U.S. Department of Education. Components of the project included use of cooperative learning methods to accomplish inservice training, use of coaching to promote the transfer of training and to refine early intervention skills, and development of instructional materials related to specific early intervention competencies. Learning teams were established in each of the seven regionally based early intervention agencies across the state. Initial instruction on specific early intervention topics (e.g., communication skills, conflict management, assessment, interviewing, developing outcomes and objectives) was accomplished with teams using cooperative learning techniques. Following initial instruction, peer coaching was employed to facilitate the transfer of targeted skills to interactions with families and young children with disabilities. Early interventionists on learning teams also used coaching to refine skills and practices that they had individually identified as priorities and that related to their delivery of home-based services. Throughout the project, professionals on learning teams served as coaches for other team members as well as for additional interested professionals in their organizations. Instruction on coaching was provided using a "train-the-trainer" approach; learning team facilitators were instructed to implement a six-step coaching cycle (Gallacher, 1995).

A cognitive coaching model was implemented during 1990–1995 by early intervention practitioners affiliated with the Hope Infant Family Support Program in California. Approximately 50% of the staff were instructed on cognitive coaching methods, including individuals with various roles in the program (e.g., managers, credentialed staff, paraprofessionals). Potential coaches were selected on the basis of available time, representation from different components of the program, and years of experience with the program. Following instruction, practitioners made a commitment to coach at least twice a month. A 1½-hour block of time was scheduled for observation and conferences every other week. Coaching partners usually remained together through one coaching cycle. Because staff expressed concern regarding the time that coaching takes away from families, administrators consistently encouraged professionals to try coaching and often directly prompted staff members to use coaching by emphasizing how it would be useful in addressing particular issues or problems. It was also significant that this program was implemented without external funding support.

A coaching program offers many benefits for early intervention practitioners (Garmston, 1987; Joyce & Showers, 1983; Lyman & Morehead, 1987; Mello, 1984; Munro & Elliott, 1987; Phillips & Glickman, 1991; Raney & Robbins, 1989; Robbins, 1991; Schreiber, 1990) and helps sustain their efforts to practice unfamiliar skills or apply new knowledge by offering the support, encouragement, and reassurance of another colleague. Coaching decreases isolation and facilitates collaboration through the exchange of ideas, methods, experiences, and resources among participants. The coaching process mirrors the synergistic family–professional relationships promoted in early intervention and encourages staff to adopt a self-correcting perspective, which promotes continued learning and improvement in professional practices by fostering the perspective that an individual's skills should be examined, discussed, and refined because they are tools of the early intervention profession. (See Chapter 17 for a description of another application of coaching using a family practicum model.) In addition, the coaching process empowers practitioners to direct their own continued professional development. Implementing a coaching program affects an organization because it provides an opportunity for professionals to obtain support and encourages the belief that practitioners help and care about each other. Coaching promotes the development of trust and helps build collegial relationships. Support, caring, trust, and collegiality are characteristics that contribute to an organization's sense of community and create a positive climate within which practitioners commit to helping each other achieve continued growth and development (Johnson & Johnson, 1989; Johnson, Johnson, & Holubec, 1991).

Components of Coaching

In one model of coaching designed for early intervention professionals (Gallacher, 1995), participants implement the coaching process by interacting around a cycle of six steps. Sometimes each step occurs during separate interactions, while at other times, steps occur almost simultaneously within a single interaction or across a few meetings. The duration of various steps depends on participants' wishes and the scope of the early intervention practitioner's interests. The six essential steps of the cycle are the following:

1. **Initial Interest** A practitioner either participates in a formal learning activity or discovers a current early intervention practice he or she wants to refine and, consequently, becomes interested in forming a coaching partnership.
2. **Planning** The coach and the early intervention practitioner meet to formulate a plan for the coaching cycle.
3. **Information Gathering** The inviting professional demonstrates or offers information regarding a targeted skill or early intervention practice, and the coaching partner gathers requested information through an observation, a face-to-face interaction, a review of audio- or videotape, or a review of written products.
4. **Analysis** Partners individually analyze information gathered in Step 3 (Information Gathering) and consider how to proceed to accomplish the practitioner's goals.
5. **Conferencing** The coaching partner solicits the practitioner's reflection on Step 3 (Information Gathering) and Step 4 (Analysis), describes the information collected, and reviews his or her analysis of the information. The partners discuss implications

of the analysis, consider courses of action the practitioner might take, and discuss whether to repeat the coaching cycle to pursue a related question or interest.

6. **Coaching Review**   The partners discuss the effectiveness of the coaching cycle they have just completed and consider what to do differently next time.

During the coaching cycle, the inviting practitioner determines what is to be learned or practiced, selects the methods or strategies for learning and practice, communicates how he or she prefers the coaching process to occur, and evaluates whether coaching has achieved his or her goals. The coaching partner and the early intervention practitioner complete specific tasks to accomplish the purpose of each particular step (Gallacher, 1995). These tasks are outlined in Table 8.3.

As they execute all steps of the coaching cycle, partners must demonstrate respect and trust for each other. However, a number of other characteristics, qualities, and competencies are displayed by both the coach and the inviting practitioner (Fitzgerald, 1993; Hutto et al., 1991; Lyman & Morehead, 1987; Mello, 1984; Robbins, 1991; Schreiber, 1990; Swarzman, 1993). These include a willingness to take risks, an openness to new ideas and other points of view, flexibility in thought and action, effective communication skills, systematic problem solving, focused observation, and efficient planning and organization. To effectively facilitate the coaching process, coaches use several specialized techniques to encourage their partner's independence and self-direction, offer support and encouragement, build trust, give descriptive feedback, complement the partner's style of learning, and promote reflection.

The coaching process unfolds more comfortably when the coach matches the inviting practitioner's style. Matching the practitioner's style relative to the degree of self-direction requires the coaching partner to modify the level of support and direction provided depending on the level of assistance the partner requests and on the amount of support the coach perceives is needed to accomplish the coaching process. The practitioner's degree of self-direction often is influenced by several contextual variables, including knowledge and understanding of the topic or content, technical skills regarding a particular topic, sense of personal competence, and the context of the learning event (Candy, 1991). Thus, the degree of self-direction that inviting practitioners demonstrate varies from individual to individual and across settings or situations.

Providing descriptive feedback is an essential component of coaching that helps coaches and inviting practitioners maintain effective coaching relationships. Tips for giving descriptive feedback have been outlined by Gallacher (1995), Hutto et al. (1991), Schreiber (1990), and Wolfe (1994). The general guidelines for feedback include the following: 1) be descriptive, not evaluative or judgmental; 2) be specific rather than general; 3) describe observable events or behaviors rather than give opinions; 4) focus on behavior rather than the person; 5) share information rather than give advice; 6) explore alternatives rather than give the answer or solution (use "provisional" language); 7) begin with positive information; 8) describe observed relationships between behaviors or events so the partner can make cause-and-effect inferences; and 9) offer the amount of information the receiver can use rather than the amount one would like to give.

Complementing the inviting practitioner's behavioral style or preferences is another specialized skill that coaches employ in matching the practitioner's style. The techniques needed to complement another practitioner's style are based on the framework for personal preference and type (Kroeger & Thuesen, 1988, 1992; Myers & Briggs, 1962; Myers & McCulley, 1985). Use of this framework allows coaches to consider their partner's style and preference regarding interaction, the process for receiving information, the kind of information that would be most salient, methods for decision making, and ways to struc-

TABLE 8.3. Tasks for inviting practitioners and coaches

Inviting practitioners	Coaches
Tasks of the partners during step 1: Initial interest	

Inviting practitioners	Coaches
Decide whether they would benefit from forming a coaching partnership to help them refine their early intervention practices.	Thoughtfully respond when a colleague approaches them to ask them to be a coach.
Decide who in their professional network or organization might function as a coach.	Schedule time to meet for planning. Maintain a record of the coaching process.

Tasks of the partners during step 2: Planning

Inviting practitioners	Coaches
Determine their focus.	Help determine the focus.
• Select topic/skill/practice.	• Provide the support and assistance necessary for the practitioner to define focus and purpose.
• Clarify purpose/goal they would like to accomplish.	• Encourage the practitioner's self-reflection.
• Clarify the specific information/behavior they want the coach to gather/observe.	
Determine where, when, and how the information will be gathered as well as where, when, and how the results will be conveyed/shared.	Ask for enough details to understand the context for coaching, practitioner's practice of the skill or procedure, and the information-gathering process.
• Describe purpose for the information gathering, what will occur, and what has previously occurred.	Help make decisions about where, when, and how the information will be gathered as well as where, when, and how the results will be conveyed/shared.
Build rapport and trust with one another.	Build rapport and trust with one another.
• Discuss concerns/apprehensions about coaching.	• Encourage practitioner to discuss concerns; work to decrease apprehension regarding coaching.
Share expectations regarding coaching.	• Be predictable and respectful.
• Describe the role of the coach.	Share expectations regarding coaching.
• Propose the "ground rules" they prefer.	• Clarify the role that inviting practitioner wants them to play.

Tasks of the partners during step 3: Information gathering

Inviting practitioners	Coaches
Conduct a session or facilitate a specific interaction as planned.	Gather information carefully and objectively.
• Describe in detail the use of a particular skill or practice, the occurrence of a particular interaction, or the existence of a particular situation.	• Collect information or record data using methods that were previously agreed on.
• Participate in a role play or reflect on a case study; or provide written products or other records.	• Notice details that reflect the effect of practitioner's use of the skill, practice, or behavior with participants in the session, role-play, and so forth.
Observe the ground rules that were developed with their partner in the planning step for this event.	Observe the ground rules for coaching that were developed with inviting practitioner in the planning step.
	• Maintain focus on the skill, practice, topic, or issue that was practitioner's identified concern.

(continued)

TABLE 8.3.   *(continued)*

Inviting practitioners	Coaches
Tasks of the partners during step 4: Analysis	
Organize the information that has been gathered in the previous step to describe what has occurred.	Organize the information that has been gathered to describe what has occurred.
• Consider whether what occurred was what they intended.	• Identify possible factors that may have influenced what occurred.
• Determine what factors influenced what happened.	• Look for patterns and themes, specifically as they relate to practitioner's focus for the coaching partnership.
• Look for patterns and themes, specifically as they relate to their focus for the coaching partnership.	• Consider incidental information and determine whether it was significant enough to mention.
• Consider incidental information and determine whether to discuss it with their partner.	• Decide whether the information was consistent with what inviting practitioner intended.
Consider what they might do differently the next time.	Plan how they will facilitate the conference to be most productive for practitioner.
Plan the issues they will discuss with the coach during conferencing.	• Think about recommendations or suggestions they could make if practitioner asks for their ideas.
Tasks of the partners during step 5: Conferencing	
Receive support, encouragement, and affirmation regarding their competencies, effective behaviors, and resources.	Provide support, encouragement, and affirmation regarding inviting practitioner's competencies, effective behaviors, and resources.
• Express their perceptions and reflections about what occurred, what went well, and what was difficult.	• Ask for perceptions and reflections regarding the skill or practice about which information has been gathered and regarding what occurred.
Get feedback regarding their use of a specific skill or practice based on information gathered.	• Offer their own perceptions and reflections.
• Compare their behavior, practice, or procedure with what they intended.	Provide feedback regarding targeted skill or practice based on information gathered.
• Listen carefully and nondefensively to feedback.	• Avoid making inferences or judgments regarding inviting practitioner's behavior, skill, or practice.
• Interpret the information/data provided by their partner and request clarification if necessary.	• Describe what they saw or heard.
Reflect on their performance, the situation, the effects of the use of the skill or practice, and their own decision making.	Facilitate inviting practitioner's reflection on his or her performance, the situation, the effects of the skill or practice, and his or her own decision making.
• Describe their feelings.	• Use questions that encourage thinking.

(continued)

TABLE 8.3. *(continued)*

Inviting practitioners	Coaches
Tasks of the partners during step 5: Conferencing	
Refine or adapt their use of a skill or practice.	Assist practitioner to refine or adapt his or her use of the targeted skill or practice.
• Generate their ideas/options regarding things that might be done differently.	• Invite practitioner to problem-solve and consider what might be done differently.
• Request ideas/suggestions from their coach regarding alternatives or strategies.	Determine plans for continued practitioner development and the coaching partnership.
Develop plans for their continued practitioner development and participation in the coaching partnership.	• Assist practitioner to conceptualize what next steps could be taken to continue his or her professional development and to decide whether coaching partnership will continue.
Tasks of the partners during step 6: Coaching review	
Review, reflect on, and consider how the coaching occurred.	Review, reflect on, and consider how the coaching occurred.
• Identify what went well and what has been difficult.	• Identify what worked well and what has been difficult.
• Consider what they have contributed to the successes and difficulties of the coaching cycle.	• Consider what they have contributed to the successes and difficulties of the coaching cycle.
• Decide whether this coaching cycle has achieved their goals for the coaching partnership.	• Ask for descriptive feedback from inviting practitioner regarding what he or she perceives they might do to make the coaching process more productive and effective for him or her.
• Give coach feedback regarding what they perceive he or she might do to make the coaching process more productive and effective.	Contemplate whether the coaching process could be altered in some way to make it more effective.
Contemplate whether the coaching process could be altered in some way to make it more effective.	• Identify what barriers have existed to completing the coaching process.
• Identify what barriers have existed to completing the coaching process.	• Suggest changes that will make the coaching process more productive and effective.
• Suggest changes that will make the coaching process more productive and effective.	

ture or organize coaching activities. For example, inviting practitioners with a sensing style often prefer that coaching partners provide details about how the coaching will occur; give clear, step-by-step explanations; and offer several examples of how the coaching process unfolded for others. However, partners with an intuitive style typically prefer to receive information about the component parts of coaching, the "big picture," and the theory of coaching first before they receive any details. Methods for identifying a partner's style and suggestions for modifying the coach's behavior and the coaching process to more effectively complement the partner's style are outlined by Kroeger and Thuesen (1988, 1992) and summarized in *Coaching Partnerships: Refining Early Intervention Practices* (Gallacher, 1995).

Promoting reflection is central to the coach's role across the coaching cycle. Reflection is a powerful impetus for continued personnel development and self-directed learning. The coach prompts and facilitates the inviting practitioner's analysis of his or her individual learning objectives, performance, and decision making regarding the use of particular techniques or practices. Through reflection, the practitioner examines the effectiveness of particular methods or practices, interprets situations or events, and considers how values, expectations, and beliefs influenced his or her choices and the situation. The coach promotes reflection by encouraging the inviting practitioner to recall a specific event in detail, examine feelings associated with the experience, and contemplate what he or she would do differently to be even more effective. Specific methods for promoting reflection are described in Boud (1987) and in Swarzman (1993).

Sustaining coaching long enough for it to be embedded in the structure of the organization presents several challenges. First, making coaching successful requires consistent efforts to create the necessary foundations for coaching within the organization. Otherwise, the context, the organization's climate, and the principles of coaching may be in conflict. As a result, coaching efforts will be less successful. Moreover, lack of commitment to ongoing personnel development, whether on the part of an individual or an organization, frequently is a serious barrier to successful coaching. Second, successful coaching requires continued orientation, instruction, and follow-up for coaches and partners. Coaches must continue to refine the coaching process, and additional staff members must be given the opportunity to be involved as coaches and learners.

Third, if administrators are involved in coaching, they must strive to keep their role as performance evaluators separate from their role as coaches. This requires that administrators clearly articulate to individuals when they are coaching and when they are supervising or evaluating them, that administrators' behaviors are congruent with the role they are performing, and that trust exists between the parties (Garmston, 1987). Other authors (e.g., Hargreaves & Dawes, 1990; McFaul & Cooper, 1984; Pusch, McCabe, & Pusch, 1985) emphasized the need to separate coaching from supervision and performance appraisal if coaching is to be accepted by practitioners.

Fourth, readiness and trust must be developed between individuals who will participate in the coaching process to reduce the "threat" individuals may feel. Coaches must make efforts to avoid being judgmental and evaluative. Participants often are more comfortable if the coach is a peer who shares common experiences (Neubert & Bratton, 1987). Coaching will be met with resistance if participation is mandated rather than voluntary. This becomes an especially delicate issue when the primary function of coaching shifts from refining professional practices through continued personnel development to remediation of performance deficits. In the latter case, essential principles of coaching likely will not be present (e.g., learner control of the content and process of coaching). Hargreaves and Dawes (1990) suggested that the contrived collegiality created when coaching is strongly encouraged or mandated by administrators actually reduces the trust, support, and collaboration that exist in an organization.

Fifth, participants must be helped to manage the time demands that coaching creates. This includes finding time in the schedule to regularly participate in discussion, observation, and conferencing; addressing competing time demands; and conveying that coaching is a valued activity (Sparks & Bruder, 1987). It also includes a sensitivity to the pace with which a coaching program may be infused in an organization. The greater the number of current demands and pressures on practitioners who may be involved in coaching, the slower the adoption of a coaching program must be to avoid creating stresses that ultimately undermine coaching efforts (Hargreaves & Dawes, 1990).

Research regarding clinical supervision suggests that many practitioners lack the willingness or ability to substantively analyze a peer's performance (McFaul & Cooper, 1984). Although practitioners often execute a form of clinical supervision similar to coaching (e.g., preobservation conferences, observation, postobservation conferences), the discussion during these interactions frequently is perfunctory without careful probing of the concerns, observations, interpretations, or alternatives. McFaul and Cooper argued that an analytical focus is crucial, and instruction for practitioners to analyze their own performance is necessary. Effective models for peer coaching continue to evolve (see Joyce & Showers, 1995, for more information).

CONCLUSION

Supervision, mentoring, and coaching all offer opportunities for practitioners to obtain needed support and to refine their practices. Each may be accomplished through various models incorporating both basic and specialized skills. A consistent theme is the need for these mechanisms to be routinely included as part of a comprehensive personnel development package, even though perceived lack of resources to adequately support these activities continues to be a barrier. In addition, the effectiveness of each of these processes appears to be correlated with the instruction and skills that the facilitator (i.e., supervisor, mentor, or coach) possesses. Specialized instruction and continued personnel development must be a priority for individuals who supervise, mentor, and coach. Furthermore, the organizational foundations, supports, and resources needed to promote and sustain effective supervision, mentoring, and coaching are similar. Unfortunately, many organizations may conclude that such foundations and supports are too costly in this time of dwindling resources. Sustaining direct services and supports to families and young children will likely be a higher priority for many agencies. Although such a decision is reasonable, in the long run, adequate supervision, mentoring, and coaching are part of a critically important infrastructure that makes quality services and supports for families and young children possible.

The connections among effective supervision, mentoring, and coaching are significant. Interest in the techniques and methods of effective supervision, mentoring, and coaching continues to grow as practitioners and organizations incorporate components of these processes into early intervention. Various models and descriptive materials must be examined carefully to illuminate the similarities and differences. Additional research is needed to identify important variables that are directly associated with improved professional practices.

RESOURCES

Bellm, D., Whitebook, M., & Hnatiuk, P. (1997). *The early childhood mentoring curriculum.* Washington, DC: National Center for the Early Childhood Work Force. Cost: $39.90. (202) 737-7700.

This is a comprehensive, flexible set of tools for mentors and mentor trainers in center-based and family child care programs. Two separate volumes, *A Trainer's Guide* and *A Handbook for*

Mentors, contain good information, along with clearly thought out and visually appealing learning activities, handouts, checklists, and supplementary readings.

Fenichel, E. (Ed.). (1992). *Learning through supervision and mentorship to support the development of infants, toddlers and their families: A source book.* Arlington, VA: ZERO TO THREE/National Center for Clinical Infant Programs. Cost: $18.95. (800) 899-4301.

Key issues and successful strategies for incorporating supervision and mentoring into training and practice institutions and systems.

Gallacher, K. (1995). *Coaching partnerships: Refining early intervention practices.* Missoula: Montana University Affiliated Rural Institute on Disabilities. Cost: Contact source. (406) 243-5467.

Designed to assist in the development and implementation of effective coaching partnerships. Manual includes six sections that define coaching; describe program development; examine the coaching process; describe roles, responsibilities, and potential modifications; and offer additional resources.

Robertson, S.C. (1992). *Find a mentor or be one.* Rockville, MD: American Occupational Therapy Association. Cost: $10.00. (301) 948-9626.

Structure, forms, and examples for successfully organizing mentoring relationships.

REFERENCES

Able-Boone, H., Sandall, S., & Loughry, A. (1989). Preparing family specialists in early childhood special education. *Teacher Education and Special Education, 12*(3), 96–102.

Acheson, K.A., & Gall, M.D. (1987). *Techniques in the clinical supervision of teachers: Preservice and inservice applications* (2nd ed.). White Plains, NY: Longman.

Ackland, R. (1991). A review of the peer coaching literature. *Journal of Staff Development, 12*(1), 22–27.

Anderson, R.H. (1993). Contingency supervision: Basic concepts. In R.H. Anderson & K.J. Snyder (Eds.), *Clinical supervision: Coaching for higher performance* (pp. 157–167). Lancaster, PA: Technomic Publishing Co.

Arredondo, D.E., Brody, J.L., Zimmerman, D.P., & Moffett, C.A. (1995). Pushing the envelope in supervision. *Educational Leadership, 53*(3), 74–78.

Bellm, D., Whitebook, M., & Hnatiuk, P. (1997). *The early childhood mentoring curriculum.* Washington, DC: National Center for the Early Childhood Work Force.

Bernard, J.M. (1994). Multicultural supervision: A reaction to Leong and Wagner, Cook, Priest, & Fukuyama. *Counselor Education and Supervision, 34,* 159–171.

Bogenschild, E.G., Lauritzen, P., & Metzke, L. (1988). *A study of teacher attrition.* Reston VA: National Clearinghouse for Professions in Special Education, The Supply/Demand Analysis Center, The Council for Exceptional Children.

Borders, D., Bernard, J.M., Dye, H.A., Fong, M.L., Henderson, P., & Nance, D.W. (1991). Curriculum guide for training counseling supervisors: Rationale, development, & implementation. *Counselor Education and Supervision, 31,* 58–80.

Boud, D. (1987). A facilitator's view of adult learning. In D. Boud & V. Griffin (Eds.), *Appreciating adults learning: From the learners' perspective.* Surrey, Great Britain: Biddles Ltd.

Bozarjian, B., Curry, D., Garner, B., Geary, K., Goodall, A., Hohn, M., & Uvin, J. (1993). *Workplace Education Mentoring Pilot Project final report.* Malden: Massachusetts Department of Education.

Brown, C., Hanft, B., & Browne, B. (1993, August/September). Of elephants, ethics, and relationships: Tools for transforming in the training of early intervention service providers. *ZERO TO THREE, 14*(1), 26–31.

Burke, P.J., McLaughlin, M.J., & Valdiviesco, C.H. (1988). Preparing professionals to educate handicapped infants and young children: Some policy considerations. *Topics in Early Childhood Special Education, 8*(1), 73–80.

Campbell, P.H. (1990). Meeting personnel needs in early intervention. In A.P. Kaiser & C.M. McWhorter (Eds.), *Preparing personnel to work with persons with severe disabilities* (pp. 111–134). Baltimore: Paul H. Brookes Publishing Co.

Candy, P.C. (1991). *Self-direction for lifelong learning: A comprehensive guide to theory and practice.* San Francisco: Jossey-Bass.

Carter, M., & Curtis, D. (1994). *Training teachers: A harvest of theory and practice.* Highland Park, NJ: Gryphon Press.

Cogan, M.L. (1973). *Clinical supervision.* Boston: Houghton Mifflin.

Colorado Speech and Hearing Association (CSHA). (n.d.). *CSHA mentorship program,* 1–6.

Costa, A., & Garmston, R. (1985). Supervision for intelligent teaching. *Educational Leadership, 42,* 70–80.

Daloz, L.A.P., & Edelson, P.J. (1992). Leadership and staff development: A mentorship model. *New Directions for Adult and Continuing Education, 56,* 29–37.

Daresh, J.C. (1989). *Supervision as a proactive process.* White Plains, NY: Longman.

Daresh, J.C., & Playko, M.A. (1991). Preparing mentors for school leaders. *Journal of Staff Development, 12*(4), 24–27.

Division for Early Childhood Task Force on Recommended Practices. (1993, August). *DEC recommended practices: Indicators of quality in programs for infants and young children with special needs and their families.* Reston, VA: Division for Early Childhood of the Council for Exceptional Children.

Fenichel, E. (1991). Learning through supervision and mentorship to support the development of infants, toddlers, and their families. *ZERO TO THREE, 12*(2), 1–6.

Fenichel, E. (Ed.). (1992). *Learning through supervision and mentorship to support the development of infants, toddlers and their families: A source book.* Arlington, VA: ZERO TO THREE/National Center for Clinical Infant Programs.

Fenichel, E., & Eggbeer, L. (1990). *Preparing practitioners to work with infants, toddlers and their families: Issues and recommendations for educators and trainers.* Arlington, VA: National Center for Clinical Infant Programs.

Fenichel, E., & Eggbeer, L. (1993). Zero to Three's TOTIS (training of trainers intensive seminar) and city TOTS (training of teams) initiatives. *ZERO TO THREE, 14*(1), 3.

Fitzgerald, J.H. (1993). Cognition and metacognition in coaching teachers. In R.H. Anderson & K.J. Snyder (Eds.), *Clinical supervision: Coaching for higher performance* (pp. 183–204). Lancaster, PA: Technomic Publishing Co.

Fukuyama, M.A. (1994). Critical incidents in multicultural counseling supervision: A phenomenological approach to supervision research. *Counselor Education and Supervision, 34,* 142–151.

Gallacher, K. (1995). *Coaching partnerships: Refining early intervention practices.* Missoula: Montana University Affiliated Rural Institute on Disabilities.

Garman, N.B. (1986, April). *From technique to practice in clinical supervision.* Paper presented at annual meeting of the American Educational Research Association, San Francisco.

Garmston, R.J. (1987). How administrators support peer coaching. *Educational Leadership, 44,* 18–26.

Garmston, R.J. (1989). *Effective school characteristics.* Sacramento: California State University.

Geiger-DuMond, A.H., & Boyle, S.K. (1995). Mentoring: A practitioner's guide. *Training & Development, 3,* 51–54.

Glatthorn, A. (1984). *Differentiated supervision.* Alexandria, VA: Association for Supervision and Curriculum Development.

Glatthorn, A. (1987). Cooperative professional development: Peer-centered options for teacher growth. *Educational Leadership, 45,* 31–35.

Glatthorn, A.A. (1990). *Supervisory leadership: Introduction to instructional supervision.* New York: HarperCollins.

Glickman, C.D. (1985). *Supervision of instruction: A developmental approach.* Needham, MA: Allyn & Bacon.

Goldhammer, R. (1969). *Clinical supervision: Special methods for the supervision of teachers.* New York: Holt, Rinehart & Winston.

Gordon, S. (1991). *How to help beginning teachers succeed.* Alexandria, VA: Association for Supervision and Curriculum Development.

Gordon, S. (1992). Perspectives and imperatives: Paradigms, transitions, and the new supervision. *Journal of Curriculum and Supervision, 8*(1), 62–76.

Graham, B. (1994). Mentoring and professional development in careers services in higher education. *British Journal of Guidance and Counseling, 22*(2), 261–271.

Guskey, T.R. (1986). Staff development and the process of teacher change. *Educational Research, 15,* 5–12.

Hall, G.E., & Hord, S.M. (1987). *Change in schools: Facilitating the process.* Albany: State University of New York Press.

Hargreaves, A., & Dawes, R. (1990). Paths of professional development: Contrived collegiality, collaborative culture, and the case of peer coaching. *Teaching & Teacher Education, 6*(3), 227–241.

Henry, J.S., Stockdale, M.S., Hall, M., & Deniston, W. (1994). A formal mentoring program for junior female faculty: Description and evaluation. *Journal of NAWE, 56*(2), 37–45.

Hersey, P., & Blanchard, K. (1988). *Management of organizational behavior: Utilizing human resources.* Englewood Cliffs, NJ: Prentice Hall.

Hord, S.M., Rutherford, W.L., Huling-Austin, L., & Hall, G.E. (1987). *Taking charge of change.* Alexandria, VA: Association for Supervision and Curriculum Development.

Howey, K. (1988, December). Mentor-teachers as inquiring professionals. *The Education Digest,* 19–22.

Howey, K.R., & Zimpher, N.L. (1987). The role of higher education in initial year of teaching programs. In G.A. Griffin & S. Millies (Eds.), *The first years of teaching.* Chicago: University of Illinois.

Huling-Austin, L. (1989). Beginning teacher assistance programs: An overview. In L. Huling-Austin, S.J. Odell, P. Ishler, R.S. Kay, & R.A. Edelfelt (Eds.), *Assisting the beginning teacher* (pp. 5–18). Reston, VA: Association of Teacher Educators.

Hunter, M. (1984). Knowing, teaching, and supervising. In P.L. Hosford (Ed.), *Using what we know about teaching* (pp. 169–192). Alexandria, VA: Association for Supervision and Curriculum Development.

Hutto, N., Holden, J., & Haynes, L. (Eds.). (1991). *Mentor training manual for Texas teachers.* Dallas: Texas Education Agency.

Johnson, D.W., & Johnson, R.T. (1989). *Leading the cooperative school.* Edina, MN: Interaction Book Co.

Johnson, D.W., Johnson, R.T., & Holubec, E.J. (1991). *Cooperation in the classroom* (5th ed.). Edina, MN: Interaction Book Co.

Joyce, B., & Showers, B. (1983). *Power in staff development through research on training.* Alexandria, VA: Association for Supervision and Curriculum Development.

Joyce, B., & Showers, B. (1995). *Student achievement through staff development* (2nd ed.). White Plains, NY: Longman.

Kadushin, A. (1985). *Supervision in social work* (2nd ed.). New York: Columbia University Press.

Kasunic, D.K. (1993). The mentoring plan for the 90's: A plan for business. In *Diversity in mentoring: Full text proceedings & executive summaries* (pp. 228–237). Atlanta, GA: Western Michigan University.

Killion, J.P., & Todnem, G.R. (1989). Mentorship through journal writing as a means of professional development for staff developers. *Journal of Staff Development, 10*(3), 22–26.

Kontos, S., & Dunn, L. (1989). Characteristics of the early intervention workforce: An Indiana perspective. *Early Education and Development, 1,* 141–157.

Kontos, S., & File, N. (1992). Conditions of employment, job satisfaction, and job commitment among early intervention personnel. *Journal of Early Intervention, 16*(2), 155–165.

Krajewski, R.J. (1993). The observation cycle: A methodology for coaching and problem solving. In R.H. Anderson & K.J. Snyder (Eds.), *Clinical supervision: Coaching for higher performance* (pp. 99–111). Lancaster, PA: Technomic Publishing Co.

Kram, K. (1983). Phases on the mentor relationship. *Academy of Management Journal, 26,* 608–625.

Kroeger, O., & Thuesen, J. (1988). *Type talk.* New York: Dell Publishing.

Kroeger, O., & Thuesen, J. (1992). *Type talk at work.* New York: Dell Publishing.

Krupp, J. (1985). Mentoring: A means of sparking school personnel. *Journal of Counseling and Development, 64,* 154–155.

Lawrenson, G.M., & McKinnon, A.J. (1982). A survey of classroom teachers of emotionally disturbed: Attrition and burnout factors. *Behavioral Disorders, 8,* 41–49.

Lyman, L., & Morehead, M. (1987). Peer coaching: Strategies and concerns. *Thrust,* 8–9.

Mark, J.H., & Anderson, B.D. (1985). Teacher survival rates in St. Louis, 1969–1982. *American Educational Research Journal, 22,* 413–421.

McCollum, J.A., & McCartan, K. (1988). Research in teacher education: Issues and some future directions for early childhood special education. In S.C. Odom & M.B. Karnes (Eds.), *Early intervention for infants and children with handicaps: An empirical base* (pp. 269–286). Baltimore: Paul H. Brookes Publishing Co.

McCollum, J.A., Yates, T.J., & Lueke, A. (1995, December). *Matching them up for mentoring: An alternative approach to staff development.* Paper presented at the DEC Conference, Orlando, FL.

McFaul, S.A., & Cooper, J.M. (1984). Peer clinical supervision: Theory vs. reality. *Educational Leadership, 40,* 4–11.

Meisels, S., Harbin, G., Modigliani, K., & Olson, K. (1988). Formulating optimal state early childhood intervention policies. *Exceptional Children, 55,* 159–165.

Mello, L. (1984). *Peer-centered coaching: Teachers helping teachers to improve classroom performance.* Idaho Springs, CO: Associates for Human Development. (ERIC Document Reproduction Service No. ED 274 648)

Morey, A.I., & Murphy, D.S. (Eds.). (1990). *Designing programs for new teachers microform: The California experience.* San Francisco: Far West Laboratory for Educational Research and Development, and San Diego State University.

Munro, P., & Elliott, J. (1987). Instructional growth through peer coaching. *Journal of Staff Development, 8*(1), 25–28.

Munson, C.E. (1993). *Clinical social work supervision* (2nd ed.). New York: Haworth Press.

Murray, M. (1991). *Beyond the myths and magic of mentoring: How to facilitate an effective mentoring program.* San Francisco: Jossey-Bass.

Myers, I., & McCulley, M. (1985). *Manual: A guide to the development and use of the Myers-Briggs Type Indicator.* Palo Alto, CA: Consulting Psychologists Press.

Myers, I.B., & Briggs, K. (1962). *The Myers-Briggs Type Indicator.* Princeton, NJ: Educational Testing Service.

Neubert, G.A., & Bratton, E.C. (1987). Team coaching: Staff development side by side. *Educational Leadership, 44,* 23–26.

Newby, T.J., & Heide, A. (1992). The value of mentoring. *Performance Improvement Quarterly, 5*(4), 2–15.

Palsha, S.A., Bailey, D.B., Jr., Vandiviere, P., & Munn, D. (1990). A study of employee stability and turnover in home-based early intervention. *Journal of Early Intervention, 14*(4), 342–351.

Phillips, M.D., & Glickman, C.D. (1991). Peer coaching: Developmental approach to enhancing teacher thinking. *Journal of Staff Development, 12*(2), 20–25.

Professional Development Center. (1994, October). *Essentials of management.* Presented for the Western Montana Comprehensive Development Center, Missoula.

Pusch, L., McCabe, J., & Pusch, W. (1985). Personalized on-site coaching: A successful staff development project at Swift Current. *Education Canada, 25*(3), 36–39.

Raney, P., & Robbins, P. (1989). Professional growth and support through peer coaching. *Educational Leadership, 5,* 35–38.

Reid, B.J., & Bross, M. (1993). Project TRAIN: Training rural area interventionists to meet needs. *Rural Special Education Quarterly, 12*(1), 3–8.

Robbins, P. (1991). *How to plan and implement a peer coaching program.* Alexandria, VA: Association for Supervision and Curriculum Development.

Robertson, S.C. (1992). *Find a mentor or be one.* Rockville, MD: American Occupational Therapy Association.

Robiner, W.M., & Schofield, W. (1990). References on supervision in clinical and counseling psychology. *Professional Psychology: Research and Practice, 21*(4), 297–312.

Rowan, L.E., Thorp, E.K., & McCollum, J.A. (1990). An interdisciplinary practicum to foster infant–family and teaming competencies in speech-language pathologists. *Infants and Young Children, 3*(2), 58–66.

Schlechty, P., & Vance, V. (1981). Do academically able teachers leave education? The North Carolina case. *Phi Delta Kappan, 63,* 106–112.

Schreiber, B. (1990). Colleague to colleague: Peer coaching for effective in-house training. *Education Libraries, 15*(1–2), 30–35.

Sergiovanni, T.J. (1991). *The principalship: A reflective practice perspective* (2nd ed.). Needham, MA: Allyn & Bacon.

Seyforth, J.T., & Bost, W.A. (1986). Teacher turnover and the quality of worklife in schools: An empirical study. *Journal of Research and Development in Education, 20*(1), 1–6.

Smith, N., & Acheson, K. (1991). *Peer consultation: An analysis of several types of programs* (Vol. 34, 6). Eugene: University of Oregon, Oregon School Study Council.

Smith, R.D. (1993). Mentoring new teachers: Strategies, structures, and successes. *Teacher Education Quarterly, 20*(4), 5–18.

Sparks, G.M., & Bruder, S. (1987). Before and after peer coaching. *Educational Leadership, 45*(3), 54–57.

Stott, K., & Walker, A. (1992). Developing school leaders through mentoring: A Singapore perspective. *School Organization, 12*(2), 153–164.

Swarzman, J.B. (1993). Communication and coaching. In R.H. Anderson & K.J. Snyder (Eds.), *Clinical supervision: Coaching for higher performance* (pp. 113–134). Lancaster, PA: Technomic Publishing Co.

Thurman, S.K., Brown, C., Bryan, M., Henderson, A., Klein, M.D., Sainato, D.M., & Wiley, T. (1992). Some perspectives on preparing personnel to work with at risk children birth to five. In L.M. Bullock & R.L. Simpson (Eds.), *Critical issues in special education: Implications for personnel preparation* (ERIC Reproduction Service No. ED 343 342, pp. 97–101). (Available from Programs in Special Education, University of North Texas, Post Office Box 13857, Denton, Texas 76203)

U.S. Department of Education. (1992). Personnel preparation in the 21st century: Response to Simpson, Whelan, and Zabel. *Remedial and Special Education, 14*(2), 23–24.

Wildman, T.M., Magliaro, S.G., Niles, R.A., & Niles, J.A. (1992). Teacher mentoring: An analysis of roles, activities, and conditions. *Journal of Teacher Education, 43*(3), 200–204.

Wolfe, B. (1994). *Coaching as follow up to training.* Unpublished manuscript, Portage Project, Region V Resource Access Project, Eau Claire, WI.

Wolfe, P., & Robbins, P. (1989). *Opening doors: An introduction to peer coaching.* Alexandria, VA: The Association for Supervision and Curriculum Development.

Wright, K.S. (1992). From the odyssey to the university: What is the thing called mentoring? *ACA Bulletin, 79,* 45–53.

Yoder, D.E., Coleman, P.P., & Gallagher, J.J. (1990). *Personnel needs—Allied health personnel meeting the demands of Part H, PL 99-457.* Chapel Hill: University of North Carolina at Chapel Hill.

III STRATEGIES FOR APPLYING RECOMMENDED PRACTICES TO SELECTED CONTENT AREAS

Part III has been designed as a "hands-on" section. The content covered in this part reflects topics important in early intervention. Program directors want employees who are competent in these areas, practitioners request help and support in developing competencies in these areas, and university and community college instructors are being asked to provide instruction in these areas. Each chapter provides a brief overview of broad areas of knowledge and competency within the particular content area being addressed, including implications for preservice and inservice content and instructional processes. The primary focus of each chapter is to offer concrete ideas, activities, and resources for personnel development in the content area. A goal for this section is that each reader should discover instructional ideas and activities to try.

9

FROM MONOLOGUES TO SKILLED DIALOGUES

Teaching the Process of Crafting Culturally Competent Early Childhood Environments

Isaura Barrera
Lucinda Kramer

We must learn of the simplest craftsman a parable. We all know the difference between the carpenter who is really an artist and the man who can knock a bookcase together if he needs one. There is no doubt which of the two is master and maker; you watch with admiration the almost miraculous obedience of tool and material to the craftsman's will, but you notice that it is not he who asserts with every gesture his will to dominate; it is the hedge carpenter who wrenches and forces and blusters and drives the wood to obey him against the grain. There is no great art without reverence. The real [craftsman] has great technical knowledge of materials and tools; but the bungler might still have that and still be a bungler. The real [craftsman] has something much more; he has the feel of the wood; the knowledge of its demands in his fingers; and so the work is smooth and satisfying and lovely because he worked with the reverence that comes of love. (Vann, 1960, p. 19)

Though it is, perhaps, not fashionable to speak of reverence and love in relation to education, Vann's quote captures two aspects of craft that underlie the authors' concept of cultural competence as presented in this chapter: 1) craft as something that lies somewhere between art and prescribed methodology, and 2) craft as a dialogic process. This dual perspective is particularly critical in this type of chapter, which runs the risk of misrepresenting the very topic on which it seeks to enlighten.

Cultural competence is a complex topic, referred to in a variety of ways (e.g., cultural responsiveness). The term *cultural competence,* with which some may take issue, has been chosen by the authors. Whatever the term, it is essential to be clear about its referent. The authors do not use the term to refer to a discrete set of skills needed only for certain populations deemed to be "diverse" or to a knowledge of customs and values of these "others," as compared with "us." They use the term in a broader sense to refer to the ability of service providers to respond optimally to all children and families, understanding both the richness and the limitations of the sociocultural contexts in which children and families, as well as the practitioners themselves, may be operating.

The scope of this chapter permits only summary descriptions and discussions of the need for and challenges of cultural competence. The first section highlights issues that research and experience indicate are critical to an adequate understanding of both need and challenges. To compensate for the limited scope of the discussion, certain words are in bold type, cuing the reader to topics on which additional references are provided (see Table 9.1). Activities to promote development of necessary attitudes, understandings, and skills in preservice and inservice settings are provided, as are resources to supplement these activities.

PERSPECTIVES ON CULTURE AND CULTURAL DIVERSITY

The term **cultural competence,** as it is typically used, presumes an understanding of **cultural diversity,** which, in turn, presumes an understanding of **culture.** Without a solid understanding of culture, cultural diversity can be, and all too often has been, reduced to simply mean *certain characteristics of certain people associated with certain ethnic groups.* From this perspective, cultural competency can too easily become understood as the body of knowledge deemed, a priori, to be necessary for communicating with these "diverse" people.

Two problems ensue from this understanding. One is that cultural competency is restricted to *knowing about,* rather than *knowing.* As a consequence, "they" (those identified as diverse) become objects to know about, rather than individuals with whom to enter into a relationship. A second, related problem is that the *knowing about* becomes largely restricted to *knowing about them* (the populations identified as diverse). Important aspects of "us" (the populations not identified as diverse) are overlooked, and an insidious remedial perspective is communicated, intentionally or otherwise.

The understanding of cultural competence described in this chapter takes a different perspective, one that focuses on understanding self in a cultural context so as to successfully enter into reciprocal relationships with others from dissimilar cultural contexts. Key information on the concepts of culture and cultural diversity is summarized here. The reader is referred to Table 9.1 for references containing more detailed discussions.

Culture

"Culture is not a nominal variable to be attached to every child in the same way that age, height, or sex might be" (Weisner, Gallimore, & Jordan, 1993, p. 61). With this statement, Weisner et al. made reference to one of the most difficult challenges posed by the concept of culture when used in psychological and educational environments. Although cultural competence requires the recognition of culture, it also requires that people not be stereotyped (i.e., defined by the culture[s] within which they participate).

At its deepest level, culture is a shared social process that both connects and distinguishes groups. At the same time, individual, psychological processes coexist that cannot be overlooked. Understanding culture requires "the capacity to move between data on individuals and particulars to summaries of shared patterns for behavior" (Weisner et al., 1993, p. 61). Culture shapes contexts and environments within which individuals develop; it is equally shaped by individuals' actions within and on these environments.

At another more superficial level, culture is embedded in clusters of behaviors, customs, values, and other such characteristics that first catch our attention when we meet someone different from ourselves. To look only at this level, however, is literally to take culture out of context. All research points to behaviors, customs, and values as seamless expressions of the deeper meanings and processes held by particular communities. Berger and Thompson (1995), for example, stated,

> Understanding the cultural context of human development requires much more than marveling at cultural differences in children and their care. It involves understanding how specific practices arise from deeper values and traditions, which, in turn, are part of the overall social context. (p. 10)

TABLE 9.1. References correlated to key terms

Term	Articles/readings	Media
Culture	Hall, E.T. (1977). *Beyond culture.* Garden City, NY: Anchor Books/Doubleday. Haviland, W.A. (1993). *Cultural anthropology.* Orlando, FL: Harcourt Brace College Publishers. Weisner, T.S., Gallimore, R., & Jordan, C. (1993). Unpackaging cultural effects on classroom learning: Hawaiian peer assistance and child-generated activity. In R.N. Roberts (Ed.), *Coming home to preschool: The sociocultural context of early education* (pp. 59–90). Norwood, NJ: Ablex Publishing Co.	*CD-ROM* *Material world: A global family portrait* Source: StarPress Media San Francisco, CA
Cultural diversity	Hall, E.T., & White, W.F. (1979). Intercultural communication: Human organization. In C.D. Mortenson (Ed.), *Basic readings in communication theory* (pp. 355–370). New York: Harper & Row. McLeod, D. (1995). Self-identity, pan-ethnicity and the boundaries of group identity. *Multicultural Education, 3*(2), 8–11. Spradley, J.P. (1972). Foundations of cultural knowledge. In J.P. Spradley (Ed.), *Culture and cognition: Rules, maps, and plans* (pp. 3–38). Prospect Heights, IL: Waveland Press.	*Video* *Valuing diversity:* *Multicultural communication* Source: Learning Seed Lake Zurich, IL
Cultural competency	Barrera, I. (1993). Effective and appropriate instruction for all children: The challenge of cultural/linguistic diversity and young children with special needs. *Topics in Early Childhood Special Education, 13*(2), 461–488. Bowers, C.A., & Flinders, D.J. (1990). *Responsive teaching: An ecological approach to classroom patterns of language, culture, and thought.* New York: Teachers College Press. Gonzalez-Mena, S. (1993). *Multicultural issues in childcare.* Mountain View, CA: Mayfield Publishing. Lynch, E.W., & Hanson, M.J. (1992b). Steps in the right direction: Implications for interventionists. In E.W. Lynch & M.J. Hanson (Eds.), *Developing cross-cultural competence: A guide for working with young children and their families* (pp. 355–370). Baltimore: Paul H. Brookes Publishing Co.	*Videos* *Cross cultural communication in diverse settings* *(GSU-103)* Source: Insight Media New York *Social interaction in diverse settings (GSU-102)* Source: Insight Media New York *Ten keys to culturally sensitive childcare* Source: Far West Laboratory Sacramento, CA

(continued)

TABLE 9.1. *(continued)*

Term	Articles/readings	Media
Principles of sound pedagogy	Bowers, C.A., & Flinders, D.J. (1990). *Responsive teaching: An ecological approach to classroom patterns of language, culture, and thought.* New York: Teachers College Press.	*Videos* *E.C. Curriculum and developmental approaches* Source: ASCD Alexandria, VA
	Bullivant, B.M. (1989). Culture: Its nature and meaning for educators. In J.A. Banks & C.A. Banks (Eds.), *Multicultural education: Issues and perspectives* (pp. 27–46). Needham, MA: Allyn & Bacon.	*Cooperative learning/learning to work together* Source: ASCD Alexandria, VA
	Tharp, R.G., & Gallimore, R. (1988). *Rousing minds to life: Teaching, learning and schooling in social context.* Cambridge, MA: Cambridge University Press.	
Culture's influence on development	Bowman, B.T. (1992). Who is at risk for what and why. *Journal of Early Intervention, 16*(2), 101–108.	*Videos* *Development & diversity—Worlds of children* series Source: GPN Lincoln, NE
	Bronfenbrenner, U. (1979). *The ecology of human development.* Cambridge, MA: Harvard University Press.	
	Greenfield, M.E., & Cocking, R.R. (Eds.). (1994). *Cross-cultural roots of minority child development.* Hillsdale, NJ: Lawrence Erlbaum Associates.	*Family influences* Source: Insight Media New York
	Harkness, S. (1992). Cross-cultural research in child development: A sample of the state of the art. *Developmental Psychology, 28,* 622–625.	
Self-reflection	Ayers, W. (1989). *The good preschool teacher.* New York: Teachers College Press.	
	Lynch, E.W., & Hanson, M.J. (Eds.). (1992a). *Developing cross-cultural competence: A guide for working with young children and their families.* Baltimore: Paul H. Brookes Publishing Co.	
	Schön, D.A. (1987). *Educating the reflective practitioner.* San Francisco: Jossey-Bass	

Category	References	Media Resources
Critical inquiry and decision-making skills	Bowers, C.A., & Flinders, D.J. (1990). *Responsive teaching: An ecological approach to classroom patterns of language, culture, and thought.* New York: Teachers College Press. Brookfield, S.D. (1987). *Developing critical thinkers.* San Francisco: Jossey-Bass. de Bono, E. (1995). *Mind power.* New York: Dorling Kindersley.	*Videos* *Tactics for thinking* Source: ASCD Alexandria, VA *Introduction to creative problem solving* Source: GCT, Inc. Mobile, AL
Trauma or chronic poverty	Desking, G., & Steckler, G. (1996). *When nothing makes sense: Disaster, crisis, and other effects on children.* Minneapolis, MN: Fairview Press. Donovan, D.M., & McIntyre, D. (1990). *Healing the hurt child: A developmental-contextual approach.* New York: Norton. Koplow, L. (Ed.). (1996). *Unsmiling faces: How preschools can heal.* New York: Teachers College Press. Miller, A. (1994). *Drama of the gifted child.* New York: Basic Books.	*Videos* *Psychological maltreatment of children: Assault on the psyche* Source: Penn State University Park, PA *Child abuse: It shouldn't hurt to be a child* AIMS Media Van Nuys, CA
Demographics	*Challenge of change: What the 1990 census tells us about children.* (1992). Washington, DC: Center for the Study of Social Policy. Figueroa, R.A., & Garcia, E. (1994). Issues in testing students from culturally and linguistically diverse backgrounds. *Multicultural Education, 2*(1), 10–19. National Center for Health Statistics. (1990). *Vital Statistics of the United States, 1990,* Vol. 1. U.S. Report of Health & Human Services, Public Health Service, Centers for Disease Control and Prevention. Hyattsville, MD: Author.	*CD-ROM* *Discovering multicultural America* Source: Gale Research Detroit, MI
Social positioning and power differences	Darder, A. (1991). *Culture & power in the classroom: A critical foundation for bicultural education.* Westport, CT: Greenwood Publishing Group. Delpit, L. (1995). *Other people's children: Cultural conflict in the classroom.* New York: New Press. Kozol, J. (1991). *Savage inequalities: Children in America's schools.* New York: Crown Publishers. McIntosh, P. (1989, July–August). White privilege: Unpacking the invisible knapsack. *Peace & Freedom,* 10–12.	*Videos* *White identity: Theory, origins, & prospect* Source: Microtraining, Inc. North Amherst, MA *The color of fear* Source: StirFry Productions Oakland, CA

Key understandings of culture include the following:

- Culture is composed of the socially generated and socially sanctioned ways of perceiving, believing, evaluating, and behaving shared by members of particular communities and transmitted across generations.
- The aspects of culture most easily perceived (e.g., food, behavior) are only the surface level of culture and are inextricably tied to and generated from deeper values, beliefs, and worldviews, which form culture's primary level.
- Culture functions both to set parameters that both connect and separate people and communities and to transmit from one generation to another ways of perceiving, believing, evaluating, and behaving deemed to be critical to personal and group survival.
- Everyone's ways of perceiving, believing, evaluating, and behaving come from somewhere. That is, everyone participates in one or more cultures, some of which may be identified by ethnic labels, some by other labels, and others that may have no easy labels.
- Culture influences ways of perceiving, believing, evaluating, and behaving in three developmental or curricular domains: 1) personal-social, 2) communicative-linguistic, and 3) sensory-cognitive. Specific parameters within each of these domains that are particularly sensitive to culture are listed in Table 9.2. These parameters are further discussed in the following section on cultural diversity.
- Experiences of **trauma or chronic poverty** can inhibit the degree to which children and families freely express ways of perceiving, believing, evaluating, and behaving common to their cultural heritage and traditions.

Cultural Diversity

How culture is defined and perceived has a significant effect on how cultural diversity is defined and perceived. Many disagreements around cultural competence ensue as a result of equating culture with ethnicity and focusing only on its more superficial level. Cultural diversity then becomes something that is inherently characteristic of only some groups. However, cultural diversity is not an inherent characteristic; it is a relative term that requires a normative referent. To make the dominant Euro-American culture that referent is to perpetuate, implicitly or explicitly, the very challenges and inequities that cultural competence is designed to address.

Cultural diversity as addressed in this chapter, therefore, is not defined by membership in a particular group. Rather, the authors of this chapter define cultural diversity according to the degree of probability that, "in interaction with a particular child or family, [the provider] will attribute different meanings or values to behaviors or events than would the family or someone from that family's environment" (Barrera, 1996, p. 71). A Spanish-speaking Puerto Rican practitioner working with an Amish family would meet this criterion, as would a practitioner with an English, French, and Scottish background working with the same family. A young early intervention practitioner from a middle-class background working with a homeless family would also meet this criterion, even if ethnic backgrounds were similar.

Thus, the issue of cultural diversity is broader than simply acknowledging ethnicity. It is, at its core, an issue of effective connections and communications between people with varying degrees of individual expressions of sociocultural similarities and differences. Cultural diversity, as an educationally relevant variable, requires a thorough understanding of the sociocultural parameters associated with each of the three domains within which

TABLE 9.2. Sociocultural parameters associated with developmental/curricular domains

Developmental/ curricular domains	Parameters
Communicative-linguistic	Language(s) of child's caregiving environments
	Child's relative language proficiency (degree of proficiency in English and other languages used in caregiving environments)
	Patterns of language usage in child's caregiving environments (e.g., what is language used for, who initiates communication with whom in what circumstances)
	Patterns of nonverbal interaction and communication
	Relative value placed on verbal and nonverbal communication
	Relative status associated with non-English language and bilingualism
Personal-social	Degree of enculturation/acculturation
	Sense of self (e.g., relative weight given to independence, dependence, and interdependence)
	Identity and competence
	Roles and rules associated with parenting and child rearing
	Knowledge and experience related to power and social positioning
	Values and beliefs associated with instrumental and emotional support
Sensory-cognitive	Funds of knowledge (e.g., relative value placed on different types of knowledge)
	Learning strategies (e.g., preference for modeling versus direct questioning)
	Problem-solving and decision-making strategies
	Worldview (e.g., how events are interpreted and explained)

Adapted from Barrera (1996).

culture operates: communicative-linguistic, personal-social, and sensory-cognitive. These parameters affect all aspects of self and behavior (see the following discussion and also Table 9.2; see also Barrera, Macpherson, & Kramer, in press, for a list of specific questions to direct information gathering within each of these parameters).

Communicative-Linguistic Parameters   Communicative-linguistic   parameters such as the language used in the home, the communication patterns, and the values underlying those patterns affect every aspect of how we learn about ourselves and the world around us. These parameters form a critical medium for early intervention; and when practitioners have a different understanding of them than do families, it becomes difficult, if not impossible, to establish rapport and convey needed information (Harry, 1992).

Personal-Social Parameters   Closely aligned to communicative-linguistic parameters are those that define the personal-social domain, which addresses how we come to know who we are and how we are expected to operate in social environments. Roles and rules associated with parenting and child rearing, for example, are critical parameters for defining our understanding of both families and children (Gonzalez-Mena, 1993). Knowledge and experiences related to power and social positioning are another such parameter. Families with a history of experiences that have generated feelings of disempowerment will define themselves, and others, differently from the ways that families with experiences that have generated feelings of empowerment (see also the section, Children's Needs for Mirroring and Validation).

Sensory-Cognitive Parameters   No less powerful are parameters associated with how we perceive and process information (i.e., sensory-cognitive domain). A clear example of these parameters was given by Bowers and Flinders (1990) in their text *Responsive Teaching: An Ecological Approach to Classroom Patterns of Language, Culture, and Thought.* Questions triggered by an understanding of this domain and its parameters include the following: What areas of knowledge are valued and supported by the family? What are the child's/family's preferred strategies for acquiring or prompting new learning? How does the family tend to events such as their child's developmental difficulties? A family's worldview and preferred strategies for problem solving are often embedded in their cultural values and experiences.

In the authors' experience, it is practitioners' lack of knowledge of the range and diversity of these parameters that often underlies the difficulties faced by children and families in early intervention environments. Issues of power and social positioning (e.g., majority–minority issues) come into play in understanding providers' lack of knowledge. As stated by McLeod (1995), "Members of majority groups usually encounter a relatively good fit between their experience of the world and the definitions they encounter in the mass media or in cultural symbols and representations," and "Where our experience of the world is consistent with the norm of society at large the frame of identity tends to blend with the background and disappear" (p. 9). The felt need to learn about the range of diversity in interaction rules or learning strategies, for example, tends as a consequence to be lower for members of majority groups than for members of groups who do not encounter a similarly "good fit between their experience of the world" and the definitions and symbols that surround them. Issues of power and social positioning cannot be separated from understandings of culture and cultural diversity. When both deep and surface levels of culture are understood, and when cultural diversity is perceived as more than ethnically derived differences, power and social positioning become key dynamics both within and across cultural environments.

Key concepts related to cultural diversity include the following:

- Cultural diversity is a relative term; it depends on who is involved.
- Ethnic differences are only one indicator, and seldom a reliable one, of cultural diversity.
- Cultural diversity, when not acknowledged and addressed, can significantly disrupt both learning and communication.
- An individual's culture, no matter how different from others, is never in and of itself the cause of such disruption. It is the response to that culture by others that gives a

culture its negative or positive consequences. Within a social environment where an individual's culture is shared by those around him or her or is accepted and validated, even when different, learning and communication need not be disrupted.

• The scope of interpersonal diversity is defined by much more than culture and its related parameters. Personality, trauma, gender, experiential histories, and many other factors also contribute to the degree of diversity among individuals.

NEED FOR CULTURAL COMPETENCE

An adequate understanding of and response to cultural parameters, as they affect teaching, learning, and interactions with children and families form the bedrock for **cultural competency** in early intervention. But why is this understanding and its corollary response essential in early childhood settings? Although the scope of this chapter prohibits an in-depth answer, significant insight can be gained from examining three areas: 1) shifting population demographics, 2) children's need for mirroring and validation, and 3) pedagogical principles.

Demographics

Great emphasis has been placed on **demographics** as a primary determinant of need for cultural competency. The majority of articles on cultural competence, in early childhood and in other areas, describe shifts in U.S. demographics since the mid-1980s. Figueroa and Garcia (1994), for example, stated that "from 1981 through 1990 some 7,388,062 people have immigrated to the United States, marking a 63 percent increase in the immigrant population over the previous decade" (p. 10) (see also Table 9.1).

An emphasis on demographic change as a primary driver of the need for cultural competence tends to overshadow two significant facts: 1) the need to understand and support cultural and linguistic parameters goes beyond simply assisting the transition of immigrant children and their families into U.S. culture; it also, and perhaps primarily, includes the need to acknowledge the contributions and dignity of U.S.-born Native American, African American, Hispanic, and other populations; and 2) development, learning, and teaching are socially structured realities reflective of the particular cultures within which they occur.

In overlooking these two facts, the emphasis on demographic change sends two implicit, but nonetheless negative, messages. The first message might read something like this: "We need to attend to cultural parameters different from our own only when there is a critical mass." Does that mean that there is no need to attend to cultural and linguistic parameters when no such critical mass exists? Does it mean that when the likelihood is that the practitioner will encounter only one or perhaps two children and families with diverse cultural parameters the need is less? A second message sent by the corollary lack of emphasis on other sources of need is, "Addressing cultural parameters diverse from our own is unrelated to sound pedagogy and children's needs." After all, if it were related, wouldn't these also be emphasized? "In general," this message might read, "the role of culture in structuring development, learning, and teaching is negligible and need not be considered."

Although the role of changing demographics in creating a need for cultural competence cannot be overlooked, it should be addressed as only one of several factors. Responding to children's needs for mirroring and validation and upholding sound pedagogical principles are other factors that generate an equally strong, if not stronger, need for cultural competency. These factors should be addressed with similar, or greater, emphasis than demographics. Perhaps they are less dramatic, but they yield rich data to inform early interventionists' perceptions and applications of cultural competence.

Children's Needs for Mirroring and Validation

Although demographic change has brought a greater range and degree of diversity to the attention of early intervention personnel, cultural diversity has always been present in the United States (Takaki, 1993). Generations of learners acquired skills and strategies to participate successfully in home communities only to find, upon entering educational environments, that these skills and strategies were ineffective or devalued and criticized. The stories of these generations, and the price they paid for the dissonance between their skills and strategies and those valued in educational settings, are still emerging (e.g., Riley, 1993; Skutnabb-Kangas & Cummins, 1988).

The role of adult behavior and feedback in child development has been well documented. Gonzalez-Mena and Eyer (1993), for example, discussed the need for adult caregivers to learn each child's unique ways of communicating, respect infants and toddlers as worthy people, and build security by teaching trust. An ability to understand and respectfully respond to the behaviors and skills that a child brings to the early intervention setting underlies these three needs. For example, it is difficult to teach trust to a child who finds little or no resonance between the way he or she has learned to operate and the way he or she is required or expected to operate in an early intervention setting. It is equally difficult to develop and maintain a sense of worth in that child. Children need to be respectfully mirrored and validated if their abilities are to unfold as fully as possible. Although lack of cultural competency is only one impediment to mirroring and validation, it is no less detrimental than other impediments, such as parental limitations and developmental delays.

Two developments have contributed significantly to the emerging recognition of children's needs for mirroring and validation and to the consequences of not responding to those needs: 1) an increased awareness and application of a social constructivist paradigm, which highlights the social nature of identity and the dynamics of social positioning and power differences; and 2) the increasing presence of violence and other signs of social stress or breakdown of social skill development and community. Although the effect of each of these developments has been different, the results have similarly substantiated the need for cultural competence in responding optimally to children. Each of these developments is discussed briefly here.

Social Constructivist Paradigm   Since the 1980s, educational and psychological literature has increasingly reflected a conceptual shift from the mechanistic or behavioral paradigm common to psychology to a paradigm that acknowledges the role of environment and social context (i.e., social constructivism) in all aspects of living and development. One of the primary assumptions of social constructivism is that "the terms in which the world is understood are social artifacts, products of historically situated interchanges among people" (Gergen, 1985, p. 5). The social constructivist paradigm is shaped by ecological, ethnographic, and critical feminist perspectives. An early reference to it was made by Super and Harkness (1981), who stated, "The bias of this [behavioral, individualistic] approach lies not in the imposition of arbitrary cultural values (though this is . . . a problem), but rather in the exclusive use of a paradigm that does not recognize the central role that culture plays in human functioning" (p. 75). Bronfenbrenner (1979) also generated an ecological perspectives model to describe the multiple and interactive contexts that affect human functioning. The concept of knowledge and life patterns as socially constructed is referred to by Kessler and Swadener (1992) and Mallory and New (1994). These researchers validated the critical need that children have to find optimum degrees of consonance between themselves and their environments. Koplow (1996) put it succinctly in relation to her area of research:

> At-risk children need to experience their affective expressions as understood and valued before they will be able to take in affective information from others. Without mastering this fundamental form of communication, children may have difficulty moving toward more sophisticated forms of communication and learning. (p. 17)

In addition to highlighting children's needs for mirroring and validation, the recognition of knowledge and life patterns as socially constructed artifacts has also opened the door to conversations about **social positioning and power differences** and their role in either enhancing or diminishing the mirroring and validation available to children. Social privilege and power differences are not easy topics to examine or to teach. Some research (e.g., Skutnabb-Kangas & Cummins, 1988; Soto & Smrekar, 1992) is beginning to uncover the differential role that these two variables play across cultures, a role that disproportionately diminishes the richness and appropriateness of some children's environments and development.

Ogbu (1995) made an important point regarding this inequity by stating that "minority status [which is accorded to many groups identified as culturally diverse] involves complex realities that affect the relationship between the culture and language of the minority and those of the dominant groups" (p. 585). One of these complex realities is the difference between what he termed *primary cultural differences* and *secondary cultural differences*. Primary cultural differences are differences in language, behavior, and other variables that exist independent of negative contact with other cultures (e.g., lack of proficiency in English). These differences typically are grounded in positive self-concepts; that is, there is no shame or anger associated with them. Secondary cultural differences tend to have shame and anger associated with them. These latter differences, though inclusive of many of the same aspects of language, behavior, and other variables characteristic of primary differences, have one critical distinction: Secondary differences are colored by the experiences and effect generated by negative contacts with other cultures that fail to mirror or validate primary differences. For example, a Native American family might have both types of differences, with the first rooted in the different language and values of its community and the second rooted in a pool of experiences in which that language and those values have been rendered invisible or "not as good" as those reflected and promoted in educational settings. Family stories of being forcefully removed from home and enrolled in boarding schools, for example, might highlight this family's secondary cultural differences.

Increased Violence and Social Stress Feelings of shame and anger arising from membership in particular groups are not limited to particular cultural backgrounds. Increasing social stresses such as violence and unemployment are, however, inhibiting the access of growing numbers of families to full participation in both their own culture and the broader social culture of power. Without such access, the children of these families are at risk for a variety of developmental disruptions. One source, for example, cited statistics that "3.3 million children witness parental abuse every year" (PACER, 1995). The impact on development of the consequent trauma and family disruption is being documented with greater frequency (Donovan & McIntyre, 1990; Weissbourd, 1996). Although there is increasing recognition of the truth of the African proverb "it takes a village to raise a child," there are fewer and fewer "villages" to provide children with the human and environmental supports they need, supports that are generated and maintained through cultural dynamics.

The dilemmas posed by this social reality challenge all caregivers to understand culture as the primary *container* of community. It is culture in its myriad forms that generates patterns of community. It is culture that shapes and contains the channels through which all children, not just those identified as culturally diverse, learn the linguistic, social, cognitive, and other knowledge and skills they need to become healthy, productive participants in adult communities. **Culture's influence on development** is critical. Super and Harkness (1981) developed the concept of a "developmental niche" to describe this influence: "At each [developmental] period the niche reflects the physical and social settings, the relevant cultural customs, the ethnopsychology of other people about one's presumed motivations, one's reasonable needs and responsibilities, and the value and significance of particular behaviors" (pp. 82–83). Bowman (1992) made two statements that are relevant here: "A culture functions to limit and expand, constrict and free, value and disdain the intrinsic potential of a child" (p. 102), and, more specifically, "The second dimension [of developmental structures] is culturally defined. . . . This dimension responds to what a particular culture makes available to support and enlarge development, such as the qualities of the physical and interpersonal development" (p. 101). Price-Williams and Gallimore (1980) stated, "Such studies [referring to cross-cultural research] show clearly the implausibility of explanations of child behavior that ignore social, cultural, economic, environmental and other macro systems factors" (p. 178).

Understanding the consequences of social stress and violence brings an enriched understanding of cultural competence as needed for more than simply responding to a few children and families designated as culturally diverse. Rather, cultural competency is understood as necessary to respectfully and fully support *all* children's growth and learning, both within their home cultural context and within the other cultural contexts common to environments outside their home. If culture's richness and diversity are not protected, every community experiences the loss in diminished learning opportunities and supports for its children.

Pedagogical Principles

There is a third, equally critical, source of need for cultural competence: **principles of sound pedagogy.** Pedagogical principles espouse attention to variations in teaching and learning formats and strategies. If principles such as "all children need positive reinforcement" and "all learning starts with motivated engagement" are to be followed, then the diverse modes and meanings of reinforcement and motivated engagement must be carefully assessed. The meanings attached to children's behaviors and interactions, the contexts for supporting these behaviors and interactions, and the modes for stimulating their development are significantly shaped by culture. Harwood (1992), for example, studied perceptions of desirable and undesirable attachment behavior in middle- and lower-class Anglo mothers and lower-class Puerto Rican mothers. She first used open-ended probes to elicit indigenous concepts and then constructed culturally sensitive vignettes to which the mothers were asked to respond. She found, among other things, that "the Anglo mothers demonstrated greater concern with qualities that enable a child to cope autonomously in an unfamiliar setting, whereas Puerto Rican mothers showed a greater concern with qualities that allow a child to maintain dignity and proper demeanor in a public context" (p. 831). Motivating each group of these mothers to support their child's "autonomy" would, as a consequence, necessitate quite different strategies.

In addressing the need to assist children's performance, Tharp and Gallimore (1988) made the point that "patient, contingent, responsive and accurately tuned adult assistance" (p. 41) requires that "the assistor . . . be in close touch with the *learner's* relationship with the task" (p. 42, emphasis added). It is a point echoed by other researchers: "The interaction of the teacher's self-understanding with the student's self-understanding, given the formative and vulnerable stage of development that the latter is undergoing, is perhaps one of the most significant aspects of the power/knowledge relationship under the teacher's control" (Bowers & Flinders, 1990, p. 163).

Thus, the need to address cultural competence as an essential skill for service providers is based on more than just demographics. It is also based children's developmental and learning needs. Ultimately, cultural competency is essential to serving any child or family optimally, as there are culturally generated factors in everyone's behaviors and beliefs. Learning to be mindfully responsive to these factors, whether similar to or diverse from our own, is not an easy task. The stimulation and development of cultural competency cannot be embodied in a clear sequence of prescriptive steps. Rather, as discussed in the next section, cultural competency evolves from a more circular and complex process.

TEACHING CULTURAL COMPETENCE

"The metaphors through which we organize our work have a powerful influence on both what we perceive and what we do" (Freedman & Combs, 1996, p. 1). Similarly, Bowers and Flinders (1990) stated that "as people make new associations words take on new meanings and thus help to constitute new interpretative schemata" (p. 11). The metaphor of "craft" for cultural competency is chosen for several specific reasons: 1) it counteracts the relatively mechanistic, linear paradigm that tends to prevail in some areas of psychology and education (e.g., to do X, follow these steps in sequence); 2) it highlights the creative, intuitive dimensions of cultural competency; and 3) it emphasizes the personal involvement and activities characteristic of the constructivist paradigm, which underlies much of the cultural data and perspectives at the cutting edge of cultural applications to education, for example, Vygotsky's "zone of proximal development" material (Hedegaard, 1990) and Feuerstein's "mediated learning experience" concepts (Jensen & Feuerstein, 1987; Lidz & Thomas, 1987).

Cultural Competency as Craft

Cultural competence, as understood by the authors of this chapter, involves the crafting of reciprocal and, thus, *dialogic,* interactions between practitioners and children and their families to ameliorate or eliminate the cultural and linguistic "bumps" that can result from diverse worldviews, languages, behaviors, skills, and funds of knowledge. The term *bump* is used because it is descriptive of what happens: people literally "bump up against" worldviews, languages, behaviors, skills, or knowledge that are unfamiliar, uncomfortable, or even distasteful to them. The cognitive and affective dissonance generated by these bumps then inhibits or disrupts desired communication and learning. *Cultural competence is the skillful, creative, and sometimes intuitive application of knowledge and skills to determine the source of cultural and linguistic dissonance and reestablish the desired communication and learning.*

Requisite Competencies

Promoting the development of the competencies needed to become culturally competent is not an easy task. Acquisition of these competencies often challenges all that lies at the core of how we define ourselves (e.g., worldviews, values). It also challenges the objective, mechanistic paradigm that generates our certainty that knowledge is something to be transmitted from teacher to learner rather than coconstructed between expert and novice (or, as is often the case with cultural competence, between novice and novice). Augsberger's (1986) description of cross-cultural competency, though focused on counseling, captured a key aspect of cultural competency that he termed "interpathy":

> Interpathy enables one to enter a second culture cognitively and affectively, to perceive and conceptualize the internal coherence that links the elements of the culture into a dynamic interrelatedness, to respect the culture (with its strengths and weaknesses) as equally valid to one's own. (p. 14)

The distinction between interpathy and either sympathy or empathy is an important one, which Augsberger described in a table that has been reprinted in this chapter (see Table 9.3).

From the context of the sources referenced throughout this chapter, as well as from their own experience and research, the authors have identified 12 competencies they believe to be essential to the crafting of culturally competent environments (see Table 9.4). Seven of the competencies address the acquisition of knowledge and understanding, and five address the development of particular skills. A corollary list of reflective questions is also presented to assist providers in assessing themselves in relation to each set of competencies. The activities mentioned in the next section and offered at the end of the chapter and the additional resources are designed to assist readers in developing the identified competencies themselves and promoting their development in others.

ACTIVITIES AND RESOURCES

The activities, as well as the overall perspective presented in this chapter, are drawn from Barrera's experiences in journeying from a transmission model to a reciprocal one, sometimes prompted gently by the results of multiple dialogues, both unskilled and skilled, with teachers and other practitioners across the United States. The journeying generated data indicating that 1) certain critical elements need to underlie the specific strategies and activities used to promote cultural competency in preservice and inservice settings, and 2) three levels of learning need to be addressed. These elements and levels are now reviewed. An annotated listing of additional resources and sample activities is provided at the end of this chapter.

Critical Elements

The primary element necessary for learning to craft culturally responsive environments is the **experience of such an environment** in preservice or inservice settings. That is, it is essential to model, not just talk about, cultural competency. Respectful dialogue is an essential component of this modeling. Freedman and Combs (1996) characterized this type of dialogue: "When we meet people for the first time, we want to understand the meaning of their stories *for them*. This sort of understanding requires that we listen with focused attention, patience, and curiosity while building a relationship of mutual respect and trust" (p. 44). It is precisely this type of understanding that children and families require and that caregivers must experience if they are to successfully craft culturally competent environments.

Self-reflection is another element that needs to be supported. Self-reflection is a necessary tool for understanding the contexts, behaviors, and values that define who we

TABLE 9.3. Boundaries among sympathy, empathy, and interpathy

Sympathy	Empathy	Interpathy
Sympathy is a spontaneous affective reaction to another's feelings experienced on the basis of perceived similarity between observer and observed.	Empathy is an intentional affective response to another's feelings experienced on the basis of perceived differences between observer and observed.	Interpathy is an intentional cognitive and affective envisioning of another's thoughts and feelings from another culture, worldview, [and] epistemology.
In sympathy, the process of "feeling with" the other is focused on one's own awareness of having experienced a similar event.	In empathy, the process of "feeling with" the other is focused on imagination, by which one is transposed into another, in self-conscious awareness of another's consciousness.	In interpathy, the process of knowing and "feeling with" requires that one temporarily believe what the other believes, see as the other sees, value what the other values.
In sympathy, I know you are in pain and I sympathize with you. I use my own feelings as the barometer; hence I feel my sympathy and my pain, not yours. You are judged by my perception of my own feelings. You are understood by extension of my self-understanding. My experience is both frame and picture.	In empathy, I empathically make an effort to understand your perceptions, thoughts, feelings, muscular tensions, even temporary states. In choosing to feel your pain with you, I do not own it; I share it. My experience is the frame, your pain is the picture.	In interpathy, I seek to learn a foreign belief, take a foreign perspective, base my thought on a foreign assumption, and feel the resultant feelings and their consequences in a foreign context. Your experience becomes both frame and picture.
Sympathy is a kind of projection of one's own inner feelings upon another, as inner feelings are judged to be similar to experiences in the other.	Empathy is the perception of a separate other based on common cultural assumptions, values, and patterns of thinking that provide a base for encoding and decoding percepts.	Interpathy is the experience of a separate other without common cultural assumptions, values, and views. It is the embracing of what is truly other.

From Augsberger, D.W. (1986). *Pastoral counseling across cultures.* Philadelphia: Westminster Press, p. 31. Copyright 1986 by David W. Augsburger. Used by permission of Westminster John Knox Press.

are and how we interact with the environment around us. "Self-awareness is the first step on the journey toward cross-cultural competence" (Lynch & Hanson, 1992, p. 37). Self-awareness must not, however, be restricted to just those aspects associated with cultural diversity (e.g., ethnic background, beliefs).[1] To effectively promote and support cultural competence, self-reflection must encompass multiple aspects of how we identify and maintain the boundaries that both connect us to and separate us from the people with whom

---

[1]Several caregivers have expressed concern to the authors about self-awareness activities at multicultural workshops that they believed validated stereotypes and reenacted, for them, past experiences with such stereotypes.

TABLE 9.4. Essential competencies for crafting culturally competent early childhood environments

Competency	Reflective assessment questions[a]

I. *Knowledge and understanding*
  a. of culture and cultural dynamics on general level and as apply to self and others
  b. of cross-cultural research on diverse patterns of child rearing, developmental support, and teaching/learning in various cultural contexts
  c. of knowledge construction, paradigms, and diverse worldviews (e.g., "objective scientific," "social constructivist")
  d. of cultural diversity (i.e., definitions, components, impact on children's learning and development)
  e. of power and social positioning dynamics that affect behavior and performance across cultural boundaries
  f. of elements of effective teaching for children who are culturally and linguistically diverse
  g. of mediation as a tool for culturally responsive intervention
	Am I able to perceive my cultural dynamics in interactions with others?
	Can I describe diverse child-rearing and developmental support patterns valued in a variety of cultural contexts and situations?
	Can I describe a variety of teaching/learning strategies as used in differing cultural contexts and situations?
	Can I describe reality from more than one perspective?
	Am I aware of historical events that have affected the experiences and perceptions of various cultural groups?
	Am I knowledgeable of the elements of effective teaching and can I relate them to working with culturally/linguistically diverse children and families?
	Can I identify how adults in children's environments are mediating experiences for children?

II. *Abilities/skills*
  a. reconsider one's role and understandings in light of different paradigms and cultural parameters
  b. locate early intervention within professional culture and community
  c. understand and respect children and family's understandings, especially when they differ significantly from my own
  d. creatively and collaboratively problem-solve with colleagues, families, and children to find best ways for bridging or mediating between understandings
  e. use these ways to mediate interactions and learning situations for children and communications and interactions with families
	"Am I situating my opinions in my [culture and] personal experience?"
	"Am I being transparent about my context, my values, and my intentions so that this person can evaluate the effects of my biases?"
	"Am I listening so as to understand how the [family's] experiential reality has been socially constructed?"; how it "makes sense" within their context?
	"Whose language [and worldview] is being privileged?" "Am I evaluating this person, or am I inviting her/him to evaluate a wide range of [possibilities]?"
	Am I focused on curiously examining "puzzlements" or on determining needs and gaps?
	Am I being responsive to cultural/linguistic parameters as I structure children's experiences?
	Am I being mindful: listening with focused attention, patience, and curiosity?
	Am I building relationships of mutual respect and trust?

[a]Questions in quotes are taken from Freedman, J., & Combs, G. (1996). *Narrative therapy: The social construction of preferred realities* (pp. 40–41). New York: Norton.

we interact (Hall & du Gay, 1996). Self-reflection on our actions is "central to the 'art' by which practitioners sometimes deal well with situations of uncertainty, instability, uniqueness, and value conflict" (Schön, 1983, p. 50). Without self-reflection, decision making in complex situations becomes merely reactive rather than responsive.

A third element is an explicit focus on **critical inquiry and decision-making skills.** The adage "If you give people fish, they will eat for a day; if you teach them how to fish, they will eat forever" captures the essence of this third element. There are no *fish,* no easy preset cookbook of steps to achieving cultural competence. The combinations of variables present in any particular interaction are too complex to be predetermined (e.g., two Native American children, even if from the same community, may reflect significantly different funds of knowledge and levels of acculturation). Assessing needs and developing appropriate interventions in specific situations require critical inquiry and decision-making skills to assess appropriateness of generic information, obtain additional information, and evaluate options.

Levels of Learning

The activities described in this chapter are organized around three levels of learning that the authors have found essential in teaching the craft of cultural competence: 1) a theoretical knowledge or "learning about" level; 2) a situated learning experiences or "learning with" level; and 3) a mediated applications or "learning through" level, in which learners are asked to apply their knowledge and skills to specific cases and situations. These levels are not sequential but are interwoven according to learner needs, preferences, cultural influences, and other circumstances. A short description of each level is given in the next section, followed by examples of activities designed to promote professional development at each level.[2]

Theoretical Knowledge Level   Activities at the theoretical knowledge level focus on developing and assessing mastery of literature and research related to culture, cultural diversity, and cultural competence. Of special importance is cross-cultural research and literature, with its rich descriptions of child rearing and child development in diverse contexts. This level of knowledge serves several purposes: 1) it affirms and validates the range and value of diversity; 2) it challenges "the validity of our current assumptions about human behavior and . . . [frees] . . . us from our own unconscious ethnocentrism" (Nugent, 1994, p. 3); and 3) it provides practitioners with the rationale to support culturally competent practices in the face of questions or criticisms (see Activities 1.1–1.3).

Situated Learning Experiences Level   The term *situated learning* is borrowed from Lave and Wenger (1991). In describing their understanding of the term, they stated, "In contrast to learning as internalization, learning as increasing participation in communities of practice concerns the whole person acting in the world" (p. 49). Learning at the theoretical level is essentially internalized learning. It is only when that learning, along with other existing knowledge, is situated in "communities of practice" that it becomes real. Barrera's experience has demonstrated that theoretical knowledge comes alive only as it is personalized through joint discussions and explorations with others in contexts that reflect a range of cultural diversity. However, situated learning experiences are not

---

[2]These activities are intended only as brief illustrations of each level. Many sources of additional activities are available (see Resources section), though Levels 1 and 3 are less represented in these sources than is Level 2. Many activities can, however, be adapted to meet the goals of Levels 1 and 3. It is recommended that this be done when possible, as the authors' experiences have demonstrated that addressing only Level 2 is insufficient for optimal development of cultural competency.

artificially contrived situations. Learners are not asked to simply role-play; rather, they are asked to participate in activities and contexts that reflect diverse paradigms, with people who reflect diverse cultures. Structured, "safe" opportunities to interact with people different from ourselves on topics that are emotionally and politically volatile are not all that common. Yet structured opportunities to ask questions such as "What is your experience of being African American?" or to simply share information on worldviews and experiences provide one of the strongest sources for developing understanding and interpathy. Cultural competency needs to be developed in a relational context if it is to involve true knowing and not merely knowing about (see Activities 2.1–2.3).

Mediated Applications Level   The mediation of learning experiences has been addressed almost exclusively in relation to young children:

> Mediated learning experience is that which takes place when an initiated human being, a mother, father, or other care giving adult, interposes himself or herself between the organism and the stimuli impinging on it and mediates, transforms, reorders, organizes, groups, and frames the stimuli in the direction of some specifically intended goals and purpose. (Feuerstein & Jensen, 1980, p. 409, as cited in Mearig, 1983)

Tharp and Gallimore (1988) elaborated on this concept, terming it "assisted performance": *"Teachers themselves must have their performance assisted* if they are to acquire the ability to assist the performance of their participants" (p. 43, emphasis added). The mediated applications level focuses on structuring opportunities for mediated, or assisted, practice as providers begin to apply new information and skills. *Note:* The sample activities chosen provide some alternatives to case studies, the primary type of activity for this level. Case studies should be drawn from situations with which participants are familiar and may be written or videotaped. Many of the discussion questions used at this level and at earlier levels can then be used to discuss various aspects of the cases (see Activities 3.1–3.3).

CONCLUSION

This chapter provided an overview of key issues and concepts related to cultural diversity and cultural competency and provided examples of activities and resources that may be used to enhance the understanding and skills of early childhood providers interested in becoming more responsive to the challenges posed by cultural diversity. Delpit (1995) provided a strong image of these challenges:

> We all carry worlds in our heads, and those worlds are decidedly different. We . . . set out to teach, but how can we reach the worlds of others when we don't even know they exist? Indeed, many of us don't even realize that our own worlds exist only in our heads and in the cultural institutions we have built to support them. *It is as if we are in the middle of a virtual reality game, but the 'realities' displayed in various participants' minds are entirely different terrains.* When one player moves right up a hill, the other player perceives him as moving left and into a river. (p. xiv, emphasis added)

The material in this chapter does not answer all the questions associated with reaching the worlds of others who are diverse from ourselves. The authors' intent was to initiate the dialogues that are essential to providing answers suitable for specific contexts. As Delpit (1995) concluded, "The answers, I believe, lie not in a proliferation of new reform programs but in some basic understandings of who we are and how we are connected to or disconnected from one another" (p. xv).

RESOURCES

Alta Mira Specialized Family Service, Inc. (1995). *Project Ta-kos: Understanding family uniqueness through cultural diversity.* Albuquerque, NM: Author. Cost: $85 plus shipping. (505) 842-9948.

Project Ta-kos instruction in cultural sensitivity is formatted in four workshop sessions. The first workshop examines self-awareness, cultural exclusiveness, and consciousness raising; the second, heightened awareness; the third, overemphasis; and the fourth, integration and balance. Each workshop builds on the previous workshop. This instructional program for service providers reflects a strong emphasis on the participants' identifying and examining their own unique cultural backgrounds.

BUENO Center for Multicultural Education. (1994). *BUENO modules for bilingual special education.* Boulder: University of Colorado School of Education. Cost: $150 each module. (303) 492-5416.

The BUENO modules provide a flexible resource that can be used in whole or in part for preservice or inservice courses, as well as for shorter institutes and workshops, addressing the needs of culturally and linguistically different students with learning and behavior problems in the classroom. Presentation notes, handouts, and overheads are included.

Carter, M., & Curtis, D. (1994). *Training teachers: A harvest of theory and practice.* St. Paul, MN: Redleaf Press. Cost: $32.95. (800) 423-8309.

This instructional monograph invites teachers of young children to become autonomous learners, responsive planners, and problem solvers in their classrooms through a narrative format. The text is presented in the theoretical framework that the authors actually use in their instructional sessions. The instruction is presented in sequential chapters: 1) overview of adult learning; 2) sample strategies for instructional topics; 3) and 4) effective teaching and instructional roles in addressing culturally sensitive and antibias practices; 5) an inclusive approach to workshop planning and staff development; 6) an outline of a project approach for teacher instruction on child-centered curriculum practice in an ongoing setting; and 7) tips on instructor resources, organization, and effective practices.

Center for Peace Education. (1995). *Dealing with differences: A training manual for young people and adults on intergroup relations, diversity, and multicultural education.* Carrboro, NC: Author. Cost: $60. (919) 929-9821.

This extensive manual is designed for individuals who are interested in facilitating workshops and classes on understanding diversity, promoting multicultural education, and improving intergroup relations. The manual provides a conceptual framework and detailed instructions for activities and allows the learners to see explicit connections to their own lives.

Quality Educational Development, Inc. (1994). *The diversity game.* New York: Author. Cost: $195. (202) 724-3335.

This board game is designed to raise awareness of diversity and encourage communication and interaction with individuals of differing cultural and linguistic backgrounds in the workplace. Three key concepts frame the game: 1) a diverse culture means a diverse workplace, 2) valuing diversity, and 3) valuing individuals leads to an effective work force. Questions on the category cards explore demographics, jobs, legislation, and society.

Seelye, H.N. (Ed.). (1966). *Experiential activities for intercultural learning.* Yarmouth, ME: Intercultural Press. Cost: $29.95. (207) 846-5168.

This monograph provides instructional materials in cross-cultural instruction and intercultural education. The emphasis is on the development of intercultural awareness and cross-cultural sensitivity, the dimensions of intercultural communication, cross-cultural human relations, and cultural diversity. Included are simulations, case studies, role plays, critical incidents, and individual and group exercises. Activities are organized by objectives, materials, setting, time, background/rationale, procedures, and resources for further reading.

Taylor, T. (1992). *Moving toward cultural competency: A self-assessment checklist.* Washington, DC: Georgetown Child Development Center. $2. (202) 687-8635.

A self-administered checklist for personnel who provide services to young children. The checklist provides a profile of the cultural competence of their programmatic setting.

York, S. (1991). *Roots and wings: Affirming culture in early childhood programs.* St. Paul, MN: Redleaf Press. Cost: $22.95. (800) 423-8309.

This book is written for early childhood teachers, program directors, teachers, instructors, and parents. Three objectives frame this practical text: 1) an understanding of multicultural education, with an emphasis on culture, ethnicity, and race; 2) practical ideas for implementing multicultural education in early childhood settings; and 3) providing useful information about multicultural education outside textbooks and professional journals.

REFERENCES

Alta Mira Specialized Family Service, Inc. (1995). *Project Ta-kos: Understanding family uniqueness through cultural diversity.* Albuquerque, NM: Author.

Augsburger, D.W. (1986). *Pastoral counseling across cultures.* Philadelphia: Westminster Press.

Ayers, W. (1989). *The good preschool teacher.* New York: Teachers College Press.

Barrera, I. (1994). *Cultural/linguistic diversity and young children with special needs: A skeleton guide to development of appropriate services.* Unpublished material prepared for full-day inservice workshop.

Barrera, I. (1996). Assessment of infants and toddlers from diverse sociocultural backgrounds. In S. Meisels & E. Fenichel (Eds.), *New visions for developmental assessment* (pp. 69–84). Washington, DC: ZERO TO THREE/National Center for Clinical Infant Programs.

Barrera, I., Macpherson, D., & Kramer, L. (in press). *Cultural competence: A handbook for early childhood service providers.* Baltimore: Paul H. Brookes Publishing Co.

Berger, K.S., & Thompson, R.A. (1995). *The developing person: Through childhood and adolescence.* New York: Worth Publishing.

Bowers, C.A., & Flinders, D.J. (1990). *Responsive teaching: An ecological approach to classroom patterns of language, culture, and thought.* New York: Teachers College Press.

Bowman, B.T. (1992). Who is at risk for what and why. *Journal of Early Intervention, 16*(2), 101–108.

Bronfenbrenner, U. (1979). *The ecology of human development.* Cambridge, MA: Harvard University Press.

Brookfield, S.D. (1987). *Developing critical thinkers.* San Francisco: Jossey-Bass.

BUENO Center for Multicultural Education. (1994). *BUENO modules for bilingual special education.* Boulder: University of Colorado School of Education.

Bullivant, B.M. (1989). Culture: Its nature and meaning for educators. In J.A. Banks & C.A. Banks (Eds.), *Multicultural education: Issues and perspectives* (pp. 27–46). Needham, MA: Allyn & Bacon.

Carter, M., & Curtis, D. (1994). *Training teachers: A harvest of theory and practice.* St. Paul, MN: Redleaf Press.

Center for Peace Education. (1995). *Dealing with differences: A training manual for young people and adults on intergroup relations, diversity, and multicultural education.* Carrboro, NC: Author.

Challenge of change: What the 1990 census tells us about children. (1992). Washington, DC: Center for the Study of Social Policy.

Darder, A. (1991). *Culture & power in the classroom: A critical foundation for bicultural education.* Westport, CT: Greenwood Publishing Group.

de Bono, E. (1995). *Mind power.* New York: Dorling Kindersley.

Delpit, L. (1995). *Other people's children: Cultural conflict in the classroom.* New York: New Press.

Desking, G., & Steckler, G. (1996). *When nothing makes sense: Disaster, crisis, and other effects on children.* Minneapolis, MN: Fairview Press.

Devito, J.A. (1995). *The interpersonal communication book.* New York: HarperCollins.

Donovan, D.M., & McIntyre, D. (1990). *Healing the hurt child: A developmental-contextual approach.* New York: Norton.

Figueroa, R.A., & Garcia, E. (1994). Issues in testing students from culturally and linguistically diverse backgrounds. *Multicultural Education, 2*(1), 10–19.

Freedman, J., & Combs, G. (1996). *Narrative therapy: The social construction of preferred realities.* New York: Norton.

Gergen, K.J. (1985). Social constructionist inquiry: Context and implications. In K.J. Gergen & K.E. Davis (Eds.), *The social construction of the person* (pp. 3–18). New York: Springer-Verlag.

Gonzalez-Mena, J. (1993). *Multicultural issues in childcare.* Mountain View, CA: Mayfield Publishing Co.

Gonzalez-Mena, J., & Eyer, D. (1993). *Infants, toddlers, and caregivers.* Mountain View, CA: Mayfield Publishing Co.

Greenfield, M.E., & Cocking, R.R. (Eds.). (1994). *Cross-cultural roots of minority child development.* Hillsdale, NJ: Lawrence Erlbaum Associates.

Hall, E.T. (1977). *Beyond culture.* Garden City, NY: Anchor Books/Doubleday.

Hall, E.T., & Hall, M.R. (1990). *Understanding cultural differences.* Yarmouth, ME: Intercultural Press.

Hall, E.T., & White, W.F. (1979). Intercultural communication: Human organization. In C.D. Mortenson (Ed.), *Basic readings in communication theory* (pp. 355–370). New York: Harper & Row.

Hall, S., & du Gay, P. (1966). *Questions of cultural identity.* Beverly Hills: Sage Publications.

Harkness, S. (1992). Cross-cultural research in child development: A sample of the state of the art. *Developmental Psychology, 28,* 622–625.

Harry, B. (1992). Developing cultural awareness. *Topics in Early Childhood Special Education, 12*(3), 333–350.

Harwood, R.L. (1992). The influence of culturally derived values on Anglo and Puerto Rican mothers' perceptions of attachment behavior. *Child Development, 63,* 822–838.

Haviland, W.A. (1993). *Cultural anthropology.* Orlando, FL: Harcourt Brace College Publishers.

Hedegaard, M. (1990). The zone of proximal development as basis for instruction. In L.C. Moll (Ed.), *Vygotsky and education: Instructional implications and applications of sociohistorical psychology* (pp. 349–371). New York: Cambridge University Press.

Jensen, M.R., & Feuerstein, R. (1987). The learning potential assessment device: From philosophy to practice. In C.S. Lidz (Ed.), *Dynamic assessment: An interactional approach to evaluating learning potential* (pp. 379–402). New York: Guilford Press.

Kessler, S.A., & Swadener, B.B. (Eds.). (1992). *Reconceptualizing early childhood education curriculum: Beginning the dialogue.* New York: Teachers College Press.

Koplow, L. (Ed.). (1996). *Unsmiling faces: How preschools can heal.* New York: Teachers College Press.

Koslow, D.R., & Salett, E.P. (1989). *Crossing cultures in mental health.* Washington, DC: SIETAR International.

Kozol, J. (1991). *Savage inequalities: Children in America's schools.* New York: Crown Publishers.

Landrine, H. (1992). Clinical implications of cultural differences: The referential versus the indexical self. *Clinical Psychology Review, 12,* 410–415.

Lave, J., & Wenger, E. (1991). *Situated learning: Legitimate peripheral participation.* Cambridge, MA: Cambridge University Press.

Lidz, C.S., & Thomas, C. (1987). The preschool learning assessment device: Extension of a static approach. In C.S. Lidz (Ed.), *Dynamic assessment: An interactional approach to evaluating learning potential* (pp. 288–326). New York: Guilford Press.

Lynch, E.W., & Hanson, M.J. (Eds.). (1992a). *Developing cross-cultural competence: A guide for working with young children and their families.* Baltimore: Paul H. Brookes Publishing Co.

Lynch, E.W., & Hanson, M.J. (1992b). Steps in the right direction: Implications for interventionists. In E.W. Lynch & M.J. Hanson (Eds.), *Developing cross-cultural competence: A guide for working with young children and their families* (pp. 355–370) Baltimore: Paul H. Brookes Publishing Co.

Mallory, B.L., & New, R. (Eds.). (1994). *Diversity and developmentally appropriate practices: Challenges for early childhood education.* New York: Teachers College Press.

Markus, H.R., & Kitayama, S. (1991). Culture and self: Implications for cognition, emotions, and motivation. *Psychology Review, 98*(2), 224–253.

McIntosh, P. (1989, July–August). White privilege: Unpacking the invisible knapsack. *Peace & Freedom,* 10–12.

McLeod, D. (1995). Self-identity, pan-ethnicity and the boundaries of group identity. *Multicultural Education, 3*(2), 8–11.

Mearig, J.S. (1987). Assessing the learning potential of kindergarten and primary-age children. In C.S. Lidz (Ed.), *Dynamic assessment: An interactional approach to evaluating learning potential* (pp. 237–267). New York: Guilford Press.

Miller, A. (1994). *Drama of the gifted child.* New York: Basic Books.

National Center for Health Statistics. (1990). *Vital statistics of the United States, of 1990, Vol. 1.* U.S. Report of the Health & Human Services, Public Health Service, Centers for Disease Control and Prevention, Hyattsville, MD: Author.

New York State Education Department. (n.d.). *Teaching culturally linguistically diverse students with handicapping conditions.* Albany, NY: Office of Education of Children with Handicaps.

Nugent, J.K. (1994). Cross-cultural studies of child development: Implications for clinicians. *Zero to Three, 15*(2), 1–8.

Ogbu, J.U. (1995). Understanding cultural diversity and learning. In J.A. Banks & C.A. Banks (Eds.), *Handbook of research on multicultural education* (pp. 582–593). New York: Macmillan.

PACER. (1995). *Risky situations: Vulnerable children.* Minneapolis, MN: Author.

Paradise, R. (1994). Traditional style and nonverbal meaning: Manzahua children learning how to be separate-but-together. *Anthropology and Education Quarterly, 25*(2), 156–172.

Price-Williams, D., & Gallimore, R. (1980). The cultural perspective. *Advances in Special Education, 2,* 165–192.

Quality Educational Development, Inc. (1994). *The diversity game.* New York: Author.

Riley, P. (1993). *Growing up Native American.* New York: Avon.

Rogoff, B., Mistry, A., Göncü, A., & Mosier, C. (1993). Guided participation in cultural activity of toddlers and caregivers. *Monographs of the Society for Research in Child Development,* Serial No. 235(8), 58.

Schön, D.A. (1983). *The reflective practitioner.* New York: Basic Books.

Schön, D.A. (1987). *Educating the reflective practitioner.* San Francisco: Jossey-Bass.

Seelye, H.N. (Ed.). (1966). *Experiential activities for intercultural learning.* Yarmouth, ME: Intercultural Press.

Skutnabb-Kangas, T., & Cummins, J. (1988). *Minority education: From shame to struggle.* Philadelphia: Multilingual Matters.

Soto, L.D., & Smrekar, J.L. (1992). The politics of early bilingual education. In S. Kessler & B. Swadener (Eds.), *Reconceptualizing the early childhood curriculum: Beginning the dialogue* (pp. 89–101). New York: Teachers College Press.

Spradley, J.P. (1972). Foundations of cultural knowledge. In J.P. Spradley (Ed.), *Culture and cognition: Rules, maps, and plans* (pp. 31–38). Prospect Heights, IL: Waveland Press.

Stewart, E.C., & Bennett, M.J. (1991). *American cultural patterns: A cross-cultural perspective.* Yarmouth, ME: Intercultural Press.

Storti, C. (1994). *Cross-cultural dialogues: 74 brief encounters with cultural difference.* Yarmouth, ME: Intercultural Press.

Super, C.M., & Harkness, S. (1981). Figure, ground, and gestalt: The cultural context of the active individual. In R.M. Lerner & N.A. Busch-Rossnagel (Eds.), *Individuals as producers of their development* (pp. 69–86). New York: Academic Press.

Takaki, R. (1993). *A different mirror: A history of multicultural America.* Boston: Little, Brown.

Taylor, T. (1992). *Moving toward cultural competency: A self-assessment checklist.* Washington, DC: Georgetown Child Development Center.

Tharp, R.G., & Gallimore, R. (1988). *Rousing minds to life: Teaching, learning and schooling in social context.* Cambridge, MA: Cambridge University Press.

Thompson, B., & Tyagi, S. (Eds.). (1996). *Names we call home: Autobiography on racial identity.* New York: Routledge.

Valdés, G. (1996). *Con respecto: Bridging the differences between culturally diverse families and schools.* New York: Teachers College Press.

Vann, G. (1960). *Heart of man.* Garden City, NY: Image Books.

Weisner, T.S., Gallimore, R., & Jordan, C. (1993). Unpackaging cultural effects on classroom learning: Hawaiian peer assistance and child-generated activity. In R.N. Roberts (Ed.), *Coming home to preschool: The sociocultural context of early education* (pp. 59–90). Norwood, NJ: Ablex Publishing Co.

Weissbourd, R. (1996). *The vulnerable child: What really hurts America's children and what we can do about it.* Reading, MA: Addison-Wesley.

York, S. (1991). *Roots and wings: Affirming culture in early childhood programs.* St. Paul, MN: Redleaf Press.

ACTIVITY 1.1

THEORETICAL KNOWLEDGE LEVEL: CONCEPT MAPPING

Objectives:

- To stimulate thinking around particular concepts
- To compare and contrast participants' formulations of these concepts

Materials

- Large sheets of paper
- Markers
- Sample concept maps (see Figure 9.1, and the following readings [if doing follow-up]: Hall & Hall, 1990; Stewart & Bennett, 1991; Storti, 1994)

Instructions:

NOTE: The sequence of this activity is designed to first elicit participants' concepts as they exist before reading specific information on them.

1. Identify a concept(s) (e.g., family, culture) for participants to map. This activity works best when all participants map the same concept and when there are diverse backgrounds represented in the audience.

2. Explain to the participants that a concept map is a visual word depiction of how a person structures a concept, similar to webbing (if they are familiar with that technique). The map is composed of circles within which words are written. The circles are connected by lines on which linking words are written. A concept map is hierarchical from top to bottom; that is, the primary concept is on top and subconcepts or components are below the primary concept (see examples in Figure 9.1).

3. Give participants paper, markers, and the following directions:
   a. Think about what you think this concept (e.g., family) means as you understand it. If you had to explain or define it for someone from another planet, how would you do so? What components, functions, or other aspects would you include?
   b. Now, I would like you to map this concept, following these rules: your map must be hierarchical from top to bottom; you must include linking words on all lines; when you are done, someone reading your map should be able to understand your understanding of the concept.

4. Allow 15–20 minutes for participants to map the chosen concept. Ask participants to tape their map on the wall when they are done; they may or may not sign it.

5. When all participants are done, allow participants 5–10 minutes to walk around and review the maps. Ask them to notice both content (what was included or not included) and structure (visual and hierarchical organization).

6. Discuss similarities and differences in how each person has depicted the same concept.

7. As a follow-up activity, assign readings from Hall and Hall (1990), Stewart and Bennett (1991), and Storti (1994). When these are completed, discuss how culture influences how we each structure our concepts. Bring the maps back out and ask each student to discuss what experiences or learning influenced him or her to structure the concept in a particular way. Can any cultural influences be identified? What other influences are identified?

Comments:

One of the challenges of becoming culturally competent is learning to think in a pluralistic, both/and fashion, rather than in a polarized, either/or fashion. This activity helps participants learn that concepts can be validly structured in multiple ways. Initial responses sometimes center on which map is right or most correct. (Discussion on whether maps need to be judged in this fashion can be an important part of this activity.) Other times there is surprise at the variety of ways a concept can be structured even in a group considered nondiverse.

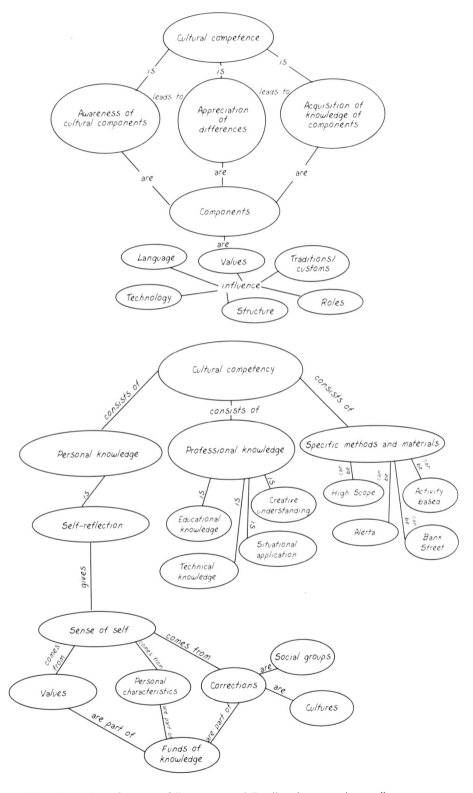

Figure 9.1. Examples of maps of the concept "cultural competency."

ACTIVITY 1.2

THEORETICAL KNOWLEDGE LEVEL: FUNDS OF KNOWLEDGE

Objective:

- To assist participants to identify how cultural values and beliefs influence perceptions of children and children's roles

Materials:

- A selection of children's books reflective of various cultures and countries (include some in languages other than English if there are participants who can read and translate them)

- Funds of Knowledge worksheet (prepared by activity leader)

- Readings: Chapter 1 from Rogoff, Mistry, Göncü, and Mosier (1993), and Chapter 2 from Bowers and Flinders (1990)

Instructions:

1. Before initiating the activity, prepare Funds of Knowledge worksheets: Take a sheet of paper and divide it into eight spaces. Label each space with one of the following categories: concepts, experiences, story grammar (e.g., event sequence, plot), social environments, family/community composition and organization, approaches to problem solving, language, other (e.g., values). Type the following instructions on the top: "Select and read a children's story. After reading it, identify the fund(s) of knowledge it reflects (i.e., the types of knowledge it assumes as normative). Use the categories below as a guide to the different aspects of the story's fund of knowledge."

2. Assign readings; include others you may be familiar with that may also seem appropriate. (This activity follows concept mapping well.)

3. After readings are completed, bring children's books to class. Ask participants to form small groups of two to three and select two books they would like to review.

4. Give each group of participants a Funds of Knowledge worksheet and ask them to complete it (20–30 minutes).

5. When completed, ask groups to present their findings to the class and discuss how they completed each part of the worksheet.

6. After all groups have reported, ask participants to relate their findings to their readings.

Comments:

This activity has proved helpful in sensitizing participants to how cultural beliefs and values are transmitted; it also helps them identify and prevent possible cultural bumps. Rogoff et al. (1993) discussed how different communities emphasize different behaviors in keeping with their developmental expectations and social goals. Can participants find evidence of this in the stories they read? Bowers and Flinders (1990) stated that the "language is not a neutral tool for the expression of ideas preformed in the mind of the individual" (p. 33). Can participants find support for this statement as a result of their activity?

ACTIVITY 1.3

THEORETICAL KNOWLEDGE LEVEL: AGREE/DISAGREE

Objective:

- To assist participants to identify how cultural values and beliefs influence perceptions of children and children's roles

Materials:

- Agree/disagree signs (strongly agree, agree somewhat, disagree somewhat, strongly disagree) (should be big enough to read comfortably from across the room)

- Three belief statements (you may use those listed below or develop others)

- Readings: Gonzalez-Mena (1993) and Rogoff et al. (1993)

- Belief statements: 1) Culture is the most significant influence in shaping your behavior, beliefs, and values; 2) intervention should always use the child's home language; and 3) culture is the most significant influence in determining the content of the curriculum used in early intervention settings.

Instructions:

1. Before session, place agree/disagree signs in room, one at each corner.

2. Before session, prepare transparencies, one statement per transparency.

3. Once session starts, place statements one at a time on overhead. Ask participants to stand under the sign that best represents their position on that statement.

4. Tally participants under each sign by number and/or name. Allow time for participants to observe ratio of positions on each statement.

5. Choose the statement that elicited the most diverse responses. Repeat this statement and ask participants to return to the position they took on that statement. Form small groups in the following proportions: one person from each "strongly" group and two people from each "somewhat" group.
   (NOTE: If no statement elicited a significant degree of diversity of responses, participants may be "assigned" to positions and asked to role-play them.)

6. Groups are instructed to reach consensus according to the following procedure: Within each group, the "agree" people are asked to be "persuaders" while the "disagree" people listen. This is done for 5 minutes. Then "persuaders" and "listeners" change roles: The disagree people are given 5 minutes to persuade. At the end of the 10 minutes, both sides are given 3 minutes to reach consensus.

7. Ask small groups to share and discuss their process and decisions with the total group. Were they able to reach consensus? How did they feel as they reversed roles from "persuader" to "listener"? If positions were changed, what most influenced the change?

8. As a follow-up, assign readings. When completed, ask participants to discuss their positions once again in light of the information they have read. Did the information support their position? Did it promote a shift in position?

Activity 1.3 is adapted from one presented in *Teaching Culturally and Linguistically Diverse Students with Handicapping Conditions*, a training manual developed by the New York State Education Department, Office of Education of Children with Handicapping Conditions, Albany.

Comments:

This activity can lead to insights related to the range of positions people can hold and the correlation of these positions to literature and research. A significant portion of a person's beliefs regarding culture and cultural diversity is based on personal experiences and emotionally laden values rather than on carefully thought-out arguments based on research. For this reason, discussion of these beliefs is important, as is learning that consensus need not always be reached. Another application of this exercise is to use it as a simulation of traditional Native American problem-solving practices within which consensus, not majority, decides actions to be undertaken.

ACTIVITY 2.1

SITUATED LEARNING LEVEL: IDENTITY CIRCLES OR "NAMES WE CALL HOME"

Objective:

- To assist participants to become familiar with their own and others' identities and the role culture has played in structuring these (i.e., to bring culture home)

Materials:

- Paper

- Markers

- Readings: Part I of Koslow and Salett (1989); Landrine (1992); Markus and Kitayama (1991)

Instructions:

1. Ask participants to find a partner. Once in pairs, ask one student to ask the other, "Who are you?" five times. The other student has 30 seconds to reply each time. Replies should be written down by the student doing the questioning. Once one student has given five answers, ask them to switch roles and repeat, with the other student answering. Discuss results briefly (this part is optional, depending on available time).

2. Tell participants they are now to get their five responses from the questioner and add any others of which they may have thought. Then tell them to draw a circle and divide it into as many parts as they have identifiers, writing one identifier in each part. Make the size of each part representative of the relative weight of that identifier (e.g., the part in which "student" is written might be smaller than the part in which "Vietnamese" is written).

3. Once this activity is completed, ask participants to discuss their circles, either in small groups or as a whole class (e.g., Were identifiers directly cultural such as "Indian"? Were they role related such as "student"?). Ask them to discuss the possible role of culture in defining each of the identifiers. Compare and contrast identifiers across participants. Can they be categorized? Into which categories?

4. As a follow-up, assign readings, then ask participants to reexamine their circles and discuss how the "names" they chose to "call home" relate to the information in their readings.

Comments:

Culture is not only about what we believe and do, it is also about who we are and how we define ourselves. Respecting distinctions in how identities are constructed and understanding that they *are* constructed is an important aspect of cultural competency. This activity stimulates rich discussions, especially when done with a diverse group.

"Names We Call Home" is a title borrowed from a book of the same name (Thompson & Tyagi, 1996).

ACTIVITY 2.2

SITUATED LEARNING LEVEL: DRAWING CONVERSATIONS

Objectives:

- To stimulate conversations about boundaries and the role of culture in shaping them

- To increase participants' awareness about their interactional patterns and habits

Materials:

- Large sheets of drawing paper

- Markers of assorted colors

- Reading: Units 1–2 of Devito (1995)

Instructions:

1. Tell students they are to have a nonverbal conversation in which they are to draw, instead of talk, back and forth. Who starts and how turns are determined are to be decided nonverbally; no talking is allowed. Each should respond to what the other does according to how he or she feels and how he or she interprets the drawing, as would happen in a verbal conversation.

2. Ask participants to pair off and find a place to sit facing each other. Each pair receives a sheet of drawing paper, and each student in the pair chooses two markers of different colors.

3. You may time the activity, or allow it to follow its own time, typically anywhere from 10 to 30 minutes.

4. Once "conversations" are concluded, ask dyads to tape them to the wall. Typically, some pairs end up with one full-page picture, others end up with multiple images or small pictures. Once drawings are on the wall, ask participants to discuss the following points:

   - What the process felt like

   - How they made decisions about start, content, and turn taking

   - Any instances in which one partner's behavior felt intrusive to or out-of-sync with the other

   - How each tried to control, adapt, or, in some other fashion, respond to the other

   - The degree to which various messages from familial, cultural, or educational contexts influenced their behaviors and responses

5. As a follow-up, assign reading and ask participants to discuss how it did or did not apply to their "conversation."

Comments:

This activity is one strategy for eliciting aspects of interactional patterns that may not be conscious. It is important to have established some trust with participants for them to share freely.

ACTIVITY 2.3

SITUATED LEARNING LEVEL: THERE'S ALWAYS A THIRD CHOICE

Objective:

- To stimulate cognitive flexibility in cultural contexts

Materials:

- Third Choice Worksheets (use scenarios given below or generate others based on your own and others' experiences)
- Readings: Stewart and Bennett (1991) (especially pp. 52–55)

Instructions:

1. Assign readings to participants. Prepare Third Choice Worksheets by taking the following scenarios and placing them on transparencies or separate sheets of paper:

    Scenario 1. Practitioner A likes to establish rapport with parents by spending time chatting with them before initiating work with their child. Parent B believes that this is a waste of time and that the practitioner needs to "get to the point."

    Choice 1: Practitioner can explain her behavior to parent and continue to chat as before.

    Choice 2: Practitioner can stop chatting in deference to parent's wishes.

    Choice 3: ?????? [Generate one or more alternative choices.]

    Scenario 2. Parent A believes that infancy is a time to play with few demands from adults. Provider B believes that although play is important, structured intervention is necessary to prevent developmental delays from worsening.

    Choice 1: "Educate" parent as to rationale for early intervention.
    Choice 2: Limit structured intervention to times when working with infant without the parent present.
    Choice 3: ?????? [Generate one or more alternative choices.]

    Scenario 3. Practitioner A believes that all intervention should adhere to family's culture and non-English language as much as possible. Practitioner B believes that both child and family need to learn skills necessary to succeed "in the mainstream"; after all, they can continue with their culture and language at home.

    Choice 1: Match intervention to family's culture and non-English language in all instances.
    Choice 2: Explain to family that early childhood providers will use English and will follow set curriculum and strategies, as for all other children.
    Choice 3: ?????? [Generate one or more alternative choices.]

2. Discuss the tendency of American culture and language to perceive and emphasize dichotomies (e.g., good/bad, near/far) compared with other cultures.

3. Ask participants to form groups of two to three. Give each group a Third Choice Worksheet and ask them to brainstorm words to generate additional options (or use overhead and work as a total group).

Activity 2.3 is based on a workshop presented by Gonzalez-Mena (1996), which was attended by one of the authors of this chapter.

4. After activity is completed, or at end of assigned time (typically 15–30 minutes is sufficient), ask groups to share the results of their brainstorming. A master worksheet may be drawn on an overhead or on a large piece of paper for posting on the wall; results can be entered on this worksheet.

5. Ask groups with greatest difficulty and with least difficulty in completing activity what factors they believe contributed to their ability to find appropriate third choices.

Comments:

This activity works well in conjunction with Activity 3.1 (Cultural Bumps). Although it is important to respect children's and families' values and preferences, it is not always possible to model them in an early childhood setting (e.g., close physical contact and caring for 5- and 6-year-olds). The ability to develop third choices can help prevent these situations from becoming unequal "win–lose" power situations. The ability to playfully explore paradigms other than those that are most familiar to us is a key aspect of connecting across cultural boundaries.

ACTIVITY 3.1

MEDIATED APPLICATIONS LEVEL: CULTURAL BUMPS

Objective:

- To stimulate cognitive flexibility in cultural contexts

Materials:

- Scenarios from the Third Choice Worksheet (as in Activity 2.3)
- Readings: Chapter 9 of Valdés (1996), especially pages 200–205; Paradise (1994)

Instructions:

1. The focus of this activity is on the scenarios themselves rather than on the resulting choices. These may be copied from the Third Choice Worksheet and placed on transparencies or on separate sheets to give to participants.

2. Discuss the concept of cultural bumps (p. 229, this chapter). Ask participants to think about times when they experienced negative emotions or a communication breakdown with someone.

3. Tell participants to form small groups of three. Give each group a sheet with scenarios (from Activity 2.3) or copy each scenario on a transparency to discuss as a total group. Ask participants to read scenarios and discuss differences in positions between family or child and service provider(s), then ask participants to role-play one or more of the situations.

4. Debrief activity, asking groups to discuss how they felt and what insights were triggered by the activity. Can behaviors be easily changed? Can different behaviors reflect similar values and beliefs?

5. Have each group present its solutions to the large group. If large group includes members who are currently in early childhood settings, they can then discuss strengths and weaknesses of the solutions for settings and situations with which they are familiar.

Comments:

This activity works well as a follow-up to the Third Choice activity, bringing it to a more concrete level. Though the readings are specific to particular communities, their conclusions are the same: Behaviors are deeply rooted in underlying values and beliefs. Simply changing a behavior without addressing these values and beliefs can often worsen rather than improve a situation.

ACTIVITY 3.2

MEDIATED APPLICATIONS LEVEL: MEDIATION PRACTICE

Objectives:

- To develop abilities to identify aspects of intervention strategies that research indicates are culturally influenced

- To modulate the same strategies according to cultural variations of these aspects

Materials:

- Various materials for selected intervention activities as chosen by the participants

- Reading: Rogoff et al. (1993)

Instructions:

1. Ask participants to read Chapter 1 of Rogoff et al. (1993), paying particular attention to the section, "Cultural Variation in Guided Participation" (pp. 9–16).

2. Tell participants to form small groups of three to four and select an intervention goal and a related activity that they would like to use (they may draw from their experiences, or you may give them curriculum guides to review).

3. They are then to identify mediation strategies appropriate for that goal and activity (e.g., if activity is puzzle completion, will they model or let child use trial and error? What cues or feedback might they use?). If participants have not had a lot of intervention experiences, videotape of early intervention settings and activities may be used. Questions would then be answered in relation to activities viewed.

4. Once strategies are identified, ask participants to brainstorm, using the following questions as guides:

   - "To what degree are strategies verbal/direct or nonverbal/proximal?"

   - "To what degree are they child–peer focused or child–adult focused?"

   - "To what degree are strategies embedded in child's social context; to what degree do they have an individual or dyadic focus?"

5. Following the brainstorming of these questions, ask participants to generate suggestions to modify strategies (e.g., if primarily verbal/direct, how could they be modified to be more nonverbal/proximal?).

6. To conclude, ask small groups to demonstrate the various strategies and modifications they generated. They may simulate with each other or could videotape lessons with children. Debrief on their experiences and, if used with children, on the range of responses to strategies.

Comments:

This activity is not a simple one and may need several sessions to be completed. Sensitizing participants to the culturally driven aspects of interactions is a key skill for working across cultural boundaries.

ACTIVITY 3.3

MEDIATED APPLICATIONS LEVEL: PROCESS STUDIES

Objective:

- To increase awareness of perceptions and expressions of cultural competence

Materials:

- Magazines for obtaining pictures
- Scissors
- Glue
- Videotaped interactions with children and families (generated by participants, taken of master teachers, or commercially available tapes of various early intervention environments)
- Videotapes of movies involving cross-cultural interactions

Instructions:

1. Ask participants to compose a collage of images and words that express or describe culturally competent intervention as they understand it. This part of activity is best done ahead of time, though it can also be done in small groups during class time.

2. Using videotapes of providers interacting with children and families, ask participants to view tapes and record specific instances in which behavior or language reflects an image or a word in their collage (e.g., if "skilled relationship" was such an image or word, what behavior or language in the tape would reflect that?).

3. After tapes are viewed and instances recorded, debrief using the following questions as guides:

   - What words or images seemed to be reflected most often?
   - Were any words or images not reflected at all?
   - Did they think of any words or images they'd like to add to the collage after viewing the video?

Comments:

Relating what we believe cultural competence to be to concrete behaviors is the focus of this activity. Using a collage has proved to be effective in that it elicits more global, intuitive images rather than more verbal strategies.

10 GUIDING PRACTITIONERS TOWARD VALUING AND IMPLEMENTING FAMILY-CENTERED PRACTICES

Susan L. McBride
Mary Jane Brotherson

Families have always been an integral, important aspect of early intervention services. Historically, families have advocated for and developed services for their children with disabilities (Turnbull & Turnbull, 1997). During the first few years of life, families are considered the primary caregivers and have a profound influence on their children's development. Their role in intervention has been valued and expected. Nevertheless, there has been a major shift in the roles of families in the intervention process. In the past, early intervention services were primarily focused on the developmental needs of the child; family roles in intervention processes tended to be those prescribed by professionals. In the 1990s, recognition of the complex nature of families and their lives (Beckman, Robinson, Rosenberg, & Filer, 1994; Hanson & Carta, 1995) has changed dramatically how early intervention services for families are conceptualized, with more emphasis on supporting family participation in planning and implementing intervention.

Three major influences have resulted in services that more broadly address the needs of the child within the context of the family. First, it is increasingly recognized that when social or economic factors interfere with a family's ability to carry out child-rearing functions, early intervention services will be effective only if they first enable the family's capacity to facilitate the child's development (Raab, Davis, & Trepanier, 1993). Thus, the focus of services has been extended to include all family members as well as the child (Krauss, 1990). Second, family systems theory suggests that family members have significant reciprocal influences on each other. It follows that intervention will be more effective when information, emotional support, and strategies for effectively interacting with the child with a disability are available to significant people in the child's life. Third, as services are expanded to meet the broader needs of families, the form, content, and intensity of services must be individualized for each family to be appropriate for their concerns and priorities (Thorp & McCollum, 1994). It is assumed that services will be more effective and family participation more successful if families have choices about their involvement with early intervention services.

Family-centered practices recognize that families are central to the lives of their children and that families are both responsible for and need support in meeting the needs of young children (Summers, Lane, Collier, & Friedebach, 1993). Family-centered early intervention services are based on the premise of full partnership with families and are designed to maximize the family's capacity to meet their child's special needs. This switch from professionally determined to family-driven services requires practitioners to have skills in collaborating, supporting, and negotiating to enhance family competence.

The components of family-centered services are embedded in early intervention law (e.g., the Individuals with Disabilities Education Act Amendments of 1991, PL 102-119) and in recommended practice (e.g., Division for Early Childhood Task Force on Recommended Practices, 1993). However, research has indicated that although many practitioners accept the principles of family-centered care, establishing family-centered practices is harder to achieve (Bailey, Palsha, & Simeonsson, 1991; Mahoney, O'Sullivan, & Fors, 1989; McBride, Brotherson, Joanning, Whiddon, & Demmitt, 1993). Full implementation of the intent and spirit of the law and quality early intervention services for families and children will depend on service providers who have the values and skills to implement these practices (Bailey, 1992).

This chapter provides strategies for preservice and inservice instruction to develop and enhance the knowledge and skills of early interventionists to provide family-centered intervention. A strong philosophical framework is important and necessary for good practice and should also undergird instructional efforts (McCollum, Rowan, & Thorp, 1994). The framework to support the instructional strategies and activities outlined in this chapter defines family-centered practice as a combination of beliefs and practices that views families and early intervention services as interrelated systems and requires particular ways of working with families that are consumer driven and competency enhancing (Dunst, Trivette, & Deal, 1988). However, the cornerstone of family-centered practice is individualizing intervention for each family and their child; what might be family centered for one family may not be for another. Thus, instructional goals must include process skills for early interventionists working with families so that they can provide flexible, individualized services (Thorp & McCollum, 1994). This content includes knowledge of family systems and the effect of disability on families, recognition of family-centered values, and specific skills for communicating and problem solving with families. Before presenting instructional strategies related to family-centered practice, however, it is necessary to set the context by considering challenges that influence instruction related to this topic.

CHALLENGES TO TEACHING FAMILY-CENTERED PRACTICES

There are several unique challenges for instruction related to family-centered practice. Consideration of these issues will provide information that instructors can use to problem-solve and best address the issues in their own settings.

Dealing with Systems Change

Any significant change in practice is a lengthy process that often begins with unclear understandings of the meaning of the change; ambivalence about the change may be pervasive (Fullan, 1991, 1993). For professionals who, like Janet in the case study in Chapter 1, were instructed in child-centered services, providing family-centered services is a radical change. Although the importance of families has always been acknowledged, knowledge and skills for working with families has not been the focus of instructional efforts. For seasoned practitioners, the change to family-centered services may be a dramatic and emotional shift in perspective and values. However, individuals just entering the field of early intervention also have their expectations and perspectives challenged when confronted with the range of process and communication skills that they must acquire to be effective with young children and their families. At the same time, preservice faculty are facing a new and challenging framework for preparing interventionists to provide services to children and families. They may be teaching content areas and skills in which they themselves have had little experience or instruction. How the subjective realities and interpretations of the change to family-centered practice are addressed for both preservice and inservice audiences is important if the intended outcome of this change is to be achieved (Fullan, 1991). In addition, for change to occur, a systematic, planned interface between preservice and inservice instruction is necessary. For instance, students in preservice instruction must be exposed to recommended practices within the realities and demands of community-based settings, whereas existing programs must reexamine their policies and practice in light of new theory and recommended practice.

Providing Opportunities for Supervised Practice

To develop effective skills for working with families, opportunities to practice family-centered skills are essential for gaining competency. This issue is particularly salient for preservice instruction. Practicum experiences that provide opportunities for students to interact with a variety of families, apply their knowledge, and practice skills are challenging to develop and supervise. It takes time and effort to develop relationships with providers and families who are willing to take risks in providing these experiences for students. In rural areas, access to families in terms of distance and diversity is challenging. Sometimes difficulty is encountered locating providers who are using recommended practices and who can provide adequate supervision of students. Providers also may believe they need to "protect" families from the intrusion of students. However well intentioned, this protection of families is often unfounded and deprives families of the opportunity to contribute to the instruction of those who will be working with them or other families like them in the future. It also deprives students of opportunities for supervised and structured interactions with families. Partnerships among instructional entities (e.g., universities, colleges, public and private training efforts), early intervention providers, and parent organizations are necessary to ensure good opportunities for practical experiences.

Recognizing Cultural Diversity

Although instruction for family-centered practice is difficult in and of itself, at the core of family-centered practice is the principle that all families are different and services and interactions must be individualized for a particular family. Families from diverse cultures present additional challenges to learning to be family centered. Knowledge of different cultures, understanding of processes of acculturation, and acknowledgment of different values demand skills in flexibility and sensitivity (see Chapter 9). Increased self-awareness is necessary so that differences are accepted as individual diversity rather than as right or wrong (McWilliam & Bailey, 1993). In addition, recognizing the need for and knowing how to learn more about families from different backgrounds is important.

Addressing Expanding Roles

The nature of early intervention service delivery systems and the roles of early interventionists are changing to address the demographic characteristics of U.S. society (Hanson & Carta, 1995). The demographic profile of the family is changing as a substantial number of children are spending all or part of their childhood in single-parent households, with more teens becoming parents and more women delaying marriage and childbearing. Societal trends such as the increase in participation in the work force by women who have young children, increases in substance abuse and exposure to violence, and the increase in the rate of poverty despite low unemployment may result in family stress. Hanson and

Carta (1995) suggested that although all families face challenges throughout their life span, many families confront multiple risks that consume their physical energy and undermine their sense of control and competence.

As a result of the changing needs of families and the multiple challenges many families encounter, the roles of all early interventionists are expanding to support family functioning across a broad arena of family issues, including basic needs and emotional well-being. This may involve roles of service identification and coordination for which interventionists have not been previously trained. Interventionists are also challenged to provide services in settings other than the home or early intervention center. For example, some professionals are already working as consultants with child care providers or coordinating their own intervention efforts with those of other interventionists. In addition, the role of the interventionist is changing from one of direct provider of services to the child alone to one of facilitating caregiver–child interaction to foster development within the child's everyday environment. These roles of collaborator, consultant, and facilitator are essential new roles for providing family-centered early intervention services.

Responding to Individual Characteristics of Participants

Instructional efforts must also be designed to meet the needs of participants. All individuals have some reference point when talking about "families": their own family. This common ground also provides a perspective about what families are and how they work that is formed and influenced by individual experiences. As discussed in Chapter 5, preservice and inservice audiences may differ substantially in both experience and depth of understanding. Thus, needs will vary, depending on each person's experience and background. Younger or less experienced participants may need to be provided with more practical, hands-on opportunities, whereas more experienced participants can spend more time with case studies and reflective discussion. Inservice participants can practice and implement skills almost immediately with families with whom they are working, whereas preservice students often have to store information for later use. These issues and challenges related to the audience must be considered in designing effective instructional activities for family-centered practice.

TEACHING STRATEGIES AND ACTIVITIES FOR DEVELOPING FAMILY-CENTERED PRACTICES

A family-centered approach to intervention should be evident in all aspects of service delivery, including first contacts, assessment of child and family concerns, development of outcomes to support achievement of family-identified needs, identification of comprehensive services and supports, service coordination, and program evaluation. The content areas that could be considered important for developing family-centered competencies are broad and diverse; thus, three core areas of instruction have been selected for discussion in this chapter. Competency in these core areas provides a working model that can be used to apply family-centered practices across all early intervention services. For the purpose of this chapter, the focus is on the following instructional areas for family-centered practice: 1) understanding family systems, 2) acquiring family-centered values, and 3) using communication and problem-solving skills. Other chapters in this book (e.g., Chapters 11 and 17) illustrate the critical nature of family-centered perspectives to many areas of service delivery.

The organization of the information for each of these areas is similar. First, an introduction and rationale for each area is provided. Second, specific teaching strategies for the area are presented. Suggestions for both preservice and inservice instruction are addressed in each section. Table 10.1 includes possible learning outcomes for each area.

Family Systems and Influence of Disability on Family

Family systems theory provides a conceptual framework for understanding the interrelatedness of family members, the effect of disability on family members, and the effects of

TABLE 10.1. Learning outcomes for instruction related to family-centered practice

Learning outcomes related to family systems and influence of disability on family

- Demonstrate understanding of roles, responsibilities, and relationships of families in caring for and educating young children with disabilities, including recognition of strengths and resources that families contribute to child's development.
- Demonstrate awareness of the diversity and individuality of family functioning.
- Describe potential impact of child with disability on caregivers and other family members.
- Demonstrate awareness of the effect of early intervention services on the child and family and the potential need for support services for all family members.
- Recognize that family members should participate in all aspects of early intervention services, including policy development, participation in staff instruction, and program implementation and evaluation.

Learning outcomes for values related to family-centered practices

- Describe the values and principles of a family-centered philosophy.
- Compare and contrast family-centered principles with traditional or child-centered views of early intervention.
- Describe how family-centered practices can accommodate individual and changing family needs.
- Apply the principles of family-centered practices to realistic situations through discussion and exercises.
- Evaluate family-centered program practices on a continuum of family-centered services.
- Recognize the benefits of modeling family and professional partnerships in instruction about family-centered practices through the use of family members as instructors.

Learning outcomes related to communication and problem solving

- Identify benefits and barriers of family-centered communication in early intervention settings with children and families.
- Identify effective listening and questioning skills related to positive interactions with families, and participate in a videotaped role-play situation to demonstrate effective use of listening and questioning skills.
- Identify effective skills for reflecting content and feelings to families and participate in a videotaped role-play situation to demonstrate effective use of these skills.
- Demonstrate the ability to evaluate one's own family-centered communication skills through self-rating and self-assessment.
- Describe how problem solving can be used to facilitate family-centered communication and decision making with families.
- Recognize the benefits of using family members to help instruct participants in effective communication and problem-solving skills.

intervention on the family system (Bronfenbrenner, 1977; Carter & McGoldrick, 1980). Turnbull, Summers, and Brotherson (1986) proposed a family systems framework that delineates family systems concepts as they relate specifically to families of children with disabilities. The four components of family systems that they addressed are 1) *family characteristics* such as socioeconomic and geographic structural characteristics of the family, personal characteristics of family members, and characteristics of the disability; 2) *family interactions* among subsystems, including marital, parent, and sibling relationships, and quality of interactions, including adaptability and cohesion; 3) *family functions* such as processes related to daily functioning, including recreation, work, socialization, affection, and education; and 4) *family life cycle*, including the stage of family development and tasks and challenges associated with each.

These concepts are described in four chapters in *Families, Professionals, and Exceptionality: A Special Partnership* (Turnbull & Turnbull, 1997). This reading provides crucial background material for discussing family systems and the implications for providing family-centered practice. The instructional strategies described in the next section will assist participants in understanding the complexity of family systems and the interrelatedness and reciprocal influences of the family systems and early intervention services. (See Chapter 18 for a description of family practicum experiences that also assist students in understanding family systems and the effect of disability.)

Analysis of Family Systems Through Literature

Family stories provide a mechanism for connecting theory to practice, give meaning and purpose to practice, and challenge assumptions about family–professional collaboration (Marchant & McBride, 1994; Walizer & Leff, 1993). There are many books written by parents or family members of children with disabilities that describe the activities of daily life, joys and struggles of parenting, and experiences with early intervention services. Some of the most interesting are written by parents who were writers by profession and thus provide the reader with a well-written, compelling account of their lives and family story. One such book, *Loving Rachel* (Bernstein, 1988), is an account of the family's first 3 years with their child who has visual impairments and other associated neurological problems. Written from the perspective of Rachel's mother, the book is also particularly sensitive to and rich in describing the effect that Rachel's disability has on all family members and is at times both distressing and moving as the family's reactions and relationships are described as they struggle with discovering, acknowledging, and adapting to Rachel's disability. The detail and sensitivity to family reactions and relationships provide a rich source of information for analyzing the components of the family system as discussed by Turnbull and Turnbull (1990). Such an analysis provides an opportunity for the participant to define different aspects of family systems theory and to use Rachel's family to demonstrate the concepts.

A book analysis project may best be used with students in preservice instruction by having them read the book as homework as lectures and discussions related to family systems are presented in class. Students can be asked to give examples from the book that illustrate the family systems concepts being discussed, providing a common source of information for the students. Another strategy is to have students read a variety of literary accounts and contribute examples of concepts from various stories. Figure 10.1 provides a framework for students to engage in a more individual synthesis of these same concepts by writing a paper. Students could also be expected to compare and contrast several family stories. A book analysis project provides an opportunity for students to read an enjoyable book while applying a family systems perspective to one family's experience (see p. 273 for a list of additional titles suitable for use in this activity).

Instruction for inservice professionals may not allow significant time for participants to read entire novels. McWilliam and Bailey (1993) developed a set of case studies that

BOOK ANALYSIS USING FAMILY SYSTEMS PERSPECTIVE

The purpose of this assignment is to help you gain an understanding of a family systems perspective and particularly how a child with a disability may affect the family system. For this project you will read the book *Loving Rachel*, the story of a family that has a child with a disability. Your task will be to analyze the family's situation using a family systems perspective. Use the following outline to organize your paper. Please give specific examples from the book to support your statements about these areas (reference page numbers where appropriate).

A. Structure of the family: Please describe the characteristics of the Bernstein family *and what effect these characteristics have on their response to Rachel's disability*. You will want to include the family structure and subsystems; nature of Rachel's disability (include severity and demands that affect family members); characteristics of the family and *how it shapes their response to the situation—size and form, cultural background, socioeconomic status, geographic location; and personal characteristics of family members such as health status, values, cognitive abilities, and skills that influence their response*.

B. Family interactions: Discuss the family subsystems (i.e., marital, parental, sibling, extrafamilial) in terms of their interactions using the concepts of cohesion and adaptability. *Please define these concepts and provide specific examples in the book to illustrate family interactions that demonstrate these concepts.* Remember, families change and are on a continuum for each of these concepts.

C. Family functions: What are this family's resources, concerns, and priorities related to family functions (e.g., financial, physical, health, socialization, education, affection, recreation, family identity)? *Which functions do you think are resources/strengths for this family? Which functions do you think are most affected by Rachel's disability and thus may be a concern or priority for this family?*

D. Life cycle: Describe the stage of the family life cycle in which the family is presently. *What are their major concerns at this time; what do you anticipate to be concerns at later stages of the life cycle?*

E. Coping resources of family members: Describe the coping styles used by various members of this family. *Define internal coping strategies (e.g., passive appraisal, reframing) and external coping strategies (e.g., social supports, spirituality) and provide specific examples illustrating these coping strategies.*

F. Early intervention: In this family, what was the role of early intervention and the impact of early intervention professionals on this family's experience? What was supportive? What was not supportive? *How, if at all, could family-focused services have been supportive of this family?*

G. Your reactions: Reflect on what you learned from reading this book. *What can you apply to your role as an early interventionist?*

Figure 10.1. Outline for book analysis.

provide alternative stimulus material for discussing concepts of family systems and allow for diversity not found in one literary work. Case stories can effectively pose real-life situations and dilemmas that participants must problem-solve; these also can be used for role play, providing opportunities to practice communication and decision-making skills. Another resource is *Exceptional Parent* magazine, publishing brief but poignant articles written by mothers, fathers, brothers and sisters, and grandparents of individuals with disabilities. The vignettes and stories provided in this publication often express alternative points of view that might otherwise be left untold. When using family stories, participants need to be guided by questions or points to consider as they read to facilitate their interpretations of the stories and to maximize their learning.

Using literature provides a safe environment for discussing family systems issues. Telling of family stories in person by family members is also an effective strategy for instruction about the importance of a family systems perspective in providing early intervention services. The following strategies provide information for including families in instructional efforts.

Coinstruction   The participation of family members in the instructional process is a logical activity because parents are the primary recipients of service and will be most affected by the knowledge and skills of personnel who work with them and their children. Efforts have increased in the 1990s to include family members extensively in both inservice (Bailey, Buysse, Smith, & Elam, 1992; Bailey, McWilliam, & Winton, 1992; Gilkerson, 1994) and preservice (Hains & Whitehead, 1994; McBride, Sharp, Hains, & Whitehead, 1995) instruction.

Coinstruction, or the collaboration of family members and providers in a sustained instructional effort, has been accepted and encouraged as recommended practice (Jeppson & Thomas, 1994; Midwestern Consortium for Faculty Development, University of Minnesota, 1994; Winton & DiVenere, 1995). If parents are involved in instructional efforts, it is more likely that the effectiveness and acceptability of family-centered intervention efforts will be enhanced (Bailey, Buysse, Edmondson, & Smith, 1992). McBride et al. (1995) identified three goals of coinstruction. First, coinstruction is an effective strategy for modeling the collaborative family–provider partnerships that are essential for developing and implementing family-centered intervention services (Gilkerson, 1994). Coinstruction provides an opportunity for participants to observe the development of family–provider relationships and the importance of effective communication to this relationship. Opportunities to observe disagreement, negotiation, and problem solving are often provided within the context of instructional activities and discussions.

Second, family stories and experiences provided by parents promote an affective understanding of family-centered practices. When participants have the opportunity to hear family members describe how a child's disability affected them and their relationships with other family members, with all the emotion, dilemmas, and complexity that their life experiences bring, family systems theory is brought to life. An affective appreciation of the family perspective also provides a foundation for defining family-centered practice. For example, if we hear the pain or frustration that parents feel as they describe being left out of a crucial decision related to their child's care, we question existing practices and are stimulated to discuss options that provide families with choices and power to make decisions.

Finally, parent coinstructors can infuse a family-centered perspective throughout the course or curriculum. Sustained instructional efforts, across a preservice course or a series of inservice instructional sessions, provide an opportunity for exploring issues related to family-centered practices across a variety of topics. In addition, family input can be used in the development, implementation, and evaluation of instructional programs. This is facilitated by having parents participate on advisory boards that review program curricula and course syllabi (Hains & Whitehead, 1994) or as members of personnel preparation committees responsible for planning instructional efforts at local and state agency levels.

Coinstruction models vary extensively and provide a variety of roles for parents and other family members in the instructional process. These roles range from sharing personal family stories to planning and teaching some of the course content. (See McBride et al. [1995] for a description of issues and strategies for implementing coinstruction and Whitehead and Sontag [1993] for a descriptive case study of coinstruction.)

Family Panel Presentations   A difficult issue in instruction is providing knowledge and experiences related to understanding and interacting with families from diverse backgrounds. Although coinstruction involves the in-depth commitment and participation of one parent, additional family perspectives are essential. Inviting several family members to participate in panel discussions provides a forum for this diversity, which must include the dimensions of a range of family constellations (e.g., single parent, blended families, foster families), various family members (e.g., brothers and sisters, grandparents, aunts and uncles), socioeconomic and cultural/linguistic diversity, and diverse experiences (e.g., homelessness, gay and lesbian parents, low income, teen parents, parents with cognitive limitations or specific disabilities). Including these people in instruction requires extensive preparation and support. Partnerships with community early intervention and early childhood programs can provide access to potential families who would participate in instructional activities.

The Wisconsin Personnel Development Project has developed an instructional videotape for parents to assist them in feeling comfortable telling their story (King, 1994) and a list of suggestions for instructors who are interested in inviting family members to participate in instruction (Whitehead, 1994). Single family members or panels of individuals can be asked to "tell their story," or very specific questions or guidelines can be provided to address specific topics (e.g., "Please tell us some ways that interventionists/programs have been supportive and ways that they have not been helpful to your family," "Please tell us about how your child's disability created opportunities or discouraged you from participating in your community"). Involvement of family members as mentors to participants for more in-depth instructional experiences is also very desirable (see Chapter 17 for a discussion of this strategy).

Eco-Mapping   The process of visually portraying family relationships and representations of the family's associations with informal (e.g., friends, extended family) and formal (e.g., early intervention, community services) supports is an excellent exercise for understanding the need for a family systems perspective. Developing eco-maps with families is a strategy that interventionists can use to learn whom families consider in their membership and to identify whom and what resources they consider to be sources of support. A map is constructed by putting the immediate family in a large center circle and drawing connecting lines to other resources such as friends, school, health care providers, social services, or religious institutions (see Figure 10.2). The strength and quality of these relationships can be depicted by using different types of connecting lines. For example, stressful relations could be symbolized by hatched lines; bold lines could represent strong, helpful relationships; dashed lines could represent weaker relationships; or arrows might indicate the flow of resources.

Dunst, Trivette, and Deal (1994) suggested that the identification of resources should be done within the context of a family-identified need to ensure that the identification of resources and supports is not intrusive to the family. In preservice settings students can

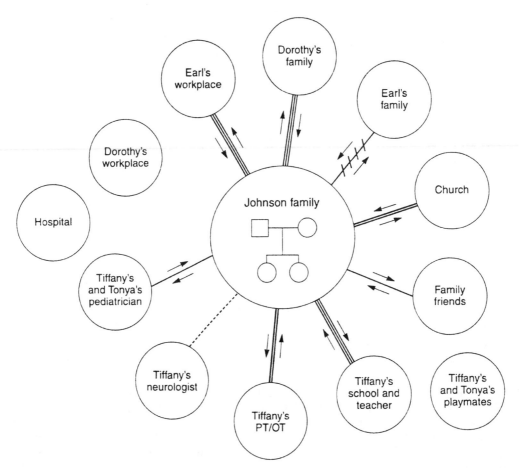

Figure 10.2. A family eco-map illustrating the family system within a social context. (From Rosin, P., Whitehead, A.D., Tuchman, L.I., Jesien, G.S., Begun, A.L., & Irwin, L. [1996]. *Partnerships in family-centered care: A guide to collaborative early intervention*, p. 42. Baltimore: Paul H. Brookes Publishing Co.; reprinted by permission.)

be paired and asked to use interviewing skills with each other to assist in developing a map of their own family of origin. In this case, the identification of supports outside the family and the relationship to community resources might be more general. Case studies could then be used for students to role-play other types of families and develop an eco-map around an identified need. For example, if a family identified the need for transportation to early intervention services, an eco-map may assist the family in identifying a natural support system of friends or relatives available for assistance rather than immediately contacting a community service. Students in practicum settings with families may want to develop eco-maps to better understand the family system and the complexity of the family's interactions with service systems.

With professionals in inservice training, the instructor might engage a parent in developing an eco-map for the entire group to observe. Follow-up discussion about strategies for eliciting information and use of the eco-map with a family is helpful. Participants can also be given the opportunity to develop and practice communication and interview skills for developing eco-maps with volunteer families before they use this strategy in their work. Although some families may find this an intrusive intervention activity, others may find it very useful. It can be used to assist students in understanding the family system and its relationship to support systems. For more information about family mapping, see Hartman and Laird (1983); for examples of using eco-maps for identifying sources of support and resources for the development of individualized family service plans (IFSPs), see *Developing Individualized Family Support Plans*, by Bennett, Lingerfelt, and Nelson (1990).

Values Related to Family-Centered Practices

To provide family-centered services, early intervention professionals must have an understanding and internalization of the values and principles that define family-centered services. A set of clear values provides a road map for attaining family-centered practices. There are a number of models that describe family-centered values and principles (Bailey et al., 1986; Dunst et al., 1988; McGonigel, Kaufmann, & Johnson, 1991; Shelton, Jeppson, & Johnson, 1987; Shelton & Stepanek, 1994); these are remarkably consistent in their characterization of family-centered practices. McBride et al. (1993) reviewed the literature and identified three major values that encompass family-centered practices:

1. *Establishing the family as the focus of services.* The first value of family-centered practices recognizes and accommodates the impact that special needs may have on the entire family system. It recognizes the strengths of the family and ensures sensitivity to the family's emotional needs.
2. *Supporting and respecting family decision making.* The second value of family-centered services acknowledges and encourages the family as equal partners on the team and as primary decision makers. It seeks to help empower families to make decisions and to develop a sense of control.
3. *Providing intervention services designed to strengthen family functioning.* The third value of family-centered practices recognizes the diversity of families and seeks to provide services that support and enhance the family's capabilities and family functioning. It focuses on assisting families to mobilize their resources and competencies to meet the changing needs of all family members.

Family-centered practice is not defined by a particular set of forms or procedures. Rather, it is a willingness to embrace values that are respectful of and collaborative with families. Many professionals who work directly with children may not approach families as the primary decision makers and the focus of service. Moreover, when professionals try to implement family-centered practices in their programs, they may encounter long-entrenched system barriers that thwart their efforts (Bailey, Buysse, Edmondson, et al., 1992).

The following instructional activities can be used to help participants explore and internalize values of family-centered practice.

Recognizing Family-Centered Practices Students in preservice instruction may be entering their profession with the idea that they will be working only or primarily with children. Having them reflect on the family as a recipient of services when children are very young may stimulate the revelation that they will often be working with other adults in the best interests of the child. Once this is acknowledged, these students may not experience the resistance to change that individuals whose instruction was primarily child focused may experience. It is helpful for the students to understand this shift from child-to family-oriented services and the difficulty that this change presents. They may see professionals in their practica struggling with this and may later be working with colleagues having difficulty operationalizing the shift.

A useful activity for helping participants recognize family-centered practices and their differences from child-centered and system-centered approaches to delivering services is "Recognizing family-centered care" in *Getting on Board* (Edelman, 1991). After a review of key concepts of family-centered practices, participants are provided with a 15-item list of statements (e.g., "A family must bring their child to the office for service coordination") and asked to decide whether the statements reflect system-centered, child-centered, or family-centered practices. Participants can then discuss the answers, with the instructor reinforcing family-centered practices. Alternatives to services identified as child centered or system centered can be explored through questions about alternative approaches and how they might be implemented. Ideas for small-group and large-group discussion, sample overheads, discussion questions, and next steps are provided with the list. To tailor the activity to local needs, the list could be modified to reflect urban or rural service delivery issues.

Participants in inservice instruction have an extensive background from which to draw for examples of family-centered practices; however, preservice students may lack these experiences. In a preservice setting, the use of videotapes such as *Heart to Heart* (Fullerton, 1992) by the Kentucky Developmental Disabilities Planning Council, or *Family-Centered Care* by the Association for the Care of Children's Health (1988), can help students see examples of family-centered practices in a variety of settings. *Heart to Heart* is 30-minutes long and includes the perspectives of several families and early intervention providers. The families give examples of the need to focus on the family as a unit and not just on the child with a disability. This videotape also emphasizes the need to build on family strengths, to provide choices to families, and to communicate openly and honestly with families. *Family-Centered Care* is 38-minutes long and also focuses on the need to see the family, not just the child, as the recipient of support and services. This videotape, however, focuses more on the family's relationship with medical services and providers. Parts or all of either film can be used effectively to provide a context for students to observe and identify practices that either support or provide barriers to family-centered practices. Participants can also be asked to identify those video segments where parents share how they want services to be family centered. A handout of the key elements of family-centered care, such as the one shown in Table 10.2, can then be used to highlight or reinforce key concepts.

Another activity for helping participants recognize family-centered practices and apply the principles to realistic situations through discussions and exercises is the use of the family vignettes from *Delivering Family-Centered, Home-Based Services* (Edelman & Cosgrove, 1991). After a review of principles for delivering family-centered services, participants are provided with one or more short videotapes, or "family stories," to apply the principles when delivering home-based services. There are five family vignettes to select from, all based on real incidents. Each vignette is about 30 minutes and begins with the provider *not* delivering family-centered services. The videotape is then turned off and the participants have an opportunity to discuss what went wrong and what should have been done. The videotape is structured to be turned on again to watch as the characters reflect on their experiences from a family-centered perspective. However, the greatest value of this activity is in the discussion and analysis after each section; this can be done effectively without seeing the taped debriefing episodes. Instructors are encouraged to recruit parents to be included as participants or coinstructors. The instruction can be more

TABLE 10.2.   Key elements of family-centered care

- Incorporating into policy and practice the recognition that the *family is the constant in a child's life*, while the service systems and support personnel within those systems fluctuate

- Facilitating *family/professional collaboration* at all levels of hospital, home, and community care:
  - –care of an individual child
  - –program development, implementation, evaluation, and evolution
  - –policy formation

- *Exchanging complete and unbiased information* between families and professionals in a supportive manner at all times

- Incorporating into policy and practice the recognition and *honoring of cultural diversity*, strengths, and individuality within and across all families, including *ethnic, racial, spiritual, social, economic, educational, and geographic diversity*

- Recognizing and respecting *different methods of coping* and implementing comprehensive policies and programs that provide *developmental, educational, emotional, environmental, and financial supports* to meet the diverse needs of families

- Encouraging and facilitating *family-to-family support* and networking

- Ensuring that *hospital, home, and community service and support systems* for children needing specialized health and developmental care and their families are *flexible, accessible, and comprehensive* in responding to diverse family-identified needs

- *Appreciating families as families* and children as children, recognizing that they possess a wide range of strengths, concerns, emotions, and aspirations beyond their need for specialized health and developmental services and support

Reproduced with permission of the Association for the Care of Children's Health, 7910 Woodmont Ave., Suite 300, Bethesda, MD 20814, from Shelton, T.L., & Stepanek, J.S. (1994). *Family-centerd care for children needing specialized health and developmental services.* Bethesda, MD: Association for the Care of Children's Health (pp. vii); reprinted by permission.

effective if parents, as recipients of services, have an opportunity to share their insights, observations, and personal experiences.

 Applying Principles of Family-Centered Practice   To assist in understanding family-centered practices, Dunst, Johanson, Trivette, and Hambry (1991) described four models for working with families on a continuum of family centeredness (i.e., professional centered, family allied, family focused, family centered). The terms family centered and family focused are often used interchangeably; however, defining these models on a continuum assists professionals in evaluating change toward family-centered practices. McBride et al. (1993) combined these four models of working with families with three major values that encompass family-centered practices and provided examples of indicators of practice that can be used to evaluate where programs fall on the continuum of family-centered services. For instance, for the value of considering the family (versus only the child) as the focus of service, a professional-centered model might limit services to directly working with the child; a family-allied model would acknowledge family resources as helpful in achieving professionally defined goals for the child; a family-focused model would consider outcomes and services for the family but would be restricted to the child's development; and a family-centered model would consider the concerns, resources, and priorities of all family members in determining outcomes and service delivery.

 An activity to help participants clarify the often subtle differences in models is to apply the values of family centeredness to realistic family scenarios. Participants could be asked, "How would you work with this family from each of the four models on the continuum (i.e., professional-centered, family-allied, family-focused, and family-centered models)?" The following is a sample scenario:

Mr. and Mrs. Russell are torn about which way to proceed with their son John. John is 30 months old and has moderate cerebral palsy. Mrs. Russell wants to take John to a city 38 miles away so that he can get daily special therapy in addition to early intervention services. She believes that if she can give him intensive special services he will develop faster. But Mr. Russell's parents have told Mrs. Russell (again and again), "There is nothing wrong with our grandson; don't spend so much time away from your husband and other two children. He'll walk when he is ready." Mr. Russell wants to believe his own parents, and neither Mr. nor Mrs. Russell is sure what to do. Describe how you would work differently with this family from the perspective of each of the four models.

Scenarios could be tailored to reflect the issues that are unique to particular inservice or preservice settings, including cultural diversity, delivering services in a rural area, or assisting interdisciplinary teams to work together to implement family-centered practices. Parents as participants or coinstructors are vital to enhancing the quality of discussions, as they are uniquely qualified to present insightful observations and experiences. The involvement of family members in discussions can greatly add to the understanding of issues and barriers to applying family-centered practices.

Evaluating Family-Centered Practice   After recognizing and applying principles of family-centered practice to hypothetical situations, participants will be ready to examine practice in the field. Murphy, Lee, Turnbull, and Turbiville (1995) identified at least 12 instruments for assessing family-centered practice and developed the *Family-Centered Program Rating Scale* for this purpose. These instruments can be used to assess and monitor changes toward family-centered programs and professional skill development. They are also useful in assisting participants to internalize principles of family-centered practice as they evaluate various practices from the perspective of these principles.

Another useful resource for helping professionals determine the extent to which their interactions, practice, and policies are family centered is *Brass Tacks* (McWilliam & Winton, 1992). Two instruments, one focused on individual interactions and one focused on program policies and practices, provide a self-rating process to examine early intervention in four areas: 1) first encounters with families, 2) identifying goals for intervention, 3) intervention planning for children and families, and 4) day-to-day service provision. These instruments are designed primarily for inservice use with professionals who have regular contact with families. Structures and strategies are provided for prioritizing and tracking program or individual movement toward more family-centered practices. A companion instrument for obtaining families' reactions is also available (McWilliam, 1992). These instruments may be used by professionals in the field to evaluate their own practice, adapting the recommended practice to their own geographic location, cultural environment, and availability of resources. Preservice students could use these same instruments to discuss the practices they are observing or in which they are participating in their practicum settings. It is important, however, to assist them in these discussions and not have them use these tools to judge the site in a manner that may alienate their cooperating professionals.

Communication and Problem-Solving Skills

The third area discussed in this chapter is the communication and problem-solving skills that are vital to delivering family-centered services. These skills are the cornerstones of developing family-centered partnerships with families. Sharing information and feelings, team building, negotiating, reaching consensus, and resolving conflict all depend on the ability of professionals to communicate and problem-solve effectively with families and with each other. Effective communication and problem-solving skills, although vital to family-centered services, are not easily acquired. Gaining competency in these skills requires ongoing practice. Assisting families to be competent communicators and problem solvers can help them gain a greater sense of control over their environment. However, before professionals can deliver family-centered services and assist families in developing skills of communication and problem solving, they must themselves be competent in these areas.

Preservice and inservice instruction in communication and problem-solving skills must include much more than a didactic approach (Carkhuff, Kratochvil, & Friel, 1968). An interactive experiential approach that provides students with a variety of opportunities to observe and practice effective communication skills is needed. Following a review of the literature on experiential methods for teaching these skills, Winton (1988) discussed two critical components that must be contained in instruction: 1) the broad areas of communication and problem solving must be broken into component skills to be taught separately, both through the use of dialectic material and videotaped or live examples of each component; and 2) participants or students must have opportunities to practice communication and problem-solving skills in role-play situations with each other or cooperating family members. The exercises and interviews should be either audio- or videotaped to provide constructive evaluation and feedback to participants.

A number of types of instructional activities can be used to help participants acquire both problem-solving and communication skills. The case method of instruction (McWilliam & Bailey, 1993) can be an excellent strategy for promoting skills in problem solving. By using family situations, participants can discuss or role-play the process of promoting successful partnerships and supporting families in the problem-solving process. Participants will have varying degrees of communication skills. Particularly at the inservice level, participants should be given the opportunity to determine their own instructional needs; some may want a review of basic skills, and others may want more in-depth instruction. Both preservice and inservice participants can benefit from involving family members in the problem-solving process. Their experiences, perceptions, insights, and knowledge can add greatly to the instruction. Participants should be given the opportunity to conduct self-assessments and to receive performance evaluations of their skills from their peers.

Communication Skills   Based on reviews by Winton (Winton, 1988; Winton & Bailey, 1988), communication skills can be thought of as divided into the following four critical components.

Listening   The greatest percentage of time in communication is spent listening. Listening involves focusing on and following what a family member has to say using both verbal and nonverbal listening skills. Good listening skills convey acceptance and understanding of another person and help build trusting relationships. These skills are especially critical at the beginning of building family-centered relationships and are the starting point for both inservice and preservice instruction.

Questioning   Questioning is used primarily to gather information about a family and promote understanding and decision making. The act of questioning, in and of itself, however, may constitute an intervention with the family. Therefore, questioning must be considered both a way of collecting information and a form of intervention. Novice practitioners and students often use a large number of closed-ended questions and may be uncomfortable with the amount of silence that families may need before responding.

Instruction for participants should provide opportunities to practice a variety of effective questioning skills (Winton, 1991a).

Reflecting Feelings   Reflecting involves the ability to identify a family member's feelings and reflect those back accurately and sensitively (Evans, Hearn, Uhlemann, & Ivey, 1984). It is the ability to communicate understanding of the world as the family perceives it. When feelings are reflected back to families, they can become more aware of how they feel and examine those feelings in relation to their problem solving and decision making. In this component, novice participants must be careful not to give advice or to overinterpret or overstate a family's feelings.

Reflecting Content   Reflecting content is the ability to restate the content of a family member's message using skills of paraphrasing and summarizing. These skills are important because they let a family know that their message is being accurately understood. Turnbull (1987) described the opportunity for families to reflect on their feelings, needs, strengths, and resources as the key to the problem-solving process. Participants at both the preservice and inservice levels need varied opportunities to practice each of the four component skills of effective communication.

One manual that provides communication activities for both inservice and preservice instruction is *Communicating with Families in Early Intervention: A Training Module* (Winton, 1991a). This module provides suggested teaching activities in the four components of communication and several scripted role plays and family stories. Participants are given examples of different types of questioning scripts and through discussion can identify how ineffective the interventionist was when he or she tried to generate goals based on what he or she thought ought to happen with families. Appendices provide examples of specific questions to elicit information on family resources, priorities and concerns, and family outcomes. Directions for role plays with several families are included along with The Family Interview Rating Scale. This scale can be used by group participants as a vehicle for self-assessment and feedback on the videotaped role plays. Other self-analysis and feedback questions are provided for participants, as well as master copies for overhead transparencies on communication and interviewing.

Another resource for helping participants develop communication and interviewing skills is the *Family-Focused Interview Videotapes* and *Family-Focused Interview: Supplemental Workbook* developed by the SKI*HI Institute (Winton, 1991b). The videotapes demonstrate the five phases of family-focused interviewing and effective listening and questioning skills (Winton & Bailey, 1988). Examples are provided of both traditional and family-centered approaches to services for two families of children with hearing impairments. Included in the supplemental workbook are multiple choice, true/false, and discussion questions for evaluation and group discussion. The workbook also includes a role-playing demonstration using four different approaches to questions. The discussion summary highlights how reflexive and open-ended questions can help gather information to identify strengths, needs, and goals of families in an ongoing process.

"As family-centered communication is put into practice, services more effectively reflect families' priorities; interventions with children are more successful; and service providers find their jobs more rewarding" (Edelman, Greenland, & Mills, 1992, p. 9). This statement is part of the introduction to another manual on communication skills, *Family-Centered Communication Skills: Facilitator's Guide*, developed through Project Copernicus (Edelman et al., 1992). This instructional manual provides nine different activities designed to help participants identify benefits and barriers to family-centered communication and to practice active listening and communication skills. The manual provides outlines and overhead transparency and handout masters for the instructors. It also provides ideas to help transfer skills to the job for inservice participants; however, many of the activities are basic communication activities and might be used best in a preservice setting. Several of the activities draw family situations from the videotape *Delivering Family-Centered, Home-Based Services* (Edelman & Cosgrove, 1991). This video of five family vignettes was discussed previously in relation to recognizing family-centered practices. The video could be used with a checklist of communication strategies (see Table 10.3) to structure the identification of ineffective or good communication practices by the participants.

Two additional resources that can be used to help participants identify and develop communication and interviewing skills are videotapes from the American Association of Marriage and Family Therapy, entitled *Building a Family Partnership* (1995a) and *Exploring Family Strengths* (1995b). The goals of the videos are to help early interventionists recognize complex systems and relationships in families and find a balance between strengths and concerns when working with a family. The videos show diverse families with a variety of issues and children with disabilities. The emphasis is on conversations with families, not interviews, and the focus is on letting the family talk to identify their own strengths and struggles. An instructor with good communication and interviewing skills is needed to help participants recognize the multiple issues raised in the videotapes and to help participants to focus on strategies for partnerships with the entire family.

Problem-Solving Skills   Since the 1980s, early intervention with children with disabilities and their families has changed from a child-centered system to a family-centered system. There has also been a shift from a deficit model of the child and family to a view that all families have strengths and resources and should be recognized as the ultimate decision makers. Within this new approach, early interventionists have recognized the

TABLE 10.3.   Strategies for clear and respectful communication

- Avoid making assumptions
- Avoid jargon and explain technical terms
- Share complete, honest, and unbiased information
- Offer your opinions, but be sure the family knows these are suggestions and not the only options
- Answer questions directly if you know the answer, or say, "I don't know"
- Avoid patronizing language and tone
- Consider differing abilities to understand
- Clarify mutual expectations
- Clarify next steps
- Realign the power
- Respect cultural differences
- Recognize time and resource constraints
- Pay attention and respond to nonverbal cues
- Create an environment for open communication

From Edelman, L., Greenland, B., & Mills, B.L. (1992). *Family-centered communication skills: Facilitators' guide* (pp. 69–70). Baltimore: Kennedy Kreiger Institute, Project Copernicus; reprinted by permission.

futility of working in uncoordinated service systems and are beginning to make systems more responsive to the needs of children and families. Changes and shifts in approaches can be difficult and time consuming; there are ongoing obstacles and barriers to change. Often, professionals see their role as solving problems or providing solutions for families. Using a family problem-solving process can give families greater control of decision making and focus on what the family wants and perceives as solutions, not on what the professional has to offer. Using effective communication skills of listening, questioning, and reflecting is critical to increasing the likelihood that the family's perspectives and goals are elicited and understood in a family-centered problem-solving process.

Students and instructors also need support and help in becoming agents of change; in addition, they need instruction on how to be effective problem solvers when they work with families in negotiating the complexity of the early intervention system. The problem-solving process is a proactive approach that can meet the challenges of supporting families through interventions and facilitate systems change (Summers et al., 1993). With effective communication skills, professionals can work with families to clearly define their needs, strengths, and resources and then creatively help families achieve the outcomes they desire for themselves and their children.

The process of problem solving involves several steps, including defining the problem, brainstorming alternatives, evaluating possible alternatives, selecting an alternative, implementing the alternative, and evaluating the alternative. A more detailed explanation of the steps can be found in Goldfarb, Brotherson, Summers, and Turnbull (1986) and Summers et al. (1993).

In *Working Together with Children and Families: Case Studies in Early Intervention*, McWilliam and Bailey (1993) present case studies specifically designed to provide participants with opportunities to practice the problem-solving process. Each case study depicts a family situation or dilemma in the area of early intervention; however, the ending is not provided. After reading the case, students can be guided through the steps of problem solving to generate one or more possible outcomes. Another strategy is to separate participants into several groups and give them the same case study to illustrate the variety of well-reasoned outcomes that may be possible for one situation. These case studies can be discussed by a large group, or participants can role-play the characters and the next step in the story, thus allowing them to practice their problem-solving and communication skills.

Another activity uses both problem-solving and communication skills to help develop child and family outcomes for the IFSP. The problem-solving steps with suggested family discussion questions are included in Figure 10.3 (Brotherson & McBride, 1992). By using a problem-solving process, families can be actively engaged in discussing their needs or desired outcomes and alternative resources to address those needs. Open-ended questions can help families clarify their desired outcomes and how they will be able to measure their success in reaching those outcomes. This process helps families to take the "driver's seat" in developing IFSPs and creates a supportive process to help families examine their values, resources, and strengths within that process. Participants can be asked to use family scenarios to role-play and practice this process with their peers.

CONCLUSION

Recommended practice in any field is an evolving process; the goals for instructional efforts will necessarily change. One major challenge will be the evolving definition of

1. What are your needs or concerns?

   How are things going for _____?

   What would you like to accomplish in the next 4 months?

   If you could focus your energy on one thing, what would that be?

2. What can your family and the program do? (Brainstorm alternatives)

   What are some ways to accomplish this?

   Can you think of another time when you needed _____? What worked for you then?

   What are some ways of getting to where you want to go?

3. Think it over and decide. (Examine family values, resources, and impact.)

   Let's talk about our ideas. How would _____ work for you?

   Who else in your family could help with these ideas?

   How would that affect others in your family?

   Describe for me which ideas you are most comfortable with.

4. What is your desired outcome?

   What specific changes do you want to see for your child or yourself?

   Describe what you would like to see happen for your child or family.

5. Tasks to do and persons responsible. (Strategies and activities)

   What do you think needs to be done to make this happen?

   What would you like for me or the therapist to do?

   Who needs to be involved in getting done what you want to do?

   Progress notes:

6. How is it working? (Criteria and time lines)

   How will you know when you're done?

   How long do you think it will take to _____?

   How long would you like it to take?

   How will you be able to tell if you (we) are successful at reaching this outcome?

Figure 10.3. Activity form: Problem-solving process for developing child and family outcomes. (Originally adapted from Goldfarb, Brotherson, Summers, & Turnbull [1991] and Winton [1991a]; from Brotherson, M.J., & McBride, S.M. [1992]. *Problem-solving process for developing child and family outcomes*. Unpublished teaching material. Ames: University of Iowa, Department of Human Development and Family Studies; reprinted by permission.)

family-centered practice. What was considered family-centered practice in 1990 is not what is recommended practice now. As Garland (1995) suggested, we must constantly ask ourselves "what do we see here that is family-centered and what do we see that could be more family-centered?"(p. 20). This ongoing process of recalibration, adjusting practice to reflect current knowledge, though frustrating, will also be healthy. Research efforts will assist in determining practices that have significant effects on the well-being and development of children and families, which will bring about changes in recommended practice that will require modifications in both preservice and inservice instruction. Thus, continuous monitoring, rethinking of concepts, and need for ongoing instruction will be required. Ongoing discussion through focus groups (Brotherson, 1994) with families and providers representing diverse locations and socioeconomic and cultural groups is essential for continuing to refine concepts of family-centered practice and to assess the status of instructional needs.

A second challenge will be the expansion of family-centered practice across disciplines. For instance, in the area of early childhood education there are an increasing number of states that are adopting unified licensing standards (early childhood and special education) that span the range from birth to age 8. This will require that instructional efforts in family-centered practice be infused into new curriculum areas and with older children. Faculty and instructors who are knowledgeable in this perspective or have developed instructional strategies for this content may not be readily available.

A third challenge will be to provide support for the interventionists who are taking new roles and implementing new skills in family-centered practice. For service delivery systems that are based on a specific philosophical or value-driven perspective such as family-centered practice, staff supervision is a key element to the quality and integrity of practice (Gilkerson & Young-Holt, 1992). To provide this support, instruction is needed for administrators and supervisors in the consultation and clinical skills necessary to support the practitioners who are learning new ways of providing services to children and families. Administrators and supervisors will need to be knowledgeable about family-centered practice and the dilemmas and complexities that their staff members are facing as they implement new ways of providing services. This need is pervasive across all disciplines and will require an instructional focus on administrative and supervisory personnel in the field and new content and instructional strategies for preservice programs. Continual recalibration and collaboration among families, instructors, and practitioners will be needed to maintain effective instruction in family-centered practice.

RESOURCES

Edelman, L. (Ed.). (1991). *Getting on board: Training activities to promote the practice of family-centered care.* Bethesda, MD: Association for the Care of Children's Health. Cost: $18 plus shipping/handling. (301) 654-6549.

A collection of instructional activities designed to promote the skills, knowledge, and attitudes required to practice in a family-centered manner. Designed for interdisciplinary preservice and inservice audiences, the materials include all necessary instructions, overheads, transparencies, and discussion questions.

Edelman, L., & Cosgrove, K. (1991). *Delivering family-centered, home-based services: Facilitator's guide to accompany the videotape.* Baltimore: Kennedy Krieger Institute, Project Copernicus. Cost: $98 plus shipping/handling. (410) 550-9700.

These five videotape vignettes, which show different examples of service delivery that is not family centered, can be used to provide participants with opportunities to watch each scenario, discuss how these scenes might have occurred in a more family-friendly manner, and develop alternative applications through facilitated discussion and role playing. Accompanying print information provides overheads, handouts, and ideas for additional activities and applications.

Edelman, L., Greenland, B., & Mills, B.L. (1992). *Family-centered communication skills: Facilitator's guide.* Baltimore: Kennedy Krieger Institute, Project Copernicus. Cost: $15. (410) 550-9700.

Materials and step-by-step instructions for conducting family-centered communication instruction for interdisciplinary audiences. Activities focus on use of positive language, active listening techniques, and strategies for communicating clearly and respectfully.

Evans, D., Hearn, M., Uhlemann, M., & Ivey, A. (1984). *Essential interviewing: A programmed approach to effective communication* (2nd ed.). Monterey, CA: Brooks/Cole Publishing. Cost: $27 plus 6% shipping and handling. (606) 525-2230 for multiple copies, (800) 842-3636 for single copies.

Programmed text defines and demonstrates how to use a group of core communication skills essential to interview anyone.

McWilliam, P.J., & Winton, P. (1992). *Brass Tacks: Part I—Program policies and practices and Part II—Individual interactions with families.* Chapel Hill: University of North Carolina at Chapel Hill, Frank Porter Graham Child Development Center. Cost: $10. (919) 966-7532.

Instruments designed to assist groups and individuals in determining the extent to which their interactions, practices, and policies are family centered. As part of inservice or preservice instruction, Brass Tacks can be used to facilitate examination of early intervention practices (e.g., first encounters with families, identifying goals for intervention, intervention planning for children and families, day-to-day service provision) and to identify specific areas for change.

Winton, P.J. (1992). *Communicating with families in early intervention: A training module.* Chapel Hill: University of North Carolina at Chapel Hill, Frank Porter Graham Child Development Center. Cost: $15. (919) 966-7532.

Objectives, readings, and teaching activities related to communication skills, as well as role-play vignettes, strategies for videotaping self-assessment and peer feedback, and an observational rating scale.

The following is a listing of suggested literature to be used in the book analysis project for family systems and effect of disability as described on pages 258–260.

Bernstein, J. (1988). *Loving Rachel.* Boston: Little, Brown. (Available from Coyne & Chenoweth, Box 81905, Pittsburgh, PA 15217).
Dorris, M. (1989). *The broken cord.* New York: Harper & Row.
Featherstone, H. (1978). *A difference in the family.* New York: Basic Books.
Greenfield, J. (1972). *A child called Noah.* New York: Holt, Reinhart & Winston.
Kupfer, F. (1986). *Before and after Zachariah.* New York: Delacorte Press.
Massie, S., & Massie, R. (1966). *Journey.* New York: Alfred A. Knopf.
Park, C.C. (1967). *The siege: The first eight years of an autistic child.* Boston: Little, Brown.
Walker, L.A. (1986). *A loss for words: The story of deafness in the family.* New York: Harper & Row.

REFERENCES

American Association of Marriage and Family Therapy. (1995a). *Building a family partnership* [Videotape]. (Available from AAMFT Foundation, 1100 17th Street, NW, Suite 901, Washington, DC 20036)
American Association of Marriage and Family Therapy. (1995b). *Exploring family strengths* [Videotape]. (Available from AAMFT Foundation, 1100 17th Street, NW, Suite 901, Washington, DC 20036)

Association for the Care of Children's Health. (1988). *Family-centered care* [Videotape]. (Available from the Association for the Care of Children's Health, 7910 Woodmont Ave., Suite 300, Bethesda, MD 20814)

Bailey, D. (1992.) *Carolina Institute for Research on Infant Personnel Preparation (Year 5 Final Report)*. Chapel Hill: University of North Carolina at Chapel Hill, Frank Porter Graham Child Development Center.

Bailey, D.B., Buysse, V., Edmondson, R., & Smith, T.M. (1992). Creating a family focus in early intervention: Professionals' perceptions of typical practices, ideal practices, and barriers to change. *Exceptional Children, 14,* 196–203.

Bailey, D.B., Buysse, V., Smith, T., & Elam, J. (1992). The effects and perceptions of family involvement in program decisions about family-centered practices. *Evaluation and Program Planning, 15,* 23–32.

Bailey, D.B., McWilliam, P.J., & Winton, P.J. (1992). Building family-centered practices in early intervention: A team-based model for change. *Infants and Young Children, 5,* 73–82.

Bailey, D.B., Palsha, S.A., & Simeonsson, R.J. (1991). Professionals' skills, concerns, and perceived importance of work with families in early intervention. *Exceptional Children, 58,* 156–165.

Bailey, D.B., Simeonsson, R.J., Winton, P.J., Huntington, G.S., Comfort, M., Isbell, P., O'Donnell, K.J., & Helm, J.M. (1986). Family-focused intervention: A functional model for planning, implementing, and evaluating early intervention. *Journal of Early Intervention, 10,* 156–171.

Beckman, P.J., Robinson, C.C., Rosenberg, S., & Filer, J. (1994). Family intervention in early intervention: The evolution of family-centered services. In L.J. Johnson, R.J. Gallagher, M.J. LaMontagne, J.B. Jordan, J.J. Gallagher, P.L. Huntinger, & M.B. Karnes (Eds.), *Meeting early intervention challenges: Issues from birth to three* (2nd ed., pp. 13–31). Baltimore: Paul H. Brookes Publishing Co.

Bennett, T., Lingerfelt, B.V., & Nelson, D.E. (1990). *Developing individualized family support plans.* Cambridge, MA: Brookline Books.

Bernstein, J. (1988). *Loving Rachel.* Boston: Little, Brown. (Available from Coyne & Chenoweth, Box 81905, Pittsburgh, PA 15217)

Bronfenbrenner, U. (1977). Toward an experimental ecology of human development. *American Psychologist, 32,* 513–531.

Brotherson, M.J. (1994). Interactive focus group interviewing: A qualitative research method in early intervention. *Topics in Early Childhood Special Education, 14,* 101–118.

Brotherson, M.J., & McBride, S.M. (1992). *Problem-solving process for developing child and family outcomes.* Unpublished teaching material. Ames: Iowa State University, Department of Human Development and Family Studies.

Carkhuff, R., Kratochvil, D., & Friel, T. (1968). Effects of professional training: Communication and discrimination of facilitative conditions. *Journal of Counseling Psychology, 15,* 68–74.

Carter, E.A., & McGoldrick, M. (Eds.). (1980). *The family life cycle: A framework for family therapy.* New York: Gardner Press.

Division for Early Childhood (DEC) Task Force on Recommended Practices. (1993). *DEC recommended practices: Indicators of quality in programs for infants and young children with special needs and their families.* Reston, VA: Division for Early Childhood of the Council for Exceptional Children.

Dunst, C.J., Johanson, C., Trivette, C.M., & Hambry, D. (1991). Family-oriented early intervention policies and practices: Family-centered or not? *Exceptional Children, 58,* 115–126.

Dunst, C.J., Trivette, C.M., & Deal, A.G. (1988). *Enabling and empowering families: Principles and guidelines for practice.* Cambridge, MA: Brookline Books.

Dunst, C.J., Trivette, C.M., & Deal, A.G. (1994). Resource-based family-centered intervention practices. In C.J. Dunst, C.M. Trivette, & A.G. Deal (Eds.), *Supporting and strengthening families: Methods, strategies and practices* (pp. 140–151). Cambridge, MA: Brookline Books.

Edelman, L. (Ed.). (1991). *Getting on board: Training activities to promote the practice of family-centered care.* Bethesda, MD: Association for the Care of Children's Health.

Edelman, L., & Cosgrove, K. (1991). *Delivering family-centered, home-based services: Facilitator's guide to accompany the videotape.* Baltimore: Kennedy Krieger Institute, Project Copernicus.

Edelman, L., Greenland, B., & Mills, B.L. (1992). *Family-centered communication skills: Facilitator's guide.* Baltimore: Kennedy Krieger Institute, Project Copernicus.

Evans, D., Hearn, M., Uhlemann, M., & Ivey, A. (1984). *Essential interviewing: A programmed approach to effective communication* (2nd ed.). Monterey, CA: Brooks/Cole Publishing.

Fullan, M.G. (1991). *The new meaning of educational change.* New York: Teachers College Press.

Fullan, M.G. (1993). *Change forces: Probing the depths of educational reform.* Bristol, PA: The Falmer Press.

Fullerton, T. (1992). *Heart to heart* [Videotape]. (Available from the Developmental Disabilities Planning Council, 275 East Main Street, Frankfort, KY 40621)

Garland, C.W. (1995). DEC recommended practices: Who uses them? *Journal of Early Intervention,* *19,* 18–20.

Gilkerson, L. (1994). Supporting parents in leadership roles. *Zero to Three, 14*(4), 23–24.

Gilkerson, L., & Young-Holt, C.L. (1992). Supervision and management of programs serving infants, toddlers and their families. In E. Fenichel (Ed.), *Learning through supervision and mentorship* (pp. 113–119). Arlington, VA: National Center for Clinical Infant Programs.

Goldfarb, L.A., Brotherson, M.J., Summers, J.A., & Turnbull, A.P. (1986). *Meeting the challenge of disability or chronic illness: A family guide.* Baltimore: Paul H. Brookes Publishing Co.

Hains, A.H., & Whitehead, A. (1994, July). *Actualizing the rhetoric: Linking research and practice for quality field-based/clinical experiences.* Paper presented at the Ohio Early Childhood and Special Education Higher Education Consortium, Maumee State Park, OH.

Hanson, M.J., & Carta, J.J. (1995). Addressing the challenges of families with multiple risks. *Exceptional Children, 62,* 201–212.

Hartman, A., & Laird, J. (1983). *Family-centered social work practice.* New York: Free Press.

Individuals with Disabilities Education Act Amendments of 1991, PL 102-119, 20 U.S.C.§1400 *et seq.*

Jeppson, E., & Thomas, J. (1994). *Essential allies: Families as advisors.* Bethesda, MD: Institute for Family-Centered Care.

King, S. (1994). *Telling your family story....Parents as presenters* [Videotape and guide]. (Available from University of Wisconson–Madison, Wisconsin Personnel Development Project, Waisman Center, Madison, WI 53705)

Krauss, M. (1990). New precedent in family policy: Individualized family service plan. *Exceptional Children, 56,* 388–395.

Mahoney, G., O'Sullivan, P., & Fors, S. (1989). The family practices of service providers of young handicapped children. *Infant Mental Health Journal, 10,* 75–83.

Marchant, C., & McBride, S. (1994). Family stories. *Journal of Early Childhood Teacher Education, 15,* 7–11.

McBride, S.L., Brotherson, M.J., Joanning, H., Whiddon, D., & Demmitt, A. (1993). Implementation of family-centered services: Perceptions of families and professionals. *Journal of Early Intervention, 17,* 414–430.

McBride, S.L., Sharp, L., Hains, A.H., & Whitehead, A. (1995). Parents as co-instructors in pre-service training: A pathway to family-centered practice. *Journal of Early Intervention, 19,* 377–389.

McCollum, J.A., Rowan, L.R., & Thorp, E.K. (1994). Philosophy as training in infancy personnel preparation. *Journal of Early Intervention, 18,* 216–226.

McGonigel, M.J., Kaufmann, R.K., & Johnson, B.H. (1991). *Guidelines and recommended practices for the individualized family service plan* (2nd ed.). Chapel Hill, NC: National Early Childhood Technical Assistance System and the Association for the Care of Children's Health.

McWilliam, P.J. (1992). *The family report.* Chapel Hill: University of North Carolina at Chapel Hill, Frank Porter Graham Child Development Center.

McWilliam, P.J., & Bailey, D.B., Jr. (Eds.). (1993). *Working together with children and families: Case studies in early intervention.* Baltimore: Paul H. Brookes Publishing Co.

McWilliam, P.J., & Winton, P. (1992). *Brass Tacks: Part I—Program policies and practices and Part II—Individual interactions with families.* Chapel Hill: University of North Carolina at Chapel Hill, Frank Porter Graham Child Development Center.

Midwestern Consortium for Faculty Development, University of Minnesota. (1994). *Information Exchange Newsletter, 3*(1).

Murphy, L.D., Lee, I.M., Turnbull, A.P., & Turbiville, V. (1995). The Family-Centered Program Rating Scale: An instrument for program evaluation and change. *Journal of Early Intervention, 19,* 24–42.

Raab, M.M., Davis, M.S., & Trepanier, A.M. (1993). Resources versus services: Changing the focus of intervention for infants and young children. *Infants and Young Children, 5,* 1–11.

Rosin, P., Whitehead, A.D., Tuchman, L.I., Jesien, G.S., Begun, A.L., & Irwin, L. (1996). *Partnerships in family-centered care: A guide to collaborative early intervention.* Baltimore: Paul H. Brookes Publishing Co.

Shelton, T.L., Jeppson, E.S., & Johnson, B. (1987). *Family-centered care for children with special health care needs.* Washington, DC: Association for the Care of Children's Health.

Shelton, T.L., & Stepanek, J.S. (1994). *Family-centered care for children needing specialized health and developmental services.* Bethesda, MD: Association for the Care of Children's Health.

Summers, J.A., Lane, V., Collier, T., & Friedebach, M.A. (1993). *First steps: Early intervention for infants and toddlers with special needs and their families: An interdisciplinary training curriculum* [Training manual]. Jefferson City, MO: Department of Elementary and Secondary Education.

Thorp, E.K., & McCollum, J.A. (1994). Defining the infancy specialization in early childhood special education. In L.J. Johnson, R.J. Gallagher, M.J. LaMontagne, J.B. Jordan, J.J. Gallagher, P.L. Huntinger, & M.B. Karnes (Eds.), *Meeting early intervention challenges: Issues from birth to three* (2nd ed., pp. 167–183). Baltimore: Paul H. Brookes Publishing Co.

Turnbull, A. (1987, May). *Accepting the challenge of providing comprehensive support to families.* Paper presented at Early Childhood Development Association of Washington annual conference, Seattle, Washington.

Turnbull, A.P., Summers, J.A., & Brotherson, M.J. (1986). Family life cycle: Theoretical and empirical implications and future directions for families with mentally retarded members. In J.J. Gallagher & P.M. Vietze (Eds.), *Families of handicapped persons: Research, programs, and policy issues* (pp. 45–65). Baltimore: Paul H. Brookes Publishing Co.

Turnbull, A.P., & Turnbull, H.R. (1997). *Families, professionals, and exceptionality: A special partnership* (3rd ed.). Englewood Cliffs, NJ: Prentice Hall.

Walizer, E., & Leff, P. (1993). Personal narratives and the process of educating for the healing partnership. *Zero to Three, 14,* 21–30.

Whitehead, A. (1994). *The parent perspective: A parent consultant directory* (2nd ed.). Madison: University of Wisconsin, Wisconsin Personnel Development Project, Waisman Center.

Whitehead, A., & Sontag, J.C. (1993). *Co-instruction: A case study.* Madison: University of Wisconsin, Wisconsin Personnel Development Project, Waisman Center–UAP.

Winton, P.J. (1988). Effective communication between parents and professionals. In D.B. Bailey & R. Simeonsson (Eds.), *Family assessment in early intervention* (pp. 207–228). Columbus, OH: Charles E. Merrill.

Winton, P.J. (1991a). *Communicating with families in early intervention: A training module.* Chapel Hill: University of North Carolina at Chapel Hill, Frank Porter Graham Child Development Center.

Winton, P.J. (1991b). *The family-focused interview: Videotapes and supplemental workbook.* Logan, UT: SKI*HI Institute, and Chapel Hill: University of North Carolina at Chapel Hill, Frank Porter Graham Child Development Center.

Winton, P.J., & Bailey, D.B. (1988). The family focused interview: A collaborative mechanism for family assessment and goal setting. *Journal of the Division for Early Childhood, 12,* 195–207.

Winton, P.J., & DiVenere, N. (1995). Family–professional partnerships in early intervention preparation: Guidelines and strategies. *Topics in Early Childhood Special Education, 15,* 296–313.

11

SERVICE COORDINATION IN EARLY INTERVENTION

Competencies, Curriculum, Challenges, and Strategies

Peggy Rosin
Elizabeth Hecht

True or false?

- Service coordination is an opportunity to work in partnership with families with young children who have special needs in a manner that is empowering and a way to create needed systems change.
- Service coordination is a Band-Aid on a set of dysfunctional health, educational, and social service systems.
- Service coordinators in early intervention may come from a variety of professional or experiential backgrounds.

Answering "false" to any of these statements indicates a need for instruction in early intervention service coordination. However, many people do not have a handle on the competencies associated with being a service coordinator. The case study of Janet in Chapter 1 shows her struggle with feelings related to her competency in providing family-centered, coordinated, community-based, interdisciplinary speech-language services. Many individuals in early intervention react similarly to Janet when providing service coordination.

Service coordination has revolutionized early intervention. Every state in the United States has agreed to fully implement a statewide system of early intervention for eligible infants and toddlers as mandated by the early intervention legislation (Part H) of the Individuals with Disabilities Education Act (IDEA) of 1990, PL 101-476. Service coordination is a required component of this early intervention system. Early intervention legislation also calls for states to ensure that qualified personnel provide early intervention services that best support the needs of infants and toddlers with disabilities and their families. Opportunities are needed for parents, service providers, and students from numerous disciplines involved in early intervention to enhance their knowledge and skills in the multiple and complex functions of service coordination.

The definition of recommended practice in service coordination has evolved and changed to reflect a family-centered philosophy. Approaches to service coordination in the 1990s challenge those who were instructed as "case managers" to reexamine their approach as effective help givers (Bailey, 1989; Buysse & Wesley, 1993; Dunst, Trivette, & Deal, 1994). Whitehead (1996) recognized that new approaches to working with families must stress family strengths and capabilities and acknowledge the reciprocal nature of the family–provider relationship:

> The philosophical shift represented in Part H deliberately broke with the traditional model of case management, a model that presumes dependency and helplessness. Part H replaces case management with a variety of innovative models of service coordination that support the interdependence, independence, capabilities, and decisions of the person and/or family receiving services and are therefore more consistent with the family-centered philosophy of Part H. (p. 209)

For many in early intervention, whether teacher, therapist, or health professional, there may not be opportunities to learn about service coordination, even though these professionals may be asked to serve as service coordinators. A number of studies have documented that professionals working in early intervention graduate from college and university programs without the competencies needed to work successfully as early intervention service coordinators (Bailey, Palsha, & Huntington, 1990; Bailey, Simeonsson, Yoder, & Huntington, 1990; Bruder & Nikitas, 1992; Hanson & Lovett, 1992).

Those graduating from training programs in the era before Part H will need new skills to implement models of helping built on empowerment and partnership. As Johnson (1994) stated, "Whether we call it the service coordinator or case manager, there is a new set of skills and a much broader professional orientation than we have been accustomed to in the past" (p. 7). Service coordination is viewed as a partnership with families, assisting them in locating, accessing, financing, coordinating, monitoring, and advocating for the services, resources, and supports needed to address their concerns and priorities. Most families receive service coordination or coordinate service for their child with disabilities by necessity, not by choice. In the early stages of involvement with early intervention, parents often do not realize that they are receiving service coordination or that they are doing it themselves. Both families and professionals need to learn skills to navigate the systems serving young children with disabilities and their families. All service coordinators need to enhance and expand their knowledge and skills to meet existing and emerging practices.

Inservice instruction in service coordination is consistently rated as a top priority at both the state and national levels (Bruder & Nikitas, 1992; Hanson & Lovett, 1992; McCollum & Bailey, 1991). In a 1994 survey of faculty, inservice instructors, and parents conducted by the Midwestern Consortium for Faculty Development (1994), service coordination was the highest-ranked instructional need across 13 states, giving evidence of a broader national need for instruction and technical assistance in this area. In Wisconsin, service coordination appears yearly on needs assessments of direct service providers conducted as part of the state's comprehensive system of personnel development (Hains & Brown, 1990; Irwin & Pflugrad, 1989; Tuchman, 1991; Wisconsin Division of Health, 1994; Wisconsin Personnel Development Project, 1989, 1991, 1992, 1994).

This chapter addresses the instructional needs of two groups: 1) existing service coordinators who are learning on the job or through inservice training opportunities and 2) future service coordinators who will need to enter the field feeling prepared and confident to meet the myriad challenges associated with early intervention service coordination. This chapter provides the following: an overview of the competencies needed by individuals who provide service coordination; concrete ideas, instructional activities, and resources that compose an approach to service coordination instruction; a delineation of instructional challenges and strategies; and consideration of future needs in service coordination instruction. The information in this chapter is based heavily on the Pathways Service Coordination Project, which is federally funded and administered through the Early Intervention Program at the Waisman Center of the University of Wisconsin–Madison. The interdisciplinary, professional, and parent staff of this project developed competencies and implemented and evaluated an options-based curriculum for instruction in service coordination.

AREAS OF KNOWLEDGE AND COMPETENCY
IN EARLY INTERVENTION SERVICE COORDINATION

What knowledge and skills do service coordinators need to meet their responsibilities and the challenges they encounter? This question underlies the development of competencies for instruction in service coordination. To develop core competencies, the following sources were tapped: 1) needs assessments and focus groups with a variety of stakeholders, including family members, service coordinators, program coordinators, higher education faculty, and local and state agency representatives; 2) state and national advisory committees; 3) current literature and resources in early intervention (see Appendix A at the end of this chapter for a list of topics for service coordination instruction drawn from the literature); 4) several field tests of the Pathways Service Coordination Project's curriculum using a variety of instruction options (e.g., for-credit university courses, 2- to 3-day institutes, workshops) with feedback on curriculum and instructional events from each group of participants; and 5) input from early intervention programs in four communities that helped to validate the areas of competency.

A distillation of the information gathered from these sources shaped the competencies and resultant curriculum. Fundamental to being a competent service coordinator are the attitudes and values brought to the job. Curricula need to allow for self-examination of and reflection on attitudes and values, especially as they relate to service coordination practice with families and others who may have perspectives and values different from the service coordinators' values. In addition to the value-based content and activities, personal and job-related skills and knowledge emerged as two predominant categories in the curriculum, as noted in Table 11.1. These competencies form the basis for what service coordinators need to know and do to be effective in working with families in the early intervention process. The competencies form the basis for the content and activities for the approach to service coordination instruction in the next section.

AN APPROACH TO SERVICE COORDINATION INSTRUCTION

The approach described in this section can assist instructors in providing much-needed inservice and preservice instruction for parents and personnel involved in early intervention service coordination. Instructors are encouraged to model the targeted competencies throughout each instructional session, include parents at multiple levels in instruction, and be responsive to the individualized needs of participants. The approach is consistent with Winton's (1990, 1994) thesis that professional development be synergistic with practices in early intervention. She strongly advocates that instructional procedures closely reflect the content of instruction. Thus, if the intent is to instruct service coordinators to enhance parental decision making, then participants also must be afforded frequent opportunities to make decisions and be supported in their decisions.

General Principles of the Instructional Approach

The instructional approach is participant centered and builds on parent–professional partnerships, which can be fostered through employing parents as staff members and con-

TABLE 11.1.   Competencies for service coordination

Personal skills and knowledge

- Working in partnership with families

- Effective communication strategies: one to one, team, interagency

- Teamwork: roles and process

- Conflict and crisis management and strategies

- Taking care of yourself: personal safety, grief issues, stress

- Leadership and change agent skills

Job-related skills and knowledge

- Understanding federal and state rules and regulations related to Part H of IDEA

- Understanding of the early intervention system and its relationship to the broader community

- Knowing the components and time lines related to the individualized family service plan (IFSP) document and the importance of the process surrounding its development, implementation, and evaluation

- Understanding the various approaches to service coordination and the impact the use of different approaches may have on service coordination practice

- Knowing the importance of and differences among services, resources, and supports and how each may assist a family and child in meeting IFSP outcomes

- Having strategies for locating, gaining access to, and financing services, resources, and supports on the IFSP

- Applying effective techniques when coordinating early intervention services

- Providing appropriate follow-along while monitoring and evaluating the IFSP process

- Advocating for services with families

- Managing multiple priorities and responsibilities of the job

- Setting personal boundaries; knowing program and agency boundaries

sultants, modeling parent and professional teams in instruction, inviting and supporting parents to be advisors in the instructional process, and supporting parents as learners along with their professional colleagues. Parents are experts on the needs of their family and children. Their collaboration in the design, planning, and implementation of personnel development activities ensures that all materials and practices fully recognize the critical, varied, and changing roles that parents play.

The participant-centered orientation can be achieved through tailoring experiences to meet individual participant's needs and offering options so that participants exercise control and choice over their learning. Even though the format for organizing and disseminating content and activities can vary (e.g., for-credit course, correspondence course, workshop), some methods can be applied across formats, including 1) self-assessment and learning plans, 2) agenda-setting and action plans, 3) accommodating learning styles using principles of adult learning, and 4) applying a problem-solving approach to instruction.

Self-Assessment and Learning Plans   One method of achieving the participant-centered orientation is through a self-assessment of strengths, concerns, priorities, and resources. Based on the self-assessment, the participant develops an individualized learning plan (ILP) listing desired outcomes from the instruction. Field-based experiences selected by the participants assist them in meeting these outcomes (see Appendix B at the end of this chapter for examples of field-based experiences). The ILP guides the selection of field-based experiences as well as any final project or product completed by the participant. A course facilitator acting as a service coordinator and mentor for the participant provides information, support, and access to material and human resources. This support is provided at a level determined by the participant to meet selected learning outcomes.

Agenda Setting and Action Plans The participant-centered orientation can be used in workshops and institutes with activities such as agenda setting (e.g., participants are asked to write what they hope to learn and the questions they want to discuss) at the beginning of the event and a Next Steps or a Commitment to Action at the end. This encourages participants to reflect on their accomplishments during the instruction and to set future outcomes. It also prompts participants to continue the learning process beyond the time limits of the specific event.

Accommodating Learning Styles Using Principles of Adult Learning A participant-centered orientation threads principles of adult learning through all elements of personnel development. In addition to the options that accommodate participants' desired outcomes, a variety of instructional techniques accommodate their preferred learning styles. These techniques reflect the basic assumptions about how adults learn and optimize the likelihood that the content is relevant and practical. Based on these assumptions, information is presented in a variety of forms, including articles, overheads, handouts, lecture, panel presentation, discussion, skits, role plays, videotapes, case stories, vignettes, and games. Participants can be asked to explore the information individually, in small and large groups, and through field-based experiences.

Applying a Problem-Solving Approach to Instruction A problem-solving approach using case studies or stories is a powerful technique for moving from theory to practice in service coordination. These complex accounts highlight the issues and challenges confronting parents and service coordinators as they navigate multiple systems. A problem-solving approach affords participants an opportunity to do the following: practice problem solving and decision making, discuss real situations that may be unfamiliar or challenging, examine and practice interpersonal skills, ground theoretical learning into practice, and explore personal values and beliefs (McWilliam & Bailey, 1993).

An Instructional Framework and Sample Instructional Activities

A framework for service coordination instruction and activities that can be applied to address the service coordination core competencies are provided in this section. This framework for organizing a curriculum divides service coordination into four phases of activities that reflect the type of interaction that might occur between a service coordinator and a family. These phases are not necessarily sequential. For example, a family may experience a number of transitions during early intervention or may never experience what they consider to be a crisis. The framework, however, conceptualizes the individualized family service plan (IFSP) process for instructional purposes and assists in targeting specific skills and knowledge.

The four phases (Rosin, Green, Hecht, Tuchman, & Robbins, 1996) are 1) *getting started* in early intervention, which includes the initial contact through the development of the IFSP; 2) *follow along* with families, which covers the implementation and monitoring of the IFSP; 3) facing *immediate needs or crisis*, which reflects a time for the family or service coordinator when there is an urgent and immediate need for support and problem solving; and 4) facilitating *transition*, which represents the sharing of information across the interface between early intervention and a system of community supports and services for children and families.

Using this framework, Figure 11.1 provides instructional activities that can be selected and tailored to meet participants' needs in each of the four phases of service coordination. Activities 1–4, which can be found at the end of the chapter, are a sampling of detailed activities that correspond to each of the four phases.

These activities can be used with individual, small and large group, and field-based activities in both preservice and inservice instruction. Many of the individual activities involve personal reflection and self-examination but can be followed by large-group sharing. Individual activities focus on finding a reference point in personal experience as a stepping-off point on the topic. For example, an instructor might ask participants to think of an experience in which they felt supported, cared for, or listened to. Then ask them to reflect on the elements of that interaction that made it work for them. Subsequent discussion can highlight how the participants can adapt this personal experience into their work with families.

Group activities usually involve four to six trainees. These small groups can share their ideas with the larger group, looking for common threads and pooling new information. Small groups are opportunities for participants to draw on personal experience as a basis for problem solving. Each person's struggles and successes are validated by similar experiences of other members of the group, allowing an opportunity for participants to benefit from the collective expertise of the group.

Field-based experiences are often pursued by an individual but also can be completed by two or more people with similar interests or concerns. Participants' choices for field-based experiences are closely tied to the ILP. Excellent learning opportunities can be developed with families and community agencies that work with families. In general, families and agency personnel welcome an opportunity to share their knowledge and experience. Preservice participants may need more structured field-based experiences. For example, participants can be paired with a family mentor as a long-term practicum experience or shadow a family for a day (see Appendix B at the end of this chapter for additional examples of field-based experiences).

All activities presented in Figure 11.1 were evaluated by participants in the Pathways Service Coordination Project activities. Participants consistently rated the following as the most beneficial: 1) group discussion, particularly small groups in which participants were given time to share and benefit from each others' expertise and experience; 2) the diversity of instructional staff and participants, in particular parents as participants; 3) the use of case studies for brainstorming and problem solving; 4) the opportunity for networking; and 5) parent panels and guest speakers. Participants clearly preferred those learning activities that allowed for individual sharing and validation of experience and expertise and those techniques that provided a context for new information within their own experiences. This summary of preferred instructional techniques can help instructors develop future curricula for instructing service coordinators.

CHALLENGES AND STRATEGIES IN SERVICE COORDINATION INSTRUCTION

Successful instruction in service coordination relies on the same principles that underlie any good instruction. The Pathways Service Coordination Project curriculum infuses principles of parent–professional collaboration and the participant-centered approach into all aspects of instructional content and process. However, a number of challenges emerged

Core competencies	Activities		
	Individual	Group	Field-based
PERSONAL SKILLS			
Communication • One-to-one • Team • Interagency	Work Style Inventory[1]	Values exercise[2] Two-person role play[3]	Observe and reflect on successful communications in your home or work environment.
Conflict management • Personal strategies for avoiding conflict • Finding common ground • Strategies for managing conflict	Reflect on a conflict you were involved with that had a positive outcome. What happened?	Video segment[4] Parent Panel[5] General ideas about working with conflict[6]	Attend a team meeting and observe how the team problem-solves together and in which situations they have difficulty reaching agreement. Record your observations.
Taking care of yourself • Personal safety • Grief counseling • Establish healthy boundaries • Stress reduction	List what you do when stressed.[7]	Videotape segment[8] Discussion—How can you do more of what you like?[9] Skit[10]	Visit a local law enforcement representative and discuss staff safety concerns.
Leadership and change agent skills • Leadership styles • When to lead and when to follow • Creating a vision • "Keep your eye on the prize"	SELF Profile[11]	Draw your vision. Ask the group to draw their vision of a system of services and resources for children and families.[12]	Attend a local Interagency Coordinating Council meeting or other forum for discussions around policy development.

(continued)

Figure 11.1. Training activities for learning core competencies in service coordination. (The numbers next to an activity correspond to a description of that activity at the end of the figure on pp. 286–287.)

Figure 11.1.   *(continued)*

SPECIFIC SKILLS AND KNOWLEDGE

Federal and state rules and regulations • Legislation and service coordination • Due processes and procedural safeguards	Ask participants to describe what they do as a service coordinator under current early intervention legislation.	Role-play on presenting rights and procedural safeguards to family members.	Call the state early intervention coordinator for a copy of your state's rules and regulations.
The IFSP • System entry through transition • Partnerships • Coordinating the evaluation process • Completing the IFSP document • Collaborative outcomes	Write three strategies for including parents before, during, and after the IFSP process.	Scenarios/role plays on developing collaborative outcomes.[13]	Shadow a family or a service coordinator through the IFSP process.
Approaches to service coordination • What are the different approaches? • Why choose one approach or another? • Co-service coordination	Reflect on the advantages and disadvantages of the model of service coordination in which you work.	The Great Debate[14]	Visit or talk with early intervention personnel about their approach to service coordination.
Resources versus services • Informal supports • Creating options • Community inclusion	Draw an eco-map of your own family.[15]	Work together in a group and draw an eco-map using a case study. Panel of experts[16]	Attend a home visit or a family support group meeting as an observer. Think about the families' connectedness to each other and the community as you listen.

(continued)

Figure 11.1.   *(continued)*

Locating, obtaining, and financing services, resources, and supports • Mapping resources • Billing and documentation	How do you organize your resources? Find and review three resource guides related to community options for families.	Design a dynamic resource file.[17]	Find out what types of recreational activities are available to children with disabilities in your community.
Coordinating early intervention services • Time management • Transferring skills • Facilitating meetings	Explore an analogy. Write how service coordination is like a river. . . .	Chopsticks[18]	Review written materials about the components of a well-run meeting and then attend a meeting and look for those components. What happened?
Monitoring and evaluating the IFSP process • Monitoring child and family outcomes • Program evaluation and parent satisfaction	Develop three questions to ask parents regarding their thoughts on progress toward the outcomes written in their IFSP.	Fish Bowl[19]	Talk with personnel at a local early intervention program about how they assess parent satisfaction or attend a parent support meeting or a parent advisory meeting.
Advocating for services • How to get services and supports • State and national advocacy groups	Think about the targets for your advocacy efforts: parents, your program, or your agency and what that means in light of limited resources.	Discuss and pool your ideas for advocacy services in your community.	Call several advocacy services and find out more about them.
INTEGRATING THE ACTIVITIES AND FUNCTIONS OF SERVICE COORDINATION[20]	Case method	Case method	Attend an interdisciplinary team staffing and then write down the contributions differing perspectives had on the discussion.

(continued)

Figure 11.1.   *(continued)*

Description of Activities in Figure 11.1

[1]The Work Style Inventory (*How to be a more effective trainer.* [1991]. Boulder, CO: Career Tracks, Inc.) is one tool for looking at personal communication styles and how different styles can interact together (available in Rosin et al., 1993).

[2]Compose a list of true or false questions (e.g., Families who use alternative medicine are not taking their child's health care issues seriously; the service coordinator should not be expected to go into an unsafe neighborhood) relevant to the topic being discussed. There are no right or wrong answers. Participants are then asked to form groups based on their answers and discuss with each other their choice and listen to the other groups' reasons for their choice. Participants are also asked to reflect on how it felt to "take a stand" and be in the minority or majority.

[3]Develop a skit (Rosin, Green, et al., 1996) that involves a first time meeting between a parent and a service coordinator. Model poor communication skills such as not asking open-ended questions. Have the trainees stop the action and discuss what is happening and what should be changed. Then continue the role play with the audience modifying the interactions at will.

[4]Scenario I from the *Pathways in Early Intervention Service Coordination* videotape (Rosin, 1996) depicts the interaction between a service coordinator and two parents, divorced, who have different ideas about early intervention services. Discuss the scenario and decide on a plan of action using the problem-solving format provided on the videotape.

[5]Invite three or four parents to come and talk with participants about their experiences with partnerships in early intervention. Prepare questions for the parents to respond to (e.g., What has helped? What have they found challenging?). Allow time for questions to discuss reactions to the panel afterward.

[6]Groups are asked to think about conflict in one area (e.g., working with families, teams, or agencies). The issue is structured so it is not too general. Each person writes down his or her conflict on the outside of an envelope and passes it to the next person in his or her group. Each person in the group writes down strategies on a card in the envelope and passes it to the next person. Each person reads the previous strategies and adds any thoughts. The small group then discusses the suggestions with each other.

[7]Progressive relaxation visualization (Rosin, Whitehead, et al., 1996).

[8]Scenario II from the *Pathways in Early Intervention Service Coordination* videotape (Rosin, 1996) depicts an interaction between a program director and a service coordinator concerning competing priorities and time management. Use a problem-solving format to discuss the issues.

[9]Group members are asked to reflect on what each likes or looks forward to about their job as a service coordinator. What would they like more time to do? What strategies can they use to organize themselves to do more of what they like? Groups then share their strategies with the large group.

[10]Develop a skit in which a parent, a service coordinator, and a program administrator are interacting with each other around daily issues as an entirely different internal dialogue is expressed concerning stress.

[11]Use the SELF Profile (National Press Publications, 1987) as a tool to increase awareness about personal leadership styles and how different styles interact.

[12]Provide chart paper and many color markers. Ask groups to share their vision of the early intervention system. Depending on the focus, a variety of discussions can follow: What do families want? What is a seamless system? How do service systems integrate with the community?

[13]Present a family story to the group. Assign roles (e.g., mother, father, speech-language pathologist, service coordinator, early interventionist). Ask the group to develop

(continued)

Figure 11.1. *(continued)*

two to three collaborative outcomes for the IFSP based on the story and their specific perspectives. Have the group reflect on their process used to arrive at the outcomes (e.g., How did they reach agreement on the outcomes they focused on? What did they do when there was not agreement? Was everyone's perspective heard? Did they have a process for making sure everyone's perspective was heard?)

[14]The Great Debate: An exploration of the different approaches to service coordination. Prepare a description of three different approaches to service coordination (e.g., interim, dedicated, parent, direct provider). Ask small groups to discuss the advantages and disadvantages of a particular approach. Have a group spokesperson present the advantages to the large group and be prepared to debate the merits of their approach. Follow with a large-group discussion. (Adapted from Hurth, J. [1991]. *Providing case management services under Part H of IDEA: Different approaches to family-centered services coordination.* Chapel Hill, NC: National Early Childhood Technical Assistance System.)

[15]The eco-map is a picture that tells how a family interacts with the outside world. Map components are drawn in circles with lines connecting them showing the strength of the interaction. The map can reflect how a family experiences their resource network and support systems, the costs and benefits of interactions with people and resources, and sources of stress and relief. The process and the resulting picture can be both fun and informative (Rosin et al., 1993).

[16]Invite three to five community and agency personnel who are well informed about resource and funding issues (e.g., Social Security Income, child protective services, public health, medical assistance billing).

[17]Resource guides are often out of date by the time they are published. Generate ideas for ways to 1) keep a resource file system current and 2) record the experiences of program staff using the resource (e.g., key contacts, good times to call). Think about organizing resources based on the needs of families in your community (Rosin, Green, et al., 1996).

[18]Chopsticks is an activity that allows pairs to explore how they share new skills with another person and how they like to learn new skills. Choose an array of objects that can be picked up with chopsticks (e.g., paper, pencils, paper clips). Vary the kinds of chopsticks, the containers objects are placed in, and the visibility of participants by using blindfolds or sunglasses. Have people work in pairs as they learn to manipulate the objects they are given. Each pair decides who wants to teach and who wants to learn. Then share with the group impressions, frustrations, and what worked. You can use this activity as a point to talk about how skills are shared with families in a supportive way, based on what people found helpful in learning to use chopsticks.

[19]Three trainers assume parts in an improvisational team role play as the rest of the group makes observations about what happened and what might have happened. The role play centers on a 6-month IFSP review in which the service coordinator, parent, and early interventionist are present. Those observing the role play make specific observations related to roles people play, decision making, facilitation, and strategies used to ensure the family members are included. The role play can be a catalyst for discussion of any one of these people.

[20]The seven functions of service coordination are discussed within the context of four clusters of service coordination activities:

1. Getting started in the IFSP process
2. Follow along and implementation of the IFSP
3. Responding to immediate, unexpected needs
4. Transition—issues and challenges are illustrated

Use the case method of instruction to explore the four clusters of activity. Use a story from the references provided. Each story includes a parent–provider scenario and embeds skill building and problem solving. Each story ends with the service coordinator needing to resolve a dilemma. Use a problem-solving format to assist the participant in developing a plan of action (McWilliam & Bailey, 1993; Rosin, Green, et al., 1996).

during the field testing of the Pathways Service Coordination Project curriculum. A discussion of these challenges and possible strategies to address them can guide others preparing service coordination instruction.

Many of the challenges encountered in instructing service coordinators are similar to those faced when teaching any content area in early intervention. Table 11.2 outlines three categories of challenge: 1) support, 2) membership, and 3) instructional content and process challenges. Because support and membership challenges in service coordination instruction are comparable for any early intervention content area, they will not be elaborated on; however, several instructional content and process challenges specific to service coordination deserve further elaboration.

Presenting the Family-Centered Care Philosophy

Understanding and actualizing the philosophy of family-centered care in service coordination practice are critical. Participants often report that they understand what family-centered care means and do not need to hear more about the philosophical underpinnings of early intervention. However, sometimes participants' comments or actions are incon-

TABLE 11.2.   Inservice and preservice personnel development challenges

Support challenges

- **Time**—sufficient time allocated

- **Funding and incentives**—money and other incentives to make personnel development a priority

- **Administration**—support for personnel development and its application to practice

Membership challenges

- **Families**—family members included in all stages of personnel development

- **Teams**—focus on team versus isolated individuals

- **Comprehensive system of personnel development (CSPD)**—efforts are coordinated with and integrated into the state's CSPD

- **Service coordinators**—preplanned with service coordinators to ensure that needs of participants and of the field are met

- **Diverse representation**—diversity represented in instructors and participants, including families

Instructional content and process challenges

- **Varying needs of participants**—service coordination conducted by people from varying backgrounds with varying abilities and needs (e.g., discipline, values, knowledge, skills, life experience, education, parent and providers training together); therefore, personnel development needs differ

- **Breadth of content**—service coordinators called on to have a range of personal skills and abilities specific to the job

- **Depth of content (awareness, knowledge, skill practice)**—ongoing opportunities for practice and feedback needed to learn a new skill

- **Personal skill training**—many aspects of service coordination related to individual values

- **Field-based experiences**—needed to provide context or practica that give real-world experience to participants

gruous with family-centered care. For example, they may nod in agreement about empowerment and family-centered care while saying, "Yes, that is all well and good but what about 'those' families," with "those families" eventually being defined as families who have different concerns, priorities, and resources from the participant. Strategies for infusing the philosophy of family-centered care into instruction include the following:

- Embed the principles of family-centered care into every instructional activity.
- Support parents as participants and co-instructors.
- Use the "technical" aspects of the content such as the IFSP as a focus of the activity while incorporating philosophy into process discussions about the activity.
- Stress that service coordination is different for every family by giving examples or asking how certain approaches to service coordination practice might work for one family versus another.
- Bring discussion about obstacles or barriers in providing service coordination back to the question "What would this practice/service/resource/program look like if it were family centered?"
- Keep the vision of family-centered, interdisciplinary, comprehensive, community-based, culturally competent services in the foreground.

Focusing on Relationship as the Basis for Service Coordination

A service coordinator develops relationships with families, other team members, and agency personnel. At the heart of any relationship are personal and interpersonal skills. Communication is the thread that unites the skills that make service coordination effective. Having myriad communication strategies and techniques is important in daily conversations with families, teammates, and agency personnel but critical in other situations such as eliciting a family's concerns, priorities, and resources for their child and themselves; resolving situations of conflict; negotiating with agencies; or facilitating a meeting. These are skills that must be practiced to be learned. Strategies include the following:

- Model the personal skills that are central to service coordination competencies throughout all instruction (e.g., question asking, open-ended comments, problem-solving format, empowering participants).
- Make clear to participants that many of the skills that underlie service coordination relationships or partnerships can be practiced and learned.
- Assign participants to teams to practice skills. Depending on whether the instruction is ongoing and on the objective, these teams could be kept constant or membership can change.
- Ask the participants to reflect on the communication aspects of any team activity.
- Explore cultural diversity and its potential influences on developing relationships. Families, teams, and agencies each have a culture that influences how a service coordinator approaches and interacts with them.

Enhancing Personal Skills

Enhancing personal skills is a form of self-improvement. A sense of self and values is inextricably linked. As service coordinators, it is essential to understand that values motivate responses and color perceptions of people and situations. It is necessary for participants to self-examine, self-reflect, and see situations and issues from other perspectives as they learn personal skills. This requirement for self-assessment and disclosure of areas of need and priority for skill enhancement can feel uncomfortable. Many participants may be less than forthcoming in a group situation or in a situation in which there may be a perceived imbalance of power. For example, in a preservice setting the university student may not want to expose his or her limitations to a professor. In an inservice setting, a service coordinator may have a program supervisor acting as instructor and may not feel comfortable talking about areas needing growth. Several strategies can be applied to help alleviate some of this discomfort, including the following:

- Sequence the curriculum so that any type of personal skills work occurs after a level of trust is established.
- Allow participants options for participating in activities that can accommodate their comfort level, cultural background, and learning style.
- Acknowledge that personal skills instruction can be intimidating to participants.
- Discuss ground rules and generate with the group ways to create a safe place for participants to talk about values and feelings.
- Acknowledge that everyone sees things through his or her own perceptual filters, and investigate points of difference in a nonjudgmental way.
- Stress the importance of the language as reflecting participants' thoughts. This may increase sensitivity to using words and descriptions with which people are comfortable.

Understanding that Service Coordination May Have Unintended Negative Consequences for Families

The intent of service coordination is to assist families in early intervention, at their desired level, to locate, reach, and receive the services, resources, and supports they need for their child and themselves. Even though service coordination is conceived as a helpful service, it may have adverse effects on families. Bill Schwab (personal communication, September 1994), a pediatrician, professor in the Department of Family Medicine at the Medical School of the University of Wisconsin–Madison, and parent of a child with disabilities, extended warnings about service coordination by citing some possible unintended negative consequences, including the following:

- Service coordination acts as a filter between the family and the system. The family members may not learn directly whom to contact and how to find resources and services. Conversely, service systems become less responsive to families because they do not work with them directly.
- Service coordinators are intermediaries between the family and the services and can make unintentional mistakes (e.g., making arrangements for others is difficult, making inaccurate assumptions).
- Service coordination is built on an assumption that it will bring consistency to families' lives by knowing who can support them in having access to the system. Numerous factors work against consistency in early intervention service coordination (e.g., positions are often entry-level positions, with high turnover of staff or transitions; multiple agencies and funding sources competing for case management or service coordination).

The reality is that the health, educational, and social service systems are not easily negotiated; therefore, service coordination can be a beneficial service. Ideally, as service coordinators work to make the system accessible and empower families, the need for service coordination will diminish. The following strategies could be used to help clarify this issue:

- Explore with participants the positive and negative aspects of service coordination.

- Encourage the participants to reflect on the process of empowerment by keeping in mind the family's desired outcomes and how the outcomes can be achieved through a partnership.
- Have participants develop strategies for transferring knowledge to parents about the system at a pace and level that is comfortable for the family.

Defining Roles and Boundaries in Service Coordination

Service coordinators need to set personal boundaries and understand discipline, program, and agency boundaries. Developing partnerships with families can lead to friendship and emotional connections with them. It is important for each service coordinator to know his or her own boundaries in working with families. These boundaries often relate to the service coordinator's personal resources (e.g., emotional, financial, time). How does the service coordinator respond during a home visit when a family has run out of diapers for the baby and there is no money in the house? Is it all right for families to call the service coordinator on weekends? Many of these questions may be individually decided, or, in some cases, there may be existing program policies.

Knowledge of program and agency roles and boundaries is equally important. In early intervention the service coordinator is responsible for coordinating a team composed of the parents and a wide range of professionals. The service coordinator needs to understand the roles of all the providers with whom he or she interacts during early intervention. This knowledge helps the right people to be involved in the critical decisions made throughout the process. What is the early intervention program responsible for in relationship to the needs of the child and family? What are the responsibilities of other agencies, and how and when should they be involved? When coordinating services, resources, and supports across agencies, the service coordinator should know whether formal or informal interagency agreements exist. Strategies to assist participants in thinking about these roles and boundaries include the following:

- Explore the meaning of partnership and point out how it differs from friendship.
- Examine the notion of empowerment and how it relates to service coordination as a helping profession.
- Encourage participants to reflect on their own comfort level in setting personal boundaries.
- Provide an opportunity to distinguish between the roles of various providers and agencies.
- Review the contents of sample interagency agreements.

Moving Beyond the IFSP Form

The service coordinator is responsible for many aspects of the IFSP and its development, implementation, and evaluation. It is essential that the coordinator know the mandated components of the IFSP, associated time lines, and parents' rights and procedural safeguards in the process. Among other things, the IFSP document reflects the child's current developmental status and needs, outcomes desired, and strategies to meet those outcomes. Helping service coordinators view the IFSP in a broader context of family and community can be challenging. Strategies to help participants move beyond the IFSP form include the following:

- Provide participants with the legal aspects of the document and examples of IFSPs at the beginning of the instruction.

- Discuss the IFSP document, and answer questions related to the more concrete responsibilities of the form and process.
- Practice setting collaborative outcomes and consensus building.
- Use an eco-map, community mapping, or other strategy to show how the child and family fit into a much broader context and the family's connections and interactions with their community-at-large.
- Explore with participants how early intervention services may be just one way to meet the desired IFSP outcomes and that there are many other formal and informal resources and supports for meeting these outcomes.
- Demonstrate various methods for eliciting family concerns, resources, and priorities, emphasizing conversation as the basis for eliciting this information.

Keeping Current in a Changing System

The service coordinator is responsible for having a broad system perspective. A frequent challenge is keeping track of changing health, education, and social service systems (e.g., managed care, welfare reform, the reauthorization of IDEA). In service coordination instruction, some strategies to address this challenge include the following:

- Share and discuss methods to map community agencies, services, and resources.
- Provide a needs-based taxonomy that shows the areas of need frequently cited by families.
- Assist participants with strategies for organization that work for them personally or that meet the early intervention program's needs and resources.
- Develop methods for contacting key agency personnel with knowledge about various systems.
- Give samples of journals, newsletters, and Internet Web sites that can help service coordinators keep up to date.

Having Methods of Support for the Service Coordinator

A statewide group of parents, service coordinators, program administrators, faculty, and state agency representatives were asked, "What information, instruction, or resources do service coordinators need to have to be able to address the challenges they are likely to face?" An unexpected category of response emerged—taking care of one's self or support for the service coordinator. In subsequent staff development efforts, the need for incorporating this topic area into the curriculum was reaffirmed. Service coordination can be a stressful job and service coordinators (parents and providers) need to stay healthy to meet the challenges of collaboration in coordinating services. The service coordination instruction could include a discussion of ways to

- Explore personal support systems within and outside the program.
- Develop formal or informal peer networks.
- Establish mentor relationships within the program.
- Build resources into the program for staff development and support.

Assisting Service Coordinators in Their Role as Change Agents

Service coordination can be viewed as an opportunity for systems change. The service coordinator is in the position to see what policies and practices work for families and which limit or set up barriers to families participating in early intervention. The service coordinator often may feel overwhelmed by the idea that in addition to all the other tasks of the job they now need to change the system too. Spending time on the topic of service coordinator as change agent can make the role appear less threatening. Some strategies include the following:

- Acknowledge that change is a constant in all aspects of life.
- Define systems change.
- Show the wide range of activities that can have an effect on systems.
- Provide a framework and strategies for noting aspects of the system that are and are not working for families.

These strategies address some challenges facing service coordinators and are offered for consideration as instructors prepare both inservice and preservice participants to be competent in the provision of early intervention service coordination.

CONCLUSION

Future needs in service coordination personnel development parallel the daunting and complex challenges for coordinating the services, resources, and supports of families. Service coordinators work within a variety of systems (e.g., family, early intervention, health, social services, education) and need competencies in understanding the culture of systems and strategies for collaborating with and bridging systems. In the current political climate, there are dwindling resources for human services, making systems collaboration imperative. Service coordinators and program and agency personnel need to join forces with families to create a family-centered system with a shared vision that crosses boundaries and builds connections. This will encourage creative methods in reaching family outcomes, such as blending funding streams across programs or using informal community supports.

For service coordinators to gain competencies and to meet the challenges, a variety of accessible staff development options needs to be available. Some options include self-directed study and correspondence courses with the possibility of receiving continuing education or university credit. Instructional materials need to be developed that can be used for multiple purposes (e.g., orientation of new staff; ongoing training for staff development; working in a supervisory, mentor, or peer-to-peer relationship [see Chapter 8]; self-study modules, tutorials). The use of distance education technology (e.g., tele-conferencing, compressed interactive two-way video, satellite television [see Chapter 19]) and computer-mediated communication systems (e.g., Web site on the Internet with a home page and links to relevant resources on the Web, e-mail, Listserve, discussion or chat groups) offer accessible options for the future. However, these methods also provide new challenges for instructors.

The diversity of people using the early intervention system is continuously adding to its complexity. In the 1990s, American children and families are in transition. According to the National Commission on Children (1991), dramatic demographic, social, and economic changes have transformed the meaning of family in the United States. Four sources of diversity offer particular challenges in early intervention. First, growing numbers of families seeking early intervention services come from ethnic and cultural backgrounds different from those of many early intervention service providers. Second, structural changes in families mean that fewer children live in two-parent families with mothers who are full-time homemakers. Third, the proportion of infants and toddlers living in poverty is increasing. And fourth, the number of families headed by parents with disabilities is growing (Rosin, 1996). Service coordinators need knowledge and skills to promote culturally competent attitudes, actions, and policies within themselves and the agencies and systems in which they work.

Diversity is a key concept for people responsible for providing inservice and pre-service instruction on service coordination. In this context, diversity extends to the participants learning about service coordination; the families with whom service coordinators work; the teams, agencies, and systems with which service coordinators collaborate; and the instruction options and formats used to meet the instruction needs for personnel preparation for early intervention service coordination. The challenges are many in preparing competent service coordinators. The success of this chapter is in the reader understanding more clearly the challenges, strategies, and lessons learned in providing service coordination instruction.

RESOURCES

Edelman, L., Elsayed, S.S., & McGonigel, M. (1992). *Overview of family-centered service coordination: Facilitator's guide.* St. Paul, MN: Pathfinder Resources, Inc. Cost: $12. (612) 647-6905.

Specific activities and materials for facilitating instruction about service coordination. Step-by-step guide provides purpose, time required, learning strategies, and specific materials needed for each of eight activities on key issues (e.g., specific roles/activities associated with service coordination).

McWilliam, P.J., & Bailey, D.B., Jr. (Eds.). (1993). *Working together with children and families: Case studies in early intervention.* Baltimore: Paul H. Brookes Publishing Co. Cost: $27 plus postage and handling. (800) 638-3775.

Edited collection of cases exemplifying the application of recommended practices in early intervention for use in preservice and inservice instruction. Text includes unsolved case dilemmas for use in teaching/instructing, decision making, and problem solving.

Rosin, P. (1996). *Pathways in early intervention service coordination* [Videotape]. Madison: University of Wisconsin–Madison, Waisman Center. Cost: $80. (608) 265-2063.

Videotape illustrates challenges faced in the provision of early intervention service coordination through four videotape scenarios. Accompanying guide highlights key issues and important skills and provides discussion questions and activities for promoting the development of skills in each area.

Rosin, P., Green, M., Hecht, L., Tuchman, L., & Robbins, S. (1996). *Pathways: A training and resource guide for enhancing skills in early intervention service coordination.* Madison: University of Wisconsin–Madison, Waisman Center. Cost: $35. (608) 265-2063.

Curriculum designed to enhance skills and knowledge of service coordination for preservice and inservice audiences. Content is divided into four sections: 1) getting started in the IFSP process; 2) follow-along and implementation of the IFSP; 3) responding to unexpected, immediate needs or crises; and 4) facilitating transitions. Materials were designed to be used in conjunction with the *Pathways in Early Intervention Service Coordination* videotape.

Rosin, P., Whitehead, A., Tuchman, L., Jesien, G., Begun, A., & Irwin, L. (1993). *Partnerships in early intervention: A training guide on family-centered care, team building, and service coordination.* Madison: University of Wisconsin–Madison, Waisman Center. Cost: $38. (608) 265-2063.

Useful instructional guide with information, activities, and teaching materials on three aspects of early intervention service delivery (family–professional partnerships, interdisciplinary and interagency team building, and service coordination). Materials were designed to be used in conjunction with the *Parents and Professionals: Partners in Co-service Coordination* videotape.

Rosin, P., Whitehead, A.D., Tuchman, L.I., Jesien, G.S., Begun, A.L., & Irwin, L. (1996). *Partnerships in family-centered care: A guide to collaborative early intervention.* Baltimore: Paul H. Brookes Publishing Co. Cost: $39. (800) 638-3775.

The three sections of this book focus on interrelated early intervention instruction themes: family-centered care, team building, and service coordination. Each section features a story, which is intended to facilitate creative problem solving on issues raised, as well as a variety of instructional aids (e.g., objectives, activities, discussion questions) skillfully interwoven with the content.

Whitehead, A., Rosin, P., & Bodolay, R. (1993). *Parents and professionals: Partners in co-service coordination* [Videotape]. Madison: University of Wisconsin–Madison, Waisman Center. Cost: $39. (608) 265-2063.

Twenty-minute videotape uses stories of three families with young children representing diversity in ethnicity, family structure, and disability to illustrate key concepts in service co-coordination. Accompanying discussion guide will facilitate the use of this videotape with differing inservice and preservice audiences.

Zipper, I.N., Hinton, C., Weil, M., & Rounds, K. (1993). *Service coordination for early intervention: Parents and professionals.* Cambridge, MA: Brookline. Cost: $7. (800) 666-2665.

Monograph designed as a resource to assist family members. It has definitions, basic facts, and useful strategies for seeking, recognizing, or advocating for effective service coordination.

REFERENCES

Able-Boone, H. (1993). Family participation in the IFSP process: Family or professional driven? *Infant and Toddler Intervention: The Transdisciplinary Journal, 3*(1), 63–71.

Bailey, D.B. (1989). Case management in early intervention. *Journal of Early Intervention, 13,* 87–102.

Bailey, D.B., Palsha, S.A., & Huntington, G.S. (1990). Preservice preparation of special educators to serve infants with handicaps and their families: Current status and training needs. *Journal of Early Intervention, 14*(1), 43–54.

Bailey, D.B., Simeonsson, R.J., Yoder, D., & Huntington, G. (1990). Preparing professionals to serve infants and toddlers with handicaps and their families: An integrative analysis across eight disciplines. *Exceptional Children, 57*(1), 26–35.

Baroni, M.A., Tuthill, P., Feenan, L., & Schroeder, M. (1994). Technology-dependent infants and young children: A retrospective case analysis of service coordination across state lines. *Infants and Young Children, 7*(1), 69–78.

Beckman, P.J., & Bristol, M. (1991). Issues in developing the IFSP: A framework for establishing family outcomes. *Topics in Early Childhood Special Education, 11,* 19–31.

Bolton, R. (1979). *People skills: How to assert yourself, listen to others and resolve conflicts.* New York: Simon & Schuster.

Brown, C.W., Perry, D.F., & Kurland, S. (1994). Funding policies that affect children: What every early interventionist should know. *Infants and Young Children, 6*(4), 1–12.

Bruder, M.B., & Bologna, T. (1993). Collaboration and service coordination for effective early intervention. In W. Brown, S.K. Thurman, & L.F. Pearl (Eds.), *Family-centered early intervention with infants and toddlers: Innovative cross-disciplinary approaches* (pp. 103–127). Baltimore: Paul H. Brookes Publishing Co.

Bruder, M.B., & Nikitas, T. (1992). Innovative practices: Changing the professional practice of early interventionists: An inservice model to meet the service needs of Public Law 99-457. *Infants and Young Children, 16*(2), 173–180.

Buysse, V., & Wesley, P.W. (1993). The identity crises in early childhood special education: A call for professional role clarification. *Topics in Early Childhood Special Education, 13*(4), 418–429.

Clifford, R.M., & Bernier, K.Y. (1993). Systems of financing early intervention. In D.M. Bryant & M.A. Graham (Eds.), *Implementing early intervention: From research to effective practice* (pp. 313–335). New York: Guilford Press.

Covey, S. (1990). *Seven habits of highly effective people: Powerful lessons in personal change.* New York: Simon & Schuster.

Dinnebeil, L.A., & Rule, S. (1994). Variables that influence collaboration between parents and service coordinators. *Journal of Early Intervention, 18*(4), 349–361.

Dunst, C., & Trivette, C. (1989). An enablement and empowerment perspective of case management. *Topics in Early Childhood Special Education, 8,* 87–102.

Dunst, C.J., Trivette, C., & Deal, A. (1994). *Supporting and strengthening families: Vol. 1. Methods, strategies and practices.* Cambridge, MA: Brookline Books.

Edelman, L., Elsayed, S.S., & McGonigel, M. (1992). *Overview of family-centered service coordination: Facilitator's guide.* St. Paul, MN: Pathfinder Resources, Inc.

Elsayed, S.S., Maddux, L.E., & Bay, C.S. (1993). *Family and the IFSP process: Training in family-centered approaches* [Facilitator's guide and videotape]. Baltimore: Kennedy Krieger Community Resources.

Gilbert, M.A., Sciarillo, W.G., & Von Rembow, D.L. (1992). Service coordination through case management. In M. Bender & C.A. Baglin (Eds.), *Infants and toddlers: A resource guide for practitioners* (pp. 69–84). San Diego: Singular Publishing Group.

Hains, A., & Brown, L. (1990). *Parent surveys.* Madison: Wisconsin Personnel Development Project.

Hanson, M., & Lovett, D. (1992). Personnel preparation for early interventionists: A cross-disciplinary survey. *Journal of Early Intervention, 16*(2), 123–135.

Harbin, G.L. (1993). Family issues of children with disabilities: How research and theory have modified practices in intervention. In N.J. Anastasiow & S. Harel (Eds.), *At-risk infants: Interventions, families, and research* (pp. 101–112). Baltimore: Paul H. Brookes Publishing Co.

Harry, B. (1992). Developing cultural self-awareness: The first step in values clarification for early interventionists. *Topics in Early Childhood Special Education, 12*(3), 333–350.

Hausslein, E.B., Kaufmann, R.K., & Hurth, J. (1992, February). From case management to service coordination: Families, policy making, and Part H. *Zero to Three,* 10–12.

Herman, P., & Murphy, M. (1990). *Parent involvement resource manual.* Madison: Wisconsin Council on Developmental Disabilities.

Hurth, J. (1991). *Providing case management services under Part H of IDEA: Different approaches to family-centered service coordination.* Chapel Hill, NC: National Early Childhood Technical Assistance System.

Individuals with Disabilities Education Act (IDEA) of 1990, PL 101-476, 20 U.S.C. § 1400 *et seq.*

Irwin, L., & Pflugrad, D. (1989). *A survey of Wisconsin families in early intervention.* Madison: Wisconsin Personnel Development Project.

Jesien, G.S. (1996). Interagency collaboration: What, why, and with whom? In P. Rosin, A. Whitehead, L.I. Tuchman, G.S. Jesien, A.L. Begun, & L. Irwin, *Partnerships in family-centered care: A guide to collaborative early intervention* (pp. 187–201). Baltimore: Paul H. Brookes Publishing Co.

Johnson, L. (1994). Challenges facing early intervention: An overview. In L.J. Johnson, R.J. Gallagher, M.J. LaMontagne, J.B. Jordan, J.J. Gallagher, P.L. Hutinger, & M.B. Karnes (Eds.), *Meeting early intervention challenges: Issues from birth to three* (2nd ed., pp. 1–12). Baltimore: Paul H. Brookes Publishing Co.

Kelker, K.A. (1987). *Making the system work: An advocacy workshop for parents.* Portland, OR: Portland State University, Regional Research Institute for Human Services.

Kinder, H.S. (1988). *Managing disagreement constructively.* Los Altos, CA: Crisp Publications.

Locke, D.C. (1992). *Increasing multicultural understanding: A comprehensive model.* Beverly Hills: Sage Publications.

Lowenthal, B. (1992). A new role for the early interventionist: Case manager. *Infant and Toddler Intervention: The Transdisciplinary Journal, 1*(3), 191–198.

Lynch, E.W., & Hanson, M.J. (Eds.). (1992). *Developing cross-cultural competence: A guide for working with young children and their families.* Baltimore: Paul H. Brookes Publishing Co.

Maddux, R.B. (1988). *Team building: An exercise in leadership.* Los Altos, CA: Crisp Publications.

Mahoney, G., O'Sullivan, P., & Robinson, C. (1992). The family environments of children with disabilities: Diverse but not so different. *Topics in Early Childhood Special Education, 12*(3), 386–402.

McCollum, J.A., & Bailey, D.B. (1991). Developing comprehensive personnel systems: Issues and alternatives. *Journal of Early Intervention, 15*(1), 57–65.

McGonigel, M.J., Kaufmann, R.K., & Johnson, B.H. (Eds.). (1991). *Guidelines and recommended practices for the individualized family service plan* (2nd ed.). Bethesda, MD: Association for the Care of Children's Health.

McWilliam, P.J., & Bailey, D.B., Jr. (Eds.). (1993). *Working together with children and families: Case studies in early intervention.* Baltimore: Paul H. Brookes Publishing Co.

Melaville, A.I., & Blank, J.J. (1991). *What it takes: Structuring interagency partnerships to connect children and families with comprehensive services.* Oak Brook, IL: The North Central Regional Educational Laboratory.

Melaville, A.I., & Blank, J.J. (1993). *Together we can: A guide for crafting a profamily system of education and human services.* Washington, DC: U.S. Department of Education and U.S. Department of Health and Human Services.

Midwestern Consortium for Faculty Development. (1994, Summer). *Summary of higher education training needs.* Paper presented at the Midwest Consortium on Higher Education Faculty Development Institutes, Minneapolis, MN.

Miller, D.W. (1991). *Strategies for getting teams unstuck.* Unpublished manuscript. American Speech-Language-Hearing Association's Infant Project Institute III. Potomac, MA: Phoenix International.

National Commission on Children. (1991). *Beyond rhetoric: A new American agenda for children and families.* Washington, DC: Author.

National Press Publications. (1987). *SELF profile.* Overland Park, KS: Rockhurst College Continuing Education Center, Inc.

Rosin, P. (1996). *Pathways in early intervention service coordination* [Videotape]. Madison: University of Wisconsin–Madison, Waisman Center.

Rosin, P., Green, M., Hecht, L., Tuchman, L., & Robbins, S. (1996). *Pathways: A training and resource guide for enhancing skills in early intervention service coordination.* Madison: University of Wisconsin–Madison, Waisman Center.

Rosin, P., Whitehead, A., Tuchman, L., Jesien, G., Begun, A., & Irwin, L. (1993). *Partnerships in early intervention: A training guide on family-centered care, team building, and service coordination.* Madison: University of Wisconsin–Madison, Waisman Center.

Rosin, P., Whitehead, A.D., Tuchman, L.I., Jesien, G.S., Begun, A.L., & Irwin, L. (1996). *Partnerships in family-centered care: A guide to collaborative early intervention.* Baltimore: Paul H. Brookes Publishing Co.

Salisbury, C.L., & Dunst, C.J. (1997). Home, school, and community partnerships: Building inclusive teams. In B. Rainforth & J. York-Barr, *Collaborative teams for students with severe disabilities: Integrating therapy and educational services* (2nd ed., pp. 57–87). Baltimore: Paul H. Brookes Publishing Co.

Scholtes, P.R. (1988). *The team handbook: How to use teams to improve quality.* Madison, WI: Joiner Associates.

Swan, W.W., & Morgan, J.L. (1992). *Collaborating for comprehensive services for young children and their families: The local interagency coordinating council.* Baltimore: Paul H. Brookes Publishing Co.

Tuchman, L. (1991). *Catch the Spirit! Summary of focus group information on issues in family-centered service coordination: Approaches to case management in early intervention.* Madison: Wisconsin Personnel Development Project.

Tuchman, L.I. (1996). Team dynamics and communication. In P. Rosin, A. Whitehead, L.I. Tuchman, G.S. Jesien, A.L. Begun, & L. Erwin, *Partnerships in family-centered care: A guide to collaborative early intervention* (pp. 145–185). Baltimore: Paul H. Brookes Publishing Co.

Wayman, K.I., Lynch, E.W., & Hanson, M. (1990). Home-based early childhood services: Cultural sensitivity in a family systems approach. *Topics in Early Childhood Special Education, 10*(4), 56–75.

Whitehead, A.D. (1996). Service coordination and models of coordination. In P. Rosin, A.D. Whitehead, L.I. Tuchman, G.S. Jesien, A.L. Begun, & L. Irwin, *Partnerships in family-centered care: A guide to collaborative early intervention* (pp. 205–222). Baltimore: Paul H. Brookes Publishing Co.

Whitehead, A., Rosin, P., & Bodolay, R. (1993). *Parents and professionals: Partners in co-service coordination* [Videotape]. (Available from the Waisman Center, 1500 Highland Avenue, Room

231, Madison, WI 53705)

Winton, P.J. (1990). A systemic approach for planning inservice training related to Public Law 99-457. *Infants and Young Children, 3*(1), 51–60.

Winton, P.J. (1994, May). Early intervention personnel preparation: The past guides the future. *Early Childhood Reporter,* 4–6.

Wisconsin Division of Health. (1994). *Wisconsin children with special health care needs: Statewide needs assessment summary report.* Wauwatosa, WI: Great Lakes Hemophilia Foundation, Inc.

Wisconsin Personnel Development Project. (1989). *Statewide survey of task force members.* Madison: Wisconsin Personnel Development Project.

Wisconsin Personnel Development Project. (1991). *County early intervention program's needs assessments.* Madison: Wisconsin Personnel Development Project.

Wisconsin Personnel Development Project. (1992). *Focus group on inservice training needs.* Madison: Wisconsin Personnel Development Project.

Wisconsin Personnel Development Project. (1994). *Evaluation and needs assessment questionnaire summary.* Madison: Wisconsin Personnel Development Project.

Zipper I.N., Hinton, M., Weil, M., & Rounds, K. (1993). *Service coordination for early intervention: Parents and professionals.* Cambridge, MA: Brookline Books.

ACTIVITY 1

PHASE 1: GETTING STARTED

"What's Wrong with This Picture"

Objective:

- Participants explore ways of giving information to parents in a clear and sensitive manner and have an opportunity to look at strategies that draw parents into the conversation.

Instructions:

1. The participants watch a role play (script below). They freeze the action and offer suggestions to align the interaction with developing a partnership and good communication skills. They freeze the action simply by yelling, "Freeze."

2. The role play is introduced. The setting is an initial meeting between a parent and the service coordinator to ask about the parent's concerns, priorities, and resources.

   - Peggy is the service coordinator; Liz is the parent. Peggy exhibits problems in communication: too much, too fast, not checking for clarification, taking control, not negotiating tasks, asking yes/no questions, and making assumptions. She is writing while Liz is talking, shuffling papers, not making eye contact. Liz exhibits problems in communication of not offering, not asking for clarification or repetition, and silence.

The Role Play:

Peggy: Well, Ms. Hecht. Hi, I'm glad to finally meet you. As you know, I am the service coordinator from the Gateway early intervention program. We are a program that . . . (give long explanation of program). Any questions?

Liz: No.

Peggy: During your daughter's recent visit to the doctor's office, you expressed a concern about your child's development. The nurse completed a Denver Developmental Screening Test (Frankenburg, Dodds, Fandal, Kazuk, & Cohrs, 1975) and found that you were correct. Your child has delays in motor and speech and you made the call to our program for a more complete evaluation to determine eligibility for early intervention. Is that correct?

Liz: Uhuh. . .

Peggy: Well, let's get some information about your daughter, okay? Let's see—she was born at term, following an uncomplicated pregnancy, and was released from the hospital at 3 days, right? She has been healthy with the exception of a few bouts of ear infections and URI and is followed by her pediatrician, Dr. Flanders.

Liz: Yes.

Peggy: Your daughter is now 14 months and is having some delays in her motor and speech skills.

Activities 1–4 are from Rosin, P., Green, M., Hecht, L., Tuchman, L., & Robbins, S. (1996). *A training and resource guide for enhancing skills in early intervention service coordination.* Madison: University of Wisconsin–Madison, Waisman Center; adapted by permission.

Liz: I think so. . . .her older sister, Tammy, was doing much more at Betsy's age. She was walking and saying words.

Peggy: It is hard not to compare children, isn't it? But children do unfold at their own speed. We will take a look at her skills especially in light of her low scores on the Denver. And we have a whole team of professionals at Gateway who are experts in working with children and will be able to give you more information about Betsy's abilities. So, what are some good times for you so that I can go ahead and set up an evaluation to determine whether Betsy's delays are significant enough to make her eligible for early intervention, okay?

Liz: Yes, I do want to know if there is something I should be doing to help her.

Peggy: After the evaluation, we will be able to give you some suggestions.

Comments:

This activity can be used to talk about basic communication skills in the context of beginning a partnership with families as they enter early intervention. Participants can be asked to reflect on what they saw; how they would have felt if they were Liz or Peggy in this situation; how it feels to be listened to. They can then work together in pairs or small groups to generate a series of open-ended questions that Peggy can use to gather information and help increase Liz's participation in the conversation or ways to ask questions that ensure the information being shared is understood.

ACTIVITY 2

PHASE 2: FOLLOW ALONG

"The Resource Map"

Objective:

- To develop an organizational framework for information and materials on early intervention resources and programs in the community that remains up to date, is specific to a program, and is easy to use regardless of an individual's knowledge of the system. The goal is to build on the cumulative knowledge of the people in a program who are gaining access to and manipulating resources for families and to develop a strategy that uses the file to add information and experiences for that community. This helps familiarize a new service coordinator with local resources and allows veteran staff to benefit from each other's experiences related to specific disabilities and resources.

Instructions:

Have participants work together in small groups to develop a taxonomy (see Appendix C at the end of this chapter for an example of a needs-based taxonomy) for organizing information about resources, services, and community programs for a new service coordinator in an early intervention program. In designing the system for use, think about how to gather and organize the information in a way that involves the entire group, and consider strategies to keep such a collection of information up to date.

ACTIVITY 3

PHASE 3: FACING IMMEDIATE NEEDS OR CRISIS

"Help, I'm in Over My Head"

Objective:

- To practice problem solving when the participants are not under pressure and to have an opportunity to receive others' perspectives on the unresolved crisis.

Instructions:

- Divide participants into groups of five or six. Ask each group to sit in a circle. Provide a small blank envelope with 1–2 blank notecards inside for each participant. Ask each individual to describe an existing crisis situation or a past but unresolved crisis in writing on the outside of his or her envelope. Participants should not put names on their envelopes.
- Ask the participants to pass their envelope to the person to their right. When participants have received a new envelope with someone else's crisis, ask them to write suggestions down on the notecards inside the envelope. Put the notecards back in the envelope, and pass them to the right again to enable participants to generate a variety of suggestions for resolving each different crisis. Continue passing the envelopes around the circle until all participants have had the opportunity to write down ideas about each crisis.
- When the originator gets the envelope, provide time for the participants to read the comments and get clarification and additional input. Ask participants to discuss what supports they use when they feel "in over their head."
- When this activity is used in an inservice setting, ask participants to present a crisis situation specific to their work.

ACTIVITY 4

PHASE 4: FACILITATING TRANSITION

"Transition Guide"

Objective:

- To think about the components of a written, family-friendly transition guide that a program could use to organize the transition process for both service coordinators and families.

Instructions:

- Based on the following ideas about what families find helpful in the transition process, design a written transition guide that meets the requirements of current early intervention legislation (federal and/or state) and addresses the needs most commonly expressed by families. What would the table of contents look like? Some things to consider including are a time line that identifies the responsible person, a glossary of terms, community resources, information on IDEA, and child care options.

What Helps Families:

- Plan in advance.
- Explore all options.
- Prepare parent and child for separation.
- Learn about the new setting, make a personal contact.
- Create open lines of communication, formal and informal.
- Identify supports needed for child.
- Provide access to educational opportunities.
- Identify helpful people/programs to support child/family after transition.
- Identify other families with whom to talk.

A TOPICS TO INCLUDE IN AN INSTRUCTIONAL CURRICULUM

Current literature and recommended practices suggest that the following topics should be included in an instructional curriculum on service coordination:

- Definition for service coordination as stipulated in current early intervention legislation with related functions and responsibilities
- Service coordination models or approaches with a historical perspective of the concept's evolution (Bailey, 1989; Dunst & Trivette, 1989; Hausslein, Kaufmann, & Hurth, 1992; Whitehead, 1996)
- Roles of service coordination (Bruder & Bologna, 1993; Dunst, Trivette, & Deal, 1994; Gilbert, Sciarillo, & Von Rembow, 1992; Hurth, 1991; Whitehead, 1996)
- Interagency coordination and collaboration (Jesien, 1996; Lowenthal, 1992; Melaville & Blank, 1991, 1993; Swan & Morgan, 1992)
- Personal skills such as communication skills and team building, including building partnerships between the family and the service coordinator (Bolton, 1979; Bruder & Bologna, 1993; Dinnebeil & Rule, 1994; Harbin, 1993; Herman & Murphy, 1990; Kinder, 1988; Maddux, 1988; Miller, 1991; Rosin, 1996; Salisbury & Dunst, 1997; Scholtes, 1988; Tuchman, 1996)
- IFSP process and development (Able-Boone, 1993; Beckman & Bristol, 1991; Elsayed, Maddux, & Bay, 1993; McGonigel, Kaufmann, & Johnson, 1991; Rosin, 1996)
- Family diversity (Harry, 1992; Locke, 1992; Lynch & Hanson, 1992; Mahoney, O'Sullivan, & Robinson, 1992; Rosin, 1996; Wayman, Lynch, & Hanson, 1990)
- Gaining access to and financing services and resources (Brown, Perry, & Kurland, 1994; Clifford & Bernier, 1993; Covey, 1990)
- Advocacy for families and the services needed for the integration of services around family priorities and preferences (Baroni, Tuthill, Feenan, & Schroeder, 1994; Edelman et al., 1992; Kelker, 1987; Zipper, Hinton, Weil, & Rounds, 1993)

B EXAMPLES OF POSSIBLE FIELD-BASED EXPERIENCES

You are encouraged to select field experiences that will assist you in achieving your course outcomes. The following are examples of activities that could help you gain skills to meet your outcomes:

- Accompany a family to a medical appointment or other type of evaluation. Join the family members in their home before the appointment, and learn what is involved in preparing for the appointment. Observe the communication skills throughout the day. Think about waiting time for families.
- Provide respite for a family. Get a feel for what it's like to be with a child in his or her home.
- Observe a team meeting, and analyze interactions from various perspectives. How would you describe the parent and professional interactions? How are parents supported? How do professionals from different agencies and disciplines interact with each other?
- Conduct a pre-assessment planning session with a family to identify their preferences for participation in their child's evaluation or assessment.
- Work with a team to conduct an arena evaluation or assessment. Practice role-release skills: 1) Let a professional from another discipline and a parent know what information you would like and 2) practice getting information for a professional from another discipline.
- Volunteer to join or observe a team that will be working with a new family. Participate in the planning process for new referrals. Get involved with the development and monitoring of the IFSP.
- Meet with family members to learn about their concerns, priorities, resources, and preferences for their child. Practice interviewing and other communication skills required for getting to know a family. Keep a journal about the experience. What promoted communication? Where did communication break down? What strategies and questions guided the process?
- Participate in the transition-planning process for a child who is turning 3. Attend planning meetings; visit receiving programs; and work with a family to identify their concerns, priorities, and preferences related to their child's transition.
- If you do not frequently facilitate team meetings, volunteer to facilitate a meeting. Ask one or more members of the team for feedback on your performance.
- Shadow a service coordinator. Learn about the roles and functions of the job.
- Meet with and interview personnel from an agency providing early intervention services to learn about the agency's involvement in early intervention (e.g., philosophy, policies, practices, specialties, key contact people).

- Visit a neonatal intensive care unit (special care nursery). Talk with a family who has a child who spent time in a special care nursery. Find out what it was like for them.
- Visit an early intervention program. Observe and meet with parents and staff. Identify the program's philosophy and practices. Which practices reflect recommended practices in early intervention?
- Investigate options in your community for integrated child care. Find out if any preschool programs integrate children with disabilities. Visit the program and talk with staff. Identify programs that may want to integrate children with disabilities. Talk about how your programs could work together to support children and families.

C A NEEDS-BASED TAXONOMY FOR RESOURCE ORGANIZATION

Resource files can be organized in a variety of ways. Resource directories are organized by agency, by disability, or alphabetically. Often knowledge of an agency's structure is needed in order to use the directories. The following organizational framework is based on the needs of families being served by a particular program. This may be easier to use because service coordinators respond to family needs but may have widely varying knowledge about the community and the agencies responsible for services to meet these needs.

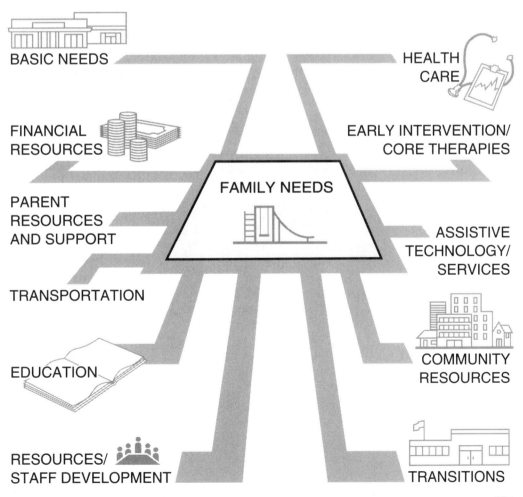

BASIC NEEDS

FINANCIAL RESOURCES

PARENT RESOURCES AND SUPPORT

TRANSPORTATION

EDUCATION

RESOURCES/ STAFF DEVELOPMENT

FAMILY NEEDS

HEALTH CARE

EARLY INTERVENTION/ CORE THERAPIES

ASSISTIVE TECHNOLOGY/ SERVICES

COMMUNITY RESOURCES

TRANSITIONS

AN EXPANDED TAXONOMY FOR RESOURCE ORGANIZATION

BASIC NEEDS

housing

respite

24-hour emergency

food (Women, Infants & Children, food
   stamps)

furniture

Social Services—Alcohol & Other Drug
   Abuse, Child Protective Services

utilities

emotional

spiritual

counseling

literacy/GED

child care

HEALTH CARE

well baby

medical specialties

Public Health Nurse

pediatricians

specialty clinics

Maternal & Child Health—lead
   screening program

home health care agencies

diagnostic services

Health Check (Early Periodic Screening,
   Diagnosis & Treatment [EPSDT])

personal care providers

emergency service

Healthy Start

nutrition

FINANCIAL RESOURCES

private insurance

EPSDT

fund-raising

Community Options Program

Family Support Program

Health Check

Medical Assistance Waiver
Programs

Supplemental Security
Income

EARLY INTERVENTION/ CORE THERAPIES

communication

occupational therapy

psychological

special instruction

audiology

physical therapy

social work

vision

IFSP

assessment/evaluation

TRANSPORTATION

car seat

ASSISTIVE TECHNOLOGY/ SERVICES

home safety

communication

mobility

customized adaptations

carpenter/architect

accessibility

vendors

home modifications

PARENT RESOURCES AND SUPPORT

advocacy

parent to parent

newsletters

financial planning

residential care

foster care

educational materials

training opportunities

legal issues

bibliography

national organizations

(United Cerebral Palsy
Associations, The Association for
Retarded Citizens)

legal rights for foster parents

disability information

parenting classes

COMMUNITY RESOURCES

recreation

camps

activities

child care

playgrounds

TRANSITIONS

neonatal intensive care unit

surgery

schools

materials

RESOURCES/ STAFF DEVELOPMENT

national

training

state

skill building

EDUCATION

transition

individualized education program

IDEA

12 PREPARING PRACTITIONERS FOR GETTING THE MOST OUT OF CHILD ASSESSMENT

Elizabeth R. Crais

Child assessment is a universal step that all children with special needs and their families take during the early intervention process. Sometimes it is a step that leads to hope and confidence for families and professionals and is the exciting beginning (or continuation) of a long-lasting and rewarding set of experiences in early intervention. Other times, it is disappointing and difficult for both families and professionals and may serve only to create confusion and frustration (Olson, 1988; Poyadue, 1988). For some families, assessment is the entry point into the early intervention system and can be the "template" for what family members perceive as their role(s) in future intervention services (Crais, 1993; McWilliam, 1996). Assessment experiences also may affect how the family views both the child and their own skills in meeting their child's needs.

The advent of IDEA and the requirement that all children undergo evaluation and assessment have heightened the focus on these activities and their key roles throughout the early intervention process. The need to determine eligibility; identify the concerns, priorities, and resources of the family; gather developmental information; plan for intervention; and monitor progress places burdens on both families and professionals to accomplish these tasks usefully and positively for both groups. The movement toward family-centered services that acknowledge family members as the primary decision makers for themselves and their children, the transition to more ecologically valid evaluation and assessment activities, the facilitation of more active roles for family members in evaluation and assessment, and the changing roles and responsibilities for professionals and family members present many challenges. Although much has been written regarding broad principles to guide assessment practices, little information is available to help practitioners make needed changes in their day-to-day delivery of assessment services. Thus, because of the barriers to making changes, practitioners may hesitate or put off making the modifications to their assessment practices that they believe could be useful. Faculty and others with personnel development responsibilities encounter similar barriers.

Change is not an easy process and may be more difficult when it involves highly practiced behaviors and routines, such as those that may surround child assessment. Asking practicing professionals to modify their assessment practices and the tools and techniques they have used for years or asking trainees to embrace a different model from ones they may have encountered in field placements or other courses may indeed test trainers' creativity. Because many professionals engage in some type of assessment activities, however, there may be frequent opportunities to modify these practices and enhanced motivation to learn more effective methods. Professionals often seek practical information in inservice activities that can be applied directly to their work settings, and the provision of explicit techniques and strategies for assessment is often an inservice priority (Crais, Geissinger, & Lorch, 1992). Thus, for instructors, assessment may be a primary means through which to address issues of moving toward family-centered and culturally sensitive practices. Both students and practicing professionals may be more receptive to these issues when they are embedded within the assessment process rather than as principles presented in isolation (see Chapters 5 and 21 for more detail on principles of adult learning).

To ultimately affect how assessments are conducted (and how instruction is provided regarding assessments), this chapter focuses on both issues and practices that need consideration when planning and conducting assessments. The chapter first addresses the issues of defining the terms *evaluation* and *assessment* and recognizing the need for ecologically valid assessments, then examines traditional and family-centered approaches to assessment with a focus on encouraging participants to analyze their own beliefs and practices regarding assessment. Finally, three key components of the assessment process—preassessment planning, family roles in assessment, and reciprocal sharing of results—are highlighted to illustrate collaborative, family-centered assessment procedures. Each section provides a rationale for why changing practices or beliefs is important, presents learner outcomes related to the content, and outlines teaching strategies and materials that can be used to achieve the learner outcomes.

ISSUES IN PLANNING AND CONDUCTING CHILD ASSESSMENTS

Two issues seem particularly critical when planning and conducting assessments. First is the way that professionals define assessment, particularly its scope and format. Second is the issue of how professionals ensure that the assessment is relevant to and valued by the family. Both issues can be directly addressed by instructors.

Defining Evaluation and Assessment

Federal regulations governing Part H of IDEA (Early Intervention Program for Infants and Toddlers with Disabilities, 1993) specify that **evaluation** must be conducted to determine the child's initial and continuing eligibility, including identifying the child's level of functioning across a variety of developmental domains. The regulations further specify that the evaluation must be comprehensive, nondiscriminatory, and conducted by qualified personnel. In contrast, the regulations define **assessment** as the ongoing procedures used throughout the child's eligibility to identify the child's unique needs; the family's concerns, priorities, and resources related to the development of the child; and the nature and extent of the early intervention services needed by the child and family (McLean & McCormick, 1993). At times, the two sets of activities may be performed separately. For example, in some states, select teams of professionals evaluate children and determine eligibility, whereas other professionals assess the children over time to plan and provide intervention services. In contrast, in other states and with a number of professionals, evaluation and assessment activities overlap, and the same professionals perform both types of activities. As suggested by some authors (Bricker, 1993; Crais, 1995; McWilliam, 1996), the federal guidelines may create artificial boundaries between these activities when they are most effectively joined together and provided within a continuum of early intervention services.

What are the differences between evaluation and assessment on a day-to-day level, and what impact do these differences have on children, families, and professionals? Traditionally, evaluations are more likely to be conducted within a structured format, use standardized instruments, and conclude within a limited time frame. Comparatively, assessment activities are typically less formal in structure, use multiple tools and methods, last over a longer period of time, and are based on a closer relationship between families and professionals. Although the legislated mandate for evaluation is to determine initial and ongoing eligibility, many families are interested in far more than a broad overview of their child. Families may report dissatisfaction with evaluation because it did not accomplish what the family hoped to gain from the process, and more time was spent on what was "wrong" with their child than on what to do to help their child (Olson, 1988; Poyadue, 1988).

Ideal practices would include evaluation and assessment as part of a continuous process; thus, "assessment" is used throughout this chapter to include both sets of activities. Many of the issues and instructional strategies presented can be applied to activities throughout the entire assessment process.

Conducting Ecologically Valid Assessments

Across a variety of disciplines, the issue of the ecological validity of assessment practices has been addressed. In considering the ecology of the child, many professionals refer to Bronfenbrenner's (1979) concept of the child nested within the family, which is itself embedded within a larger community system. Taking an ecological perspective, Bronfenbrenner advised that understanding human development meant going beyond observation of one or two people in the same location. He urged the examination of multiple people interacting across multiple settings. In considering the child's differing ecologies (e.g., home, child care setting, center-based program), the child's interactions across these settings and the facilitators and constraints inherent in those settings must be examined. Professionals who have used the child's existing ecologies for assessment *and* intervention have noted an increased ability of the child to transfer or generalize information, enhanced opportunities for people important to the child to learn about and be involved in intervention, and increased maintenance of skills (Bailey, 1989; Halle, 1988; Mirenda & Calculator, 1993). Furthermore, ecologically based assessment may serve to enhance the interactions among caregivers by recognizing the differences in expectations, roles, and interactions of these caregivers and providing an avenue for open discussions and individual modification if necessary.

As suggested by Bailey (1989), if we are to take an ecological approach to assessment, we must include all caregivers as significant partners in the assessment process; take a child's cultural background, economic status, and family value system into account to avoid cultural bias and the planning of activities that do not fit with the family's value system; focus heavily on naturalistic observation of play and daily routines to ensure awareness of the child's use of skills within meaningful contexts; and plan for the child's immediate and future placements, and analyze the skills necessary for the child to function in these settings.

Instructional Strategies to Identify and Highlight Assessment Issues

In addressing the issues regarding assessment terminology and the ecological validity of assessments, there are a number of materials and strategies available to instructors and faculty. Articles for defining and contrasting evaluation and assessment include McLean and McCormick (1993) and Turnbull (1991); readings relevant to ecological validity include Bailey (1989) and Crais (1995). Other instructional strategies could include discussion of the components of ecologically valid assessment practices, case studies that present less than ecologically valid assessment practices and discussions centered around how these practices could be modified to enhance ecological validity, and small-group discussions of the barriers to ecological validity and possible modifications in participants' practicum or work settings. Expected learner outcomes related to assessment terminology and ecological validity can be seen in Table 12.1.

EXAMINING TRADITIONAL ASSESSMENT AND FAMILY-CENTERED APPROACHES

As the field of early intervention shifts toward providing more family-centered assessment services, it is often helpful to examine both our past or our current practices and those we might seek to implement. It is particularly important to identify the impact that these varied assessment practices have on children and families.

Traditional Assessment Practices

As suggested by Bailey, McWilliam, Winton, and Simeonsson (1992), traditional assessments are often conducted exclusively by professionals, rely primarily on formal testing under standardized conditions, result in scores and diagnostic labels, and involve the identification of child limitations. As a result of these characteristics, traditional assessments may have several limitations that need consideration when planning more useful assessment activities. Bailey, McWilliam, et al. (1992) have suggested that traditional assessments could reinforce parental incompetence versus professional expertise, lead to parents' feeling disenfranchised, result in goals that are not functional, focus on limitations rather than on strengths, and result in minimal parental follow-through. In addition, Crais (1994) suggested that traditional assessment often results in professionals primarily sharing their assessment findings rather than families and professionals sharing results and may lead to professionals making most (or all) of the recommendations rather than consensus building between family members and professionals. As an alternative or in addition to traditional approaches, many have argued for a shift toward more family-centered practices in assessment (Bailey, McWilliam, et al., 1992; McLean & Crais, 1996; McLean & McCormick, 1993).

Family-Centered Principles Related to Assessment

Although many practitioners may believe in and support family-centered principles, full implementation of family-centered practices is in its infancy (Bailey, Palsha, & Simeons-

TABLE 12.1. Learner outcomes focusing on issues in child assessment

Defining evaluation and assessment

- Compare and contrast "evaluation" with "assessment" requirements.
- Describe the different ways these activities may be performed separately or together.
- Identify pros and cons for professionals and families of performing evaluation and assessment activities together.

Conducting ecologically valid assessment activities

- List the components of ecologically valid assessments as proposed by Bailey (1989).
- Discuss the impact that each component could have on the assessment process.
- Describe how the facilitation of each component could be achieved in the work or practicum setting.
- Discuss the barriers in the work or practicum setting that would make achievement of these components difficult.

son, 1991; Crais & Wilson, 1996; McBride, Brotherson, Joanning, Whiddon, & Demmitt, 1993). Professionals and families are just beginning to translate these principles into actual practice and to understand the profound effect that these changes can have on service delivery. In addition, although there has been abundant literature regarding general principles, there has been less written on the actual use of these principles in assessing young children. For example, attention has been given to terms such as empowerment, which implies the need to enhance the family's ability to make decisions and to control the types of services received by the child and family. Yet how do practitioners empower families in the assessment process, especially when this is the family's first assessment experience? Furthermore, how can families direct the assessment process if they do not know what tools and strategies are available? Thus, for many practitioners, the translation of family-centered principles to actual assessment practices may be difficult.

In two different surveys of practicing professionals (Bailey, Buysse, Edmondson, & Smith, 1992; Crais & Wilson, 1996), the most frequently mentioned barriers to working more closely with families were "system" (e.g., lack of time, caseload size) and "family" (e.g., lack of interest or education by family, cultural/value differences) factors. In these studies, "professional" factors such as lack of experience or instruction were not as frequently mentioned.

These findings have important implications for conceptualizing and conducting personnel preparation. Instructors may be faced with practitioners who espouse a belief in family-centered practices but who may not be implementing them for a variety of reasons (least of which, reportedly, are lack of training issues). Therefore, in both preservice and inservice instructional efforts focusing on assessment, instructors must first help participants analyze their existing beliefs (and practices, if inservice participants) and consider the outcomes for children and families that may result from them. Second, instructors must introduce or encourage discussion and discovery of approaches that are more family centered. Third, practitioners need guided opportunities to explore how family-centered approaches may be applied within their own work settings. (For an overview of family-centered principles, refer to Chapter 10.)

In analyzing actual practices and gaining awareness of family-centered alternatives, it is often helpful for students and practicing professionals to examine traditional assessment practices and compare those with family-centered strategies. Providing participants with examples of family-centered practices used within the assessment process can facilitate the translation of these ideas to practice in their own settings. The following section provides instructional strategies, materials, and learner outcomes to help guide the translation of family-centered principles to practice.

Instructional Strategies for Examining
Traditional and Family-Centered Assessment Practices

One strategy to help learners identify the content and issues to be examined within assessment practices is the use of videotaped examples. Video examples can illustrate and provide professional and parent perspectives on traditional and family-centered approaches. One particularly useful video is entitled *First Years Together: Involving Parents in Infant Assessment* (Project Enlightenment, 1989). This video provides a discussion by a narrator (and video illustrations) of characteristics of traditional approaches, comments by parents and professionals contrasting assessment practices, and discussion and video illustrations of an alternative, more family-centered approach. A second resource for examining assessment practices is the *Heart to Heart* (Fullerton, 1992) video, which provides parent and professional interviews and commentary on assessment services. In one clip, a professional relates the frustration of some families with assessment services:

That's why we have families pay $2,000 for multidisciplinary assessments and then they call here and say "what do I do now?" They have a label, they know the deficits, they have a name for what they have feared about what's happening for their child. And now they feel worse than they ever did . . . because they still don't know what to do when that baby doesn't sleep through the night. (Sandy Mlinarcik in Fullerton, 1992)

Two additional videos, Edelman's (1991) *Delivering Family-Centered, Home-Based Services* and *The Family and the IFSP Process* (Project Copernicus, 1993), include vignettes of families and service providers role playing interactions that occur around assessment activities. Both videotapes illustrate what happens when professionals fail to use family-centered practices. For example, Edelman's (1991) video shows a less than desirable interaction (i.e., service provider is late to parent's home; child is sleeping; and when talking to parent about child, the service provider discounts what the parent has to say about the child). The video can be stopped after viewing for group discussion, then the instructor can show segments of the individual comments made by the parent and service provider describing how they felt about the interaction. The video on the individualized family service plan (IFSP) process (Project Copernicus, 1993) uses before and after segments (e.g., first contacts; identifying concerns, priorities, and resources; IFSP development) to demonstrate how a particular activity might be performed in a more traditional mode versus a family-centered approach.

A very powerful and direct strategy for examining assessment approaches is to have family members (one or a panel) talk about their experiences. When using this approach, it is important to be specific in asking family members what to address (e.g., What were some things that were very positive about the assessments your child has had? What things were not helpful? What suggestions do you have for professionals about how to make assessments better?). Another strategy is to arrange for preservice students to interview families about their assessment experiences and then compare and contrast their findings with other students in class. A recent Division for Early Childhood presentation (Kilgo, Davis, Gamel-McCormick, & Brittain, 1995) demonstrated an effective strategy for using family perceptions on assessment. The purpose of the session was to introduce participants to an assessment approach focusing on family and professional collaboration. As the professional presenters discussed each step in their model, the parent presenter discussed her experiences and reactions to each step. The presentation was a blend of professional and family information sharing and could serve as a model for both preservice and in-service activities focusing on introducing an effective assessment or intervention model to others. The point/counterpoint approach might also be useful in presenting contrasting viewpoints on a shared event such as assessment practices.

Additional strategies include having small- or large-group discussions on a variety of assessment issues. In structuring the discussions, materials that could be used include the Bailey, McWilliam, et al. (1992) instructional manual *Implementing Family-Centered Services in Early Intervention: A Team-Based Model for Change.* This manual provides activities to facilitate changes across a variety of early intervention services, including child assessment. Provided in the manual are content areas and outlines for presentations, small- and large-group discussion activities, reading lists for participants and instructors, challenge questions to stimulate discussion and help identify areas in need of change, and masters for handouts and overhead transparencies (including characteristics and limitations of traditional assessment).

An additional (or alternative) strategy may be to show an overhead of family-centered principles and to generate a list of family-centered goals that parents and professionals may set for assessments. As adapted from Bailey, McWilliam, et al. (1992), possible goals may include identifying the family's concerns, priorities, and resources for enhancing the child's development; identifying the child's strengths and needs; identifying areas for assessment; identifying areas and settings for intervention; gaining consensus between professionals and family members on these issues; reinforcing parents' feelings of competence and worth; and creating ownership of decisions and plans by all interested parties. Small- or large-group discussions may be used to highlight possible goals and/or to compare them with goals that may be set using more traditional approaches.

Across all of these activities for examining assessment practices, participants could also be asked to document, from their own experiences or, in the case of students, those of others they observe, the kinds of activities that represent more traditional assessment practices and then to generate a list of modifications that could be accomplished to use more family-centered approaches. Common modifications include asking parents to identify the best time and location for assessment, providing parents with more choices throughout assessment, encouraging parents to take part in the assessment, and jointly identifying activities that will bring out the best in the child. Confidentiality and feelings should be respected when team members are attending inservice activities together or when students may be reporting about their practicum placements and supervisors. In addition, instructional strategies should encourage examination but not make participants feel uncomfortable or defensive about their existing practices. As suggested by Crais and Cripe (1996), participants should be encouraged to view the transition to more family-centered practices as an incremental process rather than as a set of completely new skills. The addition of family-centered practices may be seen as enriching the options available for the types of assessment services provided.

A practical strategy for having participants examine their own practices is to use a self-assessment tool. A comprehensive self-assessment tool for examining the degree to which one's practices are family centered is *Brass Tacks* (McWilliam & Winton, 1990). *Brass Tacks* has two sections—one for individual practitioners, one for entire teams—to be used to examine a variety of practices, including child assessment. The format allows individuals and/or teams to identify the degree (i.e., never, seldom, sometimes, usually, always) to which they perform certain activities (e.g., Do you conduct assessments at times convenient for families?). Then participants are asked to identify whether a change is needed, to prioritize the need, and to generate specific types of changes desired in that area. A second tool adapted from *Brass Tacks,* entitled *The Role of Parents in Child Assessment* (Crais & Wilson, 1996), is a short checklist of behaviors specific to assessment that can be completed by individual practitioners or teams to help them identify their own practices within assessment. It includes three broad areas within assessment: 1) preparing for assessment, 2) performing assessment, and 3) sharing assessment results. These types of self-assessments can also be used as a pre- and postinstruction activity to gauge the beliefs and practices of the participants at the beginning and the end of the instruction to help them document changes in their own perceptions. Learner outcomes for examining traditional and family-centered assessment approaches are listed in Table 12.2.

KEY COMPONENTS IN CHILD ASSESSMENT

In translating family-centered principles into practice, three components in the assessment process seem critical to facilitating a move to more family-centered assessment activities: preassessment planning, the roles available to families in assessment, and the sharing of assessment results. The following sections provide a rationale for each component, an

TABLE 12.2.   Learner outcomes in examining traditional and family-centered assessment practices

- Identify several characteristics of traditional assessment approaches.

- Identify several limitations of traditional assessment approaches.

- Demonstrate awareness of family members' perceptions regarding assessment services.

- Identify key family-centered principles that need to be taken into account when planning and conducting child assessments.

- Identify goals for assessment that represent a traditional approach.

- Identify goals for assessment that represent a family-centered approach.

- Demonstrate the ability to categorize one's own assessment practices (or those of others observed) as to their degree of family centeredness.

- Identify the kinds of barriers that may inhibit practitioners from using family-centered practices in current practicum or job setting.

- Identify a few family-centered practices that may be implemented in your current setting.

- Identify some of the things (e.g., resources, activities) that may need to happen to make those types of modifications possible.

overview of possible strategies and materials, specific issues and suggestions for preservice and inservice instruction, and learner outcomes.

Preassessment Planning

In an effort to individualize assessments for each child and family, preassessment planning can make a substantial difference in how assessments are conducted and perceived by both families and professionals. Preassessment planning is a process through which families and professionals set the many parameters of an upcoming assessment (Crais, 1993, 1996b; Kjerland & Kovach, 1990; McGonigel, Kaufman, & Johnson, 1991). It is a time to gather information from and provide information to families to facilitate collaborative decision making. Crais (1994) described common goals for preassessment planning as including identifying what families want and/or need from assessment, identifying family priorities and preferences for assessment, identifying areas and activities of strength for the child, and determining the roles that family members might take in assessment.

Professionals can begin by gathering information about parent concerns or questions and identifying what parents wish to gain from assessment. For children who have been assessed previously, it is helpful to ask the family about the kinds of activities that were performed, the types of activities that provided the most information, and what information from the previous assessment was most useful to them. Other information gathered can include the best time(s) and location(s) for the upcoming assessment, preferences for formal versus informal approaches, the child's favorite activities or toys, other people to include, and the order in which the activities will be performed. Part of the preassessment planning activities also typically include gathering information on the child's background (e.g., birth, medical, developmental histories) and current issues or behaviors.

For issues or behaviors of concern to families, initial information could be gained about the characteristics of the concerns, when and where problems occur or do not occur, any contributing health problems and physiological influences. Following the suggestions of Winton and Bailey (1993), families can also be asked to describe what they have tried in these situations and what worked or did not work. Asking families about the advice they have received from others regarding these situations can also be informative. During the early phases of information gathering, it is also helpful to ask family members what happens when activities go well (e.g., when the child is able to indicate needs, when challenging behaviors do not occur). A detailed description of the activity and what led to the successful interaction can be useful. In addition, asking who was present and what they did can give families and professionals an idea of how the child responds to the efforts of others.

Using the preassessment planning time to identify the family's preferences for their roles and responsibilities in assessment is important. As the parameters of the upcoming assessment are set (e.g., informal versus formal approaches, identification of observation contexts, others who will be involved), professionals and families can discuss the options available and decide which roles and responsibilities they each will take. Once the parameters have been set, the family and professionals can identify the order of the activities (e.g., parent–child interaction, then professional–child interaction; hearing screening, then free play with toys and materials) to build the assessment plan collaboratively. Throughout the assessment, it is important that family members are familiar with each task before its introduction to the child. This familiarity must extend beyond the content of the activity to its relevance in determining those issues that originally prompted the assessment (Crais & Calculator, in press). The preassessment phase is an excellent time to discuss each assessment task and its relevance.

Throughout the assessment planning, it is important to consider the sociocultural beliefs and values of the families. Some families may readily take an active role in assessment planning and implementation, whereas others may be more hesitant and want the professionals to take the lead. Winton and Bailey (1993) suggested that the types of questions and how they are asked can influence the degree to which families take an active role in planning for their child. When professionals take the time to explore and honor the knowledge that family members have about their child, the results can be far reaching.

During the preassessment planning phase, time should also be spent discussing the "how, when, and where" of sharing assessment results. Family members can be asked their preferences in this regard, if there are others who may benefit from hearing and/or contributing to the results, and whether an additional follow-up meeting would be useful for the family or others who cannot be present. Families who will be performing observations or assessments themselves can be asked whether they feel comfortable sharing their findings during the postassessment meeting. Ideas for organizing these findings can be discussed, or summary forms can be provided for families to organize their results. In addition, some families may want to meet with one or more professionals before the actual sharing of results to discuss their findings and how these might be presented to the team. Families also need to be given the option of whether the assessment sharing and the development of the IFSP are combined into one meeting or whether a follow-up meeting will be held to actually generate the IFSP.

Instructional Strategies Focusing on Preassessment Planning

To begin instructional activities related to preassessment planning, the instructor needs to identify whether the targeted impact on participants will be at the knowledge, skill, or values level. Activities at the knowledge, or awareness, level could include a brief discussion of the basic purposes of preassessment planning and small- or large-group generation of goals and/or lists of information sought in preassessment planning. A further means of knowledge development for trainees is to have them first read about preassessment planning, including articles or book chapters by Crais (1993, 1996a, 1996b), Kjerland and Kovach (1990), or McWilliam (1996). Practical materials that can demonstrate different methods for gathering preassessment information include written forms or checklists and videotapes. A popular tool used in preassessment planning is the Project Dakota preassessment planning form that appears in Bailey, McWilliam, et al. (1992) and McGonigel et al. (1991). This form has basic questions such as "What kinds of concerns do you or others have?" "Where would you like the assessment to take place?" and "What are your child's favorite toys or activities to help him become focused, motivated, and comfortable?" Other tools that can be useful in preassessment planning include the *AEPS Family Interest Survey* (Bricker, 1993), which provides questions to identify areas in which the family may have an interest (e.g., knowing more about the child's current strengths and needs, learning to talk and play with the child). At an awareness level, copies or overheads of these tools could be shared with participants to enhance their knowledge of the availability of the tools. Participants can then be asked to discuss what additional methods are (or could be) used in their work or practicum settings to gather this type of information.

Video examples that include preassessment discussions with families can be used to target both knowledge and skill levels within preassessment planning. Two available videos are the *Transdisciplinary Arena Assessment Process*: *A Resource for Teams* (Child Development Resources, 1992) and the first contacts portion of *The Family and the IFSP Process* (Project Copernicus, 1993). In addition, participants can familiarize themselves with several communication strategies for preassessment planning, such as those suggested by Crais (1996a) and those provided in Table 12.3. After some exposure to questions to ask or strategies useful in gathering preassessment information, participants can watch the videotapes to look for various communication strategies used by the professionals and then comment on their effectiveness. Once the major information to be sought during preassessment planning and some basic "how-to's" have been discussed, participants can be asked to perform role-play activities (e.g., Activity 1 at the end of the chapter) using the suggested communication strategies.

The role plays can begin with detailed histories of the child and family or with only minimal information provided, such as in Activity 1. It may be easier for participants to perform the role plays if they do not have too many child or family facts to remember and can focus on the process. Because the participants will typically have opportunities to gather basic background information (e.g., child developmental, medical histories) in their practicum or work settings, this role-play activity does not focus specifically on this type of information gathering; however, it could be included if practice is needed. In a large group, the participants can first be asked to identify what they would want to accomplish in preassessment planning. Then, in four-person role plays (two professionals, one parent, and one observer), they can plan collaboratively an assessment for the child with the mother. The participants can later report to the large group their experiences and what they learned and can rate the effectiveness of different strategies they used.

An additional way for participants to gain experience in planning assessments is to enlist families they already work with or know (or are known to the instructor) who might be willing to let them practice this type of planning. Preservice students can also participate in actual preassessment meetings with "new" families to plan an upcoming initial assessment. Videotaping these sessions for later viewing and discussion by the professionals and students (and family) on the aspects of the meetings that promoted collaborative planning can be useful. With students (or inservice participants who will be seen

TABLE 12.3. Communication strategies for use in child assessment

Domains of interest	Questions[a]
Understanding family priorities for assessment	What are the areas in which you would like more information about [child]?
	What kinds of information would be most useful to you regarding [child]?
	What is it you want out of the assessment process?
Understanding family preferences for assessment	Where and when would be the best place and time that we can gather and share some information about [child]?
	Are there other locations that you believe would be important to include in our information gathering?
	Are there other people who you might like to have participate in the information gathering and sharing?
	Who would you like to be a part of helping [child] in the future?
Understanding child's interests and strengths	What are things [child] enjoys doing?
	What are things [child] is really good at doing?
	What kinds of toys does [child] enjoy playing with?
	How can we see [child] at his [or her] best?
	What activities have been tried with [child] before?
	Which ones worked and which ones didn't work?
Understanding family priorities for participation	Which activities would you like to be a part of (e.g., stay with [child], sit and observe, demonstrate what [child] likes and is able to do, fill out checklist or testing, confirm professional observations)?

From Crais, E. (1994). *Increasing family participation in the assessment of children birth to five* [Continuing education manual and audiotapes]. Chicago: Applied Symbolix; adapted by permission.

[a]These questions might be used in determining family participation in assessment.

again), direct observation assignments can also be made, and participants can be asked to identify preassessment practices used in their own or their practicum settings. Tools such as *Brass Tacks* (McWilliam & Winton, 1990) or *The Role of Parents in Child Assessment: Self-Evaluation by Practicing Professionals* (Crais & Wilson, 1996) can be used in a checklist format for participants to note whether particular preassessment information was typically gathered from families and what format was used. Participants can also be encouraged to identify ideas or to try to use strategies in their practicum or job settings and then to report to the class their efforts and results.

One activity that may bring about changes in the beliefs and values of participants is to ask family members to talk about their assessment experiences; this may be particularly powerful if families have experienced different types of assessment. To hear family members contrast different assessment practices and talk about the benefits they experienced when they had the opportunity to plan their child's assessment collaboratively with professionals can be quite striking.

Certain communication skills are vital to successful interactions within preassessment planning, as in all other parts of the assessment process. There are a number of resources available to encourage participants to examine their own communication skills and to begin to use more family-centered ones (see Chapter 10). The opportunity to apply these skills within an assessment framework provides participants with a realistic way to practice. Activities aimed toward enhancing communication skills in pre- and postassessment interactions and in interactions during assessment can provide a variety of opportunities. Learner outcomes associated with preassessment planning appear in Table 12.4, along with outcomes for other key components.

Family Roles in Assessment

There are numerous reasons that families are critical to the assessment process. Family members have unique knowledge about the child that is often unavailable to professionals (Bailey, 1989; Crais, 1993; McLean & McCormick, 1993). For example, family members can describe the child's interactions with a variety of people, in different settings, and under varied conditions. Through the combined efforts of family members and professionals, a larger sample of behaviors may be available for analysis.

Families and professionals may also contribute different information to the assessment process. For example, Morrow, Mirenda, Beukelman, and Yorkston (1993) looked at parents', teachers', and speech-language pathologists' contributions to choosing vocabulary for children using augmentative systems. The authors noted that although there were many similarities in the words selected across the informants, each informant also contributed words that were unique to his or her interactions with the child. These findings indicate that no one informant group should have been left out of the vocabulary selection process.

In addition to what families can contribute to the assessment process, families can also gain from their participation in assessment. Taking care of a child with disabilities may be stressful and at times may place additional demands on families (Turnbull & Turnbull, 1990). The family's awareness, knowledge, and understanding of the child's special needs are important factors in their overall adjustment to the child (Barber, Turnbull, Behr, & Kerns, 1988). As families participate more fully in assessment and receive adequate support and information, they may gain increased understanding of their child's special needs. In addition, as they work together with professionals to build on their existing resources and generate strategies addressing their concerns, they may increase their ability to deal with stressful caregiving issues and to plan more effectively for their child (Dunst, Trivette, & Deal, 1988).

In addition to contributing to the family's understanding of the child's special needs and their ability to plan for their child, participation in assessment may also prompt awareness in specific areas. As indicated by the work of Bloch and Seitz (1989), Bricker

TABLE 12.4.   Learner outcomes related to three key components of assessment

Preassessment planning

- Identify the benefits of preassessment planning for both professionals and families.
- Identify the purposes of preassessment planning.
- Gain practice in conducting a preassessment planning meeting.
- Demonstrate the ability to examine one's own practices (or those of others observed) for evidence of preassessment planning.
- Describe different strategies that could be used for conducting preassessment planning (especially under different work setting constraints).

Family roles in assessment

- Identify several reasons that family input to the assessment process is invaluable.
- Identify several benefits that families may gain by participating in the assessment process.
- List some drawbacks to assessments that occur without participation by family members.
- Describe how the assessment process may lead to positive or negative feelings of the family toward the child.
- Identify the benefits of having a variety of assessment roles available to family members.
- Contrast the historical roles of family members with those available currently.
- Identify tools and techniques that may facilitate family participation for each role in assessment.[a]
- Identify necessary skills for family members to fulfill each role in assessment.
- Recognize one's own biases about family members' abilities to evaluate the child.
- Gain awareness of recent findings and reasons for the findings relative to parents as evaluators.
- Recognize the need to honor family preferences in their assessment roles.

Reciprocal sharing of assessment results

- Describe the importance of sharing assessment results to family–professional relationships and the remainder of the early intervention process.
- Identify characteristics of traditional sharing of assessment results.
- Identify more family-centered alternatives to sharing assessment results.

[a]See Figure 12.1 for an illustration of family roles in assessment.

and Squires (1989), and Brinckerhoff and Vincent (1987), asking family members to complete a developmental assessment of their child helped the family to increase their awareness of current and future developmental milestones, pinpoint the child's strengths and needs, and take a greater role in intervention planning.

With the increased focus on service delivery models that encourage professionals to take a more consultative role, using families in an expanded assessment role is efficient for many reasons. At both a screening and an assessment level, the input of families not only enhances the assessment process but also shortens it. Thus, using families as assessors is not only valuable for what it provides and promotes but can also be viewed as an efficient strategy for gaining a greater amount and variety of information.

Many professionals have been exposed to the abundant literature that has reported that parents typically "overestimate" their child's skills or skill levels compared with professional judgments (Gradel, Thompson, & Sheehan, 1981; Sexton, Hall, & Thomas, 1983; Sheehan, 1988). As indicated by Bailey (1989), however, reliability between professionals and parents is often a multifactored process dependent on demographic variables, the skill area assessed, and the age of the child. Furthermore, Bailey questioned whether parent–professional agreement is always an outcome to be desired; in contrast, Bailey supported the notion of using varied perspectives when assessing a young child.

A variety of professionals (Beukelman & Mirenda, 1992; Crais, 1991, 1995; Dunst, Trivette, et al., 1988) have suggested that the assessment process should be viewed as a series of consensus-building activities. Beukelman and Mirenda (1992) argued that a major goal of initial assessment should be the development of long-term consensus building and management. Dunst, Trivette, et al. (1988) focused on the lack of consensus building by professionals as a major reason for parent and professional conflict regarding early intervention services and the failure of families to follow professionally prescribed recommendations. Dunst and colleagues suggested that consensus building needs to take place around three critical points: 1) the nature of the presenting concern, 2) the need for treatment, and 3) the course of action that should be taken. The participation of family members in assessment may provide opportunities for consensus building that may facilitate current and future interactions between families and professionals.

Without active participation of families in the assessment process, not only will valuable information be missed, but families also may not assume ownership of the decisions made or the interventions planned (Beukelman & Mirenda, 1992). Furthermore, as suggested by Beukelman and Mirenda, if families have been excluded from the assessment phase when team dynamics and interaction styles are established, they may not learn to participate as team members and may not feel like part of the team.

If assessment and intervention activities are to be owned by families, the activities must match families' perceptions of what is appropriate and important. Therefore, throughout the planning process, families' cultural backgrounds, economic status, and value systems must be taken into account. In doing so, professionals may avoid cultural bias and the planning of activities that are not understood, are misunderstood, and are not supported by families (Bailey, 1989). The active participation of all of the child's family can enhance both the validity and reliability of the assessment through collaborative planning and implementation.

Given that families are most often the primary intervention agents, their participation in assessment can enhance both the intervention planning and the implementation process. For some families, however, the role of primary interventionist may require too much time and energy, thus causing guilt and stress (Dunst, Leet, & Trivette, 1988; Tannock & Girolametto, 1992). As Tannock and Girolametto suggested, part of the assessment process should include consideration of the family's and other caregivers' roles in intervention. Professionals need to ensure that the intervention program does not overwhelm the family or other caregivers. The active participation of families in both assessment and intervention planning is one means of ensuring that the interventions planned match the family's preferences and priorities.

Since the late 1980s, increasing attention has been paid to the explicit roles that family members take in assessment activities and specifically to increasing the participation of family members throughout the assessment process (Bailey, 1989; Crais, 1993; Kjerland & Kovach, 1990; Neisworth & Bagnato, 1988; Sheehan, 1988). Historically, families' roles in assessment have been limited to that of observer or informant of background information (Bailey, McWilliam, et al., 1992). The advent of arena assessment and the use of naturalistic assessment settings have provided increased opportunities for family members to play a more active part in the assessment of young children. For practicing professionals and students who were instructed in more traditional approaches, however, the transition to more active participation by family members may not be easy.

Instructional Strategies Focusing on Family Roles in Assessment

Activities such as parent panels, family interviews, or videos that focus on family perceptions of assessment can also be used to raise awareness of the importance of family participation in assessment. The video by Project Enlightenment (1989) provides comments by parents and professionals about the vital role that families play in child assessment. Books and articles written by parents of children with disabilities that touch on assessment issues include Butler (1983) and Failey (1993). In addition, articles or book chapters discussing family roles in assessment include those by Bailey, McWilliams, et al. (1992), Crais (1993), Crais and Calculator (in press), Kjerland and Kovach (1990), and McLean and McCormick (1993). Learner outcomes specific to family roles and recognizing what families can provide to and gain from child assessment appear in Table 12.4.

One way to introduce the idea of varied participation of family members in assessment is to talk about a continuum of less to more active roles as suggested by Bailey, McWilliam, et al. (1992), adapted by Crais (1994), and illustrated in Figure 12.1. To introduce the concept of family roles at an awareness level, the Bailey, McWilliam, et al. (1992) materials describe and provide characteristics of some of the roles on the continuum. Students or professionals can be asked to identify the strengths and limitations of each of the roles, particularly if only one role is offered to family members. An additional activity to highlight parental roles in assessment is to talk about the types of assessment tools and techniques that facilitate parents' taking each role. Through small- or large-group activities, participants (supplemented by the instructors) can generate a list of sample tools and techniques that may promote each of the roles identified. For tools that may be new to participants, overheads of protocols and video examples may be used to demonstrate the ways parents may take part in assessment. Crais (1993) discussed varied roles and described available tools and techniques for assessing both the overall development and the communication skills of young children. A brief annotated list of tools for increasing family and teacher participation in assessment is provided in Table 12.5.

An issue that often arises in both preservice and inservice groups concerning parental roles in assessment is that of the competence of parents as reporters and evaluators of their children's behaviors. One way to broach the topic of parental competence to fulfill various roles is to ask participants to generate a list of skills necessary to perform each role listed in Figure 12.1. Invariably, as they discuss the roles, they identify a core set of characteristics of family members or factors that might promote family participation in

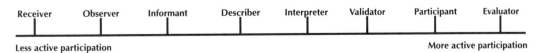

Figure 12.1. An illustration of less to more active roles of family members in assessment. (Adapted from Bailey, McWilliam, et al. [1992].)

TABLE 12.5. Tools and techniques for increasing family–professional participation in assessment

---

Bagnato, S., & Neisworth, J. (1990). *System to Plan Early Childhood Services (SPECS)*. Circle Pines, MN: American Guidance Service.

Judgment-based assessment by professionals and family members of children ages 2–6 years across communication, sensorimotor, physical, self-regulation, cognition, and self/social areas. Focuses on team assessment and program planning through consensus bulding.

Bricker, D. (Ed.). (1993). *Assessment, Evaluation, and Programming System (AEPS) for infants and children: Vol. 1. AEPS Measurement for birth to three years*. Baltimore: Paul H. Brookes Publishing Co.

Criterion-referenced assessment, evaluation, and family participation components. Areas include fine motor, gross motor, adaptive, cognitive, social-communication, and social. Also includes a Family Report for parents to assess their child; a Family Interest Survey to gain information on child, family, and community interests; a Data Recording Form to record child progress; and a Child Progress Record for parents and caregivers to keep track of their child's progress. Volume 2 includes curricular materials.

Bricker, D., Squires, J., Mounts, L., Potter, L., Nickel, R., & Farrell, J. (1995). *Ages & Stages Questionnaires (ASQ): A parent-completed, child-monitoring system*. Baltimore: Paul H. Brookes Publishing Co.

Set of 11 developmental questionnaires periodically sent to parents of children at risk between 4 and 48 months. Areas screened include fine motor, gross motor, communication, personal-social, and problem solving. A Spanish version is also available. Squires, Potter, and Bricker (1995) provides guidance for using the questionnaires.

Cardone, I., & Gilkerson, L. (1989). Family Administered Neonatal Activities. *Zero to Three, 10*(1), 23–28. Washington, DC: Bulletin of the National Center for Clinical Infant Programs.

Uses the Neonatal Behavioral Assessment Scale (Brazelton, 1973) to involve parents in observing and interpreting their newborn's actions and reactions. Focus is on confirming parents' perceptions of the newborn through observations.

Fenson, L., Dale, P., Reznick, S., Thal, D., Bates, E., Hartung, J., Pethick, S., & Reilly, J. (1993). *MacArthur Communicative Development Inventories*. San Diego: Singular.

Parent report instruments used to determine child's comprehension and production vocabularies (including single and combined words, gestures, imitations) for children 8–16 months using words and gestures, and production vocabulary for children 16–30 months using single words and word combinations. Dale (1991) describes the use and results of the instruments.

Ireland, H. (1992). *Child Development Inventories*. Minneapolis, MN: Behavior Science Systems.

Parent-completed instrument used to identify a child's skills across fine motor, gross motor, social, expressive language, language comprehension, general development, self-help, letters, and numbers. Age range covered is 15 months to 6 years. Other associated tools include a parent interview format and screening tools for infant development (birth to 15 months), ages 1–3 and 3–6, and kindergarten readiness.

Variety Pre-Schooler's Workshop. (1987). *Parent/Professional Preschool Performance Profile (5 P's)*. Syosset, NY: Author. (Available from Variety Pre-Schooler's Workshop, 47 Humphrey Drive, Syosset, NY 11791)

(continued)

TABLE 12.5. *(continued)*

Behavior scales for children from 6 to 60 months designed for home–school collaboration. Areas include social, motor, cognitive, self-help, language, and classroom adjustment. Parents and teachers complete the assessment based on their own observations of the child's performance, respectively, at home and school. Then the parents and teachers meet to discuss ways to facilitate desired behaviors seen at home or school in the other setting. Available in English and Spanish.

Wetherby, A., & Prizant, B. (1993). *Communication and Symbolic Behavior Scales.* Chicago: Riverside.

Developed for 9 to 24-month-old preverbal to verbal chldren. Observation, interaction, and parent interview. Measures communicative functions and means, reciprocity, social-affective signaling, and verbal symbolic and nonverbal symbolic behavior. Includes eight communication temptations; unstructured, directed, and combinatorial play; and comprehension items. Also includes Caregiver Perception Rating form for caregivers to complete after the assessment to gain their perceptions of the child's behavior and performance during the assessment.

From Crais, E. (1994). *Increasing family participation in the assessment of children birth to five* (pp. 67–69). Chicago: Applied Symbolix; adapted by permission.

assessment (e.g., interest in their child, opportunity to observe the child, ability to express their ideas about their child to others, time to meet with others, parents encouraged to choose their own level and type of participation). As the discussion continues, factors that participants may initially have thought were paramount (e.g., parental education level, instruction and experience with assessment measures) begin to lose prominence as counterarguments or individualized strategies are identified. For example, small- or large-group discussions often lead to comments such as, "Assessments can be tailored to most educational levels or cultural expectations," "A lower educational level should not be assumed to preclude active participation if desired by parents," "Most parents are interested in and care about their child despite their circumstances," and "Sometimes parents, although interested, just don't have the time or energy to participate very actively." In addition to the practical ideas that students or professionals may generate, there is an emerging body of literature and research on parent participation of which participants may not be aware. The following are three findings since 1989 from this literature:

1. High correlations between family members' concerns about their child's developmental status and the outcome of developmental screening measures (Bricker & Squires, 1989; Glascoe, McLean, & Stone, 1991)
2. High correlations between maternal and professional estimates of the developmental status of the child (Bloch & Seitz, 1989; Sexton, Thompson, Perez, & Rheams, 1990)
3. High correlations between family members' judgments of vocabulary and syntax levels and professional assessment using standardized testing and language sampling (Dale, 1991; Dale, Bates, Reznick, & Morisset, 1989)

One of the challenges for instructors is how to raise the awareness of participants to current findings related to these issues. A means used in both preservice and inservice instruction is to talk first about the traditional bias against family members as accurate reporters of information. It may be helpful to illustrate this by using personal examples (e.g., "I was instructed not to trust parents and to ask sensitive information at least twice for verification"). Asking participants to share the biases they were taught can also raise a number of these issues. Throughout the discussion, it is important to reiterate that many professionals were taught these ideas because of the predominant findings in the literature. For example, in a review of empirical studies from 1950 to 1983, Sheehan (1988) reported that in 75% of the studies parents rated their child's performance higher than did the professionals. In addition, these beliefs were acquired because of practitioners' own experiences in asking parents to report when their child performed certain behaviors (e.g., rolled front to back, began to babble). It is now recognized that it is difficult for anyone to be accurate in remembering specific details about some behaviors (particularly those performed years ago).

To provide a contrast with traditional views of parent reliability, an overhead of the findings provided above can be shown and participants asked to generate the reasons they think these findings are in such contrast to more traditional findings. Often arising from the discussion are issues such as the variations in the types of instruments used (e.g., standardized versus criterion referenced), the use of recognition (e.g., "Does your child now do X?") versus recall (e.g., "When did your child do X?") formats, the conditions of testing (e.g., formal versus informal), the use of arena and play-based assessment, the increased regard for family members' unique knowledge of the child, the broader and more ecologically valid view of children in assessment (i.e., child in context rather than decontextualized), and the importance of gaining multiple sources and perspectives in assessment (Bailey, 1989; Meisels & Provence, 1989; Neisworth & Bagnato, 1988). Depending on the familiarity of the participants with newer assessment techniques and tools, the instructor may need to provide examples from current instruments and techniques (see Table 12.5).

At a skill-building level, several of the videotapes mentioned previously can be used to encourage participants to identify roles family members play in assessment and to begin a discussion of ways to facilitate increased opportunities for a variety of roles offered throughout assessment. To help participants identify areas in need of change, Brass Tacks (McWilliam & Winton, 1990) or The Role of Parents in Child Assessment: Self-Evaluation by Practicing Professionals (Crais & Wilson, 1996) can again be used. In inservice activities, small-group discussions can be used regarding the changes professionals can make to facilitate a greater variety of roles for families in assessment. Participants may often provide examples of creative ways to offer increased roles to families in assessment. The role play in Activity 1 can also be used to develop the skills of participants in working collaboratively with a family to identify and clarify their roles in assessment. Families who are experienced at the assessment game may also be willing to work with participants to provide them with "safe" practice opportunities. Finally, participants may be encouraged to try some of these ideas in their practicum or work settings and in particular may use videotaping as a means to review their interactions and identify strengths and areas in need of modification.

Issues that always need attention in instruction on family roles are that families will vary in the type and amount of participation they want in their child's assessment and that professionals need to honor these preferences. Both practicing professionals and students can be asked to generate a list of factors that might preclude some families from wanting or being able to take a more active role in the assessment of the child. Examples of factors include parents who are burned out from years of early intervention activities, lack of transportation or travel distance when assessments do not occur in the home, working parents who are unable to meet during the day, or parents who want unbiased opinions of their child without their presence. A discussion of each factor, how it may affect the assessment, what strategies may be used to attempt to lessen the factor, and how family decisions can be honored by professionals may be useful. A quote by Sheehan (1988) on parental involvement in educational decision making can be a helpful reminder: "This different perspective is an awareness that parental involvement is not a universal good for all parents, for all children, or for all schools. Rather, it is an activity that has benefits for some parents, many children, and most schools" (p. 85). Learner outcomes for family roles in assessment are provided in Table 12.4.

Sharing of Assessment Results

Although instruction on new assessment methods and tools may be fairly common, less attention in both preservice and inservice instruction seems to be given to the sharing of the information gathered by families and professionals. As suggested by Olson (1988), discussing sensitive assessment information is perhaps one of the most difficult tasks associated with providing services to young children with disabilities, yet few professionals have received formal instruction in this area. As a means of continuing to build consensus between families and professionals, this step cannot be underestimated. Families who have been dissatisfied with their assessment experiences often report that it is not the gravity of the information shared but the way the information was shared (Martin, George, O'Neal, & Daly, 1987; Tarran, 1981). The type and amount of information that is shared and the way it is shared may have an impact on not only the follow-up decisions made but also on how families and professionals feel about the assessment process.

As with other phases, it is recommended that all those who can contribute to and gain from the sharing of the assessment information be present. In recognizing the wisdom of Beukelman and Mirenda (1992) in their suggestion to develop strategies to encourage participation by all team members during the assessment, the same suggestion may hold during the postassessment meeting. In contrast with traditional approaches in which professionals do most of the reporting, alternatives have included beginning the discussion by asking families to give their impressions of the assessment activities, addressing the parent's concerns first, and asking families what they view as the child's strengths or needs. Families and others who have played a more active role in assessment (e.g., performing observations, completing checklists, conducting assessment activities) may be asked to provide an overview of their assessment results. Families that have played a greater role in planning and assessing are more likely to be active in the sharing of results. Brinckerhoff and Vincent (1987) demonstrated this principle by asking families to complete a family profile, a developmental checklist, and a daily routine inventory before their child's individualized education program (IEP) meeting. These families also met with a school liaison before the IEP meeting to help organize their assessment findings. The families who were more actively involved in assessment were more likely to contribute to intervention planning and decision making compared with a control group of parents who were not asked to participate in the above activities before the IEP meeting.

As suggested by McLean and Crais (1996), whether or not families participate directly in assessment, they may be offered additional options that could help them prepare for the sharing session. For example, families may be encouraged to think about or write down characteristics of the child, what they would like the child to do in the next month or year, and what ways they see possible to help their child achieve in these areas. When there is time between the assessment activities and the sharing session, families may be given a list of questions to consider before the discussion (e.g., "What were your overall impressions of the assessment?" "What were the assessment activities that went well?" "What were the activities that did not go as well?" "What area would you like to discuss first?"). Consensus building can also be greatly facilitated by engaging families in a process of validating assessment findings and corresponding interpretations of results. Families are encouraged to support as well as challenge the examiner's impressions, comparing these data to their own impressions. This is also a time in which results of assessment tasks can be tied to parental anecdotes, thus supporting the generalizability of results and others' abilities to relate what might otherwise be perceived as abstract impressions to daily interactions and outcomes with a particular child (Crais & Calculator, in press).

Another strategy that may build consensus and contribute to a collaborative relationship is to share assessment information in an ongoing manner throughout the assessment process. As each task, tool, or series of tasks is completed, families and professionals can discuss their findings and begin generating a list of ideas for either further assessment or later intervention planning. The ongoing sharing of assessment results may also reduce the amount of information that needs to be shared at the end (or at any one time), thus resulting in more accurate perceptions and understanding of what is shared.

Whether information is shared throughout or after the assessment, it is important that sharing be performed in a way that is useful to families in decision making, that promotes competence and hope, and that facilitates consensus building. It may be useful at the end of an assessment to ask families if their concerns and priorities were addressed and what, if anything, they still need from professionals. Returning to families' original concerns expressed at the beginning of the process may be a way to revisit these issues and to direct further efforts to areas not addressed satisfactorily or still in question. This may be particularly important for professionals who perform evaluations for eligibility purposes where little intervention planning actually takes place. In some of these instances, families may leave with little information on what specifically to do next with their child or with any immediate suggestions for ways to deal with their initial concerns. Ideally, in these situations, time could be spent initially addressing the family's immediate concerns even though more thorough planning will take place later. At the very least, family members should be well aware of the constraints of the evaluation setting so that they have realistic expectations of what they are likely and not likely to receive.

Instructional Strategies Focusing on Sharing Assessment Information

In considering instructional strategies at an awareness level, participants may again examine more traditional approaches to sharing assessment information and more family-centered approaches. Small- and large-group discussions are often useful to identify characteristics of traditional approaches, such as professional team members meeting and discussing their findings without the parents, team members giving lengthy reports with little time for questions or discussion by parents, professional "jargonese" being used that parents may not understand, and parents not being involved in decisions about what and how to share assessment findings. For identifying alternative practices, individual or panels of parents can be asked to relate some of their own experiences with the sharing of assessment results, particularly what they appreciated and valued. One strategy to raise the awareness level of participants is to use video- and audiotapes of parents talking about their experiences. In addition to the previously described videos, two other videos that include information of this type are *Improving the Post-Assessment Process: Families and Teams Together* (Moore, Ferguson, & Eiserman, 1995) and *Interdisciplinary Teamwork: A Guide for Trainers and Viewers* (Virginia Institute for Developmental Disabilities, 1990). Two videos that deal exclusively with the sharing of assessment information and how it is perceived by family members are *On This Journey Together: Part I. The Early Years* (Family First, 1991) and *Breaking the News*, developed by the Institute for Families of Blind Children (1990). In addition, *Breaking the News* also provides insight into the anguish experienced by professionals when having to share devastating news. This type of video is particularly useful with parent–professional audiences and acknowledges professionals' feelings and the awareness of the existence of these feelings by parents.

Written materials describing more family-centered approaches and strategies for sharing assessment results include book chapters by Kjerland and Kovach (1990) and Murphy (1990); a monograph by Olson (1988); a book by McWilliam, Winton, and Crais (1996); and an instructional curriculum that includes a focus on sharing and interpreting assessment results (Summers, Lane, Collier, & Friedebach, 1993). Crais (1994) also included a module devoted to identifying strategies to facilitate mutual sharing of assessment results.

Once some awareness-level activities have taken place (e.g., discussion, video viewing, reading), activities aimed more at skill building can occur. At a skill-building level, participants can be encouraged to identify characteristics or behaviors in the videos that either promote or inhibit mutual sharing of assessment information. Role-play activities using actual experiences of the participants can also be quite informative, as illustrated in Activity 2.

In trying variations of this activity for both preservice and inservice, scenarios created by the participants as well as prepared ones can be used. Although the prepared ones help the activity begin faster, the participant-created ones seem to work better. When the participants use their own experiences, they have background information to share before and after the role play regarding the scenario, and they also seem to gain from learning someone else's perspectives and ideas for alternative approaches.

In considering the gradual move toward more family-centered assessment practices, the importance of sharing assessment information cannot be underestimated. No matter how family centered an assessment is, if sharing assessment information and further decision making are not very family centered, then the original purpose has been defeated. Learner outcomes for reciprocal sharing of assessment information are provided in Table 12.4.

CONCLUSION

The benefits of planning, performing, and sharing the findings of assessment in a collaborative manner cannot be overestimated. First, benefits may come from the relationship and the roles and expectations developed among the families, professionals, and others who interact routinely with the child. When families and professionals work collaboratively in assessment, they set the tone for future interactions and begin the process of continuous consensus building. In addition, when families are actively engaged in planning and conducting the assessment, the activities and results should better represent both the child's typical functioning and the families' views of the child. As suggested by Crais (1995), collaboratively planned assessments should also provide families with more of what they want and need from assessment and, therefore, be more useful to families than traditional assessments. Thus, active participation of families within the context of assessment becomes a beginning point for collaborative efforts throughout the intervention process. Although there is evidence that some professionals are offering more active roles to families in assessment (Crais & Wilson, 1996), there are still many tasks and activities that could be performed by family members desiring an active role, if provided the opportunity, the appropriate format, and the necessary support.

RESOURCES

Bailey, D.B., McWilliam, P.J., Winton, P., & Simeonsson, R. (1992). *Implementing family-centered services in early intervention: A team-based model for change.* Cambridge, MA: Brookline Books. Cost: $19.95. (800) 666-2665.

Resources (goals, handouts, transparencies) for and description of a team-based decision-making workshop for implementing family-centered services. Materials included were developed to support instruction on the elements of a family-centered approach to identifying, establishing, and tracking family-centered plans.

Child Development Resources. (1992). *Transdisciplinary arena assessment process: A resource for teams* [Videotape]. Norge, VA: Author. Cost: $149.95 (videotape and print viewing guide). (804) 566-3300.

A 43-minute videotape demonstrating a six-step, family-centered transdisciplinary approach to arena assessment and IFSP development. Viewing guide includes forms, activities, and materials suitable for teaching/instruction about the process as a whole or the component parts (e.g., preassessment planning).

Crais, E. (1994). *Increasing family participation in the assessment of children birth to five*. Chicago: Applied Symbolix. Cost: $59. (800) 676-7551.

Workbook and audiotapes sharing information and strategies related to facilitating active participation by all caregivers in planning, conducting, analyzing, reporting, and interpreting assessment activities and results. Overviews are provided of main issues, along with detailed handouts, examples, and references suitable for use in preservice or inservice instruction.

Edelman, L. (1991). *Delivering family-centered, home-based services* [Videotape]. Bethesda, MD: Association for the Care of Children's Health. Cost: $98 plus shipping and handling. (301) 654-1205.

Videotape includes five vignettes, each of which illustrates what happens when service providers fail to practice family-centered principles. Each vignette illustrates a different interaction (e.g., home-based assessment, an IFSP meeting) and provides instructors with material that can be used for awareness (e.g., identification of practices that are not family centered), knowledge (e.g., of alternative, desirable practices), and application (e.g., through role playing).

Family First. (1991). *On this journey together: Part 1. The early years* [Videotape]. Columbus, OH: Author. Cost: $10.95. (800) 875-2723.

A 22-minute videotape loaded with teaching/instructional examples provided by 16 Ohio families. Messages focus on initial reactions to diagnoses and labels, interactions with professionals that have been helpful or hurtful, and strategies for making collaboration around assessment more productive.

Fullerton, T. (Ed.). (1992). *Heart to heart* [Videotape]. Frankfort: Kentucky Developmental Disabilities Planning Council. Cost: $10. (800) 928-6583.

A 45-minute videotape of parents and professionals discussing their roles and frustrations while exploring approaches for developing productive working relationships. There are approximately 25 different clips within this film that could be used to highlight and explore issues related to jargon, information sharing, decision making, program planning, and expectations.

Graham, M.A. (1993). *Evaluation and assessment of infants and toddlers: Creating family-centered, developmentally appropriate evaluations*. Tallahassee, FL: Center for Prevention and Early Intervention Policy Studies. Cost: $27. (904) 644-6166.

Materials designed to convey to individuals involved in the screening, evaluation, and/or assessment of infants and toddlers the necessary information for creating family-centered, developmentally appropriate, multidisciplinary evaluations at the community level. Instructor's guidebook is thorough and well organized, offering pre- and posttests, overheads, handouts, activities, and references on a variety of assessment-related topics (e.g., "Review of Instruments," "Alternative Evaluation/Assessment Processes").

Institute for Families of Blind Children. (1990). *Breaking the news* [Videotape]. Los Angeles: Author. Cost: $10. (213) 913-3455.

A 15-minute videotape developed for physicians with powerful teaching messages for any group assessing young children. Handles the content of sharing difficult diagnostic information sensitively and effectively.

McWilliam, P.J., & Winton, P. (1990). *Brass tacks: A self-rating of family-focused practices in early intervention, Part I. Program practices and policies; Part II. Individual interactions with families.* Chapel Hill: University of North Carolina at Chapel Hill, Frank Porter Graham Child Development Center. Cost: $10. (919) 966-4221.

Instruments designed to assist groups (e.g., interdisciplinary professionals, family members, administrators) and individuals in examining and improving the quality and effectiveness of their interactions with families. Using a facilitated self-rating process, four areas of practice can be examined: "First Encounters with Families," "Identifying Goals for Intervention (Child and Family Assessment)," "Intervention Planning for Children and Families," and "Day-to-Day Service Provision."

Project Enlightenment. (1989). *First years together: Involving parents in infant assessment* [Videotape]. Raleigh, NC: Author. Cost: $35 plus shipping and handling. (919) 856-7774.

This 19-minute videotape accomplishes several purposes: 1) provides family perspectives on what they like and dislike about assessments, 2) demonstrates family–professional collaboration in formal and informal assessment situations, and 3) illustrates how assessment can provide opportunities to plan interventions while supporting family strengths and accomplishments.

REFERENCES

Bagnato, S., & Neisworth, J. (1990). *System to Plan Early Childhood Services (SPECS).* Circle Pines, MN: American Guidance Service.

Bailey, D.B. (1989). Assessment and its importance in early intervention. In D. Bailey & M. Wolery (Eds.), *Assessing infants and preschoolers with handicaps* (pp. 1–21). Columbus, OH: Charles E. Merrill.

Bailey, D.B., Buysse, V., Edmondson, R., & Smith, T. (1992). Creating a family focus in early intervention: Perceptions of professionals in four states. *Exceptional Children, 58*(4), 298–309.

Bailey, D.B., McWilliam, P.J., Winton, P., & Simeonsson, R. (1992). *Implementing family-centered services in early intervention: A team-based model for change.* Cambridge, MA: Brookline Books.

Bailey, D.B., Palsha, S., & Simeonsson, R. (1991). Professionals' skills, concerns, and perceived importance of work with families in early intervention. *Exceptional Children, 58,* 156–165.

Barber, P.A., Turnbull, A.P., Behr, S.K., & Kerns, G.M. (1988). A family systems perspective on early childhood special education. In S.L. Odom & M.B. Karnes (Eds.), *Early intervention for infants and children with handicaps: An empirical base* (pp. 179–198). Baltimore: Paul H. Brookes Publishing Co.

Beukelman, D.R., & Mirenda, P. (1992). *Augmentative and alternative communication: Management of severe communication disorders in children and adults.* Baltimore: Paul H. Brookes Publishing Co.

Bloch, J., & Seitz, M. (1989, July). Parents as assessors of children: A collaborative approach to helping. *Social Work in Education,* 226–244.

Brazelton, T. (1973). *Neonatal Behavioral Assessment Scale.* Philadelphia: J.B. Lippincott.

Bricker, D. (Ed.). (1993). *Assessment, Evaluation, and Programming System (AEPS) for infants and children: Vol. 1. AEPS measurement for birth to three years.* Baltimore: Paul H. Brookes Publishing Co.

Bricker, D., & Squires, J. (1989). The effectiveness of parental screening of at-risk infants: The infant monitoring questionnaires. *Topics in Early Childhood Special Education, 9,* 67–85.

Bricker, D., Squires, J., Mounts, L., Potter, L., Nickel, R., & Farrell, J. (1995). *Ages & Stages Questionnaires (ASQ): A parent-completed, child-monitoring system.* Baltimore: Paul H. Brookes Publishing Co.

Brinckerhoff, J., & Vincent, L. (1987). Increasing parental decision-making at the individualized educational program meeting. *Journal of the Division for Early Childhood, 11*, 46–58.

Bronfenbrenner, U. (1979). *The ecology of human development: Experiments by nature and design.* Cambridge: Harvard University Press.

Butler, A. (1983). There's something wrong with Michael: A pediatrician–mother's perspective. *Pediatrics, 71*(3), 446–448.

Cardone, I., & Gilkerson, L. (1989). Family administered neonatal activities. *Zero to Three, 10*(1), 23–28. Washington, DC: Bulletin of the National Center for Clinical Infant Programs.

Child Development Resources. (1992). *Transdisciplinary arena assessment process: A resource for teams* [Videotape]. Norge, VA: Author

Crais, E. (1991). Moving from "parent involvement" to family-centered services. *American Journal of Speech-Language Pathology, 1*, 5–8.

Crais, E. (1993). Families and professionals as collaborators in assessment. *Topics in Language Disorders, 14*(1), 29–40.

Crais, E. (1994). *Increasing family participation in the assessment of children birth to five.* [Continuing education manual and audiotapes]. Chicago: Applied Symbolix.

Crais, E. (1995). Expanding the repertoire of tools and techniques for assessing communication skills of infants and toddlers. *American Journal of Speech-Language Pathology, 4*(3), 47–59.

Crais, E. (1996a). Applying family-centered principles to child assessment. In P.J. McWilliam, P. Winton, & E. Crais (Eds.), *Practical strategies for family-centered intervention* (pp. 69–96). San Diego: Singular.

Crais, E. (1996b, Winter). Preassessment planning with caregivers. *Asha,* 38–39.

Crais, E., & Calculator, S. (in press). The role of caregivers in the assessment process. In A.M. Wetherby, S.F. Warren, & J. Reichle (Eds.), *Communication and language intervention series: Vol. 7. Transitions to prelinguistic communication.* Baltimore: Paul H. Brookes Publishing Co.

Crais, E., & Cripe, J. (1996, June). *Child assessment.* Presentation to the Southeastern Institute for Faculty Training OutReach Summer Institute, Highland Lake, NC.

Crais, E., Geissinger, S., & Lorch, N. (1992). Continuing education needs and preferences of speech-language pathologists working with infants and toddlers with special needs and their families. *Infant-Toddler Intervention, 2*(4), 263–276.

Crais, E., & Wilson, L. (1996). The role of parents in child assessment: Self-evaluation by practicing professionals. *Infant-Toddler Intervention, 6*(2), 125–143.

Dale, P. (1991). The validity of a parent report measure of vocabulary and syntax at 24 months. *Journal of Speech and Hearing Research, 34*, 565–571.

Dale, P., Bates, E., Reznick, J., & Morisset, C. (1989). The validity of a parent report instrument of child language at twenty months. *Journal of Child Language, 16*, 239–249.

Dunst, C., Leet, H., & Trivette, C. (1988). Family resources, personal well-being, and early intervention. *Journal of Special Education, 22*, 108–116.

Dunst, C., Trivette, C., & Deal, A. (1988). *Enabling and empowering families.* Cambridge, MA: Brookline Books.

Early Intervention Program for Infants and Toddlers with Disabilities; Final rule. (1993, July 30). 34 CFR Part 303. *58, Federal Register,* 40958.

Edelman, L. (1991). *Delivering family-centered, home-based services* [Videotape]. Bethesda, MD: Association for the Care of Children's Health.

Failey, R. (1993, June/July). Parental perspectives. *Asha, 35*, 33.

Family First. (1991). *On this journey together: Part I: The early years* [Videotape]. Columbus: The Ohio Department of Mental Retardation and Developmental Disabilities.

Fenson, L., Dale, P., Reznick, S., Thal, D., Bates, E., Hartung, J., Pethick, S., & Reilly, J. (1993). *MacArthur Communicative Development Inventories.* San Diego: Singular.

Fullerton, T. (Ed.). (1992). *Heart to heart* [Videotape]. Frankfort: Kentucky Department of Education.

Glascoe, F., McLean, W., & Stone, W. (1991). The importance of parents' concerns about their child's behavior. *Clinical Pediatrics, 30,* 8–11.

Gradel, K., Thompson, M., & Sheehan, R. (1981). Parental and professional agreement in early childhood assessment. *Topics in Early Childhood Special Education, 1*(2), 31–39.

Graham, M.A. (1993). *Evaluation and assessment of infants and toddlers: Creating family-centered developmentally appropriate evaluations.* Tallahassee, FL: Center for Prevention and Early Intervention Policy Studies.

Halle, J. (1988). Adopting the natural environment as the context of training. In S. Calculator & J. Bedrosian (Eds.), *Communication assessment and intervention for adults with mental retardation* (pp. 155–185). Boston: Little, Brown.

Institute for Families of Blind Children. (1993). *Breaking the news* [Videotape]. Los Angeles: Author.

Ireland, H. (1992). *Child Development Inventories.* Minneapolis, MN: Behavior Science Systems.

Kilgo, J., Davis, M., Gamel-McCormick, M., & Brittain, H. (1995, November). *Authentic assessment: Teaming with families to design developmentally appropriate learning experiences.* Paper presented at the Annual International Early Childhood Conference on Children with Special Needs, Orlando, FL.

Kjerland, L., & Kovach, J. (1990). Family–staff collaboration for tailored infant assessment. In E.D. Gibbs & D.M. Teti (Eds.), *Interdisciplinary assessment of infants: A guide for early intervention professionals* (pp. 287–297). Baltimore: Paul H. Brookes Publishing Co.

Martin, N., George, K., O'Neal, J., & Daly, J. (1987). Audiologists' and parents' attitudes regarding counseling of families of hearing-impaired children. *Asha, 29*(2), 27–33.

McBride, S., Brotherson, M., Joanning, H., Whiddon, D., & Demmitt, A. (1993). Implementation of family-centered services: Perceptions of families and professionals. *Journal of Early Intervention, 17,* 414–430.

McGonigel, M., Kaufman, R., & Johnson, B. (1991). *Guidelines and recommended practices for the individualized family service plan* (2nd ed.). Bethesda, MD: Association for the Care of Children's Health.

McLean, M., & Crais, E. (1996). Procedural considerations in assessing infants and preschoolers with disabilities. In M. McLean, D. Bailey, & M. Wolery (Eds.), *Assessing infants and preschoolers with special needs* (2nd ed., pp. 46–68). Columbus, OH: Charles E. Merrill.

McLean, M., & McCormick, K. (1993). Assessment and evaluation in early intervention. In W. Brown, S.K. Thurman, & L.F. Pearl (Eds.), *Family-centered early intervention with infants and toddlers: Innovative cross-disciplinary approaches* (pp. 43–79*)*. Baltimore: Paul H. Brookes Publishing Co.

McWilliam, P.J. (1996). Rethinking child assessment. In P.J. McWilliam, P. Winton, & E. Crais (Eds.), *Practical strategies for family-centered intervention: Getting down to brass tacks* (pp. 55–68). San Diego: Singular.

McWilliam, P.J., & Winton, P. (1990). *Brass tacks: A self-rating of family-focused practices in early intervention, Part I: Program practices and policies* and *Part II: Individual interactions with families.* Chapel Hill: University of North Carolina at Chapel Hill, Frank Porter Graham Child Development Center.

McWilliam, P.J., Winton, P., & Crais, E. (Eds.). (1996). *Practical strategies for family-centered early intervention.* San Diego: Singular.

Meisels, S., & Provence, S. (1989). *Screening and assessment: Guidelines for identifying young disabled and developmentally vulnerable children and their families.* Washington, DC: National Center for Clinical Infant Programs.

Mirenda, P., & Calculator, S. (1993). Enhancing curricula design. *Clinics in Communication Disorders, 3,* 43–58.

Moore, S., Ferguson, A., & Eiserman, W. (1995). *Improving the post-assessment process: Families and teams together* [Videotape]. Boulder: The University of Colorado, Department of Communication Disorders and Speech Science.

Morrow, D., Mirenda, P., Beukelman, D., & Yorkston, K. (1993). Vocabulary selection for augmentative communication systems: A comparison of three techniques. *American Journal of Speech-Langauge Pathology, 2*(2), 19–30.

Murphy, A. (1990). Communicating assessment findings to parents: Toward more effective informing. In E.D. Gibbs & D.M. Teti (Eds.), *Interdisciplinary assessment of infants: A guide for early intervention professionals* (pp. 299–307). Baltimore: Paul H. Brookes Publishing Co.

Neisworth, J., & Bagnato, S. (1988). Assessment in early childhood special education: A typology of dependent measures. In S. Odom & M. Karnes (Eds.), *Early intervention for infants and children with handicaps: An empirical base* (pp. 23–49). Baltimore: Paul H. Brookes Publishing Co.

Olson, J. (1988). *Delivering sensitive information to families of handicapped infants and young children.* Unpublished manuscript, University of Idaho, Special Education Department, Moscow.

Poyadue, F. (1988). In my opinion: Parents as teachers of health care professionals. *Child Health Care, 17*(2), 82–84.

Project Copernicus. (1993). *The family and the IFSP process* [Videotape]. Baltimore: Kennedy Krieger Institute.

Project Enlightenment. (1989). *First years together: Involving parents in infant assessment* [Videotape]. Raleigh, NC: Author.

Sexton, D., Hall, J., & Thomas, P. (1983). Multisource assessment of young handicapped children: A comparison of a diagnostician, teachers, mothers, and fathers. *Diagnostic, 9,* 3–11.

Sexton, D., Thompson, B., Perez, J., & Rheams, T. (1990). Maternal versus professional estimates of developmental status for young children with handicaps: An ecological approach. *Topics in Early Childhood Special Education, 10*(3), 80–95.

Sheehan, R. (1988). Involvement of parents in early childhood assessment. In R. Sheehan & T. Wachs (Eds.), *Assessment of young developmentally disabled children* (pp. 75–90). New York: Plenum.

Squires, J., Potter, L., & Bricker, D. (1995). *The ASQ user's guide.* Baltimore: Paul H. Brookes Publishing Co.

Summers, J., Lane, V., Collier, T., & Friedebach, M.A. (1993). *First steps interdisciplinary training curriculum.* Kansas City: University of Missouri, Institute for Human Development.

Tannock, R., & Girolametto, L. (1992). Reassessing parent-focused language intervention programs. In S.F. Warren & J. Reichle (Eds.), *Communication and language intervention series: Vol. 1. Causes and effects in communication and language intervention* (pp. 49–79). Baltimore: Paul H. Brookes Publishing Co.

Tarran, E. (1981). Parents' views of medical and social-work services for families with cerebral palsied children. *Developmental Medicine and Child Neurology, 23,* 173–182.

Turnbull, A. (1991). Identifying children's strengths and needs. In M. McGonigel, R. Kaufman, & B. Johnson (Eds.), *Guidelines and recommended practices for the individualized family service plan* (2nd ed., pp. 39–55). Bethesda, MD: Association for the Care of Children's Health.

Turnbull, A., & Turnbull, H. (1990). Family Information Preference Inventory. In A. Turnbull & H. Turnbull (Eds.), *Families, professionals, and exceptionality: A special partnership* (2nd ed., pp. 368–373). Columbus, OH: Charles E. Merrill.

Variety Pre-Schooler's Workshop. (1987). *Parent/Professional Preschool Performance Profile (5 P's).* Syosset, NY: Author. (Available from Variety Pre-Schooler's Workshop, 47 Humphrey Drive, Syosset, NY 11791)

Virginia Institute for Developmental Disabilities. (1990). *Interdisciplinary teamwork: A guide for trainers and viewers* [Videotape]. Van Nuys, CA: CHADEM.

Wetherby, A., & Prizant, B. (1993). *Communication and Symbolic Behavior Scales.* Chicago: Riverside.

Winton, P., & Bailey, D. (1993). Communicating with families: Examining practices and facilitating change. In J. Paul & R. Simeonsson (Eds.), *Understanding and working with parents of children with special needs* (2nd ed., pp. 210–230). New York: Holt, Rinehart & Winston.

ACTIVITY 1

GENERATING ASSESSMENT PLANS

Objectives:

- To give participants practice in identifying family concerns and priorities related to assessment
- To give participants practice in identifying child strengths and techniques to use in assessment
- To give participants practice in working collaboratively with families in planning an assessment process

Time: 35–45 minutes

Instructions:

1. Ask participants to divide into groups of four. Each group will take part in a role play with a "parent" and two "professionals." The fourth person will be an observer.

2. Ask each group to first assign the "roles" and take a few minutes to acquaint themselves with their tasks and to read the referral information provided at the end of this activity.

3. The "professional's" job is to gather information from the parent regarding her concerns and priorities for the child's assessment, the child's strengths and ideas/activities to help in planning assessment, and the role she would like to play in the assessment. The professionals can use the sample questions listed in Table 12.3 to help generate the dialogue. The two professionals will need to discuss briefly who will gather the various areas of information (e.g., priorities/concerns versus child strengths). The professionals may want to circle or highlight some of the questions on Table 12.3 for use in the role play.

4. The "parent's" job is to provide any additional facts about her "child" that she would like to include. This person can draw from professional or personal experiences to enhance the information about the child described in the brief referral information. The parent can share this information with the professionals before the role play begins. The parent can make up information in response to the professionals' questions as the role play continues.

5. Each group then begins a brief role play of the meeting between the professionals and the parent to discuss the upcoming assessment. Groups can "freeze frame" anytime during the role play to replay a question/response and try a different approach or to talk over issues.

6. After the role play, the observer in each group can lead a discussion about how the professionals and parent felt in their roles. Which strategies/questions were helpful and which ones were not?

Referral information:

Johnny Carter is a 14-month-old boy who was referred by his physician to the area child development center because of the physician's concerns about Johnny's overall developmental delays. Johnny is the child of a single mother (Ellen Carter) who works the night shift at the local factory so that she can spend her days with Johnny. Ms. Carter and Johnny live with her parents, and his grandmother helps take care of Johnny. In talking to Ms. Carter to set up the upcoming meeting, she noted that Johnny does not seem to be paying attention to people the way her nephew about the same age does. She said that he does not make many sounds and has trouble eating some foods. She also reported that she and her mother call him "Mr. Floppy" because he is so loose and has trouble sitting up by himself. She reported that his birth history was typical and that she did not notice anything was wrong with him until he was a few months old and he was not as active as her nephew.

ACTIVITY 2

SHARING ASSESSMENT RESULTS

Materials needed:

- Index cards

Instruction:

1. Participants can be asked to work in pairs to identify times when they had to share difficult information with families (or for students, information that they think would be hard to share).

2. Each pair is then asked to write one brief scenario on an index card. So that participants will realize they do not have to write too many details, a few examples should be given (e.g., You have to tell this family that you believe their child has autism, has a severe hearing loss, or has overall developmental delays). They can also add qualifying information to "help" the role players (e.g., "This family has had several different diagnoses for their child" "This is a young single mother" "The parents disagree on whether the child has difficulties").

3. Then ask each pair to trade index cards with another pair and role-play each other's scenarios as "professionals." In this way, the two who wrote the scenario have the opportunity to watch someone else try to share this information as they serve as the "parents." The "professional" pairs are encouraged to create any additional information/factors they want to add to the scenario (e.g., these parents have taken an active part in assessing the child, the professionals and parents have shared assessment information in an ongoing manner throughout the assessment, the parents have said that they are not interested in developmental levels but want ideas for working with their child). After the professional pairs have had several minutes to prepare, they then perform the role play and later discuss their impressions.

4. The other pair then role-plays the scenario they were given.

5. Large-group discussion following the role plays often generates a variety of approaches taken to sharing difficult information, and participants have the benefit of hearing others talk about facing some of the same issues they do.

13

PREPARING PRACTITIONERS FOR PLANNING INTERVENTION FOR NATURAL ENVIRONMENTS

Juliann Woods Cripe
Mary Frances Hanline
Steven E. Daley

Early intervention for infants and toddlers with disabilities is not a new concept (Noonan & McCormick, 1993; Peterson, 1987). Professionals and paraprofessionals from a variety of disciplines and service agencies have been concerned with the developmental and educational issues of infants and toddlers and their families for some time. There are, however, several significant differences between the traditional infant intervention programs established in the early 1960s and 1970s and those that are being implemented in the 1990s. These differences reflect the expanded knowledge base available concerning typical child development, the impact of the environment on development, the role of the family, effective curricula and intervention strategies, and the systems for delivering services. During the 1970s, visualizing recommended practices in early intervention would have yielded an image of an instructor working one-to-one with a child to stimulate the acquisition of sensory behaviors such as visual tracking or developmental milestones like stacking blocks. Instructors, often called home visitors, would be following a skills-oriented curriculum using a step-by-step prescriptive approach. The home visitor would use specially designed toys and materials to work with the child and would collect data on the child's responses while the parent observed.

Programs, and the individuals participating in the delivery of services to infants and toddlers, are now envisioned very differently. What is seen in the 1990s is a team of professionals from various disciplines (guided by family members) working together, sharing roles and responsibilities. Team members plan and integrate intervention on the child's individualized family service plan (IFSP) outcomes throughout the day in naturally occurring play, routines, and activities using the child's favorite toys and materials. Family members and other identified caregivers, such as child care providers, are found teaching while changing the child's diapers, reading a story, folding laundry, and driving to the store. Services are provided in a variety of settings, including the home, community groups, child care programs, family child care settings, and neighborhood playgroups.

Portions of this chapter were completed while the first author was funded partially by U.S. Department of Education grant #HO2493033 to the University of Kansas.

The shifts in what has traditionally been considered recommended practice in early intervention (i.e., from professionally driven to family guided, from discipline specific to interdisciplinary integrative, from developmental milestones to functional, from teacher directed to child initiated, from behavioral to contingent responsive, from skill/academically based to activity/play based) necessitate reflection by all individuals interested in the delivery of early intervention (Bricker & Cripe, 1992; Cook, Tessier, & Klein, 1996; Hutinger, 1994). A significant challenge for early intervention students and those individuals involved in preservice and inservice instruction for early interventionists is to recognize that the program processes (e.g., assessment, identification of goals and objectives, instructional methodology and approaches to team planning and implementation) provided in the past were not wrong; rather, they represented points in a continuing process of evolution. Through research and model demonstration projects, the information available about early intervention and effective program processes has expanded tremendously. Preservice and inservice personnel must address the critical need to advance innovations from research into practice. As noted throughout this text, to accomplish this advance, personnel must be willing to greet opportunities for instruction in new practices with open minds, to implement new or modified approaches and evaluate their effectiveness critically, and to share the results of these evaluation efforts with their colleagues. Specifically for planning intervention (the focus of this chapter), early interventionists must be competent observers of children and their environments. Only with an understanding of the child and the environment can the early interventionist arrange for learning opportunities related to identified skills and follow the child's lead to foster child initiation (Bricker & Cripe, 1992). Children enjoy adult attention that is focused on the child's interests and activities and will seek to maintain it, thus creating more opportunities for learning to occur.

Early interventionists must be skillful communicators with both children and adults. Family members identify "being a good listener" as an important characteristic of family-centered personnel. Teamwork requires skills in communication, including the ability to both share and receive information. Early interventionists must be able to share their knowledge with adults and to teach others to intervene with the child through an interdisciplinary approach. Finally, early interventionists must be skilled observers of their own behavior and able to reflect on what worked well and what did not as well as know how an activity could be modified or a material adapted to increase accessibility, how a strategy could be explained and demonstrated more clearly to a caregiver, and how their communications with team members could have been more efficient or effective. Through these observations and reflections, early interventionists can become contributors to the knowledge base for other team members planning intervention in natural settings.

This chapter is designed to facilitate participants' evolution toward the recommended practices that ensure the development of child-initiated, family-guided, contingently responsive, functional, activity-based, and play-based intervention within natural settings. This chapter identifies and describes processes related to planning interventions (e.g., linking assessment to intervention, writing outcomes) and describes activities that could be used for developing the knowledge base and the skills necessary for implementation of the identified processes.

LINKING ASSESSMENT WITH INTERVENTION

Planning for intervention in natural environments is part of a larger linked systems approach that supports the interconnectedness of the assessment, intervention, and evaluation components in early intervention (Bricker, 1989; Neisworth & Bagnato, 1988). A linked systems approach advocates the direct use of the information collected during assessment to formulate the IFSP goals and outcomes. The IFSP goals and outcomes guide the selection of intervention content and instructional strategies. The close relationship of activities and strategies maximizes intervention efficiency and increases the probability that the outcomes will be accomplished for the child and family (Bricker & Cripe, 1992). The evaluation of child and family progress focuses on the identified goals and outcomes and is consistent with assessment procedures by reviewing and updating the initial assessment information. Using a linked systems approach, an early intervention specialist implements a very fluid and dynamic assessment–intervention model to meet the needs of rapidly developing infants and toddlers and their families in early intervention settings (Cohen & Spenciner, 1994).

To support intervention planning in natural settings using a linked systems approach, early intervention team members must implement ecological assessment procedures; many activities for teaching these procedures are contained in Chapter 12. Ecologically valid assessment refers to collecting assessment information as the child and family participate in their daily activities (Bergen, 1994). It includes observation of the child eating, playing with brothers and sisters, getting dressed, joining a playgroup when at child care, and coping with a trip to the physician for a checkup. Ecological assessment facilitates understanding the child's cultural and community influences, the roles of various caregivers and family members, and the requirements of the family's daily schedule (Cook et al., 1996). Participation in assessment by the caregivers and team members in each environment (e.g., parents, siblings, extended family members, physicians, child care workers, Sunday School teachers, early intervention specialists, therapists) establishes the foundation for their continued involvement in the intervention planning and implementation. Authentic assessment, during which skills and behaviors are demonstrated in real-life context (Meyer, 1992), and dynamic assessment, during which the evaluator actively engages and supports the child in tasks designed to learn about how the child learns (Lidz, 1991), are additional strategies for linking assessment to intervention that provide critical information from family and other caregivers about what already works or does not work for the child in different settings (Cohen & Spenciner, 1994). These types of assessment activities help to identify intervention strategies appropriate to the child.

Portfolio assessment is a purposeful collection of a child's records to provide evidence of his or her efforts and skills (Grace & Shores, 1994) and is useful for demonstrating growth and communicating with team members. It is particularly appropriate for the development of family-guided IFSPs that portray the child within the context of his or her family and community. Within the portfolio, a variety of information may be arranged, involving the different settings and caregivers, to document the child's progress over time, thus linking assessment with intervention (Arter & Spandel, 1991; Hanline & Fox, 1994). All team members, and especially the family, have contributions for the portfolio. Photos, scribbles, or word lists are examples of items that can be collected and shared within the portfolio and that foster active participation from all caregivers in whatever setting they interact with the child.

WRITING IFSP OUTCOMES FOR INTERVENTION PLANNING

The development of a well-written, comprehensive IFSP is critical to successful intervention planning because the IFSP goals and outcomes are the link between assessment and intervention. Early intervention specialists must be able to clearly articulate the family's priorities for the child through the careful development of individual goals and outcomes.

Without the establishment of meaningful individual goals and outcomes for children, early intervention specialists and care providers lack appropriate criteria for intervention planning. If the intervention outcomes are well chosen and operationally defined, each team member's contributions to intervention efforts become clear. With meaningful goals and outcomes, the reinforcement of child-initiated action, the selection of routines, and the planning of activities is straightforward, even in various community settings with different team members.

Particularly important in embedding intervention in natural environments is providing opportunities for practicing the child's targeted goals and outcomes. Putting puzzles together or finding hidden objects, even when the activities are fun for the child, is not good intervention planning if the activities do not provide the child with opportunities to learn new skills or reinforce previous intervention targets. Play, activities, routines, and materials should be selected for intervention based on their ability to provide opportunities to practice the outcomes targeted on the IFSP. As activities proceed, their usefulness can be monitored by determining the number of times children can practice targeted emerging skills or rehearse and generalize other recently acquired behaviors (Bricker & Cripe, 1992).

Because of the critical importance of the IFSP outcomes to good intervention planning, early intervention specialists must be able to write IFSP outcomes that are meaningful and measurable based on the family's priorities. IFSP outcomes actually facilitate naturalistic interventions because they are written in the words of the family, not in professional jargon (Noonan & McCormick, 1993). An outcome statement reports what the family has identified as their priority concerns, that is, what they want to occur to enhance their child's development. It is a positive action statement that reflects change (e.g., Corrina will feed herself with a spoon; family will have respite resources available weekly; Tobias will attend child care to play with other children), rather than a description of an impairment or need (e.g., Corrina is still drinking from a bottle; Dad yells at Billy when he cries; Tobias will not share toys). Some outcome statements will directly address concerns for the child while others will focus on resources and priorities for the family.

The outcome statement must be observable to the team members so that criteria can be established to determine when the outcome has been accomplished (Notari & Bricker, 1990). One strategy for ensuring observability is for the family members to close their eyes and visualize how the child (or situation) will look when the outcome is achieved. This can be helpful when services become confused with outcomes (e.g., when family members identify physical therapy services as their priority rather than the child sitting or walking). Another strategy for writing good outcome statements is to phrase the outcome as an "in order to" statement that identifies the relationship between the process and the product (Deal, Dunst, & Trivette, 1989). Examples include the following: Autry will use sounds and gestures (process) in order to gain attention (product), Tobias will attend child care (process) in order to learn to play with other children (product), and Dalton will use a walker (process) to get in an upright position for walking (product). This strategy helps team members focus on the ultimate priority identified by the family, even when small steps must be taken to get there.

The process of outcome development enhances family leadership through the determination of their priorities when families are viewed as colleagues with the other early intervention team members. Early interventionists need to support and encourage family members in their initial efforts as team members. Few family members recognize and value their own expertise during the initial outcome- and intervention-planning efforts. Team members must provide the framework for family members to achieve the level of participation they feel comfortable with during the initial IFSP and intervention planning efforts (also see Chapter 10). Outcome identification also serves the important function of identifying the resources and sources of support necessary to accomplish the desired outcomes. Family members and caregivers are knowledgeable about the child, their existing formal and informal supports, and available resources, whereas team members are knowledgeable about options for services, additional resources, and available supports. Together, this information becomes the basis for determination of early intervention services on the IFSP.

In addition to the outcome statement, the strategies that will lead to its accomplishment are delineated. These action steps set the stage for intervention planning by providing information about team members' roles and responsibilities, as well as suggestions for activities that are congruent with child and family preferences (Johnson, McGonigel, & Kaufmann, 1989). Resources, materials, and methods are also included to assist the team's organization of the intervention plans for each outcome. Using the family's definition of what they would like to see accomplished in the outcome, an evaluation plan is identified. This establishes the criteria, the time lines, and the individuals responsible for monitoring progress. The criteria used should not be an arbitrary percentage or ratio but rather the most appropriate measure for meeting the family's definition of success. A challenge for early interventionists is to learn (or, in some cases, relearn) how to write family-friendly, yet measurable and meaningful, criteria statements. Working together, individualized, functional, and measurable outcomes and actions plans can be developed that promote intervention planning within natural environments.

Team members often find it challenging to gather assessment information from the family and develop a measurable and functional outcome that builds the foundation for intervention. To assist participants, a series of activities is included at the end of this chapter to illustrate the combined processes of linking assessment to intervention and writing outcomes for intervention planning. Activity 1, "Writing Outcomes," can be used to illustrate the points discussed previously in this chapter about writing outcomes linked to assessment. Autry, first introduced in Activity 1, is included in several illustrative activities to support participant skill development through a case study approach. In each activity, small-group discussion and problem solving supports the teamwork process as well as facilitating knowledge and skill development.

Activity 2, "Identifying Intervention Contexts and Services," can help generate discussion about the complexity of identifying services most appropriate for ensuring that the outcomes are accomplished. The discussion can follow a simulation of the team meeting with participants role-playing the various team members. Asking each "team" to develop a service plan for Autry in their community extends the application of learning. Just as there are many options for services, as illustrated in Activity 2, there are many strategies that can be identified for accomplishing the identified outcomes. An additional activity for Autry's team could be to use creative problem solving to develop implementation and evaluation strategies as suggested in Activity 3, "Writing Outcomes that Support Intervention Planning."

NATURALLY OCCURRING EVENTS AS THE CONTEXT FOR INTERVENTION

Once outcomes and initial strategies have been identified, the team translates them into intervention activities and experiences that promote learning and enhance development within the child's natural environment. For infants and toddlers, naturally occurring events include child-initiated actions and play (e.g., climbing into cupboards to play with the pots and pans, activating the mobile on the crib), daily routines (e.g., diapering, travel to child care, washing up), and planned activities (e.g., taking a trip to the store, listening at story time) (Bricker & Cripe, 1992).

Play and Child-Initiated Actions for Infants and Toddlers

Play has long served as a central organizing framework for early cognitive, social, and language development (Piaget, 1962; Vygotsky, 1962). Evidence supports the notion that children's play stimulates and supports their development in all of the learning domains (Fewell & Vadasy, 1983; Garvey, 1977; Smilansky & Shefatya, 1990; Vygotsky, 1967). Play-based approaches to both assessment and intervention with infants and toddlers with disabilities are hallmarks of practice in early intervention in the 1990s (Linder, 1993a, b). Play-based approaches provide opportunities for infants and toddlers to use child-initiated action routines to develop and practice skills with their family members and early interventionists in a positive, natural, mutually satisfying context (Cook et al., 1996).

It is within the context of play that children often initiate activities that can be used to guide their intervention plans through the selection of preferred activities and materials (Kostelnik, Soderman, & Whiren, 1993). Early interventionists must be knowledgeable of play behaviors and strategies to facilitate play development to use the child's play initiations. The child's play is assessed through observation, interaction, and discussion with care providers. Because each child has different play interests and styles, the team members must get to know the child as an initial step for planning intervention (Martin, 1994). Some children meet each opportunity with enthusiasm, whereas others are thoughtful and methodical.

The ability to follow the child's lead, a critical competency for early interventionists working with infants and toddlers, takes practice and knowledge of each child's individual patterns for learning (Linder, 1993b). This competency may be difficult for some adults to achieve because of previous professional instruction that delineated their role as the individual responsible for identification, organization, and direction of the learning activities. It will no doubt be a controversial and potentially humbling experience for early interventionists to be directed to learn from the child how to plan his or her intervention! Child-directed play is truly the most valuable learning activity for infants and toddlers and must be included within the curriculum (Kostelnik et al., 1993). It provides enjoyment for both the child and the caregiver, opportunities to explore objects and construct experiences within the environment, and opportunities to interact and negotiate with age mates; and it facilitates development of skills across developmental domains (Koralek, Colker, & Dodge, 1993). Play is the special work of young children because it gives them the opportunity for success (Rogers & Sawyers, 1988).

Daily Routines

Daily routines provide additional opportunities for developing new skills and for generalizing skills already learned with infants and toddlers. By definition, routines occur both regularly and frequently, and, as such, they provide infants and toddlers and their caregivers with a variety of different opportunities to engage in specifically targeted skills or activities. These routines may include dressing, diapering, resting, bathtime, quiet play and naptime, potty time, getting ready for child care, laundry time, meal preparation, or any of a variety of formally defined or informally identified activity sequences. Because families organize their routines based on what constitutes individual and group priorities, the use of daily routines as the setting for early intervention may be more sensitive to the cultural and social values of the family. Routines also provide opportunities for all the child's caregivers to participate in the intervention.

As professionals work with the family to deliver early intervention services in a variety of settings, it is essential that the importance of the daily routines in the life of the child and family be comprehended because these routines compose the real context within which services are provided. Obviously, daily routines will differ dramatically from child to child, family to family, one setting to another, and, perhaps, week to week. However, if early intervention services are viewed as both portable and flexible, early interventionists should have a much easier job of translating IFSP goals and outcomes into the everyday routines of the child and family in as many different environments as the child participates.

The use of daily routines and naturally occurring events as a context for early intervention services may be logically appealing, but it constitutes a relatively new approach for early intervention teams. This perspective builds directly on the functional skills approach, which has been successfully applied in work with children with severe disabilities (Cipani & Spooner, 1994; Snell, 1993), and is considered to be a developmentally appropriate practice for early childhood educators (Bredekamp, 1987; Koralek et al., 1993). Routines will exist within most natural environments for infants and toddlers. They are the mainstay of child care and preschool schedules (Kostelnik et al., 1993). Routines used for infants and toddlers in intervention should be predictable, flexible, and short and should involve repetitive actions. To facilitate participant competence, Activities 4, 5, and 6 help participants define routines and practice gathering information about routines.

The family members must guide the professionals on the early intervention team in determining which of the daily routines to include in intervention. Only the family knows their responsibilities and time commitment to home, job, and/or school; the needs of other family members; general logistics; and their comfort level. It is essential that the early intervention professionals have an understanding not only of the routines that embrace and surround the child but also of the child's preferences and family's choices for involvement in their daily activities. For example, for some families, mealtimes may not be good for embedding practice because the family values mealtime as a time to catch up on the events of each other's day or as a time for quiet conversation. For others, a sit-down meal is a rare occasion because of hectic schedules. Identifying routines that occur on a predictable basis with sufficient frequency to provide ample opportunities for practice requires a good deal of collaboration among team members. When creativity and flexibility are encouraged, routines can be identified for most families. Appreciating the challenges families face and the family's values and culture is crucial for the family-guided use of routines in intervention.

Case studies, such as the one included in Activity 7, are excellent strategies for providing participants with the opportunity to explore the complexities of everyday life for most families. At the preservice level, case studies share concrete experiences that participants may encounter. For inservice participants, case studies can be used to acknowledge the experiences and contributions of the participants. Role plays, as included in Activity 7, provide an opportunity to practice ideas and plans generated in case studies, further extending the learning into real-life situations.

Embedding intervention into routines requires identifying opportunities for practice of the outcomes in each routine. As an example, consider Xochitl, age 9 months, who is working on reaching for and grasping objects. During her busy morning at home, she has opportunities to reach for the powder bottle and hold it while her mom changes her, to reach for and hold toast at breakfast, and to reach for and hold her toys while playing with her sister. While her mom is at work, her grandmother listens for Xochitl and goes to her crib when she hears her fussing and gives her a rattle to hold. Her grandmother then takes her from the crib and changes her, offering her the powder bottle again. While her sister gives her various choices of toys to reach and grasp, her grandmother prepares a bottle. Xochitl's 13-year-old brother arrives home in time to hold out the bottle for her to grasp and then to feed her. Later, her younger sister plays with her on a blanket on the bedroom floor and offers her different clothing objects to reach for and grasp while getting her ready for bed. When her mom comes home from work, Xochitl is in her night clothes and is holding her shoe. Throughout the course of the day, she has had more than 25 opportunities to reach for and grasp objects functional to the interaction at hand. If early intervention services are to be embedded into naturally occurring event, they also must be nondisruptive to established family routines yet provided with sufficient frequency to ensure that learning will occur.

A commonly used strategy to facilitate planning is the development of an intervention schedule or matrix (Bricker & Cripe, 1992; Noonan & McCormick, 1993). The development of a schedule provides a visual reminder of the outcomes to be addressed and when and where they will be addressed throughout the child's day. It serves as a valuable form of communication between team members and assists in planning and in documentation of the number and types of opportunities. It is helpful for both caregivers at home and in group settings. It is especially useful when multiple caregivers and team members at different settings are involved in the child's program. The team can see at a glance when an outcome is not being addressed frequently enough or when additional or different routines or activities need to be developed to support progress and generalization.

Early interventionists can use the schedule matrix to support inclusion because the matrix shows how the schedule already developed at child care or preschool embeds intervention. Developing a schedule matrix with the child care provider or teacher reassures them that the intervention will not add significantly more work but will use what is already occurring. Team members from different disciplines can use the schedule matrix as a starting point for integrating therapy. They can each identify preferred times and activities for embedding specific targets throughout the day and together decide how multiple outcomes across developmental domains can be incorporated into the same routine or activity. Examples of schedules for Autry at home and in child care are shown in Figures 13.1 and 13.2. During instruction, participants could be asked to develop similar routines as part of the teaching process.

In addition to monitoring progress on the outcomes, team members should keep records that describe the family members' preferences and the specific strategies used to facilitate planning and to prevent miscommunication between team members and caregivers. Working in natural environments often involves additional participants on the team who work directly with the child. Planning for who does what and when it is done is essential to ensure an effective program for the child and to reduce the amount of redundant or conflicting questioning and consulting with the family and caregivers. Although team communication, both face to face and in writing, is often perceived as time consuming, it is essential for effective intervention. Figure 13.3, an example of an intervention planning worksheet, could be used as the basis of an instructional activity, such as Activity 3. Participants could also design a team intervention planning worksheet suitable to their current practicum or worksite or modify the one provided in Figure 13.3.

PLANNED ACTIVITIES

Planned activities are those that would not routinely occur without adult initiation (Bricker & Cripe, 1992). For infants and toddlers, planned activities typically involve simple events such as trips to the store or post office, play on a swing or at a park, or reading a book

Routines	Vocalizing with gestures	Walking with one-hand support
Car travel	Point at and name common objects or places (trucks, McDonald's) to gain Autry's attention.	Give Autry small object to carry to the car from child care. Walk beside him to the car.
Bathtime	Put favorite toys or sponges by the tub. Offer the boat or bubble pipe and wait for Autry to reach and vocalize to request.	Walk with Autry to the bathtub. After bath, walk with him to the hamper to put away towels.
Playtime	Put favorite toys on a shelf out of Autry's reach so he can point and ask for them.	Encourage Autry to help Troy walk Puddles outside holding Troy's hand.
Bedtime	Wave goodnight and blow kisses to Puddles and Troy. Tell his favorite toys and stuffed animals goodnight.	Walk Autry to his bedroom.

Figure 13.1. An example of an individual schedule for Autry.

before bed. This is in contrast to planned activities in preschool classrooms that involve sophisticated art or drama projects, sand and water science activities, or dress-up role play. Activities planned for toddlers may include dancing to music, using art materials as a process with no product expected, "tea parties," playdough, and building houses and roads with blocks (Bredekamp, 1987; Koralek et al., 1993). Water table (or sink) activities include pouring, squeezing, dumping, and dunking.

It has been common practice for the early interventionist to arrive at the child's home or child care center with a series of planned activities that disrupt the ongoing schedule of routines and play and proceed to deliver early intervention from a bag of tricks and special toys. The early interventionist would then leave after about an hour, when each

Group Schedule

Tots and Tales		AUTRY			DALTON			LARRY	
	Vocalize with gestures	Walk with one hand	Point	Early words	Pincer grasp	Drink without spills	Two-word combo	Initiate play
8:30 A.M. Breakfast	X		X	X	X	X	X	X
9:00 A.M. Blocks and Legos	X	X	X	X	X		X	X
9:30 A.M. Music circle	X	X	X	X			X	
9:45 A.M. Story	X	X	X	X	X		X	
10:00 A.M. Play in centers	X	X	X	X	X		X	X
10:25 A.M. Closing circle	X		X	X			X	

Figure 13.2. An example of a group schedule.

Family name: _____ **Date:** _____

Typical daily schedule of family:

A.M.   P.M.

_____   _____

_____   _____

_____   _____

Information to gather in a family-friendly fashion:

1. Which routine(s) do family members identify as mutually enjoyable?
   How frequently do they occur?
   What motivates the child to participate?

   _____

   _____

   _____

2. How does the caregiver currently proceed with the routine?

   _____

   _____

   _____

3. What outcome(s) should be embedded? Where and when?

   _____

   _____

   _____

Strategies to demonstrate to caregiver:
(Incorporate only 1–2 strategies per routine.)   NOTES:

- ☐ Follow the child's lead
- ☐ Provide choices
- ☐ Model appropriate response
- ☐ Give appropriate portions
- ☐ Time delay: Wait for child to request
- ☐ Interrupt sequence and wait for response
- ☐ Place materials out of reach
- ☐ Create silly situations
- ☐ Provide physical assistance

Communication strategies for caregivers:

- ☐ Speak slowly and clearly; use common words
- ☐ Focus on the child's actions/communication
- ☐ Use gestures
- ☐ Use an exaggerated/animated voice
- ☐ Take turns with actions/vocalization
- ☐ Expect a response from child
- ☐ Respond to child's initiation
- ☐ Expand on child's response
- ☐ Include a variety of attractive, interesting, and desirable objects and materials

Figure 13.3. Intervention planning worksheet. (From Cripe, J., & Graffeo, J. [1995]. Parsons: University of Kansas, KUAP–Parsons, Project FACETS; reprinted by permission.)

of the specific objectives had been addressed in directed play activities and the time allotted for special instruction on the IFSP was completed, without incorporating the planned activities into the child's schedule or routines. Planned activities for infants and toddlers should be activities that characterize the everyday life of most young children and not the elaborately scripted activities early interventionists may choose to construct as opportunities for the child to learn new skills. Planned activities also must focus on the child's specific outcomes rather than on general stimulation for maximum progress to occur. In planning activities, it is often difficult to focus on the child's intervention target(s) and easy to become overly involved in the activity. Activity 8 helps the participants practice the art of planning intervention activities for young children.

Planned activities for infants and toddlers are subject to immediate change to follow the child's lead. The lack of stability and predictability of even typical activities suggests that early interventionists need to be both flexible and responsive to unexpected changes. Although the early intervention team should plan for a balance between play, routines, and planned activities in intervention, because of the age and experiences of infants and toddlers, most time, either individually or in groups, will be spent in play or in routines.

INCREASING OPPORTUNITIES IN INTERVENTION PLANNING

During routines and planned activities, opportunities can often be increased by a team analysis of the activity sequence. Many hidden opportunities can be found during the setup and cleanup of the area or activity. Adults can involve the child in gathering and organizing the materials for snack, choosing clothing to put on, or picking up the toys after play. Interactions can often be repeated, such as in games like peekaboo or This Little Piggy, many times before the child tires, again increasing the target responses. Early interventionists must be careful not to preempt opportunities for the child to practice skills in very functional activities. Preempting can easily occur because of the desire to be helpful to the child, to be efficient and move on to another task rapidly, or because setting up and cleaning up are traditionally teacher duties. Activity 9 provides the team with practice in increasing opportunities in activities for Autry.

There are also many strategies that may facilitate increasingly complex response repertoires and child skill levels. These strategies include the use of interesting or novel materials, placement of materials out of the child's reach, and giving inadequate portions of desired materials. As shown in Figure 13.3, these strategies can be used throughout the routines or planned activities to increase the opportunities children have to practice their targeted outcomes. When applied skillfully, these strategies will offer an extra trial without detracting from the activity, disrupting the child's initiations, or interfering with the logical sequence and predictability of the routine. Activity 10 is an opportunity to role-play teaching caregivers to use various intervention strategies systematically and effectively.

CONCLUSION

Working in natural environments using naturalistic interventions does not mean that the intervention will just naturally occur. In contrast, early interventionists must plan more carefully, document more creatively, and communicate more frequently with team members to ensure the child is making optimal progress. Early interventionists in the 1990s need to know the same content of good instruction (i.e., how and when to model, to deliver prompts or cues, to reinforce, to provide physical guidance) as past early interventionists, but they also need to know how to apply the behavioral strategies within the context of naturally occurring events. It is not the principles of good instruction that have changed but the strategies for their implementation. Cues may be provided by a greeting to the child when the early interventionist enters the home rather than by a verbal prompt to "look at me." The designated number of instruction trials may be distributed throughout the day during diapering or at mealtimes rather than during a pull-out mass trial treatment session. The reinforcement of a child for practice will not be tokens or verbal praise but rather the toy requested or the turn taken by another child in a game. Early interventionists must never lose sight of why special instruction or special education is special; specialized training approaches are designed and implemented to ensure that learning occurs.

Knowing where, when, and how to intervene is essential for early interventionists, but they also need to understand why and believe in the principles of family-guided, interdisciplinary, activity- and play-based intervention in natural contexts. Without the underlying theoretical knowledge and the commitment to the values of early intervention, team members will be unable to creatively problem-solve and make decisions based on the principles. Preservice and inservice preparation must include information on the rationale for the approaches as well as application opportunities that support the team process. Implementation strategies without the theoretical framework are as unsatisfying for team members in the field as theory without practice is for students. Early interventionists who appreciate where the field has been and what it has done will also understand that the field will continue to evolve. They will prioritize their professional development to grow with and contribute to the knowledge and implementation base for the field of early intervention.

RESOURCES

Bricker, D., & Cripe, J.W. (1992). *An activity-based approach to early intervention.* Baltimore: Paul H. Brookes Publishing Co. Cost: $27. (800) 638-3775.

Shows how to use natural environments and relevant events to effectively and efficiently teach infants and young children. Useful ideas for developing individualized goals and objectives and monitoring child progress. Designed to be used in conjunction with the videotape discussed below.

Cripe, J.W. (1995). *Family-guided activity-based intervention for infants and toddlers* [Videotape]. Baltimore: Paul H. Brookes Publishing Co. Cost: $37. (800) 638-3775.

This 20-minute videotape illustrates strategies through which parents and other caregivers can take advantage of natural learning opportunities. Narration and examples are clear and provide supplemental materials for diverse audiences.

Linder, T.W. (1993). *Transdisciplinary play-based intervention: Guidelines for developing a meaningful curriculum for young children.* Baltimore: Paul H. Brookes Publishing Co. Cost: $49. (800) 638-3775.

Creative strategies for promoting cognitive, social-emotional, communication and language, and motor development. Activities and materials can support teaching and instruction and language about the design and implementation of IFSPs.

McGonigel, M., Kauffman, R., & Johnson, B. (1991). *Guidelines and recommended practices for the individualized family service plan* (2nd ed.). Bethesda, MD: Association for the Care of Children's Health. Cost: $15. (301) 654-6549.

Essential information about the IFSP process, from the federal rules and regulations to recommended practice. This book includes vignettes and family stories, as well as extensive samples, forms, procedures, and instruments for use in preservice or inservice instruction.

Rule, S. (1996). *Strategies for instruction in natural environments.* Logan: Utah State University, Center for Persons with Disabilities. Cost: $450 (includes two videotapes, instructor's manual, and participant's manual). (801) 797-1987.

Part of a five-videotape series designed to provide preservice and inservice education in instructional procedures appropriate for use in natural environments. The remaining three videotapes, *Strategies for Preschool Intervention in Everyday Settings,* will be available in CD-ROM and videotape formats in September, 1997.

REFERENCES

Arter, J.A., & Spandel, V. (1991). *Using portfolios of student work in instruction and assessment.* Portland, OR: Northwest Regional Educational Laboratory.

Bergen, D. (1994). *Assessment methods for infants and toddlers.* New York: Teachers College Press.

Bredekamp, S. (1987). *Developmentally appropriate practice in early childhood programs serving children from birth through age 8.* Washington, DC: National Association for the Education of Young Children.

Bricker, D. (1989). *Early intervention for at-risk and handicapped infants, toddlers, and preschool children.* Palo Alto, CA: Vort Corporation.

Bricker, D. (Ed.). (1993). *Assessment, evaluation, and programming system (AEPS) for infants and children: Vol. 1. AEPS measurement for birth to three years.* Baltimore: Paul H. Brookes Publishing Co.

Bricker, D., & Cripe, J.W. (1992). *An activity-based approach to early intervention.* Baltimore: Paul H. Brookes Publishing Co.

Cipani, E.C., & Spooner, F. (1994). *Curricular and instructional approaches for persons with severe disabilities.* Needham, MA: Allyn & Bacon.

Cohen, L.G., & Spenciner, L.J. (1994). *Assessment of young children.* New York: Longman Publishing Group.

Cook, R.E., Tessier, A., & Klein, M.D. (1996). *Adapting early childhood curricula for children in inclusive settings* (4th ed.). Columbus, OH: Charles E. Merrill.

Cripe, J.W. (1995). *Family-guided activity-based intervention for infants and toddlers* [Videotape]. Baltimore: Paul H. Brookes Publishing Co.

Cripe, J.W., & Graffeo, J. (1995). *Family-guided approaches to collaborative early intervention training and services (FACETS).* Parsons: Kansas University Affiliated Programs.

Deal, A.G., Dunst, C.J., & Trivette, C.M. (1989). A flexible and functional approach to developing individualized family support plans. *Infants and Young Children, 1*(14), 32–43.

Fewell, R.R., & Vadasy, P.F. (1983). *Learning through play.* Allen, TX: DLM.

Garvey, C. (1977). *Play.* Cambridge, MA: Harvard University Press.

Grace, C., & Shores, E.F. (1994). *The portfolio and its use: Developmentally appropriate assessment of young children* (3rd ed.). Little Rock, AK: Southern Association on Children Under Six.

Hanline, M.F., & Fox, L. (1994). The use of assessment portfolios with young children with disabilities. *Assessment and Rehabilitation in Exceptionality, 1,* 40–57.

Hutinger, P.L. (1994). Integrated program activities for young children. In L.J. Johnson, R.J. Gallagher, M.J. LaMontagne, & J.B. Jordan, J.J. Gallagher, P.L. Hutinger, & M.B. Karnes (Eds.), *Meeting early intervention challenges: Issues from birth to three* (2nd ed., pp. 59–94). Baltimore: Paul H. Brookes Publishing Co.

Johnson, B.H., McGonigel, M.J., & Kaufmann, R.K. (Eds.). (1989). *Guidelines and recommended practices for the individualized family service plan.* Bethesda, MD: Association for the Care of Children's Health.

Koralek, D.G., Colker, L.J., & Dodge, D.T. (1993). *The what, why, and how of high quality early childhood education: A guide for on-site supervision.* Washington, DC: National Association for the Education of Young Children.

Kostelnik, M.J., Soderman, A.K., & Whiren, A.P. (1993). *Developmentally appropriate programs in early childhood education.* New York: Macmillan.

Lidz, C.S. (1991). *Practitioner's guide to dynamic assessment.* New York: Guilford Press.

Linder, T.W. (1993a). *Transdisciplinary play-based assessment: A functional approach to working with young children* (Rev. ed.) Baltimore: Paul H. Brookes Publishing Co.

Linder, T.W. (1993b). *Transdisciplinary play-based intervention: Guidelines for developing a meaningful curriculum for young children.* Baltimore: Paul H. Brookes Publishing Co.

Martin, S. (1994). *Take a look: Observation and portfolio assessment in early childhood.* Reading, MA: Addison-Wesley.

McGonigel, M., Kauffmann, R., & Johnson, B. (1991). *Guidelines and recommended practices for the individualized family service plan* (2nd ed.). Bethesda, MD: Association for the Care of Children's Health.

Meyer, C.A. (1992). What's the difference between authentic and performance assessment? *Educational Leadership, 49*(8), 39–40.

Neisworth, J.T., & Bagnato, S.J. (1988). Assessment in early childhood special education: A typology of dependent measures. In S.L. Odom & M.L. Karnes (Eds.), *Early intervention for infants and children with handicaps: An empirical base* (pp. 23–44). Baltimore: Paul H. Brookes Publishing Co.

Newborg, J., Stock, J., Wnek, L., Guidubaldi, J., & Svincki, J. (1984). *Battelle Developmental Inventory (BDI).* Allen, TX: DLM.

Noonan, M.J., & McCormick, L. (1993). *Early intervention in natural environments: Methods and procedures.* Pacific Grove, CA: Brooks/Cole.

Notari, A., & Bricker, D. (1990). The utility of a curriculum-based assessment instrument in the development of individualized education plans for infants and young children. *Journal of Early Intervention, 14,* 117–132.

Peterson, N. (1987). *Early intervention for handicapped and at-risk children.* Denver, CO: Love Publishing.

Piaget, J. (1962). *Play, dreams, and imitation.* New York: Norton.

Rogers, C.C., & Sawyers, J.K. (1988). *Play in the lives of children.* Washington, DC: National Association for the Education of Young Children.

Rule, S. (1996). *Strategies for instruction in natural environments.* Logan: Utah State University, Center for Persons with Disabilities.

Smilansky, S., & Shefatya, L. (1990). *Facilitating play: A medium for promoting cognitive, socioemotional, and academic development in young children.* Gaithersburg, MD: Psychosocial and Educational Publications.

Snell, M.E. (1993). *Instruction of students with severe disabilities* (4th ed.). Columbus, OH: Charles E. Merrill.

Vygotsky, L.S. (1962). *Thought and language.* Cambridge, MA: MIT Press.

Vygotsky, L.S. (1967). Play and its role in the mental development of the child. *Soviet Psychology, 12,* 62–76.

ACTIVITY 1

WRITING OUTCOMES

Instructions:

1. Divide participants into small "teams" of five or six people. Team members should simulate an IFSP meeting to generate outcomes for Autry. Be sure a team member represents Katherine, Autry's mother.

2. As a team, use the "Action A will be implemented in order to accomplish Action B" approach to writing outcomes for Autry. Work to ensure the process results in outcomes that are

   - Reflective of family priorities

   - Appropriate for teaching in various settings

   - Functional and sustainable

   - Supportive of caregiver–child interactions

   - Interaction enhancing with peers and/or siblings

   - Interesting and motivating for the child

   - Developmentally appropriate

Case Study: Autry

Autry, 22 months, was referred to early intervention services after moving to Beauville with his mom, Katherine, his brother, Troy, age 13, and the family dog, Puddles. Autry received physical therapy (PT) and speech-language pathology (SLP) services at a hospital outpatient clinic three times a week in his previous program. Katherine was interested in services that would give Autry the opportunity to interact with other children yet would not conflict much with her work schedule. She also requested home visits so she and Troy could learn how to work with Autry, too.

Autry's portfolio included his baby book with photographs highlighting his progress from his premature arrival at 30 weeks and 3 pounds, 2 ounces to his current weight of 16 pounds. Eligibility of early intervention services was documented by significant delays in the motor and communication domains on the Battelle Developmental Inventory (Newborg, Stock, Wnek, Guidubaldi, & Svincki, 1984) and by his physician's diagnosis of cerebral palsy. Anecdotal records from the hospital showed progress in fine and gross motor areas with Autry currently walking with a two-wheel walker, stringing large beads, and feeding himself with a spoon with minimal spilling. The SLP reported that Autry did not verbalize in the therapy setting but used crying and hitting to communicate protests.

An Assessment, Evaluation, and Programming System (AEPS) (Bricker, 1993) curriculum-based assessment was added to his portfolio to assist in intervention planning. Using the *AEPS Family Report* and observations of Autry at play at his child care center, Katherine identified communication as her main priority for Troy's intervention so he could begin to develop friendships. She also believed that his crying and hitting were getting worse because he did not have other more effective ways to get attention and ask for things. The team agreed that continued support was necessary to maintain Autry's fine and gross motor progress. Being new to the area, Katherine requested information on resources, community programs, and parent groups. The team also prioritized transition planning for Autry. Katherine reported that Autry's preferred activities involve Troy and Puddles and being outside. The teacher from Tots and Tales Child Care Center, which Autry attends when Katherine works, identified the household and music/book centers as his favorite inside areas.

ACTIVITY 2

IDENTIFYING INTERVENTION CONTEXTS AND SERVICES

Instructions:

1. Ask participants to read the following vignette. Facilitate a large-group discussion using the questions below the vignette.

   At Autry's IFSP meeting, the team decided that he would join the Early Intervention Toddler Play Group children at the Tots and Tales Child Care Center he attends and receive bimonthly after-work home visits from the early intervention specialist. The Toddler Play Group provides integrated early intervention services to eligible children four mornings a week for 2 hours. Eight children are currently participating with three children identified as having special needs. An early intervention specialist leads each session with nursing, PT, occupational therapy, and SLP services available on a consultation basis. The SLP and PT will see Autry weekly and provide strategies for embedding his outcomes into the group activities in the playgroup, with the child care teacher, and at home. The child care center teacher agreed to incorporate learning opportunities for Autry throughout the daily routines and to participate in team planning. Troy and Puddles are anxiously awaiting a home visit so they can be involved, too!

2. As a team, debate the pros and cons of the options Autry's team chose for him.

   - Do you agree with their plan?

   - What other choices should/could have been considered?

   - What might the team consider if the Toddler Play Group were not available?

   - What are some of the potential problems that could occur with intervention occurring in so many sites across so many team members?

   - What if the PT and SLP changed on the team and were no longer willing to provide services in the child care setting? How could the team continue to plan and provide integrative therapy?

ACTIVITY 3

WRITING OUTCOMES THAT SUPPORT INTERVENTION PLANNING

Instructions:

Instruct your teams to use Autry's case study and the following example of his communication outcome to write strategies and an appropriate evaluation plan for the outcomes written in Activity 2.

Outcome Plan

Child's name: Autry
Persons responsible: Katherine (mom), Juli (SLP), Tom (early interventionist), Ruth (teacher)
Service: Early Intervention
Date: 03/01/96

Outcome statement: (What is to be accomplished?)

Autry will ask for help and indicate what he wants with gestures and vocalizations.

Strategies: (How will the outcome be accomplished? Who will be involved? When and where will the activities occur?)

Katherine and Ruth will share Autry's "best times" and routines throughout the day at the child care center and at home with Juli and Tom. Familiar routines that are fun for Autry and comfortable for Katherine and Ruth will be identified.

A team intervention activity plan will be used to share information across team members. (See Figure 13.3. on p. 346 for one example of a plan.)

During home visits, Juli will show Katherine and Troy a new strategy (e.g., modeling, pauses, choices) as appropriate that can be used to help support Autry's attempts to communicate.

The strategies will be included in daily routines using Autry's favorite toys (e.g., book, bear, train) and planned activities outdoors with Puddles and Troy.

At group time, the team will plan activities and use various naturalistic intervention strategies in routines that provide opportunities for Autry to make requests.

Katherine will post activity sheets or routine data sheets on the refrigerator for easy reference, and Ruth will include comments on Autry's communication attempts when she writes in his home–school journal.

Evaluation: (How will we know the outcome is accomplished? Who will review? When?)

Autry will gesture by pointing, waving, showing, and vocalizing for his food, toys, and materials at home and child care. Each month Juli, Tom, and Katherine will chart Autry's progress.

ACTIVITY 4

DEFINING ROUTINES

Instructions:

1. As a group, define what a routine is and list common examples on a flipchart or chalkboard. Next, ask each participant to turn to someone and identify five important routines in his or her own life. (*Important* may be defined simply as difficult to change or interrupt.) Compare similarities and differences based on personal preferences, current lifestyle, family values, logistics, and economics.

2. Take one very common routine (e.g., early morning bathroom and breakfast procedures) and have participants list in sequence the steps they follow to complete that routine. As a group, discuss how many different ways people can accomplish the same task. Ask participants to reflect on implications for practice that occurred to them as a result of this activity.

ACTIVITY 5

DELINEATING ROUTINES APPROPRIATE FOR INTERVENTION PLANS

Instructions:

1. List, as a group, typical examples of daily routines for children ages birth to 3 years. Discuss how the routines could vary in a family with six children versus two children; with extended family members as caregivers versus private child care; with a child with severe, multiple disabilities requiring assistive medical technology versus a child with a hearing loss.

2. Knowing that maintaining a family-guided approach to intervention planning requires each family to identify their preferred routines, role-play an opportunity to visit with a family to identify the specific routines that could potentially be used for intervention. Encourage the participants to look for routines that are interesting to the child, comfortable for the caregiver, completed quickly, require joint attention, involve interesting materials or desirable objects, and offer opportunities for repetition. Routines that are mutually satisfying for the child and caregiver will be undertaken with the most frequency and will meet with the greatest success.

ACTIVITY 6

ASKING THE RIGHT QUESTIONS ABOUT ROUTINES

Instructions:

1. It can be difficult to initiate a conversation with a family about their typical routines. Families new to early intervention may be suspicious of why team members are asking questions (i.e., a professional is asking questions to point out what they are doing wrong). Families may be trying to please the team and give the answers they think the team wants to hear rather than their everyday reality or they may believe the information is personal and private and choose to not respond.

2. Ask each participant to identify a family with an infant or toddler who would be willing to "practice" with them. Encourage participants to try various strategies for learning about the family's schedule and to ask the family for feedback on the different approaches.

ACTIVITY 7

CASE STUDY FOR DEFINING ROUTINES

Instructions: Read the following case study.

Case Study: Triesté and Torre

Triesté is meeting with her son's new early intervention specialist, a speech-language pathologist, to develop intervention plans. Torre, age 16 months, has just been identified with a significant bilateral hearing loss. They are scheduled to meet at the Churchill High School Child Care Center that Torre attends during the day while Triesté is in school. Triesté has her class schedule arranged to end at lunchtime. If everything goes well, Triesté and Torre get home before his naptime so Triesté has time to do her homework before she starts her evening shift as a waitress at Big Boy's at 5:00 P.M. The time that Triesté missed in school when Torre was born and had so many medical complications put her a semester behind. Now that he has a hearing problem and needs more help, she is unsure how she is going to find the time. She finds herself struggling to even get her schoolwork done and has just about given up on any hope of a scholarship for college. Working 5 hours a night at Big Boy's provides only enough money to pay for Torre's immediate needs and to pay a little back to her mother on the huge debt for medical expenses incurred at the time of Torre's birth. Triesté believes her schedule is as full as it can possibly be, and she does not want to ask her mom to do more work with Torre as she babysits him every evening. It is enough that she has to feed him, bathe him, and put him to bed after working an 8-hour shift at the factory.

The speech-language pathologist told Triesté on the phone when she set up the appointment that she would help Triesté work with Torre to learn to communicate through the use of routines and that it would be fun. Triesté does not quite see how that is going to happen!

Discussion: Ask the following questions or assign them for homework for later discussion.

- As the SLP, how would you describe the use of routines to Triesté? How would you support Triesté in using caregiver–child routines to address communication goals for Torre? How would this differ from providing individual speech therapy at the center?

- What options might be available in the natural environment for Triesté and Torre? How could you help Triesté identify the options?

- What complications in the daily schedule of Triesté and Torre must the early interventionist be especially sensitive to?

- Given this scenario, what possible routines for embedding intervention objectives could you suggest to Triesté as examples? Be creative. There is more to life than bathtime and meals!

Follow-Up: Lead participants in one or both of these activities.

- Divide the class into pairs with one member of the dyad playing the part of Triesté and the other playing the part of the SLP. Role-play the ideas you generated in your plan during the Case Study for Defining Routines for the class.

- Lead the participants in a discussion of how the planning might be different if 1) Torre had severe cerebral palsy with feeding problems instead of a hearing loss, 2) Torre were visually impaired, or 3) Torre had a diagnosis of autism.

ACTIVITY 8

DEVELOPING PLANNED ACTIVITIES

Instructions:

1. In a group discussion, pose the question, "Which comes first, the activity or the outcome?" The answer may seem very obvious: the outcome, of course. In actual practice, however, it is often the opposite. "Really cool" activities are planned based on materials available, community events, or upcoming holidays without careful consideration of their actual potential to provide opportunities for instruction.

   Explain to the participants that when planning activities, it is important to prioritize the child's intervention outcomes. The role of the early interventionist is to incorporate the outcomes into current activities or to plan activities that provide multiple opportunities for working on the targeted outcomes. It is easy to get involved in planning activities that are so fun, especially when working in small groups of toddlers, that the purpose of the activity—embedding intervention outcomes—becomes secondary to the activity. Activities that relate to themes such as pets, community helpers, and holidays often occur in preschool and community group child care settings and can be used very effectively for intervention with careful planning. Without planning, the activity may be completed without the child addressing any targeted outcomes. To ensure the activity maximizes intervention opportunities, the early interventionist working with the team should carefully examine the activity for learning opportunities.

2. Ask the participants to assume the roles of different team members (i.e., child care provider, family member, SLP, teacher) and to plan several developmentally and functionally appropriate activities for both individual children at home and for small groups of children at a child care center. Use Autry's and Torre's outcomes as examples, if needed.

3. Ask the participants to describe how their team identified activities and opportunities to embed the targets. The team may want to consider questions such as the following:

   - **Is this a preferred activity for the child?** When the activities are fun and inherently reinforcing, there is a greater probability that the child will become actively engaged and learn from them. If not, then planning may not be a good use of the team's time as the child is not likely to attend or to return to the activity. For example, making pasta necklaces can incorporate many fine motor, cognitive, communication, and social intervention outcomes if the activity is motivating and interesting to the child. If the child does not choose to spend time at table activities and prefers to play with blocks and cars, it would be better to incorporate opportunities for the child while playing with blocks and cars.

   - **Does the activity provide opportunities for the targeted outcomes without becoming contrived?** One common mistake often made when intervening in natural settings is to believe that any activity can be made into an intervention activity. For young children, it is important that the activities have an obvious and logical sequence that makes sense. They are using contextual cues and their experiences to learn; therefore, it is important to minimize unnecessary variation to include instruction on an outcome. The best rule is the following: The simpler, the better.

   - **Is this activity a part of ongoing daily activities or is it a special event?** Obviously, activities that are repeated frequently provide more opportunities for practice than special events (e.g., holiday, field trip activities) and, therefore, through repetition become familiar to the child. Activities that are repeated can also provide a framework to scaffold increasingly more difficult skill development.

- **Does the activity provide opportunities for child initiation?** Activities that provide maximum opportunities for the child to direct the play and the adult to follow will last longer and generally allow for more opportunities to practice targeted skills. Specific activities such as making a hand puppet may offer several opportunities to label objects and to make requests, to use fingers to grasp and release small objects, and to sort by size, but when the puppet is finished, the activity is logically completed. In contrast, at the water table, play can include practice on the same outcomes while floating boats, and continue when the child adds cars that sink, and still continue when wind-up fish and ducks are added. When the child takes the boats and cars to the block corner, the early interventionist can still follow the child's lead and embed instruction in the new activity.

- **Are there opportunities for peer interaction?** Play with peers provides ample reinforcement for working on targeted outcomes without the need for extrinsic reinforcers. Arranging the environment to ensure that opportunities exist for practice on targeted outcomes can facilitate child initiation and peer interaction without the need for adult direction. For example, Jacob can push the grocery cart as he practices walking with assistance to the household corner while his friends, Cara and Eric, put groceries in the cart. Adults may need to help organize the play but then need to fade their support to encourage the interactions between peers.

4. Teams may share their activity plans with each other and discuss variations that will help maintain the child's interest and help to increase complexity as the child meets the initial targeted outcomes.

ACTIVITY 9

INCREASING OPPORTUNITIES

Instructions:

This activity can be accomplished either as a team or individually.

1. Direct the participants to look at Autry's group activities (see Figure 13.2) with the intent to increase opportunities to practice his targeted outcomes. Remind the participants that the purpose of every scheduled activity is to provide learning opportunities; thus, breakfast, circle, music, story, blocks, and centers should all be considered during planning. Generate (aloud or in writing) ideas for how opportunities to practice might occur within the following activities:

   • **Setup and cleanup:** An easy but frequently overlooked strategy for increasing response opportunities is to provide opportunities for children to participate in the setup and cleanup of a routine or activity. For example, during setup children may assist in gathering and moving materials to a specified work area. Autry could carry a bucket of blocks to the center. For other children, social goals might include taking turns and interacting and cooperating with peers. Communication targets such as following directions and asking and answering questions can easily be included. At home, caregivers can include the child in setup, too. For example, Autry can get his own diaper and wipes. Cleanup offers similar response opportunities along with practice of self-help skills. Caregivers tend to preempt many opportunities for practice by having everything ready.

   • **Repetition:** Children acquire new skills through repetitive practice. Practice play occurs, for example, when children drop and retrieve items, pull to stand and fall purposefully, climb stairs, exercise sensorimotor schemes (e.g., bang blocks), and vocalize repeatedly. Repetition is easily incorporated in routines and activities with infants and toddlers simply because they enjoy it. Adding a variation to peekaboo such as blowing a kiss or making a raspberry when saying "boo" adds novelty to maintain interest and allows the interaction to be repeated again and again. Materials also support repetition in activities. Autry can vocalize and gesture to the caregiver for each block during block play rather than the caregiver giving him a bucket of blocks at one time.

   • **Imitation and role play:** Children engage in imitation and role play when they pretend to be another person or imitate the actions of another person. For example, a toddler can play the role of a parent by assisting a doll in hand washing, imitating dad stirring pudding, or driving the car like mom. Role-playing permits children opportunities to initiate and maintain interactive play, practice communication, develop problem-solving skills, and sequence actions. Use of common objects (e.g., dishes, combs, hats) facilitates role play.

ACTIVITY 10

TEACHING CAREGIVERS INTERVENTION STRATEGIES

Instructions:

There are many effective strategies for increasing response opportunities in both individual and group activities. When working in natural settings it is important not only for the early intervention specialist to know when, how, and how often to apply these strategies but also to demonstrate and explain to other caregivers how these strategies can be used. Although most strategies appear to be "common sense," the early interventionist must be cautious regarding the overuse or misuse by individuals not specifically instructed in instructional methods.

Discuss how you would teach a caregiver to use these strategies within routines and activities to practice the child's targeted outcomes. Role-play with a partner what you would say. Be sure to address the following questions:

How would you demonstrate this to a family member?
What cautions would you share?

1. **Use interesting materials:** Young children are most likely to initiate learning about the things that interest them, thus increasing opportunities for practice. Materials should be developmentally appropriate and relevant to the child's interests and routines.

    How would you demonstrate this strategy?
    What cautions are critical to share with the caregiver to ensure success?

2. **Place materials out of reach:** Placing some desirable materials within view but out of reach may encourage children to make requests to secure the materials. The effectiveness of this strategy may be enhanced by showing the child materials, naming the materials, and then waiting attentively for the child to make a request. Caregivers can use this strategy with a favorite toy or an afternoon snack.

    How would you demonstrate this to a family member?
    What cautions would you share?

3. **Give inadequate portions:** Providing small or inadequate portions of preferred materials such as blocks, crayons, or crackers is another strategy used to promote interaction. During an activity the children enjoy, caregivers can control the amount of materials available so that the children have only some of the parts needed to complete the activity. When the children use the materials initially provided, they are likely to request more from the caregiver or other children.

    How would you demonstrate this to a caregiver?
    What cautions would you share?

4. **Provide choice making:** There are occasions when two or more options for activities or materials can be presented to children. Children may be most encouraged to make a choice when one of the items is preferred. For example, the caregiver may hold up two different toys (e.g., a big red tractor and a small green block) and wait for the child to indicate his or her preference.

    How would you demonstrate this to a caregiver?
    What cautions would you share?

5. **Encourage some need for assistance:** Creating a situation in which children are likely to need assistance increases opportunities for interaction with caregivers or peers. A wind-up toy, a swing that a child needs help getting into, or an unopened bottle of bubbles are all examples of materials that can encourage interaction.

How would you demonstrate this to a caregiver?
What cautions would you share?

6. **Create silly situations:** Absurd or silly situations that violate the child's expectations can be useful to increase communication, social interaction, and problem solving. For example, an adult who playfully attempts to put a child's shoe on his or her own foot, who tries to comb his or her hair with a block, or who reads a washcloth may encourage the child to comment on the absurd situation.

How would you demonstrate this to a caregiver?
What cautions would you share?

7. **Be forgetful:** "Forgetting" can occur when the caregiver fails to provide the necessary equipment or materials or overlooks a familiar or important component of a routine or activity. Examples include not having any water in the tub at bathtime, not having cups or plates on the table for snack time, playing kickball without a "ball," or not having books for storytime.

How would you demonstrate this to a caregiver?
What cautions would you share?

14

BUILDING EFFECTIVE EARLY INTERVENTION TEAMWORK

Corinne Welt Garland
Adrienne Frank

When the Education of the Handicapped Act Amendments, PL 99-457, was enacted in 1986 and later reauthorized as the Individuals with Disabilities Education Act (IDEA), the legislation was influenced by strong support among families and within the professional community for a team approach to assessment, program planning, and service delivery. The "multidisciplinary team" defined by PL 99-457 required the "involvement of two or more disciplines or professions in the provision of integrated and coordinated services, including evaluation and assessment activities and the development of the IFSP" (IDEA Regulations, 34 CFR, Part 303.17).

However, the need to move beyond IDEA's definition of teamwork toward collaborative interaction among disciplines and agencies is clearly reflected in the professional literature of the late 1980s and early 1990s (Garland, 1994; McGonigel, Woodruff, & Roszmann-Millican, 1994; Rainforth & York-Barr, 1997) and, to a lesser extent, in the law itself. IDEA required states choosing to participate in the voluntary Part H Infants and Toddlers Grant Program to develop policies in support of interagency and interdisciplinary collaboration at state and local levels. Those policies, along with interagency agreements, have made it necessary for community-based health care, child development, education, social service, and other professionals to collaborate across agencies and disciplines and with families. The law also encouraged interdisciplinary approaches to preparing early intervention personnel (McCollum & Bailey, 1991).

This chapter offers a framework for building teamwork at both the inservice and preservice levels supported by practical resources that instructors can use. The chapter includes discussions of the nature of teamwork in early intervention, the need to prepare personnel to learn new roles on teams, and the individual and systemic characteristics that must be considered in planning for professional development. Although most of the activities included were developed for use with inservice audiences, their application to preservice settings is clear.

CHALLENGES FOR TEAM MEMBERS

Despite strong support for working as part of early intervention teams, providers are confronted by at least two obstacles to providing services. First, professionals frequently lack both the preservice and inservice preparation needed to be successful team members. Second, all too often the workplace itself serves as a barrier to interagency, interdiscipli-

363

nary, family-centered services, making it difficult for even highly skilled professionals to engage in meaningful collaboration and teamwork.

Lack of Instructional Opportunities

Professionals in research, personnel preparation, and practice have all recognized that training in teamwork is "likely to yield the greatest immediate impact on the provision of quality early intervention services" (Bailey, Simeonsson, Yoder, & Huntington, 1990, p. 34). Even the crafters of IDEA encouraged preparation of early intervention personnel on an interdisciplinary basis (McCollum & Bailey, 1991) and required states to plan for comprehensive systems of professional development.

Without a well-prepared cadre of professionals, the intent of the legislation to ensure coordinated, collaborative services for young children with disabilities will be seriously impeded; however, preservice coursework does not typically incorporate instruction in the skills needed for teamwork. Bruder and McLean (1988) found that only 10% of personnel preparation programs required coursework in the process of teamwork. Bailey et al. (1990) reported that undergraduates from a variety of intervention disciplines—special education, occupational therapy, physical therapy, speech-language pathology, social work, nutrition, and nursing—received an average of only 8.6 clock hours in teamwork and the graduate students only 11.4 clock hours. The lack of preservice instruction in teamwork is mirrored by the absence of staff development opportunities in community-based programs that provide teams and interagency groups with a chance to learn together (Bailey, 1989).

Like their colleagues in education, allied health, and human services, few physicians are prepared to be active participants on community-based early intervention teams, even though their expertise is necessary to the tasks of Child Find, assessment, and program planning for infants and toddlers with disabilities. Despite initiatives by their professional organizations, many physicians remain unaware that the infants and toddlers program of IDEA exists, let alone that it has implications for their professional practice (Cohen, Kanthor, Meyer, & O'Hara, 1990). Blackman, Healy, and Ruppert (1992) reported results of a statewide survey of pediatricians conducted by the New York State Chapter of the American Academy of Pediatrics in which only 15% of the respondents believed that they were well-informed about the infants and toddlers part of IDEA, and only 8% saw themselves as being involved in the development of the individualized family service plan (IFSP), which must include a statement of the child's physical development.

Universities struggle with internal barriers to reworking curricula to offer meaningful preparation for teamwork. Although notable exceptions exist, departmental differences in philosophies, curricula, degree requirements, competition for financial resources, and faculty positions frequently limit creative options for interdisciplinary degree programs that emphasize teamwork. Students and faculty alike "choose to enter their professions and maintain their choices based on . . . expectations about the chosen profession" (Krahn, Thom, Hale, & Williams, 1995, p. 6). Those expectations may limit their willingness to expand traditional roles in favor of teamwork. Increased specialization has created a body of professionals whom some see as being highly knowledgeable and skilled within narrow fields of study (McMahon, 1989).

Barriers to preservice preparation for teamwork are mirrored by obstacles to inservice staff development opportunities in community-based programs (Bailey, 1989). It is challenging for administrators and supervisors to plan staff development in teamwork that is appropriate to the range of knowledge and skills that both new and experienced team members bring as well as to individual learning needs and styles. Requirements for re-certification and continuing education credits frequently force people into separate disciplinary channels for inservice education rather than into programs designed to bring professionals together across disciplines to learn new skills in working together.

Organizational Barriers to Teamwork

Families and children need coordinated, collaborative services from several agencies and disciplines; however, most human services organizations have hierarchical, departmental structures that frequently separate disciplines. Departmental structures often isolate practitioners from their colleagues in other disciplines, making it difficult to establish the time and procedures needed for collaboration and communication. A service delivery system that institutionalizes the parallel functions of individual agencies and disciplines also institutionalizes, inadvertently or by design, barriers to communication, shared values and resources, and meaningful collaborative teamwork. Agencies or interagency groups needing staff development in teamwork are often hindered by the logistical barriers of varied work schedules, professional responsibilities, isolated locations, and travel distances (Ludlow, 1994).

Struggles of turf, authority, and power that occur within and across agencies compound the barriers to promoting teamwork (Garner, 1994). Social and political changes have led to increased competition for resources that have the potential to reduce and divide services. It is difficult to predict whether the battle for increasingly scarce fiscal resources will heighten the emphasis on competition or whether agencies will be forced into new, more efficient collaborative models of interaction.

Increasingly large caseloads make it difficult for teams to find time for the staff development they need to change the nature of their interactions. Personnel shortages, particularly among physical, occupational, and speech-language therapists, create unreasonably high caseloads that limit time for staff development and nurture the belief that therapists, in short supply, must focus on their traditional therapy roles rather than on the broader responsibilities of team members. High levels of staff turnover in early intervention (Hebbeler, 1994) result from low pay, social mobility, and job stress.

Although the needs of children and families often require an interagency approach to service delivery, frequent changes in membership make it especially hard for teams to establish trust, ensure communication, transfer knowledge and skills, and work together to solve problems. As personnel change, teams must repeatedly reconstitute themselves around new members, teaching them the norms, culture, and procedures that characterize their teamwork. These changes make team development a spiraling rather than linear process as experienced team members leave and are replaced by new members who may lack the most basic information about teamwork. Team members who are anxious to move forward with the development of teamwork skills may lose patience with the pace of behavioral and programmatic change slowed by the repeated loss of experienced colleagues.

To illustrate some of these challenges, vignettes drawn from three different early intervention situations typical of many communities are presented.

A private therapy practice in one community has a contract with the local early intervention team for assessment and intervention. Therapists are expected by their administrators to treat high numbers of children and to write reports for third-party payers to ensure reimbursement. Their reports contain jargon that service coordinators and parents feel is not family friendly. The pressure to see many children limits their time to meet as a team, to share information and skills with parents and other providers, and to participate in staff development related to teamwork.

A health department nurse has service coordination responsibilities for 150 families in addition to her work as coordinator of a diagnostic clinic. Families and early
childhood special educators providing early intervention services find her unwill-
ing to give the time needed to establish the close relationship of trust with the
family that characterizes successful service coordination.

A community mental health and mental retardation agency hires young, inexperienced service coordinators to serve as fiscal gatekeepers to the early intervention system, while a private, not-for-profit agency that has served children for
2 decades is responsible for implementation. Each finds the other lacking in willingness to collaborate or to share information, and both are engaged in a power
struggle with child and family at the center. For these providers, team members
in name only, staff development opportunities in teamwork are useless without
an accompanying administrative vision of and support for the systems change
that will be required.

In examining the factors that impede teamwork, and particularly the examples provided
in the previous section, it is clear that professionals who are expected to work in new
contexts with new skills and who must participate in organizational change to do so must
be given opportunities to develop those skills through both the preservice and continuing
staff development if they are to succeed. Preservice and inservice instruction cannot stand
alone in support of new team approaches to early intervention. Preservice must prepare
students for future roles as willing team members and as willing participants in organizational change. Inservice staff development must be part of a larger project of planned
change in which families, service providers, and financial and programmatic decision
makers work together to develop a vision for early intervention services and to set goals
for systems and program change. When people feel competent to do what is expected of
them, their resistance to change is diminished. Administrative support for the time it takes
for staff to learn new skills is critical to the willingness and ability of people to implement
change.

PLANNING PROFESSIONAL DEVELOPMENT FOR TEAMWORK

At both the preservice and inservice levels, the purpose of personnel preparation for
teamwork is to give early intervention providers knowledge and understanding of key
elements in the process of working as a team (Rosin, Whitehead, Tuchman, Jesien, &
Begun, 1993). Observations, internships, and practicum placements provide preservice
opportunities to see different teams at work, to examine the impact of team dynamics on
task accomplishment, and to expand students' understanding of their future roles on early
intervention teams. For community-based service providers who seek inservice opportunities to enhance their work together, both content and process of staff development should
respond to their identified needs and to the status of their team interaction, to real team
needs, and to circumstances. Whether they currently work on early intervention teams or
plan to do so in the future, adult learners will need to gain understanding of models for
team interaction; factors influencing teamwork; and strategies for decision making, problem solving, and conflict management. A simple problem-solving process can form a
structure for planning and implementing professional development in teamwork. The process for designing customized staff development in teamwork includes the following important steps: 1) define the goal through needs assessment, 2) develop and negotiate the
agenda, 3) obtain commitment to the agenda and to participation, 4) clarify expectations
and structure the environment, 5) implement professional development activities, and 6) eval-

uate the instruction. The last step serves as the needs assessment for continuing professional development. A discussion of each step in the process follows.

Define the Goal Through Needs Assessment

Setting the goal for professional development begins with determining its purpose. Have team members asked for help because of unresolved conflict on the team? Is it a new team that needs clarification of roles and procedures? Has an administrator decided that the team needs help in communication or decision making? Do preservice students need to acquire a basic understanding of concepts such as team or team dynamics? How do they perceive their own roles on early intervention teams?

One challenge for personnel developers is to use multiple measures and to tap multiple sources for needs assessment. When learning opportunities are designed for a group that already works, or wants to work, as a team, a description of current team norms is necessary. That description should include information about whether the team has a written mission statement, how the team sets and measures goals, how team members perceive the team and their individual roles, and prior staff development the team has had.

In gathering data, the instructor may collect written information from the team such as a mission statement, policies and procedures, and the program brochure. These can reveal important information about the ways in which team members work with one another and with families. Gathering information from multiple team members, including families who have received services from the team, will result in more accurate information about the participants' needs. Asking several team members about their teamwork increases their investment in staff development and its potential results. Broad participation in the needs assessment process helps teams begin the change process and decreases their hostility and resistance to proposed changes.

Several instruments can be used to assess the need for staff development in teamwork. The Team Development Scale (Dyer, 1987), the Team Effectiveness Rating Scale (Neugebauer, 1983), and the team assessment developed by Project BRIDGE (1986) can be used to measure teamwork. The Skills Inventory for Teams (SIFT) (Garland, Frank, Buck, & Seklemian, 1992) allows a team to rate its functioning in 12 areas of teamwork, using a 5-point scale (see Table 14.1). Once problem areas have been identified using the SIFT,

TABLE 14.1.   SIFT categories

- Clarity of purpose
- Cohesion
- Clarity of roles
- Communication
- Effective use of resources
- Good decision making and problem solving
- Responsibility and implementation
- Conflict resolution
- Evaluation
- Internal support
- External support for teamwork

From Garland, C.W., Frank, A., Buck, D., & Seklemian, P. (1992). *Skills inventory for teams (SIFT)*, pp. 4–8. Norge, VA: Child Development Resources; reprinted by permission.

a second section of the instrument helps the team to define needs more specifically by rating team behaviors and skills in any of the 12 categories perceived to be problematic. Simpler instruments can help the team identify needs by checking "yes," "no," or "I'm not sure" in response to statements such as "Our early intervention team needs help with . . . developing a family-centered, team assessment process" (Child Development Resources [CDR], 1995). The preservice instructor can use any of these same measures to help students rate their own skills in teamwork or to assess the teamwork observed at community programs.

Needs assessment ratings can be collected by team members or by an outside facilitator for summary and presentation as part of the inservice process. Relating the content of professional development events to needs that learners have identified creates a heightened sense of relevance for the participants. Using a needs assessment instrument both before and after a program of inservice education offers both teacher and learners a way of measuring change in how team members view the team and/or their own skills and the effectiveness of the professional development.

Needs assessments that yield numerical information offer clear summaries and are a relatively time-effective and nonthreatening approach to data collection. However, in sharing results, instructors should consider the limits of numerical data. Because mean scores may fail to represent sufficiently the perspectives of one or two strong dissenters, the presentation of a range or a distribution of scores may be helpful. For example, if a group rates the level of team cohesion as high but two members reflect that they feel little or no allegiance to the team, the team cannot ignore their alienation when planning for improved teamwork.

Numerical needs assessment data will not be as descriptive as data resulting from open-ended questionnaires, interviews, or team discussion. Simply asking each team member to identify one area for improvement and one strength of the team provides useful information on setting priorities for change. Several formats for such interviews are available for use or modification (Phillips & Elledge, 1989). Although on-site or telephone interviews can be time consuming, they offer the interviewer rich information that is especially helpful when the team is engaged in serious conflict. Transcriptions of responses can be compiled and presented to the group in such a way as to preserve confidentiality. The frequency with which major issues are identified provides information on the breadth of perceptions about teamwork.

Group interviews may be useful for teams whose members do not know each other well or do not have much time for interaction. However, only the most skilled instructor will be able to handle, in a group context, members' fears of reprisal for honesty in discussing team problems or an inclination to bypass team development activities in favor of finding immediate solutions to problems aired in the group interview.

The needs assessment allows the instructor to pinpoint and clarify learners' needs and to articulate goals for developing new skills in teamwork. For many teams, the needs assessment is an opportunity not only for planning professional development activities but also for practicing communication, decision making, and other skills needed for teamwork. Often, needs assessment and skill development, as well as process and content, are merged. (See Chapter 6 for additional discussion of these issues.)

Develop and Negotiate the Agenda

For some teams, the needs assessment process results in clearly defined agendas for team development, whereas for others priorities are divided among several team development needs. Content and methods will be influenced by needs and priorities, the length of time available for professional development, whether professional development can be provided by an individual internal to the organization or whether it requires an outside facilitator, and other logistical considerations.

The content of preservice preparation can be adjusted based on students' assessments of their needs for skill development and on their experiences with community teams. Case studies can be used to provide an inservice context to a preservice audience. Even relatively inexperienced students at the preservice level will have had some experience in teamwork—in sports; in an orchestra or band; in other extracurricular activities such as a church or synagogue group; through participating with their own families in group decision making; or in community civic, social, or political organizations. Acknowledging their experience and potential future use of teamwork skills creates relevance for adult learners who are not already part of early intervention teams (see also Chapter 11).

Obtain Commitment to the Agenda and to Participation

Inservice instructors, whether inside or external to the organization, will need to ensure that the administrators who have supervisory or programmatic responsibility for participants have sanctioned the purpose of the professional development activities and the participation of their staff and are committed to the actions that will be planned as sequelae. Instructors can submit written plans based on the needs assessment data for administrative signature across all participating agencies, or they can receive those assurances in less formal ways. A written staff development plan should specify responsibility for ensuring staff participation, including part-time staff and consultants; for authorizing and supporting, as appropriate, family participation as teachers and as learners; for supporting instructional costs; and for arranging logistics.

Having administrators participate in team development activities helps ensure their commitment and that of their staff. Their presence sends a message to service providers that administrators "endorse the activities being conducted and . . . are willing to work . . . to change program practices" (Bailey, McWilliam, & Winton, 1992, p. 75). Administrative interest can motivate participants and convey that the inservice events justify the expenditure of administrative time and resources and are important to the future of the organization. Instructors will need to ensure equal participation by all team members in activities and discussions even when administrators are present. At the same time, instructors will need to acknowledge the administrative decision-making parameters idiosyncratic to each organization and help teams cope with the realities of organizational structures. This is especially important as teams plan follow-up activities and changes in team functioning as a result of professional development activities (Winton, McWilliam, Harrison, Owens, & Bailey, 1992).

Teams will need to decide who should participate in their staff development. If the purpose is to build a team or improve team practices, participants who have the information and authority to make decisions about teamwork must be present. Teams will want to consider family members, staff from one or many agencies, and system planners at the state and local levels as potential participants. Although "ideally, the team consists of all those persons who affect or who are affected by the decisions that might be made" as a result of staff development (Winton et al., 1992, p. 50), group size affects the types of activities that can be used. Instructors will want to have some knowledge of the cultural norms and mores of the team so that expectations for participants are culturally appropriate.

The instructor at the preservice level will need to decide whose perspectives on teamwork students need to hear, considering all the sources of information that can be brought from the community into the classroom. It is as important for students entering the field to understand how administrators perceive the decision-making process as it is for them to hear from families about what they believe their role is and should be.

Bringing family members into the classroom as both instructors and learners enriches students' understanding of the early intervention team process (see Chapter 17 for more information on family participation in instruction). As team members expand their skills in airing and managing conflict productively, they can become less protective of themselves and their colleagues and more open to including families in conflict resolution. Skills in communication, decision making, and conflict resolution are essential to any team member who will participate in family-centered assessment and IFSP planning.

Groups frequently seek inservice training to identify sources of interpersonal, interdisciplinary, or interagency conflict and to improve their team relationships. Those groups may want to limit participants to those immediately involved in the conflict. Parents who are dealing with a number of stressors in their lives may experience heightened stress from participation in this kind of intense work on team building as did one Texas family who asked to be excused from a session on conflict resolution. An early intervention team in Pennsylvania decided to invite parents from another community to provide feedback on family-centered practice so that the team members would not expose the families with whom they worked to their team's conflicts.

Clarify Expectations and Structure the Environment

Successful preservice and inservice instructors will appreciate the importance of the physical and human environment and will create an atmosphere in which professional development in teamwork can succeed. The environment should be physically comfortable, setting the stage for the emotional comfort necessary for open communication. The room arrangement should be conducive to interaction so that participants can see and hear one another. When team members are in conflict, table arrangements can establish barriers and limit vulnerability. Unlike preservice education, inservice instruction is vulnerable to interruptions by beepers, telephones, and secretaries. Limiting those distractions by choosing an environment away from the workplace or by strictly honoring an agreement to refuse interruptions is important to the work of the team. Finding a site or classroom in neutral territory when conducting professional development activities with individuals from different agencies or from different disciplines may also need to be considered at both inservice and preservice levels.

Implement Professional Development Activities

The introduction to professional development can help participants understand what is expected of them and allay fears. The time in which the first participants enter the room and wait for activities to begin is typically wasted and can be altered to be more productive. This is a good time to display a flipchart or overhead with instructions such as "List five things you like about the team you work on" or "One thing I hope will change as a result of today's session is . . . ." For preservice, a statement such as "Two things that I like best about working with others are . . . " can accomplish the same purpose. Instructors can use this time to help participants focus on the task and on a positive view of their teams and themselves.

Icebreaker activities can establish a relaxed climate and help learners see their colleagues in new ways. Asking participants who do not know each other well to work in small groups to find three things they have in common and three differences among them helps people to get acquainted and to begin to see their colleagues both as unique individuals and as people not unlike themselves. Such activities work well at the beginning of a preservice course to set the tone for team learning.

Clarifying the agenda and expectations relieves anxiety and establishes a partnership of responsibility for what the instructor and the learners hope to accomplish together. The instructor is responsible not so much for ensuring that learning takes place but for what Stuart (1986) described as a facilitative role of promoting and helping the student take control of learning.

Professional development in teamwork has behavior change as its intended result. Stuart (1986) offered helpful guidelines for promoting learning that results in behavior change, including 1) acceptance by the facilitator for the climate of openness within the group, for guidance on codes of conduct, and for building group identity; 2) acceptance of the facilitator as a resource to be used by the group to clarify, organize, and promote learning; 3) awareness by the facilitator of the emotional needs of individuals within the group; 4) participation by each learner both as an individual and as a group member; and 5) acknowledgment that the learner is responsible for learning even though instructional objectives may have been determined elsewhere.

Drawing on principles of adult learning (discussed in Chapter 5), instructors will recognize that teamwork and the building of relationships cannot be taught through lecture. Although lecture can be used to present basic information or to reinforce concepts that learners may have fully or partially acquired, it must be accompanied by active-learning strategies that promote skill building and practice. In *Team Building at Its Best,* Spruell (1989) suggested the following guidelines to use in planning team-building activities: 1) choose activities that meet each team's objectives, 2) tailor activities to the conditions and needs of each team, 3) choose activities that can be managed given logistical arrangements and instructional support, 4) allow enough time not only for an activity but also for processing and discussing the results of the activity with the team, 5) try new activities before using them in training, and 6) anticipate the potential reactions of participants and be prepared for any necessary adaptations.

Several types of activities can be used to teach about teamwork. Paper-and-pencil activities that clarify team roles and values can be done by individual team members and followed by discussion in small or large groups. For example, "Who Decides" (Francis & Young, 1979), adapted by CDR's (1996) Trans/Team Outreach, provides participants with a list of decisions that early intervention teams frequently face. Participants work alone to determine how decisions are typically made by their team, ranging from authoritative to consensus-seeking modes. In the preservice context, students can use this activity to describe the methods used by teams they have observed or participated in within or outside of class. Following these activities with guided discussion in small or large groups can help learners clarify and understand their existing teamwork procedures. During discussion, the instructor may need to support the learner who is venting frustration, to manage emerging conflict, to elicit the participation of more reticent participants, and to keep the discussion focused on the agenda. Large-group discussion gives preservice students the opportunity to learn from the observations and experiences of their colleagues how a variety of community organizations make decisions.

Problem-based learning "is a teaching method that emphasizes active, student-centered learning in a small group format" (VanLeit, 1995, p. 349). Information is organized and presented as an integrated clinical problem or a case study in written form, on videotape, or in role play. For example, a written child assessment report can give a team the chance to practice reaching consensus through brainstorming, problem solving, and decision making to develop IFSP outcomes. The video *Creating a Vision: Individualized*

Family Service Plan (Colorado Interagency Coordinating Council & Colorado Department of Education, 1990) shows three short vignettes of IFSP meetings. The video can be used to have the group identify family-centered practices and brainstorm about how they might make the interactions more family centered. Project Copernicus also offers a videotape on the IFSP process that can be used in similar activities (Project Copernicus & Department for Individual and Family Resources, 1993).

Case studies in which team members engage in role play provide other opportunities for practicing the application of general principles of family-centered teamwork. Mc-William and Bailey (1993) provided more than 20 case studies in early intervention in their book *Working Together with Children and Families: Case Studies in Early Intervention.* The case "The Team Meeting" is particularly effective for generating discussion about characteristics of effective teams.

Regardless of methodology, the instructor's role is to engage participants through the use of varied learning opportunities by posing credible dilemmas and challenging the participants to respond. Instructors engage students by sharing their own knowledge to help the group clarify issues or problems, by using effective questioning skills, and by maintaining an environment that is stimulating and collegial. Bailey and colleagues (1992) observed that the skilled facilitator must be "flexible and able to think on his or her feet" (p. 79) when off-the-agenda problems arise or the emotional climate needs to be managed. Cartoons and other appropriate uses of humor can help diffuse tension and create a comfortable learning environment.

Evaluate the Instruction

Evaluating teamwork-related instruction must go beyond measuring participants' reactions. It is important to measure, over time, changes in the ways in which people work together as teams as a result of instruction (see also Chapter 7). The same instrumentation used for team needs assessment can also be used to measure outcomes. Team needs or performance before and after instruction can be examined.

Bruder and Nikitas (1992) described an inservice model that uses a variety of evaluative measures, including case studies, questionnaires, rating scales, consumer satisfaction scales, and others. Trans/Team Outreach closes each team training with the development, by the team, of a written change plan. Writing the change plan gives the team a chance to practice, with coaching and technical assistance from on-site instructors, new skills in making decisions. It provides an opportunity for the team to set priorities for improved teamwork and to choose specific strategies and time lines for implementation of its change plan. Informal follow-up interviews are helpful as are structured interviews both before and after staff development activities to measure tangible results or changes in specific team practices and to evaluate efficacy of the staff development.

Evaluation of instruction in teamwork is based on the understanding of continuing education as a catalyst for change. From its planning to its evaluation, successful professional development is based on the acknowledgment that "real change will occur only when a comprehensive, long-term, systematic approach is taken and when those who will be affected by change participate in decisions about its implementation" (Bailey et al., 1992, p. 74).

CONTENT AND RESOURCES FOR PROFESSIONAL DEVELOPMENT IN TEAMWORK

The remainder of this chapter includes a discussion of the major content areas that can be included in preparing personnel for teamwork, along with strategies and resources the instructor can use. Written needs assessments, observations of teams, interviews with key informants, and review of the team development literature have helped the authors identify six major areas in which instruction is frequently needed: 1) characteristics of an effective team; 2) definition of team mission, philosophy, and values; 3) clarification of member roles and responsibilities; 4) communication and conflict resolution; 5) decision making and problem solving; and 6) action planning and the change process.

Practical activities that can be used to teach new information and skills in each of these areas of teamwork are offered in the following sections. Many of these resources are found in the literature from the field of business leadership or organizational development and can be adapted or modified for use with early intervention teams.

Characteristics of an Effective Team

The mere existence of a group does not ensure effective teamwork. In preparing professionals and parents for teamwork, the instructor must give learners a vision of the qualities and characteristics of effective teams. Participants can often generate a lengthy list of characteristics that make a team effective, or the 12 general characteristics of effective teams used in the SIFT (Garland et al., 1992) can be used as the basis for a short lecture. Other information such as types of teams or stages of team development (Briggs, 1993) can help participants understand the complex, changing nature of teams. Activities 1–3 are designed to help learners define the characteristics of an effective team and to recognize stages in the development of teams.

Team Mission, Philosophy, and Values

Frequently, teams in the early stages of development or teams that have undergone substantial change in response to reconfiguring of service delivery systems lack a clear understanding of what it is they are to do together and what values and philosophical principles undergird their approach. Without a common understanding of mission and philosophy, the team lacks guidelines for making decisions and flounders in the critical tasks of teamwork. Questions of "Should we do this?" or "How can we do this best?" can be better answered by teams that make choices in the context of their team mission, instead, "Will this proposed action help us fill our mission of providing comprehensive early intervention services for families of children with disabilities?"

Activity 4 outlines a process for helping a team develop a mission statement. Students can examine a list of specific team or program practices for congruence with their written mission statements to learn how the mission statement can direct the work of a team.

Clarification of Member Roles and Responsibilities

Teamwork is enhanced when members understand their own and others' roles. As teams move toward more highly interactive provision of early intervention services, individual team members commit to teaching and learning from each other and to sharing roles and responsibilities based on the needs of the child and family and the skills of staff. This process is central (United Cerebral Palsy [UCP] National Collaborative Infant Project, 1976) to the transdisciplinary team model (McGonigel et al., 1994).

Team members need to know the characteristics of effective leadership and of effective team members. Parker and Kropp (1992) described an activity that asks participants to use a consensus decision-making process to rank the importance of 10 characteristics of effective team members, for example, "comes prepared," "supports other's contributions," "asks questions," or "shares ideas." Parker and Kropp also offered activities that involve asking small groups to observe behavior and provide feedback to each other. Team members work in pairs, rating their own teamwork skills and those of their partners, followed by a discussion about their roles on the team.

Dyer (1987) raised the possibility that team conflict can occur when there is a violation of role expectations. When a team asks for help in defining or clarifying job roles and responsibilities, Phillips and Elledge's (1989) module on role clarification will be useful. The module provides questions that can be used for individual role negotiation, asking an individual what he or she expects to do in his or her job, what he or she actually does, what is needed from the individual, and what the individual needs from other team members. Dyer developed a similar activity (Activity 5) to help teams eliminate discrepancies in role perceptions.

For teams needing help in identifying responsibility for leadership roles, Francis and Young (1979) offered a "Leadership Functions Check Sheet" (see Figure 14.1) that allows participants to identify who on their team performs each of 11 different leadership tasks. This activity can be adapted for both preservice and inservice instruction by asking each participant to identify the leadership tasks on the check sheet that they can perform with comfort and skill and those in which they want more practice to increase their level of skill.

If team members are ready to move beyond basic role definition to learning how to use the transdisciplinary process of role transition, instructors can use one of several activities available in the CDR Trans/Team Outreach materials (1996). The "Role Transition Examples" table is designed to increase understanding of the steps in the role transition process. This table (see Table 14.2) gives behavioral examples related to teamwork, and participants identify the step in role transition that is exemplified by each behavior. For example, given the behavior "an occupational therapist who is a specialist

---

Who on the team . . .

- brings together individual contributions?
- ensures decision making?
- begins meetings?
- checks whether objectives are set?
- ensures effective teamwork methods?
- gets the team started or unstuck?
- watches over operations?
- brings in external information?
- represents the team with other groups?
- summarizes or clarifies discussions?
- encourages contributions and/or supports members in difficult situations?

Figure 14.1. An example of a leadership functions check sheet. (Adapted from *Improving Work Groups: A Practical Manual for Team Building* [pp. 152–153, 161–162] by D. Francis & D. Young. Copyright © 1979 by Pfeiffer & Company, San Diego, CA. Used with permission.)

TABLE 14.2. Steps in role transition

Role	Description
Role extension	Self-directed study within one's own discipline
Role enrichment	Understanding basic terminology and rationale outside one's own discipline
Role expansion	Making programming judgments across disciplinary boundaries
Role exchange	Demonstrating techniques to a colleague in another discipline
Role release	Implementing, with authorization, techniques learned from a colleague in another discipline
Role support	Consultation and support or back-up therapy provided to team members across disciplines

From Child Development Resources. (1996). *Trans/Team Outreach training materials.* Norge, VA: Author; reprinted by permission.

in feeding attends a workshop on new feeding techniques," participants should correctly identify that this is an example of role extension, through which a team member increases knowledge within his or her own discipline or area of expertise. Another activity, "Daily Activities that Support Team Teaching and Learning" (CDR, 1996), helps team members identify activities during which teaching and learning can naturally take place among all members, emphasizing opportunities for family participation in the role transition process.

Communication and Conflict Resolution

Group problem solving rests on a climate that supports the free and open exchange of ideas and opinions without fear of criticism, divisiveness, or reprisal for dissent. Such a climate fosters the development of innovative, state-of-the-art treatment and program approaches (Antoniadis & Videlock, 1991; Garner & Orelove, 1994). A climate of open communication and trust is also critical to the parent–professional partnerships that are the hallmarks of family-centered teams.

There are many instruments available to help teams assess their functioning. These usually include at least one item that measures the extent to which communication on the team is characterized by openness and honesty or by guardedness and reluctance to share ideas and opinions. Dyer's Team Development Scale (1987) includes questions such as "How safe is it in this team to be at ease, relaxed, and myself?" and "To what extent do I feel 'under wraps,' that is, have private thoughts, unspoken reservations, or unexpressed feelings and opinions that I have not felt comfortable bringing out into the open?" Answers to the second, on a scale of 1–5, range from "almost completely under wraps" to "almost completely free and expressive." Francis and Young (1979) offered a Team Climate Questionnaire, which includes an item on "openness" that asks, "Are individuals open in their transactions with others? Are there hidden agendas? Are some topics taboo for discussion within the group? Can team members express their feelings about others openly?" Responses can be made on a 7-point scale from "individuals are very open" to "individuals are very guarded."

Videotapes such as *Delivering Family-Centered, Home-Based Services* (Project Copernicus, 1991) can help learners identify communication successes and problems by viewing examples of home visits or IFSP meetings. A simple but sometimes threatening way of addressing communication problems among team members is to use written messages that help members to state and address their problems. Activity 6 helps teams recognize the importance of clear communication.

Conflict is an inevitable part of working in a team and, when well managed, a positive force. Preparation for teamwork must emphasize that diverse views and perspectives are inherent in teamwork and must provide team members and leaders with ways to incorporate diverse perspectives and conflicting views in decision making and ways to use a range of ideas in creative problem solving. Finally, team members must learn a variety of productive styles and strategies for airing and managing conflict.

There are many resources available to help instructors with this topic. Clinard (1987) offered a step-by-step guide to conflict resolution that gives participants the opportunity to practice conflict resolution in role-play or real-life situations. The idea of sending a written message is a frequently used strategy, and Francis and Young provided a sample in their "From me to you, from you to me" message sheet (1979, p. 189). The message sheet provides a written framework for telling another team member, "It would be more comfortable and beneficial for me if you would . . . do the following things more or better; do (other) things less or stop doing them; continue (others); and start doing these additional things." This sheet can be given to the group as a resource for giving feedback and for handling conflict as the need occurs. Some instructors may use the form during classes or workshops as a way of having participants practice giving feedback in a supportive environment. Preservice instructors may invite feedback on their own work as a teacher, giving students another chance to practice using the form.

Francis and Young (1979) based the following activity on an idea by Roger Harrison of Development Research Associates. Message sheets are distributed to participants, who are asked to fill out one for every other team member. When the messages are completed and delivered face down, all team members read their messages and are asked to seek clarity through open discussion, asking for behavioral examples when needed. Team members are encouraged to negotiate agreements resulting in commitments such as "In the future I will . . ." (p. 188) that can be posted or recorded and distributed to the entire team as a reminder of their commitments. An extremely high level of interpersonal comfort among learners must be present to support this activity. In the absence of such trust and comfort, the instructor may instead encourage participants to use the format on a one-to-one basis, using the instructor as a resource. Conflict vignettes may also be used as the basis for less threatening role play, having the "From me to you" messages filled out by participants who play the roles of individuals in the vignettes. Case studies, such as "The Team Meeting" (McWilliam & Bailey, 1993), which illustrates a team with unresolved conflicts, are also useful catalysts for role-play activities. The video and accompanying guide *Interdisciplinary Teamwork: A Team in Name Only and Becoming an Effective Team* (Virginia Institute for Developmental Disabilities, 1992) illustrate the impact of ineffective teamwork on the family.

Phillips and Elledge (1989) offered sample flipcharts and many activities, including a conflict resolution role play. Their "Personal Definitions of Conflict" activity provides an opportunity for participants to consider their own "reactions to conflict and . . . ways of dealing with it" (p. 135). After responding to 12 open-ended statements such as "When someone disagrees with me about something important or challenges me in front of others, I usually . . ." (p. 136), participants are encouraged to work in pairs to discuss their responses. This activity helps participants understand their own and others' responses to conflict. It provides each learner with an opportunity to assess areas for personal skill development. The activity can also be used to create an awareness of how individuals respond differently to conflict and, thus, the importance of having a variety of conflict resolution strategies from which to choose. Activity 7 is also from *The Team Building Source Book* (Phillips & Elledge, 1989).

Decision Making and Problem Solving

Early intervention professionals come together because they acknowledge the advantages of group problem solving and because "a group has a greater capacity to recognize and reject poorly conceived solutions" (Rainforth & York-Barr, 1997, p. 28). However, teams frequently lack procedures for using the skills of their members in group problem-solving processes. Inservice and preservice instruction should provide team members with several strategies for group problem solving and should offer opportunities for participants to practice using new skills.

Instructors may provide information about a basic five-step problem-solving process similar to the following: 1) define the problem, 2) generate alternative solutions, 3) select alternative strategies, 4) decide and implement, and 5) evaluate and monitor solutions. Based on the needs and skills of the group, each step may need to be taught separately or can be taught in a single activity if participants have experience in group decision making.

Dyer (1987) suggested using the force field analysis problem-solving design to help team members clarify a problem or an issue. The force field method involves asking three simple questions: 1) What is our desired level of effectiveness? 2) What forces drive us toward the desired level? and 3) What forces restrain us? Once obstacles and facilitative factors in the environment are clear, the team can develop realistic and strategic plans for problem solving.

The Nominal Group Technique (Delbecq, VandeVen, & Gustafson, 1975) can help teams to practice generating solutions and setting priorities. The major steps in this procedure are working alone to write down ideas, offering and recording of ideas, clarifying ideas, ranking of strategies, and discussing the outcomes. Instructors pose problems related to early intervention service delivery or teamwork, for example, long waiting lists for physical therapy services. Participants are given the opportunity to generate creative strategies for problem solving without judgment by other team members. In practicing brainstorming techniques, instructors may want to appoint a process monitor who provides feedback, reminding people not to evaluate or discuss solutions prematurely or to provide nonverbal feedback such as rolling their eyes or nodding emphatically.

Instructors should ensure that they offer an understanding of both group and individual decision-making strategies and the advantages and disadvantages of each, particularly consensus. It is important for participants to have a good understanding of how their teams typically make decisions and to understand the parameters for acceptable change. Teams wanting to move from authoritative decisions to group decisions will need to understand that salaries, for example, are unlikely to be determined by consensus. Francis and Young (1979) provided an activity, "Who Decides," that has been adapted by Trans/Team Outreach (CDR, 1996) to help early intervention providers identify their team's typical decision-making styles. Participants circle statements that reflect how the team usually makes decisions. Three of 15 statements reflect each of five styles: 1) authoritative, 2) consultative, 3) group voting, 4) group consensus, and 5) delegated. Scores are tallied to get a group profile. As participants clarify their understanding of how their team makes decisions, they can identify areas in which collaborative group process might be more effective.

For many of the activities of early intervention teams, most especially assessment and IFSP development, the best collective judgment of the team can be reached only by open communication and by sharing perspectives and opinions. Instructors can choose from many activities designed to practice group decision making. Activity 8, adapted from *A Handbook of Structured Experiences for Human Relations Training* (Pfeiffer & Jones, 1973), can help teams practice reaching consensus using an activity of low threat to the early intervention team.

Action Planning and the Change Process

Preservice and inservice education should result in commitment by individuals and teams to make behavior change. Whether the goal of change is to increase the extent of team collaboration or family centeredness or to change the ways in which teams make decisions, it is necessary for those who serve on early intervention teams to understand the importance and nature of the change process.

In Edelman (1990), there are several activities dealing with change. In one, participants are asked to remember a time of difficult change and to draw a picture of themselves in the midst of such change. Participants are asked to look at their own pictures and to tell what they were feeling in that picture. The instructor can record the feelings on an overhead or flipchart and point out common responses to change such as fear, anxiety, anger, and isolation as well as the less frequently cited but more positive responses of hopefulness, eagerness, and excitement. Participants can be invited to tape their pictures on the walls.

Team members who already have a problem-solving framework should be able to move easily into planning for change in teamwork and in their service delivery strategies. Instructors can help teams use a consensus decision-making process to identify the results they want from their change projects. Teams can use new brainstorming skills to generate and select strategies to be used, as in Francis and Young's exercise "Creative Change" (1979, p. 249). Formats that teams can use in planning for change are found in Phillips and Elledge (1989) who suggested using action planning to bring closure to team-building training and to reinforce the progress made during. Dyer (1987) suggested that action planning should answer the following questions: 1) What specific actions should be taken to deal with (teamwork) problem areas? 2) Who should be responsible for the actions? 3) When should the actions start and end? and 4) What should be the date of the first report of results?

For teams taking on change projects, whether related to teamwork or service delivery, or in the preservice context to create an appreciation of the possibilities of positive change, the videotape *The Winds of Change* (Barr Films, 1991) is a wonderfully allegorical cartoon that brings an optimistic closure to a team-building session.

CONCLUSION

All personnel preparation, whether at the preservice or inservice level, is intended to result in changes in knowledge, attitudes, skills, or behaviors. Change is difficult for most people. Changing the ways in which people work together to provide early intervention services, similar to most change projects, is fraught with anxieties, frustrations, and fear. However, resistance to change is greatly minimized when people are confident that they will be given a chance to develop the skills needed to do new tasks or old tasks in new ways and that they will not be allowed to fail. Building skills in teamwork at both the preservice and the inservice levels is the prerequisite for the changes in early intervention service delivery that will result in coordinated, collaborative, family-centered teams.

RESOURCES

Colorado Interagency Coordinating Council & Colorado Department of Education. (1990). *Creating a vision: The Individualized Family Service Plan.* Denver, CO: Denver Early Childhood Connection. Cost: $2.40 (covers postage and handling). (303) 832-6168.

A 30-minute videotape with vignettes illustrating different applications of the IFSP process, suitable for use in inservice or preservice instruction.

Eastern Kentucky University. (1992). *The story of the goose.* Richmond: Eastern Kentucky University, Training Resource Center. Cost: $65. (606) 622-1497.

This 4-minute videotape tells the story of how geese have developed a model of teamwork and cooperation that can be an inspiration even to the most cynical.

Francis, D., & Young, D. (1992). *Improving work groups.* San Diego: Pfeiffer & Company. Cost: $34.95. (619) 578-5900.

Materials focused on the underlying concepts of working teams include 25 activities for helping teams learn to work through "blockages" and other elements that inhibit success.

Garland, C., Frank, A., Buck, D., & Seklemian, P. (1992). *Skills Inventory for Teams (SIFT).* Norge, VA: Child Development Resources. $24.95 plus postage and handling. (804) 566-3300.

An inventory of skills needed to function as a part of an early intervention team. This instrument was designed to help teams and individual team members identify key areas of need and strength regarding teamwork and can be used to complement preservice or inservice instruction. Directions and forms are provided.

Garland, C.W., McGonigel, M.J., Frank, A., & Buck, D. (1989). *Transdisciplinary arena assessment process: A resource for teams.* Norge, VA: Child Development Resources. Cost: $149.95 (videotape and print viewing guide). (804) 566-3300.

A 43-minute videotape demonstrating a six-step family-centered transdisciplinary approach to arena assessment and IFSP development. Viewing guide includes forms, activities, and materials suitable for teaching/instructing about the process as a whole or the component parts (e.g., preassessment planning).

McWilliam, P.J., & Bailey, D.B., Jr. (Eds.). (1993). *Working together with children and families: Case studies in early intervention.* Baltimore: Paul H. Brookes Publishing Co. Cost: $29 plus postage and handling. (800) 638-3775.

An edited collection of cases exemplifying the application of recommended practices in early intervention for use in preservice and inservice instruction. The text presents unsolved case dilemmas for teaching/instructing, decision making, and problem solving.

Pfeiffer, J.W., & Jones, J.E. (Eds.). (1973). *A handbook of structured experiences for human relations training* (Vol. IV). San Diego: Pfeiffer & Company. Cost: $19.95. (619) 578-5900.

A compact, portable collection of activities on teams and teamwork that are easy to use, adaptable, and reproducible.

Phillips, S.L., & Elledge, R.L. (1989). *The team building source book.* San Diego: Pfeiffer & Company. Cost: $89.95. (619) 578-5900.

Fully reproducible activities and materials for a single team-building exercise or a sequence of team-building instruction. Eleven modules of varying length (15 minutes to 3 hours) are included on aspects of teamwork, each complete with objectives, instructions, sample assessment materials, and handouts.

Project Copernicus. (1991). *Delivering family-centered, home-based services* [Videotape]. Bethesda, MD: Association for the Care of Children's Health. Cost: $98 plus shipping and handling. (301) 654-1205.

This videotape includes five vignettes, each of which illustrates what happens when service providers fail to practice family-centered priciples. Each vignette illustrates a different interaction (e.g., home-based assessment, an IFSP meeting) and provides instructors with material that can be used for awareness (i.e., identification of practices that are not family centered), knowledge (i.e., of alternative, desirable practices), and application (i.e., through role playing).

Virginia Institute for Developmental Disabilities. (1990). *Interdisciplinary teamwork: A guide for trainers and viewers.* Van Nuys, CA: Child Health and Development Educational Media. Cost: $65. (818) 994-0933.

A two-part videotape designed to illustrate and promote discussion and analysis of both positive and negative team processes (e.g., disagreement among team members, not honoring family priorities, using jargon). Viewer's guide provides background information, instructional objectives, a content outline, suggested learning activities, and discussion questions for use in preservice or inservice instruction.

REFERENCES

Anoniadis, A., & Videlock, J.L. (1991). In search of teamwork: A transactional approach to team functioning. *Infant and Toddler Intervention, 1*(2), 157–167.

Bailey, D.B., Jr. (1989). Issues and directions in preparing professionals to work with young handicapped children and their families. In J.J. Gallagher, P.L. Trohanis, & R.M. Clifford (Eds.), *Policy implementation and PL 99-457: Planning for young children with special needs* (pp. 97–132). Baltimore: Paul H. Brookes Publishing Co.

Bailey, D.B., McWilliam, P.J., & Winton, P.J. (1992). Building family-centered practices in early intervention: A team-based model for change. *Infants and Young Children, 5*(1), 73–82.

Bailey, D.B., Simeonsson, R.J., Yoder, D.E., & Huntington, G.S. (1990). Preparing professionals to serve infants and toddlers with handicaps and their families: An integrative analysis across eight disciplines. *Exceptional Children, 57*(1), 26–35.

Barr Films. (1991). *The winds of change* [Videotape]. Irwindale, CA: Barr Training and Development Films/Videos.

Blackman, J.A., Healy, A., & Ruppert, E. (1992). Participation by pediatricians in early intervention: Impetus from P.L. 99-457. *Pediatrics, 89,* 98–102.

Briggs, M.H. (1993). Team talk: Communication skills for early intervention teams. *Journal of Childhood Communication Disorders, 15*(1), 33–40.

Bruder, M.B., & McLean, M. (1988). Personnel preparation for early interventionists: A review of federally funded projects. *Journal of the Division for Early Childhood, 12*(4), 299–305.

Bruder, M.B., & Nikitas, T. (1992). Changing the professional practice of early interventionists: An inservice model to meet the service needs of P.L. 99-457. *Journal of Early Intervention, 16*(2), 173–180.

Child Development Resources (CDR). (1995). *Trans/Team Outreach needs assessment instrument.* Unpublished. (Available from Child Development Resources, Post Office Box 280, Norge, VA 23127-0280)

Child Development Resources (CDR). (1996). *Trans/Team Outreach training materials.* Unpublished. (Available from Child Development Resources, Post Office Box 280, Norge, VA 23127-0280)

Clinard, H. (1987). *Winning ways to succeed with people.* Houston, TX: Gulf Publishing.

Cohen, H., Kanthor, H., Meyer, M.R., & O'Hara, D. (1990). *American Academy of Pediatrics Survey: District II*. Valhalla: New York Medical College, The Mental Retardation Institute.

Colorado Interagency Coordinating Council & Colorado Department of Education. (1990). *Creating a vision: Individualized family service plan* [Videotape]. Littleton, CO: Mile High Down Syndrome Association.

Delbecq, A.L., VandeVen, A.H., & Gustafson, D.H. (1975). *Group techniques for program planning: A guide to Nominal Group and Delphi processes*. Glenview, IL: Scott, Foresman.

Dyer, W. (1987). *Team building: Issues and alternatives*. Reading, MA: Addison-Wesley.

Education of the Handicapped Act Amendments of 1986, PL 99-457, 20 U.S.C. §1400 *et seq.*

Edelman, L. (1990, July). *Developing change agent skills: Keeping a "people focus" during organizational change*. Paper presented at Child Development Resources' Summer Institute, Williamsburg, VA.

Francis, D., & Young, D. (1979). *Improving work groups: A practical manual for team building*. San Diego: Pfeiffer & Company.

Garland, C.W. (1994). World of practice: Early intervention programs. In H.G. Garner & F.P. Orelove (Eds.), *Teamwork in human services: Models and applications across the life span* (pp. 89–113). Newton, MA: Butterworth-Heinemann.

Garland, C.W., Frank, A., Buck, D., & Seklemian, P. (1992). *Skills Inventory for Teams (SIFT)*. Norge, VA: Child Development Resources.

Garland, C.W., McGonigel, M.J., Frank, A., & Buck, D. (1989). *Transdisciplinary arena assessment process: A resource for teams*. Norge, VA: Child Development Resources.

Garner, H.G. (1994). Critical issues in teamwork. In H.G. Garner & F.P. Orelove (Eds.), *Teamwork in human services: Models and applications across the life span* (pp. 1–15). Newton, MA: Butterworth-Heinemann.

Garner, H.G., & Orelove, F.P. (Eds.). (1994). *Teamwork in human services: Models and applications across the life span*. Newton, MA: Butterworth-Heinemann.

Hebbeler, K. (1994). *Shortages in professionals working with young children with disabilities and their families*. Chapel Hill, NC: NEC*TAS.

Krahn, G.L., Thom, V.A., Hale, B.J., & Williams, K. (1995). Running on empty: A look at burnout in early intervention professionals. *Infants and Young Children, 7*(4), 1–11.

Ludlow, B.L. (1994). Using distance education to prepare early intervention personnel. *Infants and Young Children, 7*(1), 51–59.

McCollum, J.A., & Bailey, D.B. (1991). Developing comprehensive personnel systems: Issues and alternatives. *Journal of Early Intervention, 15*(1), 57–65.

McGonigel, M.J., Woodruff, G., & Roszmann-Millican, M. (1994). The transdisciplinary team: A model for family-centered early intervention. In L.J. Johnson, R.J. Gallagher, M.J. LaMontagne, J.B. Jordan, J.J. Gallagher, P.L. Hutinger, & M.B. Karnes (Eds.), *Meeting early intervention challenges: Issues from birth to three* (2nd ed., pp. 95–131). Baltimore: Paul H. Brookes Publishing Co.

McMahon, B. (1989). Teamwork: A complete service with specialist skills. *Professional Nurse, 4*, 433–435.

McWilliam, P.J., & Bailey, D.B., Jr. (Eds.). (1993). *Working together with children and families: Case studies in early intervention*. Baltimore: Paul H. Brookes Publishing Co.

Neugebauer, R. (1983, November). Team effectiveness rating scale. *Child Care Information Exchange, 4*.

Parker, G.M., & Kropp, R.P. (1992). *50 Activities for team building*. Amherst, MA: HRD Press.

Pfeiffer, J.W., & Jones, J.E. (Eds.). (1973). *A handbook of structured experiences for human relations training* (Vol. IV). San Diego: Pfeiffer & Company.

Pfeiffer, J.W., & Jones, J.E. (Eds.). (1975). *A handbook of structured experiences for human relations training* (Vol. V). San Diego: Pfeiffer & Company.

Phillips, S.L., & Elledge, R.L. (1989). *The team building source book*. San Diego: Pfeiffer & Company.

Project BRIDGE. (1986). *Decision-making for early services: A team approach*. Chicago, IL: Center for Educational Development & Project BRIDGE, American Academy of Pediatrics.

Project Copernicus. (1991). *Delivering family-centered, home-based services* [Videotape]. Baltimore: Kennedy Krieger Institute, Project Copernicus.

Project Copernicus. (1993). *Family and the IFSP process: Training in family-centered approaches* [Videotape]. Baltimore: Kennedy Krieger Institute, Project Copernicus, Department for Individual and Family Resources.

Rainforth, B., & York-Barr, J. (1997). *Collaborative teams for students with severe disabilities: Integrating therapy and educational services* (2nd ed.). Baltimore: Paul H. Brookes Publishing Co.

Rosin, P., Whitehead, A., Tuchman, L., Jesien, G., & Begun, A. (1993). *Partnerships in early intervention: A training guide on family-centered care, team building, and service coordination.* Madison: University of Wisconsin–Madison, Waisman Center.

Spruell, G. (Ed.). (1989, January). *Team building at its best.* Alexandria, VA: ASTD Infoline Series.

Stuart, R.R. (1986). Promoting adult learning. *Programmed Learning and Educational Technology, 23,* 253–258.

United Cerebral Palsy (UCP) National Collaborative Infant Project. (1976). *Staff development handbook: A resource for the transdisciplinary process.* New York: Author.

VanLeit, B. (1995). Using the case method to develop clinical reasoning skills in problem-based learning. *The American Journal of Occupational Therapy, 49*(4), 349–353.

Virginia Institute for Developmental Disabilities. (1992). *Interdisciplinary teamwork: A team in name only and becoming an effective team member* [Videotape]. Van Nuys, CA: Child Health and Development Educational Media.

Winton, P.J., McWilliam, P.J., Harrison, T., Owens, A.M., & Bailey, D.B. (1992). Lessons learned from implementing a team-based model for change. *Infants and Young Children, 5*(1), 49–57.

Woodruff, G., & McGonigel, M.J. (1988). Early intervention team approaches: The transdisciplinary model. In J.B. Jordan, J.J. Gallagher, P. Hutinger, & M.B. Karnes (Eds.), *Early childhood special education birth–3* (pp. 163–182). Reston, VA: Council for Exceptional Children.

ACTIVITY 1

TEAMS YOU HATE

Objective:

• To help clarify the characteristics of effective teams

Time:

45–60 minutes depending on team size

Materials:

• Blank flipchart

• Markers

• List of characteristics of effective teams

Content review:

Not applicable. This is a good introductory activity that draws on the participants' experiences and helps them clarify the qualities they need for teamwork to succeed.

Instructions:

1. Tell participants that almost everyone has had some teamwork experience, whether on the job or in personal life—as a member of a committee; a PTA or church or synagogue board, youth group, sorority, fraternity or social organization; an interagency team; or even as part of a family decision-making process. The activity leader who knows something about the work experience of the participants will be able to choose the most meaningful examples.

2. Ask participants to think about the team they belonged to that they most disliked, the one whose meetings they dreaded attending. Ask them to reflect on those times and to remember what about the team they so disliked. Record their feelings on the chart or overhead.

3. The list can then be used to introduce, by comparison, the qualities of effective teams, pointing to the specific examples the participants gave and contrasting the behaviors of smooth-functioning and poorly functioning teams. For example, "Remember the team that you hated because all they did was talk and no one ever made a decision? Well the effective team is one in which the team has clear-cut procedures for making decisions and for assigning responsibility to ensure that decisions made are implemented."

Activity 1 is from Child Development Resources. (1996). *Trans/Team Outreach training materials.* Unpublished. (Available from CDR, Post Office Box 280, Norge, VA 23127-0280)

ACTIVITY 2

THE PUZZLE OF EFFECTIVE TEAMWORK

Objective:

- To increase knowledge of types of teams and characteristics of effective teams

Time:

45–60 minutes

Materials:

- Pictures of teams from magazines, for example, baseball team, Boy Scout group, cheerleaders, orchestra or band, SWAT team, firefighters, or surgical team, all glued onto cardboard and cut into 3-, 4-, or 5-piece puzzles.

- Flipchart, overhead, or worksheet given to each participant with the following questions:

  What type of team is represented by the picture in the puzzle: task team, decision-making team, or support team?

  Why does this team work together?

  Is there a designated leader? What kind of leadership is needed for this team to function?

  How dependent are team members on one another?

  What are two or three other characteristics that make a team effective?

Content:

Before this activity, the activity leader should introduce the definition of a team and descriptions of types of teams. A simple team definition is a group with a reason for working together, interdependent and committed to a cause. Types of teams include task, decision-making, and/or support team.

Instructions:

1. Count participants. Shuffle and distribute puzzle pieces, one to each participant, telling them they have pieces of puzzles that represent working teams.

2. Ask participants to assemble the puzzles by finding the participants who hold other pieces and putting the puzzle together. Have them work in small groups to answer the questions.

3. The small groups can share their responses in the large setting if time allows.

Activity 2 is from Child Development Resources. (1996). *Trans/Team Outreach Training Materials.* Unpublished. (Available from CDR, Post Office Box 280, Norge, VA 23127-0280)

ACTIVITY 3

TEAM DEVELOPMENT WHEEL

Objective:

- To help the participants determine the characteristics of their teamwork and to place their team on a continuum of team development

Time:

30 minutes

Instructions:

Before this activity, the activity leader should introduce the definition of a team and stages of team development (Briggs, 1993).

1. Place the team development wheel shown below on an overhead and distribute as individual handouts.

2. Ask individual team members to make a mark that places their team on the continuum of team development.

3. Have the members work in small groups to discuss where they placed their team and why, giving specific examples of team behaviors.

TEAM DEVELOPMENT WHEEL

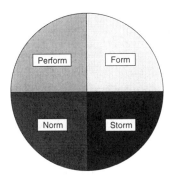

Activity 3 is adapted from Francis and Young (1979) who suggested placing a slightly different version of the team development wheel on a large flipchart and having each team member mark his or her rating directly on the chart. Each team member is asked, in the large group context, to explain his or her appraisal, giving specific examples. The facilitator helps the team to come to consensus about the developmental status of the team and to plan activities to help the team move forward in development.

ACTIVITY 4

DEVELOPING A MISSION STATEMENT

Objective:

To help a team develop a draft mission statement or to clarify its understanding of its existing mission statement

Time:

Minimum of 60 minutes to several hours, depending on clarity of purpose and whether the desired outcome is a written mission statement

Materials:

- Paper and pencils for each participant
- Flipchart, paper, markers, and masking tape

Content review:

Before this activity, the activity leader should introduce the concept of mission as an enduring and broad purpose of a team that is distinct from goals that apply to a fixed period of time and that is revised as it is accomplished.

Instructions:

1. As a full team or in small groups of fewer than eight members, ask participants to write a draft mission statement that describes what the team does and for whom. The mission statement should reveal the team's values and identify how the team relates to children, families, team, agency, and/or community. For example, CDR's mission is to provide services to young children with special needs and their families and to provide training and technical assistance for the professionals who serve them.

2. Ask each group to write a one-sentence statement of the mission of the team on flipchart paper and to post it on the wall.

3. Review each of the statements with the full group to identify common elements of all statements and underline these in the same color marker. The team may need assistance from the instructor in seeing commonalities.

4. Ask the team to identify those statements that appear to be conflicting or inconsistent among the statements (e.g., to serve children or to serve children with disabilities) and underline those in another color.

5. Lead the team in discussion to help it resolve discrepancies in the statements of mission until there is consensus around key points in the mission statement. If the team had a mission statement before it started, compare its work product with its existing statement, trying to resolve discrepancies.

6. Depending on the complexity of the task, the activity leader can bring closure by drafting a mission statement for consideration by the group, appointing a work group made up of one member from each of the previous subgroups to develop the draft, or asking the team to work on the mission statement before the next teamwork session.

7. Ask the team whose approval it will need to have for its mission statement, and develop a plan for securing that approval.

Activity 4 is from Child Development Resources. (1996). *Trans/Team Outreach Training Materials.* Unpublished. (Available from CDR, Post Office Box 280, Norge, VA 23127-0280)

ACTIVITY 5

ROLE EXPECTATIONS / CLARIFICATION DESIGN

Objective:

- To clarify job roles and responsibilities

Time:

Average time of 15–20 minutes for each role discussed. The first few may take longer than subsequent role discussions.

Instructions:

1. Ask one person on the team to volunteer to be the focus of the activity to start.

2. Ask the focal person to describe his or her role.

3. Ask the team members to tell the focal person how they perceive his or her role.

4. The activity leader helps the team come to agreement on the focal person's role.

5. Ask the focal person to tell the team what he or she needs from the team to perform the job.

6. Help the team reach consensus about the redefined role of the focal person.

The sources of Activity 5 are Dyer (1987) and Phillips and Elledge (1989).

ACTIVITY 6

TEAM-BUILDING ACTIVITY

Objective:

- To recognize the importance of clear and open communication in work groups

Time:

45–60 minutes

Materials:

- Several sets of Legos, Tinkertoys, or other colored building blocks

Instructions:

1. Divide participants into groups of 10–12 people, and divide each of those groups in two: architects and builders. The builders are asked to wait in another room. A time limit is set for each of the tasks.

2. Architects are given the necessary pieces, all the same color, and are told that they have 20 minutes in which to develop written instructions for assembling struc- ture out of the building materials for the builders. The architects may not touch the building pieces.

3. The builders' job is to assemble the structure according to the architects' plans within a specified time.

4. Architects are told that they may not talk to the builders. Architects observe how their plans are carried out by the builders.

5. After completion, large-group discussion emphasizes the importance of com- munication. The activity leader may ask, "How did builders feel when they were asked to leave the room?" Architects may be asked, "How did you feel when the builders came in and said 'Aren't you ready for us yet?'" Discussion may also be used to create an awareness of the ways in which arbitrary regulations unnecessarily hamper teamwork and of the need of teams to question and chal- lenge, when possible, those regulations. The activity informs participants about problems that may arise when policy makers or administration develops a plan or program without input from the service providers who will implement it.

Activity 6 is adapted from *A Handbook of Structured Experiences for Human Relations Train- ing,* vol. V, by J.W. Pfeiffer & J.E. Jones. (eds.). Copyright © 1975 by Pfeiffer & Company, San Diego, CA. Used with permission.

ACTIVITY 7a

CONFLICT MANAGEMENT STYLES

Objective:

- To recognize preferred styles of conflict management

Time:

45–60 minutes with discussion

Materials:

- Worksheet on the following page
- Pencils
- Additional worksheets can be found in Phillips and Elledge (1989)

Instructions:

1. Distribute worksheet(s) to small groups of fewer than eight participants.

2. Ask participants to rank the alternative courses of action on the worksheet, from the most to the least desirable way of dealing with the conflict situation. Rank the most desirable course of action "1," the next most desirable "2," and so forth, ranking the least desirable or least appropriate action "5."

3. When the large group reconvenes, discuss the experiences of participants. For example, ask, "What influenced your decision about the best course of action?" or "When would you choose a different strategy?"

Variations:

Have participants choose partners with whom to discuss their results and their responses to situations; or ask participants to share, with partners, behavioral examples of how they use their dominant conflict management style within the teamwork context. Another adaptation is found in Parker and Kropp's (1992) *50 Activities for Team Building*. Participants rate the team's dominant mode of conflict management and place their ratings on a large graph on a flipchart. The activity leader can help the team consider individual perceptions and reach consensus about the team's style of conflict management.

Activity 7a was originally adapted from *The Team-Building Source Book* by S.L. Phillips & R.L. Elledge. Copyright © 1989 by Pfeiffer & Company, San Diego, CA. Used with permission.

Activity 7a is from Child Development Resources. (1996). *Trans/Team Outreach Training Materials.* Unpublished. (Available from CDR, Post Office Box 280, Norge, VA 23127-0280)

Additional worksheets can be found in Phillips and Elledge (1989).

ACTIVITY 7b

CONFLICT MANAGEMENT STYLES ACTIVITY WORKSHEET

Instructions:

Your task is to rank the five alternative courses of action with the case below from the most desirable or appropriate way of dealing with the conflict situation to the least desirable. Rank the *most* desirable course of action "1," the next most desirable "2," and so forth, ranking the *least* desirable or least appropriate action "5." Enter your rank for each item in the space next to each choice.

Jacqueline is the coordinator of an early intervention program. Recently she noticed that one of the staff from another program in the same agency has been coming over and talking to one of her staff (*not* on break time). The efficiency of Jacqueline's staff member seems to be falling off, and there have been some deadlines missed due to her inattention. Jacqueline thinks she detects some resentment among the rest of the staff. If you were Jacqueline, you would

_____ A. Talk to your staff member and tell her to limit her conversations during on-the-job time.

_____ B. Ask the agency director to tell the coordinator of the other project to keep her staff in line.

_____ C. Confront both staffers the next time you see them together (as well as the other coordinator, if necessary), find out what they are up to, and tell them what you expect of your staff members.

_____ D. Say nothing now; it would be silly to make something big out of something so insignificant.

_____ E. Try to put the rest of the staff at ease; it is important that they all work well together.

_____ F. OTHER: _____
_____

Activity 7b is from Child Development Resources. (1996). *Trans/Team Outreach Training Materials.* Unpublished. (Available from CDR, Post Office Box 280, Norge, VA 23127-0280)

ACTIVITY 8
CONFLICT MANAGEMENT STYLES

Objective:
- To practice and examine the process of reaching consensus

Time:
45–60 minutes

Materials:
- Trustworthiness of Occupations Worksheets
- Pencils

Content review:
Review the definition of consensus and the rules for reaching consensus. Consensus means that the "right" answer is the best collective judgment of the team. The purpose is not to argue or to win but to use conflict productively. Each member must accept responsibility for hearing and being heard. In consensus, there is no voting and no horse trading. Voting only measures the surface opinion of the majority. Horse trading or bartering is concession rather than true sharing.

Instructions:
1. Participants should work alone for 5–10 minutes to rank 15 occupations: clergy, used-car salesperson, auto mechanic, physician, college professor, army general, TV repairperson, labor union organizer, corporate executive, auto mechanic, judge, politician, news reporter, lawyer, and police officer. The rank order should be the same order of trustworthiness that they think 400 people in a university study used, from "1," most trusted, to "15," least trusted.

2. After the rankings are complete, participants work in small groups of 3–5 people. Each group must choose a timekeeper, spokesperson, and recorder and work to achieve consensus on a rank-ordered list.

3. Small groups discuss the following questions: What helped the process? What impeded the process? Who was influential and in what ways? How did the group discover and use its resources?

4. Spokespersons from each of the groups report on their experiences to the large group.

Note:
In Volume IV of Pfeiffer and Jones (1973), there is a variety of similar activities on pages 58–67, including "Life Crisis" and "Dating Preference" worksheets.

Variations:
Trans/Team Outreach (CDR, 1996) has created two adaptations. The "Waiting List Worksheet" is a scenario in which an early intervention program with a waiting list considers options for dealing with a referral of a child who has a diagnosed condition that will make her eligible. Working as above, the teams must reach consensus on the ranking of the range of options. A values clarification activity gives the team another chance to practice reaching consensus around the values that drive early intervention services.

Activity 8 is adapted from Pfeiffer and Jones (1973).

15

PREPARING PRACTITIONERS TO PROVIDE EARLY INTERVENTION SERVICES IN INCLUSIVE SETTINGS

Susan Kontos
Karen Diamond

Including children with disabilities in environments with typically developing children (inclusion) is becoming increasingly common, partly in response to legislation that supports this model of providing early education services (Bricker, 1995). Development of professional skills that support inclusion has been added to the large cluster of competencies that typically define early intervention and early childhood education as professions. As have other changes in service delivery models in the 1990s, such as family-centered practices and interdisciplinary teaming, inclusion requires practitioners to develop new skills and strategies that can be applied to the process of providing specialized early childhood services. Ultimately, inclusion involves teamwork with practitioners from multiple disciplines and an evolving cycle (not a finite set) of concerns and priorities.

Although preparing personnel to function as skilled professionals or paraprofessionals is not an easy task, preparing them to engage in the complex process of inclusion becomes a special challenge. The context for early intervention/early childhood education personnel preparation changes when the focus moves from narrower, more "specialized" topics (e.g., positioning) to preparation for inclusion. Moreover, the lack of a tradition of education for inclusion means that instructors (inservice and preservice) must use common sense and educated guesses about the best approach rather than official pronouncements of recommended practice or other knowledge-based forms of guidance.

This chapter examines issues in helping practitioners learn the skills they need to work in inclusive early childhood settings by examining different theoretical frameworks and service delivery models and the ways in which these models may influence the educational needs of practitioners. Related contextual issues that affect preparation of teachers, therapists, and other staff for inclusive programs, including staffing and training issues, are considered. Next, the collective wisdom of nine experts on preservice and/or inservice personnel preparation for inclusion, interviewed for this chapter, are presented. Concrete

The authors of this chapter express their appreciation to the following people who agreed to be interviewed for this chapter: Michael Conn-Powers, Indiana University; Dale Fink, University of Illinois; Corinne Garland, Child Development Resources; Lynn Hartle, University of Florida; Judith Niemeyer, University of North Carolina–Greensboro; Patricia Snyder, Louisiana State University Medical Center; Vicki Stayton, Western Kentucky University; Patricia W. Wesley, University of North Carolina at Chapel Hill; and Barbara Wolfe, University of Wisconsin–Eau Claire.

suggestions and recommendations are provided on how to prepare personnel and for what they should be prepared. Finally, the infrastructure needs for systematically preparing personnel to support inclusionary practices are discussed.

ISSUES AND CHALLENGES IN PREPARATION FOR INCLUSION

Theoretical Frameworks

Successful inclusion of children with disabilities in regular early childhood classrooms involves practitioners from many disciplines, including some who have not traditionally practiced in classroom settings (e.g., physical therapists, speech-language pathologists). Although inclusion can take place in settings other than classrooms (e.g., swimming lessons, day camp), classrooms have received the majority of attention and effort concerning recommended practices in inclusion. Consequently, many of the challenges in instructing for and implementing inclusion are a result of varying familiarity with and differing assumptions about how children with disabilities should be served in classroom settings. These differences are reflected in the debates about recommended practice in early intervention that have taken place among educational practitioners (Carta, Schwartz, Atwater, & McConnell, 1991; Strain et al., 1992). Even though these differences have been debated primarily in educational arenas, they serve as an important backdrop for preparing any practitioner for inclusion, regardless of discipline.

Although differences in assumptions between general and special early childhood educators about recommended practices seem to be diminishing, there is no question that historically there have been major differences that continue to influence practitioners. Early childhood special education grew from a recognition of the importance of providing intervention for children with disabilities to prevent, or reduce, the impact of a disability on a child's future development. In general, "the implicit assumption within [early childhood special education] programs [has been] that the disability of the child prevents him or her from taking advantage of the typical environmental experiences that promote normal child development" (Odom & McEvoy, 1990, pp. 51–52). This assumption has been reflected in teaching practices, especially the behavioral orientation of special education that has given rise to a traditional teacher-centered approach emphasizing preacademic and adaptive skills (Wolery & Brookfield-Norman, 1988). Consequently, early childhood special education approaches have emphasized the importance of a range of services, individualized teaching plans (Odom, Skellenger, & Ostrosky, 1993), and instructional methodologies that result in skill acquisition and make the "best use of instructional time," while using "the least intrusive and most natural techniques" (Carta et al., 1991, p. 5).

In contrast, developmentally appropriate early childhood practices have grown from research with typically developing children and have reflected practices designed for children without disabilities (Bredekamp & Copple, 1997). The maturationist and constructivist underpinnings of early childhood education have led to more child-centered environments in which play, rather than direct instruction, is the medium for learning (DeVries & Kohlberg, 1987; Rogers & Sawyers, 1988).

Thus, views of recommended practice by these two sister disciplines have been at odds with each other. Despite converging viewpoints brought about by approaches that bridge the two disciplines (e.g., activity-based intervention; Bricker & Cripe, 1992), there remain significant concerns in the early intervention field regarding the viability of child-centered approaches for young children with disabilities (Carta et al., 1991) and little room for behavioral approaches to any aspect of early childhood education in the guidelines for developmentally appropriate practice (Bredekamp & Copple, 1997). In addition, as Janet in the vignette in Chapter 1 learned, education that focuses on traditional approaches to providing therapies does not adequately prepare therapists who will be expected to provide specialized treatment for young children with disabilities in inclusive settings. Integrating special therapies within activity-based options in early childhood classrooms is advocated as recommended practice in early intervention (McLean & Odom, 1988). Out-of-the-room treatment continues to be the predominant model, however, for providing therapy to young children with disabilities in early childhood programs (Graham & Bryant, 1993). It is clear that the challenge is to develop effective programming for all children that incorporates the strengths of multiple disciplines and practitioners working in early intervention and early childhood education. When this challenge has been met, education for professionals working in inclusive programs will be easier because no discipline will feel the need to compensate for the perceived limitations of another.

Evolving Models of Inclusion

Partly as a consequence of these theory- and discipline-based differences in approaches to working with young children, numerous models of inclusion or mainstreaming have been offered since the mid-1970s. These models have evolved as greater numbers of children with disabilities are receiving services in general early childhood settings and as the disciplines involved in providing these services have developed more compatible worldviews. The models reflect differences in underlying philosophies and theoretical approaches to early childhood education and early intervention as well as reflecting differences in goals for children.

When programs have adopted a behavioral or therapeutic approach, it is likely to be associated with teacher-directed, formal instructional approaches (cf. LEAP; Hoyson, Jamieson, & Strain, 1984). In many programs that reflect this behavioral approach, children with disabilities receive intervention services within a segregated setting containing relatively small numbers of children with disabilities and participate for only a portion of the day in a setting with typically developing peers. In some cases, inclusion in a preschool or child care program has been designed to supplement the child's participation in a special education program, without any specific intervention goals (Safford, 1989). Often, the "mainstream" portion of the day focuses on developing social, peer-related skills, whereas cognitive, language, and motor development are emphasized in the self-contained special education class (Klein & Sheehan, 1987; Kontos & File, 1993). Mainstreamed experiences have also included reverse mainstreaming programs in which a relatively small percentage of typically developing children are placed in classes for children with disabilities (Odom & McEvoy, 1990). In some programs, typically developing children have received special instruction as peer tutors or instructors for their classmates with disabilities (Strain, 1981). In both of these instances, the typically developing child has been included in the classroom to facilitate specific behavior changes in children with disabilities, either by serving as a model of age-appropriate behavior or by serving in the role of teacher for a child with disabilities (Young, 1981). These approaches to serving children with disabilities and typically developing children together are likely to use pull-out approaches to therapy.

Alternatively, mainstreamed or integrated approaches that have grown out of early childhood education traditions have emphasized developmentally appropriate practices for all young children. Developmentally appropriate practice approaches, which serve as the framework for teaching in many early childhood programs, emphasize the processes through which children acquire new knowledge and information, rather than assessing the child's performance on specific tasks (Bredekamp & Rosegrant, 1992). General early childhood programs may include specialized interventions, but often many do not because of a lack of funds or specially prepared staff. Therapies may be used by families separately from the classroom program as an "add-on." Thus, the focus in these programs has often been on allowing children to choose activities and to participate in the way that they prefer, without as much attention to individual goals and objectives. Each of these approaches is compatible with the history and theoretical models used in these two fields.

Inclusive programs are different from the models previously described. The goal in inclusion is to preserve individualized approaches to developing goals and objectives and assessing outcomes for children with disabilities while maintaining developmentally appropriate practices for all children. Changes in both general and special early childhood education since the late 1980s are making this type of inclusive program more feasible. Teaching strategies in early childhood special education have begun to move from directive, instructionally oriented approaches to those in which adults emphasize responsive, child-initiated styles (Mahoney, Robinson, & Powell, 1992; Odom et al., 1993). As changes have occurred in early intervention programs, they have been reflected in the ways in which specialized therapies are provided to young children in those programs. Integrating specialized therapies within ongoing classroom activities or providing therapy as an add-on to the school day are models that support inclusion (Peck, Furman, & Helmstetter, 1993).

Not only have there been changes in early intervention approaches, but the early childhood education field has begun to expand definitions of developmentally appropriate practices, particularly in the context of the needs of individual children, including children with disabilities. Such changes in early childhood education and early intervention, in conjunction with recent legislation (e.g., the Education of the Handicapped Act Amendments of 1986, PL 99-457, and its amendments; the Americans with Disabilities Act [ADA] of 1990, PL 101-336), make inclusion an increasingly common experience (Wolery et al., 1993). The definition of inclusion typically involves a child with disabilities receiving comprehensive services in a developmentally appropriate program side-by-side with typical children and participating in the same activities, with adaptations to those activities (or the child's involvement in them) as needed (Bricker, 1995).

Under these circumstances, early childhood special education, general early childhood education, and therapeutic interventions are "blended" in practice. Blended approaches to inclusion are likely to require different preparation than more traditional mainstreaming approaches, both because of curricular approaches and varying role expectations on the part of the practitioners involved.

Roles and Responsibilities

An important consequence of inclusion is that the roles of the professionals in the classroom are changing: The early childhood teacher assumes responsibility for educating young children *with* and *without* disabilities (Kontos & File, 1993), whereas the special education teacher and therapists are much more likely to serve as consultants to the classroom teacher rather than devote all of their time to providing direct services (File & Kontos, 1992, 1993). Preschool and child care teachers, classroom aides, family child care providers, and others (e.g., YMCA or YWCA workers) working with young children need to extend their existing knowledge of serving young children to include children with disabilities. Likewise, early childhood special education teachers and therapists serving in the role of consultant to community programs need to adapt their experience as direct service providers to a new role as indirect service providers, including acquiring new consultation skills. Both early childhood special educators and therapists are relinquishing some direct service responsibilities and need to learn new roles and skills. Thus, changes in intervention practices, continuing differences in theoretical and philosophical approaches to early intervention, and multiple (and changing) professional roles make preservice and inservice education for inclusion imperative.

Logistical Factors

In addition to the issues previously described, there are a variety of systems issues, including program schedules and staff turnover, that affect the ways in which inclusive programs operate and who should be prepared. Ideological differences that limit the duties of classroom teachers and interventionists (Peck et al., 1993) and assumptions about which practitioners most need preparation influence the ways in which preparation for inclusion is provided.

Scheduling   Operating schedules for early childhood programs are not uniform. Family child care homes and child care centers, whether or not they are inclusive, often provide full-day, year-round services for children and families. Family child care providers usually work alone, whereas child care center staff frequently work staggered schedules to accommodate a 10-hour day. Part-day preschool programs, whether public or private, typically operate according to an academic-year calendar and enroll children for less than a full day. Children typically attend part-day programs in either the morning or the afternoon, from 2 to 5 days per week. These differences are useful for families who have varying needs for an early childhood program but can make inservice activities difficult to schedule and coordinate. Staff in early childhood programs have little time available away from the children (i.e., either breaks or planning time), which is a further complication and means that some inservice activities will need to be scheduled for evenings and weekends when they must compete with personal and family responsibilities.

Staff Turnover   Both early intervention and early childhood education are fields troubled by high turnover rates. Annual turnover rates for early intervention staff (across personnel categories) range from 18.5% (Palsha, Bailey, Vandiviere, & Munn, 1990) to 30.5% (Kontos & Dunn, 1989). These rates have been estimated to be even higher for child care settings (41%; Whitebook, Howes, & Phillips, 1989) and family child care homes (up to 59%; National Association for the Education of Young Children [NAEYC], 1985). Staff turnover creates difficulties for any type of instructional endeavor, but especially one that is multidisciplinary. Inservice instruction should not be viewed as an antidote to turnover (evidence shows that better salaries and working conditions are more likely to address this problem). However, the turnover problem necessitates that inservice preparation be an ongoing rather than periodic activity and requires frequent orientation-type preparation for new staff in addition to ongoing education for continuing staff.

Education and Specialized Preparation

Cross-field comparisons have shown that levels of education vary between early childhood education and early intervention teachers, but not dramatically (Kontos & File, 1993). Family child care providers are, on average, about as educated as typical early intervention aides. About two thirds of child care staff in the National Child Care Staffing Study were found to have specialized preparation in early childhood education or child development (Whitebook et al., 1989), but it was not always at the college level. Although child care teachers are less likely to have a bachelor's degree than early intervention teachers, the differences are not great. Early childhood programs serving typically developing children, as well as programs serving young children with disabilities, employ significant numbers of teachers and aides without specialized preparation in either field. Two early intervention personnel surveys (Hanson, 1990; Kontos & Dunn, 1989) found that only 50% of early intervention teachers had majored in early childhood or special education. In contrast, related service providers and therapists (e.g., nurses, physical therapists, occupational therapists, speech-language pathologists) typically have received discipline-based preparation in therapeutic interventions, frequently at the baccalaureate or graduate degree level. They are unlikely, however, to have a background in the application of such interventions within typical (i.e., nonclinic) early childhood settings.

The frequently held assumption has been that the targets of preparation for inclusion should be the early childhood community receiving children with disabilities into their programs (e.g., Klein & Sheehan, 1987; Peterson, 1983; Templeman, Fredericks, & Udell, 1989) and that the experts were the early childhood special educators, therapists, and other early intervention professionals. This assumption held even if these experts' own preparation focused exclusively on traditional special education and intervention approaches and on direct service to children in self-contained settings, including clinics and special education classrooms. Data suggest that this assumption is not well founded and that for inclusion to be effective, all professionals involved need new concepts and skills on which to base their work (Giangreco, Edelman, & Dennis, 1991; Kontos & File, 1993; Peck et al., 1993).

STRATEGIES FROM THE FIELD

Numerous inservice and preservice preparation models have been developed to address the needs of practitioners who will be employed in inclusive settings. These models have grown out of local needs, state planning, and federal funding initiatives. Some of them have been disseminated widely, but most of them have not. The collective wisdom that has accumulated on preparation for inclusion has not been systematically tapped. This section suggests strategies for providing preservice and inservice education for practitioners who will be working in inclusive programs. These strategies largely reflect the results of interviews that the authors of this chapter completed with nine professionals who are leaders in preparing practitioners for inclusive programs. These nine leaders were asked to describe the most important content to include and the most effective process (method) for getting this content across during either inservice or preservice preparation for inclusion. Recommended strategies were also based on already available instructional materials. All of these strategies reflect our beliefs that inclusive programs can work well for children, families, and professionals. Students and practitioners who are, or will be, working in inclusive settings need to believe that inclusion is possible. One person noted that some students think that inclusion is easy to do, whereas others have heard rumors about inappropriate practices that have been labeled as inclusion (see McCollum & Bair, 1994). Neither of these preconceptions is completely accurate, and both perspectives need to be addressed in preparing practitioners for inclusion.

Process

This section provides an overview of the processes or methods that leaders believed to be most effective for preparation for inclusion. Recommended strategies are also provided.

Attending to Principles of Adult Learning   Although important for everyone, principles of adult learning are especially critical in programs that include either older undergraduate students or practitioners who are participating in inservice programs. These principles include increased opportunities for active learning and few lectures. According to the leaders, learners must hear about, see, and practice the skills, concepts, and relationships that are the focus of instruction in order to apply what is learned to an inclusive setting. Observing what effective inclusionary practices look like is perceived as a crucial step in learning how to use them. This may involve videotapes, simulations, role playing, or field trips. (See Chapters 5 and 21 for more information on designing training.)

Field trips to programs providing exemplary inclusionary services within the community or surrounding area may be the most effective means for preservice and inservice preparation for inclusion. Staff and children are real as opposed to images on celluloid, and there is potential for interaction with the participants in the program. Not all communities are equally well endowed with such programs, however.

In the absence of, or in addition to, exemplary programs to visit, videotapes can serve a useful purpose. Several videotapes on inclusion include *Same Time, Same Place* (Purdue University, Continuing Education Administration, 1992), *Right from the Start* (Indiana University, Institute for Developmental Disabilities, 1989), and *Just a Kid Like Me* (Child and Family Services, 1991). *Same Time, Same Place* focuses on the roles and responsibilities of multiple disciplines (including a pediatrician) in the process of inclusion for children with severe disabilities in child care centers and family child care homes. Another videotape, *Family-Guided Activity-Based Intervention for Infants and Toddlers* (Cripe, 1995), does not show inclusion but does show naturalistic strategies for working with young children with disabilities that are appropriate for inclusive settings.

Simulation or role-playing activities can reinforce what was learned in a visitation or a videotape. Participants working in small groups can identify a child with whom they are all familiar (from a classroom or a videotape) and describe that child's strengths and developmental goals and objectives. They can then identify the components of the child's routine in the classroom (e.g., group time, free play activities, self-help, nap, snack, gross motor and/or outdoor activities). The small groups can first discuss adaptations to selected routines (whether they are necessary and, if so, what), and then role-play how to accomplish them.

Modeling an Inclusionary Philosophy   Modeling of inclusive practices by higher education faculty, including team teaching and cross-department collaborations, is an important component of preservice programs, according to the leaders interviewed. Similar approaches to team teaching occur in inservice education. As one educator noted, "How can we prepare others to be inclusive, and to work together, if we don't do it ourselves?" This approach to preservice and inservice education requires people who are committed to inclusion. Modeling inclusive practices means integrating educators from different disciplines who work together to teach within a unified course. As discussed in Chapter 4, higher education administrative issues of program ownership, faculty credit for teaching, and time for meetings (as well as program development) are often roadblocks to developing critically important work across academic departments and colleges. Working across community programs to provide preparation for inclusion presents similar issues of ownership of, and credit for, the educational process.

Modeling inclusion also means including parents and family members as instructors in preservice and inservice programs. There are a variety of strategies for including families as instructors, according to the leaders we interviewed. Among these are approaches that solicit and include parent input in the development of the program, include family members as part of the teaching team, and match students with families as part of a course or practicum experience. Strategies for supporting family–professional instructional partnerships are described in Chapter 17.

Another approach to modeling inclusion is including students and practitioners from different fields in classes or workshops. Interdisciplinary experiences can occur for students in a number of different ways. In some higher education–based programs, particularly those that are team taught, students from different backgrounds (e.g., education, child development, occupational or physical therapy, speech therapy) are enrolled together in the same program. This provides important opportunities for students to learn from and support each other and offers numerous opportunities to model team-building strategies and develop collaborative skills. Similar opportunities can be found in inservice programs when all members of an interdisciplinary team attend the same program.

Follow-Up   Inclusion education leaders pointed out that having the opportunity to practice new skills requires follow-up by those offering the instruction. Follow-up implies that instructors will work on site with participants once the more didactic aspect of instruction has ended, providing them with feedback and support (Wesley, 1994). It is time consuming and expensive but is the step we can least afford to skip. If nothing else, it forces instructors to individualize education for staff in the same way they advocate individualized services for children. More information on follow-up strategies is provided in Chapter 7.

The Best Practices in Integration (BPI) Inservice Training Model, for instance, recommends initial skills assessment of staff involved in instruction as a first step toward individualized inservice preparation (see Instructional Module 2 of Klein & Kontos, 1993). The skills that were assessed in this model were collaborative consultation skills, but the strategy could be adapted to any type of skill. Sample topics and items for the BPI skills inventory are listed in Figure 15.1. Participants are asked to assess their skills before starting so that educational experiences can be better tailored to the unique needs of participants. They are asked to reassess themselves at regular intervals during the follow-up phase of preparation to distinguish skills that have been achieved and those that con-

---

Consulting skills:	Self-rating
I. *With regard to basic knowledge:* Understands the match between possible consultation approaches and specific consultant situations, settings, and needs	1 2 3 4
II. *With regard to systems change:* Is able to identify positive and negative effects that might result from efforts to change part of a system	1 2 3 4
III. *With regard to personal characteristics and skills:* Can establish and maintain a sense of rapport and mutual trust with all people involved in the consultation process	1 2 3 4
IV. *With regard to interactive communication skills:* Is perceptive in grasping and validating stated/unstated meanings and affect in communication	1 2 3 4
V. *With regard to collaborative problem solving:* Uses a team approach to identify common goals and objectives for the child's learning program	1 2 3 4
VI. *With regard to own development:* Is able to assess own effectiveness by using children's progress, parent and staff feedback, and self-ratings	1 2 3 4

Figure 15.1.   Sample items from a skills inventory for consultants. (Rating scale: 1 = I need to learn more about this skill, 2 = I need assistance in improving this skill, 3 = I can do this skill independently, and 4 = I can do this skill very well.)

tinue to need work. Thus, instruction is always focused on skills that still need work. A skills inventory can also be used as an observation tool by an instructor or other interested party to provide feedback to participants. A discussion of similarities and differences between a self-assessment and an assessment by an instructor can prove useful for participants. This is a more individualized approach to preparation than is typically seen in early intervention, but it is more likely to result in skill acquisition than the "one-size-fits-all" variety.

The leaders suggested strategies to make follow-up more practical. First, if staff from service delivery agencies participate in teaching as teams, they can provide some feedback and support for each other at their workplace. In addition, instructors can send participants back to the workplace with handouts and videos that can be referred to during the "practice" phase of instruction. Apprenticeship and/or mentoring programs (within or across service providers) can also extend the work of the instructor on site. Finally, ending preparation experiences with team action planning gives professionals a head start on applying what they learned in the workplace.

Program Evaluation   Regular, ongoing evaluation of preservice and inservice preparation programs is critical to ensure that they meet the goals specified for them. Such evaluation includes follow-up after instruction as well as evaluation during the program. If programs do not include an evaluation component, there is no way of determining whether the needs of students are being met. Self-rating checklists such as the BPI skills inventory, observations of participants focused on specific skills, or quizzes built into the didactic portion of instruction can be components of such an evaluation (see Chapter 6 for more information on evaluation).

Content

The leaders interviewed also described the content areas they believed were most important to include in preparation for inclusion. This section highlights those areas and provides strategies for addressing them.

Family-Centered Practices   Family-centered practices are a cornerstone of early intervention and an important component in educating practitioners in inclusive practices. Research is beginning to show, however, that among early intervention professionals there is a considerable gap between the "talk" and the "walk" (Bailey, 1989; McBride, Brotherson, Joanning, Whiddon, & Demmit, 1993). Moreover, although the field of early childhood education has a history of family involvement as a core value (Honig, 1979), the concept and process of family-centered services as espoused by early interventionists may be quite foreign. Thus, the leaders interviewed were in relative agreement that all professionals involved in inclusion need a better understanding of the principles and practices of family-centered services and that instruction should include all groups of professionals working with young children in inclusive settings. Chapter 10 provides strategies for addressing family-centered practices in preservice and inservice instruction.

Practices in Inclusive Early Childhood Settings   A developmentally appropriate practices (DAP) (Bredekamp, 1987) model was frequently mentioned by the leaders as an important framework for inclusive early childhood classroom programs. This reflects the assumption that, when children with disabilities are included in settings with typically developing peers, they will learn best in high-quality early childhood settings rather than in settings that adopt either a teacher-directed or "laissez-faire" approach. Developmentally appropriate early childhood programs are age appropriate and individually appropriate (Bredekamp, 1987), meaning that the curriculum is founded on child-initiated, hands-on learning experiences during play. Adults in developmentally appropriate settings play an active role by planning the learning environment and enhancing children's experiences during play through responsive (but not intrusive) involvement.

Thus, general early childhood educators need to be especially aware of the ways in which they provide developmentally appropriate inclusive programs. Early intervention specialists (e.g., early childhood special educators, speech-language therapists, physical therapists, occupational therapists) who are least likely to learn about that approach in their own disciplinary education need to become aware of strategies for working within developmentally appropriate programs. Many early intervention professionals have been instructed to use methods that are in direct conflict with DAP and, through discomfort with and/or ignorance about child-initiated approaches to working with young children, could actually (inadvertently or otherwise) sabotage inclusion efforts. Thus, it is crucial that early interventionists involved in inclusion be fully familiar and comfortable with developmentally appropriate approaches.

The National Association for the Education of Young Children (NAEYC) has published a variety of modestly priced materials that can assist in this process. For instance, there are two videotapes—*Developmentally Appropriate Practices: Children Birth to Five* and *Appropriate Curriculum for Young Children: The Role of the Teacher*—that explain and demonstrate what DAP are. These would be especially useful for introducing the concept of DAP to participants with little or no previous exposure. To encourage the application of knowledge about DAP, each participant could be given a checklist on selecting a quality early childhood program that incorporates the principles of DAP (available from NAEYC, BPI Instructional Module 1 [Klein & Kontos, 1993], or from local child care resource and referral agencies). Each participant is assigned to visit an early childhood program to complete the checklist. The results of that visit would then be the focus of a discussion at the next session with participants giving examples of practices observed that were or were not appropriate as well as some that were not easily classified. The resulting discussion helps participants deal with the nuances of DAP and understand that practices typically fall along a continuum of appropriateness.

Understanding Typical Development as Basis for Early Childhood Curricula According to the training leaders interviewed for this chapter, students and practitioners need to understand the needs of typically developing children. This forms the foundation for thinking about inclusion and strategies for working with individual children in inclusive settings. A focus on specific, disability-related information was not seen by the instructional leaders as an especially helpful focus in preparing practitioners for inclusive settings. Thus, even though some general early childhood educators may believe that what they need is to know more about specific disabilities, the consensus seems to be that other areas are much more crucial and that preparation for inclusion does *not* involve a didactic, out-of-context, introduction to all disabilities. The source of expertise about individual children with disabilities should be families and early intervention specialists and should come in the context of program planning for the child.

Individualized Interventions for Children with Disabilities Individualizing children's programs within a developmentally appropriate classroom continues to be an important issue, according to the leaders. The work of Bricker and Cripe (1992) in the development of an activity-based intervention model is an approach that can be adapted for inclusive early childhood settings. This model provides a framework for helping students develop strategies for including individual objectives for all children within the context of a developmentally appropriate early childhood program. In addition, specific teaching strategies drawn from special education practice (including strategies for modifying disruptive behavior and strategies that can be used to shape or reinforce desired behaviors) can be important tools for participants. A critical issue in preparing practitioners for inclusion, according to leaders, is integrating objectives and adapting learning activities for individual children. It is this component that helps to make inclusive programs distinct from either traditional early childhood special or general education programs.

An activity designed to assist participants to embed children's goals and objectives into ongoing routines or activities is to provide participants with a description of a child with disabilities and a list of daily routines and activities the child encounters in a typical day in the early childhood program. The participant, or a small group of participants, is given the task of selecting routines or activities in which an objective could be addressed, including adaptations that might be necessary. This activity might be accomplished more successfully if participants first viewed the videotape on activity-based intervention (Cripe, 1995). (See Chapter 13 for additional activities.)

Responsive Environments   Understanding what children's environments are like, how children fit within their environments, and how to evaluate these environments are important skills. Looking at the environment rather than the child as the challenge and developing strategies for modifying the environment to better meet the needs of children complements the more individualized focus of activity-based intervention.

Several instruments designed to alert professionals to environmental factors are available, including the Early Childhood Environment Rating Scale (Harms & Clifford, 1980), the Family Day Care Rating Scale (Harms & Clifford, 1989), and the Infant/Toddler Environment Rating Scale (Harms, Clifford, & Cryer, 1990). Giving these instruments to early intervention specialists as a way to evaluate general early childhood programs that are qualified to serve children with disabilities is neither a collegial approach to inclusion nor does it take into account family choice factors that supersede professional notions of a program worthy of inclusion. Providing these instruments to general early childhood practitioners who, as evidenced by their participation in education, are contemplating accommodations for children with disabilities can be enlightening and practical. It provides a concrete mechanism for focusing on the environment and identifies exactly the types of changes that can be made for improving it. Although none of these three instruments can assist with adaptations to the environment for a particular child, each provides common ground for practitioners from various disciplines to address environmental modifications more generally and to set the stage for addressing issues of child and environment fit.

Team Building   Collaborative consultation is gaining prominence as a strategy for supporting inclusion and was frequently mentioned by the leaders as an important component of preparation. The validity of this prominence is reflected in research showing that, when inclusion fails, it is typically due to problems between the adults involved in the process and rarely related to the children (Peck et al., 1993). Additional information on teaching about teaming is available in Chapter 14. The need for this content cuts across disciplines and roles. The role of early childhood special educators frequently moves from direct to indirect service when inclusive service delivery models are in place. Therapists are less reliant on traditional, pull-out individual therapy sessions. Early childhood educators take on early intervention direct service in addition to their original responsibilities. Together with parents, all of these professionals must collaborate to support the child's inclusion experiences. Who leads the team? Is there an expert? How can we be effective consumers of others' expertise? How are problems resolved? How are resistance and conflict handled? These are issues that can be addressed through collaborative consultation approaches.

The BPI Inservice Training Model (Klein & Kontos, 1993) includes instructional modules designed to support preparation for collaborative consultation. One activity included in the BPI Instructional Modules involves a set of five vignettes, each one depicting early intervention consultants from various disciplines (e.g., speech-language pathology, early childhood special education) working with an early childhood educator (a sample vignette is included in Figure 15.2). Participants are asked to decide if the team members in the vignettes were working collaboratively, to explain how the noncollaborative relationships might have developed, and to identify ways that collaboration could be increased. Typically, participants are very critical of the practitioners in the vignettes, but the basis for criticism is quite different across small groups. Thus, including time for sharing the results of the small-group activities with the full group is worthwhile.

STRUCTURAL CHALLENGES TO PREPARATION FOR INCLUSION

As several instructional leaders indicated in our interviews, inclusion is a type of systems change; improving teaching or therapy skills alone will not make it happen (Klein & Kontos, 1993; Wesley, 1994). There are structural factors concerning the local and regional early childhood and early intervention systems that affect how preparation for inclusion will occur.

An important issue that influences preservice educational programs is the structure of teacher certification and credentialing of related service providers within each state. We spoke with educators whose states had unified certification in early childhood/early childhood special education (with certification based on yet-to-be-determined performance criteria), states that offered separate certification in each of these areas, and states in which certification cut across the preschool age range (birth to 4 years old, and 3 years old to third grade). In some states, students graduating from dual certification (early childhood education, early childhood special education) programs had opportunities for employment in inclusive settings, whereas in others, most children with disabilities were enrolled in self-contained classes. In relatively few of these communities was the consultant model of early intervention the one used in early childhood programs. This creates a dual focus (and occasional dilemmas) for degree-granting programs: that of preparing students for

---

At his yearly professional association conference, Gordon, a speech-language pathologist, attended a workshop about a new intervention that excited him. Back at work, he was struck with the idea that he would like to try the intervention with Jackie, a child for whom he serves as a consultant. The next week he told Jackie's early childhood program teacher he wanted to teach her the intervention so she could use it with Jackie. He presented her with a plan that covered the next 3 weeks.

Questions:
1. Was Gordon working collaboratively?
2. If not, how and why did this situation come about?
3. How could collaboration be increased in this situation? Specify exactly who would need to do what.

Figure 15.2.   Sample vignette from a BPI small-group exercise.

employment opportunities upon graduation (even when these would likely not be in inclusive settings), and preparing students in inclusive approaches to early intervention so that they might not only serve children and families in these settings but also advocate for inclusion as appropriate early childhood practice.

For related service providers such as speech-language pathologists and physical and occupational therapists, credentialing is essentially "all age," and there is little or no opportunity for specializing during the degree program. States or professional organizations vary widely in their credentialing requirements for practitioners in early intervention services. Losardo (1996) noted that areas receiving the least amount of attention in bachelor's and master's programs for communication specialists include interdisciplinary teamwork, family assessment and intervention, and practicum experiences with young children and their families. Similar results have been reported for personnel preparation programs in physical and occupational therapy (McEwen & Shelden, 1996). Thus, it may be up to the individual practitioner and to the states' Comprehensive Systems of Personnel Development to determine and provide the skills that related service providers need to know to function in inclusive settings.

Several of the leaders had comments that directly or indirectly related to other types of infrastructure supports of the preparation for inclusion process. For preservice educators, there are higher education institutional barriers created by departmental structures, program ownership, faculty teaching loads, and calculation of student credit hours within and across majors (see Chapter 4 for a detailed discussion of these issues).

For inservice educators, the infrastructure barriers are a bit different but no less daunting. In many states, the general early childhood and early intervention inservice education "systems" (loosely defined) are separate and communicate little, if at all, with one another. An approach to modeling inclusion is to infuse preparation for inclusion into existing educational opportunities for early childhood educators. This makes sense for preparing general educators who are providing direct services to young children with disabilities in their classrooms, but it may not be effective if early childhood educators participate in inservice education separate from early intervention professionals. It may also be problematic if it promotes the idea that the sole or primary targets of preparation for inclusion are the general early childhood educators and that early intervention professionals already know about inclusion.

One way to avoid these problems would be to merge the early intervention and early childhood education inservice educational systems so that the expertise is shared. Accomplishing such a merger would require that all the organizations in a state that provide education to professionals who work with young children work together to establish joint educational priorities, share resources, and collaboratively prepare interdisciplinary groups of professionals. A prerequisite for such a dramatically different approach to education is effective working relationships among professional organizations representing the disciplines involved (e.g., state Association for the Education of Young Children groups, the Division for Early Childhood, state physical therapy associations), state agencies (e.g., departments of education, boards of health, child care resource and referral), and private service delivery organizations (e.g., developmental disability/rehabilitation agencies, child care programs, preschools). These types of relationships are not built overnight and require that all perceive mutual advantage to the enterprise. Several examples of in-roads being made in this area are provided by the Partnerships for Inclusion Project in North Carolina (see Chapter 3 for additional information on this project) as well as several newsletters that target instruction for both the early childhood and the early intervention communities (*All Together Now* in North Carolina and *The Training Connection* in Indiana).

CONCLUSION

Preparing personnel to engage in an ongoing process such as inclusion is a challenge under any circumstance but is particularly challenging when it is a relatively new addition to the skills and competencies required of professionals who work with young children with disabilities. The leaders interviewed for this chapter acknowledged these complexities but, through experience, had also forged strategies for overcoming them. There were consistencies in the recommendations they made for the content and process of preparation for inclusion across the inservice and preservice educators.

With respect to content, none of the leaders interviewed believed that an abundance of information on specific disabilities was either necessary or helpful in preparing professionals for inclusion. Almost all of them believed strongly that professionals need to understand inclusion as a philosophy and developmentally appropriate practice as an approach to early intervention. The blending of early childhood education and early intervention practices was frequently accomplished through the tenets of activity-based intervention (Bricker & Cripe, 1992). Family-centered services and collaborative, interdisciplinary teamwork were the two other content areas in which there was consistency across the leaders interviewed.

These leaders consistently emphasized the practice component of instruction as either dominant to (inservice) or equal with (preservice) didactic approaches. In inservice education, this is translated to simulation and hands-on activities during workshop sessions and later on-site follow-up. For preservice education, this is frequently translated to practicum experiences that supplement and enhance coursework. In either case, professionals are unlikely to apply what they learn didactically unless doing so is part of the educational process.

Although the emphasis has been on common ground, the reality is that there is no one correct way to prepare for inclusion given the diversity of students and professionals, service delivery systems, and children and families. Thus, each program, community, higher education institution, and state has the task of creating what works for it, in light of the experiences of those before it. Perhaps the best overall advice regarding preparation for inclusion is provided by Salisbury, Galucci, Palombaro, and Peck (1995): "Building on those practices [that classroom teachers believe are working] affirms and values the extant knowledge of practicing professionals and provides an efficient and naturally occurring context in which to develop future interventions" (p. 136).

RESOURCES

Bredekamp, S., & Copple, P. (Eds.). (1997). *Developmentally appropriate practice in early childhood programs* (Rev. ed.). Washington, DC: National Association for the Education of Young Children. Cost: $8. (800) 424-2460.

A well-grounded source of information for teachers/instructors, administrators, family members, and policy makers for use in instruction, program design, and program evaluation.

Child and Family Services. (1991). *Just a kid like me* [Videotape]. Hollywood, CA: DUBS, Inc. Cost: $25. (213) 461-3726.

Twenty-seven–minute video showing children with different disabilities in inclusive settings, including after-school care for primary grades.

Cripe, J.W. (1995). *Family-guided activity-based intervention for infants and toddlers* [Videotape]. Baltimore: Paul H. Brookes Publishing Co. Cost: $37. (800) 638-3775.

This 20-minute videotape illustrates strategies through which family members and providers can take advantage of natural learning opportunities. Narration and examples are very clear and provide supplemental materials for preservice or inservice instructional audiences.

File, N., & Kontos, S. (1992). Indirect service delivery through consultation: Review and implications for early intervention. *Journal of Early Intervention, 16*(3), 221–234.

Article discusses barriers to effective practice of consultation and implications for early intervention programming. Delineation of specialized instruction necessary to increase opportunities for children with disabilities to receive early childhood services in integrated settings.

Harms, T., & Clifford, R. (1980). *Early Childhood Environment Rating Scale (ECERS)*. New York: Teachers College Press. Cost: $8.95. (800) 575-6566.

An easy-to-use instrument designed to assist teachers, administrators, family members, and instructors in examining the quality features of early childhood settings. Defines quality through a scale of 37 items in seven categories (e.g., personal care routines, furnishings, gross and fine motor activities, language and reasoning). Companion instruments from the same publisher include the Family Day Care Rating Scale, Infant/Toddler Environment Rating Scale, and School-Age Care Environment Rating Scale.

Indiana University, Institute for Developmental Disabilities. (1989). *Right from the start* [Videotape]. Bloomington: Author. Cost: $38 plus shipping and handling. (812) 855-6508.

Videotape focuses on the roles and responsibilities of multiple disciplines in facilitating the inclusion of children with severe disabilities in child care centers and family child care homes.

Klein, S.M., & Kontos, S. (1993). *Best Practices in Integration (BPI) Inservice Training Model: Guide and instruction modules*. Bloomington: Indiana University, BPI Outreach Project. Cost: $17.50. (812) 855-6508.

An instructional model to prepare people delivering services for infants, toddlers, and preschool children with disabilities within community-based early childhood settings. Describes methods and provides materials (e.g., checklists, handouts, transparency masters, vignettes, case examples) for ensuring participant knowledge and skill regarding collaborative consultation. Includes resources for a technical assistance process to facilitate the integration of young children with disabilities in general early childhood programs and successful collaboration among all partners.

McWilliam, P.J., & Bailey, D.B., Jr. (Eds.). (1993). *Working together with children and families: Case studies in early intervention*. Baltimore: Paul H. Brookes Publishing Co. Cost: $27 plus shipping and handling. (800) 638-3775.

Edited collection of cases exemplifying the application of recommended practices in early intervention for use in preservice and inservice education. Text includes unsolved case dilemmas for use in teaching/instruction, decision making, and problem solving.

Partnerships for Inclusion. (1993). *Can I play too?* [Videotape]. Chapel Hill: University of North Carolina at Chapel Hill, Partnerships for Inclusion. Cost: $25 (12-minute overview version), $50 (20-minute parent and provider versions). (919) 962-7364.

Three companion videos (overview, parent, and provider versions) about inclusion of young children with disabilities in early intervention/early childhood environments. These materials have been used effectively to raise awareness in inservice and preservice instructional formats.

Purdue University, Continuing Education Administration. (1992). *Same time, same place* [Videotape]. West Lafayette, IN: Author. Cost: $18. (800) 359-2968.

Video features children with disabilities in a variety of inclusive settings. Focuses on the roles and responsibilities of multiple disciplines (including a pediatrician) in the inclusion process for children with severe disabilities in child care centers and family child care homes. Good examples for assisting participants to identify components of development, environment, and routines.

Wesley, P. (1993). *Mainstreaming young children: A training series for child care providers.* Chapel Hill: University of North Carolina at Chapel Hill, Partnerships for Inclusion. Cost: $57.50. (919) 962-7364.

Ready-to-use materials for instructors. Eight instructional modules are designed to be presented in sequence as part of a 44-hour course but can easily be used independently to address topics related to inclusion. Each module includes notes to the instructor, student objectives, a module flow guide, instructor outlines, transparencies, and handouts.

Wesley, P. (1994). Providing on-site consultation to promote quality in integrated child care programs. *Journal of Early Intervention, 18*(4), 391–402.

Describes methods and materials developed by the Infant-Toddler Care Project to provide child care programs with on-site consultation that reinforce and emphasize aspects of quality care for all children. Ideas for providing knowledge and skills to support the inclusion of infants and toddlers with disabilities.

West, J., Idol, L., & Cannon, G. (1989). *Collaboration in the schools: An inservice and preservice curriculum for teachers, support staff, and administrators.* Austin, TX: PRO-ED.

Consists of an instructor's manual and a learner's booklet. Although it was created for public school settings, its focus on communicating, interacting, and problem solving transcends setting.

REFERENCES

Americans with Disabilities Act (ADA) of 1990, PL 101-336, 42 U.S.C. §12101 *et seq.*

Bailey, D.B., Jr. (1989). Issues and directions in preparing professionals to work with young handicapped children and their families. In J.J. Gallagher, P.L. Trohanis, & R.M. Clifford (Eds.), *Policy implementation and PL 99-457: Planning for young children with special needs* (pp. 97–132). Baltimore: Paul H. Brookes Publishing Co.

Bredekamp, S., & Copple, P. (Eds.). (1997). *Developmentally appropriate practice in early childhood programs* (Rev. ed.). Washington, DC: National Association for the Education of Young Children.

Bredekamp, S., & Rosegrant, T. (1992). *Reaching potentials: Appropriate curriculum and assessment for young children* (Vol. 1). Washington, DC: National Association for the Education of Young Children.

Bricker, D. (1995). The challenge of inclusion. *Journal of Early Intervention, 19,* 179–194.

Bricker, D., & Cripe, J.W. (1992). *An activity-based approach to early intervention.* Baltimore: Paul H. Brookes Publishing Co.

Carta, J., Schwartz, I., Atwater, J., & McConnell, S. (1991). Developmentally appropriate practice: Appraising its usefulness for young children with disabilities. *Topics in Early Childhood Special Education, 11,* 1–20.

Child and Family Services. (1991). *Just a kid like me* [Videotape]. Hollywood, CA: DUBS, Inc.

Cripe, J.W. (1995). *Family-guided activity-based intervention for infants and toddlers* [Videotape]. Baltimore: Paul H. Brookes Publishing Co.

DeVries, R., & Kohlberg, L. (1987). *Programs of early education: The constructivist view.* White Plains, NY: Longman, Inc.

Education of the Handicapped Act Amendments of 1986, PL 99-457, 20 U.S.C. §1400 *et seq.*

File, N., & Kontos, S. (1992). Indirect service delivery through consultation: Review and implications for early intervention. *Journal of Early Intervention, 16*(3), 221–234.

File, N., & Kontos, S. (1993). The relationship of program quality to children's play in integrated early intervention settings. *Topics in Early Childhood Special Education, 13,* 1–18.

Giangreco, M., Edelman, S., & Dennis, R. (1991). Common professional practices that interfere with the integrated delivery of related services. *Remedial and Special Education, 12,* 16–24.

Graham, M.A., & Bryant, D.M. (1993). Characteristics of quality, effective service delivery systems for children with special needs. In D.M. Bryant & M.A. Graham (Eds.), *Implementing early intervention: From research to effective practice* (pp. 233–252). New York: Guilford Press.

Hanson, M. (1990). *Final report: California early intervention personnel model, personnel standards, and personnel preparation.* Sacramento: California Department of Developmental Services, Community Service Division.

Harms, T., & Clifford, R. (1980). *Early Childhood Environment Rating Scale* (ECERS). New York: Teachers College Press.

Harms, T., & Clifford, R. (1989). *Family Day Care Rating Scale.* New York: Teachers College Press.

Harms, T., Clifford, R., & Cryer, D. (1990). *Infant/Toddler Environment Rating Scale.* New York: Teachers College Press.

Honig, A. (1979). *Parent involvement in early childhood education.* Washington, DC: National Association for the Education of Young Children.

Hoyson, M., Jamieson, B., & Strain, P. (1984). Individualized group instruction of normally developing and autistic-like children: The LEAP curriculum model. *Journal of the Division for Early Childhood, 8,* 157–172.

Indiana University, Institute for Developmental Disabilities. (1989). *Right from the start* [Videotape]. Bloomington: Author.

Klein, N., & Sheehan, R. (1987). Staff development: A key issue in meeting the needs of young handicapped children in day care settings. *Topics in Early Childhood Special Education, 7,* 13–27.

Klein, S., & Kontos, S. (1993). *Best practices in Integration (BPI) Inservice Training Model: Guide and instructional modules.* Bloomington: Indiana University, Department of Curriculum and Instruction.

Kontos, S., & Dunn, L. (1989). Characteristics of the early intervention workforce: An Indiana perspective. *Early Education and Development, 1,* 141–157.

Kontos, S., & File, N. (1993). Staff development in support of integration. In C.A. Peck, S.L. Odom, & D.D. Bricker (Eds.), *Integrating young children with disabilities into community programs: Ecological perspectives on research and implementation* (pp. 169–186). Baltimore: Paul H. Brookes Publishing Co.

Losardo, A. (1996). Preparing communication specialists. In D. Bricker & A. Widerstrom (Eds.), *Preparing personnel to work with infants and young children and their families: A team approach* (pp. 91–113). Baltimore: Paul H. Brookes Publishing Co.

Mahoney, J., Robinson, C., & Powell, A. (1992). Focusing on parent–child interaction: The bridge to developmentally appropriate practices. *Topics in Early Childhood Special Education, 12,* 105–120.

McBride, S., Brotherson, M., Joanning, H., Whiddon, D., & Demmit, A. (1993). Implementation of family-centered services: Perceptions of families and professionals. *Journal of Early Intervention, 17,* 414–430.

McCollum, J., & Bair, H. (1994). Research in parent–child interaction: Guidance to developmentally appropriate practice for young children with disabilities. In B. Mallory & R. New (Eds.), *Diversity and developmentally appropriate practices: Challenges for early childhood education* (pp. 84–106). New York: Teachers College Press.

McEwen, I.R., & Shelden, M.L. (1996). Preparing physical therapists. In D. Bricker & A. Widerstrom (Eds.), *Preparing personnel to work with infants and young children and their families: A team approach* (pp. 135–159). Baltimore: Paul H. Brookes Publishing Co.

McLean, N., & Odom, S. (1988, June). *Least restrictive environment and social integration: Division for Early Childhood paper.* Reston, VA: Division for Early Childhood, Council for Exceptional Children.

McWilliam, P.I., & Bailey, D.B., Jr. (Eds.). (1993). *Working together with children and families: Case studies in early intervention.* Baltimore: Paul H. Brookes Publishing Co.

National Association for the Education of Young Children (NAEYC). (1985). *In whose hands? A demographic fact sheet on child care providers.* Washington, DC: Author.

National Association for the Education of Young Children (NAEYC). (1993a). *Appropriate curriculum for young children: The role of the teacher.* Washington, DC: Author.

National Association for the Education of Young Children (NAEYC). (1993b). *Developmentally appropriate practices: Children birth to five* [Videotape]. Washington, DC: Author.

Odom, S., & McEvoy, M. (1990). Mainstreaming at the preschool level: Potential barriers and tasks for the field. *Topics in Early Childhood Special Education, 10,* 48–61.

Odom, S., Skellenger, A., & Ostrosky, M. (1993, March). *Ecobehavioral analysis of activity engagement in early childhood education and special education classrooms.* Paper presented at the biennial meeting of the Society for Research in Child Development, New Orleans, LA.

Palsha, S., Bailey, D., Vandiviere, P., & Munn, P. (1990). A study of employee stability and turnover in home-based intervention. *Journal of Early Intervention, 14,* 342–351.

Partnerships for Inclusion. (1993). *Can I play too?* Chapel Hill: University of North Carolina at Chapel Hill, Partnerships for Inclusion.

Peck, C.A., Furman, G.C., & Helmstetter, E. (1993). Integrated early childhood programs: Research on the implementation of change in organizational contexts. In C.A. Peck, S.L. Odom, & D.D. Bricker (Eds.), *Integrating young children with disabilities into community programs: Ecological perspectives on research and implementation* (pp. 187–205). Baltimore: Paul H. Brookes Publishing Co.

Peterson, N. (1983). Personnel training for mainstreaming young handicapped children. In J. Anderson & T. Black (Eds.), *Mainstreaming in early education* (pp. 23–43). Chapel Hill, NC: Technical Assistance Development System.

Purdue University, Continuing Education Administration. (1992). *Same time, same place* [Videotape]. West Lafayette, IN: Author.

Rogers, C., & Sawyers, J. (1988). *Play in the lives of children.* Washington, DC: National Association for the Education of Young Children.

Safford, P. (1989). *Integrated teaching in early childhood: Starting in the mainstream.* White Plains, NY: Longman, Inc.

Salisbury, C., Galucci, C., Palombaro, M., & Peck, C. (1995). Strategies that promote social relations among elementary students with and without severe disabilities in inclusive schools. *Exceptional Children, 62,* 125–138.

Strain, P. (Ed.). (1981). *The utilization of classroom peers as behavior change agents.* New York: Plenum.

Strain, P., McConnell, S., Carta, J., Fowler, S., Neisworth, J., & Wolery, M. (1992). Behaviorism in early intervention. *Topics in Early Childhood Education, 12,* 121–142.

Templeman, T., Fredericks, H., & Udell, T. (1989). Integration of children with moderate and severe handicaps into a day care center. *Journal of Early Intervention, 13,* 315–328.

Wesley, P. (1993). *Mainstreaming young children: A training series for child care providers.* Chapel Hill: University of North Carolina at Chapel Hill, Partnerships for Inclusion.

Wesley, P. (1994). Providing on-site consultation to promote quality in integrated child care programs. *Journal of Early Intervention, 18*(4), 391–402.

West, J., Idol, L., & Cannon, G. (1989). *Collaboration in the schools: An inservice and preservice curriculum for teachers, support staff, and administrators.* Austin, TX: PRO-ED.

Whitebook, M., Howes, C., & Phillips, D. (1989). *Who cares? Child care teachers and the quality of care in America.* Oakland, CA: Child Care Employee Project.

Wolery, M., & Brookfield-Norman, J. (1988). (Pre)Academic instruction for handicapped preschool children. In S.L. Odom & M.B. Karnes (Eds.), *Early intervention for infants and children with handicaps: An empirical base* (pp. 109–128). Baltimore: Paul H. Brookes Publishing Co.

Wolery, M., Holcombe-Ligon, A., Brookfield, J., Huffman, K., Schroeder, C., Martin, C., Venn, M., Werts, M., & Fleming, S. (1993). The extent and nature of preschool mainstreaming: A survey of general early educators. *Journal of Special Education, 27,* 222–234.

Young, C.C. (1981). Children as instructional agents for handicapped peers: A review and analysis. In P. Strain (Ed.), *The utilization of classroom peers as behavior change agents* (pp. 305–326). New York: Plenum.

16 EARLY INTERVENTION PUBLIC POLICY ANALYSIS

Issues and Strategies in Personnel Preparation

Barbara Hanft
Patricia Place

There are five primary reasons why practitioners, administrators, and families must analyze early intervention policies and practices. First, policies should promote services that are meaningful to consumers and effective in achieving desired outcomes. Second, federal, state, and local laws and regulations affect programs and practices in both dramatic and subtle ways that practitioners must learn to recognize. Third, by understanding the basic provisions of early intervention law and regulations, practitioners and families can discourage misinformation and incorrect interpretations that may be incorrectly held out as "the law." Fourth, if early intervention policies are monitored and analyzed as they are developed by governing bodies, they will better reflect recommended practices. Finally, as public policies are implemented, careful evaluation can highlight beneficial aspects of the policy as well as those requirements that need modification.

This chapter defines a policy as a statement of goals and principles that govern actions to address and solve issues affecting groups of people. Political scientists argue that the term *policy* should be reserved for "statements of intention and direction of a relatively high order" (Starling, 1977, p. 128), which is "commonly used to designate the *most* important choices made either in organized or in private life" (Lasswell, 1951, p. 5). Furthermore, the authors of this chapter view policies as the rules and standards that are established to allocate public resources to meet a particular social need. Viewed in this perspective, early intervention policies for young children with disabilities are key goals and guiding principles that reflect the political, economic, and societal values of a specific time period regarding how to care for and provide services to children with special needs and their families. These goals and principles take the form of laws, regulations, guidelines, and administrative directives.

This chapter identifies three key competencies needed to analyze early intervention policies: 1) understanding the context for the development of an early childhood policy, why it was needed, and how it evolved; 2) critiquing the policy to understand its provisions and how it will affect all stakeholder groups; and 3) influencing public policy during its development and implementation by contributing to draft policies and modifying existing ones. The text is organized in four major sections. First, challenges to teaching public policy analysis are described. Then three instructional sections, each targeted to one of the key competencies, are presented. Each instructional section includes strategies for teaching the content, skills, and values of each competency. Selected teaching resources for instructors and recommended readings for participants are included in tables in each of the three instructional sections.

CHALLENGES TO TEACHING PUBLIC POLICY ANALYSIS

Teaching students and practitioners to analyze early intervention public policy is a complex task. One of the factors that contributes to this complexity is that there is no comprehensive public policy for children in the United States. As Gallagher (1981) pointed out, "Public policy around any broad dimension of American society such as the family will be done in piecemeal, issue-by-issue, decision making" (p. 38). Early childhood policies cover health, education, public welfare, housing, child care, and economic issues; no one state or federal agency has responsibility for all of these. Table 16.1 identifies the key laws to consider in early childhood personnel preparation activities. Students and practitioners should understand the provisions and effects of each of these laws as well as their implementing regulations and any accompanying guidelines. Smith (1996) provided a comprehensive listing of federal programs serving children with disabilities.

A second challenge in personnel development is that early intervention is a relatively new policy arena. Before the early 1900s there were no national health or social policies for children (with or without disabilities), reflecting the values and perspectives that children were possessions of their parents, without rights until they matured (Hanft, 1991). Children did not receive specialized pediatric care because they were viewed as miniature adults without unique developmental or health needs of their own. This instructional challenge is addressed by suggesting strategies to assist participants in understanding the political, social, and economic factors that influence the development of a specific policy in the section on understanding the context for policy development.

A third challenge in teaching many participants to analyze early intervention public policy is their lack of awareness and experience in three key areas: 1) family members' desires for their children, 2) day-to-day program operations, and 3) atypical child development. Participants at both preservice and inservice levels must learn to critically review public policy; however, a major difference exists between these two groups. Practitioners working in the field directly experience how a new or revised policy will affect the families they serve as well as their own professional services; preservice students generally do not have these experiences on which to base their analysis. The suggested instructional strategies in this chapter emphasize ways to dramatize how policies affect both professional and family life.

A final instructional challenge is that policy development is often perceived as an invisible process that is very difficult to influence. Many people do not understand the process of drafting or revising laws and regulations and feel powerless to change them. They view their daily existence as separate from the legislative or regulatory process and have little interest in contacting state or federal policy makers. The instructional section on influencing public policy focuses on learning to communicate effectively with all policy makers.

UNDERSTANDING THE CONTEXT FOR PUBLIC POLICIES

Understanding why a policy is needed and how it evolved is essential to analyzing the policy's impact on children and their families. This requires a thorough understanding of

TABLE 16.1.   Federal laws authorizing services for children with disabilities and their families

Law	Target group	Provisions for children with disabilities
Individuals with Disabilities Education Act (IDEA) of 1990, PL 101-476		
Part B enacted in 1975 (the Education for All Handicapped Children Act, PL 94-142)	Children 3+ years with disabilities	Special education and related services in the least restrictive environment
Part H enacted in 1986 (the Education of the Handicapped Act Amendments, PL 99-457)	Infants birth to 2 years and family members	Developmental and related family services in natural environments
Economic Opportunity Act Amendments of 1972, PL 92-424 (Head Start)	Children birth to 5 years from low-income families including:	
	Preschoolers with disabilities who meet IDEA eligibility or state definition of developmental delay	Preschool enrichment, special education and related services
	Infants and toddlers with disabilities less than 3 years of age	Comprehensive child development and family support services; prenatal care
Americans with Disabilities Act (1990), PL 101-336, and Section 504 of the Rehabilitation Act (1973), PL 93-112	All children and adults in programs receiving federal funds; disability viewed as a physical or mental impairment (or perception of such impairment) that substantially limits a major life activity	Prohibits discrimination on the basis of disability; mandates reasonable accommodations in all public and private schools, child care, work settings, and so forth
Medicaid Title XIX of the Social Security Act Amendments of 1965, PL 89-97	All low-income families who receive Aid to Families with Dependent Children (AFDC) or Supplemental Security Income (SSI) or meet other state criteria	Access to federally mandated medical, social, psychological, and health services; optional state services can be offered such as home and community waivers to care for children with disabilities outside of institutions

(continued)

TABLE 16.1. *(continued)*

Law	Target group	Provisions for children with disabilities
Title V of the *Social Security Act of 1935,* PL 74-271		
Maternal and Child Health (MCH)	All children and families	Federal grants to states for health services such as prenatal care, well baby clinics, immunizations
Programs for Children with Special Health Care Needs (initially titled "Crippled Children's Services")	Children with physical and mental disabilities	Rehabilitation, social service, and medical services
Developmental Disabilities Assistance and Bill of Rights Act (1975), PL 94-103	Individuals who meet the definition of a developmental disability before age 18	Federal grants to states to support protection and advocacy; university affiliated programs for evaluation and intervention services; Developmental Disability Planning Councils

Note: Original enactment dates are identified; laws are generally amended every 3–5 years.

the climate or context for policy development, that is, the social, economic, and political factors that influenced the development and implementation of a particular policy. The political context refers to the jurisdiction and responsibility of federal, state, and local government for providing services to young children. The social context includes the values and mores regarding all children's and families' rights in general as well as those of individuals with special needs. The economic context relates to how monetary and human resources are allocated and used for services for children with disabilities within the overall context of national, state, and local funding priorities.

The following example describes the context for the enactment of the Early Intervention Program for Infants and Toddlers with Disabilities (Part H) in the Individuals with Disabilities Education Act (IDEA) and serves as a model for understanding why other laws identified in Table 16.1 were enacted. Understanding the context for the development of a policy is part of the process of policy analysis and sets the stage for critiquing its impact once it is implemented.

Why the Early Intervention Program Was Enacted

At the beginning of the 20th century, the United States was in the grips of the eugenics movement, which viewed people with disabilities, particularly mental or emotional disabilities, as "deviant." Intervention for these individuals focused on compulsory sterilization and institutionalization in large, isolated state facilities. Millions of children with disabilities were denied access to public schools as late as the 1970s because they were considered uneducable, even though public schooling had been provided by the states to "typical" children since the 1800s (Riley, Nash, & Hunt, 1978).

Several political, social, and economic factors reversed these policies in the 1970s. On the political front, organizations of parents and advocates began to demand services for children with disabilities. In landmark legislation prompted by a lawsuit filed by a parent advocacy group in 1971, the Supreme Court ruled that children with mental retardation could not be denied access to public education (*Pennsylvania Association for Retarded Children [PARC] v. the Commonwealth of Pennsylvania*, 1971). Furthermore, the Supreme Court ordered that this education must take place in the least restrictive environment, forcing the widespread deinstitutionalization of children who had been "warehoused" in large segregated state schools. A related case (*Mills v. Board of Education of the District of Columbia*, 1972) expanded this right to all students with disabilities. Congress responded to the demands of parents and advocates by passing the Education for All Handicapped Children Act of 1975, PL 94-142, which required all states to provide eligible children with a free and appropriate public education if the states wanted certain federal education funds (Turnbull, 1986).

One of the key social trends that emerged during the 1970s and 1980s was the active role of parents in their children's education and health care. A convincing body of early childhood research demonstrated that parents could positively affect their child's educational achievement (e.g., Bowlby, 1969; Werner, Bierman, & French, 1971). Previously, parents of children with disabilities were viewed as passive recipients of intervention and often had no say about the type or amount of services their children received in school or health settings (Pizzo, 1990). This perspective shifted to one of parents as proactive team members, critical to the decision-making process. This shift in the social climate is reflected in the provisions of IDEA requiring the schools to develop an individualized education program for each student in conjunction with parents and guaranteed due process rights for parents related to the identification, evaluation, and placement procedures for their children. Likewise, in the health arena, the family-centered care movement emphasized that family members were the central decision makers for their children's intervention (Shelton, Jeppson, & Johnson, 1989).

In the 1980s, research also documented the economic effectiveness of providing services at a young age (Lazar & Darlington, 1982; Shonkoff & Hauser-Cram, 1987). Early intervention was shown to improve the developmental outcomes for children with disabilities and was considered cost effective because it minimized the need for services and supports at a later age. Providing early services made for sound social and economic policies.

Thus, in 1986, the evolution of early intervention public policy progressed with the enactment of the Education of the Handicapped Act Amendments, PL 99-457, creating the Early Intervention Program for Infants and Toddlers with Disabilities and extending entitlement for special education and related services to preschoolers. These amendments to IDEA reflected the political, social, and economic contexts of the family and disability advocacy movement, judicial decisions ensuring education for individuals with disabilities, the realization of the importance of family participation in decision making, and recognition of the effectiveness and cost benefits of early intervention. Understanding this context enables participants to identify the social, political, and economic reasons for the development of a specific policy such as the early intervention program of IDEA.

Teaching Strategies: Understanding the Context

The following strategies can assist participants to identify and analyze the context for policy development. They are designed to develop knowledge (e.g., analyze economic trends), skills (e.g., identify and argue positions in court cases), and values (e.g., adopt the perspective of parents of children with disabilities). Table 16.2 outlines the purpose and identifies faculty and student resources for each of the following strategies.

Creating Context Collages To gain an overview of the context in which the early intervention program of IDEA was enacted, participants can develop a pictorial or print collage depicting the social, political, and economic context during landmark periods in the enactment of specific legislation for children (see Table 16.1). (For the early intervention program in IDEA, these landmarks are 1975 and 1986.) To understand the social context, participants can review high school and college yearbooks; the style, society, or living pages in newspapers and magazines; musical hits; and popular television shows. For a review of the political context, newspaper headlines can identify the issues of the times and the pressures on Congress and the President. Finally, the economic context can be understood by reviewing past editions of *The Wall Street Journal, Business Week,* and economic reports issued by public and private organizations. As participants develop their collages, they should correlate education and health policies implemented during the identified landmark periods with the political, social, and economic contexts of each period. This activity has also been successfully used as an inservice activity by grouping participants into "decades." Each group takes a 10-year period starting in the 1940s through the 1990s and identifies the key contextual markers based on their own knowledge and experience of each period (Bergman, 1995).

Conducting Court Debates Once an entitlement for public education for all school-age children was established in the 1970s, early intervention policy evolved to include children at younger ages via statewide, interagency programs mandated in IDEA. Participants can gain insight regarding the political context in the 1990s by examining landmark court decisions from the past. After reviewing relevant decisions, for example, *PARC v. Commonwealth of Pennsylvania* (1971) or *Mills v. Board of Education of the District of Columbia* (1972), teams are assigned to argue on behalf of the student and family or state perspective. The entire class can then discuss their attitudes and reactions to the courts' decisions.

Demystifying Legislation Some participants may be intimidated at the thought of reading and analyzing actual legislation. Before reading a law or regulations, participants can review the report that accompanies proposed legislation (see Table 16.2 for information on how to obtain congressional committee reports). Reviewing the report will familiarize participants with the context for the legislation and the inspiration for provisions in more understandable terms than the formal legislation. For instance, participants might review the 1986 report accompanying the U.S. House of Representatives' draft of PL 99-457 (U.S. House of Representatives, 1986). After they have read this report, participants will be better prepared to analyze the early intervention provisions of IDEA as well as the related regulations. This activity can be concluded by having participants debate the arguments for authorization of the early intervention program in IDEA and suggest why particular provisions were included.

Adopting a Family Perspective IDEA defined the family as having a primary role in decision making for the provision of early intervention services. Many students as well as new practitioners may assume that family members were always given a role in planning and decision making. Table 16.2 recommends readings for students that focus on parent and advocate narratives describing their experiences caring for and securing services for children with disabilities. To supplement or replace these readings, family advocates can be invited to address the group to share their perspectives on how the role of family members evolved from passive recipient to active partner since the 1970s.

TABLE 16.2. Resources for guiding participants to understand the context for early intervention public policy

Strategy	Purpose	Recommended faculty resources(s)	Student resources
Creating context collages	To gain an overview of the social context influencing the passage of IDEA	"Early childhood intervention: The evolution of a concept" (Shonkoff, 1990) "Impact of federal policy on pediatric health and education programs" (Hanft, 1991)	"The politics of mental retardation during the Kennedy administration" (Berkowitz, 1980) "The Education for All Handicapped Children Act of 1975 (PL 94-142): Its history, origins and concepts" (Zettel & Ballard, 1982)
Conducting court debates	To examine and interpret court cases as they affect policies and programs in the 1990s	*Free Appropriate Public Education* (Rapport, 1996; Turnbull, 1986)	"Interpreting the rights of exceptional citizens through judicial action" (Smith & Barresi, 1982)
Demystifying legislation	To become proficient in understanding policy by interpreting laws, regulations, and reports and debating specified topics	*Legal and Political Issues in Special Education* (Cremins, 1983) Internet addresses for draft legislation and hearing schedules for federal government: U.S. House of Representatives: http://www.house.gov U.S. Senate: http://www.senate.gov	Copies of legislation, regulations, and congressional committee reports may be available from a depository library for U.S. government publications (contact a local library or the Office of Depository Services, U.S. Government Printing Office, (202) 512-1109, to locate the closest depository library)

(continued)

TABLE 16.2. (continued)

Strategy	Purpose	Recommended faculty resources(s)	Student resources
			Federal reports, laws, and regulations are available for purchase from the U.S. Government Printing Office, Post Office Box 6015, Gaithersburg, MD 20877 (202) 512-1800, fax (202) 512-2250, and are listed in the *Monthly Catalog of United States Government Publications*, found in many libraries
Adopting a family perspective	To understand the evolution of parental roles in decision making for their children	"Parent advocacy: A resource for early intervention" (Pizzo,1990) "A brief history of family support programs" (Weissbourd, 1987)	*Parents Speak Out: Then and Now* (Turnbull & Turnbull, 1985) "Vision and empowerment" (Vohs, 1989)
Scanning the environment	To analyze the impact of political, economic, and social trends affecting a specific early intervention program	*Strategic Planning in Education: Unleashing Our School's Potential* (Newberry, 1992)	"Environmental scanning is vital to strategic planning" (Poole, 1991)

Scanning the Environment An environmental scan, a process of collecting data about trends and events that may affect a program or organization, is an excellent strategy for understanding the context for existing policies (Bryson, 1995; Newberry, 1992). Teams of participants can assess the impact of political, economic, technological, and social trends affecting a specific early intervention program by reviewing the larger community and national context in which the program operates. Reviewing all stakeholder attitudes and beliefs regarding the provision of early intervention services is also an essential component of this activity. Participants can gather information for their environmental scan by talking with the local chamber of commerce and community and business leaders. They can also review school board and county council reports and newspaper articles. Teams scan or review these data to identify political trends (e.g., upcoming elections, pending legislation, leadership), social trends (e.g, population served by the program, demographics of the entire community, attitudes and values of stakeholders), provider characteristics (e.g., education and experience, profession, instructional needs, personnel shortages), and the economic picture (e.g., funding sources for the program as well as revenues and businesses in the community). Once this information is collected, teams of participants can prepare charts for each category, separating the identified trends into supports and challenges for implementation of a specific early childhood policy within a community.

Because the development of an environmental scan requires some research, it is best assigned between classes or in preparation for an inservice workshop. When there is limited time for data collection, a guest speaker, such as an early intervention program director, can be invited to describe a particular program in the participants' community. Key demographic data describing the community in general and the population served by the early intervention program can be distributed on fact sheets for participants to review as they complete their scan. Inviting a guest speaker can also provide a helpful focus when trainees come from different programs or lack professional work experience (Hanft & Feinberg, 1995).

CRITIQUING EARLY CHILDHOOD POLICIES

To analyze the effect of early intervention policies, participants must first understand the provisions and intent of a particular policy. To accomplish this, participants must have a framework to guide their analysis. Gallagher (1989) described a seven-step model for analyzing the impact of a policy once implementation has begun. He used PL 99-457 to illustrate his model (see Table 16.3).

Framework of Policy Analysis

The first two steps of the model (i.e., the issues that led to the creation of the particular policy and a brief history of the present policy) are incorporated in the previous section

TABLE 16.3. Model of policy analysis

Steps for analyzing policy
1. Define the issues leading to the creation of the policy.
2. Summarize the history of the present policy.
3. Recognize the value base for the policy.
4. Examine how the policy has been implemented.
5. Identify how program objectives have been achieved.
6. Describe challenges and barriers to policy implementation.
7. Formulate recommendations for action.

Adapted from Gallagher (1989).

on understanding the context for public policies. Steps 3–7 are also essential considerations in critiquing policies and are discussed in the following sections.

Recognizing the value base of a particular policy is the third step of Gallagher's model for critiquing policies. Although the value base for a policy may be communicated in a statement of need or vision, it is more often an implicit assumption or understanding. The values underlying early intervention policies, however, should be unambiguous to ensure effective implementation and communication among stakeholders (Moroney, 1981). Some major assumptions underlying the early intervention program of IDEA include the following: 1) when it comes to intervention, the earlier, the better; 2) if help is not available to infants and toddlers who need it, society will bear the costs of disabilities that might have been remedied or ameliorated; 3) intervention should do no harm; 4) family involvement is important in developing plans for the child; and 5) development is a continuous process (Paul, Gallagher, Kendrick, Thomas, & Young, 1992). Values contrary to these (e.g., we should not expend money on children who, at best, will make little contribution to society) may also be held by some stakeholders and will challenge or even derail the implementation of a specific policy, such as the early intervention program of IDEA (Gallagher, 1989).

Examining the implementation of a policy is the fourth step in policy analysis. Key questions to ask when reviewing the provisions of an early intervention policy and accompanying regulations are identified in Figure 16.1. Participants must understand the specific provisions of a policy to be able to understand its impact on each of three major early intervention stakeholder groups: 1) children who need specific services to grow and develop and their family members; 2) community agencies and early intervention person-

---

1. What services and programs does the policy provide for families and children, and who is eligible to participate?

2. What rights and protections does this policy guarantee for children and families?

3. How will current early intervention services/programs be affected by this policy, and what changes in operations and procedures will practitioners and administrators need to make?

4. Who will oversee the implementation of this policy and administer any services/programs?

5. What federal, state, and local resources (e.g., funding and personnel development) will be available to carry out this policy as mandated?

6. What benefits and/or challenges will this policy bring to families and children, early intervention providers, and administrators?

Figure 16.1.   Key questions to ask when reviewing an early intervention policy.

nel who provide specialized services to children and families; and 3) administrators and legislators who authorize, fund, and oversee community programs and services.

The fifth step, identifying program objectives, focuses on evaluating whether basic policy objectives have been achieved. Typically, reviewers accomplish this through a literature search, personal interviews, questionnaires soliciting stakeholders' assessments and perspectives, or on-site review of specific programs and services to children and families established by the policy.

The sixth step identifies the challenges and barriers to policy implementation. Possible barriers include institutional (e.g., agencies, preexisting laws, bureaucratic procedures), psychological (e.g., personal, religious, or cultural beliefs of key individuals who implement the policy), sociological (e.g., values and mores of particular stakeholder groups), economic (e.g., funding sources, revenue, programmatic costs), political (e.g., challenges from established groups such as different levels of government or a professional organization), and geographic (e.g., rural versus urban, state and local boundaries, physical barriers such as mountains or rivers). Knowing the context for the formulation of a policy may provide indicators of challenges or barriers affecting implementation. For example, the political and social context for the 1986 reauthorization of IDEA provided strong support for extending the mandate for special education and related services down to age 3 but not to birth. Understanding this context enables participants to identify a major challenge to implementation of IDEA in having two sets of programs to administer the services, that is, early intervention services for the birth to 2-year-old population and school-based services for children with disabilities age 3 years and older. A particular challenge is faced when children make the transition from early intervention to school-based services.

The seventh and final step is to formulate recommendations for action. After evaluating whether policy objectives have been achieved, there are three possibilities for future action, specifically, acceptance, or partial or total revision of the policy under study. Strategies to assist participants in learning how to persuade policy makers to make changes as they draft and modify early intervention policies are discussed in the third instructional section on influencing public policy.

Teaching Strategies: Critiquing Early Childhood Policies

The following instructional strategies operationalize Steps 3–6 of Gallagher's model of policy analysis. These activities will assist participants in learning to analyze public policies during their implementation. Table 16.4 outlines the purpose and provides faculty and student resources for each of the strategies.

Identifying Stakeholder Values   The following activity will assist participants in understanding values and perspectives of early intervention stakeholders (e.g., families, practitioners, administrators). After reading family narratives (see Table 16.4 for suggestions) and/or talking with guest speakers to understand family perspectives, participants can be divided into small groups to discuss how personal and societal values affect the implementation of a policy, such as the early intervention program of IDEA. To illustrate, one concern for many families is finding cost-effective early intervention services in their own communities. Participants should consider how culture, ethnicity, and religion contribute to the values held by different families as they cope with the financial issues of paying for specialized services for their child. For example, participants might consider the differing values contained in statements such as, "My child's delay is God's will; He will take care of us somehow" or "I cannot ask others for help and must work harder to get what my child needs." Participants should consider how such personally held values

TABLE 16.4. Resources for guiding trainees to critique public policy

Strategy	Purpose	Faculty resource(s)	Student reading
Identifying stakeholder values	To understand the values and perspectives of major stakeholder groups (e.g., families, practitioners, administrators)	*Handbook for Ethical Policy Making* (Paul et al., 1992). "The place of principles in policy analysis" (Anderson, 1979)	"Parental perspectives on the system of care for two birth weight infants" (Willis, 1991) *Reflections on Growing Up Disabled* (Jones, 1982)
Understanding IDEA provisions	To understand the early intervention provisions of IDEA via innovative and entertaining strategies	Copies of IDEA and its regulations (CFR: Title 34; Education; Part 300–399) are available from Superintendent of Documents, U.S. Government Printing Office, Washington, DC 20402 (202) 783-3238 *Part H Updates.* (National Early Childhood Technical Assistance System, 1996). Available from: NEC*TAS, 500 NationsBank Plaza, 137 E. Franklin St., Chapel Hill, NC 27514 (919) 962-2001	*Families on the Move* (Institute for Child Health Policy, 1992), available at no cost from the National Center for Education in Maternal and Child Health, 2070 Chain Bridge Rd., Suite 450, Vienna, VA 22182 (703) 821-8955 ext. 254 *Road Trip* (Sloop, 1994) diagrams, for the car parts, are available from the Partnerships for Inclusion Project, Frank Porter Graham Child Development Center, CB 8180, UNC, Chapel Hill, NC 27599. Henderson (1992) includes informational materials about early intervention legislation and playing the game *Jeopardy* (Frank Porter Graham Child Development Center).
Interviewing policy makers	To demonstrate an awareness of various policies by framing interview questions and conducting interviews of stakeholders	"A functional analysis of the evolution of public policy for handicapped young children" (Meisels, 1985)	"From dream to reality: A participant's view of the implementation of Part H of PL 99-457" (Apter, 1994)

422

Evaluating policy effectiveness	To identify the format and methods used by policy analysts	An annual listing of all reports and testimony (including policy evaluations) published by the U.S. General Accounting Office (GAO) can be obtained from the GAO Document Ordering System (202) 512-6000. Example: *Home Visiting: A Promising Early Intervention Strategy for At-Risk Families* (GAO/HRD-90-83) The National Maternal & Child Health Clearinghouse also distributes policy reports (703) 821-8955. Example: *Health Policy and Child Health: Expansions of Coverage, Managed Care Creates New Outreach Challenges*	"Effects of family support intervention: A ten year follow-up" (Seitz, Rosenbaum, & Apfel, 1985) *The Increasing Array of Early Care and Education Policies: An Argument for State and Local Control* (Smith, 1992). (Available from Allegheny-Singer Research Institute, 320 East North Ave., Pittsburgh, PA 15212)
Analyzing vignettes	To evaluate the intricacies of potentially ambiguous or complex aspects of public policies	"The case method of instruction: Teaching application and problem solving skills to early interventionists" (McWilliam, 1992) "Problem-based learning: A review of literature on its outcomes and implementation issues" (Albanase & Mitchell, 1993)	*Working Together with Children and Families: Case Studies in Early Intervention* (McWilliam & Bailey, 1993)

support or challenge the societal values for early intervention programs identified on page 420.

Understanding IDEA Provisions   Before reviewing how a policy is implemented, participants must understand the content of the early intervention provisions of IDEA. The following three activities provide an interesting complement to readings about provisions of IDEA:

1. *Families on the Move*   A 10-minute video, *Families on the Move* (Institute for Child Health Policy, 1992) was filmed from a family perspective and provides a general introduction to the early intervention program in IDEA. The video illustrates 14 basic components of the law by linking each provision with the analogous parts of a bicycle, for example, the bicycle handlebars are representative of the family's role in steering the individualized family service plan.

2. *Road Trip*   An educational game for teams, *Road Trip* (Sloop, 1994) was developed by a parent advocate to compare the basic components of the early intervention provisions of IDEA to the parts of a car. For instance, the steering wheel of a car is analogous to the role of the lead agency in coordinating or driving the statewide system of services. Replicas of car parts can be distributed to groups or pairs of participants as a prompt to discuss how their assigned car parts represent an aspect of the law. Teams can work to move a car across a map of their state by winning points for accurately describing their assigned IDEA provisions.

3. *Jeopardy*   A humorous strategy to reinforce understanding of the major provisions of the early intervention program of IDEA is to play a version of the popular television game show *Jeopardy* (Rush & Martin, 1995). An "emcee," who dresses up in colorful clothes, gives each small group of participants a different statement describing a specific provision of the early intervention program. Each group must compose the corresponding question to win a point. For example, the correct question to the statement "This administrative group is responsible for ensuring that an IFSP is developed and implemented" is "What is a lead agency?" Descriptive materials about the law, as well as a copy of the legislation and implementing regulations, should be available to participants to use in forming the correct question. In preparation for this activity, each participant can write 10 statements with corresponding questions for the emcee to present.

Interviewing Policy Makers   Participants can use the questions posed in Figure 16.1 to assist them in understanding the provisions of a specific policy in several ways. Practitioners can review newly implemented legislation, regulations, or administrative directives with a focus on how stakeholders from their particular agency or program will be affected both positively and negatively. Preservice students can use the questions as interview prompts to elicit the views of administrators, practitioners, and families involved in early intervention regarding the positive and negative impact of a specific policy. Guest speakers or a panel with respondents representing families, administrators, and practitioners could also be invited to class to discuss the questions.

Evaluating Policy Effectiveness   Another strategy for teaching participants to evaluate the effectiveness of a public policy is to study reports completed by policy analysts. Participants can identify the structure and methods used, sources of information, key sections of the report, how analysis is presented, and recommendations for modification. Sources for early intervention reports available to the public are suggested in Table 16.4.

Analyzing Vignettes   Role playing and/or discussing narratives of family situations gives participants the opportunity to grapple with the ambiguity and complexity of evaluating the supports as well as challenges to an early intervention policy. The following vignette was presented to key constituents during a case study of policy development for the early intervention program. Participants may want to compare results of their discussions with those of these policy makers (see Place & Gallagher, 1992).

A mother living in a rural region of your state goes into delivery very early in her pregnancy, and complications develop with the infant after her birth. The baby is air-evacuated to the nearest neonatal intensive care unit (NICU). Because the baby meets the eligibility requirements for your early intervention program, a service coordinator is assigned and contacts the family, explaining that the early intervention program includes services to enhance the capacity of the family to meet the special needs of their child. The service coordinator asks family members what they need. They immediately say that the mother wants to see her baby. They do not have a car, nor do they have the money to go by public transportation. The mother explains, "My baby needs to be held by her mom. That's what she needs to get well and grow strong."

Sometimes the very ambiguity of the language of the law can create a challenge to interpretation and implementation. Various policy makers did express dramatically different points of view regarding the state's responsibility to provide early intervention services. Participants may answer the following questions on their own and provide a rationale for their answers based on the law and regulations: 1) Does the early intervention system sponsored under IDEA have a responsibility to provide the mother with transportation to a distant city where her infant is being treated in an NICU? and 2) If the parent then says she cannot pay for a hotel room, what is the responsibility of the system? Conclude this activity by holding a debate so that participants can articulate their positions and discuss inconsistencies in interpretations. Sources for additional narratives regarding family and state administrator perspectives are suggested in Table 16.4.

INFLUENCING PUBLIC POLICY

The final step in policy analysis is formulating recommendations for future action. This action will involve influencing policy makers to maintain support for existing programs; influence the passage or revision of legislation, regulations, or other guidelines affecting services; and prevent the adoption of policies that may hinder the ultimate effectiveness of early intervention services for families and children. To fulfill the role of advocating for a certain policy, participants must demonstrate sophisticated analyses and communication. They should be able to look beyond the surface of what a policy states and evaluate testimony and evidence regarding its impact.

Teaching Strategies: Influencing Public Policy

Effective policy advocates need to communicate effectively with influential policy makers. This requires being able to analyze positions, frame ideas, develop persuasive arguments, and convey these recommendations in an effective and respectful manner. The following strategies will assist participants to learn and practice the skills of a successful policy advocate. Table 16.5 outlines the purpose and provides faculty and student resources for these strategies.

TABLE 16.5. Resources for teaching participants to influence public policy

Strategy	Purpose	Faculty resource(s)	Student resources
Conducting a mock hearing	To adopt the perspectives of key policy makers by taking on the roles of congressional representatives and witnesses at a hearing	*Congressional Procedures and the Policy Process* (Oleszek, 1984) *The Dance of Legislation* (Redman, 1973)	*Anatomy of a Hearing* (League of Women Voters of the United States, 1972)
Evaluating oral testimony	To evaluate the oral testimony of key policy makers by attending a public hearing	*Present Yourself* (Gelb, 1988)	"Public hearings: Make sure your testimony is heard" (Glomp, 1982) "How to get your congressman to listen to you" (Kiplinger, 1972)
Gaining insight about influence	To gain insights from policy makers about factors that influence their decision making and to learn how to positively influence decision makers	*Lions Don't Need to Roar* (Benton, 1992) *People Skills* (Bolton, 1979)	*Written by Herself: An Anthology of Women's Autobiographies* (Ker Conway, 1992) "Influencing others: Skills are identified" (Goleman, 1986)
Developing persuasive arguments	To consider a position from all sides and to practice debating pros and cons	*Presentation for Decision Makers: Strategies for Structuring and Delivering Your Ideas* (Holcombe & Stein, 1983)	"The clinician as advocate for sensory integration" (Hanft, 1987)
Writing letters to policy makers	To become capable of drafting succinct and persuasive letters to policy makers	*How to Write Your Congressman and the President* (Friends Committee on National Legislation, 1991). Address: 245 Second St., N.E., Washington, DC 20002 (202) 547-6000	*Special Education and Related Services: Communicating By Letter Writing* (Ferguson & Ripley, 1991)

Conducting a Mock Hearing   This activity focuses on conducting a mock hearing with participants assuming the roles of congressional committee members and witnesses. The success of this activity is dependent on some preparation by the instructor and participants. The instructor should monitor when congressional hearings relevant to early intervention are scheduled to videotape specific televised proceedings from networks dedicated to broadcasting congressional news (see Table 16.2 for the Internet address for hearing schedules). Copies of written testimony may also be requested from witnesses by contacting them immediately after the committee hearing (committees also may keep transcripts on file for several weeks after hearings). After viewing the videotape and reading any hearing documents obtained, participants can critique the witnesses' oral and written testimony and modify their testimony in ways they think will enhance the impact of their positions. Participants are then prepared to reenact the hearing, role-playing congressional members and witnesses viewed in the tapes. Participants not involved in the mock hearing can critique the effectiveness of the oral presentations to the committee. Participants will benefit from analyzing testimony and witnessing an actual congressional hearing but will also gain experience in making persuasive speeches before an authoritative body.

Evaluating Oral Testimony   Local hearings or meetings can be identified for participants to attend (e.g., school board meetings, public hearings at the state capitol, the recreation subcommittee of the local city council). Participants should note the following in journals or oral presentations to the class: Who presented before the policy board? Whom did they represent? Why were these people invited or allowed to testify? How did the policy makers interact with each witness, and what influenced these varying interactions? What points did particular hearing witnesses make? How effective were they? Once the participant has analyzed the hearing, he or she can rewrite one witness's testimony to enhance its effectiveness. In addition to giving participants exposure to actual public debates, this exercise necessitates that participants analyze all the subtle influences crucial to testifying in a hearing. Finally, the task requires detailed analysis of testimony and recommendations for improving the presentation.

Gaining Insight About Influence   A key community leader, such as a county supervisor, the chair of the school board, or parent activist, may be invited to participate in an interview conducted by participants focusing on how to influence policy makers. Before the guest arrives, trainees should reach consensus about the interview questions (e.g., how to identify key decision makers for specific issues, how to gain access to policy makers, how to phrase comments, what influences this particular policy maker positively, what hazards can the guest warn the participant to avoid). Have a stand-up mike, if necessary, and assign or ask for volunteers to present questions to the interviewee. Ask the policy guest to offer tips and stories to guide the participants to become more effective at influencing policies.

The participants might also be interested in how the guest became an influential person. What led them to become interested in policy development, implementation, or influence? What instruction did they seek? What important life choices or events led to this outcome? For example, readings from *Written by Herself: An Anthology of Women's Autobiographies* (Ker Conway, 1992) will assist participants in understanding how women have attained positions of influence in professions from which they traditionally have been excluded (see Table 16.5).

Once questions are selected, a mock press conference or interview can be conducted. Participants could write a one-page press release based on what they learned from the interview. This activity gives participants the experience thinking about and framing essential questions to ask an influential policy guest. It also gives them an opportunity to interview an influential guest in a formal manner in front of an audience and to summarize complex information succinctly.

Developing Persuasive Arguments   When considering the implications of a policy, it is important to consider its impact from all perspectives. Participants can make a grid of all key stakeholder groups and summarize the pro and con perspectives of each group. This will help participants develop their argument to present to policy makers as well as anticipate the opposition's points by answering the question, "What does this policy mean for my group as well as other stakeholders?" (Scott & Acquaviva, 1985). To illustrate, assume a group of early intervention program managers has convened to suggest revisions to state Medicaid policy regarding payment for early intervention services in community settings outside of hospitals. Chart the key issues (pro and con) for each of three groups—families, practitioners, and state administrators—in regard to expanding the Medicaid coverage for the birth-to-3 population. Using this stakeholder perspective chart as a base, participants can develop their argument for or against this proposal. Remind them that effective proposals anticipate and answer the opposing views with objective data.

Writing Letters to Policy Makers   Participants can be divided into groups of three and asked to reach a consensus about a local issue they would like to see policy makers address. Participants should organize their thoughts in a concise and persuasive letter to key decision makers (sources for effective letter writing to influence policy makers are listed in Table 16.5). To practice letter writing, issues need not be confined to early intervention and may address issues such as asking the city council or county board of directors to install a new traffic light at a dangerous intersection or requesting that university administrators implement a new policy of having security guards accompany students to their cars or dorms after 10 P.M. to ensure their safety. More experienced participants may write to state and federal policy makers regarding issues of personal or professional concern.

Many participants will receive a response, especially if they are members of the policy makers' constituency. Responses should be shared with the group. Some groups may not receive a reply. Participants should be reminded that the purpose of the task is to identify a policy that needs change, learn what constitutes an effective policy request, and draft such a letter. The response from policy makers is not essential to accomplish the desired goals for this task.

CONCLUSION

This chapter has provided faculty of personnel development programs with strategies for teaching participants to analyze public policy effectively. Students in preservice programs as well as practitioners in the field must receive instruction in policy analysis to understand the laws, regulations, and other policies that govern early intervention programs as well as clarify administrative directives regarding how best to conduct early intervention programs and services. Three key competencies have been identified that participants must acquire to analyze policies effectively: 1) understand the political, social, and economic context contributing to the development of the policy; 2) critique the provision of the policy and evaluate its effectiveness; and 3) influence policy makers to draft or revise policies.

As we approach the 21st century, many long-standing policies affecting children with disabilities and their families will come under scrutiny as the political, social, and economic context for providing early intervention services to children and families changes.

Debates about federal and state responsibility for services, limited financial resources for health care and education, and manpower shortages will continue to raise complex questions regarding whom to serve and what programs are needed and desirable. These complex questions are not answered simply, nor are policies understood solely through a review of their provisions. Policy analysis is a complex process that goes beyond a simple understanding of the provisions of a specific policy. Participants must be prepared to engage in a comprehensive analysis of the issues, values, and impact of a policy to make rational recommendations and influence the implementation of key early intervention policies for children and their family members.

> (Early) intervention is not a monolithic phenomenon.... The idea that there is a "right" way to intervene with infants is outmoded.... We must design models that account for greater diversity of needs; offer more respect for individual differences; embody different governance structures; foster different approaches to training; contain totally different roles for families; rely on different levels of responsibility and leadership from diverse social services; and generally reflect different relationships between recipients of services, professionals, lay professionals, researchers, and policy makers. (Meisels, 1992, p. 5)

REFERENCES

Albanase, M., & Mitchell, S. (1993). Problem-based learning: A review of literature on its outcomes and implementation issues. *Academic Medicine, 68*, 52–81.

Americans with Disabilities Act of 1990, PL 101-336, 42 U.S.C. §12101 *et seq.*

Anderson, C. (1979). The place of principles in policy analysis. *The American Political Science Review, 73*, 711–723.

Apter, D. (1994). From dream to reality: A participant's view of the implementation of Part H of PL 99-457. *Journal of Early Intervention, 18*(2), 131–140.

Benton, D. (1992). *Lions don't need to roar: Using the leadership power of professional presence to stand out, fit in and move ahead.* New York: Warner Books.

Bergman, A. (1995, March). *Evolution of common sense and disability policy: From institutional to community and facility-based services to support individuals and families in inclusive communities.* Paper presented to the Think Tank on Therapeutic Services for Children with Disabilities, United Cerebral Palsy Associations, Inc., Washington, DC.

Berkowitz, E. (1980). The politics of mental retardation during the Kennedy administration. *Social Sciences Quarterly, 61*, 128–143.

Bolton, (1979). *People skills.* New York: Simon & Schuster.

Bowlby, J. (1969). *Attachment and loss* (Vol. 1). New York: Basic Books.

Bryson, J. (1995). *Strategic planning for public and nonprofit organizations.* San Francisco: Jossey-Bass.

Cremins, J. (1983). *Legal and political issues in special education.* Springfield, IL: Charles C Thomas.

Developmental Disabilities Assistance and Bill of Rights Act of 1975, PL 94-103, 42 U.S.C. §6000 *et seq.*

Economic Opportunity Act Amendments of 1972, PL 92-424, 42 U.S.C. §2921 *et seq.*

Education for All Handicapped Children Act of 1975, PL 94-142, 20 U.S.C. §1400 *et seq.*

Education of the Handicapped Act Amendments of 1986, PL 99-457, 20 U.S.C. §1400 *et seq.*

Ferguson, S., & Ripley, S. (1991). *Special education and related services: Communicating by letter writing.* Washington, DC: National Information Center for Children and Youth with Disabilities.

Friends Committee on National Legislation. (1991). *How to write your Congressman and the President* (How-to series #4). Washington, DC: Author.

Gallagher, J. (1981). Models for policy analysis: Child and family policy. In R. Haskins & J. Gallagher (Eds.), *Models for analysis of social policy: An introduction* (pp. 37–77). Norwood, NJ: Ablex Publishing Co.

Gallagher, J.J. (1989). The implementation of social policy: A policy analysis challenge. In J.J. Gallagher, P.L. Trohanis, & R.M. Clifford (Eds.), *Policy implementation and PL 99-457: Planning for young children with special needs* (pp. 199–215). Baltimore: Paul H. Brookes Publishing Co.

Gelb, M. (1988). *Present yourself.* Rolling Hills Estate, CA: Jalmar Press.

Glomp, D. (1982). Public hearings: Make sure your testimony is heard. *Association Management*, 34.

Goleman, D. (1986, February 18). Influencing others: Skills are identified. *The New York Times, Science Times*.

Hanft, B. (1987). The clinician as advocate for sensory integration. *Occupational Therapy in Health Care*, 4(2), 137–146.

Hanft, B. (1991). Impact of federal policy on pediatric health and education programs. In W. Dunn (Ed.), *Pediatric occupational therapy* (pp. 273–284). Thorofare, NJ: Charles B. Slack.

Hanft, B., & Feinberg, E. (1995, July). *Early intervention/early childhood summer institute.* Presented at the George Washington University, Department of Teacher Preparation and Special Education, Washington, DC.

Henderson, L. (1992). *Legislation regarding a family-focused approach to early intervention.* Chapel Hill: University of North Carolina at Chapel Hill, Southeastern Institute for Faculty Training, Frank Porter Graham Child Development Center.

Holcombe, M., & Stein, J. (1983). *Presentations for decision makers: Strategies for structuring and delivering your ideas.* Belmont, CA: Lifetime Learning Publications.

Individuals with Disabilities Education Act (IDEA) of 1990, PL 101-476, 20 U.S.C. §1400 *et seq.*

Institute for Child Health Policy. (1992). *Families on the move* [Videotape]. (Available from the National Center for Education in Maternal and Child Health, 2070 Chain Bridge Road, Suite 450, Vienna, VA 22182)

Jones, R. (1982). *Reflections on growing up disabled.* Reston, VA: Council for Exceptional Children.

Ker Conway, J. (Ed.). (1992). *Written by herself: An anthology of women's autobiographies* (Vol. 1). New York: Random House.

Kiplinger, W. (1972, July). How to get your congressman to listen to you. *Association Management*, 24.

Lasswell, H. (1951). The policy orientation. In H. Lasswell & D. Lerner (Eds.), *The policy science* (pp. 5–8). Stanford, CA: Stanford University Press.

Lazar, I., & Darlington, R. (1982). Lasting effects of early education: A report from the Consortium for Longitudinal Studies. *Monograph of the Society for Research in Child Development*, 47(2–3, Serial No. 195).

League of Women Voters of the United States. (1972). *Anatomy of a hearing.* Washington, DC: League of Women Voters Foundation.

McWilliam, P.J. (1992). The case method of instruction: Teaching application and problem solving skills to early interventionists. *Journal of Early Intervention*, 16(4), 360–373.

McWilliam, P.J., & Bailey, D.B., Jr. (Eds.). (1993). *Working together with children and families: Case studies in early intervention.* Baltimore: Paul H. Brookes Publishing Co.

Meisels, S. (1985). A functional analysis of the evolution of public policy for handicapped young children. *Educational Evaluation & Policy Analysis*, 7(2), 115–126.

Meisels, S. (1992). Early intervention: A matter of context. *Zero to Three*, 12(3), 1–6.

Mills v. Board of Education of the District of Columbia, 348 F. Supp. 866 (D.C.C. 1972).

Moroney, R. (1981). Policy analysis within a value theoretical framework. In R. Haskins & J. Gallagher (Eds.), *Models of policy analysis* (pp. 78–102). Norwood, NJ: Ablex Publishing Co.

National Early Childhood Technical Assistance System. (1996). *Part H updates.* Chapel Hill, NC: Author.

Newberry, A. (1992). *Strategic planning in education: Unleashing our school's potential.* Vancouver, CA: EducServ Inc.

Oleszek, W. (1984). *Congressional procedures and the policy process.* Washington, DC: Congressional Quarterly.

Paul, J., Gallagher, J., Kendrick, B., Thomas, D., & Young, J. (1992). *Handbook for ethical policy making.* Chapel Hill: University of North Carolina at Chapel Hill, Carolina Policy Studies Program, Frank Porter Graham Child Development Center.

Pennsylvania Association for Retarded Children (PARC) v. Commonwealth of Pennsylvania, 334 F. Supp. 1257, 343 F. Supp. 279 (E.D. Pa 1971, 1972).

Pizzo, P. (1990). Parent advocacy: A resource for early intervention. In S. Meisels & J. Shonkoff (Eds.), *Handbook of early childhood intervention* (pp. 668–678). Cambridge, MA: Cambridge University Press.

Place, P., & Gallagher, J. (1992). *Part H policy development for families: A case study report.* Chapel Hill: University of North Carolina at Chapel Hill, Carolina Policy Studies Program, Frank Porter Graham Child Development Center.

Poole, M. (1991). Environmental scanning is vital to strategic planning. *Educational Leadership, 7,* 40–41.

Rapport, M.J.K. (1996). Legal guidelines for the delivery of special health services in school. *Exceptional Children, 62*(6), 537–550.

Redman, E. (1973). *The dance of legislation.* New York: Simon & Schuster.

Rehabilitation Act of 1973, PL 93-112, 29 U.S.C. §701 *et seq.*

Riley, D., Nash, H., & Hunt, J. (1978). *National incentives in special education: A history of legislative and court actions.* Alexandria, VA: National Association of State Directors of Special Education.

Rush, D., & Martin, V. (1995, May). *Training parents, providers and faculty as inservice and preservice trainers for Part H.* Workshop presented at the CSPD annual conference, Arlington, VA.

Scott, S., & Acquaviva, J. (1985). *Lobbying for health care.* Rockville, MD: American Occupational Therapy Association.

Seitz, V., Rosenbaum, L., & Apfel, N. (1985). Effects of family support intervention: A ten year follow-up. *Child Development, 56,* 376–391.

Shelton, T., Jeppson, E., & Johnson, B. (1989). *Family-centered care for children with special health care needs.* Bethesda, MD: Association for the Care of Children's Health.

Shonkoff, J. (1990). Early childhood intervention: The evolution of a concept. In S. Meisels & J. Shonkoff (Eds.), *Handbook of early childhood intervention* (pp. 3–32). Cambridge, England: Cambridge University Press.

Shonkoff, J., & Hauser-Cram, P. (1987). Early intervention for disabled infants and their families: A quantitative analysis. *Pediatrics, 80*(5), 650–658.

Sloop, S. (1994). *Roadtrip* [Game]. (Available from the Partnerships for Inclusion Project, NCMB Plaza, Frank Porter Graham Child Development Center, University of North Carolina, Chapel Hill, NC 27599).

Smith, B. (1992). *The increasing array of early care and education policies: An argument for state and local control.* Pittsburgh, PA: Allegheny-Singer Research Institute.

Smith, B., & Barresi, J. (1982). Interpreting the rights of exceptional citizens through judicial action. In J. Ballard, B. Ramirez, & F. Weintraub (Eds.), *Special education in America: Its legal and governmental foundations* (pp. 65–82). Reston, VA: Council for Exceptional Children.

Smith, C. (1996). Selected federal programs serving children with disabilities. In R. Behrman (Ed.), *The future of children* (Vol. 6, pp. 162–173). Los Altos, CA: David and Lucile Packard Foundation.

Social Security Act of 1935, PL 74-271, 42 U.S.C. §301 *et seq.*

Social Security Act Amendments of 1965, PL 89-97, 42 U.S.C. §101 *et seq.*

Starling, G. (1977). *Managing the public sector.* Homewood, IL: The Dropsy Press.

State Legislative Leaders Foundation. (1995). *State legislative leaders: Keys to effective legislation for children and families.* Centreville, MA: Author.

Turnbull, R. (1986). *Free appropriate public education.* Denver, CO: Love Publishing Co.

Turnbull, R., & Turnbull, A. (1985). *Parents speak out: Then and now.* Columbus, OH: Charles E. Merrill.

U.S. House of Representatives. (1986). *Education of the Handicapped Act Amendments of 1986* (Report 99-860). Washington, DC: U.S. Government Printing Office.

Vohs, J. (1989). Vision and empowerment. *Infants and Young Children, 2*(1), vii–x.

Weissbourd, B. (1987). A brief history of family support programs. In S. Kagan, D. Powell, B. Weissbourd, & E. Zigler (Eds.), *America's family support programs* (pp. 38–56). New Haven, CT: Yale University Press.

Werner, E., Bierman, J., & French, F. (1971). *The children of Kauai: A longitudinal study from the prenatal period to age ten.* Honolulu: University of Hawaii Press.

Willis, W. (1991). Parental perspectives on the system of care for two birth weight infants. *Infants and Young Children, 3*(4), v–x.

Zettel, J., & Ballard, J. (1982). The Education for All Handicapped Children Act of 1975 (PL 94-142): Its history, origins and concepts. In J. Ballard, B. Ramirez, & F. Weintraub (Eds.), *Special education in America: Its legal and governmental foundations* (pp. 11–22). Reston, VA: Council for Exceptional Children.

IV MODELS FOR PERSONNEL PREPARATION

How have others addressed the personnel preparation challenges that are described throughout this book? Part IV provides information about specific models that have been developed, implemented, and evaluated to deal effectively with the issues introduced in Part I and the challenges described in subsequent sections. The information in Part IV has application at state, community, program, university, and community college levels and across all disciplines. The focus is on practical information that will assist agencies and individuals in making changes that affect the way that personnel preparation is implemented. The final chapter addresses the nuts and bolts of "putting it all together," drawing on instructional strategies and examples from the previous chapters.

17

PARENT–PROFESSIONAL PARTNERSHIPS IN PRESERVICE AND INSERVICE EDUCATION

Angela Capone
Karla M. Hull
Nancy J. DiVenere

Another doctor's appointment, probably the tenth this month. It's amazing that a 7-month-old baby who has been through as much as Chris has can still maintain an easy disposition. Although the physicians comment on his easygoing nature, it seems as though no one cares about what it takes to support an infant whose skin is raw from eczema, who can't take more than three sips from a bottle without coughing due to asthma, and who has had three surgeries and countless trips to an emergency room, all prompted by difficulties related to his circumcision. As Angela, Chris's mother, thinks back on the past 7 months, she tries to figure out why she has such uneasy feelings about the medical profession. For the most part Chris's medical needs have been addressed (not always in a timely fashion, but always ultimately addressed), but there is something unrewarding about each visit.

First came the medical student, "Tell me about Chris. Why are you here?" (as if the red, oozing lesions on his face weren't visible). You know the typical questions. With all his questions answered, he told us that the doctor, a pediatric dermatologist, would be in in a minute. At least Dr. Krusinski always talked to Angela, played with Chris, and had his secretary call to see how they were doing. He had also been honest enough to share that two treatments prescribed by other doctors had caused more harm than benefit (honesty is definitely an endearing quality). As Dr. Krusinski and the medical student entered the room, Chris looked up, quieter than usual and with no smile.

"Oh, Chris, what has happened to you? Don't worry, we'll get you better." Dr. Krusinski looked at the medical student and said, "This is typically one of the happiest little boys I see; clearly his eczema is out of control, and we need to readjust his medication." What a treat—Dr. Krusinski knew who Chris was and incorporated that knowledge into the diagnosis. He then turned to Angela and asked her to talk about how she was taking care of Chris's skin. After completing her litany of "lotions and potions" (a routine rivaled only by a professional masseuse), he turned to the medical student and said, "It's so important to ask the parent(s) what they've been doing—it makes your job so much easier. Angela has just described the perfect scenario, and look at Chris; it's obviously not working. There isn't a doubt in my mind that they need a higher-level cream." At this point Dr. Krusinski answered a number of Angela's questions about eczema and skin infections, prescribed an antibiotic, and then began to talk to her about how to make decisions on working with the antibiotic and the three levels of skin

creams Chris now has. As he ended the visit, he reminded her that his secretary would call in 2 days to see how things were going.

Once they were alone, Angela sat with Chris and thought, "This must be what family-centered care feels like." They had both been the recipients of a great deal of respect. Chris was not just an infant with a skin ailment; he was a happy little boy whose skin was having a dramatic impact on his disposition. She wasn't simply the person holding Chris; she was the person who cared for this little boy, who had a routine of care, who had observations, and who had expertise. Dr. Krusinski clearly acknowledged that he couldn't do his job without her. He gave Angela the information and tools that would allow her to care for Chris in the best possible manner. In addition, he communicated that he saw her as a decision maker in Chris's treatment. He taught her how to observe and use the various "lotions and potions" effectively and responsively. How amazing—she was seen as a partner in Chris's care. This is what had been missing!

Partnership may well be remembered as a hallmark of the 1990s. It is a concept that is reshaping how America wants to deliver goods and services (Kagan, 1991). Across the United States, families and professionals are establishing partnerships. Parents are participating as members of task forces and advisory boards, mentors for other families, grant reviewers, participants in quality improvement initiatives, and as instructors for preservice and inservice activities (Jeppson & Thomas, 1994c).

We have learned that when parents and professionals work in partnership the results are dramatic. Parent–professional partnerships have been attributed with "humanizing the service delivery system, improving outcomes for children, contributing to greater satisfaction for both parents and professionals" (Jeppson & Thomas, 1994b, p. 1) and "creating an atmosphere in which the cultural traditions, values, and diversity of families are acknowledged and honored" (Bishop, Woll, & Arango, 1993, p. 29). The vignette about Chris and his mom exemplifies the impact of authentic partnerships between parents and professionals on the lives of children and their families. The partnership Dr. Krusinski established with Angela clearly illustrates what can happen when a professional steps out of a traditional approach to service delivery and views a parent as an essential partner in the delivery of services. A closer look at this partnership reveals the following key elements of parent–professional partnerships:

- Dr. Krusinski clearly acknowledged Chris as a person with a pleasant disposition that was being affected by a medical condition. His actions communicated to Angela that treatment for the condition, although related to the medical problem, was, more important, linked to helping Chris get back to his old self.
- Dr. Krusinski acknowledged that Chris's eczema was being treated on an ongoing basis by Angela; therefore, he was neither the sole provider of medical treatment nor the only individual with information that would help Chris.
- Dr. Krusinski clearly communicated that he needed Angela's expertise in dealing with Chris's condition to make an appropriate next-step decision.
- Dr. Krusinski gave Chris and Angela new information as well as a new treatment, and then reviewed how this new treatment fit with all the other information and treatments they were already using.
- Dr. Krusinski also set up a "check-in" visit that was not primarily related to Chris's skin needing medical attention but was designed to provide an opportunity for Angela and Dr. Krusinski to reflect on both how Chris was doing and how the treatment felt to Angela.

FACILITATING PARENT–PROFESSIONAL PARTNERSHIPS IN PRESERVICE AND INSERVICE EDUCATION

Preservice and inservice training opportunities that facilitate the preparation of professionals who are able to practice in partnership with families are grounded in family-centered principles. Such opportunities require considerable reflection and evaluation on the part of professionals as well as a commitment to an ongoing, developmental process: a journey undertaken in partnership with families. Since the 1970s, families have become increasingly involved in preservice and inservice instruction, and much has been learned from the reflections of families and professionals who have engaged in instructional partnerships. Bishop et al. (1993) described seven principles that provide the foundation for family–professional collaboration:

1. Promotes a relationship in which family members and professionals work together to ensure the best services for the child and family
2. Recognizes and respects the knowledge, skills, and experience that families and professionals bring to the relationship
3. Acknowledges that the development of trust is an integral part of a collaborative relationship
4. Facilitates open communication so that families and professionals feel free to express themselves
5. Creates an atmosphere in which the cultural traditions, values, and diversity of families are acknowledged and honored
6. Recognizes that negotiation is essential in a collaborative relationship
7. Brings to the relationship the mutual commitment of families, professionals, and communities to meet the needs of children with special needs and their families

These principles can be put into practice by including the family at the ground level of instructional activities, using innovative ways to identify and recruit families for participation in the instructional partnership, creating partnerships with parent organizations to ensure continuity and ongoing support to both families and professionals, maintaining an array of instructional opportunities in which families can participate, and acknowledging and responding to logistical challenges in creative ways.

Involving Families as Partners in Preservice and Inservice Education

Parent–professional partnerships are the vehicle that can change the traditional culture of preservice and inservice instruction. These partnerships set a context for the preparation of family-centered practitioners by modeling the qualities of a collaborative relationship between families and professionals. Partnerships model the belief that families are valued consumers of, and competent partners in, the design, implementation, and evaluation of early intervention services. More important, partnerships communicate the need for the expertise of both families and professionals to develop and implement appropriate services for young children with disabilities and their families. Parent–professional partnerships for preservice and inservice instruction provide one of the best means of communicating the family-centered philosophy. These partnerships reinforce a belief in family centeredness and strengthen programs, practices, and practitioners. Partnerships become the enduring quality of successful preservice and inservice instruction, and they sustain family-centered practitioners.

Although parent–professional partnerships have a positive impact on all levels of the service delivery system, they are not a natural phenomenon. When they do exist these partnerships reflect a deliberate effort to include families in arenas typically dominated by professionals (Jeppson & Thomas, 1994b). Since the late 1980s, inservice and preservice instructional programs have made great strides toward establishing authentic partnerships between parents and professionals (Bailey, Palsha, & Huntington, 1990; Favrot, Steele, & Worthington, 1993; Winton & DiVenere, 1995). A report on early intervention personnel preparation programs (Campbell, 1994) indicated that U.S. universities have begun to address the need to prepare family-centered practitioners by providing students with op-portunities to learn with and from families. Responses to a written survey from 100 graduate- and undergraduate-level early intervention personnel preparation programs representing 38 states and the District of Columbia suggest three distinct trends. First, parents are becoming involved in the personnel preparation process; 81% of the programs reported that parents participate as guest lecturers, and 19% of the programs reported that parents co-teach with faculty. A second trend relates to opportunities for students to spend time with families in their homes. Seventy-seven percent of the programs reported that students complete at least one assignment with a parent of a young child with a disability in the family's home, and 45% of the programs reported students complete a practicum of at least 20 contact hours over a semester or term with families in their homes. Finally, the role of families in the personnel preparation process is expanding. Forty-nine percent of the programs identified unique ways in which families are involved in personnel prep-aration, including participation on advisory boards ($n = 22$), supervision of students ($n = 24$), involvement in practicum ($n = 16$), and participation in a parent mentoring program ($n = 16$).

The Nature of Parent–Professional Partnerships

> Successful partnerships are characterized by an exchange of ideas, knowledge, and resources. Partners form a mutually rewarding relationship with the purpose of improving some aspect of education. The relationship must be based on the identification and acceptance of compatible goals and strategies. In addition, the partners should respect the differences in each other's culture and style, striving to apply the best of both worlds to achieve established goals. (Grobe, 1993, p. 7)

A number of concrete steps can be taken to involve family members as equal partners in preservice and inservice training. In the following sections, these steps are illustrated with a parent's voice.

Maintaining an Array of Options　Winton and DiVenere (1995) identified four types of roles that parents may fill, including instructors, practicum supervisors, team participants in staff development, and planners and policy makers. Each role translates into a broad array of actions that increases the potential of capitalizing on the expertise each family has to offer. The uniqueness of each family and family context enhances participants' opportunities to understand the intricacies of a family-centered philosophy as it relates to different situations. The extent to which families have opportunities to participate as instructors directly affects participants' opportunities for learning. Table 17.1 identifies sample activities that can be associated with each role.

The journey toward creating partnerships with families must be driven by constant attention to the ways in which families are included in training activities. In a study by Capone (1995), 52 parents who had been involved in preservice and inservice training activities were interviewed and participated in follow-up focus groups to describe their

TABLE 17.1. The roles of families in parent–professional partnerships in training

Families as instructors

- Participation on panels
- Teaching a module
- Co-instructor for a course
- Co-instructor for a workshop

Family practica experiences

- Pairing students and families for a home visit
- Participation in semester-long practicum experiences

Families as participants in a team-based model of staff development

- Participating as decision-making partners in defining how programs can move toward more family-centered practice

Families members as personnel preparation policy makers and planners

- Membership and leadership roles on state interagency coordinating councils
- Participation on personnel subcommittees of the interagency coordinating council
- Participation as paid consultants and staff on various innovative instructional grants funded federally or locally

perceptions of the role of parents in training activities. Parents in this study discussed a desire to participate as equal partners, whereby they are partners in all aspects of the instructional activities in which they are asked to participate (i.e., planning, implementing, evaluating). The phrase that was used frequently by parents during the interviews was "involvement at the time of conception."

> Parents are advocates for children; they have information about strategies that work for kids as well as strategies that can help the system function in a more efficient and responsive manner. Parents' experiences have tremendous potential for not only informing, but also promoting system change. It is, however, very difficult to be in a reactive stance. For example, it's difficult when someone else has already established the goals, and often developed the materials for a training session, and then asks you to please provide your perspective on these goals and materials. It would feel so much more like a partnership to be involved from the beginning—to be a part of identifying the goals and developing the materials. (Capone, 1995)

When parents state, "At all levels and in all activities parents should be viewed as equals in the partnership," they are describing a frustration that stems from not being provided with an opportunity to understand the larger whole. When parents are not included as partners at the point of conception, it limits the potential value of the knowledge and experience they have to share with professionals.

> What I do and say, as a parent, can and should depend on the format of the presentation and what my experiences have been. I have a great deal to share beyond "what my family story is." In order for this to happen I need the same tools: perhaps encouragement, but most definitely information. Information about the overall goals of the training. Information on who else is speaking and what they are going to say. Information on how to best organize my presentation. In short, parents would like to be involved in the total process: planning and imple-

menting as well as being prepared to participate in training, not so that they will be professionals, but so that the parent perspective will be presented well. (Capone, 1995)

Parents in this study also applied the concept of participating as equals in the partnership to the evaluation process occurring at the end of most training sessions.

> Professionals appear to have specific "expectations" relative to parent performance. If I knew what they were I would be better able to meet them. Perhaps, a mentorship system could be set up to support parents as trainers (e.g., visiting other parent training sessions), or perhaps, when we think of supporting parents as training partners we can also think of support as the opportunity to explore the training issues with others who are also involved in the training. (Capone, 1995)

Parents are speaking about what might be described as "mutual obligations and expectations," a partnership in which all participants understand the goals and objectives as well as their specific role in realizing those goals. Therefore, participation in evaluation of the activity provides an opportunity for dialogue and trust building, two key elements in establishing equality among partners.

Partnerships are most successful when all presenters are included in all phases of the instruction, from planning and implementation to evaluation and follow-up. Including families at all levels increases the effectiveness of the instruction and ensures that family-centered principles are clearly reflected in instructional partnerships. In one study (Capone, 1995), parents spoke about the issue of respect: respect for what parents have to say, respect for their experience, and respect for their commitment. Respect, as parents discussed it, can take many forms: payment, scheduling accommodations (e.g, doing instruction when it is most convenient for the parent, including options to support child care during the instruction), being involved as an equal partner (e.g., knowing what everyone else knows), and the opportunity to have equal time to present. When parents participate in instructional activities, attention should be given not only to the content of a presentation but also to the whole presentation, from logistics, to introductions, to summarizations. When introducing parents during instruction, even the tone and the attitude expressed are reflective of the level of partnership that exists between parents and professionals: "Being introduced [by someone with a] 'This is the Parent' tone implies much to the audience" (Capone, 1995).

It is important that family partners have numerous and varied ways of sharing their perspectives and experiences. Family input can be as formal as creating paid staff positions or as informal as holding a coffee hour on a hospital unit for families to share their perspectives on the hospital experience (Jeppson & Thomas, 1994b). In a family focus forum on parent–professional partnerships in instruction, parents expressed the view that every interaction with professionals is an instructional opportunity (Capone, 1995).

Recruiting Families　The effectiveness of instructional partnerships is largely dependent on including families from diverse backgrounds with a wide range of experiences. Attention should be given to including families who are existing consumers of services as well as experienced families and ensuring that the families in the partnership reflect the composition of the community in which the instruction occurs. Family members (Capone, 1995) have spoken of the diverse perspectives that they have to offer based on their backgrounds, the age of their children, their experience as instructors, and their particular role in their family (e.g., mother, father, sibling). Almost all parents noted the need to ensure that instruction provides participants with opportunities to hear varying perspectives on any given issue: "One parent was always approached because of being a 'black, visible parent.' It is an asset to have culturally diverse parent representation, especially in a region like New York" (Capone, 1995).

There are a variety of ways to identify and recruit families, keeping in mind the importance of including a diversity of parent perspectives. The following list was adapted from one described in "Essential Allies: Families and Professionals Working Together to Improve Quality of Care" (Jeppson & Thomas, 1994b):

- Contact local or statewide Parent to Parent organizations.
- Post notices on community bulletin boards and in medical, educational, recreational, and social service programs.
- Contact organizations that serve particular cultural groups.
- Develop radio, newspaper, or television public service announcements in the languages of the communities being served.
- Use cultural mediators (i.e., knowledgeable individuals within cultural communities).

Ensuring Support Through Parent Organizations   Establishing partnerships with parent organizations strengthens as well as supports a network of families as instructional partners. In addition, many parent organizations have resources to support families before, during, and after their involvement in instructional experiences. As the quote suggests, parents will face a variety of new issues and emotions as they begin to share their experiences in new and different arenas. It is essential that support be available to assist them in both naming and working through those issues.

> Parents could use support to explore their role in the partnership. As parent–professional partnerships become more complex, with parents assuming more responsibilities, parents need support to reflect on issues/concerns around a perceived sense of loss of identity as a parent. (Capone, 1995)

Winton and DiVenere (1995) described three categories of support for parents: 1) emotional support, 2) informational support, and 3) instrumental support. One of the roles of a parent organization is to support parents in the ways they have identified as essential to facilitating their parent voice. One example of the kinds of support available to families before a presentation is provided by Parent to Parent of Vermont, which created a set of guidelines to assist families in planning and organizing presentations for preservice and inservice instruction (see Figure 17.1).

Parent to Parent of Vermont suggests that professionals who have invited families to make presentations offer to help families prepare for their presentations. It is important to talk with families about issues that may arise during a presentation such as how to cope with unexpected emotions and how to answer personal questions. It is also important to remember that each parent presenter is different. Professionals should develop an array of strategies to ensure that parents feel comfortable and supported in assuming the role of instructional partner. Furthermore, Parent to Parent of Vermont urges professionals to call families shortly after their presentation to thank them and offer feedback: "Hearing from participants that my participation broadened and enhanced an understanding of disability and chronic illness of individuals and their families lets me know I am making a difference!" (Capone, 1995).

Responding to Logistical Barriers   One barrier that is frequently raised is the ability of professionals to have access to appropriate reimbursements for their training partners. The types of preferred reimbursement should be explored with the family. In addition to offering stipends, many professionals offer families access to fax machines, telephones, child care, and mileage reimbursements. Most universities have discretionary funds in their departmental budgets that can be allocated for family partners. In addition, universities can offer free coursework, access to the gymnasium (with pool and exercise equip-

HOW TO ORGANIZE A PRESENTATION

1. Invitation to participate in preservice and inservice instruction.

2. Determine request:

✓ Will you be presenting alone or with a partner?

✓ How much time is available?

✓ How many participants? What are their needs for information?

✓ How experienced are participants?

✓ Who requested the information? (Is the need for information unanimous, or do some people believe they "already know/do this"?)

✓ Is there a common philosophy among participants?

✓ Is this a one-time-only opportunity to meet? (Depending on their needs, it might be helpful to schedule a follow-up 4–6 weeks after the initial session to problem-solve and discuss issues after they have had a chance to try out information/philosophy.)

✓ Discuss stipend and travel expenses.

✓ Send written confirmation of your understanding of the request, time, place, date, and so forth.

3. Prepare the presentation:

✓ Review all the instructional materials available to you.

✓ If the presentation is to be "solo," select appropriate materials based on #2 above.

✓ If you are presenting with an instructional partner, allow time to discuss/select materials and roles for collaborative presentation.

✓ Be sure you will have access to equipment (e.g., VCR, slide projector), if you will be using them.

✓ Prepare handouts, overheads, agenda for the day. (Try to add humor using overheads and other equipment.)

✓ Practice exercises that are not familiar to you. Imagine questions that may arise. Think about how you would respond to questions.

4. The day before the presentation:

✓ Review your materials.

✓ Be sure you have everything you will need: nametags, markers, masking tape, flipcharts, and so forth.

✓ Call for directions if you are unfamiliar with the area.

✓ Consider bringing along a picture of your child or family.

(continued)

Figure 17.1. Guidance for families involved in preservice and inservice instruction. (Adapted from Winton & DiVenere, 1995.)

Figure 17.1. *(continued)*

---

5. The day of the presentation:

√ Allow plenty of time for travel.

√ Be yourself.

√ Help people feel relaxed.

√ Make an effort to learn and remember people's names. Refer to participants by name (if possible) when they ask questions.

√ Use your sense of humor.

√ Remain nonjudgmental.

√ Involve the audience. When questions are raised, turn them over to the entire group before answering yourself.

√ Have fun!

---

ment), access to the library, and other gifts that would support the important work of family instructional partners.

Parent–professional partnerships encourage a different way of thinking about the design, implementation, and evaluation of preservice and inservice training opportunities. Instead of asking the question "How can parents be a part of the delivery of a specific curriculum content?" professionals need to consider how the planning and implementation of the instructional opportunities facilitate and model communication, cooperation, and teaming among parents and professionals.

In summary, the discussions about the qualities of effective partnerships support the need for parents to be involved in all aspects of instruction, from conception to evaluation; to be provided the support necessary to accomplish their task effectively; to represent a diversity of experiences; and to be treated with respect. The parent voices used to illustrate these points mirror Kagan's (1989) definition of a collaborative partnership; that is one that is characterized by intense joint planning and a sharing of resources, power, and authority. This kind of partnership means more than ensuring that parents and professionals appear together at training sessions. It challenges parents and professionals to engage in ongoing, honest discussions to develop a shared understanding of each partner's role in the development, implementation, and evaluation of preservice and inservice instructional opportunities. Figure 17.2 provides guidelines for considering different approaches to establishing and maintaining parent–professional partnerships for preservice and inservice education.

TWO PRESERVICE MODELS FOR PARENT–PROFESSIONAL PARTNERSHIPS IN INSTRUCTION

Two programs at the University of Vermont provide examples of parent–professional partnerships in preservice training. The first model, The Medical Education Project, represents a collaboration between the University of Vermont College of Medicine and Parent to Parent of Vermont. The second model is a partnership between the Early Childhood Special Education Master's Program at the University Affiliated Program of Vermont, in the University of Vermont College of Education, and Parent to Parent of Vermont. Both programs represent a partnership between parents and professionals in preservice training.

1. **Include families at the ground level of instructional activities.**
   A. Families are included at the conception and planning level of instruction.
   B. Families are given information necessary to support their role.

2. **Use innovative ways of identifying and recruiting families for participation as instructional partners.**
   A. A variety of options exists for identifying and recruiting families.
   B. We have identified families who are current consumers as well as veterans.
   C. Our instructional partners reflect the composition of the community in which our personnel preparation occurs.

3. **Create partnerships with parent organizations to ensure continuity and ongoing support for families and professionals and to acknowledge and respond to logistical barriers in creative ways.**
   A. Families are supported before, during, and after their involvement in instructional experiences.
   B. Families are provided with emotional, informational, and instrumental support based on their preferences and needs.
   C. We have developed partnerships with parent organizations in our area.
   D. We have explored a variety of options for reimbursing family partners.

4. **Maintain an array of instructional opportunities.**
   A. There are both formal and informal opportunities for families to participate in personnel preparation.
   B. We have included opportunities for family involvement in each area of our instructional experiences from conception to implementation to evaluation.

Figure 17.2. Guidelines for involving families as partners in preservice and inservice instruction.

Medical Education Project

The Medical Education Project, a collaboration between the University of Vermont's College of Medicine and Parent to Parent of Vermont, was established in 1985 as a required component of the clinical rotation in pediatrics for all medical students. Created long before the concept of family-centered care was an established approach, this project relied on families as teaching partners. The Medical Education Project was founded on the belief that families are experts in the care of their children and that individuals with disabilities are competent, experienced advocates for their health care.

Goals   The goals of this project, developed collaboratively by families and physician faculty, guide each of the four sessions:

- To give medical students an opportunity to step out of their student role and into the role of a parent
- To give medical students an opportunity to learn the art as well as the science of practicing medicine
- To help medical students recognize and acknowledge their own biases and personal beliefs to avoid imposing them on a family or person with a disability or illness
- To give medical students an opportunity to see beyond an individual's illness or diagnosis—to see the person at home, in his or her own community

Description of the Sessions   Students are required to attend four sessions that are designed to promote dialogue and decision making that enable students to understand the following: 1) the importance of providing accurate, unbiased information to families;

2) the need to meet with, and be supported by, immediate and extended family members and friends as part of the decision-making process; and 3) the ways values and beliefs affect how decisions are made.

Before students arrive for the first session, they have been randomly "matched" with a family. Students are given the names of the family and the child and are asked to make contact with their family early in the rotation and to set up a meeting time convenient for the family. Students are not provided with any information about the child's diagnosis or disability because they are not there to interview, assess, or evaluate but rather to listen and learn from the family. Families wanting to participate are sent a letter of welcome (Figure 17.3).

Each session encourages students to take on a parental perspective. During Session 1 students are asked to make a decision—a decision every parent who has a child born with hypoplastic left heart syndrome must make. Students are asked to return the following day with their decision and the reasons they chose either compassionate care, transplantation, or a three-part surgery called the Norwood Procedure. Following this discussion, facilitated by the two pediatricians who have been with the project since its inception, students are asked to decide which of four diagnoses (i.e., Down syndrome, third-degree burns that include the child's face, cystic fibrosis, and meningomyelocele) they would find most difficult and least difficult as a parent and why. As students discuss their decisions, they are supported to explore how those decisions reflect their values, biases, and attitudes about disabilities. In addition, faculty from Parent to Parent encourage students to explore the relationship between their personal attitudes about parenting a child with a disability and their interactions with parents. During the final session, students reflect on their home visits and consider their experience in the context of the entire seminar. Because families direct the discussion during the home visit, students come away with unique learning experiences, which they in turn share with colleagues during the final session.

Role of Families   Families involved in the Medical Education Project participate in an orientation meeting, agree to host a medical student for an evening or an afternoon, and identify at least three points they want students to take back with them. Following the home visit, families are asked to complete a Parent Feedback Sheet (see Figure 17.4).

Role of Parent to Parent Staff   An essential component to the success of this project is the opportunity to process and discuss each part of the seminar. Medical students appreciate not only the lessons learned during the home visit but also the willingness of physician faculty and Parent to Parent staff to talk about ethical dilemmas, values, and beliefs. Students are also extremely impressed by witnessing the impact of an ongoing health condition or disability on all family members and the critical role of family members in providing and advocating for health care. Parent to Parent staff participate in all aspects of this seminar. The staff write to families following the last session, sharing comments from medical students' testimony that the home visit made a difference.

Families continuously report that the reason they participate is because they know their experiences and those of their children are listened to and learned from. This collaborative model has launched additional parent–professional partnerships.

Early Childhood Special Education Program

The Family-Based Practicum Experience for Early Childhood Special Education Master's students at the University of Vermont College of Education was collaboratively designed by university-based faculty and faculty from Parent to Parent of Vermont. This year-long practicum provides students with in-depth experience with a family of a child with a special health care and/or educational need and incorporates a variety of opportunities for interns and family members to interact.

Dear Fellow Parents:

Welcome to the Medical Education Project. As parents, you are the best resource in providing accurate information to medical students regarding the qualities you and your family find most helpful in a physician. Since 1985, families have graciously agreed to bring students into their lives. During these visits students have learned directly from families in the relaxed and informal atmosphere of their homes.

In addition to home visits, medical students are required to attend three lecture/discussion sessions taking place at the beginning and the end of their 8-week pediatric rotation. In preparation for the home visits, you are requested to attend one orientation session. The orientation is held to introduce you to some of the families already involved in the Project; meet with Drs. David Stifler and Don Swartz, our two physicians involved in the Project, to help you consider the points you would like to get across to students; and to help you structure your home visit. Information about the dates and times of the orientation, along with a response card, is enclosed.

I wanted to share comments from medical students with you to let you know how important your participation in this project is. The following comments are from students who have completed their home visit with a family:

"I think that the home visit was important. It gave me an opportunity to see that families with children who have chronic illnesses live very normal lives and that their medical problems are a small part of their everyday life."

"I feel that these home visits are invaluable not just because I met some wonderful people who gave me some insight as to what it is like to take care of and keep abreast of the needs and potential of a chronically ill child, but because I learned and saw for myself the human side of medicine and how people deal with illness and emotional needs outside of the hospital setting. I plan to see my family again because they have become friends. Thank you!"

Based on feedback from family and student participants in the past, it is recommended that you give careful thought to how the visit will be structured. Consider what has been significant, both positive and negative. Remember that as parents you are a vital resource in providing helpful information. For instance, if you have a lot of thoughts you would like to share regarding your family's experiences, being at the dinner table with an active family may not be the best arrangement. However, if your message is to have the student experience firsthand how your household functions, being in the midst of the juggling scene of a family dinner may be just the right setting. Above all, do what is best for you and your family!

Before the visit we ask that you formulate three points that you want to communicate during the visit. Think back to your initial contact with physicians, for instance, and what your family would have appreciated (e.g., language used, information shared).

The benefit of having an ongoing program of this kind is that we can make adaptations over time, as necessary. For this purpose, your feedback is of great value to us here at Parent to Parent. Your comments have a great impact on the implementation of the project and are given the utmost attention. Please return the attached forms in the envelope provided. Feedback is to be sent in as soon as you have had your home visit. We know your time is precious and are grateful for all your efforts!

If you have any questions at any point about your experience in the Medical Education Project, please call us anytime at 555-5290.

Sincerely,

Nancy DiVenere
Director

Figure 17.3. Medical Education Project welcome letter.

1. Explain how you feel the visit went overall. Was it a positive experience for you and your family? If not, why not?

2. You thought about specific points you wished to convey to the student during the visit. Based on the student's reactions or comments, do you believe you got your point(s) across?

3. Do you believe that these home visits are an important component to the medical student's experience on his or her pediatric rotation?

Figure 17.4. Medical Education Project: Parent feedback sheet.

Goal The experience was designed to prepare family-centered practitioners and provide students with the opportunity to learn directly from a family rather than from reading or attending lectures about families.

Description of Practicum The experience (Phase I) begins in the fall semester, in a somewhat unique and definitely unsettling manner. Student interns are asked to enter the family without a role. Students are prepared to listen and respond to families from the heart. In conversations with families, students learn what is important for the child and family. Students accompany families to meetings with health care providers, educators, and advocacy groups. The goal is for students to experience the complexity of issues and concerns facing families and meet the myriad professionals involved in the lives of families whose children have a special health care and/or educational need. Because this practicum experience is guided and directed by the families themselves, students experience the lives of families from a vantage point different from that typically available to students in traditional professionally driven practica opportunities. Based on the relationship established during the first semester, students and families design an action plan for the second semester (Phase II) that outlines goals and activities that consider both the family's priorities and the intern's learning needs. The following are two examples of second semester action plans:

- Developing a videotape of a preschool child with disabilities that shows the child effectively functioning in a variety of community settings (e.g., child care, gymnastics); this videotape was then used by the family for transition meetings as their son entered kindergarten
- Creating a home-care book that outlined the variety of medical procedures, preferences, and so forth of one young child so that the family could quickly and easily orient a new caregiver to the important routines and characteristics of their child

The activities that students implement during Phase II facilitate the acquisition of an understanding of the elements of a family-centered approach. These experiences develop the intern's ability to incorporate the elements of the family-centered approach into all aspects of his or her practicum requirements and to develop an understanding of ways in which existing systems and policies can become more responsive to family concerns and priorities. The partnerships students establish with families have proven to be essential components of their master's program. Students rely on their relationship with the family as a safe place to explore family issues and begin to define themselves as family-centered practitioners.

Role of Parent to Parent Staff   The Family-Based Practicum Experience provides a vehicle for modeling parent–professional partnerships in two critical ways. First, Parent to Parent staff identify, recruit, and help nurture the families who participate in the Family-Based Practicum Experience. The second critical component is the supervision provided by Parent to Parent of Vermont. Parent to Parent staff maintain close contact with both families and students. In their role, Parent to Parent staff have helped students and families "negotiate" their relationship, and, perhaps more important, Parent to Parent staff help students relate the relationship established with a family in their family-based experience to the types of relationships they establish with families in the more professionally driven early intervention system. Parent to Parent supervisors bring a perspective to this practicum experience that could not be provided by other members of the instructional team.

Although students enter this practicum experience without a defined role, they report that it is through this experience that they develop an understanding of their role as an early interventionist. The appendix at the end of this chapter presents an outline of the Family-Based Practicum Experience.

CONCLUSION

Partnership—such a simple word for some very complex and challenging activities. Partnerships are established so that final products are enriched by the expertise of separate individuals, but in true partnerships, the individuals work in such concert that the group perceives itself as one. As people become more skilled in working together, sharing expertise, and moving toward collaboration, incredible things can be accomplished.

Parent–professional partnerships in preservice and inservice education can take a variety of forms, from participation on panels to co-teaching courses. The partnership sets a context for preparing family-centered practitioners, by modeling the belief that families are valued consumers of, and competent partners in, the design, implementation, and evaluation of services. Such a partnership communicates that it requires the expertise of both families and professionals to develop and implement appropriate services for young children with disabilities and their families.

RESOURCES

Jeppson, E.S., & Thomas, J. (1994). *Essential allies: Families as advisors.* Bethesda, MD: Institute for Family-Centered Care. Cost: $10. (301) 652-0281.

Lots of very practical information, illustrations, and resources for supporting family involvement in leadership roles, including instruction. Developed to "help bridge the gap between providers' past training and new expectations of collaboration and partnerships with families" (p. 1).

McBride, S.L., Sharp, L., Hains, A.H., & Whitehead, A. (1995). Parents as co-instructors in preservice training: A pathway to family-centered practice. *Journal of Early Intervention, 19*(4), 343–355.

Describes benefits and challenges, based on experiences of several teams with family–professional coinstruction in preservice settings. Addresses the following: recruitment and selection of family members, preparation for coinstruction roles, student evaluations of coinstruction experiences, supports for family members and faculty in coinstruction roles, and diversity issues.

Winton, P.J., & DiVenere, N. (1995). Family–professional partnerships in early intervention personnel preparation: Guidelines and strategies. *Topics in Early Childhood Special Education, 15*(3), 296–313.

Article describes types of and rationale for some of the roles family members can play in personnel preparation efforts and offers guidelines and strategies for facilitating family participation in ways that model collaborative family–professional partnerships. Strategies provided apply across multiple contexts (e.g., preservice, inservice, policy making).

REFERENCES

Bailey, D.B., Palsha, S., & Huntington, G. (1990). Preservice preparation of special educators to work with infants with handicaps and their families: Current status and training needs. *Journal of Early Intervention, 14*(1), 43–54.

Bishop, K., Woll, J., & Arango, P. (1993). *Family/professional collaboration for children with special health needs and their families.* Burlington: University of Vermont, Department of Social Work and the Division of Services for Children with Special Health Needs, Maternal and Child Health Bureau.

Campbell, P. (1994). *Report from the Northeast Regional Faculty Training Institute on Personnel Preparation.* Philadelphia, PA: Temple University, College of Education, Department of Curriculum, Instruction, and Technology in Education.

Capone, A. (1995). *Parent–professional partnerships in preservice and inservice training: A parent's perspective.* Manuscript in preparation. University of Vermont.

Favrot, K., Steele, S., & Worthington, R. (1993). *Developing parent trainers to participate in training about inclusion: A model to empower parents.* Symposium presentation at Zero to Three National Training Institute, Washington, DC.

Grobe, T. (1993). *Synthesis of existing knowledge and practice in the field of educational partnerships.* Washington, DC: Office of Educational Research and Improvement, U.S. Department of Education.

Jeppson, E.S., & Thomas, J. (1994a, Fall). Essential allies: Families and professionals working together to improve quality of care. *Advances in Family-Centered Care, 1*(2), 1.

Jeppson, E., & Thomas, J. (1994b). *Essential allies: Families as advisors.* Bethesda, MD: Institute for Family-Centered Care.

Jeppson, E.S., & Thomas, J. (1994c, Fall). Involving families in advisory roles: Eight steps to success. *Advances in Family-Centered Care, 1*(2), 2–6.

Kagan, S. (1989). Early care and education: Tackling the tough issues. *Phi Delta Kappan, 70*(6), 433–439.

Kagan, S. (1991). *United we stand: Collaboration for child care and early education services.* New York: Teachers College Press.

Shelton, T.L., & Stepanek, J.S. (1994). *Family-centered care for children needing specialized health and developmental services.* Bethesda, MD: Association for the Care of Children's Health.

Winton, P., & DiVenere, N. (1995). Family–professional partnerships in early intervention personnel preparation: Guidelines and strategies. *Topics in Early Childhood Special Education, 15*(3), 296–313.

APPENDIX

EARLY CHILDHOOD SPECIAL EDUCATION MASTER'S PROGRAM

Family-Based Practicum Experience

The family-based experience provides interns with the opportunity to learn directly from a family rather than from reading or attending lectures about families. This practicum component provides interns with an in-depth experience with a family of a child with a special health care and/or education need(s). Through this experience, interns will acquire an understanding of the elements of a family-centered approach and knowledge of the ways in which existing systems and policies can become more responsive to family concerns and priorities.

Each intern has a Parent to Parent supervisor who is available to provide resources and support. A minimum of two meetings with each intern will be held during each of the fall and spring semesters. However, the Parent to Parent supervisor will be available to meet with individual interns on a weekly basis to discuss any issues regarding the implementation of a family-centered approach. It is the responsibility of the intern to communicate any additional supervision needs to the Parent to Parent supervisor.

Family-Centered Care for Children Needing Specialized Health and Developmental Services (Shelton & Stepanek, 1994) is an excellent resource for this activity. Parent to Parent of Vermont, located at the Champlain Mill, also has a lending library with many valuable resources.

GUIDELINES

The family-based experience has been designed to be implemented in two phases. The requirements and written components of each phase are described here.

Phase I: (Fall Semester) Getting to Know the Family

1. Maintain a log of the time spent with the family.

    You will be asked to submit a log of the time you spent with the family throughout the year including a brief description and a brief reflection of each activity. Phase I activities include the following:

    A. Initial visit with the family

B. Ongoing contact with the family (weekly or on a schedule that meets the family's needs)

C. Attending a physician's appointment

D. Attending an IFSP or other conference held with the school

E. Observing the child in a setting where services are being provided (school, child care, home, therapy)

F. Having a meal with the family

G. Providing respite (spend enough time with the children so that the parents will have time to "get out of the house" if they would like to)

H. Selecting two additional experiences that you and the family identify as valuable (e.g., attend a parent support group meeting, attend a birthday party)

2. Reflect on your experience.

A. Identify an aspect of your experience with the family and write a reaction paper discussing your perspective on this experience.

B. Facilitate a discussion (during practicum seminar) regarding the experience you discussed in your paper.

3. Set goals for Phase II (spring semester).

Together with your family, identify the goals and activities you will engage in during Phase II. The goals and activities should be mutually beneficial and should consider the intern's learning needs and the family's own priorities. You will also want to develop a time line for your goals and activities. The goals and time lines should be written and handed in with your reflection paper on the assigned date at the end of the fall semester. You may also want to discuss the ways in which you and the family "negotiated" the goals and activities for Phase II.

Phase II: (Spring Semester) Implementing a Plan

Phase II activities require you to spend 48 hours with your family over the course of the semester. The goals and activities addressed during these 48 hours are those that were identified with the family in the fall. Your 48 hours can be divided to allow you to accomplish these mutually determined goals. In the past interns and families have been very creative in defining their goals and activities for Phase II of the Family-Based Experience. These ideas have included but are not limited to the following:

• Developing a "Fun and Care Book" that the family could share with baby-sitters about their child

• Providing child care for the child and/or siblings

• Assisting a family in applying through Medicaid for wheelchair funding

1. Maintain a log of the time spent with the family.

Submit a log of the time you spent with the family throughout the year, including a brief description and a brief reflection of each activity.

2. Reflect on your experience.

A. Identify an aspect of your experience with the family and write a reaction paper discussing your perspective on this experience. You will want to discuss any changes you made in your original plan for Phase II. How were those changes "negotiated"?

B. Facilitate a discussion (during practicum seminar) regarding the experience you discussed in your paper.

18 DESIGNING AND IMPLEMENTING INNOVATIVE, INTERDISCIPLINARY PRACTICA

Sharon E. Rosenkoetter
Vicki D. Stayton

Janet's story, as presented in Chapter 1, reflects the changing roles that personnel in early intervention are expected to perform. Her experience has implications for designing personnel programs that prepare individuals for these new roles. This young professional would have been better prepared to work as a team member if her professional preparation program had included mentored opportunities to collaborate with students from other disciplines via one or more interdisciplinary practica.

The following are elements of an interdisciplinary practicum as the term is used in this chapter:

- Supervised field experiences with children and families
- Adherence to family-centered philosophy and inclusion of family members during all phases of developing and implementing the field experience
- Involvement of students, faculty, and service providers from two or more disciplines
- Student participation and active membership on an interdisciplinary team
- Systematic supervision to help students reflect on their skills as team members

Disciplines may include nutrition, psychology, speech-language pathology, early childhood education, early childhood special education, nursing, physical therapy, occupational therapy, social work, audiology, and others. Interdisciplinary practica have been recommended in the early intervention literature (McCollum, Rowan, & Thorp, 1994; McCollum & Stayton, 1996; Stayton & Miller, 1993), encouraged by the U.S. Department of Education in its funding of innovative personnel preparation programs, and increasingly implemented across academic departments in a variety of higher education institutions.

RATIONALE FOR INTERDISCIPLINARY PRACTICA

Interdisciplinary practica are beneficial in a variety of ways. Faculty involvement in interdisciplinary experiences builds the professional knowledge and skills of individual par-

Portions of this chapter were completed while the authors were funded partially by U.S. Department of Education grants #HO29Q30013 and #HO24D30046 to the Associated Colleges of Central Kansas and #H029Q10067 and #H029Q20121 to Western Kentucky University; however, the content does not necessarily reflect the position of the U.S. Department of Education, and no official endorsement should be inferred.

ticipants as they learn firsthand about the discipline-specific roles, philosophy, and language of other disciplines and as they reflect on, practice, and explain their own skills. Moreover, shared faculty supervision of students allows for elimination of duplication and pooling of resources across disciplinary programs. Most important, the faculty team has the opportunity to evaluate and model interdisciplinary practices for students, increasing the effectiveness of both faculty and students in this important area. Like their faculty mentors, students in an interdisciplinary practicum can begin to appreciate the discipline-specific roles, philosophy, vocabulary, and methods of other disciplines. Such a practicum creates a setting in which students can continue to learn about early intervention and to apply related collaborative skills under supervision. Given the diversity among students (McCollum et al., 1994; McCollum & Stayton, 1996; Stayton & Miller, 1993), practicum participants often can learn from one another's previous employment, practica, or volunteer experiences in early childhood settings.

This chapter describes the results of a national survey of practicum practices, defines critical factors necessary for successful practicum implementation, identifies persistent challenges and ways to address them, and makes recommendations to personnel developers and policy makers regarding interdisciplinary practica. Practicum models from diverse settings illustrate the process of developing and implementing an interdisciplinary practicum.

SURVEY OF EXISTING PRACTICES

We used three strategies to gather the information reported in this chapter on interdisciplinary practica: 1) literature review, 2) reflections on personal experiences, and 3) a survey of university personnel preparation programs that prepare professionals for early intervention. A list of potential informants was generated by noting all institutions holding grants to develop innovative personnel preparation programs for early childhood services from the U.S. Department of Education, Office of Special Education Programs; these projects are intended to prepare students from a variety of disciplines to work in early intervention. This project list was supplemented with help from the Council for Exceptional Children, which provided addresses for all institutions with programs leading to certification in early childhood special education (ECSE) or its equivalent. We reasoned that ECSE was likely to be a partner in most interdisciplinary personnel preparation for services to infants and toddlers with special needs and their families. A total of 289 institutions were identified in this manner.

A six-page, 24-item questionnaire was prepared seeking answers to frequently asked questions about interdisciplinary practica. The survey included both open-ended and multiple-choice questions. The survey was sent to contact people at each of the 289 institutions. Responses were received from 155 of the 289 schools, yielding a participation rate of 54%. Faculty personnel in different roles completed the survey. Of the 155 respondents, 58 institutions (38%) indicated that they sponsor interdisciplinary practica, though not necessarily with all the components previously listed. The characteristics of survey respondents are summarized in Table 18.1. Many respondents sent additional supportive information (e.g., practicum handbooks, curriculum guides, evaluation forms) to amplify their answers. Data from the survey, including quotations from participants and supportive materials they contributed, were used to inform this chapter and illustrate its key concepts.

The institutions that reported sponsoring such field experiences vary widely in the degree to which students and faculty members from multiple disciplines collaborate with

TABLE 18.1.   Demographics of survey respondents

Institutional sponsorship	Location of institution	Size of student body	Credit given for interdisciplinary practicum
Public university—44	Rural—10	12,000+—38	Graduate—27
	Suburban—5	5,000–12,000—9	Undergraduate and graduate—20
Private university—11	Urban—21	2,000–5,000—2	Undergraduate only—3
	Two of above locations—8	less than 2,000—5	
	All three locations—12		

Note: When all responses in a column do not total 58, some respondents did not answer the question.

service providers and families in planning, implementing, and evaluating shared practicum experiences. Most respondents see their interdisciplinary collaboration for practicum as "under development," "unfinished," or "in process," which is not surprising as the majority of these projects reportedly began around 1990.

ORIGINS OF INTERDISCIPLINARY PRACTICA

Most interdisciplinary practica began in response to one or more of the following influences, as described by survey respondents:

- Recommended practices by professional organizations that espouse interdisciplinary training, in many cases involving families (e.g., Division for Early Childhood [DEC] Task Force on Recommended Practices, 1993)
- Funding priority given to interdisciplinary personnel preparation projects, including interdisciplinary field experiences, by federal and state agencies and foundation grants officers
- Encouragement of interdisciplinary practica by regional faculty training institutes of the Early Education Program for Children with Disabilities and by presenters at national conferences: "At the Institute, they convinced us we needed to try this."
- Leadership by the state's university affiliated program (UAP), whose mission, in part, is to provide interdisciplinary training: "We were teaching about interdisciplinary service."
- Existing models for community-based services that feature interdisciplinary and transdisciplinary service delivery, which require competence in interdisciplinary collaboration on the part of higher education's graduates (McGonigel, Woodruff, & Roszmann-Millican, 1994; Stayton & Karnes, 1994)
- Desire by university faculty to model the collaborative skills they describe during class presentations (McCollum & Stayton, 1996): "Our department made a commitment to teaching **and utilizing** the transdisciplinary approach."
- Expressed needs by program graduates to appreciate the knowledge base and specialized expertise of colleagues in related human services professions: "The practicum is essential for students to develop better understanding of the perspectives of professionals from different disciplines."

- Desire to help students develop greater sensitivity to families as team members (McCollum & Stayton, 1996): "Working with families to develop our interdisciplinary practicum has affected our whole program in a positive way."
- Assertiveness by a single faculty member—typically the one most directly involved in early intervention training—who took the lead in seeking other faculty, bolstering their understanding of early intervention, defining common objectives for field experiences, and inviting participation in planning and implementing an interdisciplinary practicum: "It seemed silly to have a speech-language pathology program and an ECSE program in the same department and not have interdisciplinary efforts."

KEY CONCEPTS OF INTERDISCIPLINARY PRACTICA

Common Philosophy as a Foundation

Most significant in developing, implementing, and evaluating an interdisciplinary practicum, according to respondents, is the establishment of a shared philosophy (McCollum et al., 1994). It is desirable for all groups with a role in the practicum (i.e., students, practicum site staff, university administrators and faculty from multiple departments, families) to participate in writing its philosophy. At a minimum, the philosophy should be jointly developed by all faculty involved in the practicum and then critiqued by other participants. For example, Western Kentucky University's philosophy statement was jointly developed by its interdisciplinary faculty and is shared with students and on-site practicum staff as part of their orientation (see Figure 18.1).

Important or significant features of a philosophy statement include outlining consensus on both content and process for the practicum. Specifically, the philosophy statement conveys the team's understanding of the terms early intervention, family centered, and interdisciplinary. Furthermore, the statement delineates the significant outcomes desired for students and describes how those outcomes are to be achieved (e.g., "This practicum will embody family-centered services," "It will provide practice in inclusive settings," "The student will experience interdisciplinary team membership").

ONE UNIVERSITY'S PHILOSOPHY STATEMENT

1. Current research and best practice suggest that social work, psychology, and speech/communication disorders professionals must develop knowledge and skills specific to young children with disabilities to be adequately prepared to work in early intervention programs.

2. Young children with disabilities and their families receive services from a variety of professionals who must be trained to work as team members.

3. Services for young children must exemplify a family-centered approach, with personnel having knowledge and skills in a family systems model.

4. Young children with disabilities benefit from placement in integrated settings, and professionals require integrated training to work in such settings.

5. Research concerning adult education points to the importance of adults' being actively involved in the learning process, with course work having the flexibility for students to make choices about their learning experiences.

Figure 18.1. The philosophy statement that guides Western Kentucky University's interdisciplinary early childhood program. (Reprinted by permission of Western Kentucky University.)

According to survey respondents, the faculty and students who come together to develop, implement, and evaluate an interdisciplinary practicum must collaborate on a regular and ongoing basis regarding roles on the team; strategies for decision making; and responsibilities of students, faculty, administrators, and practicum site staff for accomplishing practicum activities and achieving desired outcomes (Stayton & Miller, 1993). Commitment to this shared responsibility should be stated in the philosophy statement. The philosophy statement then influences the attitudes displayed by practicum leaders and shapes the knowledge and skill competencies to be taught. It guides the selection of specific activities to achieve those competencies during the practicum experience. This philosophy statement should be shared among students, service providers, and practicum leaders and should regularly be used to guide practicum decisions. When disagreements arise, revisiting the philosophy statement can often serve to build consensus. Respondents to the survey varied greatly in the degree to which they have developed and are using local philosophy statements to guide their interdisciplinary work.

Faculty and Students from Diverse Disciplines

By definition, an interdisciplinary practicum involves faculty and students from more than one discipline. According to survey results, the most commonly involved disciplines are psychology, speech-language pathology, early childhood education, early childhood special education, physical therapy, occupational therapy, nursing, and social work. Most respondents did not describe family members as a "discipline" among their practicum collaborators, though many use family consultants to help plan, conduct, and/or evaluate their practicum.

Although 2–12 disciplines reportedly participate in interdisciplinary practica on various campuses, the most frequently cited number of disciplines is 2. Moreover, 8 of the 11 universities with two disciplines link early childhood education (ECE) and ECSE as the collaborating disciplines, with no other related disciplines participating. The next most frequently cited number of disciplines partnering for practicum is four, with 7 institutions indicating that number. Across the survey's 58 respondents, only two programs, other than those that pair ECE and ECSE, have identical combinations of participating disciplines. Interdepartmental collaboration appears to be guided by local factors, such as the discipline-specific programs offered on campus and the disciplines typically represented in nearby early intervention services.

The following practicum model illustrates how a practicum can be organized across six different disciplines.

UAP-Initiated Practica Across Six Disciplines

Virginia Commonwealth University (VCU) is a public, state-supported university enrolling more than 21,000 undergraduate, graduate, and health professional students on its two campuses in Richmond, Virginia. Through its university affiliated program (UAP), VCU has offered a unique interdisciplinary option for graduate students in psychology, ECSE, physical therapy (PT), occupational therapy (OT), nursing, and social work for approximately 9 years. An Interdisciplinary Steering Committee, comprising faculty from these six disciplines, plans and oversees the coursework, practica, and seminars that constitute this interdisciplinary program in early intervention/education. The committee meets at least quarterly to plan and discuss issues related to the program and to promote interdisciplinary co-operation and collaboration within the university's programs.

Twelve to 15 students per semester participate in the interdisciplinary program in early intervention/education. Students from the disciplines of OT, PT, psychology, nursing, and social work complete 12 graduate hours over a 1-year period, in addition to the regular graduate program in their home discipline. The early

intervention program consists of three courses, four seminars, required program tasks (competencies), and an interdisciplinary practicum in a program serving infants and toddlers with disabilities and their families. One of the courses, "Interdisciplinary Teamwork," addresses issues related to effective team building. The other two courses provide content specific to providing family-centered services to young children with disabilities and their families. ECSE students enroll in "Interdisciplinary Teamwork," attend the seminars, and participate in the practicum, but they do not enroll in the other two courses because this content is fully covered elsewhere.

Before initiating this program, university faculty made an extensive study of potential practicum sites to locate ones with positive interdisciplinary practices. Most students in the interdisciplinary program are placed in one of these practicum sites with a cooperating professional from their own discipline. ECSE students are occasionally supervised on site by a cooperating professional from a discipline other than education, especially in infant-toddler programs where few educators are employed. Students are typically placed individually at different locations. Faculty from each student's home discipline provide university supervision for field-based experiences.

Cooperating professionals are oriented to the interdisciplinary practicum via individual meetings with the university supervisor. One very successful aspect of the VCU experience is that individualized contracts are jointly developed by the university supervisor, student, and on-site cooperating professional. Each contract addresses unique site and student characteristics and clearly specifies interdisciplinary tasks to be completed. Students and cooperating professionals believe that this contract helps to set clear expectations for interdisciplinary performance and guide the accomplishment of defined tasks.

The field-based experience is formally evaluated in several ways. Students complete pre– and post–self-assessments of their knowledge and skills in defined areas, and these self-assessments are compared. University supervisors and cooperating professionals write at least three formal evaluations during each practicum and provide feedback to students. At the conclusion of the placement, the student completes an evaluation of the university's procedure and the supervisor's performance.

Institutional Support for Innovation

Faculty responding to this survey agreed that administrative support is essential for the effective implementation of an interdisciplinary practicum, just as it is for other interdisciplinary efforts (McCollum & Stayton, 1996; Stayton & Miller, 1993). The type and level of support reported by survey respondents varied across institutions. The most basic need is for verbal acceptance of the interdisciplinary effort by deans and department heads, along with their willingness to permit faculty decision making and flexibility in implementing the practicum. One respondent referred to this basic approval as "iron-clad administrative support." At a more significant level of commitment, survey respondents identified other administrative contributions, including funding for continuing education and travel, secretarial assistance, space for meetings, instructional materials, teaching assistants, hiring of qualified supervisors, minigrants to practicum sites to prepare staff for practicum roles, and support for a new course to support the innovative practicum concept. Release time for faculty to collaborate in initiating the practicum is an especially significant contribution that the institution can make to encourage the development of a quality practicum experience.

However, 29 of the 58 survey respondents provided no information about the types of administrative support they receive. Because many of the participants in this survey receive grant support for their practica, it may be that specific administrative support has not yet been an issue. Experience suggests that this issue will increase in importance as federal grants end and universities address the need to institutionalize their interdisciplinary practicum without grant support (Rooney, 1995).

Flexibility of Practicum Participants

Flexibility, flexibility, and more flexibility—this factor is stressed as critical in the sparse literature, professional presentations, and survey results collected for this chapter.

Faculty   Faculty involved with interdisciplinary practica must be open to considering new concepts from early intervention as well as to examining challenges to the assumptions and standard routines represented in their own disciplines. Faculty may need to address the following issues: different definitions of familiar terms; varied ways to supervise students; disagreements about how to involve students in planning; and diverse methods of assessment, intervention, and reporting. Expectations of family members on the intervention team, students, and site supervisors may vary across departments. These must be reconciled with one another and with the requirements of accrediting organizations. Creativity and careful explanation are needed to help the latter understand how local arrangements address their standards. Time lines for an unfamiliar collaborative effort are likely to require flexibility. Faculty must be willing to commit the hours required to resolve challenging issues.

Students   Flexibility is also an important attribute for students. Although practicum students are still learning their own discipline's philosophy, language, and roles, an interdisciplinary practicum experience requires them simultaneously to assimilate practices from other disciplines and also to engage in advanced skills such as role exchange and role release. Students must also learn to collaborate with numerous unfamiliar individuals such as family members, staff at the practicum site, and faculty and students from other departments. Students encounter unaccustomed routines and unexplained regulations. Respondents to the survey emphasized that undergraduates particularly need discipline-specific support and guidance in conjunction with their interdisciplinary supervision. The prepracticum orientation that many faculty provide to new students can draw attention to the elements of flexibility needed during the practicum.

Site Supervisors and Other Staff   The flexibility required of staff in supervising practicum students at the practicum site constitutes yet another juggling act. Staff must be able to grasp what faculty members hope to accomplish in the practicum, even though this experience is likely to differ from traditional practicum expectations. Site staff need to take the perspective of faculty and students to orient them to the expectations, policies, and procedures of the site. In addition, staff must communicate with faculty and students from multiple disciplines, articulate clearly their own needs, and release some responsibility to individuals who may have less education and experience in early intervention than they do. All of these elements will happen more quickly when site supervisors have worked out trusting relationships and information exchange across the disciplines providing services at the site on an ongoing basis.

Families   As with others on the service team, families are called on to be flexible in the practicum relationship. Families at participating sites will be asked to accept a new, less-experienced person on their child's team, as the university student learns to implement family-centered intervention. Some families may resist new personnel, no matter how carefully the student is introduced, and their feelings must be honored. For those family members who choose to participate on the practicum planning team, there is a need to look beyond their individual family situation to issues of students, professors, site supervisors, and other families and to discuss intervention questions at some distance from their immediate family's concerns.

Within the new relationships that result from the interdisciplinary practicum, a family may confront some unfamiliar questions. Family members may choose to rethink the nature and amount of their investment in early intervention with their own child and, more broadly, in the community's advocacy. The personal reflection that results can have positive outcomes or negative consequences. For example, one family who interacted considerably with a faculty–student team decided, as a result, to become more involved in advocacy groups in the state. Another mother decided to return to school to study social work to enter the field of early intervention. A third family tired of the frequent interaction with so many students and faculty and decided to end participation in their center's parent support groups.

The Institution   Flexibility is needed from university administrators in terms of examining traditional practices for student registration and faculty supervision; fostering cross-department, or even cross-college, decision making; and encouraging locally appropriate solutions to the challenges of interdisciplinary efforts. Flexibility can also assist administrators in scheduling practica and supportive coursework, assigning faculty to practica, allowing release time for ongoing development activities, assigning space for use by multiple programs, fostering collaboration with community programs, allocating resources to support the practicum, and negotiating with external accrediting agencies to accomplish the positive, if nontraditional, aims of practicum planners. For example, one administrator released faculty from other teaching responsibilities during the summer that the interdisciplinary practicum was instituted to give them time to develop a quality experience that could be replicated in the future.

Contextual Sensitivity

When multiple disciplines come together across university and community early intervention programs, a variety of relationships (i.e., contexts) for learning may overlap or even conflict. All practicum participants need to develop sensitivity to the local situation, which includes at least five significant components: 1) the multiple disciplines represented by the university faculty; 2) the university–community program relationship; 3) the nature of teaming among staff at the intervention site; 4) service provider–family relationships; and 5) relationships among faculty, students, and site staff. The language, values, and work styles of the various practicum participants must be understood and considered in building the overall practicum plan as well as the plans of individual students or teams of students. When students see faculty and site supervisors discussing the collaborative relationship in order to improve their work together, this presents a powerful model for students.

In addition to the personalities, discipline-specific preparation, roles, and previous experiences of the practicum participants, practicum planners must consider many other variables, as listed in Figure 18.2. Any interdisciplinary practicum must be responsive to its local context to survive and accomplish the goals of the institution.

Use of Quality Practicum Sites

To achieve desired outcomes, practicum sites must provide quality services; that is, they must model appropriate relationships among families and professionals. They must also practice intervention strategies recommended specifically by the participating disciplines as well as generally by leaders in early intervention. They must regularly evaluate the impact of their services and refine service delivery in accord with consumer feedback.

Practicum sites may be required to support students in an ongoing manner or during just one period of the year, such as a summer session. The majority of respondents indicated that practica occur over a full semester with the credit hours granted varying from

1. Which university departments are available?
2. Which university departments want to be involved?
3. What philosophy will undergird the interdisciplinary practicum?
4. What university and community structures (e.g., Educational Policies Committee, local interagency coordinating council), as well as other resources, are available to assist practicum development?
5. What early intervention programs might participate as practicum sites?
6. How well might each of the potential sites model teaming and collaboration?
7. What type of inservice training might be necessary for university faculty during practicum development?
8. What type of inservice training might be necessary for site staff during practicum development?
9. What type of orientation might be helpful for families prior to the practicum?
10. Which students (based on level, previous coursework, previous employment experience, etc.) could be involved in the practicum?
11. What students want to be involved in the practicum?
12. Will students be placed individually or in interdisciplinary teams?
13. What time of year (school year, between semesters, summer, combination) is available for interdisciplinary practicum, considering student schedules, site schedules, and faculty supervisors' schedules?
14. What shared expectations pertain for the practicum among
    Faculty from different departments?
    Personnel at the practicum site from various disciplines?
    Students from different disciplines and at different stages in career development?
    Families to be served?
15. What procedures will be followed for student placement, orientation, supervision, communication, and grading?
16. How will the practicum be evaluated by each of the participants, including
    Students?
    Families?
    Site personnel?
    Faculty from participating departments?
    University administrators?
    Accrediting agencies?
17. What formative and summative evaluation procedures will be used to assess the effectiveness of the practicum?

Figure 18.2.   Questions to consider in evaluating the local context.

1 to 8 and the days of the week varying from 1 to 5. Practica in a few programs, however, continue across two semesters, whereas others include only a few weeks during a semester or a shorter summer term. Practicum sites seem to be selected based on the following variables: 1) their location—community based or university based, 2) the number and characteristics of children and families served, 3) program philosophy, 4) staffing patterns, 5) types of services offered, and 6) relationship with the university. Ten programs among the 56 survey respondents employed university-based sites for some of their practicum experiences. Various community-based sites, including hospitals, child care centers, Head Start, public schools, and evaluation centers, were also used. Some settings served only young children with disabilities, whereas others were inclusive. Respondents to the survey emphasized that programs were selected as practicum sites because they offered family-centered, team-based services. Another factor in the selection of practicum sites was staff willingness to accept students and to participate in their supervision.

Whatever the structure of potential interdisciplinary practicum sites, it is desirable for them to exemplify the philosophy(ies) of both the university's institutional programs and that developed by the practicum planning team. Programs must actively welcome family leadership in both their own individualized family service plan (IFSP) development and in the decision making that occurs regarding agency policies. Students should be allowed to work with families functioning in both of these roles during the practicum. Personnel at the practicum site should demonstrate expertise in collaborative skills as well as in those required by their individual disciplines to model appropriate behaviors for students. Team members must be open to innovation and change, showing students the flexibility necessary to meet family needs. Stability in staff is desirable to provide cohesive team functioning as well as informed leadership for students.

Respondents' comments, as well as the authors' personal experience, suggest that this list of quality descriptors cannot always be satisfied in arranging practicum sites. Furthermore, there is a need to respect agencies' limits for student supervision and not overload the exemplary programs. University faculty are advised to determine their basic requirements (e.g., respect for families, team functioning) and then to support agency change in positive directions through providing staff development opportunities, sharing videotapes and reading materials, and, if tactfully done, modeling appropriate practices. The dilemma of insufficient numbers of quality practicum sites remains, and survey results show that this dilemma is widespread across the United States.

Evaluation of the Practicum

Both formative and summative evaluations are critical to improving the interdisciplinary practicum. Formative evaluation can be used to identify potential problems that the appropriate team needs to address in an ongoing fashion during the course of the practicum. Summative evaluation provides information on the overall effectiveness of the practicum in achieving its goals. Survey respondents reported involving students, on-site staff, parents, and university faculty in overall evaluation of the practicum. Students also evaluated themselves and their on-site supervisors. On-site supervisors and faculty typically evaluated students. Five programs provided no response to the survey's evaluation questions. Of the 58 respondents, 23 (39%) indicated that parents are not involved in the evaluation process. Overall, it appears that evaluation data collected for interdisciplinary practica were similar to those used in other practicum situations. The most common data collection methods appeared to be pre- and postassessment of competencies/objectives by students, postevaluation questionnaires regarding the practicum, and direct performance observations with written feedback. Some programs required journals with self-reflection about the interdisciplinary experience. One program employed a team self-evaluation tool on a weekly basis, and another program used a team roles survey before and after the practicum as well as a questionnaire on team functioning as a follow-up evaluation measure. Three universities reported using external evaluation.

Challenges and Solutions

An interdisciplinary practicum brings together a variety of participants with different histories of education and professional service. Creating an effective learning experience for students, while also rewarding site personnel and families for their contributions, can be a challenging task. Success in this endeavor requires specific actions before and during the practicum as well as initial and ongoing attention to the relationships involved.

Assembling the Interdisciplinary Team to Plan the Practicum   One of the challenges inherent in interdisciplinary practica is the task of bringing together people who have not worked together before. This frequently requires crossing departmental, even college, lines. To mirror early intervention, the university's interdisciplinary team must go beyond ECE and ECSE to include other disciplines. Developing collaborative relationships with representatives of disciplines such as nursing, social work, allied health, psychology, and nutrition will simulate for faculty the experiences of practitioners who work daily on interdisciplinary teams. One strategy for identifying who should be on the planning team is to determine which disciplines are typically included on early intervention teams within the community; identify the parallel personnel preparation programs represented within the university, community, or region; and establish procedures for involving faculty and students from those disciplines within the practicum.

Faculty representing all participating disciplines may not be present in the same location. The following practicum model illustrates a creative approach to offering interdisciplinary practica when higher education disciplines are limited.

When Higher Education Disciplines Are Limited

One personnel preparation program in ECSE exists within a consortium of six small liberal arts colleges ranging in size from 200 to 700 students. The colleges lie within a diamond approximately 75 miles by 85 miles in a rural area of the Great Plains. The consortium, called the Associated Colleges of Central Kansas (ACCK), has operated a collaborative program in special education since 1972 and a certification program in ECSE since 1987. Although the ECSE program is designed as an undergraduate offering in terms of credit, it attracts a significant percentage of students with bachelor's or master's degrees, who enroll in the 33-hour program seeking endorsement to teach children birth to age 8 and their families. In 1995, 15 graduates received Kansas certification. With the help of federal grants since 1990, ACCK has developed an Infant Specialization to be taken concurrently with the core ECSE program. Last year 13 graduates completed the Infant Specialization. A number of practicing professionals in the area also participated.

Although committed to offering interdisciplinary field experiences, the ACCK faculty has been challenged in implementing them. The small colleges of the consortium contain no departments of school psychology, speech-language pathology, nutrition, school administration, occupational therapy, or physical therapy. Two schools among the six sponsor undergraduate nursing programs with a life-span emphasis. Two of the colleges include undergraduate social work programs, also with a life-span orientation. Opportunities for cross-departmental practica are limited in this context.

The ECSE faculty are themselves a diverse group, with initial preparation in psychology, ECE, special education (mental retardation, trainable level; learning disabilities), and educational administration. They bring these diverse backgrounds, along with many years of experience as ECE/ECSE teachers, to practicum supervision.

Given the rural location of the ACCK colleges, potential practicum sites are limited in number. However, available practicum sites accurately reflect the settings most program graduates will enter for employment. Students complete a total of three ECSE practica, totaling at least 12 weeks, in addition to their 8-week student teaching placement in general education. They are placed for practica chiefly within a 115-mile by 170-mile diamond. All students take a course on collaboration skills, all participate in five seminars per year led by professionals from a variety of disciplines, and all student practica require experiences with and reflection on interdisciplinary decision making. In addition to placement in community- or school-based intervention programs, students may request a hospital, institution, or specialized intervention program placement for their third practicum. They may also request to specialize in interdisciplinary experiences. The following examples illustrate the diversity of practicum settings experienced by students:

- A team of four students spent 2 weeks at the University of Kansas Medical Center's Child Developmental Unit, assigned to diagnostic and intervention teams representing multiple disciplines.
- A student with previous certification in hearing-impaired education and extensive experience in early intervention with deaf infants spent 4 weeks at a Wichita medical center. Her supervision was shared by the ACCK supervisor in ECSE and the hospital's pediatric audiologist, a child life specialist, and a neonatal intensive care unit (NICU) nurse. This student spent a great deal of her time with the interdisciplinary team, interpreting the hospital's assessments to parents and developing collaborative transition plans from hospital to community for babies with multiple impairments.
- A young undergraduate who aims to practice in a rural area was assigned to an intensive care nursery at a hospital in Garden City, Kansas, with supervision from an ECSE-trained Infant Specialist and NICU nurses.
- Other undergraduates regularly are placed in a community program with an innovative hospital-based program to monitor infants at risk. The team to which these students are assigned includes a speech-language pathologist, a physical therapist, a special educator, a nutritionist, a social worker, and a nurse.

Interdisciplinary practicum experiences are highly individualized, matching the practicum context and supervision with each student's needs, preferences, and previous experience. Types of interdisciplinary activities vary considerably from student to student. Nevertheless, the emphasis on interdisciplinary collaboration, transdisciplinary service delivery, and family-centered services is constant for all students. Although imperfect and certainly still evolving, ACCK's practicum plan is one example of using available resources creatively to accomplish interdisciplinary practica.

Developing Common Understandings of Early Intervention Faculty from diverse disciplines may differ in various ways. Some faculty members and service providers have focused attention on infants, toddlers, and young children throughout their careers, whereas others have worked with an older age group or have a life-span perspective. Similarly, some professionals operate from a medical model, diagnosing impairments and prescribing remediation or cure, whereas others employ an empowerment model that collaborates with families to identify strengths and build on them. Some identify themselves as behavioral in approach, whereas others emphasize their developmental orientation. Furthermore, some professionals are most comfortable with clinical, highly specialized forms of service delivery, whereas others have adopted ecological approaches and transdisciplinary service delivery. Different disciplines, as educated in various regions of the United States, may bring idiosyncratic approaches to early intervention as well as to the planning process for an interdisciplinary practicum. Despite this potential diversity, it is essential for faculty to develop a shared philosophy of early intervention to communicate effectively with students.

Existing differences in perspective need to be acknowledged and discussed within a climate of respect and honest exploration. One strategy for initiating such discussions is to ask representatives from each department to share articles from their disciplines' early intervention literature for group study. Another strategy is to invite an expert in the field to meet with the faculty group and help them clarify the key early intervention concepts in their own language. It is also valuable for faculty to attend state or regional early childhood meetings together and discuss presentations.

Reconciling Different Understandings of the Roles of Families in Early Intervention By law and by recommended practice, families are at the heart of early intervention; however, this concept tends to be understood and applied differently. To speak to students with a single voice, faculty for the interdisciplinary practicum need a common understanding about family roles in early intervention. Again, joint study of articles and books on family-centered practices can be useful (see also Chapter 10). Panel discussions by families with children in early intervention or by representatives from the state's parent training and information center can expedite the development of shared understanding. Better yet, inclusion of experienced parents on the practicum's planning team will positively shape its actions.

Creating a Shared Plan for Team Functioning Some members of the practicum planning team will be experienced and highly skilled at collaborative planning, whereas others will not. Established ways of interacting within the university's or practicum site's governance may need to be modified to develop procedures for shared decision making and joint supervision across departments and even across colleges. Societal emphasis on differential respect for individuals according to their salary and educational level must be openly acknowledged but deemphasized while contributions according to individual and shared expertise are rewarded. For example, family members and community-based early childhood program staff can make significant contributions to the planning and evaluation processes for the practicum and even to other university functions, such as student admissions decisions and course development, even though these individuals may not have graduate degrees. It is essential for university faculty to experience with cooperating professionals at the practicum site the concept of teaming and horizontal decision making that they seek to model for students. Members of the faculty team must recognize that as a team they will experience the same stages of team development (SkillPath, Inc., 1991) and assume similar team roles (Handley & Spencer, 1986) as will their students. Reflection and discussion about team process as well as practicum content are essential for the practicum planning team.

Useful strategies include discussion of shared readings (see Chapter 14) and safe exploration of the concepts of collaboration in both university and practicum settings. One respondent stated, "Focus on trust, humor, openness, flexibility, and a climate that supports risk taking and change. This interpersonal component is the highest priority."

Determining the Aims of the Interdisciplinary Practicum What is it designed to teach? What is it not designed to teach? What must students experience, and what "would be nice if . . . "? In short, what are the priorities, and which are the "attractive incidentals" for the practicum experience? Without a clearly articulated focus and defined instructional priorities, the practicum is destined to mean different things to different participants, and some will undoubtedly become disillusioned.

A strategy identified by several respondents is to determine specific practicum goals before the practicum in collaboration with families, service providers, and students and to define how their achievement will be measured. If faculty are divided in their aims for the practicum, this disagreement should be reconciled before initiating the experience. Everyone involved with the practicum should have a clear understanding of the outcomes desired, and the expectations for each role and the daily activities that are planned should flow from the previously agreed-upon philosophy. Programs should identify one set of core competencies for all disciplines involved in the practicum placement; unique competencies may be added for specific disciplines. An illustration of an interdisciplinary practicum with clear focus and priorities is provided in the following practicum model.

Practicum Teams Across Four Disciplines

Western Kentucky University (WKU), a regional university in south-central Kentucky, has an enrollment of 15,000 and draws students from both rural and suburban areas. WKU has had a master's-degree program in Interdisciplinary Early Childhood Education, Birth through Kindergarten (IECE,B–K) since the summer of 1991. This program, partially grant supported, attracts approximately 15 new students per year with a variety of professional backgrounds and formal education. In addition, since the fall of 1993, WKU has offered, with federal support, a specialization in early intervention for up to five students per year in each of the disciplines of social work, school psychology, and speech-language pathology. Students in the latter two programs are enrolled in graduate programs and tend to have matriculated directly from an undergraduate to a graduate program. The social work students are undergraduates. Students must apply to participate in this program and are selected partly based on career interests in early intervention.

Students complete several discipline-specific practica as part of their respective degree programs. In addition, they complete a 5-week cross-disciplinary summer practicum together. Students are assigned to teams of five to six people at the beginning of the spring semester and then participate with their teams in a variety of activities (e.g., studies, role plays, simulations) during preparatory seminars. The goal is to have at least one student per discipline represented on each team. The teams are then assigned to infant-toddler or preschool settings based on students' interests and their work or practicum experiences.

One full-time faculty member from each of the participating disciplines is involved in planning, implementing, and evaluating the practicum. Depending on the number of IECE,B–K students involved in the practicum, additional faculty-level supervisors may be required. These individuals, typically graduates of the IECE,B–K program with extensive experience in early childhood settings, are supported with grant and departmental monies. Faculty have dual roles, serving on both the faculty team and a student team. Faculty provide supervision for both their student team and for students in their own discipline. Although the faculty have formal education in their respective disciplines, they also have previous early childhood experience such as counseling for Head Start, developing an inclusive child care program, assessing young children, teaching in Head Start and other preschool programs, and providing home-based intervention. The common faculty interest in early childhood services unifies the committee that designed the IECE,B–K program and continues to stimulate collaborative projects related to the early years.

The setting for the 5-week practicum is the WKU Child Care and Head Start Center. It was selected because it already existed on campus and operated during the summer, it was NAEYC accredited, its staff were flexible in meeting the needs of the practicum teams, and it serves children with and without disabilities. The center serves approximately 70 children in one infant classroom, one toddler classroom, and two preschool rooms. Classroom staff join with the student–faculty teams during the practicum. Four coordinators (i.e., education, disabilities, family services/mental health, nutrition/health) assist program staff and the practicum teams.

Students are expected to have the knowledge base to apply core competencies in the practicum setting. This knowledge base has been acquired through discipline-specific coursework, interdisciplinary coursework, and seminars. At least three seminars are scheduled in the preceding fall and spring semesters, and five in the 5-week summer term before the practicum; special seminars are also held during the practicum to support team functioning. These seminars are designed to introduce or expand on content with involvement from all practicum students and faculty. Topics include an introduction to the program of study and its philosophy, the IFSP process, arena assessment, collaboration and teaming, early childhood curriculum, integrating objectives into the daily routine, and CPR instruction. Summer seminars also include a general orientation to the practicum for students and an orientation for both center staff and practicum students.

Practicum requirements are individualized based on program competencies with each student and supervisor developing a practicum plan. At minimum, each student must function as service coordinator for one child and family, plan and implement activities with children and families, participate in an arena assessment, and chair at least one of the required weekly team meetings. Each student completes a portfolio.

WKU offers an interdisciplinary practicum experience for students from four disciplines who participate as teams at a campus-based early childhood center. For institutions of higher education with several compatible disciplines and a suitable practicum site on campus, this model may be beneficial (McCollum & Stayton, 1996; Stayton & Miller, 1993). Its success depends on strong administrative support, recognition of the interdisciplinary process as part of faculty evaluation, commitment of faculty to the program, flexibility of professors in playing multiple roles, commitment of university funds after grant funds cease, broad-based participation of family members in developing the program, and comprehensive program evaluation consistent with all facets of the model.

Finding Time for Communication Among the Responsible Parties   Almost every survey respondent who had implemented an interdisciplinary practicum commented on the time factor: "It would be easy to underestimate the time required to build bridges to other departments." Useful strategies include regularly scheduled meeting times that are held "sacred" by participants; study sessions for interdisciplinary discussions of early intervention and supervision; travel together to professional conferences dealing with personnel preparation in early intervention; and time lines that include considerable consultation time at all phases of practicum development, implementation, evaluation, and refinement.

Furthermore, university personnel need to commit considerable time to spend on site at the early intervention program if they are to develop a quality interdisciplinary practicum experience. "Two visits a semester," as described by one survey respondent, will not accomplish a worthwhile outcome. Some of the necessary on-site time is spent mentoring the student(s), some is spent supporting and sharing expertise with the service providers, and some is spent analyzing the practicum process to improve it. The payoff for the time commitment by faculty is likely to be a cadre of competent faculty to "cover the range of needed supervision" and help all to adjust satisfactorily to the ebbs and flows of student enrollment in field experiences.

Finding/Creating Quality Practicum Sites   Survey respondents emphasized the importance of careful decision making regarding practicum sites. They suggested, "Go and observe well-established, existing programs." "Observe potential sites several times." Then "focus on ones that really value family members as primary players and team members." Choosing sites that already follow many recommended practices is a good strategy.

But what if few options are available, as in many rural areas, and each of the alternative sites has some limitations? As early intervention has been changing rapidly, many agency personnel have not had access to professional development opportunities in collaboration and family-guided service delivery, or, even with exposure to these concepts, they have not made the necessary applications. University personnel must evaluate the potential for growth of available programs and consider the most promising, collaborative means for supporting their adoption of recommended practices (Rosenkoetter & Mann-Rinehart, 1994).

Partnership in staff development may yield quality practicum sites in the long term as well as build mutually supportive relationships between early intervention providers and university faculty, relationships valuable for a variety of purposes. Faculty may invite program personnel to join them in study groups, in inservice presentations, or in class or conference sessions to exchange knowledge and skills. Professors may initiate joint visits to model programs that follow recommended practices and then discuss informally what has been observed. They may share books or videotapes or bring in outside experts to work as consultants with both program personnel and university faculty in designing the new interdisciplinary practicum. Site personnel may visit other practicum sites to learn from and contribute to their evolving practices and eventually to share ideas with faculty.

Faculty must respect the expertise of the program staff and the families in the community they serve. They must allow adequate time to nurture collaboration among agency personnel, university faculty, and families to build the infrastructure for the practicum. The quality of agency leadership, including hospitality to university faculty and general openness to change, along with the flexibility of student practicum participants is vital to making a practicum work in a less-than-ideal location.

The issue of site quality may also arise when one or more professional members of a program's team are not exemplary in their disciplinary competence for early intervention. Faculty personnel then need to determine how to support the service provider in achieving new knowledge and skills, to supplement the student's practicum experience beyond this agency, or to find another practicum site for the placement. Students should not be responsible for changing inappropriate practicum sites or supervisory personnel. Rather, differences of opinion between agency and university personnel must be worked out in their supervisory collaboration.

Two alternatives for using community-based practicum sites that may prove to be attractive to some faculty planners are using university-sponsored child care centers or establishing special playgroups. On some campuses, National Association for the Education of Young Children (NAEYC)–accredited, university-sponsored centers for infant-toddler care incorporate early intervention services under the leadership of professionals and graduate students (McCollum & Stayton, 1996). Although not fully real world, such locations may be advantageous because of their quality staff and their preexisting relationship to the university's programs. In such a setting, students may encounter fewer challenges to recommended practices, allowing them to focus on learning new intervention strategies. The setting may, however, limit their opportunities to observe conflict resolution.

A second alternative involves inviting a group of young children, including some eligible for early intervention, to participate as volunteers in special playgroups established for the express purpose of the interdisciplinary practicum (Rowan, Thorp, & McCollum, 1990). In such an arranged setting, faculty and students will not encounter service providers with philosophies different from their own. This makes practicing agreed-upon skills easier, but preparing students to function in real-world agencies, such as the one that Janet entered (see Janet's story in Chapter 1), may then need to be addressed through other practica.

Meeting Accreditation Standards of National Professional Organizations and Satisfying State Licensure/Certification Requirements   Many states (e.g., New Mexico, North Carolina, Washington) include in their licensure requirements for early intervention professionals a number of competencies related to interdisciplinary teaming and family-guided services. Similarly, the standards published by many professional organizations (American Speech-Language-Hearing Association, 1990; Division for Early Childhood of the Council for Exceptional Children, National Association for the Education of Young Children, & Association of Teacher Education, 1996; National Association for the Education of Young Children, 1995; University of Kentucky College of Nursing, 1993) incorporate these two domains. A well-designed interdisciplinary practicum is an excellent strategy for addressing these competencies. Said one respondent, "Many problems that arise are due to the rigid, disciplinary nature of service systems." Advised another, "Be prepared to defend the adequacy of training students at least partially under a professional outside their field. The coordination necessary and the politics of pulling it off can be tremendous."

Necessary strategies include the following:

- Careful research about licensure/certification requirements for each discipline involved in the practicum
- Documentation of time spent by each of the relevant disciplines in collaborative development of the practicum experience ("They wanted to know that our discipline had been involved throughout the planning")
- Monitoring of proposed changes in standards for licensure
- Education of state and national leaders of the professions about ways that interdisciplinary field experiences motivate student learning of essential competencies (cf. Merrill-Palmer Institute, 1994)
- Advocacy to move the field as a whole and one discipline in particular toward embracing this concept

In situations in which strict supervisory guidelines prevent students from participating in interdisciplinary practica, faculty can develop opportunities for students to spend time in community-based interdisciplinary services as a part of their required coursework.

Recruiting Understanding and Support from University Administrators Administrators with broad responsibilities may be unaware of the importance of interdisciplinary practica for the preparation of early intervention personnel. Education about this new field, its importance to the university's programs, and the opportunity for the school to provide exemplary training across disciplines must be shared with administrators initially and through repeated brief updates on the progress of the effort. Comments and outcome data from graduates, information about publicity accruing to the university from the interdisciplinary practicum project, copies of published manuscripts, lists of professional presentations, and testimonials from involved faculty can contribute to the ongoing information sharing. Where support is needed (e.g., release time to implement the initial effort, secretarial assistance, encouragement from administration to minimize cross-college red tape), it should be concisely requested and explained.

Respecting Differences in Personalities and Styles of Student Supervision Among Participating Faculty Variation in work styles, supervision practices, and personalities is a necessary concomitant of shared leadership, and it parallels the team situations in which students are being prepared to function. Diversity can strengthen the team's ultimate product, the practicum experience, as long as it is recognized, aimed toward the common goal, and used to support student learning.

One respondent commented, "Examine a variety of models for supervision and a host of supervisory practices" before deciding how students will be mentored. The interdisciplinary practicum offers an opportunity for faculty and service providers to grow in their leadership skills while challenging them to supervise in ways appropriate to individual students' needs. It also offers students an opportunity to learn from faculty from other disciplines. Yet the survey results indicated that only 11 of the 56 responding programs employ cross-discipline supervision. Strategies for accommodating varied personal styles include attending to the collaboration process and communication styles, as well as the outcomes, of the interdisciplinary practicum; developing common statements of goals, procedures, and time lines to frame all practicum elements; using partnering and/or role-playing supervision techniques to provide modeling for colleagues; and establishing open, respectful discussion of differences to strengthen team functioning.

Planning and Implementing Program Evaluation Activities   As with any other component of the personnel preparation program, the practicum must be evaluated to determine its effectiveness in relationship to the resources expended. Empirical evidence is essential to document the need for institutionalization of the practicum. Data may differ from those to be collected for other practica; needs should be determined based on the philosophy and goals for the interdisciplinary practicum.

All practicum participants should contribute to the evaluation process. The survey shows a widespread weakness here: Although one rationale for an interdisciplinary experience is to prepare students to provide more family-centered services, only 59% of the universities responding definitely included parents in their practicum evaluation process. The authors have found many parents willing to complete satisfaction surveys and to participate in focus groups. Only one program reported follow-up contact with employers. That institution has been gathering such data since 1988 and has found them very useful in refining the institutional experience. Lack of more widespread data gathering from employers may be due partly to the relative "newness" of many interdisciplinary practica. Evaluation data can be collected from employers via questionnaires, focus groups, and interactions with advisory groups.

CONCLUSION

Survey results suggest that interdisciplinary practica have largely developed since 1990. They are designed to improve student preparation to contribute effectively in early intervention. It is unclear from the survey results, however, how many universities are actually offering interdisciplinary practica. Surveys were sent to 289 institutions, and 155 of those responded, yet only 38% of the respondents (20% of the total sample) reported interdisciplinary practica. Programs that do offer an interdisciplinary practicum are likely to be in larger, publicly funded institutions with graduate programs. Many of these programs, although we cannot provide a specific number, have received financial support through U.S. Department of Education personnel preparation grants.

If interdisciplinary practica are truly critical to ensure that students acquire the skills to provide collaborative, interdisciplinary, family-centered early intervention services, then mechanisms must be developed to encourage more universities with a variety of disciplines to provide interdisciplinary practicum experiences. Those respondents who have participated in interdisciplinary practica as students, faculty, or site supervisors were universally positive about the experience; they also identified some significant challenges to implementing the concept. However, the potential benefits outweigh the drawbacks.

The following nine recommendations are based on the authors' and respondents' experiences with interdisciplinary practica:

1. Recognize that an interdisciplinary practicum involves more than students' achieving separate competencies furnished by two or more departments. Faculty need to do the

hard work of deriving *one* set of competencies that pertains for early intervention across disciplines (cf. Florida Consortium of Newborn Intervention Programs, 1991; Merrill-Palmer Institute, 1994). Discipline-specific outcomes may be added to the foundational list.

2. Recognize that interdisciplinary practica involve more than mere exposure of students to personnel from different disciplines. Rather, collaboration needs to be consciously practiced, evaluated by students and their multidisciplinary supervisors, and reflected on throughout the practicum experience.

3. Recognize that interdisciplinary practica for early intervention should go beyond the fields of ECE and ECSE to include some of the 15 other disciplines mentioned in the Individuals with Disabilities Education Act. Which disciplines and which departments must be determined within the local context.

4. Recognize that the special expertise of family members needs to be included on the interdisciplinary teams that develop, implement, and evaluate interdisciplinary practica for students. Most programs surveyed for this chapter appear to be making minimal use of families' expertise in providing field-based experiences for students.

5. Recognize that personnel in community-based early intervention programs, family members, and students are valuable partners in developing interdisciplinary practica. They bring different perspectives from those of faculty, and their observations will strengthen the practicum design. "Allow planning time to permit all parties to feel committed to the process. Continue setting aside time to ensure good and continuous communication among all parties."

6. Further work is needed to refine the concept of interdisciplinary practica and expand its applications. Formal research can be shared through professional journals. Equally important is the informal sharing of implementation experiences that helps to improve the development of interdisciplinary practica across the United States. Discussion sessions at professional meetings are useful for this purpose. Especially valuable is the sharing of ways to overcome common dilemmas.

7. Systematic evaluation of what students learn, and fail to learn, under different practicum conditions will help higher education planners choose the practicum configuration(s) that will best fit with the resources and constraints of local families, students, faculty, and service programs.

8. Dissemination concerning the concept of interdisciplinary practica needs to occur across the disciplines that serve young children with disabilities and their families. It also needs to occur through media that reach university administrators, who can provide the resources essential to support the development of interdisciplinary practica.

9. Along with community service providers, faculty members from various departments are likely to need technical assistance, inservice instruction, or external facilitation to develop their own skills in interdepartmental communication and collaboration. Survey respondents repeatedly emphasized that shared values and beliefs about early intervention and student learning, common understandings of language, and sufficient time to talk and learn together are essential for faculty members to achieve a successful practicum plan.

RESOURCES

American Speech-Language-Hearing Association. (1990). The role of speech-language pathologists in service delivery to infants, toddlers, and their families. *Asha, 32*(Suppl. 2), 31–34, 94. (301) 897-5700.

A description of expectations that fall within the professional scope of practice and expertise of speech-language pathologists in serving young children with disabilities and their families. The document is also designed to provide health care providers, educators, and the general public with an awareness of the services that speech-language pathologists can provide.

Division for Early Childhood of the Council for Exceptional Children, National Association for the Education of Young Children, & Association of Teacher Educators. (1995, June). *Personnel standards for early education and early intervention: Guidelines for licensure in early childhood special education.* Washington, DC: Authors.

Describes the knowledge and skills necessary for effective work with all young children, including those with special needs. This publication helps distinguish the roles of educators in both early childhood education and early childhood special education and outlines recommendations for licensure for early childhood special educators serving children with disabilities in a variety of settings.

Division for Early Childhood (DEC) Task Force on Recommended Practices. (1993). *DEC recommended practices: Indicators of quality in programs for infants and young children with special needs and their families.* Reston, VA: Division for Early Childhood of the Council for Exceptional Children. Cost: $20 plus shipping. (800) 232-7373.

Recommended practices for programs designed to meet the special needs of infants and young children. Aspects of early intervention that are examined include assessment; family participation; individualized family service plans and individualized education programs; interventions for children who are gifted; and interventions to foster cognitive, communication, social, adaptive behavior, and motor skills. Suggestions for service delivery models, supporting transitions, developing personnel competence, and evaluating programs are also included.

McCollum, J.A., & Stayton, V.D. (1996). Preparing early childhood special educators. In D. Bricker & A. Widerstrom (Eds.), *Preparing personnel to work with infants and young children and their families: A team approach* (pp. 67–90). Baltimore: Paul H. Brookes Publishing Co. Cost: $45 plus shipping and handling. (800) 638-3775.

An examination of the contributions and responsibilities of early childhood special educators working with young children and their families in a team approach. The authors describe the skills and knowledge that early childhood special educators bring to the field of early intervention, along with personnel preparation programs and recommended practices.

McGonigel, M.J., Woodruff, G., & Roszmann-Millican, M. (1994). The transdisciplinary team: A model for family-centered early intervention. In L.J. Johnson, R.J. Gallagher, M.J. LaMontagne, J.B. Jordan, J.J. Gallagher, P.L. Hutinger, & M.B. Karnes (Eds.), *Meeting early intervention challenges: Issues from birth to three* (2nd ed., pp. 95–131). Baltimore: Paul H. Brookes Publishing Co. Cost: $30 plus shipping and handling. (800) 638-3775.

Addresses the importance and challenges of using a transdisciplinary team approach to serving infants and young children in family-centered early intervention. The authors examine three team approaches, including a transagency team model.

Rowan, L.E., Thorp, E.K., & McCollum, J.A. (1990). An interdisciplinary practicum for infant–family related competencies in speech-language pathology and audiology. *Infants and Young Children, 3,* 58–66.

Insights from the implementation of an interdisciplinary instructional practicum for two graduate programs, Speech and Hearing Science and Early Childhood Special Education. Describes the instructional programs and approaches in terms of philosophy, implementation, challenges, and outcomes.

Stayton, V.D., & Miller, P.S. (1993). Combining early childhood and early childhood special education standards in personnel preparation programs: Experiences in two states. *Topics in Early Childhood Special Education, 13,* 372–387.

A rationale for the integration of early childhood special education and early childhood education programs as a strategy for promoting more cohesive and effective preservice training. Two unified programs are described, along with the barriers and facilitators.

University of Kentucky College of Nursing. (1993). *National standards of nursing practice for early intervention services.* Lexington: Author. Cost: Free while supplies last. (606) 233-5406.

An overview of the Education of the Handicapped Act Amendments of 1986, PL 99-457, and what it means to nursing professionals. Delineation of the scope of practice and standards of care for nurses, as well as standards of professional performance and guidelines for specialty practice.

REFERENCES

American Speech-Language-Hearing Association. (1990). The role of speech-language pathologists in service delivery to infants, toddlers, and their families. *Asha, 32*(Suppl. 2), 31–34, 94.

Division for Early Childhood of the Council for Exceptional Children, National Association for the Education of Young Children, & Association of Teacher Educators. (1995). *Personnel standards for early education and early intervention: Guidelines for licensure in early childhood special education.* Washington, DC: Author.

Division for Early Childhood (DEC) Task Force on Recommended Practices. (1993). *DEC recommended practices: Indicators of quality in programs for infants and young children with special needs and their families.* Reston, VA: Division for Early Childhood of the Council for Exceptional Children.

Florida Consortium of Newborn Intervention Programs. (1991). *Competencies for professions serving at-risk and disabled infants, toddlers, and their families.* Tallahassee: Florida Department of Education.

Handley, E.E., & Spencer, P.E. (1986). *Decision-making for early services: A team approach.* Elk Grove, IL: American Academy of Pediatrics.

McCollum, J.A., Rowan, L.E., & Thorp, E.K. (1994). Philosophy as training in infancy personnel preparation. *Journal of Early Intervention, 18,* 216–226.

McCollum, J.A., & Stayton, V.D. (1996). Preparing early childhood special educators. In D. Bricker & A. Widerstrom (Eds.), *Preparing personnel to work with infants and young children and their families: A team approach* (pp. 67–90). Baltimore: Paul H. Brookes Publishing Co.

McGonigel, M.J., Woodruff, G., & Roszmann-Millican, M. (1994). The transdisciplinary team: A model for family-centered early intervention. In L.J. Johnson, R.J. Gallagher, M.J. LaMontagne, J.B. Jordan, J.J. Gallagher, P.L. Hutinger, & M.B. Karnes (Eds.), *Meeting early intervention challenges: Issues from birth to three* (2nd ed., pp. 95–131). Baltimore: Paul H. Brookes Publishing Co.

Merrill-Palmer Institute. (1994). *Interdisciplinary competencies: Final report of the interdisciplinary personnel preparation committee to the Michigan state interagency coordinating council.* Detroit, MI: Wayne State University.

National Association for the Education of Young Children (NAEYC). (1995). *Guidelines for preparation of early childhood professionals: Associate, baccalaureate, and advanced levels.* Washington, DC: Author.

Rooney, R. (1995, April). *Implementation of interdisciplinary personnel preparation programs for early intervention.* Paper presented to the Comprehensive System of Personnel Development Conference, Arlington, VA.

Rosenkoetter, S.E., & Mann-Rinehart, P. (1994, June). *Developing and nurturing practicum sites.* Paper presented at the Midwest Symposium on Faculty Development, Minneapolis, MN.

Rowan, L.E., Thorp, E.K., & McCollum, J.A. (1990). An interdisciplinary practicum for infant–family related competencies in speech-language pathology and audiology. *Infants and Young Children, 3,* 58–66.

SkillPath, Inc. (1991). *Coaching and team-building skills.* Mission, KS: Author.

Stayton, V.D., & Karnes, M.B. (1994). Model programs for infants and toddlers with disabilities and their families. In L.J. Johnson, R.J. Gallagher, M.J. LaMontagne, J.B. Jordan, J.J. Gallagher, P.L. Hutinger, & M.B. Karnes (Eds.), *Meeting early intervention challenges: Issues from birth to three* (2nd ed., pp. 33–58). Baltimore: Paul H. Brookes Publishing Co.

Stayton, V.D., & Miller, P.S. (1993). Combining early childhood and early childhood special education standards in personnel preparation programs: Experiences in two states. *Topics in Early Childhood Special Education, 13,* 372–387.

University of Kentucky College of Nursing. (1993). *National standards of nursing practice for early intervention services.* Lexington: Author.

19 DISTANCE EDUCATION IN EARLY INTERVENTION PERSONNEL PREPARATION

Mary-alayne Hughes
Sue Forest

Acute shortages of qualified personnel have arisen as states have strived to fully implement the early intervention legislation of the Education of the Handicapped Act Amendments of 1986, PL 99-457. Historically, personnel have been prepared through conventional preservice models in which students attend classes on a university campus. The advantages of this model include the students' in-depth study of the components of early intervention through participation in coursework and supervised practica and research experiences. In addition, students have physical access to faculty, peers, and numerous information resources via libraries, computers, and writing labs. However, this model of instruction is not available to a large body of employed individuals who may not reside within daily commuting distance of a university or whose full-time employment limits their ability to attend traditional classes on campus. Given these constraints, employed individuals often receive training through inservice models (e.g., seminars, conferences, workshops) in which they travel to a centralized site. The inservice program usually is of short duration and typically addresses more narrowly focused content; follow-up instruction or technical assistance often is not provided (see Chapter 7 for more information on follow-up), and college credit typically is not available.

Although both preservice and inservice models serve a particular function in personnel preparation, neither model in its conventional form is sufficient to address early intervention's current shortages of qualified personnel, either in the breadth of individuals who need to be trained or retrained or in the depth of content in which these individuals need training. Distance education as a mode of instruction may be one answer to this quandary.

This chapter explores the issues and challenges associated with distance education within the context of personnel preparation in early intervention. The chapter begins by outlining the history of distance education (including its various definitions) and providing information concerning its efficacy. This is followed by a discussion of the practical issues and challenges associated with implementing a distance education program, including those issues specific to an applied field such as early intervention. The focus of this discussion concerns preservice programs that grant college degree credit in a distance education format for individuals who must use a nontraditional form of education due to family, employment, or geographic distance constraints. However, much of this discussion would also apply to inservice programs designed for this same type of participant.

DEFINING DISTANCE EDUCATION

Distance education is used as an instructional mode in numerous countries around the world (e.g., Australia, China, India, Norway, United States, West Africa). A variety of subject matter is taught in education, engineering, business, allied health, natural sciences, and liberal arts. Internationally, there are more than 1,500 distance-teaching institutions (Holmberg, 1989). Some of the more well-known include Athabasca University (Canada), Everyman's University (Israel), Open Universiteit (Netherlands), Open University (United Kingdom), University of the Air (Japan), and Universidad Nacional de Educacion a Distancia (Spain). The International Council for Distance Education estimates that approximately 10 million people worldwide study at a distance annually (Kaye, 1988). In addition to preservice opportunities through institutions of higher education, the military and the corporate world (e.g., automotive, petroleum, health care industries) use distance education to provide employees with continuing education opportunities. For example, Voluntary Hospitals of America (VHA), the largest alliance of hospitals and multihospital systems in the United States, has signed a contract with the VTEL Corporation to offer VTEL's interactive telecommunications equipment to VHA's 900 not-for-profit hospitals. The equipment will facilitate continuing medical education to health care professionals and also provide opportunities for cross-hospital communication concerning patient diagnosis and treatment (Klinck, 1993). Given these examples, the use of distance education for a variety of preservice and inservice educational purposes seems boundless.

But what exactly is distance education? In the United States, the earliest forms of distance education were correspondence study programs that were established in the late 1800s at Illinois Wesleyan College and the University of Chicago. In 1919, the University of Wisconsin started the first federally licensed educational radio station. Educational television broadcasting originated at the University of Iowa between 1932 and 1937 (Verduin & Clark, 1991).

Internationally, the Open University of the United Kingdom served as a model for distance education programs and heralded the modern era in distance education when it first began teaching students in 1971. In the United States, coursework through distance education has been offered for many years by departments and divisions within conventional universities. However, the Annenberg/CPB Project was a catalyst for the development of many of these programs. In 1981, the Annenberg School of Communications at the University of Pennsylvania committed $150 million to the Corporation for Public Broadcasting to support projects that enhance the use of telecommunications and information technologies in higher education. Thus, this project is a major funding source that supports the development of innovative distance education course materials and technologies (Moore, 1987).

There also has been growth in networks and consortia of institutions that provide distance education (e.g., National Technological University, a consortium of 15 universities from the Association for Media-Based Continuing Education for Engineers). However, distance education in the United States is not as formalized as it is in other countries where centralized policy-making bodies and distance education systems have been established (Moore, 1987).

Distance education is changing rapidly because of the burgeoning growth in telecommunications technologies. Several problems are associated with its evolution and international application. First, the terminology associated with distance education is inconsistent and thus confusing. For example, the term *distance education* is often used interchangeably with nontraditional education and open learning, and yet many have argued that these terms are not synonymous (Keegan, 1986; Verduin & Clark, 1991). In addition, terms used in English for this field of education include (but are not limited to) correspondence study, home study, external studies, independent study, teaching at a distance, and off-campus study (Keegan, 1986). Distance learning and distance teaching also are commonly used referents; however, Keegan (1986) suggested that distance education is a more suitable term as it brings together both the teaching and learning aspects of the process. Moreover, the International Council for Correspondence Education changed its name to the International Council for Distance Education at its 1982 world conference, thus formally adopting this term and providing international sanction for its use (Moore, 1990).

Second, there continues to be debate concerning the definition of distance education as part of the ongoing attempt to delimit it as a field of study. Some definitions have stressed the structural characteristics of the separation of teacher and learner (Holmberg, 1985) whereas other definitions have focused on the use of technical media (Moore, 1973) and the industrialization of the teaching process (Peters, 1973, as cited in Keegan, 1986). Keegan (1986) reviewed the literature and synthesized various characteristics of previous definitions into five interdependent elements. Although his definition gained general acceptance, a more minimalist definition of three elements was proposed (Garrison & Shale, 1987): 1) the majority of educational communication between teacher and learner occurs noncontiguously, 2) communication between teacher and learner is two-way communication, and 3) technology is used to mediate the two-way communication.

All of these definitions emphasize the geographic aspects of distance and focus on the noncontiguous mediated communication between teacher and learner. However, Moore (1983) suggested that physical distance may not be the most critical factor and proposed the concept of transactional distance. Moore defined transactional distance as the interplay between the variables of dialogue (i.e., the extent to which teacher and learner can interact with one another) and structure (i.e., the extent to which the program is responsive to the learner's individual needs). Both of these variables exist on a continuum from high to low, and a more distant program would be one in which there is a negative correlation between dialogue and structure, that is, low dialogue (not much opportunity for teacher–learner interaction) and high structure (program is tightly structured and not responsive to individual needs).

Although it is important to consider both the geographic and instructional aspects of distance, developing a definition of distance education is not as simple as it first appears. Even a minimalist definition seems too restrictive with its focus on the separation between teacher and learner, and none of the existing definitions allow for possible variations in how the physical distance is defined. For example, there are programs in which students travel to campus on the weekends to receive instruction or faculty travel to off-campus sites to teach a class. Moreover, there are programs in which there is some combination of travel (i.e., part of the instruction is physically face to face) and mediated communication (i.e., part of the instruction is through technological means). Would these programs be defined as examples of distance education?

Shale (1990) argued that the debate over definition has outgrown its usefulness and that there is no need for a special definition. However, others find the debate important and use working definitions to clarify their research (Moore, 1990). In this chapter, we view distance education as an instructional mode whose purpose is to provide access to education to those individuals who otherwise would not have access because of family, employment, or logistical constraints. Furthermore, we have chosen to discuss the issues associated with both the distance and education components of distance education as those components apply to the instruction of early intervention personnel.

EFFICACY OF DISTANCE EDUCATION

Is distance education an effective instructional mode? How does it compare with more conventional modes of teaching? A survey of the literature reveals a large body of research concerning the effectiveness of distance education. The reader is referred to Moore (1990) and Verduin and Clark (1991) for a more comprehensive review; however, several summary points can be made.

Wagner (1990) enumerated four features of distance education literature: 1) a large body exists as papers or conference presentations; 2) it tends to be conceptual (i.e., provides direction for action) rather than theoretical; 3) it tends to be descriptive (e.g., observational data, case study, surveys); and 4) it has an international orientation, with much of the literature produced by countries other than the United States. Both Moore (1990) and Wagner (1990) stated that the majority of the research in distance education has evaluated the effectiveness of various types of technical media, although a review by Gibson (1990) also included literature on student characteristics (e.g., demographics, educational background, cognitive personality style, learning style motivation) and effects on the learner of modifications in the educational environment (e.g., tutorials, telephone contacts, peer tutoring, use of the mail system to provide learner support). However, it should be noted that the subject matter of the courses evaluated in these studies is typically that of factual content (e.g., natural sciences, psychology, business) compared with applied content, although some research has targeted instruction in skill-based areas such as natural sciences laboratory work, photography, mechanics, and airplane equipment troubleshooting (Verduin & Clark, 1991). Those who have studied this research suggest that "distance education methodology appears to achieve cognitive outcomes equal to those achieved by the more traditional means of education delivery for adults. In many cases, the scale even tips toward distance education" (Verduin & Clark, 1991, p. 117). However, all agree that much more research is needed, particularly in applied fields.

With regard to teacher education, a database on distance education is beginning to emerge. A perusal of the ERIC abstracts for 1982–1994 under the rubric of "distance education and teacher education" revealed a total of 138 records. Although many of these records referred to international programs in personnel preparation (e.g., Australia, China, South Africa), there were numerous entries concerning inservice and preservice teacher preparation programs in general education and special education across the United States (e.g., Alabama, Alaska, California, Iowa, Kansas, Maine, Nevada, New Jersey, Texas, Utah, West Virginia, Wisconsin, Wyoming). Many of these entries are descriptive and provide information about the way in which the program is structured, including advantages and disadvantages. Some include evaluative data on consumer satisfaction, cost-effectiveness, and the comparative effectiveness of various technical media (e.g., videotape, audiotape). In general, the rural states appear to be leading the way in the use of distance education as an instructional mode of delivery. Almost every program cited (except for the international programs) concerned teacher preparation in special education; and most programs offered a combination of technical media and/or physical face-to-face program options.

ISSUES AND CHALLENGES OF IMPLEMENTING DISTANCE EDUCATION

Given the differences between conventional forms of education and distance education, there are numerous issues and challenges associated with the implementation of a distance education program. These challenges appear in varying degrees and in various manifestations in both preservice and continuing education settings. In this chapter, issues and challenges related to the college or university setting are considered; however, these issues also apply to settings in which distance education is used as an avenue for continuing professional development.

Organizational Structures

The organizational pattern and administrative practices of a university are based on the educational philosophy and mission of that institution as well as some economic and political restrictions (Verduin & Clark, 1991). A major issue for effective distance education is in what type of university the program is located and how the administrative infrastructure supports that program.

Rumble (1986) identified three models that reflect ways in which distance education can be administered in a university setting. In one model, the university has distance education as its sole responsibility. An example of this is the Open University of the United Kingdom in which all courses are offered in a distance education mode. This model can be effective because there is a clear focus on the distance students; however, this administrative model is not prevalent in the United States.

At the other end of the continuum is the consortium model of distance education. In this model, several institutions pool their resources and collaborate in implementing distance education. Although the collaborative efforts enable the consortium to provide the distance education program, the collaborative process also is the major obstacle to effective implementation. Philosophical and administrative differences, unequal contributions by the institutions, distrust, and difficulties in sharing costs and materials are some of the problems that may arise (Verduin & Clark, 1991).

A more common arrangement is the model in which both distance education and conventional education occur as a mixed mode (Keegan, 1986). A variety of organizational designs is possible. For example, individual departments may offer distance education courses, or a distinct unit may be created to offer distance education across a variety of areas. A variety of administrative designs also is possible, including the use of the university's central administration or the creation of a specialized administrative unit to oversee and provide support for distance education programs (e.g., office of extramural programs, division of continuing education). According to Verduin and Clark (1991), the major advantage of this model is that it can draw on the resources of the resident faculty and administrative infrastructure that already exist. However, there are numerous problems associated with this model (Verduin & Clark, 1991).

First, there may be a lack of parity of esteem between distance education and campus-based instruction, resulting in second-class status for the distance education program. This may deter faculty participation, particularly if there is no administrative recognition of how the additional time requirements of distance education preparation and instruction may affect progress toward tenure. Second, there may be a lack of faculty participation due to the amount of preparation required for teaching at a distance. This may place an unfair burden on the course loads of junior faculty, or the distance education courses may be relegated to less effective instructional faculty. Third, there may be a lack of effective distance education instruction due to the inability of faculty or lack of support for faculty to change their conventional campus-based teaching strategies. For example, lecturing is a common form of conventional instruction, but it becomes a "talking head" phenomenon when used in a video teleconference format in which there is no built-in mechanism for two-way interaction between lecturer and student. Fourth, there may be a lack of administrative recognition and/or planning for the monetary costs associated with the initial implementation and maintenance of the chosen distance education technology. Although distance education programs can reach a wider audience, they are not necessarily less expensive than conventional education, even from a long-term perspective. For example, equipment must be purchased, maintained, and upgraded, and the instructional faculty may need additional clerical, administrative, and technical staff support to implement the program. Rumble (1986) also suggested that, depending on the type of technology used, the cost structure of distance education is different from conventional education (i.e., there may be significant investment in course development and materials before students are enrolled), and traditional approaches to budgeting and staffing levels may be ineffective when planning and implementing distance education programs.

Given these factors, one key to effective distance education is the provision of administrative support and resources for the instructional faculty. For example, faculty may need additional clerical staff to help with the dissemination of class materials and exams and to respond to inquiries concerning the program. Depending on the type and sophistication of the distance education technology, typically there are needs for additional technical staff such as on-site facilitators to set up and troubleshoot equipment, distribute materials, facilitate group activities and student discussions (Willis, 1993), collect assignments, and proctor exams. Administrative support also encompasses staff development. This may include instruction in effective distance education teaching strategies (Stewart, 1987) and training in the use of technical equipment in addition to equitable workloads and recognition toward tenure (Dillon, 1989).

Administrative flexibility is another key factor in the successful accommodation of distance education students. For example, responsiveness of the system can be seen in flexible admission practices (Holtzclaw, 1988) and procedures that allow flexible time lines for the initiation and completion of coursework outside of the usual semester boundaries (Paul, 1986). In addition, the registration process is a particularly important activity as it can facilitate the smooth entry of students or can be a barrier to student enrollment. It is crucial that faculty maintain communication with the administrative offices responsible for registration, and it is helpful if there is some administrative flexibility so that the process is user friendly for students. For example, are distance education students required to register on campus? If so, are there evening and weekend walk-in hours? Can registration be conducted through the mail or by telephone? Can students pay by credit card (Toby Levine Communications, Inc., 1994)?

Learner Characteristics

In addition to the administrative differences between distance education and conventional education programs, the students who participate in distance education tend to be different from conventional college-age students. Demographic data available from several large national studies of adults studying for college credit (Aslanian & Brickell, 1988; Brey & Grigsby, 1984) show that the majority of students are female, married, employed full time, and older than typical college-age students. The implications of these demographic characteristics are that many of these students have other responsibilities outside of school (e.g., family, job) that place demands or constraints on their time and their level of commitment to school. In addition, these students may be returning to school after a gap of several years, and they may lack confidence in their ability to succeed (Stewart, 1987). Moreover, they may have weak literacy skills, inadequate study habits, and ineffective time management skills (Paul, 1986). However, adults are often motivated, pragmatic, and self-directed learners who bring a wealth of real-life experience to the classes they take. Given time, support, and practice, deficient skills can be remediated, although this necessitates a commitment to make faculty time and institutional resources available and accessible to the distance education student. For example, counseling and advisory services (Gladstone, 1987; Paulet, 1987) may be beneficial to those students who are having difficulty with family and time commitments or who need additional psychological and emotional support to succeed in an academic environment.

Other support services include the provision of student access to information. In many institutions, there are extramural or continuing education offices that have resources for helping students to locate and gain access to journal articles, books, and other sources of information from the university library. Some libraries also offer additional services to distance education students, including consultation services, user instruction designed for the distance education student, assistance in nonprint media and equipment, reciprocal and contractual borrowing, interlibrary loan services, and access to reserve materials (Toby Levine Communications, Inc., 1994). Some institutions may also provide a toll-free telephone number to reduce student costs in gaining access to these faculty and institutional resources.

Provision of these types of resources and support services helps distance education students handle what may be an unfamiliar and challenging environment. Furthermore, a supportive atmosphere may help curb student attrition, a significant problem in many distance education programs (Cookson, 1990).

Communication and Interaction

The geographic and transactional distances between teacher and learner pose significant challenges for distance education. Although communication is essential in any educational endeavor, it is of prime importance in distance education. Unlike conventional instruction in which teacher and student are in face-to-face contact, the interaction that occurs in distance education is usually mediated by some form of technology that, in turn, imposes constraints on the form, frequency, and immediacy of the interaction (Garrison, 1989).

Impact of Technology   Table 19.1 delineates the advantages and disadvantages of several types of telecommunications technologies that are often used in distance education programs, should the program choose to use technology as part of its design. (Weekend on-campus study is included in the table for purposes of comparison.)

Faculty must be aware of the strengths and limitations of the technology that they are using and the effect of that technology on the communicative transaction between teacher and student. Of particular consequence for communication are the types of sensory modes used and the direction of the telecommunicative signal. Some technologies provide multiple sensory cues (e.g., interactive television) whereas others are limited to one sensory mode (e.g., audioconferencing). In addition, some types of telecommunication are one-way systems in which communication flows in one direction only (usually from the teacher to the student) whereas other types are two-way interactive systems in which communication flows between teacher and student. However, combinations of sensory cues and signal direction are also possible. For example, two-way audio/one-way video teleconferencing, during which students can be heard but not seen, is one of the most common formats because it is much lower in cost than two-way audio/two-way video

TABLE 19.1. Delivery modes

Mode	Technology Used	Advantages	Disadvantages
Telecourses — Courses are offered via television			
1. live — Students can watch the course and simultaneously call in on phone to talk with other students/faculty or call in after the broadcast.	• Television • Telephones • Telephone lines • Microphones	• Convenient • Flexible • Reaches students across large geographic areas • Can be used with printed materials	• Expensive • Requires access to television • Requires some planning and scheduling • Limits teaching methods
2. taped — Students can either watch the telecast or videotape the course for later viewing.	• Television • Video recorder	• Convenient • Flexible • Reaches students across large geographic areas • Can be used with printed materials	• Expensive (not for frequent use) • No interaction • Requires some planning and scheduling • Limits teaching methods
Video teleconferencing (interactive television) — Courses are broadcast to two or more interactive television sites. Faculty and students from several locations can view and verbally interact with each other with no delay in broadcasting. Generally only one site at a time can actively interact with another site.	• Television • Television channel • Satellite hookup • Telephone lines	• Interactive • Visual and audio • Massive coverage • Convenient (satellites at public facilities) • Suitable for large audience • Satellite less expensive than fiber optic • Allows for more flexible teaching methods	• Expensive (not for frequent use) • Requires access to equipment at each site • Requires operator at each site • Requires planning and preparation

Compressed videoconferencing — Courses are broadcast to two or more interactive television sites. However, there is a delay between broadcast and signal, so individuals will see mouths move and then will hear sounds several seconds later.	• Television • Camera for each site • Control unit for panning, tilting, and zooming • Codec (video encoder and decoder) • Two digital telephone lines • Site linkage mechanism	• More cost-effective than interactive television • Interactive • Convenient (can reach many different sites) • Allows for more flexible teaching methods	• Requires having access to equipment at each site • Requires planning and preparation • Instructor requires training in using the equipment • Requires second person to operate control unit • Requires technician to service equipment • Not as effective for long lectures/discussions
Correspondence study — Courses are packaged with reading materials and assignments. Audiotapes of lectures are provided with the modules as well as commercial videos that cover specific topic areas.	• Textbook • Study guide • Audiotapes • Videotapes	• Convenient, portable • Flexible • Inexpensive • Start any time during the year • Students control learning pace	• No face-to-face interaction • Limited feedback • Need to make testing arrangements • May require access to audio- or videotape player • Limits method of instruction
Audioconferencing — Students and faculty interact via the telephone at regularly scheduled times. Students are responsible for reading and completing assignments before the telephone conference.	• Telephone or speaker telephone • Conference call service	• Convenient • Cost-effective • Eliminates travel • Minimum equipment needed • Interactive • Reaches students across large geographic areas	• No face-to-face interaction • Need to identify each person as he or she speaks • Some planning required • Ineffective for long lectures • Limits method of instruction

(continued)

TABLE 19.1. (continued)

Mode	Technology used	Advantages	Disadvantages
Weekend on-campus study — Students come to campus and take courses from faculty on the weekend.	• None	• Convenient • Inexpensive • Allows for more flexible teaching methods • Interactive	• Requires travel by students • Faculty teach late evenings and weekends • Support services not readily accessible on weekends
Computer conferencing — Students work individually or in groups to respond to assignments/tasks on the computer. Faculty respond over the computer with students. Telephone lines link terminals enabling two or more to interact simultaneously.	• Computer with modem • Telephone lines • Software links	• Convenient • Cost-effective • Flexible • Eliminates travel • Students can provide anonymous input • Reaches students across large geographic areas • Students get feedback from students and instructor	• Requires access to equipment • Limits method of instruction • Instructor requires some training in using the equipment • No face-to-face interaction
Audiographic conferencing — Faculty and students connect through telephone lines, an electronic pad and pen, and computer so they can interact verbally, draw text or graphics on-line, and/or in writing.	• Telephone • Conferencing call service • Computer with modem • Software • Electronic tablet and pen	• Convenient • Cost-effective • Eliminates travel • Interactive (talk on telephone while sending messages) • Reaches students across large geographic areas • Uses visual aids • Several students can share each computer	• Same as audioconferencing • Requires access to equipment • Instructor requires some training in using the equipment
Videotape distribution — Courses offered on-campus are videotaped and distributed to students. Students are responsible for listening to videotapes and completing assignments, reading, and/or tasks.	• Videotapes • Video camera (for instructor) • Videotape player (for students)	• Convenient for students • Flexible	• Requires access to equipment • More costly to distribute to large numbers of students • No interaction • Need person to operate video camera • Instructor and operator require some training in using the equipment

teleconferencing (Azarmsa, 1987). Compressed videoconferencing also is becoming more popular because it is less expensive than other options. However, there is a time delay between the video and audio signal so that participants see the picture a few seconds before they hear what is being said. This can affect the interaction between teacher and student as well as student-to-student interaction if multiple sites are participating.

The synchrony of the communication also affects the interaction between teacher and student. Real-time communication (e.g., two-way audio, picture telephone) allows for synchronous conversation between teacher and student. Time-delayed communication (e.g., facsimile machine, electronic mail, some forms of computer conferencing) allows teacher and student to converse without having to be "on" at the same time (Toby Levine Communications, Inc., 1994). Decisions must be made about which components of the program are better served by real-time communication versus time-delayed communication.

In addition to considering the types of sensory modes, direction of the telecommunication signal, and synchrony of the communication, several other factors can affect the communication between teacher and student when using distance education technologies. Even if the technology is the most interactive format available (e.g., two-way video/two-way audio), the teacher may be interacting with the television camera. This may be disconcerting because nonverbal feedback from students (e.g., eye contact, facial expression, body language) provides teachers with important information about their teaching effectiveness, pacing, and student learning (Zvacek, 1991). One way to address this communicative challenge is to have a live audience participating on-site.

Student-to-student interaction may also be limited, especially if multiple sites are participating in a class session. Many teachers begin the first class with a discussion of the impact of the technology on teacher–student and student–student interactions and what constitutes appropriate communication etiquette. Also, teachers can personalize the mediated communicative process by meeting face to face with each student at least once during the time period in which the class is offered (Willis, 1993), distributing photographs of the participants before the first class, providing time for extended introductions during the first class, and injecting humor throughout the class sessions.

Another communicative challenge is the sensitivity of the chosen technology. Many systems are so sensitive that the noise from a fallen soda container may trigger the system to bring that particular site on camera. This can be very distracting and disconcerting to the teacher, and students may or may not be aware that they are now on camera.

Accessibility   Communication between teacher and student also is affected by each student's accessibility to the teacher as well as to other students. Outside of the class sessions, there may be diminished opportunities for students to receive social support from faculty and their peers (Stewart, 1983). From the teacher's perspective, it is more difficult to support students with academic, social, or familial problems that affect their academic work. For example, in difficult situations, face-to-face discussion is the preferred mode of communication; however, the distance education teacher cannot simply ask the student to make an appointment during office hours. Situations must be handled over the telephone, yet nonverbal cues and feedback are missing and it may be difficult, if not impossible, to reach the student in a timely fashion.

Another aspect of accessibility is student accountability. Although teachers struggle with questions of accountability in conventional education, it becomes more of an issue when there is physical separation between teacher and student. How will the teacher know if the assignment or project is the student's own work? Will students take exams? Will an honor system be used, or will a proctor be provided on site? Who will supervise and monitor off-campus applied experiences and practica? The challenge is to address these questions in creative and innovative ways.

Instructional Effectiveness

The teaching effectiveness of the faculty is critical to the success of a distance education program. Several variables must be considered, including course design, instructional materials, teaching strategies, and interpersonal skills.

Regardless of the type and sophistication of the technology, teaching a distance education course is not a simple matter of teaching a conventional course in a distance education format (Willis, 1993). When designing the course, faculty must consider the impact of geographic and transactional distance between themselves and their students. For example, will assignments or other products be required? Because of geographic distance, there will be a time delay in the exchange of these products. If the products are designed to build on one another, or if it is important to give students an opportunity to correct and revise various products, how will this time delay affect that process?

Course design also must incorporate the needs and desires of the students targeted for the course. A needs assessment is an effective planning tool when making decisions about course format and technology because faculty may discover important characteristics about their student population that, in turn, may impinge on the selection of technology (Ho, 1991). For example, do the targeted students spend large amounts of their time traveling by car to deliver early intervention services in rural areas? If so, the use of audiotapes might be preferred over videotapes. A needs assessment may also provide faculty with a framework to develop examples, case studies, and other activities that are contextually relevant to the students, thereby enhancing student learning (Ho, 1991).

Because of the altered communication between student and teacher, the quality of the instructional materials plays a large role in the effectiveness of distance education (Stoffel, 1987). Faculty must consider the types of materials to be used and the impact of the chosen technology on the use of materials such as overheads and instructional videos. In addition to materials used in class, faculty must consider whether students will require additional materials to facilitate their participation (e.g., study guides) and what type of media or combination of media will be most effective (e.g., print, audio, video). Print materials often compose a large portion of items mailed to students, and it is important that these materials are clear, concise, neat, well organized, and error free (Ho, 1991). Nonprint materials such as audiotapes and videotapes also may be used, but two questions in particular should be addressed. First, are there back-up tapes in case of loss, and second, will someone be responsible for checking the clarity and quality of the tapes before they are mailed to students?

In addition to course design and materials, the instructional effectiveness of the faculty is paramount. From his review of the research literature, Willis (1993) suggested that the following components have a positive impact on general instructional effectiveness: Understand the demographic and cultural diversity of the students, and use contextually relevant examples in class discussions; provide informative feedback in a timely fashion (see also Stoffel, 1987); encourage interaction between students, and foster face-to-face contact (to the extent possible) between teacher and students; provide an on-site facilitator as a bridge to link student and teacher; enhance student motivation; help students keep up with assignments, thereby discouraging attrition; realize that family support is critical to the success of the student; and be prepared to handle technical difficulties with the equipment.

Distance education also challenges the faculty to consider and evaluate the appropriateness of particular teaching strategies and techniques within the bounds of the chosen technology. Lecture, guest speaker, panel, interview, demonstration, simulation, group discussion/report, and role play are effective techniques that may be used singly or in combination (Ho, 1991). Willis (1993) also suggested that faculty consider the following strategies: Provide course goals and objectives both verbally and in writing, develop strategies for student review and remediation, realistically assess how much course content can be covered per session, diversify activities and vary the pace, humanize the course in as many ways as possible and personalize instructor involvement through opportunities for face-to-face contact, provide a strong print component, and use contextually relevant examples. (Although further detail is outside the scope of this chapter, several sources provide additional information on general teaching strategies [Willis, 1993], interactive television [Ho, 1991], compressed formats [Breckon, 1989], and student motivation [Zvacek, 1991].)

Final consideration also must be given to the interpersonal skills of the faculty. Although there is no extant research literature in this area, anecdotal report suggests that faculty play many roles, including facilitator, encourager, problem solver, counselor (Holmberg, 1989; Moore, 1987), and technocrat. In addition, effective instruction via distance education requires that faculty be flexible in their teaching strategies and in their interactions with students; innovative and willing to try new strategies, techniques, and technologies; persistent in their quest to overcome instructional and administrative barriers; and well organized to make the best use of limited time with students. They must possess skills in communication, problem solving, decision making, and self-evaluation to handle the diversity of students and challenges associated with distance education.

Choosing a Technology

Choosing the appropriate technology is another challenge of distance education. The needs of students and faculty and the existing resources and technology that are available and accessible are some of the factors that must be considered when choosing a distance education technology (Verduin & Clark, 1991). In addition, the advantages and disadvantages of the various technologies must be weighed in conjunction with the economic costs. Willis (1989) suggested that the technological systems that have lasted have similar characteristics, including "ease of teacher/student control and use, high interactivity, and low maintenance—with flexible interaction being the most critical factor by far" (p. 33).

Implementing Applied Experiences

A major challenge for distance education programs that require applied practical experiences, internships, or student practica is the provision of supervision or mentorship. At the present time, the amount of supervision for distance education students enrolled in early intervention practica appears to vary widely across programs. For instance, in 14 early intervention distance education preservice programs surveyed by the authors (see the appendix at the end of this chapter), some students receive no supervision, some receive minimal supervision via telephone contact and/or minimal on-site visits, some do their internship with their own work caseload and are supervised by a local professional who may or may not be experienced, and some are required to take time off from their job to do an internship or practicum with supervision provided by the university or college distance education program.

Given the range of possible experiences, it is obvious that student participation in practicum and the supervision of that experience present unique challenges for distance education programs in applied fields such as early intervention. Cost is a major factor, as many programs have limited staff available for on-site supervision of students or have limited funds that preclude hiring off-campus supervisors from the student's local community. Some programs may choose to have students videotape themselves as they work with children and families and then submit those tapes for supervisory feedback; however, students must have access to video cameras, and families must be willing to be videotaped.

The challenges associated with this issue call for innovation and creativity in the design and implementation of applied experiences. Students must be challenged to be accountable for their learning, and faculty must be flexible in their approach to supervision.

EDUCATION FOR LIFELONG LEARNING

Distance education can be used by many different individuals in various settings (e.g., agencies, schools, hospitals, universities, homes) for many different purposes. Thus, it is uniquely suited as a delivery mode for inservice and other types of lifelong learning opportunities. For instance, there are many programs that provide individuals with the opportunity to communicate with others, thereby gaining peer support and access to information. These include programs such as the Colorado Meeting Place (a public access computer network for disability issues) and the MCH-Net-Link (a national telecommunications network for maternal and child health information dissemination). In addition, more professional organizations are taking advantage of the continuing education opportunities afforded by telecommunications technologies by hosting distance education vehicles such as national satellite teleconferences and videoconference series.

Each state also offers unique opportunities for distance education, although they vary by amount and sophistication. Out of necessity, rural states (e.g., Montana, New Mexico, North Dakota) seem to be leading the way as they implement distance education systems to reach their geographically dispersed populations. However, more states are beginning to take advantage of burgeoning technological opportunities and are developing distance education systems or collaborating with other states (via consortia) to share the costs of such systems. As the logical site for much of this activity and often in conjunction with state agencies and organizations, colleges and universities are taking the lead in using distance education for continuing education purposes. For example, the University of Georgia is launching an Interactive Teaching Network that will offer teleconferences augmented by support materials and wraparound activities on such topics as inclusive schools, attention-deficit disorders, and vocational special needs. The Paraprofessional Training Project is a collaborative effort of the Minnesota Department of Education, Hutchinson Technical College, Minnesota Board of Technical Colleges, and the University of Minnesota to provide distance education (via interactive television) to special education and rehabilitation paraprofessionals in Minnesota. Ohio State University hosts the Center for Advanced Study in Telecommunications, which facilitates national networking and interdisciplinary research on telecommunications and its application to distance education. These examples represent only a few of the myriad programs available.

For applied fields such as early intervention, distance education may offer opportunities for consultation from related service personnel and others who hold specialized expertise but may be in short supply (e.g., physical therapists, occupational therapists). For instance, Rule and Stowitschek (1991) described an inservice program in which distance education technology was used to provide consultation to classroom teachers as they taught preschoolers with disabilities. Through the interactive capabilities of the technology, consultants observed what was happening in the classroom and provided immediate feedback to the teachers.

Whether the focus is preservice or inservice, the general issues and challenges associated with distance education remain the same and must be considered in program design. However, the factor that makes distance education technology most appealing for inservice programming is the ease with which it can be extended over time. There is no reason to provide one-time instruction without follow-up sessions. In addition, if an interactive technology is used, individuals can be observed at their worksite and specific feedback can be given without the need for travel or time away from the worksite. However, as with preservice programs, inservice distance education programs require a supportive infrastructure, and teamwork is a necessity. At a minimum, instructors must be prepared to troubleshoot the equipment (unless a technician is available) and understand how the technology impinges on their interaction with the local participants. In addition, local on-site facilitators can help by making advanced logistical arrangements and facilitating the on-line session(s). It also is particularly crucial that the local participants are part of the planning process so that the instruction can be individualized to meet their particular needs. Ongoing evaluation also provides pertinent information concerning the appropriateness and effectiveness of the inservice program.

CONCLUSION

Distance education is an effective instructional mode to reach individuals who may lack access to more traditional forms of education. Those who are contemplating the use of distance education are encouraged to consider the advantages and disadvantages of the various technologies and to investigate what type of telecommunications options and distance education opportunities are available in their state and local community. Resources for this type of information include the following in each state: early intervention lead agency, early intervention interagency coordinating council, and the department of education. Local universities and colleges and state chapters of professional organizations also may be informational sources.

In addition to these state-level sources, the appendix at the end of this chapter provides information on 14 early intervention distance education preservice and inservice programs. These programs were identified in two ways. First, numerous directories were culled for information (e.g., the Directory of University Affiliated Programs and Early Intervention Initiative Projects). Second, the early intervention coordinators in all states were asked for information concerning distance education preservice and inservice programs in their respective states. The resulting 14 programs represent a range of distance education approaches along a continuum of technology, from weekend on-campus study in which no special technology is required to interactive video teleconferencing. Each program serves as an example of a design that addresses the unique needs of its students while using available resources and technology. In surveying these programs, we found that they were willing to share information about their respective programs, including the advantages, disadvantages, costs, development phases, implementation strategies, and evaluation data.

Distance education is one of the keys to addressing the shortages of qualified personnel in early intervention by enabling us to broaden our preservice and inservice efforts. Careful consideration of the numerous issues associated with distance education and thoughtful planning concerning participant needs can lead to an effective program that can potentially reach all early intervention personnel who are interested in enriching their knowledge and skills. We encourage you to consider "going the distance" in early intervention personnel preparation!

RESOURCES

Moore, M. (Ed.). (1990). *Contemporary issues in American distance education.* Elmsford, NY: Pergamon. Cost: $81. (800) 366-2665.

A multipurpose text providing information about types of distance education, relevant research, sources of funding, critical design factors, and instructional issues to assist in effective and efficient use of the technology.

Nevada State Department of Human Resources. (1990). *Project NETWORC final reports.* Sparks, NV. (ERIC Document Reproduction Service No. ED 329 073) Cost: $15.88 plus shipping and handling. (800) 443-3742.

Describes a model designed to deliver instruction to preservice and inservice personnel in rural areas. The model used an audio-teleconferencing system, an instructional television system, and facsimile transmitters to link three pilot sites and three replication sites to deliver a four-course series of classes. Information is also provided on curriculum development, student and facilitator evaluations, and cost comparisons.

Rule, S., & Stowitschek, J.J. (1991). Use of telecommunications for inservice support of teachers of students with disabilities. *Journal of Special Education Technology, 11*(2), 57–63.

Describes a distance education project developed to reach personnel in early childhood special education at geographically distant locations. The project included the use of two-way, full-motion video with interactive audio communications delivered to the preschool classroom.

Toby Levine Communications, Inc. (1994). *Going the distance: A handbook for developing distance degree programs using television courses and telecommunications technologies.* Arlington, VA: PBS Adult Learning Service. Cost: Free. (703) 739-5360.

Identifies steps involved in establishing distance degree programs, issues to examine before beginning the process, and the main issues involved in program development. Provides detailed information regarding faculty, student, and financial issues involved in establishing a distance degree program. Several examples of established distance degree programs are also provided.

Verduin, J.R., Jr., & Clark, T.A. (1991). *Distance education: The foundations of effective practice.* San Francisco: Jossey-Bass. Cost: $32.95. (415) 433-1767.

Describes various methods of distance education delivery and the advantages and disadvantages of each. Identifies organizational and administrative issues to consider in developing a distance education program and the opportunities and challenges for distance education in the future.

REFERENCES

Aslanian, C.B., & Brickell, H.M. (1988). *How Americans in transition study for college credit.* New York: College Entrance Examination Board.

Azarmsa, R. (1987). Teleconferencing: An instructional tool. *Educational Technology, 27*(12), 28–32.

Breckon, D.J. (1989). Teaching college courses in compressed formats. *Lifelong Learning: An Omnibus of Practice and Research, 12*(4), 19–20.

Brey, R., & Grigsby, C. (1984). *Annenberg/CPB project: A study of telecourse students (executive summary) and telecourse student survey.* Washington, DC: Corporation for Public Broadcasting. (ERIC Document Reproduction Service No. ED 264 825)

Cookson, P. (1990). Persistence in distance education: A review. In M. Moore (Ed.), *Contemporary issues in American distance education* (pp. 192–204). Elmsford, NY: Pergamon.

Dillon, C. (1989). Faculty rewards and instructional telecommunications: A view from the telecourse faculty. *American Journal of Distance Education, 3*, 35–43.

Education of the Handicapped Act Amendments of 1986, PL 99-457, 20 U.S.C. §1400 *et. seq.*

Garrison, D.R. (1989). Distance education. In S. Merriam & P. Cunningham (Eds.), *Handbook of adult and continuing education* (pp. 221–232). San Francisco: Jossey-Bass.

Garrison, D.R., & Shale, D. (1987). Mapping the boundaries of distance education: Problems in defining the field. *American Journal of Distance Education, 1*(1), 7–13.

Gibson, C. (1990). Learners and learning: A discussion of selected research. In M. Moore (Ed.), *Contemporary issues in American distance education* (pp. 121–135). Elmsford, NY: Pergamon.

Gladstone, C. (1987). Advising the nontraditional student: Putting theory into practice. *Lifelong Learning: An Omnibus of Practice and Research, 10*(6), 7–9.

Ho, C.P. (1991). Instructional strategies for interactive television. *Journal of Special Education Technology, 11*, 91–98.

Holmberg, B. (1985). *Status and trends of distance education.* Lund, Sweden: Lector.

Holmberg, B. (1989). *Theory and practice of distance education.* New York: Routledge.

Holtzclaw, L.R. (1988). Flexible admission practices for adult learners. *Lifelong Learning: An Omnibus of Practice and Research, 11*(6), 9–11.

Kaye, A. (1988). Distance education: The state of the art. *Prospects, 18*(1), 43–54.

Keegan, D. (1986). *The foundations of distance education.* London: Croom Helm.

Klinck, N.A. (1993). Back to school at work. Training strategies for the 90's. *Tech Trends, 38*(6), 32–34.

Moore, M. (1973). Toward a theory of independent learning and teaching. *Journal of Higher Education, 44*, 66–79.

Moore, M. (1983). The individual adult learner. In M. Tight (Ed.), *Education for adults: Vol. I. Adult learning and education* (pp. 153–168). London: Croom Helm.

Moore, M. (1987). University distance education of adults. *Tech Trends, 32*(4), 13–18.

Moore, M. (1990). Introduction: Background and overview of contemporary American distance education. In M. Moore (Ed.), *Contemporary issues in American distance education* (pp. xii–xxvi). Elmsford, NY: Pergamon.

Nevada State Department of Human Resources. (1990). *Project NETWORC final reports.* Sparks, NV. (ERIC Document Reproduction Service No. ED 329 073)

Paul, R. (1986). Access to failure? The challenge of open education at Athabasca University. *Community Services Catalyst, 16*(2), 18–22.

Paulet, R. (1987). Counseling distance learners. *Tech Trends, 32*(4), 26–28.

Rule, S., & Stowitschek, J.J. (1991). Use of telecommunications for inservice support of teachers of students with disabilities. *Journal of Special Education Technology, 11*(2), 57–63.

Rumble, G. (1986). *The planning and management of distance education.* London: Croom Helm.

Shale, D. (1990). Toward a reconceptualization of distance education. In M. Moore (Ed.), *Contemporary issues in American distance education* (pp. 333–343). Elmsford, NY: Pergamon.

Stewart, D. (1983). Distance teaching: A contradiction in terms? In D. Stewart, D. Keegan, & B. Holmberg (Eds.), *Distance education: International perspectives* (pp. 46–61). New York: St. Martin's Press.

Stewart, D. (1987). Staff development needs in distance education and campus-based education: Are they so different? In P. Smith & M. Kelly (Eds.), *Distance education and the mainstream* (pp. 156–174). London: Croom Helm.

Stoffel, J.A. (1987). Meeting the needs of distance students: Feedback, support, and promptness. *Lifelong Learning: An Omnibus of Practice and Research, 11*(3), 25–28.

Toby Levine Communications, Inc. (1994). *Going the distance: A handbook for developing distance degree programs using television courses and telecommunications technologies.* Arlington, VA: PBS Adult Learning Service.

Verduin, J.R., Jr., & Clark, T.A. (1991). *Distance education: The foundations of effective practice.* San Francisco: Jossey-Bass.

Wagner, E. (1990). Instructional design and development: Contingency management for distance education. In M. Moore (Ed.), *Contemporary issues in American distance education* (pp. 298–312). Elmsford, NY: Pergamon.

Willis, B. (1989). Distance education and academic policy: Making it all fit. *Tech Trends, 34*(3), 32–33.

Willis, B. (1993). *Distance education: A practical guide.* Englewood Cliffs, NJ: Education Technology Publications.

Zvacek, S.M. (1991). Effective affective design for distance education. *Tech Trends, 36*(1), 40–43.

APPENDIX

DISTANCE EDUCATION PROGRAMS

The following list of distance education programs was compiled in January 1995.

Program	Location/telephone #	Method of distance education used	Undergraduate or graduate program	Preservice or inservice focus	Supervision provided	Student financial support	Grant funded
Center for Persons with Disabilities Utah State University	Utah State University Logan, UT 84322-6800 (801) 750-1981	Mail correspondence/ interactive television	Graduate/ undergraduate	Preservice/ inservice	Yes	Stipends	Yes
Department of Special Education and Communicative Disorders Arkansas State University	P.O. Box 1450 State University, AR 72467-1450 (501) 972-3061	Interactive television	Graduate	Preservice	No	No	No
Department of Special Education West Virginia University	Research & Office Park 955 Hartman Run Rd. Morgantown, WV 26505 (304) 293-3450	Live telecourse	Graduate	Preservice	No	Tuition	Yes
Department of Special Education University of Alaska at Anchorage	ECSE Program School of Education 3211 Providence Dr. Anchorage, AK 99508 (907) 786-4435	Audioconferencing Mail correspondence Taped telecourses	Graduate	Preservice/ inservice	Yes	Stipends	Yes
Department of Special Education University of Kentucky	229 Taylor Education Bldg. University of Kentucky Lexington, KY 40506 (606) 257-7909	Live telecourse Compressed video-conferencing	Graduate	Preservice	Yes	Tuition	Yes
Early Childhood Special Education Program University of Maine	Merrill Hill College of Education University of Maine at Farmington Farmington, ME 04938 (207) 778-7000	Live telecourse	Undergraduate	Preservice/ inservice	Yes	No	Yes

Program	Address	Students travel to university					
Early Intervention and ECSE Program, University of Illinois	Department of Special Education, University of Illinois, 288 Education Bldg., 1310 South Sixth St., Champaign, IL 61820, (217) 333-0260		Graduate	Preservice	Yes	Stipends; assistantships (includes tuition)	Yes
Human Development and Family Studies, Iowa State University	Iowa State University, 101 Child Development Bldg., Ames, IA 50011, (515) 294-7838	Mail correspondence	Undergraduate	Preservice	No	Tuition and books	Yes
Rural Early Intervention Training Program, Affiliated Rural Institute on Disabilities, Montana University	University of Montana, 52 Corbin Hall, Missoula, MT 59812, (406) 243-5763	Audiotapes/mail correspondence	Graduate/undergraduate	Preservice	Yes	Stipends	Yes
Special Education Department, University of North Dakota	P.O. Box 7189, Grand Fork, ND 58202, (701) 777-3144	Interactive television	Graduate	Preservice/inservice	Yes	Stipends	Yes
South Dakota University Affiliated Program, University of South Dakota	School of Medicine, 414 East Clark St., Vermillion, SD 57069, (604) 677-5311	Videotaped telecourse and instructor travels to site	Graduate/undergraduate	Preservice	Telecourse: no Seminar: yes	Stipends	Yes
University Affiliated Program, Research and Education Planning Center, University of Nevada	College of Education/MS 278, University of Nevada, Reno, NV 89557-0082, (702) 784-4921	Audioconferencing	Undergraduate	Preservice	Yes	Stipends	Yes
University Affiliated Program, University of Arkansas	1120 Marshall, Suite 306, Little Rock, AR 72202, (501) 320-3760	Interactive television	Graduate	Preservice/inservice	Yes	Stipends	No
Waisman Center Early Intervention Program, University of Wisconsin	University of Wisconsin, 1500 Highland Ave., Madison, WI 53705, (608) 263-5984	Video-teleconferencing/compressed video conferencing	Graduate/undergraduate	Preservice/inservice	Teleconferencing: no Compressed video: yes	Stipends	Yes

20

A TEAM-BASED MODEL TO IMPROVE EARLY INTERVENTION PROGRAMS

Linking Preservice and Inservice

David Sexton
Patricia Snyder
Marcia S. Lobman
Pamela Marsalis Kimbrough
Kathy Matthews

How else but through these important forums could I ever have had the opportunity to hear about the perceptions and life experiences of Victoria, the foster parent of a previously abused child with significant developmental delays who was beginning to blossom under her care, and come to appreciate what Victoria valued both for herself and her children? John and Lakeisha, whose children also attended an early intervention program, came from very different backgrounds, yet descriptions of how they experienced family-centered practices in early intervention were as similar as they were different. Verbal pictures painted by these family members, as well as by the practitioners serving these families, vividly illuminated for me the many benefits derived by engaging in dialogues across team members. These opportunities to stop and listen to the individual and collective wisdom within each of the many groups convened enhanced my sensitivity to family concerns and realities and offered me a wealth of vivid naturalistic examples essential for conveying similar insight and understanding to future students.

This chapter describes a project in Louisiana that gave faculty members, families, practitioners, administrators, and researchers an opportunity to listen to each other's stories.

Preparation of this chapter was supported in part by grants #H029Q0084 and #H029K20406, Special Education Program, Office of Special Education and Rehabilitative Services, U.S. Department of Education, and Louisiana State Department of Education grants #92-CIT3-75 and #94-CIT2-75. Views expressed in this chapter are those of the authors, not of the funding agencies.

The authors thank the members of the State Interagency Coordinating Council and the Personnel Preparation Subcommittee for their support during project implementation. Appreciation is extended to Part H program staff at the Louisiana State Department of Education and to the members of the local site teams for their ongoing dedication to personnel preparation efforts. Special thanks are extended to Frances Billeaud, Theresa Constans-Daly, Barbara Garner, and Sarintha Stricklin for providing significant contributions to model implementation efforts.

These stories were about the struggles and successes they experienced in trying to create supportive and nurturing environments for young children with disabilities. Each person's story was about a different aspect of the situation; however, a unifying theme was their shared desire to create the best possible early intervention system in their own community and the knowledge that there were changes that needed to be made in order for this to happen.

As illustrated in the opening quote, without the project we describe in this chapter, these people would not necessarily have connected with one another; and their stories would not have been shared. Each person, and the organization he or she represented, would have worked at making changes and improvements in a somewhat isolated fashion. This situation is not unique to Louisiana.

Early intervention personnel preparation efforts traditionally have been dichotomized into two separate systems: preservice and inservice. One long-standing premise has been that preservice instruction serves as an introduction to the world of practice, and inservice instruction develops, expands, or modifies the attitudes, knowledge, and skills of practitioners (Bailey, 1989). This dichotomy often is reflected at the practice level in the development and maintenance of separate systems for preparing personnel to deliver early intervention services. Lack of integration across these systems can result in a variety of negative outcomes, including wasting precious instructional resources through duplication of efforts, maintaining preservice instructors in universities where they may become isolated from real-world instructional needs, and failing to recognize that some individuals who seek preservice instruction for credentialing or licensing purposes have years of work and inservice instructional experiences. These individuals clearly are not seeking an introduction to the world of practice when they enroll in preservice coursework. In contrast to the traditional dichotomy, Fountain and Evans (1994) pointed out that preservice and inservice instruction should be viewed as a continuum that begins in higher education and extends throughout the career of an individual.

One issue faced by states participating in the federal early intervention program (Part H) is the need to develop and implement a comprehensive system for personnel development (CSPD) that reflects this continuum by maintaining systematic, meaningful linkages between preservice and inservice instructional efforts. The necessity for linkages is particularly acute for practitioners in the early intervention system who must meet established minimum entry-level standards for their profession while simultaneously providing early intervention services. Reliance on traditional personnel preparation definitions that perpetuate separate strategies for meeting instructional needs remains a major barrier to establishing linkages between preservice and inservice instruction. If personnel preparation needs are to be effectively and efficiently met, innovative instructional models and strategies must be devised and validated by service providers, consumers, faculty from institutions of higher education, and state- and local-level policy makers.

In this chapter, we describe our experiences and those of others in Louisiana who used a team-based model for change in their efforts to improve the quality of services to young children and their families. A secondary outcome of the model was to integrate preservice and inservice instructional efforts. The term *team-based model for change* refers to a set of activities designed to help early intervention teams, including families, examine current practices and set goals for change (Bailey, McWilliam, & Winton, 1992). A team-based model was chosen to guide the development and implementation of the early intervention CSPD in Louisiana because the model permitted us to design linkages between preservice and inservice efforts while emphasizing ecological, individualized, and locally directed perspectives on staff development and service quality. The model is based on the existence of a common core of recommended practice indicators that can be translated into priorities for staff development, based on local resources, needs, priorities, and concerns. From the team-based perspective, staff development is viewed as a broad systems change effort in which attention is given across all levels (i.e., individual, family, agency, region) to inputs (e.g., Who are the individuals to be instructed? Who will provide the staff development?), processes (e.g., How will staff development be designed for individuals/families/agencies? How will staff development be delivered?), and outcomes (e.g., Who evaluated the effectiveness of the staff development activities? What kinds of immediate and lasting change result from staff development?). A unique adaptation we made to the team-based model for improving local programs was to include local university faculty as members of the "team."

This chapter begins with a description of the statewide personnel preparation context in which the model operated. This section is followed by an overview of the team-based model and how we adapted the model to improve service quality and link preservice and inservice instruction. Then, fiscal assistance obtained to support and expand model implementation is described. A case study of one site at which the model was carried out is presented to illustrate site-specific components of the model; provide examples of strategies, including instruments and processes; and highlight preservice and inservice linkages. The final sections of the chapter present information about model impact and reflect on the lessons learned during implementation.

THE LOUISIANA PERSONNEL PREPARATION CONTEXT

To understand how the team-based model was used in Louisiana, we provide an overview of our personnel preparation context. Like other states, Louisiana's context has been shaped by a unique history. The descriptions of our circumstances, provided here, are useful for understanding how the model evolved in our state and may prove useful as a guide for model replication. We believe, however, that each unique personnel preparation context determines how the model ultimately emerges in other locations.

Establishing a Statewide Personnel Preparation Planning Group

Experiential and research data gathered in the late 1980s indicated that the availability of appropriately prepared and credentialed personnel would determine the extent to which quality intervention would be provided for all eligible consumers (Bailey, Palsha, & Simeonsson, 1991; McCollum & Bailey, 1991; Miller, 1992; Palsha, Bailey, Vandiviere, & Munn, 1990; Sexton et al., 1996). In 1988, a decision was made to form a ChildNet Personnel Preparation Subcommittee to advise and assist Louisiana's State Interagency Coordinating Council (SICC) and the lead agency, the Louisiana State Department of Education, in addressing two required Part H programmatic components: CSPD and personnel standards.

An open invitation to join the ChildNet Personnel Preparation Subcommittee was issued to people who represented existing local structures most concerned with personnel preparation, for example, direct service provider agencies and institutions of higher education. Other key individuals targeted for committee membership included consumers of services, program administrators, and state and local decision makers charged with policy development and implementation. Approximately 25 individuals initially volunteered to undertake the design of the CSPD and to develop personnel standards. Because of the diversity of individual and agency interests represented, committee members often had competing needs and priorities, yet shared several common goals related to personnel preparation.

Because participation on the subcommittee was the initial forum for the expression of competing interests, early efforts focused on establishing rapport, determining additional key representation, scheduling meeting dates and times, and obtaining information about similar efforts in other states. Eventually, the ChildNet Personnel Preparation Subcommittee developed a mission statement, and consensus was reached to target the 10 major objectives listed in Table 20.1.

Gathering Data to Clarify Needs and Goals

Despite the sentiment by some members of the SICC that instructional activities should begin immediately, the ChildNet Personnel Preparation Subcommittee recommended that a statewide assessment of preservice and inservice instructional needs be undertaken. These data would be used to support the design and implementation of strategies to address the adopted objectives, including establishing linkages between preservice and inservice instruction.

TABLE 20.1. Objectives of the ChildNet Personnel Preparation Subcommittee for Part H

Objective number	Description
1	Develop a plan for comprehensive, competency-based training across disciplines.
2	Develop an appropriate credentialing mechanism for service providers.
3	Promote the development of coordinated continuing education programs for currently practicing service providers.
4	Address administrative, statutory, and regulatory issues to effect the timely implementation of appropriate personnel preparation training.
5	Establish criteria for model multidisciplinary training sites for inservice and preservice purposes.
6	Establish coordination and cooperation among agencies, disciplines, and consumers in training efforts.
7	Identify and provide incentives for appropriate instruction of service providers.
8	Review and recommend adequate allocation of funds for implementation of a coordinated, multidisciplinary, multilevel, statewide personnel training effort.
9	Establish a statewide interdisciplinary consortium of key representatives from all institutions of higher education providing training specific to early intervention.
10	Monitor all matters relating to personnel preparation in all service disciplines, including certification, credentialing, and licensing standards.

With the endorsement of the SICC, the lead agency issued a request for proposals (RFP) and, in 1990, a contract was awarded to a six-member consortium of universities to conduct a statewide, multidisciplinary personnel preparation needs assessment. Many of these universities were represented on the ChildNet Personnel Preparation Subcommittee by faculty who came from various disciplines and departments.

Data were collected from 166 preservice instructional programs offering an associate degree or higher in disciplines identified as providing, or potentially providing, early intervention services. Inservice data were obtained from 296 early intervention practitioners who represented 15 different disciplines and 4 discipline-related fields. After reviewing these data, we drew implications for planning a linked instructional system to guide subsequent CSPD and personnel standard initiatives (see Sexton & Snyder, 1991).

Using Data to Guide System Development

The needs assessment data revealed that Louisiana had large numbers of early interventionists unable to meet even the most liberal entry-level requirements for their discipline. For example, many individuals providing special instruction to infants and toddlers and their families held no formal certification and, in some cases, lacked a baccalaureate degree. Becoming fully credentialed, usually a preservice function, became a common requirement in a population that also needed ongoing staff development opportunities because of new or emerging practices in the field (Winton, 1990). Linking preservice and inservice instructional experiences for these individuals, therefore, appeared to be a logical solution.

Statewide preservice data also supported linking higher education training efforts and staff development activities. The needs survey of 166 preservice programs in Louisiana found only 29.3% reporting that clinical experiences were available with families of young children with disabilities, and, perhaps more disconcerting, only 15.9% of the surveyed programs *required* clinical experience with families of infants or toddlers with disabilities (Sexton & Snyder, 1991). These data signaled the need for service providers to collaborate with faculty from institutions of higher education to link traditional preservice instructional strategies (e.g., didactic lectures) with opportunities to observe and apply information and recommended practices in early intervention settings.

Needs assessment findings had profound implications for the setting of personnel standards. At least three major issues, identified in other states as well (e.g., McCollum & Yates, 1994), had to be addressed: 1) how to ensure that personnel possessed the needed skills and knowledge to work effectively with infants and toddlers and their families, 2) how to develop reasonable and flexible standards without disqualifying large numbers of practicing early interventionists, and 3) how to link preservice and inservice instructional initiatives in ways that would facilitate access on a statewide basis.

Data from the needs assessment provided a better appreciation of the complexity and magnitude of developing a linked system. Most ChildNet Personnel Preparation Subcommittee members believed the data supported the need to design an inclusive, but flexible, instructional system. We agreed it was important to avoid a prescriptive "one-size-fits-all" approach to instruction. Efforts were undertaken to identify instructional processes and strategies adaptable and responsive to local realities. The ambitious goal set by the subcommittee was to develop an instructional system that would enable us to examine the interests and perspectives of diverse constituents; develop a shared vision across, for example, university and college faculty, early intervention service providers, and consumers; recognize and respect the uniqueness of each local context; promote transfer of instructional content to practice; build local capacities to initiate and sustain individual and systemic change; generate information useful for personnel preparation policy development and implementation; and identify, consolidate, and maximize resources. This instructional system would be part of a larger effort to improve the overall quality of services for children and families.

The majority of members on the ChildNet Personnel Preparation Subcommittee endorsed approaching personnel preparation and continuing professional development as a continuum. To meet this goal, an organizational framework was proposed to clarify the interrelationships among system levels, instructional needs, linkage strategies, and desired impacts. The framework, shown in Table 20.2, set the parameters for the subsequent adoption of the team-based model to guide personnel preparation efforts, including the development of preservice and inservice linkages.

TEAM-BASED MODEL FOR CHANGE

ChildNet Personnel Preparation Subcommittee members reached consensus that, with appropriate adaptations, the team-based model for change could be used to organize statewide early intervention personnel development. This model appeared consistent with the desired effects listed in Table 20.2. As described by Bailey, McWilliam, Winton, and Simeonsson (1992), the original model was implemented by conducting a series of workshops with early intervention teams of service providers, administrators, and family members to help them develop strategies for becoming more sensitive and responsive to the priorities and concerns of families.

Key Features of the Original Team-Based Model for Change

The stated intent of the team-based model for change, according to Bailey, McWilliam, and Winton (1992), was to improve the quality of services for children and families by implementing "a decision-making model [protocol] that provides early intervention teams a structure and framework for becoming more family centered in their work" (p. 74). This model represented an innovative alternative to traditional staff development approaches and was developed and field-tested as part of the Carolina Institute for Research on Infant Personnel Preparation at the University of North Carolina at Chapel Hill. The model encompasses three interrelated components: 1) roles played by individuals; 2) tools that can be used to inform and guide participants; and 3) processes that promote discussion, reflection, and sharing of perspectives. Key features of the model include involving entire teams, including families, in discussions about how to improve programs; conducting self-assessments of needs within the instructional context; providing information about family-centered principles and practices during instruction in the form of possibilities and alternatives; deemphasizing technical information about laws and regulations; modeling a shared decision-making process to guide team activities and instructional experiences; generating individualized action plans for implementing change that specify activities and responsible parties; and acknowledging that improving programs is cumulative and continuous, emphasizing the importance of ongoing staff development activities.

Additional guidance for implementing the original team-based model was offered by Bailey, McWilliam, and Winton (1992) and Winton, McWilliam, Harrison, Owens, and Bailey (1992). These authors described the roles that individuals on the team might assume. For example, a facilitator's role might include providing a framework and a context in which team members examine program practices as they relate to a family-centered approach. Direct service providers might describe "what their program is doing

TABLE 20.2. Organizational framework for addressing Part H personnel preparation in Louisiana

System level	Preservice needs	Inservice needs	Linkage strategies	Desired impacts
1a. Individual • Direct service providers • Service consumers • Administrators • Decision makers	• Recruit and retain sufficient numbers of fully credentialed personnel across disciplines and levels • Deliver instruction responsive to individual needs	• Improve existing practices • Facilitate emergence of needed new practices	• Identify current and projected personnel needs • Identify relevant preservice instructional programs	• Increase the number and diversity of learners • Promote enduring practice change at service level
1b. Agency • Public • Private	• Deliver instruction reflecting recommended practices • Provide support for preservice students • Provide instructional materials to faculty	• Meet standards for practice of existing personnel • Deliver instruction responsive to individual needs • Deliver instruction resulting in practice changes • Provide instruction and materials • Familiarize administrator and decision makers with ChildNet • Instruct consumers already in ChildNet system	• Identify relevant ChildNet service providers • Identify personnel standards by discipline, role, and level • Provide participant and instruction incentives • Deliver instruction at sites and in formats that are participant friendly • Identify shared instructional needs across preservice students, inservice personnel, administrators, and consumers • Write change plans for individuals and agencies	• Increase number of fully credentialed ChildNet personnel • Improve knowledge base of administrators and decision makers • Improve instructional practices at all levels for all stakeholders • Help meet the instructional needs of consumers • Increase consumer participation when developing and delivering instructional content • Build agency capacity to meet personnel development needs

(continued)

TABLE 20.2. *(continued)*

System level	Preservice needs	Inservice needs	Linkage strategies	Desired impacts
2. Interagency • Service agencies • Institutions of Higher education (IHE) • Lead agency	• Meet ChildNet entry-level standards • Develop practicum sites for preservice students • Provide opportunities for IHE faculty to develop/improve preservice course content • Facilitate IHEs support to deliver on- and off-campus coursework • Foster interagency development of opportunities to address CSPD priorities • Provide opportunities for ongoing consumer input and review	• Translate recommended practice to service delivery • Provide opportunities for personnel to observe desired practices • Provide ongoing technical support at agency level • Facilitate IHEs support to deliver on-site staff development opportunities • Foster interagency development of opportunities to address CSPD priorities • Provide opportunities for ongoing consumer input and review	• Procure resources to support interagency efforts • Form local instructional teams • Implement individual and agency change plans • Install ongoing local instructional team review and evaluation • Include lead agency personnel	• Operationalize instructional teams in all eight regions • Identify practicum sites identified in all eight regions • Increase opportunities for preservice/inservice instruction • Document improvement in instructional quality • Improve service delivery • Solicit consumer input on personnel preparation decision making • Develop interagency recommendations for CSPD

3. Policy

- Improve certification and credentialing standards
- Install efficacious resource allocation and coordination
- Install systematic consumer input and review on preservice policy issues

- Apply quality assurance standards for delivery and evaluation of staff development experiences
- Install efficacious resource allocation and coordination
- Install systematic consumer review on inservice policy issues

- Tie resource allocation to interagency efforts that link preservice and inservice efforts
- Implement ongoing monitoring of personnel preparation efforts to ensure quality of content, instructional strategies, and linkages to practice changes
- Modify CSPD changes to encourage strategies to link preservice and inservice efforts along the same continuum
- Develop CSPD to reflect detailed, systematic strategies to link preservice and inservice instructional practices

- Revise personnel preparation practices to reflect recommended content and instructional format practices
- Formulate policy at local, regional, and state levels that promotes a continuum of quality personnel preparation opportunities

4. Attitude and climate

- Demonstrate support for importance of high-quality preservice programs across disciplines and personnel levels

- Provide support for importance of widespread availability of ongoing staff development opportunities responsive to local needs and contexts

- Disseminate information about relationship between quality of personnel and quality of services provided to consumers

- Foster general society values, supports, and rewards for personnel providing quality early intervention services right now, how that compares to a family-centered approach, and whether a change is needed" (Bailey, McWilliam, & Winton, 1992, p. 76). Family members might offer their perspectives to increase the likelihood that team decisions are valued by consumers and reflect consumer values. Administrators should actively participate in or explicitly endorse team-based activities.

Several instruments were developed to facilitate implementation of the self-assessment and change processes. Two examples of these self-assessment instruments are Brass Tacks I: Program Policies and Practices (McWilliam & Winton, 1990) and Family Orientation of Community and Agency Services (Bailey, 1990). These instruments contain listings of quality indicators against which team members can evaluate existing and desired practices in an agency or program. Figure 20.1 shows a completed example of one page from Brass Tacks I. Following self-assessment, teams identify areas in which change is desired and rank priorities for change. Once priorities are identified, teams complete plans to help them structure and implement the change process. Figure 20.2 illustrates an example of a plan for change.

Bailey, McWilliam, and Winton (1992) offered guidance about how to promote discussion, reflection, and sharing of perspectives when implementing the team-based process. They suggested that team members be provided with information about recommended practices, rules and regulations that need to be followed, and a structure for group discussion and decision-making activities.

ADAPTING THE TEAM-BASED MODEL IN LOUISIANA

The ChildNet Personnel Preparation Subcommittee decided to select the team-based model for change to guide our efforts to improve early intervention programs (Lobman et al., 1994). We decided to adapt features of the team-based model so that we could involve preservice faculty in the process of improving programs. Little was known about the appropriateness of the original model for addressing recommended practices during preservice instruction or its usefulness in linking or unifying preservice and inservice initiatives.

Based on our recognition of the need to adapt selected features of the original model, we adopted what Darling-Hammond and McLaughlin (1995) labeled as top-down support for a bottom-up reform approach to staff development. School reform literature indicated that the failure of many staff development efforts targeted at change stemmed from their being top-down models that removed teachers, parents, and building-level administrators from the process (Kretovics, Farber, & Armaline, 1991). The efficacy of using locally constituted teams composed of service providers, consumers, and faculty in Part H personnel preparation efforts also had been documented consistently in early intervention preservice programs (Hanson, Hanline, & Petersen, 1987; McCollum & Thorp, 1988; Rowan, Thorp, & McCollum, 1990), in early intervention inservice programs (Eggbeer, Latzko, & Pratt, 1993; Rush, Shelden, & Stanfill, 1995; Trohanis, 1994), in the establishment of early intervention personnel standards (Hanson & Brekken, 1991), and in early intervention policy development (Samuelson, Elder, & Evans, 1990). We selected a strategy of top-down support for bottom-up change on the basis of extant literature that suggested sustainable changes are socially constructed within real-world contexts by individuals most directly affected by the innovations (Maeroff, 1993; Patton, 1987; Ragin, 1994); successful personnel preparation change initiatives require administrative involvement and support (McLaughlin, 1990; Trohanis, 1994; Winton, 1990); and multiple, often competing, stakeholders have vested interests in any change initiative (Greene, 1994; Larner & Phillips, 1994; Moss, 1994).

Area #1: First Encounters with Families (referral and program entry)

Policy or practice	How Often?					Change needed	Priority (Top 5)	Notes
	Never	Seldom	Sometimes	Usually	Always			
1. Do you ask other agencies & professionals to encourage parents themselves to make the referral to your program (i.e., parents make first phone call or write a letter)?	1	2	3	(4)	5	Yes (No)		
2. Do you make your first face-to-face contact with families within 1 week of receiving the referral?	1	2	3	(4)	5	Yes (No)		
3. Do you have someone available to spend time talking to parents at the time of the initial referral as opposed to just taking down phone numbers, addresses, and child information?	1	2	3	4	(5)	Yes (No)		
4. Do you refrain from asking parents to complete forms until after the first face-to-face contact has been made?	(1)	2	3	4	5	(Yes) No	1	All forms completed during initial meeting
5. Are application forms and other information-gathering forms fully explained before parents are asked to complete them (e.g., why you want the info., how it will be used, and who will see it)?	1	(2)	3	4	5	(Yes) No	2	I don't think families really understand why we need information
6. Do you offer parents a choice as to where & when the first face-to-face contact will take place?	1	2	3	(4)	5	Yes (No)		

Figure 20.1. An example of a completed page of Brass Tacks I. (From McWilliam, P.J., & Winton, P.J. [1990]. *Brass Tacks I & II: A self-rating of family-centered service provision in early intervention* [pp. 5–6]. Chapel Hill: University of North Carolina at Chapel Hill, Frank Porter Graham Child Development Center; reprinted by permission.)

Figure 20.1. *continued*

	1	2	3	4	5			
7. If a child is ineligible for your services, do you **actively** assist parents in obtaining other services or resources to meet their needs?	1	2	3	4	⑤	Yes ⦸No		
8. If a child is eligible for your services but your caseload is full, do you assist the parents in obtaining other services or offer temporary, alternative services until a space is available?	1	2	3	④	5	Yes ⦸No		
9. Do you make it clear to parents that they have the right to refuse your services, even if team members think the child needs the services?	1	2	3	4	⑤	Yes ⦸No		
10. Do you ask parents to decide who will be at the initial meeting between program staff and the family?	1	②	3	4	5	⦸Yes No	3	*Only if parents ask*

506

PRACTICE # *First Encounters*
(Refer to Brass Tacks Item Nos. 4 & 5)

OBJECTIVE:
(What do you specifically hope to accomplish?)
Revise and pilot intake sheet so families are not asked for redundant information and they are given options about how they want to share information with staff.

RESOURCES NEEDED FOR ACCOMPLISHMENT:
(Check all that apply and make notes)

	Resource	Notes
X	Administrative support	*Mary will review drafts*
X	Family support or involvement	*Family member will be on workgroup*
X	Team support	*Team will comment on revisions*
	Money	
X	Time	*Workgroup will need time to meet*
X	Additional skills	*Denise will help format drafts of*
X	Additional knowledge or information	*revisions to intake sheet*

ACTIVITIES FOR ACCOMPLISHING OBJECTIVE:

Activity	Person(s) responsible	Date for completion	Team member's evaluation
1. Diane will develop a revised draft for the workgroup to consider.	Diane	7/1/93	1
2a. Diane will send the draft to Denise for formatting.	Diane	7/1/93	1
2b. Denise will format.	Denise	7/15/93	1
3. Draft of revised form will be circulated to team members for review and comments.	Denise Diane	8/1/93	1
4. Workgroup will meet to review revised format and generate a second draft.	Workgroup members	8/31/93	4

Figure 20.2. Example of a completed individual agency change plan (IACP). (1 = activity completely accomplished; 2 = activity mostly accomplished; 3 = activity partially accomplished; 4 = activity not accomplished but still needed; 5 = situation changed, activity no longer needed.)

Adapting Team Composition and Roles

The adapted model was implemented in two communities. We agreed with developers of the original model that the number and roles of participants should not be prescribed or defined narrowly (Winton et al., 1992). We believed, however, that certain groups should be represented on each local team for successful implementation of the model. Individuals representing the following groups served on each of Louisiana's teams: policy makers—representatives of the ChildNet lead agency; families—those who are consumers of early intervention services; program management—those individuals responsible for overseeing and coordinating the early intervention program; program staff—individuals responsible for actual delivery of early intervention services; facilitator—person representing the ChildNet Personnel Preparation Subcommittee who would facilitate group interactions; site liaison coordinator—individual employed by local agency who would assist the team facilitator; and higher education faculty member—person employed by an institution of higher education in proximity to the local agency. We believed adding the higher education faculty member to the team was a key to the establishment of preservice and inservice instructional linkages.

Adapting Tools

In the adapted model primary emphasis was placed on using a slightly modified version of the Brass Tacks I (McWilliam & Winton, 1990). The Brass Tacks I contains 78 items divided into four program component areas: 1) initial interactions, 2) assessments, 3) intervention planning, and 4) service provision. Use of this tool permitted teams in Louisiana to focus on overall program policies and practices, determine their status, and identify needed areas for change. Site-specific staff development activities emerged naturally through use of the Brass Tacks I. We made two modifications to the measure. First, additional items were generated for a new component that we labeled transition practices. Second, we made slight adjustments to the wording of items on the Brass Tacks I to make them apply more appropriately to all team members.

We adapted the change plan developed by McWilliam and Winton (1990) by adding a column that permitted teams to specify criteria for judging the completion of activities. This adapted change plan was labeled the Individual Agency Change Plan (IACP). An example of the adapted change plan shown in Figure 20.2 illustrates how evaluative criteria were used by one team to make judgments about their activities.

As teams reviewed the Brass Tacks I, the need to identify and complete other measures that could guide staff development efforts emerged. For example, when considering the section of the Brass Tacks I concerned with day-to-day service provision, classroom teachers on one team raised issues related to structuring classroom environments for young children. In response to this staff development need, agency personnel completed the Infant/Toddler Environment Rating Scale (ITERS) for each classroom (Harms, Cryer, & Clifford, 1990) as part of their self-assessment process.

Adapting Processes

We predicted that embedding instructional linkages into a broader change initiative to improve program quality would require substantially more time than typically involved in implementing the original model. Full implementation of the adapted model involved significant, sustained investments of time and resources by university and agency personnel. All participants on the teams learned that making changes in practices requires steady, prolonged work.

We followed the general guidance offered by Bailey, McWilliam, and Winton (1992) and Winton et al. (1992) related to promoting discussion, reflection, and sharing of perspectives during implementation of the model. Team members were provided general information about recommended practices in early intervention and ChildNet (Part H) policies and procedures.

Two additional adaptations to model processes were made. First, regional large-scale inservice instruction supplemented ongoing staff development efforts within the local agencies. These instructional events, planned by the local teams, increased general awareness about selected recommended practices. Team members and individuals not directly involved in team-based processes participated in these instructional events. Second, preservice instructional courses were offered on site at the agency or at local universities. The content of these courses and selected assignments were linked, whenever possible, to ongoing team-based processes.

Fiscal Support for Implementation of the Adapted Team-Based Model

There were at least three reasons why we were able to procure lead agency and SICC support for implementation of the adapted team-based model in Louisiana. First, our needs assessment data confirmed the necessity of developing a CSPD that would forge meaningful linkages between preservice and inservice instruction. Second, personnel working in early intervention programs throughout the state were interested in staff development efforts that would help them systematically address program quality issues. These individuals wanted to become involved in ongoing personnel preparation efforts, including development of personnel standards and implementation of the CSPD. Finally, due to the existence of the ChildNet Personnel Preparation Subcommittee, we had an established infrastructure to provide leadership for model implementation efforts.

In early 1992, members of the ChildNet Personnel Preparation Subcommittee recommended that early intervention personnel preparation funds be distributed by the lead agency via an RFP to implement the model. The Human Development Center (HDC), Louisiana's university affiliated program, identified a consortium of service providers, consumers, and representatives of higher education who were interested and willing to be involved in implementing the model. The HDC developed a response to the RFP and, in December of 1992, was awarded $117,000 to implement the model in two of Louisiana's eight early intervention service regions. The majority of project funds was given to the local teams. These funds were used to support project personnel who provided on-site guidance and support, pay for agency personnel release time to attend planning meetings, contract with consumers as paid consultants, and provide release time and travel monies to support higher education faculty participation. A small percentage of the award was used by HDC to furnish facilitators and other project support staff. Beginning in January 1993, two local early intervention teams began to implement the model at their sites.

We wanted to continue activities at the two initial project sites and implement the model in other regions of the state. Due to the statewide focus and inherent nature of any sustained systems change effort, identification of additional, continuing funding sources was mandatory if continuation and expansion of model implementation were to occur. Considerable time and effort was expended by several members of the ChildNet Personnel Preparation Subcommittee toward securing additional implementation funds from the U.S. Department of Education, Office of Special Education and Rehabilitative Services. Relying on data and knowledge gained during the first phase of model planning and implementation, we were able to attract funds that enabled model implementation efforts to continue.

Funds were secured to initiate two complementary initiatives: 1) Common Infancy Core: A Collaborative Statewide Preservice Training Project, and 2) The Collaborative Model for Responsive Inservice and Outreach. During a 3-year period, each project, funded by the U.S. Department of Education, contributed more than $260,000 to efforts to improve the quality of early intervention programs and develop between preservice and inservice efforts linkages in Louisiana. During the final year of the preservice and inservice instructional projects, an additional contract from the Louisiana State Department of Education augmented the funding base by providing another year of funding ($117,000) to support the team-based model initiative.

The total amount of funding devoted to this complex statewide effort to link inservice and preservice instruction totaled almost $770,000 during 4 years. Six of eight regional teams used these funds to engage in the team-based process for 1–2 years. This reflects an average cost of a little more than $100,000 per regional team. Large percentages of these resources were used to encourage and fund comprehensive participation on local teams and to help support team-identified priorities for improving programs.

A CASE STUDY OF MODEL IMPLEMENTATION

In this section, we discuss selected aspects of how the adapted model was applied over 2½ years in one of Louisiana's eight early intervention service regions. We first describe the early intervention site where staff development activities occurred and then site-specific team composition and roles. We describe tools and processes used at this site, and discuss and describe a typical team meeting. Finally, we discuss how linkages between preservice and inservice activities were forged as an outgrowth of the team-based process at this site.

The Arc of Caddo-Bossier

The Arc of Caddo-Bossier (C-BARC) was one of the first sites to implement the adapted team-based model. The program is located in Shreveport and provides services to children and families eligible for early intervention services who reside in the northwest corner of the state (Region VII). The greater Shreveport-Bossier city area is the third largest metropolitan area in Louisiana. The remaining parts of Region VII, outside this metropolitan area, are best characterized as rural or rural-remote.

C-BARC has a long history of providing services to young children and their families. This private, nonprofit organization was founded in 1954 by a small group of parents. C-BARC was recognized as a primary provider of early intervention services in Louisiana, even before the passage of PL 99-457 in 1986.

Several features of the C-BARC program set a context for implementing the adapted model. Service delivery models in the agency had evolved over time. Many personnel working in the agency were involved in the evolutionary process, and customary ways of providing services were well established. Formal and informal program policies and procedures reflected the collective experience and wisdom of agency personnel and structured interactions among these personnel, families, and other service providers in the region. Not unlike other service providers, C-BARC personnel were challenged to examine their typical service delivery approaches to accommodate the family-centered requirements of Part H and the evolving ChildNet system in Louisiana. There also were significant numbers of personnel employed by C-BARC who were concerned about how they would meet emerging certification or licensing requirements while working full time at C-BARC.

Site-Specific Team Composition and Roles

Fifteen individuals served on the site-specific team at C-BARC during the first year of model implementation. Potential team members (e.g., service providers, faculty, family members) were identified as a result of discussions held among C-BARC personnel, members of the ChildNet Personnel Preparation Subcommittee, and grant-funded staff. Team members who were selected agreed to participate in the adapted team-based model project for at least 2 years.

The team facilitator was a member of the ChildNet Personnel Preparation Subcommittee who had primary responsibility for explaining key features of the adapted model and fostering group interactions. This individual also served as a resource to the team by providing information about early intervention recommended practices and ChildNet policies and procedures. The Children's Services Director at C-BARC served as the site liaison. She assisted the team facilitator by developing meeting agendas, disseminating information to other individuals in the agency who were not team members, and providing the team with background information about existing policies and procedures of the agency. The representative from the institution of higher education was a faculty member from the College of Human Ecology at Louisiana Tech University. This person attended team meetings to learn of real-world service delivery challenges and how she could help address identified inservice and preservice instructional needs. Three mothers of children enrolled in the C-BARC program also were members of the team. These consumers brought family perspectives to team deliberations, providing concrete examples of how program policies and procedures affected their lives, and helped revise agency policies and procedures. Family members also participated actively in the planning and delivery of large-scale inservice instructional events and served as instructors in preservice courses. Several direct service providers participated on the team. These individuals provided important information to the team about existing agency practices. Others who served on the team provided administrative endorsement for model processes, state-level policy perspectives, and linkages to other community-based agencies.

The team was expanded during the 2½ years of model implementation. Other agency administrative personnel, representatives from family service coordination agencies, and additional consumers and service providers joined the team.

Examples of Site-Specific Tools

Two primary tools were used at this site during each successive year of model implementation, Brass Tacks I and IACPs. Team members completed the Brass Tacks I independently, then engaged in team discussions about each of the 78 items. The team facilitator used a modified nominal group technique to gain consensus about priorities for change. These priorities were translated into targeted objectives with accompanying implementing activities and recorded on IACPs. A sample page of the Brass Tacks I and an IACP generated by the C-BARC team are shown in Figures 20.1 and 20.2, respectively.

A number of other site-specific tools were developed or adopted during successive years as specific staff development needs were identified. For example, in response to an identified need to build communication and teaming skills across agency personnel, two different tools were employed. Representatives of the site-specific team, with input from a national consultant, developed a screening tool to assess perspectives of agency personnel about the existing roles and relationships of team members. Figure 20.3 shows a completed example of this screening tool. A second tool, the Team Member Screening Scale, part of the Skills Inventory for Teams (Garland, Frank, Buck, & Seklemian, 1992), also was completed by C-BARC team members. This measure is designed to help individuals learn about their own teamwork skills and to assist with the planning of staff development activities that meet individual needs (Garland et al., 1992).

Both of these tools were used to implement a continuum of staff development activities occurring at C-BARC. First, members of the local team completed these measures during a regularly scheduled meeting. They believed the information generated from these tools provided valuable insights about team roles and functions. The experiences of the site-specific team served as a springboard for having all personnel who were affiliated with early intervention services in the agency complete the measures. These data helped team members plan and structure an agencywide workshop devoted to teaming issues. The measures also were completed immediately following, and 3 months after, the occurrence of the workshop. Finally, the faculty member from Louisiana Tech University

---

TEAM SCREENING SCALE

Please answer the following questions before filling out the Team Performance Scale:

1. As you go about your daily work as a Speech Pathologist, who do you believe are the people on your team?

    parents   *social worker*
    speech pathologist   *school psychologist*
    occupational therapist   *teacher*
    physical therapist   *specialized instructor*
    service coordinator   *home interventionists*

2. List 3–5 characteristics that you think are critical if teams are to function effectively:

    communication   *understanding of roles*
    compromise   *positive attitudes and responses*

3. List what you think are 3–5 barriers that prevent teams from functioning effectively in our agency:

    lack of communication
    turf guarding
    defensive attitudes

4. List what you think are 3–5 barriers that prevent teams from functioning effectively in the ChildNet system:

    guidelines and regulations
    paperwork
    lack of communication between agencies and so forth

Figure 20.3. Team screening scale.

incorporated these types of tools into her teaming course, which was taught at the local agency, in order to link preservice course content with ongoing staff development activities.

Site-Specific Processes

Initial site-specific activities concerned building awareness and interest on the part of C-BARC personnel about the team-based model. At this point, a team facilitator from the ChildNet Personnel Preparation Subcommittee was chosen to work with agency personnel to explore interests and explain model site participation. When the decision was made to begin involvement, specific members of the C-BARC team were identified. The site liaison also was identified at this time. The site liaison's initial roles were to assist with arranging places and times for the local team meetings and to promote adoption of team-based processes within the agency.

During the first meetings of the local team, participants were provided with information about the adapted team-based model for change. The team facilitator engaged participants in discussions about the commitments and resources necessary for model implementation. Team members were asked to confirm team composition to ensure that appropriate representation was achieved.

The facilitator introduced team members to the primary tools that would be used for model implementation. Each participant was given copies of the adapted Brass Tacks I and the format for developing IACPs. Written guidelines for completing the Brass Tacks I were reviewed. The facilitator presented alternatives for how these measures could be used to structure the self-assessment process. Team members reached consensus about how they wanted to proceed and chose to complete one component area of the Brass Tacks I at a time, developing IACPs for that section of the measure before proceeding to the next section. A decision was made to devote a portion of each subsequent team meeting to the self-assessment process, using these tools and others, as appropriate.

At the initial meetings, preliminary discussions began on how instructional linkages might be established within the context of overall model implementation. The facilitator challenged team members to think about how traditional instructional approaches might be changed to organize staff development on a continuum, spanning preservice and inservice instruction. For example, team members might participate in the development of preservice instructional modules that were being produced by the faculty member from Louisiana Tech University. C-BARC could serve as a practicum placement site for students from Louisiana Tech. Team members also might be asked to participate in the planning and delivery of large-scale inservice instructional events, which would be carried out with support from state and national consultants. Team members endorsed the importance of linking preservice and inservice instruction to their ongoing local staff development efforts.

For 2½ years, the adapted model was implemented at C-BARC. The local team met each month at C-BARC for at least 2 days. At the end of each month's meeting, an agenda for the next meeting was developed by the team. The site liaison assumed primary responsibility for finalizing the agenda and distributing copies to each member before each meeting. A significant portion of team meeting time was devoted to ongoing self-assessment processes. However, there were also smaller workgroups that, between monthly visits, addressed activities specified on the IACPs. Members of these workgroups were not limited to C-BARC staff and families. For example, representatives from the ChildNet Personnel Preparation Subcommittee and Louisiana Tech participated in workgroup activities. Their participation included activities such as responding by facsimile transmissions to drafts of products being developed for use at C-BARC or providing resources for recommended practices in early intervention. Summaries of workgroup accomplishments were presented to all team members at the monthly meetings. As topics appropriate for large-scale inservice instructional events emerged, portions of the team meetings were devoted to planning these events. Because of the recursive nature of the adapted team-based model, a portion of the monthly meeting time was devoted to reviewing IACPs.

An Example of a Local Team Meeting

The agenda for the meeting of October 19, 1993, is illustrated in Figure 20.4. The agenda shows several interrelated team activities. The team reviewed and completed Section IV of the Brass Tacks I, which concerns day-to-day service provision. Plans for the large-scale inservice instructional event on teaming and communication skills were finalized. Members of the team met in smaller groups to continue work on several IACP objectives. For example, one workgroup met to address an IACP objective related to evaluation of classroom environments. A second group continued work on activities associated with making first contacts with families more family centered. This IACP objective and accompanying activities were generated after a review of the first section of the Brass Tacks I,

---

**C-BARC MODEL SITE PROJECT
SCHEDULE FOR OCTOBER 19, 1993, VISIT**

I. MANAGEMENT TEAM MEETING— 9:00 A.M. until 12:00 P.M.

    A.   Review Section IV of the Brass Tacks.

    B.   Finalize plans for consultant's November visit.

    C.   Discuss the overview of planned activities for Year II.

II. SMALL-GROUP MEETINGS

    A.   Center-based program workgroup (Robert, Sandra, Ann)

        1:00 P.M.– 3:00 P.M.

        1.   Discuss consultation visit summary.

        2.   Develop plan for "next steps" with teacher.

        3.   Discuss Infant/Toddler Environment Rating Scale findings.

    B.   Intake and referral workgroup (Diane, Denise, Shirley, Mary, Sharon)

        1:00 P.M.–2:30 P.M.

        1.   Review revised intake summary form.

        2.   Develop plan for "next steps."

    C.   Home-based program workgroup (Paula, Mary, Shirley)

        2:30 P.M.–4:00 P.M.

        1.   Discuss consultation visit summary.

        2.   Develop plan for "next steps."

    D.   Family service coordination workgroup (Samantha, Terri, Peggy, Robin, Carl)

        1:00 P.M.–3:00 P.M.

        1.   Review "Baby Lanser" forms.

        2.   Discuss how to complete forms.

Figure 20.4.   A sample agenda for a meeting.

entitled "First Encounters with Families." Finally, a third workgroup met to address on-going issues related to the development of a system for family service coordination in Louisiana. This group reviewed state-level policy documents and forms to determine how this system would affect the roles and duties of selected C-BARC personnel and the activities of the local site team.

Establishing Instructional Linkages at C-BARC

Many linkages between preservice and inservice instruction, illustrated in Table 20.3, were established during model implementation. The examples shown in Table 20.3 highlight how linkages were forged at the local site. Site-specific linkages were the unique expression of the instructional parameters listed in Table 20.2. To illustrate how team processes facilitated the development of instructional linkages, a representative series of interrelated

TABLE 20.3.   Examples of instructional linkages from the local site

- Courses were taught on site by faculty member from Louisiana Tech University for C-BARC personnel seeking certification in early intervention.

- Team-based processes helped generate competencies and assignments that were incorporated into preservice coursework required for certification.

- Course instructor got a real-world appreciation for challenges related to implementing family-centered early intervention through participation in team meetings and integrated examples into her courses.

- Input from family members was used in the planning and delivery of preservice and inservice instructional activities.

- Stipend support was provided for participation in preservice and inservice instruction to C-BARC personnel and family members.

- Team members provided substantial input to the development and implementation of statewide certification standards for early intervention.

- C-BARC served as a practicum site for its own employees and other students enrolled in preservice coursework at regional universities.

- Team members planned, implemented, and participated in the evaluation of five large-scale, regional instructional events that were an outgrowth of needs identified in team meetings.

- On-site technical assistance was used as a follow-up strategy after each large-scale workshop to facilitate transfer to the practice setting and to integrate instruction with ongoing team activities.

instructional events associated with the topic of arranging classroom environments for young children is now described.

During a team review of a section of Brass Tacks I related to day-to-day service provision, members identified the need to examine classroom environments in relation to recommended practices. An IACP was developed that specified a series of staff development activities that would be undertaken to address this identified need. The first activity involved having a national consultant observe classrooms at C-BARC before conducting a large-scale regional workshop devoted to classroom environments. After the workshop, the consultant met with team members and classroom teachers to provide verbal feedback and initial recommendations. He subsequently generated a written report of his visit to C-BARC, which contained suggestions for future staff development activities related to this topic. One recommendation was to develop a mechanism for systematically examining classroom environments periodically. As a result of this recommendation, the faculty member from Louisiana Tech University provided instruction on how to use the ITERS (Harms et al., 1990). Students enrolled in her preservice course, many of whom were C-BARC employees, received this instruction. The university faculty member established interrater reliability on the ITERS with the center-based coordinator, a graduate student at Louisiana Tech. Subsequent to these staff development activities, team members reported that many classroom teachers had made significant modifications to their classroom environments. Follow-up ITERS data gathered by the coordinator and university faculty member confirmed these observations.

EVALUATING THE IMPACT OF MODEL IMPLEMENTATION

Conducting evaluation activities to document the impact of implementing the adapted team-based model presented both opportunities and challenges. We had the opportunity to collect standardized impact data from six different implementation sites using an array of evaluation strategies. Table 20.4 shows representative examples of data sources and types of data gathered and analyzed to assess impact at the agency level. Our standardized evaluation model was generic enough to substantiate major impacts, but we faced a challenge in capturing idiosyncratic impacts at each local site. We met this challenge by encouraging local teams to adopt additional evaluation techniques that honored their unique implementation context. For example, a center-based coordinator at one site conducted informal critical incident interviews with her teachers to gather their perspectives about the impact of an on-site consultation on examining classroom environments in relationship to recommended practices.

We also were very interested in determining the impact that model activities had on establishing linkages between preservice and inservice efforts. Outcomes achieved by local teams across the six sites support the conclusion that our strategy of forging instructional linkages within broader initiatives designed to improve Louisiana's Part H service system was productive. Selected impact data that substantiated positive statewide instructional linkages include the following:

- Many of the 93 students recruited and supported in preservice certification courses were working at one of the six sites.
- A total of 1,238 individuals participated in large-scale regional workshops that were planned, implemented, and evaluated by local teams.
- Site data indicated that the provision of on-site technical assistance linked to preservice and inservice instructional content helped service providers translate recommended practices to their unique work settings.
- Most certification courses were taught at agency sites, facilitating access to instruction and opportunities to practice new skills.
- Through ongoing student–instructor interactions, certification course syllabi were revised to incorporate real-world issues and challenges.
- Family members routinely became involved in the planning and conducting of staff development workshops and certification courses.

At the state level, multisite impact data provided members of the ChildNet Personnel Preparation Subcommittee, the SICC, and Louisiana's early intervention lead agency personnel with information from which to recognize and endorse additional opportunities for facilitating instructional linkages. One example of our ability to influence state policy involved the instructional needs of a large number of individuals providing special education services in Louisiana who lacked a baccalaureate degree. A previous recommendation from the ChildNet Personnel Preparation Subcommittee to develop entry-level standards for an associate early interventionist had not been adopted by the lead agency. Service agencies were facing the possibility of being unable to retain long-time employees as personnel standards became mandated, because the early intervention standards required providers to have a minimum of a baccalaureate degree. Impact data obtained during team-based model implementation ultimately convinced state-level decision makers that this large and important cadre of personnel could be incorporated into Louisiana's early intervention system. With endorsement from the SICC, the lead agency asked the ChildNet Personnel Preparation Subcommittee members to organize an ad hoc committee to make recommendations for establishing standards for associate-level personnel.

A second example of how data gathered from local sites had an impact on further linkage initiatives involves another population of special education providers who hold

TABLE 20.4.   Data sources and representative types of data analyzed to assess agency impact at the agency level

Data sources	Representative types of data gathered and analyzed
Agendas from team meetings	What topics were addressed?
	Did team members assume planned roles?
	What percentage of meeting time was devoted to various team processes?
Minutes from team meetings	What topics were addressed?
	Which groups were represented at each team meeting (e.g., family member, provider)?
	Were all agenda items addressed?
	Were there "unplanned" agenda items addressed?
	How many times, on average, did various team members speak during team meetings?
	How many team members offered comments about a particular topic?
Brass Tacks I	Did ratings of program practices improve over time?
	Were priorities for change modified over time?
	Did the number of needed changes decrease over time?
	Did team member ratings become more congruent over time?
Created or revised documents	How many new documents were created?
	How many documents were revised?
	How many people, in which roles, were involved in creating documents?
	To whom were documents disseminated?
	How did family members rate the documents on acceptability and usefulness dimensions?
IACPs	Which Brass Tacks I component areas are reflected?
	What were the average number of activities associated with each objective?
	On average, how long did it take to complete the activities associated with each objective?
	How many activities were satisfactorily achieved?
	What were the primary resources needed to accomplish the objective?
	Which people were identified as being responsible for implementing activities?
	Did team members assume planned roles?
	Were priorities for change modified over time?

baccalaureate degrees but lack certification in any area of education. The typical route taken by these individuals when employed by local education agencies was to secure "T," or temporary, certifications that were renewed annually on completion of at least 6 semester hours of credit toward early intervention certification. Many of our model sites, however, were private, not-for-profit agencies and were ineligible to request "T" certification status for their personnel. These individuals constituted another population whose jobs were in jeopardy as minimal standards for early interventionists (i.e., certification in early intervention) were mandated. In response to impact data, Louisiana's early intervention lead agency, with SICC endorsement, allocated funds to support preservice stipends for these personnel and to compensate faculty from institutions of higher education. These additional funds were used to deliver more courses at additional sites, thus expanding instructional linkages throughout Louisiana.

LESSONS LEARNED FROM MODEL IMPLEMENTATION

The adapted team-based model was implemented in six of the eight regions of Louisiana during a 4-year period and continues to be implemented formally at several local sites. Some teams have continued to operate beyond the original team-based model funding period by leveraging local resources, securing administrative endorsement and support for ongoing model implementation, and expanding the number of individuals and agencies involved in team-based processes. Other teams have been somewhat less successful in sustaining locally directed personnel preparation change initiatives beyond the original funding period. The climate, resources, and people involved help explain the variety of directions taken over time by each local team.

Many important lessons that reflect both intended and unintended outcomes have been learned. Brief discussions of these lessons may prove useful to others facing complex statewide issues associated with early intervention personnel preparation. The following sections give voice to a number of individuals directly involved in implementing the adapted team-based model. Several individuals who had actively participated in model implementation were asked to provide their written personal perspectives (the names used are fictitious).

Lesson 1: Team Members Hold Multiple and Equally Valid Perspectives About Model Implementation

Many tenets of the original team-based model indicated that different individual agendas, values, and priorities would characterize efforts to improve program practices. Although this prediction originally appeared obvious and was taken for granted, actual model implementation brought a renewed appreciation and understanding of the extremely diverse, often competing, perspectives of team members as they give meaning to the same experiences. Perhaps this lesson is best illustrated by reflecting on the experiences described by three team members who worked together for several years at one local site. These perspectives provide important insights into how multiple perspectives influence model processes.

The Consumer's Perspective   Jane has a 2-year-old daughter, Ann, diagnosed with Prader-Willi syndrome, who is enrolled in the agency's center-based services. Jane consistently has been involved in Ann's intervention and care and has a good rapport with the agency staff. Jane was contacted by an agency administrator and agreed to serve as a site team member. She reported feeling honored to be asked, voicing the view that she could help the "professionals see things from a different point of view."

Sharing her perspectives on initial team discussions about agency practices, Jane offered the following comments:

I felt uneasy and unsure of myself at first, but, as time went on, I gained confidence and became quite verbal. During discussions regarding practices and implementation of services, I spoke up from the family point of view. I was able to help the professionals see things more realistically. The professional point of view was from their extensive instruction in a school setting. I, and the other parents on the team, gave a point of view from actual experience and day-to-day living in situations the professionals could not fully understand. When the professionals stated that the families they served did not follow what they suggested and they didn't understand why, I, and the other parents, explained things to them. When you live daily in certain situations you feel, as a parent, you know best how to handle things and why some suggestions will work and some won't. This seemed to help the professionals understand why some of their suggestions were not embraced by the families they served. Everyone began to realize through this experience that it is the family who "drives the bus" so to speak and that the family is the best source of information and implementation of services in the home.

Jane particularly seemed to value opportunities for joint instructional experiences with service providers that emphasized the consumer's perspective. Sharing her perspectives on the linked instructional experiences to address agency goals on the IACP, Jane made these observations:

I really enjoyed the workshop on teaming and family–professional collaboration. I got a chance to role-play during a case study scenario at the workshop. Everyone was given a scenario to read and actively take a role as a service team member, other than the position they currently held. Individual group discussion was encouraged, and then an open discussion was held. Everyone was very surprised when they realized they did not know about a given situation. Everyone realized that they could not assume outcomes and resolutions without consulting with the other team members who were serving the family. I felt that the most important aspect realized is that the service team needed to include the parents and/or family in any discussions and all decisions to be made. I was very happy about this realization. I also felt that role playing was a great way to understand the full scope of serving families and earning mutual respect for all. I feel that so much was learned and gained through these opportunities by all who participated. I wondered if this type of instruction would be implemented on an ongoing basis. It sure would be a lot easier on everyone if this type of inservice instruction would continue and be available to all across the United States. Seeing and understanding situations and families realistically would definitely be a plus in properly serving their clients to the fullest potential.

The Administrator's Perspective Marie has spent many years working in early intervention programs. She has extensive experience in direct services provision as a teacher and has served as the agency administrator directly responsible for infant, toddler, and family services for several years. Marie has these perspectives to share on initial model implementation at her agency:

Upon our invitation to be a facility to be instructed in model site processes, and being a believer in the inherent value of quality inservice and preservice instruction, I jumped at the chance for our local program to be the recipient of instruction provided by nationally known leaders in the field of early intervention by our participation in this grant. My initial goal was very simple: to make an already

> well-respected program that much better. "How hard could that be?" I thought. "Yes, there's always room for growth, so they'll just take what we've got and build on it!" Needless to say, it was not that simple.

Marie further reflected on ongoing team processes, placing much emphasis on the team facilitator and other project staff valuing local problem identification and solving while encouraging team consensus building and decision making.

> Much time was initially spent by the grant staff conveying a positive attitude about what our program and its individual players were doing. Thus, the team members employed by the agency felt good about the prospect of working with project staff because they were already being treated as competent in their own right. The grant staff must have had to "bite their tongues" in order to avoid "jumping in" to address glaring areas of concern. For example, our developmental assessment clinic, which is well regarded across the state for its exemplary practices, did not include the parent as part of the poststaffing follow-up to clinic. This was observed immediately by project staff but not acknowledged until we stated that we needed to take a look at it, after examining our policy. The team-based model for change process is unique; it is not just filling out a needs assessment survey and developing instructional priorities. Using the Brass Tacks to develop our priorities for instruction was a key factor in the eventual success of each instructional activity. It was different from any other process in which we had participated. Allowing the local management team to jointly plan, develop, and implement instructional events helped team members "buy in" to the change process.

Marie also reported a lesson learned related to multiple perspectives and their importance to understanding team processes. She had this to say about her view of multiple perspectives gained as a result of model participation:

> One fact became very clear . . . different people from different positions have different perceptions of the self-study process. From the administrator's side, I did not in any way feel "threatened" or concerned about potential recommendations made as a result of my participation. However, several direct service providers experienced apprehension, discomfort, and even anger during their involvement. In one particular case, differing perceptions became evident during the technical assistance portion of a visit by an outside consultant. I became very much aware of the fact that although WE had targeted this subject matter as an area of interest and concern, WE were at varying degrees of acceptance when it came to making some of the changes that were the eventual outcomes of instruction. As the administrator of the program, and although I feel very positive about the experience shared, I was left to do the "repair work" at the local level while the grant staff and outside consultants had all gone home. It was as if someone had opened Pandora's box.

Marie obviously valued the link between service providers and institutions of higher education. She shared these perspectives about the benefits of such linkages:

> The higher education component of the model site project was viewed as an extremely positive resource. As the administrator of the program, I have always encouraged continuing education and professional growth for staff. In a way, the level of commitment to the change process required so much of our staff that I felt I wanted to be able to give them something in return. The agency prepaid tuition or facilitated tuition exemption stipends [for preservice courses], offered academic coursework on site, provided the site for specific course experiences, and allowed release time for on-site Child Development Associate instruction. In

addition, a pay increase upon certification completion was offered as an incentive to participants.

The Faculty Member's Perspective   Sue has 20 years of experience as a faculty member at several institutions of higher education in Louisiana. She has spent many years providing preservice education for early intervention personnel, ranging from the associate-degree level through graduate-level instruction. She also has been conducting staff development experiences for many of Louisiana's early intervention service providers.

Sue had believed that many obstacles to the implementation of effective services since the passage of the early intervention legislation in 1986 could have been averted by focusing on the personnel needs. After all, the critical relationship between the quality of early intervention services and the competence of the service providers was hardly a novel concept. Sue made the following observations:

Did we place the cart before the horse? Couldn't we have educated a sufficient number of well-prepared professionals before expecting them to offer family-centered services to infants and toddlers with disabilities and their families? Couldn't higher education instantly initiate needed coursework and new specialization programs in a variety of disciplines to large numbers of preservice students? Couldn't the essential skills needed to focus on the family unit and the ecology of the family rather than exclusively on the child be present first in all relevant curricula? Couldn't large-scale continuing education programs be mounted instantaneously to meet the new instructional needs of practitioners? Weren't we rushing headlong toward our goal of establishing a quality early intervention service system without having taken the requisite preliminary steps?

When asked to share how her team participation had changed her perspectives about personnel preparation issues, Sue had these observations:

If we had been afforded the time sufficient to design and implement preservice and inservice instructional programs in isolation from the contextual reality of the life experiences and needs of families and service providers, the resulting instruction would have been far less effective. If we had proceeded in isolation, we might never have involved all relevant people in ongoing face-to-face interactions, which set the occasion for sharing perspectives and engaging in thoughtful, collaborative exchanges. If we had not involved families on the teams who were actual recipients of services, "professional" parents who believed they possessed the perspectives needed to represent *all* families might have been the only voices heard by service providers and instructors.

Lesson 2: Different Stages of Trust Have Unique Influences on Team Processes and Outcomes

The collaborative team processes necessary to implement the model were dependent on individuals' openly communicating their values, beliefs, preferences, and priorities while inviting, valuing, and considering the perspectives of others. The time needed to establish a climate conducive to developing trust varied according to the dynamics operating within each group and service agency. As a result of different and often competing interests, group processes occasionally resulted in honest differences of opinion among team members. As different perspectives were validated by team members, individuals grew less apprehensive about their ability to make group contributions. The team's ability to discuss sensitive issues in creative, productive, and supportive ways improved over time. For example, team facilitators initially and predictably were treated as outsiders and were hesitant to raise or comment on sensitive agency issues. In situations where team facilitators consistently clarified the values expressed by team members without making value judgments, they came to be viewed as insiders and were trusted with more sensitive information.

Lesson 3: Diversity, Not Uniformity, Characterizes Model Implementation Across Sites

Model components were expressed in extremely diverse ways across different sites. For example, some sites identified specific individuals who served on the team throughout model implementation. Other sites were more flexible, allowing individuals to serve on the team for specific discussions and then replacing them with other individuals as topics changed. A third approach was to supplement team impressions of existing agency practices with data obtained from surveys mailed to constituents throughout the whole region.

The relationship between completion of the Brass Tacks I and the development of IACPs also reflected variability. Some sites elected to complete the entire Brass Tacks before developing an IACP and identifying training possibilities. These teams believed that it was best to get a total view of program practices before attempting to prioritize targets for change. Other teams decided to stop at the end of each section of the Brass Tacks and develop an IACP based on priorities for that particular program component area. For example, one team decided that consumers were not prepared for or encouraged to participate fully in the initial agency assessment process designed to determine service eligibility. Several strategies were identified on the IACP, including modification of assessment forms to make them more family friendly, production of a videotape for families to view before actually scheduling the assessment activity, work with consumers to develop content for inservice staff instruction on how to use the materials, and collaboration with the institution of higher education team representative to incorporate information about the materials into appropriate certification coursework.

Lesson 4: Our Adapted Team-Based Model for Change Appears to Be a Two-Phase Process

We realized that implementing our adapted team-based model for change would be an inherently difficult undertaking. Due partly to the established nature of early intervention service practices and preferences at the local sites, it was necessary to devote much time to the preliminary activities of acquainting all team members with the roles, tools, and processes associated with the adapted team-based model. This sustained introductory period also involved establishing a climate favorable to change, allowing team members to learn more about each other and the agency in general, discussing how team members' perspectives of existing agency practices differed, determining what resources were required to support potential options for program change, identifying additional staff development needs and strategies, modeling team-based processes, and deciding if the required level of team consensus had emerged to develop an IACP. Over time, the site teams eventually decided what needed changing and how to implement the change process. This decision appeared to signal a second phase of model activities associated with developing, implementing, and monitoring a detailed set of change initiatives specified on the IACP. Generic processes and activities associated with each of these two phases are illustrated in Figure 20.5. Those teams that implemented Phase II activities were able to sustain activities associated with the team-based model after grant funding had ended.

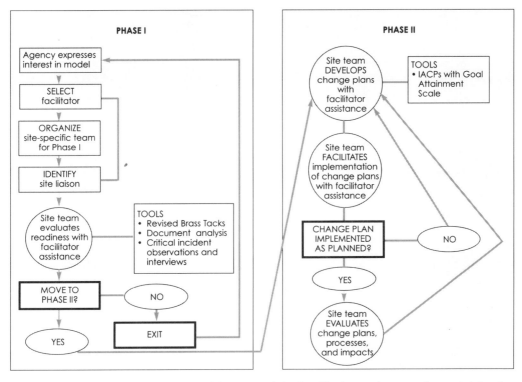

Figure 20.5. Processes and activities associated with two phases of model implementation.

However, teams that engaged only in Phase I activities still realized positive outcomes from model implementation.

Lesson 5: Linking Institutions of Higher Education with Early Intervention Service Providers Improves and Benefits Both Systems

Model processes that facilitated ongoing interactions between institutions of higher education and early intervention service agencies were extremely productive for both systems. Agency personnel benefited by gaining easier access to credit courses leading to early intervention certification. At one site, for example, a cohort of service providers was able to complete a sequence of required courses taught at their agency site by the team's higher education representative. Otherwise, these individuals would have had to drive more than 100 miles round-trip to take on-campus credit courses.

Individual faculty members were able to hear and see firsthand some of the issues facing personnel in the delivery of quality early intervention services. Such experiences benefited faculty in improving their ability to select course content and experiences that would be more easily linked to applied settings. Consider, for example, these perspectives of a team representative from an institution of higher education.

Higher education faculty may have remained in their ivory towers, gleaning information from theory and research and translating knowledge for practitioners without an authentic appreciation for the perspectives of families from diverse walks of life. I learned to appreciate the ongoing challenges we all face in translating recommended practices to the level where children and families receive

services. Offering preservice course content in isolation from real-world experiences does not promote transfer beyond university classroom walls.

CONCLUSION

We have shared the perspectives of numerous individuals, positioned at many different levels, during one state's efforts to improve early intervention services through a large change initiative. This endeavor to bridge the traditional dichotomy between preservice and inservice instruction was initiated at six local sites using teams composed of those individuals most directly affected (e.g., service providers, agency administrators, service consumers, faculty from higher education). Impact data appear to support our initial belief that the adapted team-based model for change would set a context for making program improvements and establishing instructional linkages. However, these data alone do not answer a question we frequently are asked: "Were model implementation impacts worth the time and effort expended?" Our response is a qualified "yes." Because the team-based model was not compared directly with other models, we cannot offer conclusive support for the superiority of this model over others. However, as we view the many human and non-human linkages that endure throughout our state as a result of model implementation, we continue to assert that the adapted team-based model for change is one viable alternative to traditional personnel preparation approaches.

RESOURCES

Bailey, D.B., McWilliam, P.J., & Winton, P.J. (1992). Building family-centered practices in early intervention: A team-based model for change. *Infants and Young Children, 5*(1), 73–82.

   Describes five central components of this model of instruction: team-based instruction, family participation, a decision-oriented format, guided decision-making and goal-setting activities, and effective leadership, with discussion of the methods and materials that can assist with each component.

Bailey, D.B., McWilliam, P.J., Winton, P.J., & Simeonsson, R.J. (1992). *Implementing family-centered services in early intervention: A team-based model for change.* Cambridge, MA: Brookline Books. Cost: $19.95. (800) 666-2665.

   Monograph describes a team-based decision-making workshop for implementing family-centered services in early intervention. Developed to provide the structure for a 4-day workshop in which teams (e.g., of paraprofessionals, professionals, family members, administrators) progress from identification of the elements of a family-centered approach to identifying, establishing, and tracking their plans for ensuring that positive change occurs. Goals, handouts, and transparencies are provided.

Winton, P.J., McWilliam, P.J., Harrison, T., Owens, A.M., & Bailey, D.B. (1992). Lessons learned from implementing a team-based model for change. *Infants and Young Children, 5*(1), 49–57.

   Case example of one program's experience with a team-based model for building and sustaining family-centered practices.

REFERENCES

Bailey, D.B. (1990). *Family orientation of community and agency services.* Chapel Hill: University of North Carolina at Chapel Hill, Carolina Institute for Research on Infant Personnel Preparation, Frank Porter Graham Child Development Center.

Bailey, D.B., McWilliam, P.J., & Winton, P.J. (1992). Building family-centered practices in early intervention: A team-based model for change. *Infants and Young Children, 5*(1), 73–82.

Bailey, D.B., McWilliam, P.J., Winton, P.J., & Simeonsson, R.J. (1992). *Implementing family-centered services in early intervention: A team-based model for change.* Cambridge, MA: Brookline Books.

Bailey, D.B., Palsha, S.A., & Simeonsson, R.J. (1991). Professional skills, concerns, and perceived importance of work with families in early intervention. *Exceptional Children, 58,* 156–165.

Bailey, D.B., Jr. (1989). Issues and directions in preparing professionals to work with young handicapped children and their families. In J.J. Gallagher, P.L. Trohanis, & R.M. Clifford (Eds.), *Policy implementation and PL 99-457: Planning for young children with special needs* (pp. 99–132). Baltimore: Paul H. Brookes Publishing Co.

Darling-Hammond, L., & McLaughlin, M.W. (1995). Policies that support professional development in an era of reform. *Phi Delta Kappan, 76,* 597–604.

Education of the Handicapped Act Amendments of 1986, PL 99-457, 20 U.S.C. § 1400 *et seq.*

Eggbeer, L., Latzko, T., & Pratt, B. (1993). Establishing statewide systems of inservice training for infant and family personnel. *Infants and Young Children, 5*(3), 49–56.

Fountain, C.A., & Evans, D.B. (1994). Beyond shared rhetoric: A collaborative change model for integrating preservice and inservice urban educational delivery systems. *Journal of Teacher Education, 45,* 218–227.

Garland, C., Frank, A., Buck, D., & Seklemian, P. (1992). *Skills inventory for teams.* Lightfoot, VA: Child Development Resources.

Greene, J.C. (1994). Qualitative program evaluation: Practice and promise. In N.K. Denzin & Y.S. Lincoln (Eds.), *Handbook of qualitative research* (pp. 530–544). Beverly Hills: Sage Publications.

Hanson, J.J., & Brekken, L.J. (1991). Early intervention personnel model and standards: An interdisciplinary field-developed approach. *Infants and Young Children, 4*(1), 54–61.

Hanson, J.J., Hanline, M.F., & Petersen, S. (1987). Addressing state and local needs: A model for interdisciplinary preservice training in early childhood special education. *Topics in Early Childhood Special Education, 7*(3), 36–47.

Harms, T., Cryer, D., & Clifford, D. (1990). *Infant/Toddler Environment Rating Scale.* New York: Teachers College Press.

Kretovics, J., Farber, K., & Armaline, W. (1991). Reform from the bottom up: Empowering teachers to transform schools. *Phi Delta Kappan, 73,* 295–299.

Larner, M., & Phillips, D. (1994). Defining and valuing quality as a parent. In P. Moss & A. Pence (Eds.), *Valuing quality in early childhood services* (pp. 43–60). New York: Teachers College Press.

Lobman, M., Stricklin, S., Constans, T., Barney, S., Billeaud, F., Kimbrough, P., Sexton, D., Francis, D., & Garner, B. (1994, June). *Community site development: A team-based model for change.* Paper presented at the Ninth Annual Gulf Coast Conference on Early Intervention, Point Clear, AL.

Maeroff, G.I. (1993). *Team building for school change: Equipping teachers for new roles.* New York: Teachers College Press.

McCollum, J.A., & Bailey, D.B. (1991). Developing comprehensive personnel systems: Issues and alternatives. *Journal of Early Intervention, 17,* 414–430.

McCollum, J.A., & Thorp, E.K. (1988). Training of infant specialists: A look to the future. *Infants and Young Children, 1*(2), 55–65.

McCollum, J.A., & Yates, T.J. (1994). Technical assistance for meeting early intervention personnel standards: Statewide processes based on peer review. *Topics in Early Childhood Special Education, 14*(3), 295–310.

McLaughlin, M.W. (1990). The Rand Change Agent Study revisited: Macro perspectives and micro realities. *Educational Researcher, 19*(9), 11–16.

McWilliam, P.J., & Winton, P.J. (1990). *Brass Tacks I & II: A self-rating of family-centered service provision in early intervention.* Chapel Hill: University of North Carolina at Chapel Hill, Frank Porter Graham Child Development Center.

Miller, P.S. (1992). State interagency coordination for personnel development under Public Law 99-457: Building teams for effective planning. *Journal of Early Intervention, 16,* 146–154.

Moss, P. (1994). Defining quality: Values and stakeholders. In P. Moss & A. Pence (Eds.), *Valuing quality in early childhood services* (pp. 1–9). New York: Teachers College Press.

Palsha, S.A., Bailey, D.B., Vandiviere, P., & Munn, D. (1990). A study of employee stability and turnover in home-based early intervention. *Journal of Early Intervention, 14,* 342–351.

Patton, M.Q. (1987). *How to use qualitative methods in evaluation.* Beverly Hills: Sage Publications.

Ragin, C.C. (1994). *Constructing social research: The unity and diversity of method.* Thousand Oaks, CA: Pine Forge.

Rowan, L.E., Thorp, E.K., & McCollum, J.A. (1990). An interdisciplinary practicum to foster infant–family and teaming competencies in speech-language pathologists. *Infants and Young Children, 3*(2), 58–66.

Rush, D.D., Shelden, M., & Stanfill, L. (1995). Facing the challenges: Implementing a statewide system of inservice training in early intervention. *Infants and Young Children, 7*(4), 55–61.

Samuelson, D., Elder, M., & Evans, J. (1990). A conceptual framework for state policy development. *Infants and Young Children, 2*(3), 79–86.

Sexton, D., & Snyder, P. (1991). *Louisiana personnel preparation consortium project for Part H.* New Orleans, LA: University of New Orleans.

Sexton, D., Snyder, P., Wolfe, B., Lobman, M., Stricklin, S., & Akers, P. (1996). Early intervention inservice training strategies: Perceptions and suggestions from the field. *Exceptional Children, 62,* 485–495.

Trohanis, P.L. (1994). Planning for successful inservice education for local education childhood programs. *Topics in Early Childhood Special Education, 3,* 311–332.

Winton, P.J. (1990). A systemic approach for planning inservice training related to Public Law 99-457. *Infants and Young Children, 3*(1), 51–60.

Winton, P.J., McWilliam, P.J., Harrison, T., Owens, A.M., & Bailey, D.B. (1992). Lessons learned from implementing a team-based model for change. *Infants and Young Children, 5*(1), 49–57.

21 PUTTING IT ALL TOGETHER

The Nuts and Bolts of Personnel Preparation

Camille Catlett
Pamela J. Winton

Each time learners and instructors or trainers interact, there is a precious opportunity to exchange ideas in a manner that will lead to positive and desired learning outcomes for both parties. The first 20 chapters of this book discuss the many decisions to be made about how to structure these learning opportunities from a variety of perspectives, ranging from broad systemic perspectives (Chapters 1–4) to specific models. The challenge for those responsible for planning and facilitating learning is how to select from among the possibilities to create sequences with the greatest possibility of creating desired changes.

This chapter addresses the challenges of "putting it all together" by focusing on three topics: 1) how to make good decisions about specific instructional approaches (i.e., methods and materials), 2) how to plan for the inevitable challenges that confound learning opportunities, and 3) how to use two checklists to assist with designing instructional sequences.

MAKING DECISIONS ABOUT INSTRUCTIONAL APPROACHES

Within the broader framework of content and process discussed in Chapter 5, effective instruction occurs when effective presenters use effective approaches that achieve desired learning and facilitate desired changes in practice. Wolfe's research (1992) summarized the characteristics of effective presenters as individuals who are well prepared, knowledgeable, and enthusiastic; who provide opportunities for hands-on experience; and who use a variety of techniques. From her work, we also know that effective presentations are those that are enjoyable as they provide a chance to grow, meet learner needs, and present practical content.

One area that must be considered in making decisions about what is taught is the diversity of learners. Learner diversity can be conceptualized in terms of cultural diversity (see Chapter 9), participant diversity (i.e., family members, providers representing multiple disciplines, administrators; see Chapters 5 and 20), and learner style diversity (Brookfield, 1990a; Kolb, 1985; Mezirow, 1991; Wolfe, 1993). The challenge for instructors is to use methods and materials that engage and support learning by individuals with different levels of knowledge in a manner that enables all learners to contribute and learn from each other.

Brookfield (1986) said that "the principle of diversity should be engraved on every teacher's heart" (p. 69). One of the best predictors of the merit of an instructional approach is diversity. Are a range of approaches being used to present content that diverse learners can relate to? Are multiple input channels being tapped (i.e., visual, auditory, oral, written)? Are opportunities for independent and group learning being alternated? Are lectures interspersed with more interactive techniques, such as role plays and simulations? Is time allowed for reflection and absorption of material? Prioritizing diversity of approaches to instruction serves two important purposes. First, it increases the likelihood that the content will be conveyed in the preferred learning style of most learners at some point in the instruction. Second, it introduces participants to learning modes and orientations that are new to them. Exposing learners to a variety of instructional techniques increases the likelihood that they will be successful in a variety of future learning experiences (Brookfield, 1990a). Brookfield referred to this second benefit as assisting learners to learn-how-to-learn, which is further defined by Smith (1982) as "possessing or acquiring the knowledge and skill to learn effectively in whatever learning situation one encounters" (p. 204).

In Chapter 5, McCollum and Catlett raise another important consideration in instructional design: how to match instructional approaches to desired learning outcomes expressed in terms of complexity of application, thus illustrating that instructors can select different methods and materials to achieve different levels of learning impact (e.g., awareness, knowledge, skill, attitudes/values). Table 21.1 shows how the concept of matching methods and materials with desired levels of impact applies at a more practical level and presents a description of approaches appropriate at each level of desired impact, along with examples from this book and resources for additional reading or information. Figure 21.1 and Table 21.1 in combination illustrate the importance of paying careful attention to selecting and sequencing instructional approaches; linking didactic forms to practical, field, or follow-up experiences; and balancing passive experiences with those that require more active participant involvement (Hanson & Brekken, 1991; Klein & Campbell, 1990).

At this point, it seems fitting to say a few words about lecture. Lecture has been described as the "most frequently abused" method of teaching (Brookfield, 1990a, p. 71). For many instructors it is the most familiar, and often most comfortable, vehicle for

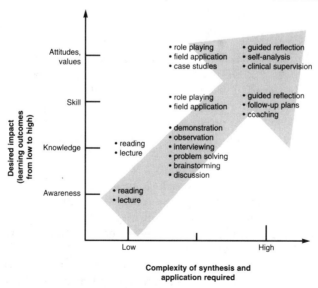

Figure 21.1. A model for matching training approach to desired training outcomes and complexity of application. (Adapted from Harris [1980].)

TABLE 21.1. Options for matching instructional approaches to desired learning outcomes

	Description	Examples in this book	Resources
Awareness-level approaches			
Environmental scan	Learners collect data (e.g., articles, pictures, personal comments, accounts) about trends and events that may affect a program, organization, or process to get a sense of the "big picture." A strategy for understanding the context for policy development.	Chapter 16, pp. 415–419	Bergman, 1995
Games	Learners play games that are constructed to address learning objectives. Can be used as icebreakers, for a change of pace, to illustrate material, for a fun way to review information, to liven up a session, or to add an element of friendly competition.	Chapter 10, p. 261 Chapter 14, p. 371 Chapter 15, p. 404 Chapter 16, pp. 416, 421	Eitington, 1989; Saunders & Hawkins, 1986
Guest presenters / panel presentations	One or more subject matter experts participate to present their viewpoints, answer questions, or discuss issues.	Chapter 10, p. 261 Chapter 11, p. 286 Chapter 12, pp. 314, 320, 323 Chapter 16, pp. 416, 421, 427–428	Meyers & Jones, 1993; Saunders & Hawkins, 1986
Lecture / lecturette	A formal discourse in which a subject matter expert develops and delivers a presentation that conveys information related to the learning objectives. Lectures can be combined with other methods to avoid learner inactivity.	Chapter 14, p. 371	Brookfield, 1990a, b; Eitington, 1989; Meyers & Jones, 1993
Models	A diagram or graphic representation gives learners a way of looking at a lot of information (i.e., the big picture) at one time. In training, models can provide a framework against which learners can test the validity of their attitudes, values, assumptions, and behaviors.	Chapter 14, Activity 3 Chapter 15, pp. 399–400	Eitington, 1989

(continued)

TABLE 21.1. (continued)

	Description	Examples in this book	Resources
Awareness-level approaches continued			
Readings	Written material to provide learners with additional information or insights. Can include articles, books or stories written by consumers, children's books, and so forth.	Chapter 9, Activity 1.2 Chapter 10, pp. 258–260 Chapter 12, pp. 318, 323, 389 Chapter 16, Tables 16.2, 16.4, 16.5	Meyers & Jones, 1993
Videotapes	Provide opportunities for participants to see actions or messages within a context. Most effective when followed by discussion, role play, or other activity to draw out and develop key concepts. Can be especially useful with audiences with limited literacy skills.	Chapter 10, pp. 261, 264, 268–269 Chapter 12, pp. 313–314, 328–329 Chapter 15, pp. 399, 402 Chapter 16, p. 424	Eitington, 1989
Knowledge-level approaches			
Brainstorming/ brainwriting	Individuals or groups generate ideas on a given theme or problem. Often uses the principles of deferring judgment, quantify breeds quality, the wilder the idea the better, and combine and improve ideas. Variation: Backward brainstorming presents a problem situation and a solution, and learners generate ideas of how the problems were solved.	Chapter 12, p. 325 Chapter 14, Activity 1, 3	Eitington, 1989
Debates	Individuals or groups choose, or are assigned, positions relative to a controversial topic. Given time to prepare, they present arguments and debate positions. Variation: At a certain point in the debate, each side is asked to reverse positions and resume the debate.	Chapter 11, p. 287 Chapter 13, Activity 2 Chapter 16, p. 416	Eitington, 1989

Method	Description	Chapter reference	Citation
Demonstrations	Learners are shown and told how something works or how to do something. Usually followed by giving the learners the opportunity to try or practice the skill with coaching and feedback.	Chapter 8 provides information on effective coaching and feedback practices, pp. 201–209	Sullivan, Wircenski, Arnold, & Sarkees, 1990
Group exercises/discussions	Small groups of learners assemble to cooperatively complete a task or process or to discuss a given topic. Groups then reconvene in the larger group to report, compare results, and articulate what has been learned from the exercise.	Chapter 9, Activity 1.2, 1.3, 2.1, 2.2, 2.3, 3.1; Chapter 12, pp. 314–315, 328; Chapter 13, Activity 3, 5, 9; Chapter 14, Activity 6, 7; Chapter 15, pp. 403–404	Brookfield, 1990a; Meyers & Jones, 1993; Saunders & Hawkins, 1986
Individual exercises/independent study	Learners spend time individually to complete a task, develop plans, develop a position, brainstorm, or reflect on the information and their response. Often followed up with small- or large-group discussion or other activity.	Chapter 11, pp. 281, 286–287; Chapter 14, Activity 8	Brookfield, 1986
Lecture/readings	See Awareness-level approaches above.		
Problem solving	A problem is identified, and an appropriate structured problem-solving method is introduced. Individuals or groups are given the opportunity to solve the problem.	Chapter 10, pp. 267, 269–271; Chapter 11, Activity 3; Chapter 14, Activity 2	Eitington, 1989
Process mapping/process studies/flowcharts	To clarify, understand, or improve procedures or protocol, the sequence of operations and key elements, images, or decisions is mapped out and reviewed or analyzed.	Chapter 9, Activity 1.1, 3.3; Chapter 10, pp. 261–263; Chapter 11, Activity 2	Deshler, 1990
Projects	Learners are given projects to complete that require understanding and application of the principles, skills, knowledge, or attitudes related to the topic. Projects can be presented for in-session use or for homework.	Chapter 14, Activity 4; Chapter 16, pp. 416, 424	Meyers & Jones, 1993

(continued)

TABLE 21.1. *(continued)*

	Description	Examples in this book	Resources
Knowledge-level approaches *continued*			
Simulations	An environment is created that models a real or anticipated situation. Combine this method with others listed in this section for introducing or practicing new material or troubleshooting around situations.	Chapter 11, p. 286 Chapter 12, pp. 318–319 Chapter 16, p. 427	Brookfield, 1990a; Meyers & Jones, 1993
Storytelling/personal incidents and perspectives	Learners share concrete experiences related to the instructional topic. Stories help provide a personal connection to the material and help learners clarify their interest, values, opinions, and stake in the topic. Listeners have the opportunity to reflect on diverse experiences.	Chapter 10, p. 260 Chapter 14, Activity 5 Chapter 16, pp. 421, 425, 427	Brookfield, 1990b
Task analysis	Individuals, small groups, or large groups break down the sequential process of a technique or procedure to understand the subtleties and interrelatedness of all the components.	Chapter 13, Activity 4, 11	Saunders & Hawkins, 1986
Write to learn/ guided reflection	Writers are given a provocative theme/question/problem/task and asked to write their thoughts before the group deals with the topic verbally. This technique helps learners get in touch with current knowledge and advance their learning more confidently.	Chapter 11, Activity 4 Chapter 13, Activity 1, 3 Chapter 16, p. 428	Hile, 1992
Skill-level approaches			
Coaching	Structured relationships for receiving support and encouragement through opportunities to review experiences, discuss feelings, describe frustrations, and check perceptions with a partner. Often a pairing of an experienced individual with a less-experienced individual.	Chapter 7, pp. 179–182 Chapter 8, pp. 201–209 Both chapters provide information on effective coaching practices	Chapters 7 and 8; Saunders & Hawkins, 1986

Field-based experiences / field applications / practica	Learners leave the structured environment of a classroom for a real-world opportunity to observe, try new things, search for information, interview people, and so forth. Specialized applications include family practica, interdisciplinary practica, and policy development practica.	Chapter 11, Appendix B Chapter 15, p. 399 Chapter 16, p. 427 Chapter 17, pp. 447–448 Chapter 18	Chapters 17 and 18; Fenichel, 1992
Follow-up plans	Specific participant-designed strategies for applying what they learned as a result of attending an educational program. Plans include a mechanism for monitoring progress in implementing plans.	Chapter 7	Chapter 7; Wolfe, 1992
Journal writing / diaries / self-reflection	Individuals write entries in a personal journal or diary as a supplement to readings and lecture. Can help participants acquire insight about their behavior, motivations, values, attitudes, and feelings. Can provide insight for instructors into impact and effectiveness of instruction.	Chapter 8, p. 208	Brookfield, 1990a, b; Lukinsky, 1990
Role playing	Situations that typify real-world experiences are presented by learners acting out assigned roles. Variations: Watch a story (videotape) that dramatizes a situation and reenact the interaction differently; carry out multiple role plays with smaller groups going on at the same time; ask players to reverse roles; let more than one learner play any given character; or use scripted role play (see below)	Chapter 11, pp. 286–287, 299 Chapter 12, Activity 1, 2 Chapter 16, p. 425	Brookfield, 1990a; Eitington, 1989
Scripted role playing	The "story" is reenacted by participants who assume the roles of characters in a situation and read from previously developed scripts. The entire group then discusses, analyzes, and problem-solves the situation that was presented. Variations: Small groups develop and present scripted role plays in the session; scripts might include the revelation of characters' thoughts as well as dialogue.	Chapter 11, Activity 1	Eitington, 1989

(continued)

TABLE 21.1. (continued)

	Description	Examples in this book	Resources
Skill-level approaches *continued*			
Self-assessment/self-analysis	Structured instruments (e.g., checklist, questions, rating scale) can be used to facilitate self-examination of attitudes/practices, followed by identification of needed/desired changes. Readministration can be used to measure progress in making targeted changes.	Chapter 10, p. 266 Chapter 11, p. 286 Chapter 12, pp. 315, 317–318 Chapter 15, p. 400	Mezirow, 1991; Saunders & Hawkins, 1986
Write to learn/guided reflection	See Knowledge-level approaches on pages 530–532.		
Attitude/value-level approaches			
Case method of instruction	Real-life situations are presented from which a group analyzes issues, applies knowledge, makes decisions, solves problems, and empathizes with the experiences of others. Also known as case studies or situation studies. Can be presented on audiotape, videotape, in writing, or live.	Chapter 10, pp. 266–267, 271 Chapter 11, p. 287 Chapter 13, Activity 7	Eitington, 1989; McWilliam, 1992; McWilliam & Bailey, 1993
Clinical supervision	The process of an experienced individual or individuals directing or guiding less-experienced individuals to accomplish clinical practice-related goals. Involves defining job requirements, counseling for improved performance, providing instruction, evaluating work, and providing feedback.	Chapter 8 provides information on effective supervision, pp. 192–196	Chapter 8; Fenichel, 1992
Field-based experiences/field applications/practica	See Skill-level approaches above		
Write to learn/guided reflection	See Skill-level approaches on pages 532–533		
Role playing	See Skill-level approaches on pages 532–533		
Scripted role playing	See Skill-level approaches on pages 532–533		
Self-assessment/self-analysis	See Skill-level approaches on pages 532–533		

Based on Edelman, L. (1995). *Learning styles, training activities, problem solving activities, and the role of training and learning.* Workshop presented at the NEC*TAS Conference on Adult Learning and Evaluation of Training and Technical Assistance, San Deigo, CA.

conveying content. But with retention rates from material delivered by lecture as low as 5% (as opposed to 50% retention from group discussion or 90% retention from teaching others), instructors need to be quite clear about why they are choosing lecture at any particular time (Parent Educational Advocacy Training Center, 1990). Most adult learners have an average attention span of 15–20 minutes, and the greatest amount of comprehension and retention occurs during the first 5 minutes (Middendorf & Kalish, 1996). Good lectures can be an efficient way to deliver specific content but need to be used judiciously. In Brookfield's (1990a) chapter entitled "Lecturing Creatively," he suggested some common reasons for selecting lecture as a preservice instructional strategy, including establishing the broad outlines of a body of material, setting guidelines for independent study, modeling intellectual attitudes for students, encouraging learners' interest in a topic, and setting the moral culture for discussions. For preservice or inservice instruction, variety may be the key to using lecture as an effective strategy. Middendorf and Kalish (1996) suggested a dozen "change-up" options, that is, instructional strategies with which to follow lecture. These include such diverse options as asking participants to write exam questions about the lecture material that was covered; posing a question about the covered content that requires analysis and synthesis, then asking learners to write and share and compare answers; and dividing participants and structuring a debate of opposing sides of an issue.

Another consideration in putting it all together is selecting instructional approaches that support desired changes on the part of participants, as illustrated in Chapter 5. Winton (1990) described this as a priority for "establishing within the [participants] the capacity to generalize skills learned . . . to refine those skills continually over time, and to teach those skills to others" (p. 56).

Specific instructional strategies can support learners in making those changes. One way is by providing instructional materials that will assist in promoting skill development and application (e.g., clear handouts, copies of relevant articles, topical reading lists, annotated bibliographies, clean copies of materials used during training that participants can copy for use). A second approach to promoting the use of new ideas is assisting participants to find material and organizational resources for ongoing use, such as libraries, special collections, electronic networks, or parent organizations. A third strategy is to employ instructional methods that give participants opportunities to practice new approaches (e.g., interdisciplinary participants working as small groups on decision making to promote effective teamwork; role plays that enable participants to "practice" skills such as interviewing or sharing diagnostic information; participating in interdisciplinary practica; participating in a mentoring relationship). The process of promoting and supporting change in early intervention personnel preparation is not easy (Winton, 1990), but individual instructors have the opportunity to make significant contributions by how they plan and implement their interactions with learners.

PLANNING FOR THE INEVITABLE
CHALLENGES THAT CONFOUND TEACHING AND TRAINING

Effective instructors who are asked to teach specific classes or workshops are capable of adapting to different responses and situations. However, even the best-prepared instructors are frequently stymied by elements beyond their control. Four common instructional challenges are lack of instructional resources, lack of fiscal resources, lack of human resources, and unanticipated variables that require instructor flexibility. Table 21.2 lists some effective strategies for addressing these challenges.

TABLE 21.2. Strategies for addressing common instructional challenges

Challenge	Strategies
Lack of instructional resources	
• Lack of resources to buy instructional materials	• Locate resources for high-quality, low-cost instructional materials. The *Resource Guide: Selected Early Childhood/Early Intervention Training Materials* (Catlett & Winton, 1996) (see Resources at the end of this chapter) lists many quality items that are readily available and inexpensive or free.
	• Explore state and local organization, parent group, and professional association resource libraries for possible materials to borrow. For example, PACER Center, a family center in Minneapolis, lends many of its videotapes for $10.
Lack of human resources	
• Lack of family members with whom to copresent	• Contact parent organizations to identify family members who may be interested.
	• Ask family members in leadership roles (e.g., interagency coordinating committees, state agency) if they would be interested or know of others who would be.
	• Contact local preschool or infant/toddler program administrators or teachers regarding family members who might be interested in personnel preparation.
• Lack of copresenters from other disciplines	• Develop partnerships with service providers from diverse disciplines and service delivery settings (e.g., home based, center based) in the community. Additional benefits for preservice audiences is that this models "tower–trench" collaboration. For inservice audiences this can underscore and reinforce the value of firsthand experiences such as their own.
Lack of fiscal resources	
• Lack of resources to support family participation	• Advocate for support from the source supporting the personnel preparation activity to include this in the budget
	• Contact organizations for families or children with special needs for possible funding for family participation.
	• Organize volunteers to support families by providing child care. At one annual early intervention conference in West Virginia, local child care providers volunteered to provide free child care to the children of participating families.
	• McBride, Sharp, Hains, and Whitehead (1995) identified a list of internal and external sources for funding parent coinstruction in higher education.

(continued)

TABLE 21.2.   *(continued)*

Challenge	Strategies
Unanticipated variables that require instructor flexibility	
• Participants are different than you expected (e.g., more sophisticated, less sophisticated, more diverse)	• Overprepare. Always prepare more activities, more examples, and more content than you can use. This will enable you to select from among possibilities in finding the best match with audience expectations and targeted outcomes.
	• If needs assessment data are not available, start with an informal needs assessment (e.g., discipline representatives? family members? administrators? settings? previous instruction or experience? expectations?). This will enable you to target content and examples to the audience.
	• Monitor the "pulse" of the participants. One way is to provide participants with Post-it notes and a feedback sheet on which they can tell you what they like and what they would change. This information can then guide any "midcourse corrections."
• Asked at the last minute to teach a class/course or provide inservice instruction	• Advocate for greater advance planning time to build in more quality features (especially interdisciplinary, team, family, and/or administrator participation).
	• Know where human resources are that can be drawn on quickly. Contact individuals who have taught similar content for ideas.
	• Know where instructional resources are and work to continuously expand your repertoire.
	• Organize materials so they can be easily located (e.g., keep three-ring binders of overheads or handouts that are indexed by topic).
	• Think like an instructor at all times. As you read an article that has a clear schematic for a particular concept, think "great overhead" or "great handout" and make a copy, with source citation, for future use.
	• Collect ideas for instructional techniques and materials at classes and workshops. By watching the process other instructors use, you'll develop an expanding repertoire of options for meeting diverse learner needs.
• Instructional design elements out of instructor control (e.g., one-shot workshop instead of a sequence of instructional interactions; lack of support for follow-up of students or participants)	• Advocate for quality features, and work to make them part of the instruction you provide.
	• Share the quality indicators with personnel preparation funders and/or planners to help them appreciate the importance and benefits of these features.
	• Share information about the importance of the quality indicators in providing instruction that will produce needed changes in knowledge and application. Winton's (1990) article has good information to support this message.

By necessity, each instructor comes prepared with preconceived objectives and expectations for each learning experience and its participants. Being prepared and organized are characteristics of effective instructors (Wolfe, 1992). But as discrepancies are noted between "the preconceptions and the realities" (Saunders & Hawkins, 1986, p. 27), flexible instructors work to diagnose the problems and make necessary changes in format, content, or delivery to meet the needs of the learners and successfully accomplish their goals. This requires creating a climate of respect and communication that will promote participant feedback and foster flexibility, thus assisting instructors in adapting to meet the needs of their audience.

It seems reasonable to presume that instructional flexibility develops as a function of experience. However, many of the strategies illustrated in Table 21.2 can be used by both new and seasoned instructors. Another message from Table 21.2 is the need to advocate for "quality" features (e.g., interdisciplinary participation, family and administrative participation) as part of the planning and support for training. The next section offers ideas for assisting instructors in looking at the big picture and designing instruction that includes the many components necessary for promoting productive change in early intervention personnel preparation.

USING CHECKLISTS TO ASSIST WITH DESIGNING INSTRUCTIONAL SEQUENCES

Trying to integrate big picture issues, such as each state's comprehensive system of personnel development (CSPD), and specific design features, such as instructional strategies or evaluation and follow-up, is a challenge for all personnel developers. With time and practice, many instructors become more proficient, constantly working to adjust their repertoire to reflect information on recommended practices and ecosystemic issues. However, it would be helpful to have one list of the key issues to work through when planning instruction.

As part of the Southeastern Institute for Faculty Training (SIFT), Winton (1996) conducted a review of early intervention personnel preparation research to discover what the literature had to say about practices that were most effective. The findings of that review are contained in an unpublished brochure (Winton, 1993) entitled *What We Have Learned About Part H Personnel Preparation,* which summarizes findings from 11 key sources (Bailey, Buysse, Edmondson, & Smith, 1992; Bailey, McWilliam, & Winton, 1992; Bailey, Simeonsson, Yoder, & Huntington, 1990; Bruder, Klosowski, & Daguio, 1989; Gallagher, 1993; Moore, 1988; Rooney, Gallagher, & Fullagar, 1993; Rooney, Gallagher, Fullagar, Eckland, & Huntington, 1992; Winton, 1990; Winton, McWilliam, Harrison, Owens, & Bailey, 1992; Wolfe, 1993). From those findings, two checklists were developed—Preservice Personnel Preparation Quality Indicators (see Table 21.3) and Inservice Personnel Preparation Quality Indicators (see Table 21.4)—to assist instructors in making decisions that are consistent with research findings. The right column of each table indicates a source in this book for information about each quality indicator, including why it is important and how to address it as a component of personnel preparation.

Designing and implementing instruction that supports learner diversity in all its forms and reflects the quality indicators of effective preservice and inservice personnel preparation is no easy task. An evaluation study conducted as part of SIFT revealed that some areas were particularly challenging (Winton, 1996). One component of SIFT was a 4-day institute designed to support the efforts of interdisciplinary groups of early intervention faculty, professionals, and families ($n = 192$) from 15 states in providing quality inservice personnel preparation in their respective states. The principles reflected in the checklist in

TABLE 21.3. Preservice personnel preparation quality indicators

Indicator	Source(s) for more information in this book
• To what extent was the instruction you provided coordinated with your state's CSPD plan?	Chapters 2–3, 6
• To what extent were certification or licensure credits available to students who participated in the instruction you provided?	Chapters 2–4
• In providing this instruction, to what extent did you work as part of an interdisciplinary instructor team?	Chapters 4, 18, 20
• To what extent did family members of children with disabilities (consumers of services) participate as part of the instructor team?	Chapters 17, 20
• To what extent was the audience interdisciplinary (at least three or more disciplines were well represented)?	Chapters 4, 18
• To what extent were experiential activities and modeling/demonstration opportunities provided as part of the instruction?	Chapters 5, 9–17, 21
• To what extent were instructional strategies used for embedding/applying the specific ideas/practices to the workplace?	Chapters 5, 7, 21
• To what extent were instructional strategies varied and sequenced in ways to support students with different learning needs and styles?	Chapters 5, 19, 21
• To what extent did students identify specific ideas/practices that they desired to try in their clinical experiences (an action plan)?	Chapter 7
• To what extent was ongoing support, monitoring, or technical assistance provided to students after the course or program ended?	Chapters 7–8
• To what extent was actual impact of instruction on practices measured or evaluated?	Chapters 6–7
• To what extent was instruction individualized according to the needs of students?	Chapters 5, 21

Adapted from Winton (1993).

Table 21.4 were emphasized throughout that event and the statewide planning that preceded it. At the end of the 4 days, the participants were asked to rate the extent to which they had incorporated each of the quality indicators into the inservice session they had provided to others during the past 6 months, using a 5-point Likert-type scale. This was considered to be a pretest measure of the quality of the inservice instruction they had provided. They were asked to respond to the same rating scale 6 months after the 4-day institute; this was the posttest measure of quality used in the study. A statistical analysis that compared their responses at these two points in time provided information about the extent to which they were able to implement the quality indicators promoted through SIFT.

The results of this comparison indicated that participants were able to make changes in the implementation aspects of personnel preparation, as reflected in statistically signif-

TABLE 21.4. Inservice personnel preparation quality indicators

Indicator	Source(s) for more information in this book
• To what extent was the instruction you provided coordinated with your state's CSPD plan?	Chapters 2–3
• To what extent were certification or licensure credits available to individuals who participated in the instruction you provided?	Chapters 2–4
• In providing this instruction, to what extent did you work as part of an interdisciplinary instructor team?	Chapter 20
• To what extent did family members of children with disabilities (consumers of services) participate as part of the instructor team?	Chapters 17, 20
• In terms of the target audience, to what extent was the instruction "team based" (included key professionals who work together on a team)?	Chapter 20
• To what extent was the audience interdisciplinary (at least three or more disciplines were well represented)?	Chapters 18, 20
• To what extent were family members involved as participants?	Chapters 17, 20
• To what extent was the instruction actively endorsed by administrators?	Chapters 3, 8, 20
• To what extent was the instruction actively attended by administrators?	Chapter 20
• To what extent were experiential activities and modeling/demonstration opportunities provided as part of the instruction?	Chapters 5, 9–18, 21
• To what extent were instructional strategies used for embedding/applying new ideas/practices to the workplace?	Chapters 3, 5, 21
• To what extent were instructional strategies varied and sequenced in ways to support different learning needs and styles?	Chapters 3, 5, 19, 21
• To what extent did participants identify specific ideas/practices that they desired to try in the workplace (an action plan)?	Chapters 3, 7
• To what extent was ongoing support, monitoring, or technical assistance provided to participants?	Chapters 7–8
• To what extent was actual impact of instruction on practices measured or evaluated?	Chapters 6–7
• How often did you provide handouts/written materials to participants?	Chapters 5, 7, 21

Adapted from Winton (1993).

icant pretest and 6-month posttest differences. Specifically, participants were more likely to provide instruction that was coordinated with their state's CSPD plan; was endorsed by administrators; included experiential activities, modeling, and demonstration opportunities; used strategies for applying instructional ideas to the workplace; and used instructional strategies that varied to meet different learning styles. However, they were unable to make changes in the planning and evaluation aspects of the instruction. For example, there were no significant differences in quality indicators related to making certification licensure credits available to participants; family participation; interdisciplinary team participation; and the provision of ongoing support, monitoring, technical assistance, or evaluation.

Participants were interviewed by telephone at the 6-month follow-up point on the barriers and facilitators that hindered or helped them accomplish individual goals for making changes in personnel preparation approaches that they identified as part of their SIFT participation. A content analysis of their open-ended responses indicated that the most powerful facilitators to making desired changes were collegial support and follow-up technical assistance from the SIFT project. The barriers they encountered were competing priorities for their time and the unexpected amount of time that it took to make their proposed changes. These follow-up interviews revealed a consistent theme of bureaucratic roadblocks to making some of the changes they perceived as important. For instance, the desire to work with families as instructional partners was tempered by the lack of money to reimburse families for their participation. Because of relationships with families that developed through the SIFT project, they believed they were able to call on families to work with them to some extent. However, they also believed that SIFT had promoted an equitable partnership, and this required reimbursement, which they were unable to secure. Therefore, the partnership they desired was fragile and sometimes not sustained because of problems with administrative support. Despite these barriers, there is evidence that some of the changes created through SIFT have been maintained and sustained within the administrative structures of the universities and early intervention systems (Winton, 1996). Additional follow-up evaluation with participants is planned with the expectation that it will provide more information about what happens after a 3-year federally funded project ends. The use of checklists for quality and evaluation strategies that track outcomes over time (Winton, 1996) are two legacies of this project that should be shared.

CONCLUSION

This chapter summarizes the nuts and bolts of designing instructional sequences that incorporate features designed to assist early intervention personnel in making needed changes. Despite the availability of information about promising practices and quality indicators, there are still some instructors who enter classrooms every day with the set of lecture notes they have used repeatedly (and ineffectively) to teach a particular course. Every day participants are lectured or "inserviced" in a manner that neither complements their knowledge and expertise nor provides useful information or resources for improving their practices. A missing piece in putting it all together is a systematic way to encourage instructors and participants to pursue opportunities to learn more about effective instructional design. This book, especially the resource sections at the end of some chapters, may provide such an opportunity.

RESOURCES

Brookfield, S.D. (1990). *The skillful teacher: On technique, trust, and responsiveness in the class-room.* San Francisco: Jossey-Bass. Cost: $29.95. (415) 433-1767.

Down-to-earth advice to all teachers—both new and veteran—on how to thrive on the unpredictability and diversity of classroom life. Particularly helpful chapters include "Lecturing Creatively," "Facilitating Discussions," "Using Simulations and Role Playing," and "Giving Helpful Evaluations."

Catlett, C., & Winton, P.J. (1996). *Resource guide: Selected early childhood/early intervention training materials* (5th ed.). Chapel Hill: University of North Carolina at Chapel Hill, Frank Porter Graham Child Development Center. Cost: $10. (919) 966-4221.

Product describes more than 300 resources that might assist in designing preservice or inservice training (e.g., curricula, videotapes, self-instructional materials, discussion guides). Resources are divided into 18 sections that correspond with key training content areas (e.g., evaluation/assessment, family–professional collaboration, teams). Emphasis is on materials that are good, readily available, and inexpensive or free.

Eitington, J.E. (1989). *The winning trainer.* Houston, TX: Gulf Publishing Co. Cost: $39.50 plus shipping and handling. (713) 520-4444.

Engaging and dynamic techniques for involving participants in the learning process, increasing retention, and promoting carryover. Sections on getting started (e.g., icebreakers, openers), using small groups effectively, role playing, games, exercises, puzzles, case method, evaluation, and transfer have broad application to preservice and inservice settings. There is even a chapter called "If You Must Lecture . . . ," describing how to make this instructional approach as effective as possible.

Saunders, M.K., & Hawkins, R.L. (1986). *The teaching game: A practical guide to mastering training.* Dubuque, IA: Kendall/Hunt Publishing Co. Cost: $32. (800) 228-0810.

A practical guide designed to assist teachers/trainers of adults. Many useful examples are provided throughout the chapters that focus on the characteristics of adult learners (and what to do about them), the characteristics of adult educators, interpersonal styles and delivery, communication between trainers and trainees, and instructional techniques. The chapter on evaluation and feedback has clear examples of how to write test questions, obtain useful feedback, and encourage self-assessment.

Winton, P. (1993). *What we have learned about Part H personnel preparation.* Unpublished brochure. Chapel Hill: University of North Carolina at Chapel Hill, Frank Porter Graham Child Development Center. Cost: Free. (919) 966-6635.

Pamphlet summarizes research related to effective practices in early intervention personnel preparation.

REFERENCES

Bailey, D., Buysse, V., Edmondson, B., & Smith, T. (1992). Creating family-centered services in early intervention: Perceptions of professionals in four states. *Exceptional Children, 58*(4), 298–309.
Bailey, D., McWilliam, P.J., & Winton, P. (1992). Building family-centered practices in early intervention: A team-based model for change. *Infants and Young Children, 5*(1), 73–82.
Bailey, D., Simeonsson, R., Yoder, D., & Huntington, G. (1990). Preparing professionals to serve infants and toddlers with handicaps and their families: An integrative analysis across eight disciplines. *Exceptional Children, 57*(1), 26–35.
Bergman, A. (1995, March). *Evolution of common sense and disability policy: From institutional to community and facility-based services to support individuals and families in inclusive communi-*

ties. Paper presented to the Think Tank on Therapeutic Services for Children with Disabilities, United Cerebral Palsy Associations, Inc., Washington, DC.

Brookfield, S.D. (1990a). *The skillful teacher: On technique, trust, and responsiveness in the classroom.* San Francisco: Jossey-Bass.

Brookfield, S.D. (1990b). Using critical incidents to explore learners' assumptions. In J. Mezirow & Associates, *Fostering critical reflection in adulthood* (pp. 177–193). San Francisco: Jossey-Bass.

Brookfield, S.D. (1986). *Understanding and facilitating adult learning.* San Francisco: Jossey-Bass.

Bruder, M., Klosowski, S., & Daguio, K. (1989). *Personnel standards for ten professional disciplines serving children under P.L. 99-457: Results from a national survey.* Farmington: University of Connecticut Health Center, Division of Child and Family Studies, Department of Pediatrics.

Catlett, C., & Winton, P.J. (1996). *Resource guide: Selected early childhood/early intervention training materials* (5th ed.). Chapel Hill: University of North Carolina at Chapel Hill, Frank Porter Graham Child Development Center.

Deshler, D. (1990). Conceptual mapping: Drawing charts of the mind. In J. Mezirow & Associates, *Fostering critical reflection in adulthood* (pp. 336–353). San Francisco: Jossey-Bass

Edelman, L. (1995, February). *Learning styles, training activities, problem solving activities, and the role of training and learning.* Workshop presented at the NEC*TAS Conference on Adult Learning and Evaluation of Training and Technical Assistance, San Diego, CA.

Eitington, J.E. (1989). The *winning trainer.* Houston, TX: Gulf Publishing Co.

Fenichel, E. (Ed.). (1992). *Learning through supervision and mentorship to support the development of infants, toddlers, and their families: A sourcebook.* Arlington, VA: ZERO to THREE/National Center for Clinical Infant Programs.

Gallagher, J. (1993, January). Carolina Policy Studies: Findings and future directions. *Frankly Speaking.* (Available from Frank Porter Graham Child Development Center, University of North Carolina at Chapel Hill, CB#8185, Chapel Hill, NC 27599-8185)

Hanson, M.J., & Brekken, L.J. (1991). Early intervention personnel model and standards: An interdisciplinary approach. *Infants and Young Children, 4*(1), 54–61.

Harris, B.M. (1980). *Improving staff performance through in-service education.* Needham, MA: Allyn & Bacon.

Hile, J. (1992, April). Getting the lead out. *Training and Development,* 9–10.

Klein, N.K., & Campbell, P. (1990). Preparing personnel to serve at-risk and disabled infants, toddlers, and preschoolers. In S.J. Meisels & M.P. Shonkoff (Eds.), *Handbook of early childhood intervention* (pp. 679–699). New York: Cambridge University Press.

Kolb, D. (1985). *Learning Style Inventory: Self-scoring inventory and interpretation booklet.* Boston: McBer and Company.

Lukinsky, J. (1990). Reflective withdrawal through journal writing. In J. Mezirow & Associates, *Fostering critical reflection in adulthood* (pp. 213–234). San Francisco: Jossey-Bass.

McBride, S.L., Sharp, L., Hains, A.H., & Whitehead, A. (1995). Parents as co-instructors in preservice training: A pathway to family-centered practice. *Journal of Early Intervention, 19*(4), 343–355.

McWilliam, P.J. (1992). The case method of instruction: Teaching application and problem-solving skills to early interventionists. *Journal of Early Intervention, 16,* 360–373.

McWilliam, P.J., & Bailey, D.B., Jr. (Eds.). (1993). *Working together with children and families: Case studies in early intervention.* Baltimore: Paul H. Brookes Publishing Co.

Meyers, C., & Jones, T.B. (1993). *Promoting active learning: Strategies for the college classroom.* San Francisco: Jossey-Bass.

Mezirow, J. (1991). *Transformative dimensions of adult learning.* San Francisco: Jossey-Bass.

Middendorf, J., & Kalish, A. (1996). The "change-up" in lectures. *FORUM, 5*(2), 1–5.

Moore, J. (1988). Guidelines concerning adult learning. *Journal of Staff Development, 9*(3), 1–5.

Parent Educational Advocacy Training Center. (1990). *NEXT STEPS: Planning for employment.* Alexandria, VA: Author.

Rooney, R., Gallagher, J., & Fullagar, P. (1993). *Distinctive personnel preparation models for Part H: Three case studies.* Chapel Hill: University of North Carolina at Chapel Hill, Carolina Policy Studies Program, Frank Porter Graham Child Development Center.

Rooney, R., Gallagher, J., Fullagar, P., Eckland, J., & Huntington, G. (1992). *Higher education and state agency cooperation for Part H personnel preparation.* Chapel Hill: University of North

Carolina at Chapel Hill, Carolina Policy Studies Program, Frank Porter Graham Child Development Center.

Saunders, M.K., & Hawkins, R.L. (1986). *The teaching game: A practical guide to mastering training.* Dubuque, IA: Kendall/Hunt Publishing Co.

Smith, R.M. (1982). Some programmatic and instructional implications of the learning how to learn concept. *Proceedings of the Adult Education Research Conference, No. 23.* Lincoln: University of Nebraska.

Sullivan, R.L., Wircenski, J.L., Arnold, S.S., & Sarkees, M.D. (1990). *A practical manual for the design, delivery, and evaluation of training.* Rockville, MD: Aspen Publishers, Inc.

Winton, P. (1993). *What we have learned about Part H personnel preparation.* Unpublished brochure. Chapel Hill: University of North Carolina at Chapel Hill, Frank Porter Graham Child Development Center.

Winton, P., McWilliam, P.J., Harrison, T., Owens, A., & Bailey, D. (1992). Lessons learned from implementing a team-based model of change. *Infants and Young Children, 5*(1), 49–57.

Winton, P.J. (1990). A systemic approach for planning inservice training related to Public Law 99-457. *Infants and Young Children, 3*(1), 51–60.

Winton, P.J. (1996). A model for supporting higher education faculty in their early intervention personnel preparation roles. *Infants and Young Children, 8*(3), 56–67.

Wolfe, B. (1992, June). *What works: What we know about effective preparation and professional development programs.* Paper presented at the National Association for the Education of Young Childrens National Institute for Early Childhood Professional Development, Los Angeles, CA.

Wolfe, B. (1993, January). *Best practices in Head Start inservice training.* Paper presented at the NEC*TAS Combined Meetings, Washington, DC.

EPILOGUE

A major challenge identified in Chapter 1 was how to connect the reforms happening in the early intervention system to reforms in personnel development systems. Certain assumptions were identified as underlying determinants of how such reforms should take place. Based on the collective wisdom and experience shared by the authors of the chapters in this book, a summary of specific recommendations for next steps and future directions follows.

INCREASE THE RESOURCES ALLOCATED TO PERSONNEL PREPARATION

Whether at the local, state, or federal level, personnel preparation falls into the budget category of discretionary spending. The term *discretionary* reflects the inherent belief that personnel development monies are expendable, fringe, and nonessential. Its importance is consistently underestimated by those who allocate resources. Research indicates that reform efforts are failing because staff development has not been emphasized (Consortium for Policy Research in Education, 1996) despite evidence that providing meaningful opportunities for professional growth is a key feature shared by successful school reform (Quellmalz, Shields, & Knapp, 1995). Personnel development systems must have the resources to address the needs of personnel who are adapting to reform efforts. As emphasized throughout this book, this does not mean more resources to support more of the same traditional approaches. It means that resources should be allocated for reforming the systems of personnel development so they can better meet the needs of existing and future early intervention personnel in nontraditional ways. This might include stipends for increasing family participation; funds to support collaboration across university departments and state agencies; resources to support community-based, on-site approaches to personnel development; and many of the other innovative approaches described throughout this book.

ADDRESS QUALITY AND EVALUATION ISSUES

Closely connected to the recommendation that more resources should be allocated to personnel preparation is the recommendation that those allocations be made on the basis of some well-defined criteria for quality and effectiveness. Accountability issues must be addressed with creativity and imagination because of the numerous challenges that arise when documenting changes in practices in an ever-changing field. However, personnel preparation will continue to be the "stepchild" in the funding arena unless solid evidence can be presented to funders that money has been well spent.

PAY ATTENTION TO THE SOCIAL AND COLLABORATIVE CONTEXT OF PERSONNEL PREPARATION

The increased emphasis in early intervention on collaborative relationships, coupled with the research that emphasizes the important role of peer and collegial support in sustaining lifelong learning and making changes, suggests that more attention should be paid to this aspect of professional growth. Creative strategies for supporting collaborative relationships are shared throughout this book. Making collaboration work to ultimately benefit the quality of programs and services provided to families requires more than just putting people together around a table, or in a meeting, or in an event. Rather, strategies for facilitating meaningful interactions and for promoting group decision making and problem solving are necessary. Supporting individual relationships over time, especially when individuals live in different parts of the community or the state, is important if collaboration is to be sustained. Research indicates that sustaining these relationships without administrative support is difficult.

CREATE A PROCESS FOR SPREADING SUCCESS

Effective models and strategies for personnel preparation have been developed, and many of these have been described in this book. However, these successes have not been shared with others systematically or effectively. Although this book addresses this problem, multiple dissemination strategies are needed to get information into the hands of those responsible for planning and implementing personnel preparation. A place to start is with the conferences and conventions sponsored by various professional organizations and agencies, as often faculty and consultants attend these for professional renewal and new information. However, the format used for conveying information in these conferences is exactly the format that this book recommends be deemphasized, that is, short, unrelated sessions that provide a superficial presentation of information or ideas. What is needed are challenging, focused, in-depth, hands-on experiences that model as well as present information about innovative instructional strategies. This is the approach taken by the Southeastern Institute for Faculty Training (SIFT) with positive outcomes in terms of short-term and long-term changes in the instructional practices of those who participated (Winton, 1996). One of the outcomes of SIFT was that some of the participating states are starting to provide comprehensive strands on personnel preparation as part of their statewide conferences. This is a start in the right direction, although more efforts of this type need to be tried and evaluated.

RECOGNIZE THAT THERE ARE NO QUICK FIXES OR SIMPLE SOLUTIONS

Reforming personnel preparation systems may be even more challenging than reforming early intervention systems. There are often more players, if the important role that universities, community colleges, and professional organizations have traditionally played in personnel development is considered. Even when successful models and strategies for personnel development have been identified, the translation to local communities requires time, patience, and effort. Financial and human resources are needed to adapt effective models to local sites, whether it be a college campus or a local community. Providing local communities and local planning or advisory boards with information and resources for personnel development must be a priority. Identifying those responsible for quality community-based personnel development efforts is a challenge associated with this recommendation. Related challenges include developing infrastructures at the state or regional level that can support college and community efforts and taking the time to systematically document progress and changes over time.

In considering these recommendations, it is clear that they are interconnected. Reforming a system that is not really a system but a collection of individual entities that share a mission to prepare personnel to serve young children and their families will require much time, creativity, and individual commitment, as well as many resources. These four items—time, resources, creativity, and individual commitment—are key components to the success of moving toward our ultimate goal of better serving young children and their families.

REFERENCES

Consortium for Policy Research in Education. (1996). *Public policy and school reform: A research summary*. Philadelphia: Consortium for Policy Research in Education Research Report Series, Report #36.

Quellmalz, E., Shields, P., & Knapp, M. (1995). *School-based reform: Lessons from a national study*. Washington, DC: U.S. Government Printing Office.

Winton, P. (1996). *A model for promoting interprofessional collaboration and quality in early intervention personnel preparation*. Chapel Hill: University of North Carolina at Chapel Hill, Frank Porter Graham Child Development Center.

INDEX

Page numbers followed by *t* or *f* indicate tables or figures, respectively.